Philipp

a travel survival kit

Jens Peters

Philippines – a travel survival kit

5th edition

Published by

Lonely Planet Publications
Head Office: PO Box 617, Hawthorn, Vic 3122, Australia
Branches: PO Box 2001A, Berkeley, CA 94702, USA
10 Barley Mow Passage, Chiswick, London W4 4PH, UK
71 bis rue du Cardinal Lemoine, 75005 Paris, France

Printed by
Singapore National Printers Ltd, Singapore

Photographs by
Krzysztof Dydynski (KD) Paul Steel (PS)
John Pennock (JPk) Tony Wheeler (TW)
Jens Peters (JP)

Front cover: Person overlooking Bangue rice terrace, Dallas & John Heaton,
Scoopix Photo Library

Illustrations by
Boy Doego Jr

First Published
February 1981

This Edition
August 1994
Reprinted with Update supplement June 1996

Although the authors and publisher have tried to make the information as accurate as possible, they accept no responsibility for any loss, injury or inconvenience sustained by any person using this book.

National Library of Australia Cataloguing in Publication Data

Peters, Jens
Philippines – a travel survival kit.

5th ed.
Includes index.
ISBN 0 86442 224 5.

1. Philippines – Description and travel – Guidebooks.
I. Title. (Series: Lonely Planet travel survival kit).

915.990447

text © Jens Peters 1994
maps © Lonely Planet 1994
photos © photographers as indicated 1994
climate charts compiled from information supplied by Patrick J Tyson, © Patrick J Tyson, 1994

Jens Peters

Jens, born in 1949 in Germany, studied advertising, communications and arts education in Berlin. Since 1970 he has travelled for several months each year in countries outside Europe. So far he has visited the Philippines (his favourite country in South-East Asia) more than 40 times and spent over seven years there. In 1977 he became involved in travel writing and has since worked as a freelance journalist for various travel magazines and published several guidebooks about tropical countries on his own.

From the Publisher

This edition was edited at the Lonely Planet office in Australia by Kristin Odijk and Sharan Kaur. Maliza Kruh was responsible for design, title page and maps, with additional maps from Marcel Gaston, Chris Lee-Ack, Sandra Smythe and Tamsin Wilson. Cover design by Tamsin Wilson.

Thanks must also go to Tom Smallman for proofreading and editorial guidance; Jane Hart for design assistance; and Rowan McKinnon who produced the index.

In addition to the many German-speaking travellers who contributed to the new German edition of Jens Peters' guide, we would also like to thank our readers (apologies if we've misspelt your name) who took the time to write in with their contributions to this guide and to *South-East Asia on a Shoestring*. These include:

Ronald Abma (NL), G R Adams (Aus), Thomas Agostin (USA), Magnus Anderberg (S), Mark Anderson, Jacob Bakker, John Bevan (UK), Harry Biddulph (USA), Eric Bloom (USA), Richard Boyle (Aus), J J Broere (NL), Nigel Brooks (UK), Ian Chaplin, Bill Chapman (Aus), Freddy Cheuk (S), Philippe Clement (F), John Collier, Alma Colubis (Phl), Meligio P Diaz (Phl), Herbert Dickmann (Aus), Alexander Divinagracia, C Donaghy, Tyrone Donnerberg (USA), Brook Downie (Aus), Steve Durnien (UK), Graham Eames (Aus), Bernard Etcheverry (Phl), Mr Etcheverry (Phl), George Finlison (USA), David Fox (UK), Jean Pierre Franck, Stephen Frazer (Aus), Daryl Gank (Aus), Marguerite Gerster (CH), Christine Godard, John M Gore (Phl), Robert Gray, Eric Gregory, Marc Gutering (B), Luc Haas (F), Jon Halle (UK), T Halma (NL), Wai Hoong Ho (HK), Jim Hobden (Phl), Johan Holmstrom (S), Richard Hunphreys (UK), David Jackson (Aus), Brigitte Jacobs (C), Steven Jacques (USA), Jeffrey James (Aus), Nils Johansson (S), R B Johnson (Aus), Christian Johnson (USA), J P R Jones (Phl), Brian Jones (NZ), Ronnie Joseph, Phillip Juntti (USA), R Kein (UK), Douglas Knight (Aus), James Lassegard, Karl Lauger (USA) Alfred Li (HK), Alex Lutzyk, Michael Mackey (UK), Paul Magee (Aus), Ralph Magro, J Mason Florence (USA) Phil Mayor-Smith, Georges Mazzocut (C), Aloysius Mesenas (S), Sedid Metzuyanim (Isr), Claudio Milletti (I), John Milne (Aus), Scott Mitchell (USA), Howard J Mlakar, Bruce Moore (T), Danilo M Morales (Phl), Glenn Morris (Aus), John Moss, Brad Newsham (USA), John O'Hagan (C), Danielle O'Loughlin (Aus), Ian Owen (Aus), Lee Ann Pasco, Colin Pearson (UK), Jo Perrett, Simonetta Po (I), Marc Poussard (USA), K Rawnsley (Aus), Marco Roebers (NL), Sanne Rokamp (Dk), Brendan Rourke (UK), Oded Salamy (USA), Alma Schurer, Robert Service (USA), Andrew Shagrin (USA), Blandine & Albert Six (NL), Renee Smit (NL), Steve Smith (Aus), Derrick Stowronski, Johan Taubert (S), Simon Watson Taylor (UK), A van Lemel (NL), Michael Vincent (Aus), Jack Vossen (NL), Mr & Mrs Will Wandt (USA), Mark Ward (Aus), John Whitney, Emyr Williams (UK), John Wolfe (Aus), Nancy Wyles (Aus), David Yu (Tai), Michael Zenobia (USA)

Aus - Australia, B - Belgium, C - Canada, CH - Czechoslovakia, Dk - Denmark, F - France, HK -

Hong Kong, Isr - Israel, I - Italy, NL - Netherlands, NZ - New Zealand, Phl - Philippines, S - Sweden, Tai - Taiwan, T - Thailand, UK- United Kindgdom, USA - United States of America

Warning & Request

Things change, prices go up, schedules change, good places go bad and bad ones go bankrupt – nothing stays the same. So if you find things better or worse, recently opened or long since closed, please write and tell us and help make the next edition better!

Your letters will be used to help update future editions and, where possible, important changes will also be included in an Update section in reprints.

We greatly appreciate all information that is sent to us by travellers. Back at Lonely Planet we employ a hard-working team to sort through the many letters we receive. The best ones will be rewarded with a free copy of the next edition or another Lonely Planet guide if you prefer. We give away lots of books, but, unfortunately, not every letter/postcard receives one.

Contents

INTRODUCTION 9

FACTS ABOUT THE COUNTRY 12

History 12
Geography 16
Climate 17
Flora & Fauna........................20
Government 25
Economy 28
Population.................................29
People 29
Art & Culture 39
Religion....................................42
Language..................................42

FACTS FOR THE VISITOR 55

Visas..55
Documents..............................56
Customs..................................56
Money.....................................56
What to Bring 59
Tourist Offices 59
Business Hours 60
Fiestas & Festivals..................60
Post & Telecommunications 64
Time 66
Electricity...................................66
Books 66
Maps 67
Media 67
Health...68
Women Travellers.....................78
Dangers & Annoyances 78
Activities 80
Accommodation.........................85
Food 86
Drinks 91
Entertainment............................91
Things to Buy............................92

GETTING THERE & AWAY 95

Air..95
Sea 98
Leaving the Philippines 98
Warning.....................................99

GETTING AROUND...100

Air..100
Bus 101
Train...103
Car Rental 103
Motorbike 104
Bicycle 104
Boat 104
Local Transport.........................107

MANILA 109

Orientation...............................109
Information 111
Rizal Park 115
Intramuros...............................117
Quiapo Church 118
Chinese Cemetery 118
Chinatown 119
Malacañang Palace..................119
Cultural Center 121
Nayong Pilipino 121
Forbes Park 121
Us Military Cemetery 121
Faith Healers............................122
Museums 122
Markets 123
Swimming 124
Places to Stay 124
Places to Eat............................137
Entertainment...........................150
Things to Buy............................153
Getting There & Away 154
Getting Around 164

AROUND MANILA 170

Bataan Peninsula 170
San Fernando (Pampanga) 170
Olongapo.................................172
Barrio Barretto & Subic 173
Around Barrio Barretto &
Subic 174
Angeles 174
Mt Pinatubo 180
Corregidor Island.....................182
Las Piñas..................................183
Cavite..183
Tagaytay (Taal Volcano) 183
Talisay.......................................184
Nasugbu & Matabungkay.........185
Batangas...................................186
Anilao..187
Lemery 187
San Nicolas 188
Calamba 188
Los Baños.................................188
Alaminos 189
San Pablo 189
Pagsanjan 190
Around Pagsanjan 192

NORTH LUZON 193

The West Coast **193**	Kabayan 218	Pagudpud 240
The Zambales Coast 193	Sagada 218	Claveria 240
Lucap & Alaminos 197	Around Sagada 221	Aparri 241
Hundred Islands 198	Bontoc 222	Gattaran 244
Bolinao 198	Around Bontoc 224	Tuguegarao 244
Lingayen 199	Banaue 226	**The East** **246**
Dagupan 199	Around Banaue 228	Roxas 246
San Fabian 201	**The North** **230**	Cauayan 246
Aringay & Agoo 202	Vigan 230	Salinas 246
Bauang 202	Bangued 235	Santa Fe 246
San Fernando (La Union) 206	Currimao 235	Baler 248
The Mountains **210**	Laoag 235	
Baguio 210	Around Laoag 239	

SOUTH LUZON 250

Lucena 250	Iriga & Lake Buhi 258	Sorsogon & Gubat 267
Atimonan & Gumaca 251	Legaspi 258	Bulan 269
Daet & Apuao Grande Island . 251	Around Legaspi 263	Bulusan & Irosin 269
Naga 255	Tabaco 267	Matnog 270
Pili 258	Tiwi 267	

AROUND LUZON 271

Batanes **271**	Santa Cruz 281	Puerto Galera Beaches 293
Batan Island 272	Torrijos 282	Calapan 296
Sabtang Island 273	Buenavista 282	Pinamalayan 296
Ibayat Island 273	Elefante Island 282	Bongabong 297
Catanduanes **273**	Tres Reyes Islands 283	Roxas 297
Virac 275	Gasan 283	Mansalay 297
Puraran 277	**Masbate** **283**	San Jose 297
Lubang **278**	Masbate 285	Apo Island & Apo Reef 299
Tilik 279	Cataingan 285	Sablayan 300
Marinduque **279**	Mandaon 285	North Pandan Island 300
Boac 280	**Mindoro** **285**	Mamburao 300
Balanacan 281	Puerto Galera 288	

THE VISAYAS 303

Bohol **304**	Punta Engaño 339	Biliran & Maripipi Islands 356
Tagbilaran 308	Olango Island 339	San Isidro 357
Around Tagbilaran 310	Liloan 340	Palompon 357
Jagna 311	Sogod 340	Ormoc 357
Anda 311	Bantayan Island 340	Baybay 359
Panglao Island 312	Malapascua Island 342	Bato & Hilongos 359
Balicasag Island 314	Talisay 343	Maasin 359
Pamilacan Island 315	Toledo 343	Liloan & Limasawa Island 360
Cabilao Island 315	Moalboal 343	**Negros** **360**
Chocolate Hills 315	Badian & Badian Island 346	Bacolod 364
Tubigon & Inaruran Island 316	Matutinao 347	Silay 369
Ubay 316	San Sebastian & Bato 347	Victorias 370
Talibon 316	Liloan 347	Lakawon Island 370
Jao Island 317	Mainit 348	San Carlos 370
Cebu **317**	Sumilon Island 348	Dumaguete 371
Cebu City 323	Montalongon 348	Around Dumaguete 375
Mt Manunggal National Park . 334	Argao 348	Maluay & Zamboanguita 375
Mactan Island 335	**Leyte** **349**	Apo Island 376
Marigondon 337	Tacloban 352	Binalbagan 376
Maribago 337	Around Tacloban 355	Kabankalan 376

Bayawan 377	Caticlan 394	Calbayog 413
Panay **377**	Boracay 394	Catbalogan 414
Iloilo City.................... 380	**Romblon** **402**	Borongan.................... 414
Guimaras Island....................384	Romblon Island.................... 403	**Siquijor** **416**
South Coast....................386	Sibuyan Island 404	Larena 416
San Jose de Buenavista 387	Tablas Island 405	Siquijor....................417
Culasi 387	**Samar**....................**409**	San Juan 418
North-East Coast 388	Allen 411	San Antonio....................418
Roxas 390	Geratag & San Jose 411	Lazi....................418
Kalibo 391	Balicuartro Islands....................411	Salag Do-Ong 418
Ibajay 394	Catarman.................... 413	

MINDANAO & SULU 419

Camiguin **419**	Marawi & Lake Lanao 441	Lake Sebu 462
Mambajao....................421	Ozamiz....................442	Cotabato....................462
Around Mambajao....................421	Oroquieta....................442	**Basilan**....................**464**
Around the Island 422	Dipolog & Dapitan....................443	Isabela....................464
Mindanao **423**	Pagadian....................444	Lamitan 465
Surigao....................428	Zamboanga....................445	**Sulu Islands** **466**
Butuan....................432	Around Zamboanga....................449	Jolo....................470
Balingoan....................434	Davao....................450	Siasi....................470
Cagayan de Oro 435	Around Davao....................455	Bongao....................470
Around Cagayan de Oro..........438	General Santos (Dadiangas) ... 459	Sitangkai 473
Malaybalay 439	Koronadel 461	
Iligan....................439	Surallah 461	

PALAWAN.. 476

Central Palawan **481**	Rio Tuba....................494	Busuanga Island 507
Puerto Princesa....................481	**North Palawan**....................**494**	Coron....................507
Around Puerto Princesa..........486	San Rafael....................494	Concepcion 508
Honda Bay 488	Roxas & Coco-Loco Island ... 495	Busuanga....................509
Nagtabon Beach 489	Port Barton....................495	Calauit Island 509
Underground River....................489	San Vicente....................497	Dimakya Island 509
Sabang....................490	Abongan & Tabuan....................497	Coron Bay....................510
South Palawan **490**	Taytay & Embarcadero..........498	Gutob Bay....................510
Narra....................490	Flowers Island....................499	Culion Island....................512
Quezon....................492	Liminangcong....................499	Cuyo Islands 512
Brooke's Point &	El Nido & Bacuit Archipelago 502	
Ursula Island....................493	**Calamian Group**....................**505**	

INDEX 515

Maps **515**	**Text** **516**

Map Legend

BOUNDARIES

—·—·—·—	.... International Boundary
—··—··—··	.... Internal Boundary
+++++++++	.... National Park or Reserve
----------	.... The Equator
··············	.... The Tropics

SYMBOLS

◉	NATIONAL	.... National Capital
●	PROVINCIAL	.... Provincial or State Capital
●	Major	.... Major Town
●	Minor	.... Minor Town
■		.... Places to Stay
▼		.... Places to Eat
⊠		.... Post Office
✈		.... Airport
i		.... Tourist Information
⊖		.... Bus Station or Terminal
66		.... Highway Route Number
☾†⊞⛪		...... Mosque, Church, Cathedral
∴		.... Temple or Ruin
✚		.... Hospital
※		.... Lookout
⚠		.... Camping Area
⌒		.... Picnic Area
⌂		.... Hut or Chalet
▲		.... Mountain or Hill
⊢⊣		.... Railway Station
		.... Road Bridge
		.... Railway Bridge
⇒ ⇐		.... Road Tunnel
↦ ↤		.... Railway Tunnel
⌢⌢⌢		.... Escarpment or Cliff
⌣		.... Pass
⊓⊔⊓		.... Ancient or Historic Wall

ROUTES

───────	.... Major Road or Highway
- - - - - -	.... Unsealed Major Road
───────	.... Sealed Road
- - - - - -	..... Unsealed Road or Track
═══════	.... City Street
+++++++	.... Railway
■─◉─■	.... Subway
- - - - - -	.... Walking Track
- - - - - -	.... Ferry Route
++++++++	.... Cable Car or Chair Lift

HYDROGRAPHIC FEATURES

	.... River or Creek
	.... Intermittent Stream
	.... Lake, Intermittent Lake
	.... Coast Line
	.... Spring
	.... Waterfall
	.... Swamp
	.... Salt Lake or Reef
	.... Glacier

OTHER FEATURES

	Park, Garden or National Park
	.... Built Up Area
	... Market or Pedestrian Mall
	.... Plaza or Town Square
	.... Cemetery

Note: not all symbols displayed above appear in this book

Introduction

Compared with other countries of South-East Asia the Philippines doesn't take up much room in the major travel catalogues – when they appear at all, that is. There's no doubt that it loses economically because of this, but this country has recently been through enough natural and political upheavals for this to be a blessing in disguise. The Philippines simply isn't ready to withstand the stresses that mass tourism and its consequences would bring.

Although travelling under your own steam through the Philippine archipelago can tax your flexibility at times, it is always a pleasure. You would have to go a long way to find people as friendly and helpful as the Filipinos. This, the Filipinos like to remind you, is 'where Asia wears a smile'.

It is the variety the Philippines offers that is so interesting for the traveller. The bustling capital of Manila contrasts with lonely islands fringed with superb beaches and gardens of coral. There are towns where you will find a thriving nightlife, but you can also visit mountain tribes who still live according to their own laws and traditions. There are huge rice terraces built eons ago with the most primitive of tools; wide sugar-cane fields with subterranean rivers and lakes; or shadowy palm forest groves and dense jungle.

Generally speaking, transport on and between the major islands is relatively frequent and of a good standard, and there are more than enough hotels, lodging houses and restaurants to choose from. If it's 'speed', 'efficiency' and 'punctuality' you're looking for, then don't expect too much here. Far better to learn to be as laid back as the Filipinos themselves!

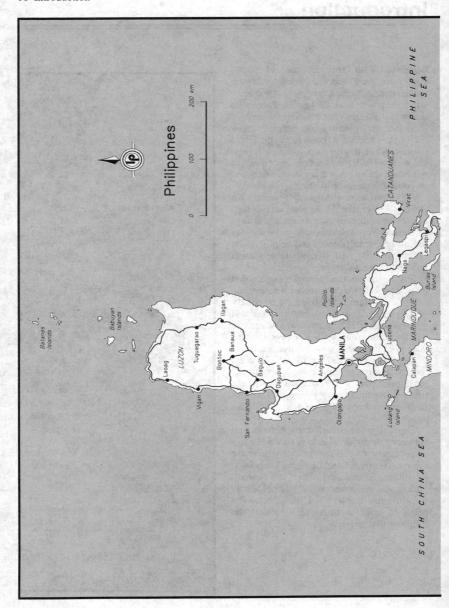

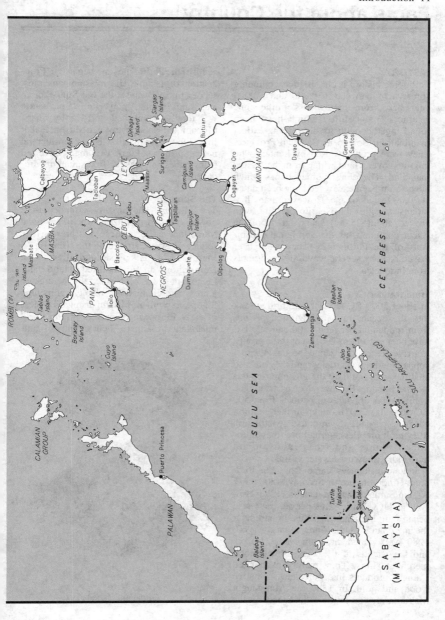

Facts about the Country

HISTORY

Philippine history is classified as beginning somewhere between 150,000 and 30,000 years ago. From this epoch stem the stone artefacts (palaeoliths) which have been found together with fossils of long-extinct mammals in Solano in Cagayan Province. They were probably used by hunters who migrated over a land bridge from the Asiatic mainland. The oldest human bones which have so far been excavated have been dated at 50,000 years of age. However, many historians consider the Negrito or Aeta, who arrived about 25,000 years ago from the Asian continent, as the aboriginal inhabitants of the Philippines. They were later driven back by several waves of immigrants from Indonesia.

Immigration

In about 5000 BC the last land bridge sank into the ocean. Five immigration periods from Indochina between 1500 and 500 BC have been recorded. The last of these groups to arrive in their long canoes brought the first copper and bronze articles, and they are also credited with building the gigantic rice terraces at Banaue (Banawe), North Luzon. The immigration of Malayan peoples from 500 BC to 1500 AD brought further cultural changes, particularly in house construction (they built on piles), agriculture (they introduced plants and trees) and animal husbandry (they used water buffalo).

Indian influences came from the Buddhist-Hindu empire of Srivijaya (800-1377 AD) in Sumatra, and Majapahit (1293-1478 AD) in Java. During this period, trade also began with Indochinese states. In particular the merchants of the Sung Dynasty (960-1280 AD) visited the main island, Luzon, and the islands of the Visayas with their merchant ships. They mainly exchanged Chinese products like porcelain for native wood and gold. In 1380 the Arab-taught Makdum arrived in the Sulu Islands in the south of the Philippines and began the 'Propagation of Islam'. His mission was most successful in Bwansa, the old Sulu capital, and Tapul Island. A powerful Islamic centre was finally established in 1475 by Sharif Mohammed Kabungsuwan, a Muslim leader from Johore. He married the very influential native princess Putri Tunoma, converted many tribes and was the first sultan of Mindanao.

The Spanish

The Muslims had already extended their power to a part of Luzon, when Ferdinand Magellan, a Portuguese seafarer in the service of Spain, arrived on the scene on 16 March 1521. His first landfall was on Homonhon, an uninhabited island near Leyte, but it was on Mactan that he erected a cross and claimed the whole archipelago for Spain – with the blissful disregard typical of early European colonisers for the local inhabitants' claim to their country. Lapu-

Ferdinand Magellan

12

Lapu, a proud Filipino chief, opposed the Spanish authority and this led to a battle in which Magellan was killed.

Ruy Lopez de Villalobos was the next to try and claim the islands for Spain. He reached the island realm with an expedition in 1543 and named it 'Filipinas' after King Philip II of Spain. The permanent Spanish colonial occupation of the Philippines began in 1565. In November of that year Miguel Lopez de Legaspi landed with his fleet at Bohol. In Tagbilaran he sealed a blood-friendship with the island ruler Rajah Sikatuna, conquered Cebu a short time later and erected the first Spanish fort in the Philippines. He was obviously very energetic.

In 1571 Legaspi conquered Manila and a year later the whole country, with the exception of the strictly Islamic Sulu Islands and Mindanao, was under Spain's domination. With the zeal typical of the Spanish at the time, churches were built and the propagation of Catholicism began.

The Push for Independence

Until 1821 the Philippines was administered from Mexico. Attempts by the Dutch, Portuguese and Chinese to set foot in the Philippines were successfully repelled by the Spanish, though the British managed to occupy Manila for a short time in 1762 during the Seven Years' War. They reluctantly handed it back to Spain under the conditions of the Treaty of Paris signed in 1763.

Dr Jose Rizal - The Philippine National Hero

Jose Rizal was born on 19 June 1861 in Calamba, Laguna. Prior to moving to Manila in 1872, where he studied painting and sculpting, he was educated by his mother and private tutors. Once at the Santo Tomas University, he started his studies in medicine, philosophy and literary science. He continued study in Madrid in 1882, where he also finally graduated. To further his education, he spent the next few years amongst others in Paris, Heidelberg, London and Berlin. During this time he came into contact with European scholars and Philippine artists and patriots of the same political persuasion as himself, who shared his dream of independence and a sense of national dignity. In 1887 his famous book *Noli Mi Tangere* (Do Not Touch Me) was published in Berlin. This socio-political work was written as a *roman à clef* and grappled with the issues of the Philippine reality and the suppressive policies of the Spanish colonial power. Although the Spanish censor banned the dissemination of the book, its stirring message achieved its aim. His second book, *El Filibusterismo*, as well as scores of inflammatory essays calling for an uprising against the Spanish were secretly distributed in the Philippines, finding a powerful resonance there.

In 1892 Rizal risked returning home and together with friends he founded the reform movement, the Liga Filipina, on 3 July. He was arrested only four days later and was exiled for four years to Dapitan on Mindanao. He used the time in exile to develop his artistic and scientific skills, and he designed various pieces of technical apparatus and equipment. He also learned several Philippine languages and worked as a teacher and doctor.

When the Philippine Revolution broke out in 1896, Rizal was condemned to death by a military tribunal in Manila for inciting people to revolt. On 30 December 1896, in front of the walls of Intramuros, now known as Rizal Park, he was executed by firing squad. ■

After the opening of the Suez Canal in 1869, many young Filipinos left their country to study in Spain and other European countries. They brought back with them new ideas and thoughts of freedom. In 1872 there was a revolt in Cavite by about 200 Filipino soldiers against their Spanish masters. It was quickly put down, but it signalled the start of a determined struggle for freedom and independence.

The spiritual founders of the independence movement were the Filipino thinkers and patriots Marcelo H del Pilar, Graciano Lopez Jaena, Juan Luna and Dr Jose Rizal. The critical writings and poems of Rizal inspired many Filipinos in their fight for freedom. When Jose Rizal founded the 'Liga Filipina' in 1892, he was exiled as a revolutionary agitator to Dapitan, Mindanao. Andres Bonifacio then founded the secret organisation Katipunan. In August 1896 the armed struggle for independence broke out, first in Manila and later throughout the country. On 30 December 1896, after an absurd mockery of a trial, Rizal was executed by the Spanish authorities. He spent the last weeks before his death in the dungeon of Fort Santiago in Manilan General Emilio Aguinaldo replaced Bonifacio as leader of the revolution in March 1897.

The USA

In 1898, as a result of a dispute over Cuba, a war between Spain and the USA broke out. Under Admiral Dewey the Spanish fleet was decisively beaten in Manila Bay. The Filipinos, seizing their chance to strike against the Spanish, fought on the side of the USA, and on 12 June 1898 General Aguinaldo declared the Philippines independent. The Americans, however, ignored the role the Filipinos had played in the war and paid the Spanish US$20 million for the latter's ex-possession: this was ratified by the Paris Peace Treaty of 10 December 1898. General Aguinaldo was not recognised as president of the revolutionary government. The Filipinos had to begin the struggle against foreign domination again – this time against the formidable USA.

After President Roosevelt recognised the newly drawn-up Philippine constitution, Manuel L Quezon was sworn in as President of the Philippine Commonwealth.

WW II

After the attack on Pearl Harbour, Japanese troops landed on Luzon and conquered Manila on 2 January 1942. The Filipino and US troops suffered defeats with high casualty rates in battles at Corregidor Island and on the Bataan Peninsula. This brought about the brutal Japanese military rule which continued until 1944, when General Douglas MacArthur fulfilled his promise to return and liberate the Philippines from the Japanese. US troops landed at Leyte and, under their lead, the islands were recaptured from the Japanese forces.

On 4 July 1946 the Philippines received full independence. The first president of the republic was Manuel Roxas. His successors were Elpidio Quirino, Ramon Magsaysay, Carlos Garcia and Diosdado Macapagal.

The Marcos Years

Ferdinand E Marcos was elected to power in 1965 and, unusually for the Philippines, was re-elected in 1969. The Marcos government found the country to be in a chaotic state. Corruption and crime had become the order of the day. People talked of the 'Wild East'.

In 1972 Marcos declared martial law and began to implement his concept of the 'New Society'. Within a short time some changes were apparent – guns disappeared from the streets, crime decreased and improvements in public health were made, but the land reform law of October 1972 only partly abolished land rents.

In foreign policy, the joining of international organisations like Economic & Social Commission for Asia & the Pacific (ESCAP), Asian & Pacific Council (ASPAC), Association of South-East Asian Nations (ASEAN) and the Colombo Plan was successful. The Philippines was also a provisional member of the General Agreement on Tariffs & Trade (GATT).

Political peace, tax abatement and low wages were reasons for foreign companies to invest money again in the Philippines from the mid-1970s on. Not all Filipinos agreed with this political peace, and communist guerrillas of the New People's Army (NPA) and members of the Moro National Liberation Front (MNLF) tried to force change through violence. The opposition parties, the Democratic Socialist Party and the Philippine Democratic Party, had no influence on internal politics. The Communist Party of the Philippines was prohibited. Although martial law was abolished in January 1981, Marcos could continue his dictatorial form of government with so-called presidential decrees.

In the presidential election of June 1981, Marcos was confirmed as head of state for another six years, but the result was contested and allegations of vote-rigging were loud and many. Parliamentary elections were held in 1984 and the opposition United Nationalist Democratic Organisation (UNIDO, an amalgamation of 12 parties) won 63 of the 200 seats. The independent candidates won eight seats, and the government party, Kulisang Bagong Lipunan (KBL) – New Society Movement , won 125, including the mandate for 17 which were directly decided by Marcos.

Cory Aquino

A deciding factor in the surprise success of the opposition was not only the dissatisfaction of a large proportion of the population over the state of the economy, but also the response of many voters to the murder of the liberal opposition politician and popular former senator Benigno Aquino upon his return from exile on 21 August 1983. This, more than anything, sharpened the political awareness of all levels of society and moved hundreds of thousands of people to protest. The snap election planned for 7 February 1986 saw the opposition unite for the first time under Aquino's widow, Corazon 'Cory' Aquino of the Philippine Democratic Party

(PDP-Laban), and her vice-presidential running mate Salvador Laurel, leader of UNIDO. They were pitted against the team of Marcos and Tolentino.

In the past Marcos had been in a position to decide more or less the outcome of the election, but this time events were being closely monitored by both internal and external sources. Cory Aquino rallied the people in a campaign of civil unrest and national protest of the nonviolent Gandhian kind. Banks, newspapers and companies favoured by Marcos were boycotted and 'People Power' began to make itself felt. The last straw for Marcos came when Defence Minister Juan Ponce Enrile and Armed Forces Vice-Chief of Staff Fidel Ramos joined the Aquino camp together with military units. Tens of thousands of unarmed civilians barricaded the streets, preventing loyalist soldiers from intervening and causing a major bloodbath.

Following the election, both candidates claimed victory and on 25 February both Ferdinand Marcos and Cory Aquino were sworn in as president in separate ceremonies. Later that same day Marcos fled into exile in Hawaii and Cory Aquino stood unopposed. She annulled the constitution and abrogated parliament.

This historic change of leadership was not really a revolution and it hardly touched the country's elite and the structures of power.

Through her ousting of the dictator, Cory Aquino became a national hero and an international celebrity. She restored democracy to the Philippines by re-establishing the political institutions of a democratic parliament and a supreme court.

Although she commanded considerable political power at the beginning of her presidency, she did not manage to bring either the military or the feudal families under control. The president could only partly fulfil the Filipinos' hopes for wellbeing and democracy. The overwhelming majority of the population, who live under conditions of appalling poverty barely above the survival line, did not profit in any way from the short-lived period of economic expansion in

1987 and 1988. Exactly the opposite: their economic misery became more pronounced from year to year. The much vaunted land reform, eagerly awaited by the numerous landless Filipinos, never really got off the ground.

During her period of office as president and commander-in-chief of the Armed Forces, Corazon Aquino survived seven attempted coups. However, it is clear she would not have survived until the last day of the six-year legislative period as head of state without the support of her Defence Minister General Fidel Ramos, and his influence on the military establishment. As a demonstration of her gratitude for his loyalty, she proposed Ramos to the Filipino voters as her candidate of choice to succeed her as president.

Fidel Ramos

As a Protestant, Fidel Ramos could not count on the support of the influential Catholic Church as he went into the election campaign which led to his narrow victory in mid-1992. The favoured candidate of the clergy, the lawyer Miriam Defensor Santiago, and the government spokesman Ramon Mitra failed to get elected, as did the candidates from the camp of the late President Marcos, who had died in exile: the magnate Eduardo Cojuanco and the eccentric Imelda Marcos.

President Ramos took office on 1 July 1992 and shortly thereafter announced his cabinet, an able group of experts in their respective fields. The goals announced by the government are ambitious. The main areas to be tackled are the creation of jobs, revitalization of the economy, reduction of the enormous foreign debt of US$32 billion and the re-establishment of a political climate in which corrupt civil servants have no opportunity to get rich by plundering the state.

In addition, a reliable electricity service has to be established as soon as possible. Since the early 1990s so-called brown-outs have paralyzed the country daily for several hours. The responsibility for this economi-cally unacceptable state of affairs lies with the antiquated and badly (if at all) serviced power stations that break down regularly. The failure of the Aquino administration to produce a far-sighted energy policy is one of the most serious negative points in the sobering catalogue of problems the President inherited from his predecessor.

On the economic front, laws have already been introduced to encourage foreign investment in the Philippines. Heads have rolled at the National Power Corporation (Napocor) and Ramos has been provided with extra decision-making powers in the energy sector. Politically, the President surprised everyone with the decision to lift the ban on the Communist Party of the Philippines which had been in effect since 1957. He saw this as a quick way to end the guerrilla war being waged in the country.

GEOGRAPHY

The Philippines officially consists of 7107 islands of which only 2000 are inhabited. Only about 500 of the islands are larger than one sq km and 2500 aren't even named. In descending order of size the biggest islands are:

Luzon	104,683 sq km
Mindanao	94,596 sq km
Palawan	14,896 sq km
Panay	12,327 sq km
Mindoro	10,245 sq km
Samar	9,949 sq km
Negros	9,225 sq km
Leyte	6,268 sq km
Cebu	5,088 sq km
Bohol	4,117 sq km
Masbate	4,047 sq km

The total area of the Philippines is 299,404 sq km. From north to south the Philippines stretches for 1850 km and from east to west for 1100 km. The highest mountain is Mt Apo, near Davao in Mindanao, at 2954 metres. Mt Pulog, east of Baguio in North Luzon, is the second at 2930 metres. There are 37 volcanoes in the Philippines, 18 of which are classed as being active, including the Mt Mayon volcano near Legaspi in South Luzon and Mt Pinatubo north-west of Manila in Central Luzon. The longest rivers are the Cagayan River, the Rio Grande de Pampanga and the Agno River in Luzon, and the Rio Grande de Mindanao and the Agusan River in Mindanao.

The islands of the Philippines can be divided conveniently into four groups. First there's Luzon, the largest and northernmost island and the site of the capital, Manila. The nearby islands of Marinduque (which is sandwiched between Mindoro and Luzon) and Mindoro are generally included with Luzon. At the other end of the archipelago is the second largest island, Mindanao. From Mindanao's south-western tip, the islands of the Sulu archipelago form stepping stones south to Borneo. Third is the tightly packed island group known as the Visayas, which fills the space between Luzon and Mindanao. Seven major islands make up this group: Panay, Negros, Cebu, Bohol, Leyte, Samar and Masbate. Cebu is the central island of the group and Cebu City is the shipping centre for the entire Philippines – from there ships run to places throughout the country. Finally, off to the west, there's the province of Palawan with more than 1700 islands. The main island is Palawan, which is long and narrow and forms another bridge from the Philippines to Borneo.

Forces of Nature

The earth's crust, the lithosphere, is only about 70 km thick and is composed of several small and large plates. Earthquakes occur depending on the amount of friction between these horizontal plates. Among the six large plates, also called continental or tectonic plates, are the Eurasian and the Pacific plates and in between is squeezed the small Philippine plate. Strong earthquakes are fairly rare, but there are light tremors from time to time.

One of the worst earthquakes to strike the Philippines this century hit large parts of the country on 16 July 1990. Measuring 7.7 on the Richter scale, the temblor killed over 1600 people and destroyed over 20,000 buildings, leaving more than 100,000 people homeless. Several strong aftershocks caused further damage to roads and houses. The worst affected cities were Baguio, Cabanatuan and Dagupan, all in northern Luzon.

The breaking points in the earth's crust are marked by deep trenches, high mountain ranges and volcanoes. The most prominent volcanic chain ('the ring of fire') leads from Alaska and the Aleutian Islands, past the Siberian Kamchatka Peninsula, the Kuril Islands and Japan to the Philippines, where there are 37 volcanoes, at least 18 of which are active. That dormant volcanoes can suddenly turn dangerously active was proved by the massive eruptions of Mt Pinatubo in June 1991. After 600 years of peace the volcano erupted again, ejecting up to 40 km into the stratospere huge amounts of ash, mud and rocks, most of which then rained down on the provinces of Pampanga, Tarlac and Zambales, causing widespread destruction in the process. Nearly 900 people lost their lives as a result of the eruption, thousands more lost everything they owned. And there will be more victims in the future when the accumulated detritus from the eruption is loosened by the monsoon rains and pours down from the slopes of the Zambales Mountains into the plains as an avalanche of mud, to bury countless villages and whole tracts of the countryside.

Luzon and the northern Visayas also lie in the typhoon belt. Some of the whirlwinds wandering from the Pacific to the Chinese mainland also affect the Philippines. Violent storms can occur from June to January, although August to November are the peak months for typhoons. Typhoons nearly always cause power failures, and fires (often caused by candles being blown over) frequently follow. Overloaded electrical points, open fires and arson are other causes of the many fires in the Philippines.

CLIMATE

The climate in the Philippines is typically tropical – hot and humid year-round. Although the weather pattern is fairly

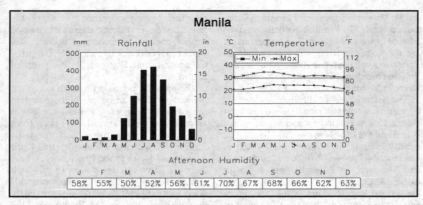

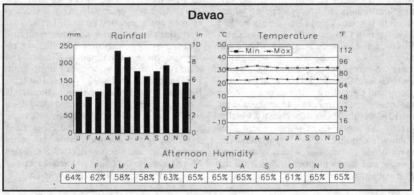

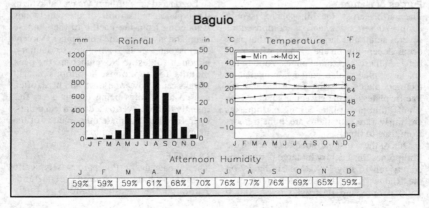

Climatic Zones

complex, it can be roughly divided into the dry season – January to June – and the wet season – July to December. January is usually the coolest month and May the hottest, but the average temperature is usually around 25°C throughout the year. However, like everywhere in the world, the Philippines weather is not 100% predictable.

December to February is the 'cool dry' period while March to May is the 'hot dry' period. You can expect rain every day in July, August and September. In May, Manila usually has daytime temperatures of 35°C to 40°C and at night it doesn't drop much below 27°C. This is the time of year when the rich citizens of Manila head for the perpetual spring of Baguio and the mountain provinces.

The best time to travel is from December to May. In December and January, however, you can expect rain on the east coast. March, April and May are the summer months. Normally, for large areas of the Philippines, the rainy season starts in June. However, for a couple of years in the mid-1980s, the rainy season came considerably late. Travelling around isn't really affected by the occasional downpour, but more by the unpredictable typhoons, which usually come with the wet monsoon season from May to November. The south-west Visayas and Mindanao lie beneath the typhoon belt, but can occasionally be hit by a crosswind. Typhoons usually blow in from the south-east.

The Pacific Ocean coastline, comprising Luzon, Samar, Leyte and Mindanao, lies in the path of the north-east tradewinds, ensuring a mild oceanic climate. The monsoon season takes place from December/January to May and brings rain to the Pacific coast but primarily dry pleasant weather to the rest of the land. In North Luzon the Central Cordillera acts as a natural climate divider. During the first weeks of the north-east monsoons in December and January, it may rain on the eastern side of this mountain range, for example, in Banaue; while a little to the west it may be dry, for example, in Bontoc and Sagada.

The south-west monsoon blows from June to December/January and brings rain. The typhoons in the Pacific region are predominantly in the Marshall Islands and Caroline Islands. They travel in a north-westerly direction to the Chinese mainland between June and November, mainly in August/September.

There are five climatic zones:

1 Typical South-East Asian monsoon climate. Long dry season from November/December to May and intense rainy period from June to November/December.
2 Short dry season from March to May. Although the rainy season from June to February is long, it is not very intense.
3 No clear-cut dry season, with rain falling during most of the year. The heaviest showers are in the months of November, December and January.
4 No clearly defined dry season. The heaviest rainfall is in the months of April to September.
5 No clearly defined wet or dry season.

FLORA & FAUNA

For many years the Philippine archipelago remained relatively isolated from the rest of the world. This meant that the existing plants and animals could evolve in their particular environment to become unique species. According to the latest estimates of fauna in the Philippines there are over 200 species of mammals, around 580 species of birds, 200 species of reptiles and 100 species of amphibious animals. Amongst those are a handful of unusual and rare species only to be found on one or two islands. It is very likely that others are yet to be discovered.

In spite of this diversity, many of the plants and animals in the Philippines can be categorised into one of three groups depending on their place of origin. These are the northern group, centred on Luzon; the southern group, centred on Mindanao but extending into the Visayas; and the western group, centred on Palawan.

The northern group claims heritage from southern China and Taiwan. The species in this group arrived in the Philippines after being blown in by monsoon winds (in the case of plant life), drifting in with the ocean tides, or by means of other natural phenomena.

The southern group includes species that originated in Australia and New Guinea. They came to the Philippines by using the islands of central Indonesia as stepping stones.

The western group, claiming a heritage from the Malay peninsula and Borneo, arrived thousands of years ago, when these areas were connected by a land bridge to several of the Philippine islands.

As with many other areas of South-East Asia, the Philippines environment suffered heavily after WW II with the introduction of large-scale logging and mining operations. Some islands, notably Cebu, were so badly damaged that many of the more vulnerable species became extinct. Most of the larger islands retain their original forest cover only on the rugged mountain tops, which form havens for the plants and animals. Other islands, like Palawan, remain relatively untouched and there visitors can still experience the original Philippines.

The flora of the Philippines presents some 10,000 species of trees, shrubs and ferns. Most common are pines (in the mountains of North Luzon), palm trees and various kinds of bamboo (along the coasts and in the flat interior). About half of the Philippine land mass is covered with forests, which makes the Philippines one of the most wooded lands on earth – for the present, that is.

In fact, tree-felling and slash-and-burn clearing have in a short time already considerably reduced these wooded expanses. Only the visible consequences of this selfish plundering of nature – erosion, soil dehydration and climatic changes – have managed to rouse the politicians from their torpor. At the beginning of 1989, all further deforestation was prohibited by law. Still, in the absence of an effective means of control, it remains to be seen whether this logging ban can bring a halt to the depredations caused by the profiteering timber industry and stop drastic deforestation by *kaingineros* (clearers so called because they create farming land through the *kaingin*, or the slash-and-burn method). On the other hand if there were not so many timber orders from industrialised countries, fewer trees would be felled and whole forests could be saved.

In 1973 the Bureau of Forest Development (BFD) was established to provide a central environmental authority to manage the remaining forested areas. This in turn has led to the recommendation or establishment of over 30 major protected areas, including 23 national parks (11 of which are classified as national recreation areas), seven national wildlife sanctuaries and three strict nature reserves.

The protected areas range from mountain peaks to lowland rainforests and coral reefs. Unfortunately, several of the protected areas are too small to maintain their wildlife populations. Other areas have been drastically reduced from their recommended size, partly due to increasing pressure from human settlements on the perimeters of such areas.

Alternative conservation efforts such as captive breeding programmes have been established as emergency measures to prevent extinction of further species.

The spectrum of tropical flowers is unique. Over 900 species of orchids are known to exist. The Cattleya orchid is seductively beautiful and the sweet-scented Sampaguita was chosen as the national flower; Filipinos like to wear chains of it around their necks.

There are no powerful predators in the Philippines, so a great number of small animals can be found, like the mouse deer in south Palawan, which is a midget deer and is also the smallest species of red deer in the world. In Lake Buhi, South Luzon, are the *sinarapan*: they are the smallest food fish in the world and are not even one cm long. The *tamaraw*, a wild dwarf buffalo with relatively short horns, lives in the mountains of Mindoro. The *tarsier*, the smallest primate in existence, and the *tabius*, the second smallest, are likewise at home in the Philippines. This is unfortunate for them because so is the *haribon*, the Philippine eagle, the largest eagle in the world, whose dietary preference is supposedly small primates. It is the country's national bird.

Parrots are mainly found in Palawan, and

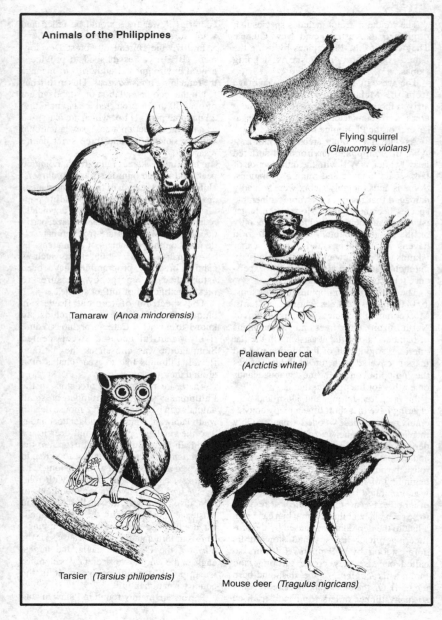

Animals of the Philippines

Flying squirrel
(*Glaucomys violans*)

Tamaraw (*Anoa mindorensis*)

Palawan bear cat
(*Arctictis whitei*)

Tarsier (*Tarsius philipensis*)

Mouse deer (*Tragulus nigricans*)

colourful butterflies abound in Cebu, Mindanao and Palawan. Also well represented in the Philippines are the ubiquitous cockroaches and mosquitoes. The latter are a favourite food of the little gecko, which is very popular as a household pet. The largest reptile of the lizard family found in the Philippines is the monitor.

Crocodiles are rare, though they still exist on Mindanao and Palawan. On the other hand, there is a great variety of snakes: especially noteworthy are the metre-long python and the poisonous sea snake.

Fish, seashells and corals are present in such a multiplicity that there isn't room to detail them here. The cumbersome water buffalo, the *carabao*, is the most important domestic animal of the Filipinos and is not called the 'farmer's friend' for nothing.

National Parks

A visit to one or more of the national parks is a must for any traveller, especially anyone who is interested in plants, animals, scenery or adventure. As with other parts of South-East Asia, many of the Philippine national parks were established only because the government yielded to local and tourist pressure to conserve these areas. Whether or not they will remain protected areas is still uncertain. Just by going to a park and signing the visitors book you will have helped to ensure that it will remain protected.

In Manila the main office of the Bureau of Forest Development (BFD) is in Diliman, Quezon City. There you can get the necessary permits for visiting selected national parks and other protected areas. These can be organised fairly easily and once you have written down your planned visits officially, you will find the permits a great help when you contact BFD representatives in the provinces to arrange your visits to specific areas. Such arrangements can include camping supplies and, where necessary, local transport and a guide. The time spent getting the permit in Manila is well worth it.

In Manila it is also useful to visit the National Museum and the Ayala Museum, where you can enquire about meetings of the Haribon Society, an active conservation group which can put you in touch with interested people who may be able to provide useful tips and contacts.

The best way to visit some of the camps mentioned here is by camping in the areas. Some camping equipment is essential and it may also be necessary at times to hire local guides. The following list of parks provides a broad cross-section of the natural beauty of the Philippines.

Mt Makiling Forest Reserve (Laguna, Luzon) This former national park is close to the campus of the University of the Philippines at Los Banos and its Forest Research Institute. As a well-studied area, it offers a good introduction to the rainforest environment. It is often visited by organised groups. If you make enquiries to the Haribon Society or the Forest Research Institute, they may put you in touch with such a group.

Quezon National Recreation Area (Quezon, South Luzon) This park is in the narrow isthmus of the Luzon Peninsula, east of Lucena. It is now an isolated patch of rainforest centred around a series of rugged limestone crags, with a trail leading to higher areas.

From this high vantage point, both sides of the peninsula can be seen. The old road that winds through the park has been bypassed, but a few buses and other vehicles still travel through the park every day.

A wide variety of wildlife can still be observed, including monkeys (macaques) and squirrels. Among the birdlife, the large hornbills are most conspicuous.

Mt Ilig-Mt Baco National Wildlife Sanctuary (Mindoro) This park is well known as the last refuge for the unique species of the Philippine dwarf buffalo, the tamaraw. After dropping to a very low level in the mid-1960s, its numbers have since been increasing. Its rescue from extinction is a success story for Philippine conservation efforts. The tamaraw are best seen in the

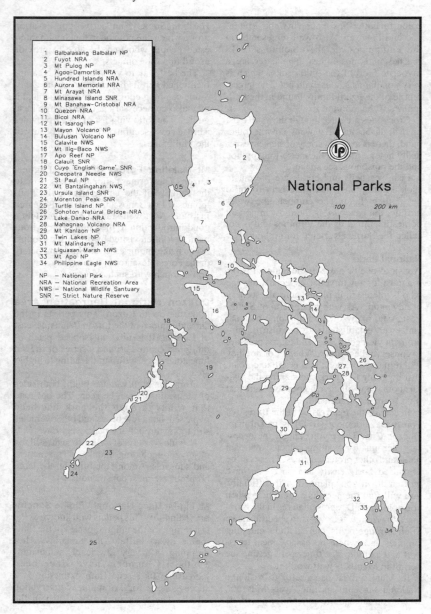

1 Balbalasang Balbalan NP
2 Fuyot NRA
3 Mt Pulog NP
4 Agoo-Damortis NRA
5 Hundred Islands NRA
6 Aurora Memorial NRA
7 Mt Arayat NRA
8 Minasawa Island SNR
9 Mt Banahaw-Cristobal NRA
10 Quezon NRA
11 Bicol NRA
12 Mt Isarog NP
13 Mayon Volcano NP
14 Bulusan Volcano NP
15 Calavite NWS
16 Mt Ilig-Baco NWS
17 Apo Reef NP
18 Calauit SNR
19 Cuyo 'English Game' SNR
20 Cleopatra Needle NWS
21 St Paul NP
22 Mt Bantalingahan NWS
23 Ursula Island SNR
24 Morenton Peak SNR
25 Turtle Island NP
26 Sohoton Natural Bridge NRA
27 Lake Danao NRA
28 Mahagnao Volcano NRA
29 Mt Kanlaon NP
30 Twin Lakes NP
31 Mt Malindang NP
32 Liguasan Marsh NWS
33 Mt Apo NP
34 Philippine Eagle NWS

NP — National Park
NRA — National Recreation Area
NWS — National Wildlife Santuary
SNR — Strict Nature Reserve

National Parks

0   100   200 km

grassland areas, especially towards the end of the dry season.

The high forests of Mindoro cover six major vegetation types, from lowland rainforest to high altitude pine forests, and contain a great diversity of wildlife. The forests there give a better picture than those on Luzon of the rugged beauty of the mountain wilderness of the northern Philippines. Visits to this park and other smaller protected areas on Mindoro can be organised from San Jose or Roxas.

Mt Kanlaon National Park (Negros Occidental) This is a large, rugged and well-forested park centred around the Kanlaon Volcano (2465 metres), which features two craters, one of which is still active with open barren areas at the higher elevations. The old crater is cylindrical and about a km wide, while the newer crater is now over 250 metres deep.

The extensive forests of the park are noted for their abundant wildlife and also feature many waterfalls and small crater lakes hidden by the trees. It is a major refuge for wildlife in the central Philippines and offers an exciting way for the more adventurous traveller to visit a rainforest.

The park's main attraction is climbing the volcano but facilities for visitors are limited. Access to the park can be organised from Bacolod and through several of the smaller towns closer to the park.

Mahagnao Volcano National Recreation Area (Leyte) This is a small park in central Leyte featuring a crater lake and diverse forest and scenic areas. It is part of the central mountain region of Leyte, extending north to the Lake Danao area, also proposed as a national park.

In 1982 the whole region was surveyed for a planned merger into one large park with trails and visitor facilities. In contrast to Negros, this region offers a relatively easy opportunity to visit a Philippine wilderness area. The main point of access is from Tacloban. Mahagnao itself is close to the Burauen area.

St Paul Subterranean National Park (Palawan) The focal point of this park, on the west coast of Palawan about 70 km from Puerto Princesa, is the Underground River, which is over eight km in length and navigable by rubber dinghy or canoe for most of its length.

The forested limestone peaks around the river area and St Paul Bay add to the park's remarkable beauty. The river cave plays host to millions of bats and swiftlets, offering spectacular viewing at dawn and dusk. It is possible to camp on the beach not far from the main entrance of the river and it is well worth spending a few days in this beautiful area. The best access to the river area is by boat from Baheli or Sabang.

Mt Apo National Park (Mindanao) This park was established in 1936 to protect the highest peak in the Philippines. Mt Apo (2954 metres) is an active volcano near Davao and its snow-capped appearance is actually caused by a thick white sulphur crust.

The most famous inhabitant of the park is the haribon, or the Philippine eagle. The numbers of this spectacular bird were once very low, but in the last 25 years have grown considerably, due in part to the experimental breeding programme at nearby Calinan. Observing this splendid bird in the wild can be an unforgettable experience. As well as scanning the sky and tree tops to see an eagle, you should listen for its piercing cry, or for the racket of smaller birds mobbing one, usually when it is resting in the tops of the larger trees near the edge of the forest.

There are several walking trails in the park, including three to the summit of Mt Apo. This park is characteristic of Mindanao's forested volcanic regions and offers spectacular scenery and wildlife. Visits can be organised from nearby Davao

GOVERNMENT
The administration of the Republic of the Philippines is subdivided into 12 regions (plus Metro Manila as the National Capital Region) consisting of 76 provinces. Every

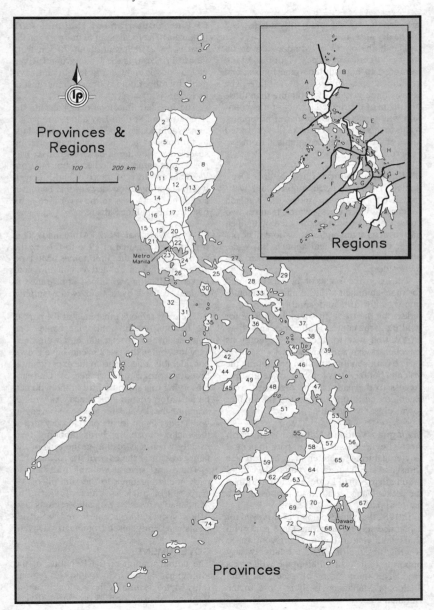

Provinces & Regions

Regions

Provinces

Provinces

1	Batanes
2	Ilocos Norte
3	Cagayan
4	Kalinga Apayao
5	Abra
6	Ilocos Sur
7	Mountain
8	Isabela
9	Ifugao
10	La Union
11	Benguet
12	Nueva Vizcaya
13	Quirino
14	Pangasinan
15	Zambales
16	Tarlac
17	Nueva Ecija
18	Aurora
19	Pampanga
20	Bulacan
21	Bataan
22	Rizal
23	Cavite
24	Laguna
25	Quezon
26	Batangas
27	Camarines Norte
28	Camarines Sur
29	Catanduanes
30	Marinduque
31	Mindoro Oriental
32	Mindoro Occidental
33	Albay
34	Sorsogon
35	Romblon
36	Masbate
37	Northern Samar
38	Western Samar
39	Eastern Samar
40	Biliran
41	Aklan
42	Capiz
43	Antique
44	Iloilo
45	Guimaras
46	Leyte
47	Southern Leyte
48	Cebu
49	Negros Occidental
50	Negros Oriental
51	Bohol
52	Palawan
53	Surigao del Norte
54	Siquijor
55	Camiguin
56	Surigao del Sur
57	Agusan del Norte
58	Misamis Oriental
59	Misamis Occidental
60	Zamboanga del Norte
61	Zamboanga del Sur
62	Lanao del Norte
63	Lanao del Sur
64	Bukidnon
65	Agusan del Sur
66	Davao del Norte
67	Davao Oriental
68	Davao del Sur
69	Maguindanao
70	North Cotabato
71	South Cotabato
72	Sultan Kudarat
73	Sarangani
74	Basilan
75	Sulu
76	Tawi-Tawi

Regions

A	Ilocos
B	Cagayan Valley
C	Central Luzon
D	Southern Luzon
E	Bicol
F	Western Visayas
G	Central Visayas
H	Eastern Visayas
I	Western Mindanao
J	Northern Mindanao
K	Southern Mindanao
L	Central Mindanao

province consists of a provincial capital and several municipalities, which in turn consist of village communities or *barangays*. A barangay with an elected head/administrator, the 'barangay captain', is the smallest socio-political administration unit in the Philippines. The term 'barangay' originates from the time the archipelago was settled between 500 BC and 1500 AD. During that time, a barangay (or balanghai) was a large seaworthy outrigger boat which could carry up to 90 passengers and was used by

Malayan peoples to migrate to the Philippines. The crews of these boats were probably social groups like village communities or extended families.

National Flag & National Anthem

The national flag of the Philippines has a white triangle on the left. On either side tapering off to the left are two stripes, the top one blue, the bottom one red. The white triangle contains three five-point stars and a sun with eight rays. The sun symbolises freedom and its eight rays represent the first eight provinces that revolted against Spanish colonial rule. The stars symbolise the three geographical divisions of the Philippines: Luzon, the Visayas and Mindanao. The blue stripe stands for the equality and unity of the people. The red stripe (placed on top in wartime) symbolises the readiness of the Filipinos to fight to the death for their country.

On 12 June 1898, General Emilio Aguinaldo declared the independence of the Philippines from the balcony of his house in Cavite. On this day the Philippine national flag was raised and the Philippine national anthem played for the first time. In the form of a march, the Marcha Nacional Filipina anthem was composed by Julian Felipe and the words were written by Jose Palma.

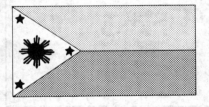

Philippine National Flag

ECONOMY

About two-thirds of Filipinos live by fishing, agriculture and forestry. A significant contribution to their diet comes from ocean, coast and freshwater fishing. Rice is the most important agricultural product. The development of new varieties of rice at the International Rice Research Institute in Los Baños, improvements in methods of cultivation and enlargement of the area of cultivation have brought the Philippines closer to self-sufficiency in food production.

The main products for export are coconuts (copra), abaca (Manila hemp), tobacco, bananas, pineapples and recently also cut flowers, including orchids.

Cattle farming is still relatively undeveloped. Poultry, pigs, sheep and goats are reared for meat, while buffaloes serve mainly as work animals. The most important minerals are chrome, iron, copper, coal, nickel, gypsum, sulphur, mercury, asbestos, marble and salt. Test drillings for oil have been only partially successful.

The Philippines, like many other Asian countries, is dependent on oil for its energy needs. Every year about US$2 billion has to be spent on crude oil imports. It is hoped that hydroelectric and geothermal power projects will go some way towards improving the energy situation. Around 20% of the total energy required is produced geothermally, which is equivalent to 8 million barrels of oil. The Philippines is second only to the USA in harnessing geothermal energy sources.

Manufacturing occurs principally in and around Manila, and consists mainly of the luxury goods, food, textile and leatherware industries, although the Philippines also manufactures automobile components.

Economic analysts are worried that the Filipino passion for grand and impressive projects, often highly capital intensive, may limit the nation's ability to come to terms with its employment problems. There is a minimum wage set by the state but this often exists only on paper. (See the following Income & Cost of Living section.) The Philippines has a large pool of skilled but underutilised labour.

Tourism is a further source of income and from 1970 to 1980 the tourist flow increased from just 14,000 visitors to over a million. In the years of political unrest from 1983 to

1986 the tourist figures declined, only to shoot up again in 1987, and in 1992 over a million tourists visited the country.

Manila had a massive increase in hotel rooms in the 1970s, but this was not followed by a similar development in provincial areas. This lack of development outside Manila may eventually limit the growth of tourism, but it does make the Philippines more enjoyable for the shoestring traveller!

Income & Cost of Living

The basic level of income is fixed by the state. According to law, the lowest possible wage of a working person is 140 pesos per day, equivalent to about US$5. Tariff rates are numerous but exist only on paper, considerably few of these being in fact observed. There are also clear discrepancies in income between city and country. Here are some examples of average wages in Manila (in the provinces the wages are on average 30% lower): restaurant staff (without tips) receive US$65 per month; teachers or labourers, US$85 per month; office workers or policemen, US$100 per month; and engineers, US$180 per month. To cover the basic necessities of life in Manila a family of six members needs at least 6000 pesos (US$215) per month.

Similarly, prices are considerably higher in the cities than in rural areas. In the country a Filipino meal costs no more than US$2. A bottle of beer (.33 litres) can be bought for the equivalent of US$0.30, and about US$0.20 is charged for soft drinks like Coca-Cola. Naturally everything is a good deal dearer in exclusive restaurants and bars. For instance, you'll pay about US$1 for a Coke at the swimming pool of the Manila Pavilion Hotel, while a beer in one of the Makati nightclubs will cost around US$2.50.

In 1993 the rate of inflation was over 10%.

POPULATION

In 1988 the population stood at 60 million. The trend is for the number of inhabitants of the Philippines to grow at a rate of 2.4% a year. The Philippines' family planning programmes are hampered not only by the strong Catholicism of the Filipinos but also by the usual Asian wish for the 'insurance' of a large family in old age. Filipinos are inclined to be very fond of children and have on average six children to a family. Consequently, you will hear of 'family planting' rather than 'family planning', although the government is putting a great deal of effort into popularising the concept of birth control.

Nearly 40% of the population of the Philippines lives in the city, while the other 60% lives in the country. Fifty-three% of Filipinos are under 20 years of age, while those who are 65 or over account for only 7% of the population. The ratio of males to females is almost even, averaging out at 100 females to 99.7 males.

Manila is the largest city with two million people, but including the suburbs of Quezon, Caloocan and Pasay, the population of Metro Manila is over 10 million. Other major cities are Davao, Cebu, Iloilo, Zamboanga, Bacolod, Angeles, Butuan and Cagayan de Oro.

PEOPLE
Cultural Minorities

Some six million Filipinos make up the so-called cultural minority groups or tribal Filipinos, which collectively comprise 12% of the total population. This figure includes the four million Muslims.

There are 60 ethnological groups altogether distributed mainly around North Luzon (Ifugao, Bontoc, Kalinga, Ilokano), central Luzon (Negrito), Mindoro (Mangyan), and western Mindanao and the Sulu Islands (Muslim). Many of these groups are looked after by the Office for Northern Cultural Communities (ONCC) or the Office for Southern Cultural Communities (OSCC). These agencies are responsible for protecting the cultural minorities' way of life and for assisting the government in bringing material and technical aid to these people to assist their integration into mainstream Philippine society. The minorities themselves decide whether to use this

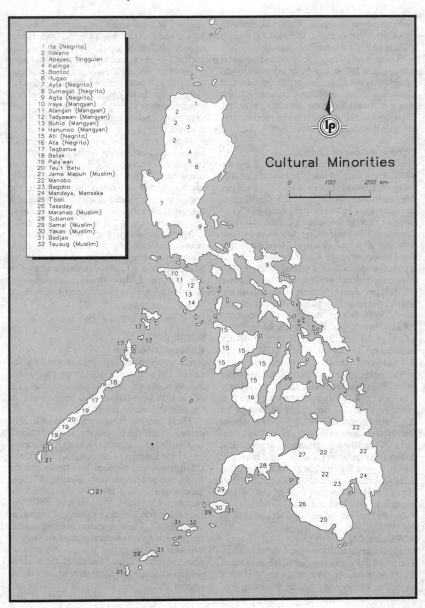

Cultural Minorities

1 Ita (Negrito)
2 Ilokano
3 Apayao, Tingguian
4 Kalinga
5 Bontoc
6 Ifugao
7 Ayta (Negrito)
8 Dumagat (Negrito)
9 Agta (Negrito)
10 Iraya (Mangyan)
11 Alangan (Mangyan)
12 Tadyawan (Mangyan)
13 Buhid (Mangyan)
14 Hanunoo (Mangyan)
15 Ati (Negrito)
16 Ata (Negrito)
17 Tagbanua
18 Batak
19 Pala'wan
20 Tau't Batu
21 Jama Mapun (Muslim)
22 Manobo
23 Bagobo
24 Mandaya, Mansaka
25 T'boli
26 Tasaday
27 Maranao (Muslim)
28 Subanon
29 Samal (Muslim)
30 Yakan (Muslim)
31 Badjao
32 Tausug (Muslim)

0   100   200 km

service, and if so what type of aid they require.

It would be beyond the scope of this book to describe all the ethnological groups in the Philippines, but a selection of those which represent an important part of the population structure and which are accessible to foreign travellers follows.

Apayao The Apayao prefer to live close to the rivers, particularly along the shores of the Apayao and Matalang rivers in the highlands of the Ilocos and Abra provinces in north-west Luzon. They call themselves *isneg* and are the descendants of the feared head-hunters in the Central Cordillera. Their leaders, named *mengal*, are celebrated, wealthy warriors with appropriately large followings. Positions of leadership are not inherited but are accorded the warrior with the greatest ability and charisma. The Apayao believe in ghosts which may take the form of people, animals, giants and monsters. They are protected by Anglabbang, the best and highest god of the head-hunters.

Apayao House

Badjao The Sulu archipelago in the south of the Philippines, as well as the coast and waters of north-east Borneo and east Indonesia, are the domain of the Badjao (or Bajau, Badjaw). They are sea gypsies, many of whom still live in small boats as extended families. Today, however, most of them have given up a nomadic way of life and have settled in houses built on stilts on coral reefs far out in the ocean or on sandbanks near the coast. No-one knows exactly how many Badjao there are, but the figure is estimated at about 30,000, two-thirds of them living in Philippine waters. They are said in legend to have originated in Johore in Malaysia.

A Badjao boat, or *lipa* (pronounced 'leepa'), is made of wood, is seven to 12 metres long, and has a removable roof over its central section. The long, thin hull is fitted with individual slats, serving as a flat base on which to stand when punting or spearing fish. The catch is then hung out to dry in the stern. There is a little oven over the stern where fish can be cooked. Apart from seafood, the mainstay of the Badjao diet is cassava: a nourishing stew that is prepared using the cassava tuber, which is rich in starch.

Sea cucumbers are gathered to be sold for use in Chinese restaurants but before they are sold they are cooked, cleaned and dried. In recent years seaweed has developed into a marketable crop. The Badjao, having adopted a settled lifestyle, have planted regular fields of seaweed grown on long stalks under the water around their homes. After the harvest it is stretched out on the platform of the villages to dry, and is later sold to chemical and pharmaceutical companies.

The Badjao try to fit in with their neighbours who, in the Sulu Islands, are the Samal and the Tausug. On the sea the Badjao consider themselves part of a mystical animist world ruled by the great god Tuhan, but many of them closer to land have adopted Islam. Despite Mecca, they are still afraid of *saitan*, the spirits of the winds, the fish, the trees, the hills and so on, because these will cause sickness if they are angry. Only the *jin*, a sort of magician or medicine man, can make contact with these spirits and try to appease them or drive them out and thereby eventually heal the sick.

A marriage celebration lasts for two days and only takes place when there is a full moon. The whole village joins in. After much clanging of *kulintangan* (xylophones), *tambol* (drums) and *agung* (gongs) men and women dance the *igal*, a traditional dance. Polygamy is allowed but is seldom practised. Couples rarely have more than five children.

The dead are buried on special islands which serve as graveyards and these are only visited for burials. Because contact with the spirits of the dead is maintained, the sea people are tied to the land. Before burial the corpse is washed and wrapped in a white sheet. As well as personal treasures, provisions are placed in the grave for the journey to the beyond.

Batak The Batak are seminomadic hunter-gatherers. They live together in many small groups in the hills and coastal regions of north-east Palawan. During the rainy season, groups join together to form larger communities. The *kapitan* (leaders) of the small groups nominate one person, also known as a kapitan, to lead the larger community during this time. The kapitan makes all the important decisions, such as choice of settlement, sharing of work and organisation of gathering activities. During this settled period the Batak also plant crops.

Encroaching civilisation and disease have tragically decimated these shy indigenous people. One can only hope that international attempts being made to stop these people disappearing entirely are successful.

Bontoc The ethnic minorities of the Central Cordillera (Apayao, Bontoc, Ibaloy, Ifugao, Kalinga, Kankanai, Tingguian) in North Luzon are often classified together as Igorot. Trinidad Pardo de Tavera, a Philippines scholar, interprets this designation as 'People of the Mountains', but, since the 200,000 mountain inhabitants differ quite considerably culturally, it is not correct to regard or discuss the different ethnic minorities collectively as Igorot. It is remarkable that in the literature on the main ethnological groups of this area now and again it is only the Bontoc who are dealt with in connection with the Igorot.

The Bontoc live in thoroughly organised village communities. Their houses are built close to the ground, and every *iti* (village) has two further important accommodation arrangements – *ato* and *olog*. The village elders live in the ato, where social and political decisions are made and religious ceremonies prepared. An ato also serves as a guesthouse and as sleeping quarters for young bachelors. Women are strictly prohibited from entering.

About 10 girls of marriageable age live in

Bontoc Houses

A	B
C	D E
F	

A (JP)
B (JP)
C (JP)
D (JP)
E (KD)
F (PS)

Top Left: On the Pagsanjan rapids, Pagsanjan, Luzon (TW)
Top Right: Woman from the Batanes Islands wearing a head covering (JP)
Bottom Left: Fire blower at the Ati-Atihan Festival in Kalibo, Panay (JP)
Bottom Right: Barbecue stand (JP)

the olog, a flat house with an extraordinarily small entrance. This building is taboo to married men: only bachelors are allowed to enter an olog and spend the night with their intended wives. Before they get that far, both partners must fulfil certain rules of the game – the man must promise to marry his partner in the event of pregnancy; if he doesn't keep his promise, he will be socially isolated and not permitted to enter the ologs again. The invitation and permission to spend the night together must be issued by the girl, and as a sign of her consent, she 'steals' a small item of his property. Every Bontoc understands this hint, and when many tobacco pouches or pipes are purloined during the day in the village, you can bet the ologs will be crowded that night.

Although the days are gone when the Bontoc were feared as head-hunters, even today this act of revenge has not been completely wiped out. Justice in the mountains is strictly 'an eye for an eye, a tooth for a tooth', or more appropriately, 'a head for a head'. *Tuf-ay* (spear), *kalasag* (shield), *kaman* (head-axe) and *sangi* (satchel) comprise the equipment of a warrior. The sangi serves as a carrier for the enemy's head. When a successful warrior returns from his expedition, there is a great celebration for two days in the village. As a sign of his heroic deed the hero is tattooed on the chest: this is known as *chak-lag* and is much coveted, as it symbolises strength and bravery. The tattooing on the arms of male and female Bontoc is called *pango. Fatek* simply means tattoo.

The Bontoc believe in a better life after death; their funerals are not sorrowful occasions and only the heads of the family are in mourning. The most important requisite of the ceremony, which lasts for several days, is a death seat, the *sungachil*. A short time after a person's death, the body is placed in an upright position in the death seat, bound fast and placed so as to be visible to all who pass in front of the house. The shroud is selected according to the status of the family. Old women sing the *anako*, the death song, and a pig is sacrificed and eaten. After nightfall, a sort of recitation begins, called *achog*, in which the life history of the dead person is reflected upon. This ritual can be quite merry as it is very difficult to get a coherent, objective account of the deeds accomplished by the deceased during their lifetime. Daybreak or exhaustion of the participants ends this part of the funeral ceremony.

The body of one of their warriors killed and decapitated by an enemy is left without ceremony in the vicinity of a track leading to the enemy village. This stands as a reminder to the enemy village that the warrior's death will be avenged.

Ifugao No other people of the Philippines apart from the Tasaday have attracted more attention than the Ifugao. They are the builders of the gigantic rice terraces of Banaue and the surrounding area. Over the last 2000 years they have shaped a technical and architectural masterpiece with bare hands and primitive tools. The imposing terraced landscape was constructed step by step from the bottoms of the valleys up to heights of 1000 metres or more. These are productive rice fields with a perfectly functioning irrigation system on the steep mountain slopes. The boundary walls have a total length of about 20,000 km. From this measurement the rice terraces of the Ifugao exceed by far those of the Bontoc and Kalinga. They are often jus-

Ibaloy House

Ifugao House

tifiably referred to as the eighth wonder of the world.

The life of the Ifugao is full of ceremonies and celebrations at which *tapuy*, a rice wine, plays an important part, whether it's at a funeral or at the carving up of a wild pig brought in by the hunters. They originally learned the rice wine manufacturing process from Chinese traders. Rice harvested under the full moon is preferred, and, in order to accelerate the process of fermentation, the rice is partly boiled in fresh, clean water. After adding a minimal quantity of sugar, the promising pot contents are emptied into an earthenware vessel, sealed and left for six months to ripen. After this period, the Ifugao can enjoy themselves over a pleasant-tasting tapuy (see the Food & Drink section in the Facts for the Visitor chapter). It is also possible that an undrinkable, sour liquid will result from mistakes made in the manufacturing process.

The Ifugao build their houses on piles; the windowless space under the pyramid-shaped roof is used as a bedroom, kitchen and storeroom. In order to please the gods, the skull of a sacrificed pig is fixed on the outside of the house. The greatest occasion for the sacrifice of a pig is the return of a successful head-hunter.

For the Ifugao, too, head-hunting is a legitimate way of executing tribal judgements. For example, in October 1977, when an Ifugao youth was run over by a bus and fatally injured, the village council decreed that either the driver or a member of his family must die, and the execution was carried out. Ten years later the driver of a bus belonging to the Pantranco line caused a serious traffic accident with fatal consequences for several Ifugao near Banaue. When the bus company refused to admit responsibility for the deaths and injuries, axes were sharpened in the villages in question. After that no bus driver would drive into the Ifugao district for fear of getting an axe in his neck, and, until the last damages payment was made Pantranco had to hand over the last 50km section of the Manila to Banaue route to local jeepneys.

The *bangibang* (war dance) is a component of this traditional vengeance. Equipped with spears, shields and axes, the warriors dance on the walls of the rice fields, their heads adorned with *katlagang*, a form of headdress made of leaves. The person who will carry out the act of vengeance is determined by using a chicken. The warriors form a circle, kill a chicken and leave it to die in the circle. The one chosen is the one closest to the chicken when it finally comes to rest after its final death throes.

Ilokano The Ilokano are of Malay ancestry. About 200 to 300 BC they came through Borneo, Palawan and Mindoro to Luzon where they settled. The most significant part of the group settled the coastal strips and the adjoining mountain regions in northern and north-western Luzon.

Already settled ethnic groups like the Isnega and Tingguian could not resist the new wave of immigration and were pushed into the hinterlands. Before the Ilokano were confronted with Christian beliefs, they had a multitiered and complicated system of gods and spirits. Only fragments of their superstitions have persisted, however, and these are mainly ornamental – such as amulets and lucky charms which are generally only worn by the inhabitants of outlying Ilokano villages.

Kalinga Houses

Kalinga The Kalinga live north of the Bontoc. They are also head-hunters. Wars and head-hunting expeditions have been largely restricted through the peace pact, *budong*, which they have worked out. This treaty declares above all that a Kalinga whose honour has been impugned does not lose the respect of the tribe if, instead of beheading the enemy, he accepts a water buffalo, for example, as payment. A significant effect of this ruling is the initiation of social and family ties between different groups.

Like the Bontoc, the Kalinga also have a house for the men and village elders. They call it *dapay*. However, there is not a typical house for marriageable girls and women. It can be any house and is indistinguishable from the others from the outside; the Kalinga name for it is the *ebgan*. Here the evening courtship takes place, the initiation songs are sung, stories told or flutes played. Successful suitors spend the night with their women in the ebgan and both partners have the opportunity to consider a common future together. If they decide to separate, the event of a pregnancy is no hindrance as there are no disadvantages for the parents or the child, who is later declared legitimate by the tribal community.

A marriage is prepared for over a long period by different ritual acts. Earthquakes, landslides and other bad omens can draw out the required ceremonies for months. When all the formalities have at last been accomplished, a house is built for the engaged couple. According to Kalinga tradition, marriages can only be celebrated in the Dadawak (the season for marriages) months of March, September or October.

Mandaya & Mansaka The Mandaya live in the north-eastern and south-eastern part of Davao del Norte on Mindanao. Mandaya means 'inhabitant of the highlands'. The Mansaka are classified ethnologically with the Mandaya. They were originally highland people who settled in clearings deep in the mountains, though today many Mansaka live in the eastern coastal regions of Davao Bay.

Animism is strongly practised by both groups, as demonstrated by the many idols carved out of wood which stand in their houses and fields. Also noteworthy are the numerous examples of silver work. Hardly any other ethnic group would use more silver to produce ornaments than the Mandaya. Even more striking than the ear adornments and finger rings are the large round chain pendants which are worn by men and women and are frequently made from coins.

Mangyan Over 50,000 Mangyan live on Mindoro. The majority of them live in the dense jungles of the mountainous interior. The Mangyan are subdivided into the Iraya, Hanunoo, Alangan, Tadyawan, Batangan, Buhid and Ratagnon.

In earlier times the majority of the Mangyan lived and fished along the coast, but later they retreated to the hills, changed their lifestyle and took up agriculture. They did not go there of their own free will but were driven back by new settlers. In their culture land belongs to everyone. If someone approaches them with deeds of title, these peace-loving people simply withdraw.

Despite the inevitable influences of civilisation, the traditions and culture of the Mangyan have survived. Distances are measured in *yells* (screams), which is the distance over which one scream is audible.

In the south of Mindoro there are settled Hanunoo who are often referred to as 'true Mangyan'. They have their own form of writing in an elaborate syllabic script. Hanunoo means 'real' and 'true'. They also have their own postal system. If they want to send messages across great distances, they carve the text into a piece of bamboo and place it into a particular bamboo post. These 'post boxes' are spread over the entire area in specially designated or well-known positions. If the Mangyan come across one of them they read all the letters and deliver those with destinations which are on their route, either personally or by placing them in a more advantageous 'post box'.

The *ambahan*, the stories told by the Mangyan, are also recorded by being carved in bamboo. A typical ambahan has each line made up of seven syllables. These poems are of a social nature. Thus they may be read to children to discipline them, or they may be given to an adult to read in cases where speaking directly with the person may be embarrassing or painful.

Maranao The province of Lanao del Sur in the north of Mindanao is the homeland of the Maranao (or Maranaw). They are the 'people of the lake' – Lake Lanao. Of all the Philippine Muslim groups, the Maranao were the last to be converted to Islam. They successfully defended themselves against all colonisation attempts by the Spaniards and Americans, for which their natural environment provided a not inconsiderable protection. Their culture and religion have both developed without interference.

Today the Maranao are concerned with preserving and maintaining their cultural identity. Marawi, lying on the northern tip of Lake Lanao, is an important spiritual centre for Muslims. Several Islamic-oriented schools and the Mindanao State University (MSU), a southern branch of the University of the Philippines, are here.

Maranao are skilled artisans and capable merchants. Cloth, wood and metal work collectively is the second most important sector of their economy; only agriculture is more important. They have a leading position in the country in the production of brass work.

Negrito There are said to be 15,000 to 50,000 pure Negrito living in the Philippines; estimates vary wildly. The number for people with Negrito blood in them, including those of mixed race, would obviously turn out much higher.

The various Negrito groups call themselves names like Agta, Alta, Ita, Ati, Ata and Aeta, which all mean 'man' or 'person'. They live dispersed over many islands but are principally found in eastern Luzon. They can be readily distinguished from all other Filipinos by their physical characteristics: they are darker and rarely taller than 1½ metres. Their hair is short and woolly-crinkly, often decorated with a bamboo ornament. Sometimes they still wear scanty clothing made out of tree bark.

The Negrito are nomads and only a few of them have settled in one place. Instead of living in solid houses, they live in huts built from twigs, branches, foliage and grass. Sometimes they lay out small fields in which they plant sweet potatoes, rice and vegetables; they also hunt and gather fruit. Bows and poison-tipped arrows are their weapons.

Seafaring Negrito are called Dumagat. You meet them occasionally on secluded beaches on the Pacific coast of North Luzon, where they settle temporarily in hastily built huts.

The Negrito do not have laws, nor do they feel themselves bound to any authority. When decisions have to be made, the decision of the head of the family is accepted and followed.

Pala'wan The Pala'wan live in the highlands of south Palawan. Their villages consist of three to 12 houses. They are led by a number of *panlima*, who are administrators and are also meant to help maintain the peace. The Pala'wan's religion has been influenced by Hindu and Islamic elements. The highest deity is Ampo, who is believed to pass on responsibility for the regulation of the affairs of humanity to his subordinate gods, the *diwats*. The practice of the religion also includes social activities such as communal dancing, singing and drinking of rice wine. A marriage is only agreed upon after lengthy negotiations between the two families concerned and is often arranged when the couple are still children.

Tasaday The Tasaday live in the mountains deep within the tropical rainforest of South Cotabato Province on Mindanao. The discovery of the Tasaday by the outside world has caused considerable controversy.

They were first discovered in the early 1960s by a hunter named Dafal, but the first 'official' meeting didn't take place until June 1971. Their good health was remarkable; from the dawn of time until their discovery, these seminaked cave and forest dwellers lived only on the fruit they gathered and the fish, frogs, tadpoles and crabs they caught. They had not yet discovered hunting or agriculture and used only primitive stone tools.

Because of their isolation, at least 50,000 years of evolution had completely passed by them. According to some reports, the 25 clan members had no contact at all with the outside world until they met Dafal. They did not even know of the existence of other groups of people outside their forest. It's worth reading John Nance's book *The Gentle Tasaday* (Harcourt Brace Jovanovich, New York, 1975; Victor Gallancz, London, 1975), which offers a fascinating eyewitness account with many photos.

However, in early 1986, Dr Oswald Iten of Switzerland, *Stern* reporter Walter Unger and Jay Ullal published some disconcerting revelations suggesting that the sensational discovery of the Tasaday had been nothing but a publicity stunt cleverly staged by Manuel Elizalde, who at the time was chief of Presidential Assistance on National Minorities (PANAMIN; the bureau has since been disbanded).

It was quite a pickle for everyone involved. Scholars and journalists from all over the world who had been convinced that the Tasaday were genuine demanded further proof and explanations. The Department of Anthropology convened an ultimately inconclusive symposium, and only a testimonial issued by the Filipino Congress, which had arranged for some Tasaday to be flown to Manila in order to clarify the question, could bring about a provisional settling of the heated debate. The authenticity of the Tasaday as an ethnic group was then officially confirmed by the highest government authorities. The most recent confirmation of the authenticity of the Tasaday was presented at the International Congress of Anthropological & Ethnological Sciences in early 1992 in Washington, DC.

Tausug The majority of Tausug live on the island of Jolo in the Sulu archipelago. They describe themselves as 'people in the current' and were the first in the Philippines to accept Islam. Nevertheless, traditional customs are still maintained. Thus a Tausug wedding, *pagtiaun*, is among the richest, most colourful festivals celebrated anywhere on the Sulu Islands. The ceremonies and celebrations last a week. An important part of the activity is the *pangalag*, a wedding dance to the sound of gongs and drums.

The Tausug love freedom and are proud of their bravery. They are renowned as skilled seafarers, diligent traders and excellent business people. Prosperity and pride have helped make the Tausug the dominant tribe from Zamboanga to Sitangkai. Their cultural wealth is exhibited through their dress, the architecture of their houses and in the style of their brass artefacts, jewellery and weapons.

Tau't Batu The Tau't Batu are referred to as 'people of the rock'. They live in caves in the Signapan Basin, north-west of Mt Mantalingajan, the highest peak in Palawan. They only leave their caves to hunt, gather fruit or harvest cassava and rice in unobtrusive fields. Other sources of nutrition, such as bats and birds, are found inside the caves. Their belief demands that nature be compensated for the death of any of the animals. Animals which have been killed will therefore be replaced by a representation in stone or wood.

A particular social custom is *bulun-bulun*, the communal living of several families brought about through the necessity to share nourishment. The Tau't Batu were not officially discovered until 1978. In order to protect the lifestyle and habitat of this peaceful group, the Signapan Basin has been declared off limits to outsiders and this is strictly enforced.

T'boli An estimated 60,000 T'boli live in about 2000 sq km in the south-western corner of Mindanao. The area is known as the Tiruray Highlands and their culture is centred in the triangle formed by the villages

Girdle (Buckle)

of Surallah, Polomolok and Kiamba, near Lake Sebu.

The T'boli do not have a village community structure. They live in houses set well apart from each other along the ridges of the highlands. In some cases, when there are close family ties, three or four houses are clustered together. Called long houses, or more colloquially, *gunu bong*, they stand on two-metre-high posts and are about 15 metres long and 10 metres wide. The T'boli are monogamous people, but polygamy is allowed and is sometimes practised by the more prosperous as a status symbol.

T'boli women have a passion for decoration and adorn themselves with ornamental combs, earrings, necklaces and chains, arm and foot bracelets, finger and toe rings and heavy, bell belts. You seldom see one without a head covering, either a *kayab*, originally a turban of abaca, more often today a simple towel; or a colourful *s'laong kinibang*, a large, round hat with a diameter of about half a metre. The traditional clothing of both men and women consists of *t'nalak* – a material woven from abaca with a dark brown background lightened by red and beige designs. It takes several months to weave, but the weaving of the *kumo*, the wedding dress, takes even longer. This typical metre-long T'boli covering has great significance in the wedding ceremony.

Yakan The Yakan mainly live on Basilan Island in the south of the Philippines,

T'boli Long House

although some have settled near Zamboanga on Mindanao. They are peace-loving Muslims who live by agriculture and cattle breeding. The most important house in a village is the *langgal*, or prayer house, which is run by an imam. All larger annual ceremonies take place here, too. Absolutely essential elements to any festival are music and games, with water buffalo fights being particularly thrilling.

The Yakan are famous as exceptional weavers. A part of their unusual traditional clothing is the *kandit*, a red belt several metres long which is wrapped around the hips to hold up skintight trousers. Adornments men wear include a colourful turban known as a *pis*, or a helmet-shaped hat called a *saruk*. Old women can still be found with overlong artificial fingernails known as *suploh*.

Warning Before you go into areas set aside for the indigenous people, please examine your motives carefully. If you just want to 'check out the natives' and take pictures for your slide night, you are very misguided. You won't be welcome, and will recognise this fact fairly promptly.

Most cultural minorities are quite friendly to strangers and foreigners. Should you be invited to eat with them, don't refuse without good (for example, religious) reasons, as it could be taken as an insult to the host. On the other hand don't eat too much as the first invitation is usually followed by a second, then a third and so on. If they sing a song for you in the evening, you should have a song on hand to sing in return. Saying that you can't sing or don't know any songs will not get you off the hook as they won't believe you. A song book may be useful if you intend visiting many minorities.

Don't refer to Muslims as Moro. The tag 'Moro' was first used by Spaniards who viewed the Muslims with contempt, probably because the Spaniards resented not being able to bring them under their yoke, as they did with the other population groups. Although many Muslims today proudly name themselves Moro, there are still some who feel discriminated against when a foreigner calls them by this name.

ARTS & CULTURE

The Philippines has developed a mixed culture from the historical blending of foreign influences with native elements. Today the Muslims and some of the isolated tribes are the only people whose culture remains unadulterated by Spanish and American influences. The ability of the Filipinos to improvise and copy is very apparent: you

---

Miss Philippines

In no other country are there so many beauty contests as on the Philippines, where the cult status of women has deep roots in Filipino culture. 'Miss' contests are a social event here, beauty queens are respected, admired and feted as celebrities wherever they go. It is said that Filipinas are amongst the most beautiful women in the world.

In the struggle for emancipation Filipinas have not modelled themselves on men's behaviour, but have sensitively and skilfully retained their femininity, which by no means implies accepting men's claim to superiority. So the Filipina not only rules the roost in the family and at home, but confidently wields power when in public office and has considerable influence in the workplace and the business world.

In the interest of getting to the top of the career ladder as quickly as possible, ambitious and beautiful young women of all social backgrounds exploit their own appearance and intelligence by presenting themselves to the public and judges in scores of beauty contests. The bigger contests at national level are always attended by VIPs, who often sit on the jury as well. Apart from good looks, a candidate in the battle for the crown and a chance at the honour of being voted the 'fairest of them all' has to be of a minimum height and be able to produce at least a high school leaving certificate. ■

need only see how the army jeeps left by the Americans were converted into colourful, shining-chrome taxis through painstaking, detailed work before the Filipinos began the serial production of these vehicles themselves.

What would a Philippine townscape be like without these unusual jeepneys? In Metro Manila about 40,000 'discos on wheels' are registered. But since 1980 most of the loudspeakers have been silenced because the 'stereo disco sound' was banned by the state. It's also rumoured that jeepneys will be replaced by the gradual introduction of buses. Something will then be missing – just as the loud, pounding rhythm of the disco music is already missing.

Pop and folk music from the West is perfectly imitated by the local bands, which is one reason why Filipino musicians are in great demand in South-East Asia from Jakarta all the way to Tokyo.

The small gallery shops in the tourist belt of Ermita reflect the high level of Filipino painting: from impressionism to realism virtually all styles are represented. Handicrafts of natural fibres, shells, brass and wood show the technical and formal crafts and the abilities of these talented people.

The ideas of the New Society propagated by Marcos really caught the national consciousness of the Filipinos in the 1970s, just as People Power did in the 1980s. People recollected their cultural heritage and began to care about their traditional arts and crafts. Consequently, the national language is strongly used today in theatre and literature and *kundimans* – romantic and sentimental love songs – are popular again. The good old folk dances, foremost among them the national dance *tinikling*, have even become a new tourist attraction. Well-known dance troupes such as Barangay, Bayanihan, Filipinescas or Karilagan have even found a spot on popular TV shows. The most successful interpreters of Philippine folk songs are the Mabuhay Singers.

National Clothing

For men, there is no obligation to wear either a tie or a suit, even at highly official political receptions. The *barong tagalog* is the sensible alternative: it is a long-sleeved shirt which lets the air through and is worn over the trousers. Underneath, it is customary to wear a T-shirt. The short-sleeved style is known as a *polo barong*. These cool, semi-transparent shirts with their fine embroidery date from the Spanish era when Filipinos were required to wear their shirts untucked, and the barong became a symbol of national consciousness. Fine barongs are made from *piña*, a fibre from the pineapple plant. The *terno* is the typical Philippine dress worn by women, recognisable by its stiff butterfly sleeves. It is only worn on formal occasions. The general fashion for women follows Western trends.

Cinema

Filipino films are produced in great number, dealing mainly with variations on the themes of violence and clichéd love stories. Productions like *Mababangong Bangungot* by Kidlat Tahimik are rare. This socially critical film was screened overseas under the title *The Perfumed Nightmare*.

In January 1981 the first film festival in Manila took place at the Philippines International Convention Center. After the success of this trial run and both first official festivals of 1982 and 1983 in the specially built film theatre, the organisers hoped that the Manila International Film Festival (MIFF) would be recognised internationally as are the festivals in Cannes, Berlin and Venice and that these cities would send their representatives. But further MIFFs, for economic and probably political reasons, have not taken place.

Sports & Games

The Filipinos are sports enthusiasts. Basketball is their favourite sport and there has been a professional league since 1975. On the popularity scale, chess and boxing are near the top. Consequently, a lot of money was wagered on the outcome of the world heavyweight boxing championship in 1975 (when Mohammed Ali fought Joe Frazier in the 'thriller in Manila'), the World Basketball Championships in 1978 and the chess championship in 1978 (between Korshnoi and Karpov).

Tennis, golf, horse racing, bicycle races and motor racing do have some followers, but are not in the category of a national sport. As a team sport in schools, volleyball is second in popularity to basketball.

Only rarely will you see a game of the once popular *sipa* being played. It's a game played with a plaited rattan ball which is kicked over a net using feet, knees, elbows or the head (a similar idea to volleyball). It is now only played in a few areas in Mindanao and occasionally in Rizal Park in Manila.

The real passion is reserved for games that involve betting. Those who wish to bet on Sunday and public holidays can go to a *sabong* (cockfight). The fights take place in a wooden arena known as a cockpit and there is great activity as early as 8 am. Before each fight several *kristos* (bookkeepers) come into the ring to encourage the spectators to part with their money and to take the bets. They use a sign language for betting and, amazingly, nothing is noted down – it's all committed to memory. Four fingers raised means P40, horizontal fingers signify hundreds and fingers pointed downwards means thousands – but check this first if you intend to participate!

While bets are being taken, the very expensive cocks are brought out and stirred up for the fight. Like boxers they fight in different weight classes. Each cock is equipped with a razor- sharp spur fastened behind the leg. This deadly spur usually brings a fight to an end after a few seconds. A 'non-pro', injured or sickly cock must be pecked twice by the winner. Only then is the fight officially over. Should the champion cock choose not to perform this concluding rite, the fight may be declared a draw. Wounded cocks are 'patched up' by experts behind the cockpit; the dead ones end up in the pot.

Filipinos & Foreigners

You can't blame the Filipinos if they are sceptical and distant towards foreigners. As history shows, foreigners have generally not come to the Philippines with friendly intentions. In spite of this, every visitor is heartily welcomed: the Filipinos are very sociable and tolerant and their natural openness surprises many visitors.

There is much to be learned by citizens of industrialised nations who like to be alone. Leisure hours which you may want to spend alone in a restaurant or pub will have to be given up. Chatty people ready to ask questions are always close at hand, especially if there is a possibility of alcohol.

It is very difficult for most foreigners to understand the psyche of the Filipino, especially, for example, when the Filipino may risk a possible 'loss of face' – a painful and embarrassing situation which the Filipino will try to avoid. As a result, they may give out completely false information quite comfortably rather than admit they don't know. Or they will just grin at you benignly pretending they didn't understand your question.

Even if a particular idiosyncrasy of the Filipinos is unpleasant or uncomfortable, you shouldn't become belligerent. You will achieve a lot more by being polite or sharing a joke. Foreigners who indulge in exaggerated reticence, arrogance or who take the opportunity to lord it over the locals financially or culturally, will never find a friend in the Philippines. They will have to make do with being ignored or mistreated.

Just like everywhere else, there are also black sheep amongst the Filipinos. For important information on this see Dangers & Annoyances in the Facts for the Visitor chapter.

Filipinos are strongly oriented towards the outside world. As a rule they don't place much store by anything produced in their own country. Imported wares are always in much greater demand than the best locally made products. They'll only make exceptions in the case of 'export quality' goods manufactured in the Philippines, which, though intended for sale abroad, sometimes appear on the local market. Try telling Filipinos that we foreigners often keep our best quality products for ourselves and export cheaper stuff far and wide and they'll stare at you in disbelief: what next!

Nevertheless, Filipino national pride is not to be underestimated. Of course they are aware that there are serious problems in their country, but they are still not prepared to listen to foreign visitors pointing those problems out and attempting to voice their criticism. This is true above all for politics.

One thing Filipinos and foreigners have in common is the discovery of the Philippines as a tourist centre. Most Filipinos know very little about their own country. There are chiefly financial and geographical reasons for this, but there's also the traditional lack of interest in one's neighbouring island. When people have the money, they prefer to fly to Hong Kong or Europe for shopping and sightseeing, or if possible go to the USA. Until recently the slogan 'See the Philippines first' was hardly able to attract a single travel-happy Filipino. But now the situation has changed noticeably. With so many foreigners streaming into the country, travelling around and to all appearances having a fine time, Filipinos are becoming curious about their long-ignored homeland. After all, if outsiders are so attracted to the islands, there must be something worth seeing.

Gifts You can bring a lot of happiness to children and adults in the Philippines through small tokens of appreciation, so take some small things to give such as ballpoint pens, cigarettes, lighters, stickers, photos of yourself or bottles of perfume and other obvious imports (possibly with well-known trademarks clearly displayed).

Filipinos are very inquisitive and interested in where the visitor comes from and what it's like there. To show them, or to offer them a gift in return for hospitality you have received, you can make good use of postcards from your country. People also like to look at pictures of your home, family,

animals and plants. These things are good conversation starters.

You will be well liked if you're friendly – it doesn't cost anything. There's a fine local saying: 'A smile gives more light than electricity'.

RELIGION

The Philippines is unique for being the only Christian country in Asia – over 90% of the population claim to be Christian, more than 80% of whom are Roman Catholic. The Spanish did a thorough job!

Largest of the minority religious groups are the Muslims (about 8%) who are found chiefly on the island of Mindanao and along the Sulu archipelago. When the Spanish arrived toting their cross, the Muslims were just getting a toehold in the region. In the northern islands their influence was only small and was easily displaced, but in the south, the people had been firmly converted and Christianity was never able to make a strong impression.

About 4% of Filipinos belong to the Philippine Independent Church, which was founded by Gregorio Aglipay in 1902 as a nationalist Catholic church. The Iglesia ni Kristo is the largest community of Protestant believers, to which 4% of the population belongs. Baptists, Methodists, Mormons, Jehovah's Witnesses and members of other religious groups and sects make up about 2%. Except for a tiny percentage of Buddhist believers, the remainder of the population are animists.

LANGUAGE
History

Historically, the waves of immigration of alien peoples (Indonesians, Chinese, Malays etc) and the structure of the country (a series of islands) have brought about a multiplicity of languages and language groups. Today there are about 80 significantly different dialects spoken.

During the period of Spanish occupation, Spanish was taught in schools and, since education is mainly a prerogative of the wealthy, it developed as the language of politicians and the business community. Though small, the influence of Spanish on the local languages is still present today (for instance, in the numerical system and in the Zamboangan language in Chavacano). Spanish was abolished in 1968 as a compulsory subject in higher schools, but is still the mother tongue of a small percentage of the population, mainly the upper class.

Since in an occupied country the language of the colonial overlord often dominates, English became very important with the beginning of the US era. Since the declaration of total independence from the USA in 1946, English has remained the language of commerce and politics in the Philippines. Newspapers, TV, radio announcements and even government statistics are evidence of this.

A National Language The concept of a national language was formed after the Spanish-American War in 1898, but it wasn't until 1936, a year after the formation of the Philippines Commonwealth, that the Institute of National Language was established. President Manuel Quezon declared Tagalog the national language in that year and the appropriate bill was incorporated into the Philippine constitution in 1946.

There were several other contenders for the role of the main language in this multi-lingual country – among them Cebuano, Hiligaynon and Ilocano. The compromises reached during the 1970s still hold; the constitution of 1973 confirms Filipino as the main language. It is based on Tagalog but contains certain linguistic elements from the other Philippine languages. Since 1978 Filipino has been taught in schools and universities.

Gestures & Signs
As well as the spoken and written language, the Filipinos use various gestures and signs. The hand movements which mean 'go away' to us signify 'come here' in the Philippines. The brief raising of the eyebrows is generally meant positively. One hisses to gain attention, for example, when calling one of the

waiters in a restaurant. The thumb is not used to indicate numbers; you indicate two beers, for example, always with the ring finger and the little finger; using your middle finger could get you into trouble. Instead of pointing with your finger, you indicate discreetly by pointing pursed lips in the direction you want. Incidentally, in a *turo-turo* restaurant (turo means 'point') there is no menu: the food is displayed and customers point to what they would like to eat. When you want to pay the bill, look out for one of the waiters and draw a rectangle in the air with your index finger and thumb. Should the waiter or waitress be looking the other way, just hiss briefly. If Filipinos don't understand a question, they open their mouths.

Communicating
It is not vital to know the local language, as English will get you through most situations, but as in any country, locals will be pleased and surprised if you have learned even a few fragments of their language. The following may help.

Some Notes on Pronunciation
In Filipino *p* and *f* are often interchanged (Filipino = Pilipino). This means that a written *p* can be pronounced as an *f*. This interchange is sometimes carried over into English by Filipinos (April = Afril) but it in no way impairs understanding.

A *w* written in Filipino is often pronounced as a *u* (Banawe = Banaue, ikaw = ikau). Double vowels are pronounced separately (paalam = pa-alam). The combination *ng* is pronounced 'nang' and *mga* is pronounced 'manga'.

The syllable *po* underlines courtesy towards elders and persons of respect (eg, *Salámat po Ginang Santos*, Thank you Mrs Santos).

Filipino
In the words and phrases below, an accent over the vowel of a syllable means that this syllable is stressed. There is sometimes more than one word given in Filipino.

Some Useful Words & Phrases

and	*at*
who (singular)	*síno*
who (plural)	*sinu-síno*
how	*paáno*
what	*anó*
when	*kailán*
why	*bákit*
How many?	*Ilán?*
How much?	*Gaáno, magkáno?*

People & Pronouns

man	*laláki, laláke*
woman	*babáe*
Mr	*Ginoó*
Mr Santos	*Ginoóng Santos*
Mrs	*Gínang*
Mrs Santos	*Gínang Santos*
Miss	*Binibíni*
Miss Santos	*Binibíning Santos*
child (general)	*batá*
child (own)	*anák*
boy	*bátang laláki*
girl	*bátang babáe*
grandmother/grand-father	*lóla/lólo*
friend	*kaibígan*
unmarried man	*binatà*
unmarried woman	*dalága*

I	*akó*
you	*ka, ikáw*
he/she	*siyá*
they	*silá*
we (I and you)	*táyo*
we (I and others)	*kamí*
you (plural)	*kayó*

old	*matandá*
young	*batá*
tall	*mataás*
short	*pandák*
happy	*maligáya*
sad	*malungkót*
intelligent	*matalíno*
drunken	*lasíng*
handsome, pretty	*pógi, guwápo/a*
ugly	*pángit*

Greetings & Civilities

hello, greetings	*mabúhay*
good morning	*magandáng umága*
good day	*magandáng tanghalí*
good afternoon	*magandáng hápon*
good night	*magandáng gabí*
goodbye	*paálam, adyós*
'bye	*bay*
thank you	*salámat*
thank you very much	*maráming salamat*
please	*pakí*
yes/no	*oó/hindí*
yes/no (polite)	*opó/hindí po*
OK	*síge*
excuse me	*ipagpaumanhín*
only, merely, simply	*lang (lamang)*
again, similarly	*namán*
always, of course	*siyémpre*
good/well	*mabúti*
also good/well	*mabúti rin*
You're welcome.	*Waláng anumán.*
Just a minute.	*Sandalí lang.*
No problem.	*Waláng probléma.*
It's all right.	*Ayós ang lahát.*

How are you?
  Kumustá (ka)?
How are you? (plural)
  Kumustá (po) kayó?
Well, thank you, and you?
  Mabúti salámat, at ikáw?
Where have you been?
  Saán ka gáling?
Where are you going?
  Saán ka pupuntá?
I'm coming from Talisay.
  Gáling akó sa Talisay.
I'm going to Bato.
  Pupuntá akó sa Bato.

Small Talk

Do you have...?
  Mayroón...?
What did you say?
  Anó po?
Who is there?
  Síno iyán?

What is your name?
Anóng pangálan mo?
How old are you?
Iláng taón ka na?
Where do you come from?
Tagásaáng bayán ka?
You are beautiful!
Magandá ka!
I like you.
Gustó kitá.
Never mind.
Hindí bále.
I don't know.
Áywan ko (hindí ko alam).
Let's go.
Táyo na (síge na).
I like (that).
Gustó ko (itó).
I don't like...
Ayaw ko...
I'll do it (I'll get it).
Akó na lang.
You do it (You get it).
Ikáw na lang.
Come here.
Halíka díto.
What a pity.
Sáyang.
It's too late.
Hulí na.
I have no time.
Walá akóng panahón.
Later on.
Mamayá.
Are you sure?
Siguradó ka ba?
That's not true (flatterer).
Boléro.
It's none of your business.
Walá kang pakíalam.
Get lost!
Alís diyán!
not yet
walá pa
maybe/perhaps
sigúro
really
talagá
fool
gágo (ka)

crazy, mad
lóko-lóko
rude, insolent
bastós
braggart
mayábang

Getting Around
left/right	*kaliwá/kánan*
straight on	*dirétso*
back	*pauróng (pabalík)*
here/there	*díto/diyán, doón*
near/far	*malápit/malayó*
turn-off	*lumikó*
stop	*pára*
aeroplane	*eropláno*
ship	*barkó*
boat	*bangká*
bus	*bus*
car	*kótse*
taxi	*taksi*
tricycle	*traysikel*
village	*báryo*
town/city	*bayán/lungsód*
road	*daán, kálye*
street corner	*kanto*
bus station	*estasyón ng bus*
airport	*airport*
petrol station	*estasyón ng gas*
police station	*estasyón ng pulis*
embassy	*embassi*
island	*puló*
ocean, sea	*dágat*
bay	*loók*
coast, shore	*tabíng-dágat*
beach	*baybáy*
river	*ílog*
river mouth	*wáwa*
lake	*láwa*
creek	*sápa*
waterfall	*talón*
hill	*buról*
mountain	*bundók*
forest, jungle	*kagubátan*
entrance	*pasukán*
exit	*lábasan*

open	*bukás*
closed	*sarádo*

where	
saán	
How far is it?	
Gaáno malayo?	
Where is the post office?	
Saán ang koréyo?	
Which is the bus for Manila?	
Alíng bus ang papuntáng Mayníla?	
Where is the bus stop?	
Saán ang hintáyan ng bus?	
Where do I catch the jeepney?	
Saán ang sasakay ng jeepney?	
Where does this bus go?	
Saán papuntá ang bus na itó?	
Where do I get off?	
Saán akó dapát babá?	
How much is the fare?	
Magkáno ang pamasáhe?	
What town is this?	
Anóng báyan íto?	
How many km to...?	
Ilán ang kilometro hanggáng...?	

Accommodation

hotel	*otél*
room	*kuwárto*
key	*susí*
bathroom	*bányo*
bed	*káma*
blanket, cover	*kubrekáma*
pillow	*únan*
mosquito net	*kulambó*
toilet	*kubíta*

room with bath	
kuwárto na may bányo	
Do you have air-con?	
Mayroón bang air-condition?	
There is no water.	
Waláng túbig.	
How much is a room?	
Magkáno ang isáng kuwárto?	
I'll take the room.	
Síge kukúnin ko ang kuwártong itó.	

Food & Drink

food, meal	*pagkaín*
breakfast	*almusál*
lunch	*panánghalían*
dinner	*hapúnan*

plate	*pláto*
knife	*kutsílyo*
fork	*tinidór*
spoon	*kutsára*
teaspoon	*kutsaríta*
glass	*báso*
cup	*tása*
serviette/napkin	*serbilyéta*

rice (uncooked)	*bigás*
rice (cooked)	*kánin*
fish	*isdá*
meat	*karné*
chicken	*manók*
soup	*sabáw*
salad	*insaláda*
vegetables	*gúlay*
potato/sweet potato	*patátas/kamóte*
onion	*sibúyas*
egg	*ítlog*
fried egg	*prítong ítlog*
soft-boiled egg	*malasádong ítlog*
bread	*tinápay*
peanut	*maní*

sugar	*asúkal*
salt	*ásin*
pepper (grains)	*pamintá*
pepper (powdered)	*pamintáng duróg*
garlic	*báwang*
onion	*sibúyas*
soy sauce	*toyó*
vinegar	*suká*

apple	*mansánas*
banana	*ságing*
coconut (ripe)	*niyog*
coconut (young)	*bukó*
guava	*bayábas*
jackfruit	*langká*
mango	*manggá*
orange	*kahél*
papaya	*papáya*
pineapple	*pinyá*

water	*túbig*
beer	*serbésa*
wine	*alak*
coffee	*kapé*
black coffee	*kapéng matápang*
milk	*gátas*
tea	*tsa*
ice, ice cubes	*yelo*
hot	*mainít*
cold	*malamíg*
sweet	*matamís*
sour	*maásim*
spicy	*maánghâng*
salty	*inasnán*
spoiled	*sirá*
delicious	*masaráp*

I am hungry.
  Gutóm akó.
I am thirsty.
  Naúuhaw akó.
I am full.
  Busóg pa akó.
I have no appetite.
  Walá akóng gana.
It is cold.
  Malamíg íto.
I want rice & fish.
  Gústo ko ng kánin at isdá.
That was a good meal.
  Ang saráp ng pagkaín.
How much is one coffee?
  Magkáno isáng kapé?
bill
  chit or *kuwénta*
The bill please.
  Ákina ang kuwénta ko (magkáno).

Shopping

money	*péra*
expensive/cheap	*mahál/múra*
too expensive	*masyádong mahál*
big/small	*malakí/maliít*
old/new (things)	*lumá/bágo*
many/all	*marámi/lahát*
several, few	*kauntí*
broken, destroyed	*sirá*
more	*kauntí pa*
less	*tamá na*

How much is this? (touch)
  Magkáno itó?
How much is this? (point)
  Magkáno iyán?
What is this/that?
  Ano itó?
When will it be ready?
  Kailán matatápos?
Do you have/is there...?
  Mayroón...?
Do you have any...?
  Mayroón ba kayong...?
Do you have anything cheaper?
  Mayroón bang mas múra?

Time & Dates

today	*ngayón*
tomorrow	*búkas*
every day	*áraw-áraw*
every night	*gabí-gabí*
tonight	*ngayóng gabí*
last night	*kahapong gabí*
anytime	*maski kailán*
a day	*isáng áraw*
a night	*isáng gabí*
day & night	*áraw-gabí*
every Thursday	*túwing Huwébes*
every afternoon	*túwing hápon*
yesterday	*kahápon*
day before yester-day	*noóng kamakalawá*
day after tomorrow	*sa makalawá*
What time is it?	*Anóng óras na?*

week
  linggó
last week
  noóng nakaraáng linggó
this week
  ngayóng linggóng itó
next week
  sa linggóng darating
month
  buwán
a month
  isáng buwán
this month
  ngayóng buwáng itó

year	
taón	
a year	
isáng taón	
every year	
taón-taón	
last year	
nakaraáng taón (nagdáan na taón)	
next year	
sa sunód sa taón	

Numbers

0	*walá*
1	*isá*
2	*dalawá*
3	*tatló*
4	*apát*
5	*limá*
6	*ánim*
7	*pitó*
8	*waló*
9	*siyám*
10	*sampú*
11	*labing-isá*
12	*labíndalawá*
13	*labíntatló*
20	*dalawampú*
21	*dalawampút isá*
22	*dalawampút dalawá*
30	*tatlumpú*
31	*tatlumpút isá*
40	*ápatnapú*
50	*limampú*
60	*ánimnapú*
70	*pitumpú*
80	*walampú*
90	*siyámnapú*
100	*isáng daán*
101	*isáng daán at isá*
200	*dalawáng daán*
201	*dalawáng daán at isá*
500	*limáng daán*
1000	*isáng libo*
5000	*limáng libo*

Days

Monday	*Lúnes*
Tuesday	*Martés*
Wednesday	*Miyérkoles*
Thursday	*Huwébes*
Friday	*Biyérnes*
Saturday	*Sábado*
Sunday	*Linggó*

Months

January	*Enéro*
February	*Pebréro*
March	*Márso*
April	*Abril*
May	*Máyo*
June	*Húnyo*
July	*Húlyo*
August	*Agósto*
September	*Setyémbre*
October	*Oktúbre*
November	*Nobyémbre*
December	*Disyémbre*

one kg	*isáng kilogram*
two pesos	*dalawáng píso*
three km	*tatlóng kilométro*
five litres	*limáng lítro*
10 cubic metres	*sampúng métro kúbiko*

one-half	*kalahatí*
one-third	*isáng-katló*
one-quarter	*isáng-kapat*

Weather

sun	*áraw*
clear, bright	*malinawág*
clouds, fog, mist	*úlap*
cloudy	*úlap, maúlap*
warm	*mainít*
cold	*malamíg*
lightning	*kídlat, lintík*
rain	*ulán*
rainy	*maulán*
thunder	*kulóg*
storm/typhoon	*bagyó*
wind	*hángin*
windy	*mahángin*

once	*minsan*
twice	*makálawá*
three times	*makatatló*
often	*madalás*
seldom	*bihirá*

For a more complete selection of phrases, basic vocabulary and grammar for travel in the Philippines, see Lonely Planet's *Pilipino Phrasebook*. A handy, easy-to-carry Filipino/English dictionary is *The New Dictionary* by Marie Odulio de Guzman (National Book Store, Manila, 1968).

An excellent Tagalog language course is available from Audio-Forum, 226 Foscote Mews, London, W9, England, UK. This extensive self-instructional language course, *Beginning Tagalog*, consists of 24 cassettes and two text books totalling 900 pages. It costs roughly UK£230.

Cebuano

Cebuano is the second most widely spoken language in the Philippines. It's spoken in the Visayas and in many parts of Mindanao.

Useful Words & Phrases

who (singular)	*kinsá*
who (plural)	*kinsá-kinsá*
how	*unsaón*
what	*unsa*
when	*kánus-a*
where	*asá*
why	*nganóng, ngáno*
How much?	*Tagpila, pila?*
What did you say?	*Unsa tó?*

People & Pronouns

man	*laláki*
woman	*babáye*
Mr	*Ginoó*
Mr Santos	*Ginoóng Santos*
Mrs	*Gínang*
Mrs Santos	*Gínang Santos*
Miss	*Dalága*
Miss Santos	*Dalagáng Santos*
grandmother/grandfather	*lolá/loló*
friend	*amígo/a*
unmarried man	*ulitawó, soltéro*
unmarried woman	*dalága, dalagíta*
child	*báta*
child (own)	*anák*
boy	*binatílo*
girl	*balagíta*

I	*akó*
you	*ikáw*
he/she	*siyá*
they	*silá*
we (I and you)	*kitá*
we (I and others)	*kamí*
you (plural)	*kamó*

old	*tigúlang*
young	*batán-on*
tall	*taás*
short	*mabú*
happy	*malipáyon*
sad	*magu-ol*
intelligent	*hawód*
handsome, pretty	*gwápo/a*
ugly	*ngíl-ad*

Greetings & Civilities

hello, greetings
 mabúhay
good morning
 maáyong búntag
good day
 maáyong udtó
good afternoon
 maáyong hápon
good night
 maáyong gabií
goodbye
 babáy, síge
thank you
 salámat
thank you very much
 daghán salámat
please
 palihóg
yes/no
 oó/díli
yes/no (polite)
 opó/dilagí
OK
 síge, síge taná
only, merely, simply
 lang
again, similarly
 napúd
always, of course
 siyémpre

no problem
walá probléma
It's all right.
Maáyo ang tanán.
good/well
maáyo
also good/well
maáyo sab/maáyo man
and
ug

You're welcome.
Waláy sapayán.
Just a minute.
Kadalí lang.
How are you?
Kumustá (na)?
How are you? (plural)
Kumustá (na) kamó?
Well, thank you, and you?
Maáyo man salámat, ug ikáw?
Where have you been?
Diín ka gíkan/Asá ka gíkan?
Where are you going?
Asá ka muadtó/Asá ka páingon?
I'm coming from Kalibo.
Gíkan ko sa Kalibo/Tayá Kalibo ko.
I'm going to Boracay.
Uadtó ko sa Boracay/Páigon ko sa Boracay.

Small Talk
Who is there?
Kinsá ná?
What is your name?
Unsay pangalan mo?
How old are you?
Píla na may ímong idad?
Where do you come from?
Tagá diíng lúgar ka?
I like you.
Gústo ko nimó.
Never mind.
Síge na lang.
I don't know.
Ámbot lang/Walá ko kahibaló.
Let's go.
Dalí na/Síge na.
I like (that).
Gustó ko (niána).

I don't like...
Díli gustó ko...
I'll do it/I'll get it.
Akó na lang.
You do it/You get it.
Ikáw na lang.
Come here.
Dalí díri.
What a pity.
Anugon.
It's too late.
Awáhi na.
I have no time.
Wa koy panáhon.
Later on.
Pagkátaud-taud.
Are you sure?
Siguradó ka ba?
not yet
walá pa
maybe/perhaps
tingáli
really
tínuod
That's not true (flatterer).
Boléro.
fool
búgok (ka), bangak
crazy, mad
lúku-lúko
rude, insolent
bastós
braggart
hambugéro, hambugéro
It's none of your business.
Walá kay labot.
Get lost!
Paháwa dihá!

Getting Around
left/right	*walá/tuó*
straight on	*dirétso*
back	*luyó, mobalík*
here/there	*dínhi/dínha, dídto*
near/far	*dúol/layó*
turn-off	*molikó, nilikó, likó*
stop	*pára*
aeroplane	*eropláne*
car	*kótse, sakyanán*
bus	*track, bus*

boat	*sakayán*
village	*báryo*
town/city	*lungsód/siyudád*
road	*dálan*
island	*puló*
ocean, sea	*dágat*
bay	*loók*
coast, shore	*hunásan*
beach	*baybáyon*
river	*subá*
river mouth	*bába sa subá*
lake	*línaw*
creek	*sápa*
waterfall	*busáy*
hill	*búngtod*
mountain	*búkid*
forest	*lasáng*

How far is it?
  Unsa kaláyo (layo)?
Where is the post office?
  Asá man ang post office?
Which bus for Cebu?
  Únsang bus ang maodtong Cebu?
Where is the bus stop?
  Asa man ang hulatán ug bus?
Where do I catch the jeepney?
  Asa ko musakay ug jeepney?
Where does this bus go?
  Asa man moadto kíning bus?
Where do I get off?
  Asa ko manaóg?
How much is the fare?
  Tagpíla ang pléte?

Accommodation

hotel	*otél*
room	*kuwárto*
bath	*bányo*
room with bath	*kuwárto nga anaáy bányo*
bed	*katré*
blanket, cover	*hábol*
key	*yáwi*
pillow	*únlan*
mosquito net	*muskitéro*
toilet	*kasílyas*

Do you have air-con?
  Nabáy air-condítion?
There is no water.
  Walá túbig.
How much is a room?
  Pilá ang usá ka kuwárto?
I'll take the room.
  Síge kuhaon ko ang kining kuwárto.

Food & Drink

food, meal	*pagkaón*
breakfast	*pamaháw*
lunch	*paniúdto*
dinner	*panihápon*
plate	*pláto*
knife	*kutsílyo*
fork	*tinidór*
spoon	*kutsára*
teaspoon	*kutsaríta*
glass	*báso*
cup	*tása*
serviette/napkin	*serbilyéta*
rice (uncooked)	*bugas*
rice (cooked)	*kanú*
fish	*isdá*
meat	*karné*
beef	*karnéng báka*
pork	*karnéng báboy*
chicken	*manók*
soup	*sabáw*
salad	*salad*
vegetables	*utan*
potato/sweet potato	*patátas/kamóte*
egg	*itlóg*
fried egg	*prítong ítlog*
soft-boiled egg	*malasádong ítlog*
bread	*tinapáy (pan)*
sugar	*asúkar*
salt	*ásin*
pepper (grains)	*pamintá (síli)*
pepper (powdered)	*pamintáng ginalíng*
garlic	*áhos*
onion	*sibúyas*
soy sauce	*toyó*
vinegar	*suká*
apple	*mansánas*
banana	*ságing*

coconut (ripe)	*lubi*
coconut (young)	*butóng*
guava	*bayábas*
jackfruit	*nangká*
mango	*manggá*
orange	*kahíl*
papaya	*kapáyas*
pineapple	*pinyá*

beer	*serbésa*
water	*túbig*
coffee	*kapé*
black coffee	*maisóg na kapé*
milk	*gátas*
tea	*tsaa*
ice, ice cubes	*ápa*

hot	*inít*
cold	*bugnáw*
sweet	*tamís*
sour	*aslum*
spicy	*hang*
salty	*parát*
delicious	*lamí*
spoiled	*pános*

I am hungry.
  Gigútom na akó/Gigútom ko.
I am thirsty.
  Guiháw ko/Guiháw na akó.
I am full.
  Busóg na akó/Busóg ko.
I have no appetite.
  Walá koy gana.
That was a good meal.
  Kalami sa pagkaón.
The bill please.
  Ang báyronon palíhog.

Shopping
money
  kuwárta
expensive/cheap
  mahál/baráto
too expensive
  kamahál, mahál kaáyo
big/small
  dako/gamáy
old/new (things)
  dáan/bágo

many/all
  dághan/tanán
several, few
  gamáy, diyútay
broken, destroyed
  gubá
less
  hustó na, diyutay
more
  gamáy pa

How much is this? (touch)
  Tagpíla na?
How much is this? (point)
  Tagpíla kaná?
What is this/that?
  Unsa ni?
When will it be ready?
  Kánus-a matápos?

Time & Dates
today
  karón
tomorrow
  ugma
every day
  káda ádlaw, ádlaw-ádlaw
every night
  káda gabií
last night
  kagabií
a day
  usá kaádlaw, úsang ádlaw
a night
  usá kagabií, úsang gabií
day & night
  ádlaw-gabií
every Thursday
  káda Huwébes
every afternoon
  káda hápon
day before yesterday
  sa úsang ádlaw
yesterday
  gahápon
day after tomorrow
  sunód ugma
What time is it?
  Unsang orása na?

week
  semána, dominggó
last week
  niáging semána
this week
  károng semanáha, károng dominggó
next week
  sa sunód semána, dominggó umáabot
month
  bulán
a month
  usá kabúlan
this month
  károng bulána
year
  tuíg
a year
  usá kátuig
every year
  tuíg-tuíg, káda tuíg
last year
  niáging tuíg
next year
  sa sunód tuíg

Days

Monday	*Lunés*
Tuesday	*Martés*
Wednesday	*Miyérkoles (Miércules)*
Thursday	*Huwébes (Juéves)*
Friday	*Biyérnes (Viérnes)*
Saturday	*Sábado (Sábao)*
Sunday	*Dominggó*

Months

January	*Enéro*
February	*Pebréro*
March	*Márso*
April	*Abril*
May	*Máyo*
June	*Húnyo*
July	*Húlyo*
August	*Agósto*
September	*Setyémbre*
October	*Oktúbre*
November	*Nobyémbre*
December	*Disyémbre*

Weather

sun	*ádlaw*
clear, bright	*háyag, kláro*
clouds, fog, mist	*pangánod*
cloudy	*pangánod, dághang*
cold	*túgnaw*
warm	*inít*
lightning	*kílat, lintí*
rain	*ulán*
rainy	*ting-ulán*
thunder	*dúgdog, dalúgdog*
typhoon	*bagyó*
wind	*hángin*
windy	*mahángin*

Numbers

0	*walá*
1	*usá*
2	*duhá*
3	*tuló*
4	*upát*
5	*limá*
6	*únom*
7	*pitó*
8	*waló*
9	*siyám*
10	*napuló*
11	*únsi*
12	*dóse*
13	*tróse*
20	*báynte*
21	*báynte úno*
22	*báynte dos*
30	*tranta*
31	*tranta'y úno*
40	*kuwarénta*
50	*singkuwénta*
60	*sayesénta, sisénta*
70	*siténta, seténta*
80	*otsénta*
90	*nobénta*
100	*usá kagatós*
101	*usá kagatós ug usá*
200	*duhá kagatós*
201	*duhá kagatós ug usá*
500	*limá kagatós*
1000	*usá kalíbo*
5000	*limá kalíbo*

1 pound (weight)	*usáng librá*	one-quarter	*upát ka tungá*
2 pesos	*duhá ka píso*		
3 km	*tuló ka kilométro*	once	*usaháy*
5 litres	*limá ka lítro*	twice	*kaduhá, ikaduhá*
10 cubic metres	*napuló ka métro kubíko*	three times	*katuló*
		often	*pirme, síge síge*
one-half	*tungá*	seldom	*tág-sa, tagsa-ón*
one-third	*tuló ka tungá*		

Facts for the Visitor

VISAS

The visa you are issued at the airport on arrival in Manila or Cebu is valid for 21 days and free of charge. However, your passport has to be valid at least six months beyond the expiry of the visa. It is possible to get an extension from the Department on Immigration & Deportation, Magallanes Drive, Intramuros, Manila, and its offices in Angeles City and Cebu City.

If you arrive in the Philippines with a visa, make sure you let the immigration officer know that you've obtained it. Otherwise you risk having only the customary period of 21 days stamped in your passport.

Visa Extensions

The cost of extensions is regulated according to the time period proposed. At the conclusion of the period stipulated by the visa, you present your extension application and passport to the various immigration officials, and these documents remain with the Immigration Office (Regular Service) for processing. You can get your extension in about one day if you pay an 'express service' fee of P250. Keep all receipts, as they are likely to be checked at the airport when you leave the country. (Incidentally, anyone applying for a visa extension dressed in thongs (flip-flops) and shorts can expect to be refused service.) A number of travel agencies and restaurants run by foreigners will offer to take care of your extension application for a reasonable sum, normally between P150 and P200.

21 to 59 Days If you wish to spend between 21 and 59 days in the Philippines, you should request a 59 day visa from a Philippine embassy or consulate in your country. This will normally be granted for about US$35. If you're unable to make your application in person, you should send a letter of request asking for the application forms, and enclose

a stamped, self-addressed envelope. Don't send in your passport straight away. You have to enter the Philippines within three months of the visa's being issued, otherwise it automatically expires.

Anyone entering the Philippines without a visa or with only a 21 day visa and wishing to remain in the country for up to 59 days must pay P500 for a 38 day extension (Visa Waiver), plus a P10 'legal research fee'.

59 Days to Six Months Anyone wishing to stay in the country for more than 59 days, but no longer than six months, has to pay the following fees:

Application and Visa Fee (P450) – not applicable in the case of previously paid visa fees.
Alien Head Tax (P200) – applicable only to persons over 16 years of age.
ACR: Alien Certificate of Registration (P400) – in the case of a second application within the same calendar year; this only costs P250.
Extension Fee (P200) – for each month of the extension period already begun.
ECC: Emigration Clearance Certificate (P500) – the fee can be paid at the airport on departure; you can also make the payment at the Immigration Office, though this must be done no sooner than 30 days before departure.
Legal Research Fee (P10) – additional to every other payable fee with the exception of the Alien Head Tax.

Six Months & Longer Anyone wishing to remain in the country over six months must, in addition to the extension fees listed earlier, pay a further P700 for a Certificate of Temporary Residence. When departing after a stay of one year or longer, there is a further travel tax to pay to the tune of P1620.

The Immigration Office can order anyone applying for a visa extension of over six months to undergo an AIDS test, and can grant or refuse the application on the basis of the result.

DOCUMENTS

It is necessary to have a valid passport. Some bus and ship companies, as well as Philippine Airlines (PAL) and Philippine National Railways, have student discounts. It is essential to have a student card. If you want to hire a car, you will need a valid driver's licence from your country of origin – the international driver's permit may not be recognised.

Make two copies of your documents and of the receipts of your travellers' cheques and leave one copy at a permanent address so you can send for it if necessary. Either exchange the other copy with your travelling companion for theirs or keep it in your luggage, quite separate from the originals. Identification problems and document replacement in the case of loss or theft will be a lot easier if you take these precautions.

If you take a personal address book containing important addresses and telephone numbers, you should make a copy of them and store them separately from the originals.

Bags kept close to you, money belts and secret pockets are further ways of protecting your money, tickets and documents.

Balikbayan

After repeated alterations to the definitions of eligibility for Travel Tax Exemptions for Balikbayan (Filipinos living abroad), the following regulations are now in force: the Filipino Civil Registration Office, or the Philippine embassy or consulate in the new country of residence will provide the applicant with a certificate affirming that no tax has been paid on any income. This can then be forwarded to the Department of Tourism for exemption from payment of the travel tax. The department's address is Room 108, Ministry of Tourism Building, Agrifina Circle, Rizal Park, Manila. The certificate of Travel Tax Exemption costs P20 at the DOT. It should be shown at the airport on departure from the country.

CUSTOMS

Personal effects, a reasonable amount of clothing, toiletries, jewellery for normal use and a small quantity of perfume are allowed in duty free. Visitors may also bring in 400 cigarettes or two tins of tobacco and two litres of alcohol free of duty.

It is strictly prohibited to bring illegal drugs, firearms, obscene and pornographic media into the country.

Visitors carrying more than US$300 are requested to declare the amount at the Central Bank counter at the customs area. Foreign currency taken out upon departure must not exceed the amount bought in. Departing passengers may not take out more than P1000 in local currency.

MONEY

Currency

The Philippine currency is the peso (P) – correctly spelt piso but always referred to as the peso. It's divided up into 100 centavos (c). There are coins of 1, 5, 10, 25 and 50 centavos and of 1 and 2 pesos. Banknotes are available in denominations of 5, 10, 20, 50, 100, 500 and 1000 pesos.

The US dollar is by far the most recognised foreign currency in the Philippines. Although the safety consideration with travellers' cheques applies as much in the Philippines as anywhere else, cash (US dollars) does, as usual, have its advantages. You will often find it easier to change a small amount of cash rather than a cheque.

Exchange Rates

A$1	=	P19.8
C$1	=	P20.6
DM	=	P15.7
NZ$1	=	P15.6
UK£1	=	P40.3
US$1	=	P27.6

In some smaller regional towns there may be no bank at all and the only possibility of changing money may be at a hotel and then at a poor exchange rate. Moneychangers are often faster and more efficient than banks, although it's wise to shop around since their rates do vary. When you do change money try to get a reasonable amount of it in smaller denominations: taxi drivers almost never have change of big notes. In more remote areas it can be difficult to change even P100 notes.

Banks

You'll get the best exchange rate in Manila. In the provinces you may lose as much as 20%. In remote districts only the peso and, possibly, the US dollar will be accepted; in those areas no other currency can be relied upon. Sometimes a bank will give you a better rate for your currency than a moneychanger, at other times the opposite will be the case. You could also be charged for a quick comparison of exchange rates.

Many provincial banks only exchange travellers' cheques to a total value of $US100 or less. Cheques for larger amounts can be cashed only with the consent of the bank manager.

You are not permitted to take more than P500 out of the country. Unused pesos can be changed only at the banking counter in the departure hall of Ninoy Aquino International Airport (NAIA); you have to produce an official yellow (or white) exchange slip. These can be obtained from a bank or a licensed money exchange office.

Opening hours in Philippine banks are Monday to Friday from 9 am to 3 pm; a few banks close at 3.30 pm.

Bank Account If you are thinking of opening an account with a Philippine bank, you should be aware that only the first P40,000 are insured. By law larger amounts do not have to be reimbursed should the bank suffer bankruptcy. Even two or more accounts at the same bank are not insured beyond a total amount of P40,000 when the holder of each account is the same person.

ATM Cards The age of automatic tellers has also reached the Philippines. If you intend to stay for an extended period in the Philippines it would be worth your effort to open a bank account there and apply for an ATM card. Holders of a plastic keycard are not limited by the opening hours of the bank if they want to withdraw money from their account.

The biggest accounting systems are BancNet (Allied Bank, Interbank, Metrobank, PCI Bank) and MegaLink (Asian Bank, Bank of Commerce, Equitable Bank, Far East Bank, Philippine National Bank, Traders Royal Bank). Several hundred branch offices have been equipped with ATMs throughout the country.

Moneychangers

You'll get a fairly good exchange rate from licensed moneychangers. In Manila these will be found on Mabini St (between Padre Faura and Santa Monica Sts) and on the corner of M H del Pilar and Padre Faura Sts. Besides your passport (a photocopy of which is taken on your first transaction), you will need to produce the receipts from your purchase of travellers' cheques showing the certified number of each cheque.

The Black Market

Compared with the official exchange rate, the black market pays only a few centavos extra for each US$100 bill. The lower the denomination the lower the exchange. A US$1 bill is worth next to nothing on the black market.

Bbeware, plenty of gullible tourists have been taken for a ride! You can be sure you won't gain anything if you let a persuasive dealer convince you to change money.

The illegal moneychangers ply their trade in the following way. To begin with they'll offer you a perfectly correct rate of exchange. You receive your pesos, the dealer takes the dollars. Then, all of a sudden, the dealer will apologise for having short changed you P50. The dealer takes the pesos back, counts them out again and ostentatiously places the allegedly missing P50 on top of the pile while stealthily removing some other notes from the bottom!

Another favourite trick is not to pay out in full the agreed sum so as to provoke the irritated customer into cancelling the deal. The customer then gets counterfeit dollars handed back while the dealer keeps the good dollars and pesos! There's no getting away from the fact that most black marketeers are consummate artists when it comes to fraud.

That also goes for the pretty young Filipinas who use their charms to lure male tourists. The tourist wanting to change money is taken in by their tale of poverty and woe, and soon finds himself dealing with their well-fed 'brothers'.

Cash

In the Philippines, unlike many other countries, the rate of exchange is somewhat higher for cash than it is for travellers' cheques. You'll get the best value for large US denominations like US$50 and US$100 bills. When selling currency, bear in mind that only clean banknotes are acceptable. Crumpled, torn or dirty ones will be rejected by moneychangers.

Travellers' Cheques

If you want to keep on the safe side of the law and are prepared to accept an exchange rate of about 5% lower, you should take travellers' cheques rather than cash with you. Travellers' cheques in US dollars issued by American Express, the Bank of America and Thomas Cook will be cashed by almost every Philippine bank, and certainly by the Philippine National Bank.

Hold on to your original purchase receipts, as most moneychangers (and sometimes banks) will not cash cheques unless you can produce this documentation.

Eurocheques

It is becoming increasingly difficult to use Eurocheques in the Philippines. Even in Manila you'll barely find a bank willing to accept this form of payment. Occasionally resident foreigners will be willing to swap their pesos for Eurocheques. You can find out about current possibilities for deals of this sort in foreign-run restaurants and businesses.

Credit Cards

Well-known international credit cards such as American Express, Diners Club, MasterCard and Visa are accepted by many hotels, restaurants and businesses in the Philippines. With your Visa and MasterCard you can withdraw cash in pesos at any branch of the Equitable Bank: there are plenty of these in Manila, for example, on the corner of United Nations Ave and Bocobo St (opposite the Manila Pavilion Hotel), Ermita. You can withdraw US dollars or travellers' cheques on your American Express card at American Express, Philamlife Building, United Nations Ave, Ermita.

It's important to remember that the Equitable Bank has brought out its own national Visa card. Many of the hotels, restaurants and businesses displaying showy posters confirming that they accept 'Visa' are actually referring to this local version of it.

Transferring Money

Having money forwarded can be time consuming. Even transfers by telex often take 10 days or longer. Presumably the banks make the money work for them first.

It's advantageous to have a safe-deposit account, as that way you can arrange for the desired sum of money to be sent by telex. Costs are in the vicinity of US$15 and the waiting time is two days.

In Manila use American Express or the Philippine National Bank – the Bank of America tends to be slow. American Express card holders can get US$1000 in travellers' cheques every 21 days on their card account but you must have a personal cheque as well. Without a personal cheque for any 30 day period, card members may not exceed US$500 (US$1,000 for Platinum Card members) or its equivalent in local currency.

Payment will be made in pesos or US dollar travellers' cheques. Most banks are unwilling to pay out dollars in bills. If anything they might offer you the amount in very small bills, which you're better off refusing.

Costs

Some examples of costs in the Philippines are:

Aspirin P20
Bottle of beer P8
Litre of milk P30
Packet of cigarettes P10

One kg rice P12
One kg potatoes P25
One kg tomatoes P30
One pineapple P25
One apple P13
One orange P15
A cheap meal P80
Soap (90g) P18
Toothpaste (25ml) P10
Shampoo (125ml) P25
Daily newspaper P3
Time magazine P60
Local telephone call P3
Ektachrome 100 P170
100 km by ordinary bus P40
100 km by air-con bus P50
One hour domestic flight P1400
Litre of petrol P10

Tipping

Just as in other countries, whether or not to tip is a personal decision. If you stay in the same hotel for a few days however, there is no doubt that hotel staff wouldn't appreciate a P20 tip.

Restaurant staff generally expect a tip (it is part of their wage), even if the menu states that a service charge is included. The money then goes into a kitty and is shared later with the cook and the cashier. If the service was particularly good, a tip of around 5% of the bill will show your appreciation.

Taxi drivers will often try to wangle a tip by claiming not to be able to give change. If the charge on the meter appears to be accurate, the passenger should voluntarily round up the amount: for example, if the fare is P44, then P50 would be appropriate.

Bargaining

When shopping in public markets or even shops, Filipinos try to get a 10% discount. They almost always succeed. Foreign customers will automatically be quoted a price that is around 20% more than normal or, in places which deal mainly with tourists, up to 50% more. On the other hand, department stores and supermarkets offer set prices, and it is not customary to bargain.

WHAT TO BRING

Bring as little as possible is the golden rule – it's almost always possible to get things you might need and that's far better than carrying too much with you. A backpack is probably the best way of carrying your gear but try to thief-proof it as much as possible and remember that backpacks are prone to damage, especially by airlines, where they easily get caught up on loading equipment. Travel packs are a relatively recent innovation that combine the advantages of a backpack and a soft carry bag. The shoulder straps either detach or can be hidden away under a zip-fastened flap so they do not catch on things.

The Philippines has enough climatic variations to require a fairly wide variety of clothing. At sea level you'll need lightweight gear, suitable for tropical temperatures. In Mountain Province or when scaling the odd volcano, you'll need warmer clothing – jumpers (sweaters) and a light jacket. Bring thongs (flip-flops) for use in hotel bathrooms and showers. A sleeping bag can be particularly useful in the Philippines, especially on overnight boat trips.

If you're a keen snorkeller, bring your mask and snorkel; there are many superb diving areas around the islands. Soap, toothpaste and other general toiletries are readily available, but out in the sticks, toilet paper can be difficult to find. A first-aid kit is useful (see the Health section later in this chapter). A padlock is always worth carrying: you can often use it to add security to your hotel room. When it rains in the Philippines, it really rains, so bring a raincoat or umbrella. Other possibilities include a sewing kit, a torch (flashlight), a Swiss army knife, a travel alarm clock and a mosquito net – the list goes on.

TOURIST OFFICES

You can often get up-to-date news and travel tips about prices, departure times and so on from other travellers.

For regional information, the representatives of the Department of Tourism are available. Don't expect too much of them –

they are friendly and helpful but not always terribly knowledgeable. Several cities which don't have an official DOT office have opened up a tourist office of their own, responsible for the local area. Usually this office can be found in the town hall.

As well as the DOT head office in Manila, there are various overseas offices and regional offices scattered around the country.

Regional Tourist Offices

Around the Philippines the regional tourist offices are at:

Baguio
    Ministry of Tourism Complex, Governor Pack Rd (☎ 7014, 5416)
Cagayan de Oro
    Pelaez Sports Complex, Velez St (☎ 3340, 6394)
Cebu City
    GMC Plaza Bldg, Plaza Independencia (☎ 91503, 96518)
Davao
    Apo View Hotel, J Camus St (☎ 64688, 71534)
Iloilo
    Sarabia Building, General Luna St (☎ 78701, 75411)
Legaspi
    Peñaranda Park, Albay District (☎ 4492, 4026)
San Fernando (La Union)
    Matanag Hall, General Luna St, Town Plaza
San Fernando (Pampanga)
    Paskuhan Village (☎ 2621, 2665)
Tacloban
    Children's Park, Senator Enage St (☎ 2048)
Zamboanga
    Lantaka Hotel, Valderroza St (☎ 3931)

In Manila there are tourist offices at NAIA and Rizal Park. See under Tourist Office in the Information section in the Manila chapter for more details.

Overseas Reps

Overseas offices of the Philippines Department of Tourism include:

Australia
    Highmount House, Level 6, 122 Castlereaugh St, Sydney, NSW 2000 (☎ (02) 267 2695/2756)
Hong Kong
    Philippine Consulate, 21 F Wah Kwong Regent Centre, 88 Queen's Rd Central (☎ (5) 8100770)

Germany
    Kaiserstrasse 15, 60311 Frankfurt/M (☎ (069) 20893/20894)
Japan
    Philippine Embassy, 11-24 Nampeidai Machi, Shibuya-ku, Tokyo (☎ (03) 3464 3630/3635)
    Philippine Tourism Center, 2F Dainan Building, 2-19-23 Shinmachi, Nishi-Ku, Osaka 550 (☎ (06) 535 5071/5072)
UK
    Philippine Embassy, 17 Albemarle St, London WIX 7HA (☎ (071) 499 5443/5652)
USA
    3460 Wilshire Blvd, Suite 1212, Los Angeles, CA 90010 (☎ (213) 4871 4527)
    Philippine Center, 556 Fifth Ave, New York, NY 10036 (☎ (212) 575 7915)

BUSINESS HOURS

Businesses open their doors to the public between 8 and 10 am. Offices, banks and public authorities have a five-day week. Some offices are also open on Saturday morning. Banks open at 9 am and close at 3 or 3.30 pm. Embassies and consulates are open for the public mostly from 9 am till 1 pm. Offices and public authorities close at 5 pm. Large businesses like department stores and supermarkets continue until 7 pm, and smaller shops often until 10 pm.

FIESTAS & FESTIVALS

There are many town fiestas which take place on the numerous national holidays over the whole year. An expensive festival is held for two or three days in honour of the appropriate patron saint. It is hard to understand how some of the families shoulder the financial burden: the enormous expenses incurred bear no relation to the poverty and hardship of everyday life in the Philippines. Food and drink are offered with lavish generosity and at the end of the fiesta some visitors even get the money for their journey home pressed into their hands. One or more bands are hired, and musicians and entertainers add to the atmosphere of a people's festival. There is also usually a beauty contest in which the contestants are heavily sponsored. Foreigners and visitors from distant towns get the same royal treatment as friends and relatives.

January

Appey This is a three-day thanksgiving festival of the Bontoc for a bounteous harvest. Countless chickens and pigs are slaughtered and sacrificed for this festival.

1 January

New Year's Day As in Western countries the new year is colourfully and loudly welcomed. Families come together to celebrate the traditional *media noche*, the midnight meal. The streets are incredibly noisy and can be dangerous: fireworks are shot off for several days before New Year, often resulting in the loss of fingers and thumbs. Every year unintended and premature explosions of illegally produced fireworks result in chaotic scenes at the hospitals. Many of those affected do not live to see the next New Year.

First Sunday in January

Holy Three Kings' Day This is the official end of the Christmas season. The children receive their last Christmas presents on this day. In Santa Cruz and Gasan on Marinduque, the imitation kings are led on horseback through the town. Spectators throw coins and sweets to the children who run alongside the procession.

9 January

Black Nazarene Procession What is probably the largest procession of the Philippines begins early in the afternoon in Quiapo at the Quiapo church. Thousands of Catholics crowd the streets in this part of Manila when the 'Black Nazarene', a life-size statue of Christ made of blackwood, is carried through the town.

Third Weekend in January

Ati-Atihan This festival in Kalibo on Panay is the Rio de Janeiro or New Orleans Mardi Gras of the Philippines. It's an important and spectacular festival, when the town rages for three days. People dance, sing and play drums. Thousands of people, outrageously costumed and cleverly masked, celebrate around the clock until the last evening, when a long procession of excited participants ends the intoxicating festivities.

The origins of the festival date back to the middle of the 13th century, when 10 Datu families had to flee from Borneo. They sailed northeast and landed on the Philippine island of Panay, where the resident Ati – small, dark Negrito people – gave them a piece of land on which to settle. A festival was celebrated and the newly arrived people blackened their faces so they would look just like the local Ati.

Many years later the Spaniards, who had converted much of the country to Christianity, used this ritual to deceive unfriendly Muslims and counter their attempts to influence Kalibo. They got the inhabitants to dye their skin black, wear warlike clothing and pretend they were Ati. The victory against the Muslims was interpreted as being achieved through the intervention of Santo Niño, the child Jesus, and thus the festival started to take on a religious significance.

Third Sunday in January

Sinulog – Santo Niño de Cebu This is the climax of the week-long festival of Pasundayag sa Sinulog. Groups of people, all dressed in costume, gather in Downtown around the junction of Colon St and Osmeña Blvd until about 9.30 am when they make their way through the streets of Cebu City, sometimes marching, sometimes dancing the peculiar Sinulog steps and shouting 'Pit Senyor'. The procession takes several hours to go past.

Sinulog is the traditional dance of the old women followers, who can also be seen dancing by themselves in front of the Basilica Minore del Santo Niño and Magellan's Cross any day of the week. 'Pit Senor' means 'viva el Señor', by which is meant 'long live Santo Niño' (the child Jesus). Hotels are nearly always booked out on the holiday weekend.

Sinulog is also celebrated in Kabankalan on Negros during this weekend. As well as the actual Sinulog on the Sunday there are also horse fights on the Saturday.

Fourth Weekend in January

Ati-Atihan in Ibajay One weekend after the festival in Kalibo, another festival takes place in Ibajay, 30 km to the north-west. According to the statements of the people of Ibajay, their Ati-Atihan is the original and only true one – maybe they're correct. At least it's fair to say that though this festival is not supported financially by commercial interests or attended by hordes of tourists, the locals, dressed in their simple but original costumes, celebrate with as much enthusiasm as the people in Kalibo.

Dinagyang This festival in Iloilo City includes parades, but the spectators are quiet and passive, unlike the crowds at the similar Ati-Atihan activities in Kalibo.

January/February

Chinese New Year Depending upon the lunar calendar, Chinese New Year celebrations take place some time between 21 January and 19 February. There are ritual and traditional dragon dances in Manila's Chinatown.

February

Saranggolahan In many villages and towns this is the beginning of the kite-flying season. People of all ages take part in competitions with kites of the most varied forms, colours and sizes.

2 February

Feast of Our Lady of Candelaria This is a town festival with processions and parades in honour of Our Lady of Candelaria, the patron saint of Jaro, a district of the city of Iloilo. It's the biggest religious event in the western Visayas.

11 February

Feast of Our Lady of Lourdes This celebration is held in memory of the appearance of the 'Lady of Lourdes' in Lourdes, France. It takes place on Kanlaon St, Quezon City, and includes processions in the evening. The feast is also celebrated in San Juan del Monte, Bulacan Province.

14 February

St Valentine's Day This is a day for lovers – an important date for the romantic Filipinos. Small gifts and valentine's cards are personally delivered or sent, and couples dress up to go to a nice restaurant, dance in a disco or go to the movies. Filipinos are deeply upset if they have to spend St Valentine's Day without a valentine.

22 to 25 February

People Power Days These are thanksgiving days for the end of the Marcos era, peacefully brought about by the people. The Epifanio de los Santos Ave (Edsa) in Quezon City was the main scene of the so-called People Power revolution, and on this wide street the reinstalment of democracy is now celebrated every year. The 25th is an official national holiday.

26 February

Dia de Zamboanga This is a festival held by and for Muslims and Christians with cultural offerings, exhibits, regattas and religious ceremonies, in which the old Spanish and Muslim traditions of the city are given expression.

March/April

Moriones Festival Around Easter there are many passion plays in the Philippines. The most popular and colourful is the Moriones Festival in Marinduque. The Roman soldier Longinus, not Jesus, is the focus of the week-long play. Longinus is blind in one eye and as he pierces the right side of the crucified Jesus with his spear, blood drops on his blind eye and suddenly he can see again with both eyes. The first thing he sees is Christ's passage to heaven; Longinus announces the incident and must flee. The Roman warriors want to stop this 'rumour' and capture him on Easter Sunday. His execution by beheading is the climax of the play.

Maundy Thursday (official holiday) Apart from Good Friday, Maundy Thursday is the most intensively celebrated day of the holy week. Deep in thought, people attend church, most of the traffic comes to a halt and a perceptible silence reigns throughout the country.

On Maundy Thursday and Good Friday almost everything is closed or stops – even Metrorail services in Manila and PAL flights. Things start again on Easter Saturday.

Good Friday (official holiday) The many crucifixions and scourges which take place throughout the country have grown into a real tourist attraction! The best known places for this are San

Fernando (Pampanga Province), Antipolo (Rizal Province), Manila and Jordan (Guimaras Island). *Easter Sunday* (official holiday) At daybreak throughout the land, church bells are rung to herald the resurrection of Christ. Also at dawn, separate mother and son processions – symbolising the risen Christ's meeting with his mother – begin, concluding under a bamboo and flower arch.

9 April

Bataan Day (official holiday) This is a national remembrance day at the Mt Samet Shrine recalling the disastrous battle against the Japanese in WW II and the degrading 'death march' on the Bataan Peninsula.

27 April

Bahug-Bahugan sa Mactan Magellan's landing and the battle which led to his death are acted out on the beach of Mactan, on Mactan Island, Cebu. There are fights in the water, but be early: some years the activities start at 8 am and are all over a couple of hours later.

28 April to 1 May

Binirayan – Handuyan Over 700 years ago 10 Malayan political fugitives from Borneo reached the Panay coast. They were made welcome by the Negrito chief, Marikado, and were allowed to settle in Malandog near present-day San Jose de Buenavista. The landing and settlement are re-enacted using time-honoured costumes and decorated boats. This festival has been celebrated since 1974, but the date has tended to vary and if it continues will probably only be held on alternate years. The most interesting part – the landing of the boats – usually starts early in the morning.

April, May or June

Turumba Festival Turumba means falling, leaping, jumping, skipping or dancing. This describes the behaviour of the participants in the procession in Pakil, Laguna Province.

1 to 30 May

Flores de Mayo – Santacruzan Throughout the whole country, processions in honour of the Virgin Mary take place in the afternoon and evening. Young girls in white dresses decorate the statues of Mary with flowers. An attractive focus of the processions in the flowering month of May are the most beautiful Filipinas of the local villages.

1 May

Labor Day This is a national holiday but no important activities are held.

3 May

Carabao Carroza Water buffalo races are held in Pavia, a few km north of Iloilo City on Panay Island. The fastest water buffaloes from the surrounding 18 *barrios* (neighbourhoods) run against each other in a final deciding race. The beauty queens are carried to the race track on festively decorated sleds. Be there by 8 am. There is a town fiesta on the following day.

6 May

Araw ng Kagitingan A day on which all Filipinos who have shown exceptional courage, either in their private lives or while serving their country are honoured. War veterans and nostalgia seekers visit the fortified island of Corrigidor in Manila Bay in memory of the battle against the Japanese (The Fall of Corregidor) in 1942.

14 & 15 May

Carabao Festival This is a two-day celebration in honour of the farmers' patron saint, San Isidro. Farmers lead decorated water buffaloes to the church square in a long procession on the afternoon of 14 May. There they kneel and are blessed. The next day the water buffalo races take place. Festivals are held in Pulilan (Bulacan Province), San Isidro (Nueva Ecija Province) and Angono (Rizal Province).

15 May

Pahiyas The patron saint San Isidro is also honoured in Lucban and Sariaya, Quezon Province. On the day of the harvest festival, the house façades are attractively decorated with agricultural products. There is a procession in the afternoon. The huge leaves and blooms, which look like coloured glass and shine in the sun, are particularly decorative on Lucban. They are made out of *kiping*, a rice dough, following a traditional recipe and method and eaten at the end of the festival, or given to the guests. The procession takes place in the afternoon.

17 to 19 May

Fertility Rites This three-day festival in Obando (Bulacan Province) is dedicated to the three patron saints of the city. The Obando Festival became famous for its procession, a series of dances based on earlier fertility rites. On 17 May young unmarried men dance through the streets in the hope of soon finding a bride. The following day, unmarried women try their luck. The last day is given to childless couples who show their desire to have children through their participation in this festival.

12 June

Independence Day This is a national holiday with military parades.

24 June

Feast of San Juan Bautista The deeds of St John the Baptist are re-enacted on this day in San Juan, Manila. Friends, relatives and curious spectators are 'baptised'. Water is thrown from, and at, passing cars – keep your camera in a plastic bag!

Parada ng Lechon In Balayan, Batangas Province, St John's Day is celebrated with a 'suckling pig parade'.

28 to 30 June

Apung Iro (Apalit River Parade) The inhabitants of Apalit (Pampanga Province) show their reverence for St Peter with a boat parade.

First Sunday in July

Pagoda sa Wawa This is a river procession with the Holy Cross of Wawa in the pagoda boat. It takes place in Bocaue, Bulacan Province, just 30 km north of Manila.

29 July

Pateros River Fiesta Pateros, a suburb of Manila, is the centre of duck breeding. From here Manila is supplied with the Filipino delicacy *balut* (see The Filipino Menu in the Food & Drink section later in this chapter). The fiesta recalls the killing of a legendary crocodile which threatened the existence of the balut suppliers.

August

Kadayawan sa Dabaw For two weeks in August, Davao on Mindanao celebrates the Orchid Festival, the Fruit & Food Festival and the Tribal Festival.

Third Weekend in September

Peñafrancia Festival The ceremonious river festival in Naga, South Luzon, has become a great tourist attraction. The climax is the spectacular boat parade on the Naga River in honour of the Blessed Virgin of Peñafrancia.

10 to 12 October

Zamboanga Hermosa This is a festival with cultural performances, religious ceremonies, exhibitions, regattas and the choosing of Miss Zamboanga. The festival is dedicated to the patron saint of the city, Nuestra Señora del Pilar.

Second Weekend in October

La Naval de Manila This procession goes along the main streets of Quezon City to the Domingo Church. It commemorates the victorious sea battle against the Dutch plunderers in the year 1646. This festival is also celebrated in Angeles in Pampanga Province.

19 October

MassKara Festival On the weekend closest to 19 October, the largest festival on Negros takes place in Bacolod. There are street dances and groups of people wearing costumes and friendly, smiling masks.

1 November

Undas (All Saints' Day) On this national holiday families meet at the cemetery and stay there the whole night and even the night before. Numerous lights, candles and flowers on the graves make an impressive sight. There are booths and stalls in front of the cemetery.

23 November

Feast of San Clemente On this feast day a boat parade takes place in Angono, Rizal Province. It is a thanksgiving by the fishing people in honour of their patron saint, San Clemente.

30 November

Bonifacio Day This is a national holiday in tribute to Filipino heroes, most especially in honour of Andres Bonifacio, who headed the Katipunan, the revolutionary movement formed to fight the Spaniards.

Late November, early December

Grand Canao This is a festival of the hill clans in Baguio, North Luzon. There are dances and rituals in which, among other things, victorious warriors are honoured and water buffaloes, pigs and chickens are sacrificed. There are also agricultural exhibitions and craft demonstrations.

8 or 9 December

Feast of Our Lady of the Immaculate Conception An impressive boat procession is held at night on the Malabon River and Manila Bay at the fishing community of Malabon in the north-west of Metro Manila. There are street processions in the afternoon.

16 to 25 December

Simbang Gabi You can hear Christmas carols practically all over the Philippines from about the beginning of November. Officially, however, the Christmas season begins on 16 December. Following the old traditions, religious Filipinos go to *simbang gabi* (night masses) which are held before dawn.

24 December

Giant Lantern Festival The most spectacular lantern parade and contest in the Philippines takes place in San Fernando, Pampanga Province. Some of the *parol* (coloured paper lanterns) are so large they must be drawn by a tractor. Be at the big church by about 8 pm and you won't miss anything. After midnight mass the most beautiful lantern will be chosen.

25 December

Christmas This family day, as in practically all Christian countries, is awaited with great excitement by children. However, grown-ups also seem to wait for a Christmas present impatiently, and ask repeatedly for a week beforehand: 'Where is my Christmas?'

28 December

Holy Innocents' Day Just as people in the West play April Fools' Day tricks on 1 April, so do Filipinos try to catch one another out on this day.

30 December

Rizal Day This is a national holiday with street parades in memory of the Filipino national hero, Dr Jose Rizal, who on this day in 1896 was executed by the Spaniards. Statues of him are decorated with flowers, and national flags are lowered to half-mast.

Muslim Festivals

There are also some important dates associated with the Muslim calendar. As the Islamic calendar is lunar, it is 11 days shorter than the Gregorian one, so these dates change each year. The Hari Raya Poasa, which marks the end of Ramadan, occurred at the end of May in 1990. In February the Hariraya Hajji is the time of pilgrimages to Mecca. Muslims spend most of the 10th day of the 12th month of their calendar in mosques. In March/April, Maulod-En-Nabi is the prophet Mohammed's birthday. It is a Muslim holiday with ceremonial readings from the Koran in all mosques.

POST & TELECOMMUNICATIONS
Postal Rates

Airmail letters (per 20g) within the Philippines cost P2 (ordinary/three weeks), P3 (special/one week) and P16 (speed/24 hours).

Airmail letters (per 10g) cost P6 to South-East Asia, P7 to Australia and the Middle East, P8 to Europe and North America and P9 to Africa and South America.

Aerograms and postcards cost P5 regardless of the destination.

Sending Mail

If you take your mail straight to the mail distribution centre near the domestic airport in Manila, it will be processed and sent out much quicker. So far all my letters have arrived home safely. If you are sending important items (such as film) out by mail, it is best to send it by registered post. Registered express letters will be delivered – all going well – within five days. Around Christmas especially, you should make sure your letters are stamped immediately so that no-one can remove your postage stamps and use them again. Even at the small post office on Mabini St, Manila, there have been numerous complaints about stamp pilfering.

Unlike the General Post Office (GPO) and the Mabini St Post Office, the Rizal Park Post Office near the Manila Hotel is less frequented, and you may only have to wait there a little while or not at all.

Top Left: Trishaw/Pedicab (JP)
Top Right: Landscape created from Mt Pinatubo eruption, near Angeles (JP)
Bottom: Black Nazarene procession in Quiapo, Manila (JP)

Top: Bullock-led cane cart, Manila (TW)
Bottom: The ubiquitous jeepney (JP)

A tip for stamp collectors: at the Manila GPO you can get special release stamps. Go to the special room at the rear on the left-hand side of the building.

Receiving Mail

The Philippine postal system is generally quite efficient. You can get mail sent by poste restante at the GPO in all the major towns. In Manila you'll find the poste restante to the left, at the back of the GPO. It's open Monday to Saturday from 8 am to 5 pm and Sunday until noon.

Ask people who are writing to you to print your surname clearly and to underline it – most missing mail is simply misfiled under given names.

You can also have mail sent to an American Express office if you're using American Express travellers' cheques or carrying an American Express card. American Express has offices in Manila, Makati and Cebu City. The Manila address is Clients' Mail, American Express, Philamlife Building, United Nations Ave & Maria Orosa St, Manila. You can get information by calling ☎ 8159311 (ask to be connected).

If you wish to send money in a letter to the Philippines, you should only do so by registered letter, otherwise its safe arrival can't be guaranteed. To keep on the safe side, camouflage the valuable item with a piece of carbon paper and then fasten the contents to the envelope with a staple on the outside: there are postal employees with X-ray vision! In fact, it's not uncommon for envelopes also stamped on the back to be opened (registered letters are known to carry valuable items!). Post office crooks are capable of removing most of the enclosed money and leaving just a token remainder; or they might switch a US$5 bill for a US$50 one before passing the letter on for 'regular' delivery. Postal money orders present no problem. These take about 10 days.

Parcels

Depending on the country, only parcels weighing less than 10 or 20 kg will be dispatched by the Philippine postal service. They must also be wrapped in plain brown paper and fastened with string. Parcels sent to Europe by surface (sea) mail take from two to four months to reach their destination.

Opening Hours

Opening hours in Philippine post offices are not the same everywhere. Many close at noon, others shut on Saturday as well. The following opening hours can usually be relied upon: Monday to Friday from 8 am to noon and 1 to 5 pm. With few exceptions, post offices are closed on Sunday and public holidays, and at the end of the year there are at least three public holidays: Rizal Day (30 December), New Year's Eve and New Year's Day. During the Christmas period, from mid-December to mid-January, mail is delayed by up to a month (see the Fiestas & Festivals section earlier in this chapter for Christmas season information).

Telephone

You do not find telephones everywhere in the Philippines; in an emergency try the nearest police station, which in many areas will have the only telephone. Telephone numbers are always changing so get hold of a local directory before calling.

In contrast to overseas calls, local calls in the Philippines are full of problems. It can take a ridiculously long time to be connected and the lines over long distances are bad. International calls are a breeze in comparison.

Long-distance overseas calls can be made from most hotels. A three minute station to station call to Europe costs about P300. It's a few pesos cheaper if you call directly from one of the offices of the Philippine Long Distance Telephone Co (PLDT). There are PLDT offices at Escolta St and Taft Ave in Manila as well as at other central locations.

Note that it is far cheaper to make station to station rather than person to person calls from the Philippines: the charges are about 25% less.

Try to call outside business hours (of the country you are ringing) when the waiting time will be considerably less. On Sunday there is a 25% reduction in the charge.

Fax

Many hotels and offices are equipped with fax machines. Sending a fax from a hotel to overseas can be quite expensive (for example, P350 for one page to Europe). On the other hand, private telecommunication companies, including Eastern Telecoms and PLDT charge about P95 for the first minute (one page) and P85 for the following minutes.

Domestic fax transmissions are relatively cheap, for example, from Manila to Cebu City the first minute costs P25 and the following minutes are P20.

Telegrams

The international telegram service is pretty prompt and reliable, but internal telegrams are likely to be delayed. There are two major domestic telegram companies: Radio Communications of the Philippines (RCPI) and Philippine Telegraph & Telephone Corporation (PT & T).

To Europe, 12-hour telegrams cost about P14 a word and to Australia they cost P15. Within the Philippines, a telegram to Cebu from Manila, for example, costs about P1.50 a word and takes five hours.

To compare, a telex to Europe costs P85 per minute (four lines) through Eastern Telecoms.

TIME

The Philippines is eight hours ahead of GMT, and two hours behind Australian Eastern Standard Time. Philippine time has a curious nature – it includes lack of punctuality and a need for patience. A rendezvous à-la-Philippine time is basically very loose. Either you are waited for, or you wait. Don't get too upset – tomorrow is another day. In the Philippines the only reliable times are sunrise and sunset. If you have been invited somewhere, do as the locals do and arrive about an hour after the arranged time. This will be considered polite and will save the host the embarrassment of a guest arriving too early.

ELECTRICITY

The electric current is generally 220V, 60 cycles, although the actual voltage is often less, particularly in some provinces. In some areas the standard current is the US-style 110V. An adapter may be needed for Philippine plugs which are usually like the US flat, two-pin type.

Blackouts are common even in the tourist centres. A pocket torch (flashlight) is very useful for such occasions.

BOOKS

Manila has a good selection of bookshops – see under Bookshops in the Information section in the Manila chapter for details. There is a fairly active local publishing industry, mainly in English. Books on the Philippines tend to fall into either the coffee-table variety or the rather dry facts and history group.

History

Among the history books is *A Short History of the Philippines* by Teodoro Agoncillo (Mentor Pocketbook, Manila, 1975); *The Philippines* by Onofre D Corpuz; and *Readings in Philippine History* by Horacio de la Costa (Bookmark, Manila, 1965), which is good if you're not too fond of formal history. *For Every Tear a Victory* by Hartzell Spence is said to be the best Marcos biography. *Shadows on the Land – An Economic Geography of the Philippines* by Robert E Huke (Bookmark, Manila, 1963) may also be of interest.

People & Society

Interesting books to look for on specific Philippine topics include *The Truth behind Faith Healing in the Philippines* by Jaime T Licauco (National Book Store, Manila, 1981). *The Yakans of Basilan Island* by Andrew D Sherfan (Fotomatic Inc, Cebu City, 1976) or *T'boli Art* by Gabriel S Casal (Filipinas Foundation Inc, Makati, 1978) will be of interest to those wanting more information on the people of Mindanao and the south. A handy, easy-to-carry Filipino/English dictionary is *The New Dictionary* by Marie Odulio de Guzman (National Book Store, Manila, 1968).

MAPS

You can get comprehensive road maps of the Philippines from Petron, Mobil and other petrol companies. Petron's *The Philippine Motorists' Road Guide* is available in bookshops. The trilingual map of the *Philippines* (Nelles Verlag, Munich) is also worth having. Detailed survey maps and sea charts can be obtained from the Bureau of Coast & Geodetic Survey (see under Maps in the Information section of the Manila chapter).

For Manila, Metro Manila and environs within a radius of 50 km, Heinrich Engeler's city map of Manila, *Metro Manila*, is recommended. You'll find it at the National Book Store. Bookmark has published four illustrated city maps which offer a bird's-eye view of the modern city's most important streets and noteworthy buildings: *Metro Manila Landmarks*, *Baguio Landmarks*, *Cebu Landmarks* and *Makati*. The lighthearted *Survival Map of Manila* gives full details on entertainment, restaurants and shopping.

MEDIA
Newspapers & Magazines

After 20 years of press censorship under Marcos, the change of government brought a flood of new national and local newspapers and magazines indulging in a marvellous journalistic free-for-all. Before, there was a group of four big government-friendly national dailies. Now about 20 publications, including the *Manila Bulletin*, the *Philippine Daily Inquirer*, *Malaya*, *The Manila Chronicle*, the *Manila Standard*, *Newsday*, *Today*, *Daily Globe*, *The Philippine Star*, *The Journal* and the *Evening Stars* fight for their share in a free market. All are in English. In contrast to the unilateral reporting during Marcos's time the media today represent a fair, critical and objective difference of opinion. *Tempo* and *Peoples* are vigorous

tabloid papers, which appear in both English and Tagalog.

A lesser role is played by the Philippine papers *Balita*, *Taliba* and *Ang Pilipino Ngayon*, in keeping with their circulation and layout. In the Sunday editions of various newspapers a magazine is included. Newspapers printed in Manila but sold outside the capital are more expensive because of transport costs. The number of comics published and read each week is quite phenomenal.

There are also a few magazines which appear weekly, amongst which the *Free Press*, with its irreverent and quite critical articles, stands out.

International events are meagerly reported or analysed in the Philippine mass media. If you want to know more you can get *Newsweek*, *Time*, *Asiaweek*, *Far Eastern Economic Review* and the *International Herald Tribune*. These and other international publications like the *Observer*, *Mail on Sunday* and *Sunday Times* can be found on sale in the larger hotels.

Both the English-language newspapers *Expat* and the *Foreign Post* appear weekly and are free of charge in many hotels. Both publications are aimed towards foreigners living in the Philippines and tourists.

Radio & TV

Radio and TV operate on a commercial basis and the programmes are continually interrupted by advertisements. There are altogether 22 TV channels. Seven broadcast from Manila, sometimes in English and sometimes in Tagalog.

FILM & PHOTOGRAPHY

Take sufficient slide film with you as there is not a lot of choice in the Philippines. This is especially true of the provinces, where the use-by date has often expired. Kodak Ektachrome 100 costs about P170, a 200 costs P215 and a 400 costs about P250. Mayer Photo on Carlos Palanca St, Quiapo, probably has the cheapest film in Manila. Around the corner on Hidalgo St there are more photo shops.

There's no problem with normal colour

film, which is often preferred by Filipinos. Development is fast and good value. High-gloss prints (nine cm by 13 cm) can be processed in an hour at a cost of P2.50 per print; cheaper processing will take longer.

Officially you are only allowed to bring five cartridges of film in with you, but the customs officials usually turn a blind eye in the case of tourists.

The usual rules for tropical photography apply in the Philippines. Remember to allow for the intensity of the tropical light, try to keep your film as cool and dry as possible and have it developed as soon as possible after exposure.

Although airport X-ray security equipment is said to be safe for films, that doesn't apply to frequent X-rays. If you're going to be passing through airport security checks on a number of occasions, it's wise to remove your film from your bag and have it inspected separately.

Remember that cameras can be one of the most intrusive and unpleasant reminders of the impact of tourism – it's polite to ask people before you photograph them. A smile always helps.

HEALTH

You probably won't get any of the illnesses described here. However, you might be unlucky or need to help others, in which case the information in this section will be a useful starting point.

Travel health depends on your predeparture preparations, your day-to-day health care while travelling and how you handle any medical problem or emergency that does develop. While the list of potential dangers can seem quite frightening, with a little luck, some basic precautions and adequate information you will experience little more than an upset stomach.

Travel Health Guides

There are a number of books on travel health:

Staying Healthy in Asia, Africa & Latin America, Moon Publications. Probably the best all-round

guide to carry, as it's compact but very detailed and well organised.

Travellers' Health, Dr Richard Dawood, OUP. Comprehensive, easy to read, authoritative and also highly recommended, although it's rather large to lug around.

Where There is No Doctor, David Werner, Hesperian Foundation. A very detailed guide intended for someone, like a Peace Corps worker, going to work in an undeveloped country, rather than for the average traveller.

Travel with Children, Maureen Wheeler, Lonely Planet Publications. Includes basic advice on travel health for younger children.

Predeparture Preparations

Health Insurance A travel insurance policy to cover theft, loss and medical problems is a wise idea. There is a wide variety of policies and your travel agent will have recommendations. The international student travel policies handled by STA or other student travel organisations are usually good value. Some policies offer lower and higher medical expense options, but the higher one is chiefly for countries like the USA which have extremely high medical costs. Check the small print:

1 Some policies specifically exclude 'dangerous activities' such as scuba diving, motorcycling, even trekking. If such activities are on your agenda you don't want that sort of policy.

2 You may prefer a policy which pays doctors or hospitals direct rather than you having to pay on the spot and claim later. If you have to claim later, make sure you keep all documentation. Some policies ask you to call back (reverse charges) to a centre in your home country where an immediate assessment of your problem is made.

3 Check if the policy covers ambulances or an emergency flight home. If you have to stretch out you will need two seats and somebody has to pay for them!

Medical Kit A good medical kit is essential, particularly if you are going off the beaten track. Because you can't always get to your main luggage when travelling, for example on a flight, it's recommended that you keep a small medical kit in your hand luggage with medications such as pain-relieving tablets, diarrhoea tablets, eye drops and perhaps

Alka Seltzer. Consult your doctor about individual medicines.

A possible kit list includes:

1 Aspirin or Panadol – for pain or fever.
2 Antihistamine (such as Benadryl) – useful as a decongestant for colds, allergies, to ease the itch from insect bites or stings or to help prevent motion sickness.
3 Antibiotics – useful if you're travelling off the beaten track. Choose a good broad-spectrum antibiotic.
4 Kaolin preparation (Pepto-Bismol) or Imodium – for stomach upsets.
5 Rehydration mixture – for treatment of severe diarrhoea, this is particularly important if travelling with children. Lomotil is also useful.
6 Antiseptic, mercurochrome and antibiotic powder or similar 'dry' spray – for cuts and grazes.
7 Calamine lotion – to ease irritation from bites or stings.
8 Bandages and Band-aids – for minor injuries.
9 Scissors, tweezers and a thermometer (note that mercury thermometers are prohibited by airlines).
10 Insect repellent, sunscreen, suntan lotion, chapstick and water purification tablets.
11 Condoms – to avoid sexually transmitted diseases.

Ideally, antibiotics should be administered only under medical supervision and should never be taken indiscriminately. Overuse of antibiotics can weaken your body's ability to deal with infections naturally and can reduce the drug's efficacy on a future occasion. Take only the recommended dose at the prescribed intervals and continue using the antibiotic for the prescribed period, even if the illness seems to be cured earlier. Antibiotics are quite specific to the infections they can treat, stop immediately if there are any serious reactions and don't use them at all if you are not sure that you have the correct ones.

In the Philippines many medicines will generally be available over the counter and the price will be much cheaper than in the West, but they may be marketed under a different name. Some medicines are supposedly available only with a prescription form, but, it seems, it's not compulsory for every pharmacy to see one. Antibiotics are available in Philippine pharmacies without prescription. Manila is the best place to buy antibiotics.

As in other developing countries, be careful of buying drugs, particularly where the expiry date may have passed or correct storage conditions may not have been followed. It's possible that drugs which are no longer recommended, or have even been banned, in the West are still being dispensed. In the bigger cities you have a better chance of getting proper medicine at a clean, well-equipped and busy pharmacy rather than at a small store which sells cigarettes and Coca-Cola as well. In small towns choose a pharmacy connected to a hospital or recommended by a doctor.

Health Preparations Make sure you're healthy before you start travelling. If you are embarking on a long trip make sure your teeth are OK: there are lots of places where a visit to the dentist would be the last thing you'd want to do.

If you wear glasses take a spare pair and your prescription. Losing your glasses can be a real problem, although in many places you can get new spectacles made quickly, cheaply and competently.

If you require a particular medication take an adequate supply, as it may not be available locally. Take the prescription, with the generic rather than the brand name (which may not be locally available), as it will make getting replacements easier. It's a wise idea to have the prescription with you to show you legally use the medication.

Immunisations Vaccinations provide protection against diseases with which you might come into contact. For the Philippines no immunisations are necessary, but the further off the beaten track you go the more necessary it is to take precautions. For the Philippines a yellow fever vaccination is necessary only if you're coming from an infected area. Nevertheless, all vaccinations should be recorded on an International Health Certificate, available from your physician or government health department.

When organising your vaccinations make

sure you plan ahead as some of them require an initial shot followed by a booster, while some vaccinations should not be given together. Most travellers from Western countries will have been immunised against various diseases during childhood, but your doctor may still recommend booster shots against measles or polio, diseases still prevalent in many developing countries. The period of protection offered by vaccinations differs widely and some are contraindicated if you are pregnant.

The possible list of vaccinations includes:

Tetanus & Diphtheria Boosters are necessary every 10 years and protection is highly recommended.

Typhoid Protection lasts for three years and is useful if you are travelling for long in rural, tropical areas. You may get some side effects such as pain at the injection site, fever, headache and a general unwell feeling.

Hepatitis A (Infectious Hepatitis) Gamma globulin is not a vaccination but a ready-made antibody which has proven very successful in reducing the chances of hepatitis infection. Because it may interfere with the development of immunity, it should not be given until at least 10 days after administration of the last vaccine; it should also be given as close as possible to departure because of its relatively short-lived protection period of six months.

Hepatitis B As in most tropical countries Hepatitis B occurs in the Philippines. Worldwide this disease kills more people in a single day than AIDS kills in a single year. The vaccine is quite expensive and you need three shots (the second shot four weeks after the first shot; the third shot six months after the second shot); a booster is necessary after every three to five years. For those people intending to spend a lot of time in the tropics, the investment is a worthwhile one.

Yellow Fever Protection lasts 10 years and is recommended if you are coming from places where the disease is endemic, chiefly Africa and South America. You usually have to go to a special yellow fever vaccination centre. Vaccination is contraindicated during pregnancy but if you must travel to a high-risk area it is probably advisable.

Basic Rules

Care in what you eat and drink is the most important health rule; stomach upsets are the most likely travel health problem but the majority of these upsets will be relatively minor. Don't become paranoid, trying the local food is part of the experience of travel after all.

Drinks Water in the cities should be safe to drink, but if you don't know for certain, always assume the worst. Ice from ice factories should be OK too, but sometimes it comes from tap water frozen in plastic bags, in which case you should be careful. Reputable brands of bottled water or soft drinks are generally fine. Take care with fruit juice, particularly if water may have been added. Milk should be treated with suspicion, as it is often unpasteurised. Boiled milk is fine if it is kept hygienically and yoghurt is always good. Tea or coffee should also be OK, since the water should have been boiled.

Water Purification The simplest way of purifying water is to boil it thoroughly. Technically this means boiling for 10 minutes, something which happens very rarely!

Simple filtering will not remove all dangerous organisms, so if you cannot boil water it should be treated chemically. Chlorine tablets (Puritabs, Steritabs or other brand names) will kill many but not all pathogens. Iodine is very effective in purifying water and is available in tablet form (such as Potable Aqua), but follow the directions carefully and remember that too much iodine can be harmful.

If you can't find tablets, tincture of iodine (2%) or iodine crystals can be used. Two drops of tincture of iodine per litre or quart of clear water is the recommended dosage; the treated water should be left to stand for 30 minutes before drinking. Iodine crystals can also be used to purify water but this is a more complicated process, as you have to first prepare a saturated iodine solution. Iodine loses its effectiveness if exposed to air or damp so keep it in a tightly sealed container. Flavoured powder will disguise the taste of treated water and is a good idea if you are travelling with children.

Food Salads and fruit should be washed with purified water or peeled where possible. Ice cream is usually OK if the brand name is

Magnolia, but beware of street vendors and of ice cream that has melted and been refrozen. Thoroughly cooked food is safest but not if it has been left to cool or been reheated. Take great care with shellfish and fish and avoid undercooked meat. In general, places that are packed with travellers or locals will be fine, while empty restaurants are dubious.

Nutrition If the food you are eating is of low nutritional value, if you're travelling hard and fast and therefore missing meals, or if you simply lose your appetite, you can soon start to lose weight and place your health at risk.

Make sure your diet is well balanced. Eggs, beans and nuts are all safe ways to obtain protein. Fruit you can peel (bananas, oranges or mandarins for example) is always safe and a good source of vitamins. Try to eat plenty of grains (eg, rice). Remember that although food is generally safer if it is cooked well, overcooked food loses much of its nutritional value. If your diet isn't well balanced or if your food intake is insufficient, it's a good idea to take vitamin and iron pills.

In hot climates make sure you drink enough – don't rely on feeling thirsty to indicate when you should drink. Not needing to urinate or very dark yellow urine is a danger sign. Always carry a water bottle with you on long trips to avoid dehydration. Excessive sweating can lead to loss of salt and therefore muscle cramping. Salt tablets are not a good idea as a means of preventing dehydration, but adding salt to food can help.

Everyday Health A normal body temperature is 37°C (98.6°F); more than 2°C higher is a 'high' fever. A normal adult pulse rate is 60 to 80 beats per minute (children 80 to 100, babies 100 to 140). You should know how to take a temperature and a pulse rate. As a general rule, when somebody has a fever the pulse increases about 20 beats per minute for each degree Celsius rise in body temperature.

Respiration (breathing) rate can also be an indicator of illness. Count the number of breaths per minute: between 12 and 20 is normal for adults and older children (up to 30 for younger children, 40 for babies). People with a high fever or serious respiratory illness (like pneumonia) breathe more quickly than normal. More than 40 shallow breaths a minute usually means pneumonia.

Many health problems can be avoided by taking care of yourself. Wash your hands frequently as it's quite easy to contaminate your own food. Clean your teeth with purified water rather than water straight from the tap. Avoid climatic extremes: keep out of the sun when it's hot, dress warmly when it's cold. Avoid potential diseases by dressing sensibly. You can get worm infections through walking barefoot or dangerous coral cuts by walking over coral barefoot. You can avoid insect bites by covering bare skin when insects are around, by screening windows or beds or by using insect repellents (an excellent insect repellent is 'Off!').

Seek local advice: if you're told the water is unsafe because of jellyfish, crocodiles or bilharzia, don't go in. In situations where there is no information, play it safe.

Medical Problems & Treatment

Potential medical problems can be broken down into several areas. First there are the climatic and geographical considerations – problems caused by extremes of temperature, altitude or motion. Then there are diseases and illnesses caused by insanitation, insect bites or stings, and animal or human contact. Simple cuts, bites or scratches can also cause problems.

Self-diagnosis and treatment can be risky, so wherever possible seek qualified help. Although treatment dosages are given in this section, they are for emergency use only. Medical advice should be sought before administering any drugs.

An embassy or consulate can usually recommend a good place to go for such advice. So can five star hotels, although they often recommend doctors with five star prices.

(This is when that medical insurance is really useful!) In some places standards of medical attention are so low that for some ailments the best advice is to get on a plane and go somewhere else.

Climatic & Geographical Considerations
Sunburn In the tropics, the desert or at high altitude you can get sunburnt surprisingly quickly, even through cloud cover. Use a sunscreen and take extra care to cover areas which don't normally see sun, eg, your feet. A hat provides added protection, and you should also use zinc cream or some other barrier cream for your nose and lips. Calamine lotion is good for mild sunburn.

Prickly Heat Prickly heat is an itchy rash caused by excessive perspiration trapped under the skin. It usually strikes people who have just arrived in a hot climate and whose pores have not yet opened sufficiently to cope with greater sweating. Keeping cool but bathing often, using a mild talcum powder or even resorting to air-conditioning may help until you acclimatise.

Heat Exhaustion Dehydration or salt deficiency can cause heat exhaustion. Take time to acclimatise to high temperatures and make sure you get sufficient liquids. Salt deficiency is characterised by fatigue, lethargy, headaches, giddiness and muscle cramps, and in this case salt tablets may help. Vomiting or diarrhoea can deplete your liquid and salt levels. Anhydrotic heat exhaustion, caused by an inability to sweat, is quite rare.

Heat Stroke This serious, and sometimes fatal, condition can occur if the body's heat-regulating mechanism breaks down and the body temperature rises to dangerous levels. Long, continuous periods of exposure to high temperatures can leave you vulnerable to heat stroke. You should avoid excessive alcohol or strenuous activity when you first arrive in a hot climate.

The symptoms are feeling unwell, not sweating very much or at all and a high body temperature (39°C to 41°C). Where sweating has ceased, the skin becomes flushed and red. Severe, throbbing headaches and lack of coordination will also occur, and sufferers may become confused or aggressive. Eventually the victims will become delirious or convulse. Hospitalisation is essential, but meanwhile get patients out of the sun, remove their clothing, cover them with a wet sheet or towel and then fan them continually.

Fungal Infections Hot weather fungal infections are most likely to occur on the scalp, between the toes or fingers (athlete's foot), in the groin (jock itch or crotch rot) and on the body (ringworm). You get ringworm (which is a fungal infection, not a worm) from infected animals or by walking on damp areas, like shower floors.

To prevent fungal infections wear loose, comfortable clothes, avoid artificial fibres, wash frequently and dry carefully. If you do get an infection, wash the infected area daily with a disinfectant or medicated soap and water, and rinse and dry well. Apply an antifungal powder like the widely available Tinaderm. Try to expose the infected area to air or sunlight as much as possible and wash all towels and underwear in hot water as well as changing them often.

Motion Sickness Eating lightly before and during a trip will reduce the chances of motion sickness. If you are prone to motion sickness try to find a place that minimises disturbance – near the wing on aircraft, close to midships on boats, near the centre on buses. Fresh air usually helps while reading or cigarette smoke doesn't. Commercial antimotion-sickness preparations, which can cause drowsiness, have to be taken before the trip commences: when you're feeling sick it's too late. Ginger is a natural preventative and is available in capsule form.

Diseases of Insanitation
Diarrhoea A change of water, food or climate can all cause the runs; diarrhoea caused by contaminated food or water is more serious. Despite all your precautions you may still have a bout of mild travellers'

diarrhoea, but a few rushed toilet trips with no other symptoms is not indicative of a serious problem. Moderate diarrhoea, involving half-a-dozen loose movements in a day, is more of a nuisance. Dehydration is the main danger with diarrhoea, particularly for children, so fluid replenishment is the number one treatment. Weak black tea with a little sugar, soda water, or soft drinks allowed to go flat and diluted 50% with water are all good. With severe diarrhoea a rehydrating solution is necessary to replace minerals and salts. You should stick to a bland diet as you recover.

Lomotil or Imodium can be used to bring relief from the symptoms, although they do not cure the problem. Only use these drugs if absolutely necessary – eg, if you *must* travel. For children Imodium is preferable, but do not use these drugs if the patient has a high fever or is severely dehydrated.

Antibiotics can be very useful in treating severe diarrhoea, especially if it is followed by nausea, vomiting, stomach cramps or mild fever. Ampicillin, a broad spectrum penicillin, is usually recommended. Two capsules of 250 mg each taken four times a day is the recommended dose for an adult. Children aged between eight and 12 years should have half the adult dose; younger children should have half a capsule four times a day. Note that if the patient is allergic to penicillin, ampicillin should not be administered.

Giardiasis The intestinal parasite *Giardia lamblia*, is present in contaminated water. The symptoms are stomach cramps, nausea, a bloated stomach, watery, foul-smelling diarrhoea and frequent gas. Giardiasis can appear several weeks after you have been exposed to the parasite. The symptoms may disappear for a few days and then return; this can go on for several weeks. Metronidazole, known as Flagyl, is the recommended drug, but it should only be taken under medical supervision. Antibiotics are of no use.

Dysentery This serious illness is caused by contaminated food or water and is characterised by severe diarrhoea, often with blood or mucus in the stool. There are two kinds of dysentery. Bacillary dysentery is characterised by a high fever and rapid development; headaches, vomiting and stomach pains are also symptoms. It generally does not last longer than a week, but it is highly contagious.

Amoebic dysentery is more gradual in developing, causes no fever or vomiting but is a more serious illness. It is not a self-limiting disease: it will persist until treated and can recur and cause long-term damage.

A stool test is necessary to diagnose which kind of dysentery you have, so you should seek medical help urgently. In case of an emergency, note that tetracycline is the prescribed treatment for bacillary dysentery, and metronidazole for amoebic dysentery.

With tetracycline, the recommended adult dosage is one 250 mg capsule four times a day. Children aged between eight and 12 years should have half the adult dose; the dosage for younger children is one-third the adult dose. It's important to remember that tetracycline should be given to young children only if it's absolutely necessary and only for a short period; pregnant women should not take it after the fourth month of pregnancy.

With metronidazole, the recommended adult dosage is one 750 mg to 800 mg capsule three times daily for five days. Children aged between eight and 12 years should have half the adult dose; the dosage for younger children is one-third the adult dose.

Cholera Cholera vaccination is not very effective. However, outbreaks of cholera are often widely reported, so you can avoid such problem areas. The disease is characterised by a sudden onset of acute diarrhoea with 'rice water' stools, vomiting, muscular cramps and extreme weakness. You need medical help, but in the meantime, treat for dehydration (which can be extreme) and, if there is an appreciable delay in getting to hospital, begin taking tetracycline. See the Dysentery section for dosages and warnings.

Viral Gastroenteritis This is caused not by bacteria but, as the name suggests, by a virus. It is characterised by stomach cramps, diarrhoea, sometimes by vomiting, sometimes a slight fever. All you can do is rest and drink lots of fluids.

Hepatitis Hepatitis A is the more common form of this disease and is spread by contaminated food or water. The first symptoms are fever, chills, headache, fatigue, feelings of weakness and aches and pains. This is followed by loss of appetite, nausea, vomiting, abdominal pain, dark urine, light-coloured faeces and jaundiced skin; the whites of the eyes may also turn yellow. In some cases there may just be a feeling of being unwell or tired, accompanied by loss of appetite, aches and pains and jaundiced skin. You should seek medical advice, but in general there is not much you can do apart from resting, drinking lots of fluids, eating lightly and avoiding fatty foods. People who have had hepatitis must forgo alcohol for six months after the illness, as hepatitis attacks the liver and it needs that amount of time to recover.

Hepatitis B, which used to be called serum hepatitis, is spread through sexual contact with an infected partner or through skin penetration. It could, for instance, be transmitted via dirty needles or blood transfusions. Avoid having your ears pierced, or tattoos or injections done in places where you have doubts about the sanitary conditions. The symptoms and treatment of type B are much the same as for type A, but gamma globulin as a prophylactic is effective against type A only. (See the earlier Hepatitis B section under Immunisations.)

Typhoid Typhoid fever is another gut infection that travels the faecal-oral route – ie, contaminated water and food are responsible. Vaccination against typhoid is not totally effective and, as it is one of the most dangerous infections, medical help must be sought.

In its early stages typhoid resembles many other illnesses: sufferers may feel like they have a bad cold or flu on the way, as the early symptoms are headache, sore throat and a fever which rises a little each day until it is around 40°C or more. The victim's pulse is often slow relative to the degree of fever present and gets slower as the fever rises, unlike a normal fever where the pulse increases. There may also be vomiting, diarrhoea or constipation.

In the second week the high fever and slow pulse continue and a few pink spots may appear on the body; trembling, delirium, weakness, weight loss and dehydration are other symptoms. If there are no further complications, the fever and other symptoms will slowly go during the third week. However, you must get medical help before this because pneumonia (acute infection of the lungs) or peritonitis (burst appendix) are common complications, and because typhoid is very infectious.

The fever should be treated by keeping the victim cool; dehydration should also be watched for. Chloramphenicol is the recommended antibiotic but there are fewer side effects with ampicillin. The adult dosage is two 250 mg capsules, four times a day. Children aged between eight and 12 years should have half the adult dose; younger children should have one-third the adult dose.

Patients who are allergic to penicillin should not be given ampicillin.

Worms These parasites are most common in humid, tropical areas. They can live on unwashed vegetables or in undercooked meat or you can pick them up through your skin by walking barefoot. Infestations may not be obvious for some time, and, although they are generally not serious, they can cause severe health problems if left untreated. A stool test is necessary to pinpoint the problem and medication is often available over the counter. If you think you might have contracted worms sometime during your travels, it's not a bad idea to have a stool test when you get home.

Diseases Spread by People & Animals
Tetanus This potentially fatal disease is found in undeveloped tropical areas. It is

difficult to treat but is preventable with immunisation.

Tetanus occurs when a wound becomes infected by bacteria which live in the faeces of animals or people, so clean all cuts, punctures or animal bites. Tetanus is also known as lockjaw, and the first symptom may be discomfort in swallowing, or a stiffening of the jaw and neck; this is followed by painful convulsions of the jaw and whole body.

Rabies Rabies is found in many countries and is caused by a bite or scratch by an infected animal. Dogs are a noted carrier. Any bite, scratch or even lick from an animal should be cleaned immediately and thoroughly. Scrub the area with soap and running water, and then clean with an alcohol solution. If there is any possibility that the animal is infected, medical help should be sought immediately. Even if the animal is not rabid, all bites should be treated seriously as they can become infected or result in tetanus. A rabies vaccination is now available and should be considered if you are in a high-risk situation – eg, if you intend to explore caves (bat bites could be dangerous) or work with animals.

Tuberculosis Although this disease is widespread in many developing countries, it is not a serious risk to travellers. Young children are more susceptible than adults, and vaccination is a sensible precaution for children under 12 travelling in endemic areas. TB is commonly spread by coughing or by unpasteurised dairy products from infected cows. Milk that has been boiled is safe to drink; the souring of milk to make yoghurt or cheese also kills the bacilli.

Diphtheria Diphtheria can be a skin infection or a more dangerous throat infection. It is spread by contaminated dust contacting the skin or by the inhalation of infected cough or sneeze droplets. Frequent washing and keeping the skin dry will help prevent skin infection. A vaccination is available to prevent the throat infection.

Sexually Transmitted Diseases (STDs)
Sexual contact with an infected partner spreads these diseases. While abstinence is the only 100% preventative, using condoms is also effective. Gonorrhoea and syphilis are the most common of these diseases; sores, blisters or rashes around the genitals, discharges or pain when urinating are common symptoms. Symptoms may be less marked or not observed at all in women. Syphilis symptoms eventually disappear completely, but the disease continues and can cause severe problems in later years. The treatment of gonorrhoea and syphilis is by antibiotics.

There are numerous other STDs, for most of which effective treatment is available, though as yet there is no cure for herpes or HIV/AIDS. The latter is becoming more widespread in the Philippines. Using condoms is the most effective preventative.

HIV/AIDS can also be spread through infected blood transfusions – note that most developing countries cannot afford to screen blood for transfusions. It can also be spread by dirty needles – vaccinations, acupuncture and tattooing can be as dangerous as intravenous drug use if the equipment is not clean. If you do need an injection, it may be a good idea to buy a new syringe from a pharmacy and ask the doctor to use it.

According to the Philippine Department of Health (DOH) there were 380 known AIDS cases in the country as of mid-1993. The number of HIV infected Filipinos at the time was estimated by the National AIDS Prevention Program to be 35,000 in all. Awareness of and knowledge about this deadly illness are not yet widespread in the Philippines; the decision to use a condom is still mostly left up to the male partner.

Insect-Borne Diseases
Malaria This serious disease is spread by mosquito bites. Symptoms include headaches, fever, chills and sweating which may subside and recur. Without treatment malaria can develop more serious, potentially fatal effects.

If you are travelling on Palawan and Mindanao where malaria is more widespread than in other parts of the Philippines, it is extremely important to take malarial prophylactics. These are available in various forms, so ask your doctor for advice. They generally have to be taken for a period of time before you depart and after your return.

Antimalarial drugs do not actually prevent the disease but suppress its symptoms. Chloroquine is the usual malarial prophylactic; a tablet is taken once a week for two weeks before you arrive in the infected area and six weeks after you leave it. Unfortunately there is now a strain of malaria which is resistant to Chloroquine and so an alternative drug is necessary. Maloprim (weekly) or Proguanil (daily) can be used to supplement the Chloroquine. Better still is Lariam which is taken once a week and is effective against Chloroquine-resistant strains.

Chloroquine is quite safe for general use, side effects are minimal and it can be taken by pregnant women. Maloprim can have rare but serious side effects if the weekly dose is exceeded and some doctors recommend a checkup after six months of continuous use. Fansidar, once used as a chloroquine alternative, is no longer recommended as a prophylactic, as it can have dangerous side effects, but it may still be recommended as a treatment for malaria. Chloroquine is also used for malaria treatment but in larger doses than for prophylaxis. Doxycycline is another antimalarial for use where chloroquine resistance is reported; it causes hypersensitivity to sunlight, so sunburn can be a problem.

Mosquitoes appear after dusk. Avoiding bites by covering bare skin and using an insect repellent will further reduce the risk of catching malaria. Insect screens on windows and mosquito nets on beds offer protection, as does burning a mosquito coil. Mosquitoes may be attracted by perfume, aftershave or certain colours – light coloured clothes are generally better than dark. The risk of infection is higher in rural areas and during the wet season.

Dengue Fever There is no prophylactic available for this mosquito-spread disease; the main preventative measure is to avoid mosquito bites. A sudden onset of fever, headaches and severe joint and muscle pains are the first signs before a rash starts on the trunk of the body and spreads to the limbs and face. After a few more days, the fever will subside and recovery will begin. Serious complications are not common.

Typhus Typhus is spread by ticks, mites or lice. It begins as a bad cold, followed by a fever, chills, headache, muscular pains and a body rash. There is often a large painful sore at the site of the bite and nearby lymph nodes will be swollen and painful.

While tick typhus is spread by ticks, scrub typhus is spread by mites that feed on infected rodents and exists mainly in Asia and the Pacific Islands. You should take precautions if walking in rural areas in South-East Asia. Seek local advice on areas where ticks pose a danger and always check yourself carefully for ticks after walking in a danger area. A strong insect repellent can help, and serious walkers in tick areas should consider having their boots and trousers impregnated with benzyl benzoate and dibutylphthalate.

Cuts, Bites & Stings

Cuts & Scratches Skin punctures can easily become infected in hot climates and may be difficult to heal. Treat any cut with an antiseptic solution and mercurochrome. Where possible avoid bandages and Band-aids, which can keep wounds wet. Coral cuts are notoriously slow to heal, as the coral injects a weak venom into the wound. Avoid coral cuts by wearing shoes when walking on reefs, and clean any cut thoroughly.

Bites & Stings Bee and wasp stings are usually painful rather than dangerous. Calamine lotion will give relief and ice packs will reduce the pain and swelling. There are some spiders with dangerous bites but antivenins are usually available. Scorpion stings are notoriously painful and can be fatal. Scorpions often shelter in shoes or clothing.

Certain cone shells found in the Pacific have a dangerous or even fatal sting. There are various fish and other sea creatures which have dangerous stings or bites or which are dangerous to eat. Again, local advice is the best suggestion.

Snakes To minimise your chances of being bitten, always wear boots, socks and long trousers when walking through undergrowth where snakes may be present. Don't put your hands into holes and crevices, and be careful when collecting firewood.

Snake bites do not cause instantaneous death and antivenins are usually available. Keep the victim calm and still, wrap the bitten limb tightly, as you would for a sprained ankle, and then attach a splint to immobilise it. Then seek medical help, if possible with the dead snake for identification. Don't attempt to catch the snake if there is even a remote possibility of being bitten again. Tourniquets and sucking out the poison are now comprehensively discredited.

Jellyfish Local advice is the best way of avoiding contact with these sea creatures with their stinging tentacles. Dousing in vinegar will deactivate any stingers which have not 'fired'. Calamine lotion, antihistamines and analgesics may reduce the reaction and relieve the pain.

Bedbugs & Lice Bedbugs live in various places, but particularly in dirty mattresses and bedding. Spots of blood on bedclothes or on the wall around the bed can be read as a suggestion to find another hotel. Bedbugs leave itchy bites in neat rows. Calamine lotion may help.

All lice cause itching and discomfort. They make themselves at home in your hair (head lice), your clothing (body lice) or in your pubic hair (crabs). You catch lice through direct contact with infected people or by sharing combs, clothing and the like. Powder or shampoo treatment will kill the lice and infected clothing should then be washed in very hot water.

Leeches & Ticks Leeches may be present in damp rainforest conditions; they attach themselves to your skin to suck your blood. Trekkers often get them on their legs or in their boots. Salt or a lit cigarette end will make them fall off. Do not pull them off, as the bite is then more likely to become infected. An insect repellent may keep them away. Vaseline, alcohol or oil will persuade a tick to let go. You should always check your body if you have been walking through a tick-infested area, as they can spread typhus.

Women's Health

Some women experience irregular periods when travelling, due to upset in routine. If you use contraceptive pills, don't forget to take time zones into account, and beware that the pills may not be absorbed if you suffer intestinal problems. Ask your physician about these matters.

Gynaecological Problems Poor diet, lowered resistance due to the use of antibiotics and even contraceptive pills can lead to vaginal infections when travelling in hot climates. Maintaining good hygiene and wearing skirts or loose-fitting trousers and cotton underwear will help to prevent infections.

Yeast infections, characterised by a rash, itch and discharge, can be treated with yoghurt, or a vinegar or lemon-juice douche. Nystatin suppositories are the usual medical prescription. Trichomonas is a more serious infection; symptoms are a discharge and a burning sensation when urinating, and if a vinegar-water douche is not effective, medical attention should be sought. Flagyl is the prescribed drug. In both cases, sexual partners must also be treated.

Pregnancy Most miscarriages occur during the first three months of pregnancy, so this is the riskiest time to travel. The last three months should also be spent within reasonable distance of good medical care, as quite serious problems can develop at this time. Pregnant women should avoid all unnecessary medication, but vaccinations and malarial prophylactics should still be taken where necessary. Additional care should be taken to prevent illness and particular attention should be paid to diet and nutrition.

Contraceptive Pills & Tampons Contraceptive pills and tampons are available in the larger towns and in tourist areas, but it's still advisable to take some with you. Tampons are hard to come by, and indeed are hardly known of, so you need to give the pharmacy staff a good description of what it is you are after when you send them off to search the shelves!

WOMEN TRAVELLERS

Many Filipinos like to think of themselves as being irrestible macho types, but can also turn out to be surprisingly considerate gentlemen. They are especially keen to show their best side to foreign women. They will address you respectfully as 'Ma'am', shower you with friendly compliments ('you are so beautiful' etc) and engage you in polite conversation.

But Filipinas too (for instance if travelling next to a foreign women on a bus) will not miss the chance to ask a few questions out of curiosity: for example, about your home country, reason for and goal of your journey, and of course about your husband, how many children you have etc. It is then not unusual for the Filipina to get out of the bus after a few km and be replaced by another one, who will then proceed to ask exactly the same questions all over again.

So it would be a good idea to be prepared and have a few polite answers ready. After a few days on the road you'll be grateful for them.

On the other hand, it is best simply to ignore drunken Filipinos if they pester you. Simulated friendliness could easily be misunderstood as an invitation to get to know each other better. If a group of Filipinos starts a drinking session in a restaurant, it is not exactly recommended practice to sit down at a table next to them. In such cases, the best thing to do is just to change restaurants.

There have been cases reported of Fil-

ipinos sexually harassing foreign women, but they are very, very rare. In the absence of alcohol, frightening naivety and simple stupidity, probably the vast majority of cases could have been avoided.

Another word of advice: inspect hotel rooms with thin walls for strategic peepholes, and remember, don't accept cigarettes, food, drinks or sweets from friendly strangers as these gifts might be drugged.

DANGERS & ANNOYANCES
Security

If you throw your money on the table in bars and restaurants, or flash large banknotes around, don't be surprised if you get mugged on the corner when you leave. Stupidity is punished and the big and small-time gangsters in Manila are waiting for opportunities, just like their counterparts anywhere else in the world.

Look after your valuables and don't even let on that you have them. You will be taken for a wealthy foreigner regardless, even if you are not well off by Western standards and have saved for ages for your trip. Irresponsible behaviour will only provoke a challenge. This is particularly the case at Christmas, when the time for love and peace mobilises a whole army of thieves and beggars to pay for their gifts with the help of money from tourists and locals alike.

Here are some hints on how to guard your possessions and look after your own safety:

Money belongs in your front trouser pockets, in a pouch worn around your neck and under your clothes, or in a concealed money belt. Don't make it easy for pickpockets, as they are often very skilful.

Keep shoulder bags or camera bags in body contact; don't let them out of your sight. Develop the habit of keeping your hand underneath them: Filipinos with razors are quiet and quick.

Avoid dark alleys at night, especially if you have been enjoying San Miguel beer or Tanduay rum.

Don't pay your taxi fare until all of your luggage is unloaded.

Deposit valuables in the hotel safe, or rent a safe-deposit box at a large bank: it will cost about P150 a year. This is recommended if you want to deposit tickets, documents, travellers' cheques or souvenirs for any length of time while travelling around the country. An important thing to remember when leaving is that all the banks are closed on public holidays. Unfortunately, it's very difficult to get an empty safe-deposit box: either they are all allocated or the bank will not accept deposits for only a short time.

Don't reveal the name of your hotel and especially not your room number to just anyone who asks for it. If necedssary, give a false address spontaneously and believably.

Look over your hotel room carefully before you check out: anything left behind becomes the property of whoever finds it.

If at any stage you should be held up – by someone on a bike in a dark alley, for instance – don't try to defend yourself. Filipinos shoot quickly.

Wherever there are tourists there are thieves: for example, pickpockets and transvestites on Ermita and amateur and professional thieves in the buses to Batangas and the Puerto Galera pier. Be particularly cautious around Ermita, especially on Mabini St and Rizal Park.

Caution, Trap!

Recently there appears to have been an upsurge of thieves who specialise in robbing travellers, so beware. Usually these situations are provoked by gullibility and misplaced trust. It's only a small percentage of Filipinos who should be avoided and if you keep your wits about you, there should be no problems. It's not necessary to become totally insecure, but the following ruses have all been used:

If someone runs up to you, anxiously advising you that your money has been stolen, stay calm and don't immediately reach for the place where you keep your money. The pickpocket is just waiting for you to give your hiding place away.

Newspaper vendors usually have a thick bundle of newspapers tucked under their arm. Pickpockets on the other hand will usually only offer one newspaper for sale, holding it up with one hand far closer than normal to their victim's face, while the other takes advantage of the cover and cleans out their pockets. Now and then these mostly youthful thieves will employ their tricks in restaurants, taking with them anything useful such as cigarettes and lighters, or even a wallet carelessly left on the table.

A low-profile, yet busy, place (ideal for tricksters to spot their victims) used to be (and maybe still is) the main Manila office of PAL on Roxas Blvd. This is usually a busy place and such activities

can go unnoticed. For instance, you may be approached by a very pregnant woman who, working together with a young man, will start chatting and later invite you to a sightseeing tour of the town, or to her home. This offer of friendship will usually end with you losing your money.

I have also had reports of fraud in Baguio and Banaue. Tourists are approached by one or two attractive young Filipinas (or two friendly Filipino men) who are well dressed and speak good English, and are invited for coffee, which tastes a bit strange (not uncommon for native coffee in this area). After five or 10 minutes the visitors are out cold, and wake up 12 hours later in a park or field somewhere with all their valuables gone.

If a complete stranger comes up to you, especially in the Ermita district (Mabini St, Fiesta Pilipino and Rizal Park) and hands you a line about remembering you (for example 'Hello my friend, do you remember me from the airport...San Fernando...I was your bus driver etc) and suggests showing you the town or inviting you to dinner, don't accept. Others may claim that they were the customs or immigration officer when you arrived at NAIA recently. They weren't. Another line is: 'We're also strangers here, but we know people who can show us the town together'. Invitations to a party from such a stranger will usually end up with you being drugged, robbed and abandoned.

Another is to claim that a sister will be flying next week to, for example, Germany, Australia or the USA and – what a coincidence – will be working as a nurse in the same town as you come from. However, before her departure she would like to be reassured by hearing something more about the country and the town. This is merely a pretext to lure you to a house and rob you. It's a well-practised trick in Baguio. Once more: always be wary of sudden invitations, even at the risk of condemning innocent Filipinos. Don't accept drinks and food from strangers, not even on bus trips (sweets can be doctored as well!).

Beware also of Westerners who either can't or don't want to go home, and talk about 'extremely promising' ideas or having good connections. They will tell you that all they need is an investor and will assure you they're not in the least worried about how small or large the investment might be.

If someone tries to get hold of the name of your bank or your account number under some pretext, be careful. If, as well, either before or after this attempt, you are asked if they can leave some of their stuff with your things, look out. Now they have an excuse to look through your things as well as theirs and possibly find your bank account number, and with this information they can telex your bank to send money to an account they have set up in your name.

Calesas (horse-drawn cabs) in the Ermita district, for example, along Roxas Blvd, are almost always on the lookout for unsuspecting tourists. The favourite trick is to invite the tourist into the cab to take a picture of him with his own camera. While this is happening two Filipinos get in and tell the driver, who is in the know, to take them on a 'city tour'. After 200 to 300 metres the 'tour' is over, and the tourist has a tough time trying to get out of paying P250 for it.

Never join a card game with Filipinos – you'll always lose. If the 'cousin' of your host allegedly works at the casino, and offers to coach you in tricks, don't be taken in. I've met people who, after losing three games, still haven't realised the syndicate was working against them.

And then there are the fake police who cruise through the tourist quarters of Manila in twos or threes in a new limousine. They stop tourists from their 'squad' car, showing them a false police badge and, on the pretext of checking for counterfeit currency allegedly in circulation, ask them to step into the vehicle for a few minutes. Then these very experienced and terribly obliging gentlemen will kindly offer to check your money to make sure it's genuine. While doing this they skilfully and swiftly help themselves to some of the cash, and on handing back the rest, will reassure you that the notes are perfectly good. And just to complete the trick, as you alight they'll helpfully draw your attention to the pickpockets and petty criminals (who get bolder every day) allegedly waiting for you on every street corner.

There are a few points you should be aware of so you'll know who you're dealing with. It is extremely rare for Filipino police officers to show a badge as ID: usually their mark of authenticity is the neatly pressed uniform or the revolver hanging loosely from their belt. Plain-clothes police officers are more likely to get about in a T-shirt, jeans and gym shoes, than in smart fashionable suits. Number plates on police cars are, as on all government vehicles, white with red letters and numbers, and the first letter is as a rule 'S'. Number plates of licensed taxis are yellow with black lettering, and those of private vehicles are white with green lettering.

As well as meeting fake police officers, you may come into contact with a related species: false immigration officials, whose favourite haunt is the Nayong Pilipino and the Intramuros/Rizal Park district. Their game is to demand to inspect tourists' passports, and then to return them only on payment of a handsome sum. In reality genuine immigration officials make only occasional random checks of tourists' passports. In

any case they are normally satisfied with a photocopy: there's no need to have the original on you night and day.

Finally, remember that there will be new ideas and variations each year. Filipino thieves do not lack ingenuity or imagination. Don't let them spoil your trip.

Drugs

Since the early 1980s the laws governing drug abuse have grown increasingly severe in the Philippines. Unauthorised people are absolutely forbidden to handle, own or traffic in drugs.

So-called dangerous drugs are divided into two categories: prohibited drugs (opium, heroin, morphine, cocaine, LSD, marijuana); and regulated drugs (pharmaceutical drugs, sleeping pills, pain killers etc).

Transgressions are punished very severely. Penalties range from six to 12 years imprisonment plus a fine of P6000 to P12,000 for possession of marijuana and go up to P14,000 to P30,000 plus the death penalty for manufacture, trafficking, or import or export of any of the prohibited drugs. The laws also impose these sorts of penalties for the abuse of regulated drugs, if possession and use is not certified by a doctor's prescription.

If a fine can't be paid in the time allowed, the accused is free to bring in a lawyer, or to obtain the services of the Legal Assistance Office – if its staff can be motivated into action!

Other

For possible fire traps see the Accommodation section later in this chapter. For problems sending and receiving mail see Post & Telecommunications earlier in this chapter.

ACTIVITIES

'Few countries in the world are so little known and so seldom visited as the Philippines, and yet no other land is more pleasant to travel in than this richly endowed island kingdom. Hardly anywhere does the nature lover find a greater fill of boundless treasure.'

This was written about 100 years ago by Fedor Jagor, a German ethnographer. Today Jagor would be astonished – basically nothing in his assessment has changed. Although the Philippines is not so unknown anymore, it still surprises adventurers and discoverers with remarkable experiences: buried gold, unexplored caves, undamaged diving holes, sunken Spanish galleons, thick jungles with rare plants and animals, primeval people, active volcanoes of all sizes and completely uninhabited paradise islands.

Caving

Judging from the number of caves in existence, only a handful could have so far been explored. This is because very few Filipinos would willingly go into the unknown depths of the earth! The reasons are fear and superstition or just plain lack of interest.

In earlier times many caves served as burial grounds. It is not unusual to find bones and skulls, although you seldom find artefacts like vessels, tools, arms or jewellery. These have all been gathered up during earlier explorations. If you shine a light in completely unknown caves you might find some war spoils left by the Japanese, which, according to the calculations of the American columnist Jack Anderson, are distributed over 172 hiding places in the Philippines and are worth close to US$100 billion.

Climbing

There are no alpine summits in the Philippines, although there are volcanoes worth climbing. The official list records 37 volcanoes, 18 active and 19 dormant, but all unpredictable. The most dangerous include Mt Mayon and Mt Taal, which are both known to be explosive and consequently destructive. Other appealing challenges for climbers are the volcanoes Mt Makiling (1144 metres) and Mt Banahaw (2177 metres) on Luzon; Mt Hibok-Hibok (1322 metres) on Camiguin; Mt Kanloan (2465

metres) on Negros; and Mt Apo (2954 metres – the highest mountain in the Philippines) on Mindanao.

All dangerous volcanoes are overseen by the Commission on Volcanology (Comvol), the centre of which is in the Philippine Institute of Volcanology, Hizon Building, 29 Quezon Ave, Quezon City. This is where you can learn whether or not an eruption is predicted in the foreseeable future. Specific questions about climbs can be answered by the Philippine National Mountaineering Association in the Tours & Promotions section of PAL, 1500 Roxas Blvd, Manila.

Deserted Islands

There are 7107 islands in the Philippines and more than 60% of them are uninhabited. One would think that this would be music to the ears of a modern-day Robinson Crusoe, but unfortunately most of these godforsaken islands are stark rocks or simply sandbanks jutting uninvitingly out of the sea. If you search for it, however, you will almost certainly find an idyllic spot with white sand and palm beaches. Try north of Bohol, or in Gutob Bay between Culion and Busuanga. I found 12 isolated islands there in one day!

To really go à la Robinson Crusoe and enjoy it you need something to do, otherwise you'll get bored very quickly in paradise. If you take few supplies, you will soon find your days filled with trying to find more. The sea offers most things: fish, crayfish, sea porcupines, mussels, snails, algae and seaweed.

After just a few days of complete isolation, most budding Crusoes come to the conclusion that it is better to be isolated in pairs or groups. Of what use is the most beautiful place in the world if there is no-one to share it with?

Diving

Diving has become a very popular activity in the Philippines and not without reason. This country possesses a large selection of major diving areas, although many underwater sites in recent times have suffered violent ecological damage. To get first class dives

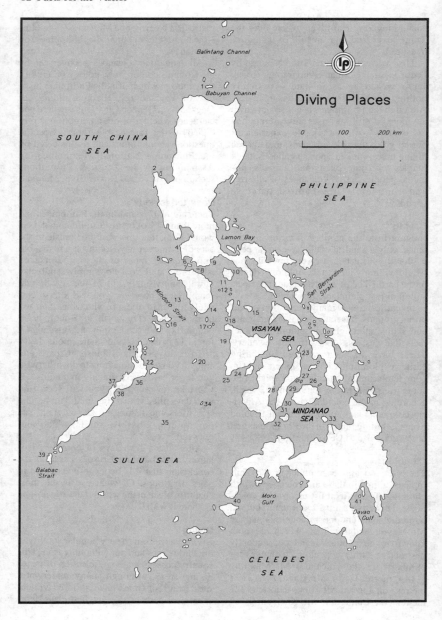

	Diving Place	Diving Season	Entry Point
1	Fuga Island	April – May	Fuga Island
2	Santiago Island	November – June	Bolinao
3	Polillo Islands	April – October	Infanta, Jomalig, Balesin
4	Nasugbu	November – June	Nasugbu
5	Lubang Islands	March – June	Catalagan (Batangas Province)
6	Balayan Bay	All Year	Anilao
7	Puerto Galera	All Year	Batangas City
8	Verde Island	All Year	Batangas City
9	Sigayan Bay	All Year	San Juan
10	Mopog Island	April – October	Lucena, Gasan
11	Tres Reyes Islands	April – October	Gasan
12	Dos Hermanas Islands	April – October	Gasan
13	Apo Reef	March – June	San Jose (Mindoro)
14	Buyallao	April – October	Mansalay
15	Cresta de Gallo	March – June	Tablas
16	Calamian Islands	All Year	Coron
17	Semirara Island	March – June	San Jose (Mindoro)
18	Boracay Island	All Year	Kalibo
19	Batbatan Island	April – June	San Jose (Panay)
20	Cuyo Islands	March – June & October	Cuyo
21	Bacuit Bay	November – June	Liminangcong, El Nido
22	Taytay Bay	April – October	Taytay
23	Capitancillo Island	April – October	Sogod
24	Cresta de Gallo	All Year	San Joaquin
25	Nagas Island	All Year	San Joaquin
26	Danajon Island	All Year	Mactan
27	Mactan	All Year	Cebu City, Mactan
28	Pescador Island	All Year	Moalboal
29	Cabilao Island	All Year	Tagbilaran
30	Panglao Island	All Year	Tagbilaran
31	Sumilon Island	All Year	Dumaguete
32	Apo Island	All Year	Dumaguete
33	Mambajao	All Year	Balingoan
34	Cagayan Islands	March – June	Cagayancillo
35	Tubbataha Reef	March – June	Puerto Princesa
36	Green Island Bay	April – October	Roxas
37	Ulugan Bay	November – June	Bahile
38	Honda Bay	April – October	Puerto Princesa
39	Balabac Island	All Year	Balabac
40	Santa Cruz Island	All Year	Zamboanga
41	Talikud Island	All Year	Davao

you should use proven diving operators who know the remaining good diving sites.

The Department of Tourism quickly recognised the growing popularity of diving and issued the informative *Discover the Philippines through Scuba Diving* guide. It lists 10 dive resorts, 11 dive shops and 16 agencies which offer excursions. For more information you can contact the addresses given in the brochure or the Philippine Commission on Sports/Scuba Diving, in the Tourism Building, Agrifina Circle, Rizal Park, Manila. A useful book is *The Diver's Guide to the Philippines* (Unicorn Books Ltd, Hong Kong, 1982) by David Smith and Michael Westlake.

Lots of diving businesses have grown over the last few years and an almost endless variety of programmes is available. During the high season (mid-March to mid-May) mobile dive bases are set up on various islands. You can hire completely equipped diving boats at any time of the year and you can rent anything you need from Manila's diving shops, although it is better to bring some of your own equipment. PAL will raise your baggage limit to 30 kg to allow for this, but any oxygen tanks you bring with you must be empty. If you need to buy diving equipment, try Aquaventure Philippines and Dive Mate, both on Pasong Tamo St, Makati, Manila. Besides locally made products they also have imported goods from Japan and the USA.

The most beautiful diving sites are far from the settled areas where the underwater scenery is likely to have been destroyed by drainage and dynamite. In the Mindoro Strait, east of the little island of Apo, you will find the Apo Reef. At low tide this reef is partly exposed and is among the most spectacular diving areas in the Philippines.

Probably the best place for diving is in the Sulu Sea on the little-explored Tubbataha Reef. Because of the long distance from the port of departure – it's about 185 km from Puerto Princesa in Palawan – and because of the resultant high costs involved, very few companies offer expeditions to this area. The Quiniluban Group is also difficult to get to. It comprises the northern section of the Cuyo Islands and is a protected area for turtles. The island world of the Calamian Group (Busuanga, Culion, Coron), the Bacuit Archipelago (El Nido) and Honda Bay (Puerto Princesa) is relatively easy to get to and is one of the most popular diving areas. Sumilon Island off the south-east coast of Cebu is a year-round favourite.

There is one thing they don't have to do in the Philippines that diving areas in other parts of the world find necessary: sinking ships deliberately, so adventure-hungry divers can have tempting targets to explore. Hundreds of years of maritime activity have made sure that the floor of the archipelago is littered with wrecks from typhoons, wars and collisions with reefs. Ideal conditions for exploration are found in the sound between the islands of Busuanga and Culion; in 1944

a fleet of 12 Japanese ships went down here, seven of them in a small protected bay, where the wrecks now lie in 30 to 40 metres of crystal clear water.

For 250 years Spanish galleons travelled between Manila and Acapulco in Mexico, laden with silver coins, gold, silk, porcelain, pearls, precious stones and other objects of value. Of the more than 30 trading vessels which were lost during this era, 21 sank in the coastal waters near the Philippines, mostly near Catanduanes, Samar and South Luzon. Fairy-tale treasures are said to be spread over the ocean floor and up to now the remains of only 14 of these wrecks have been located.

There is no law in the Philippines against searching for lost galleons. If you find one, however, you must inform the National Museum. If there is a recovery, the discoverer will get a share of the spoils. If you want to explore or photograph a known wreck, you should inform the National Museum of your intentions in writing. It is all too easy as a stranger to be charged with illegal plunder of treasure.

Gold Hunting

There is so much that wasn't found by the gold-hungry Spaniards. For over 300 years they ruled these islands, yet compared to the pillage of South and Central America, their excesses here were humble indeed. Today the Philippines has an output of 30 tonnes of pure gold annually, placing it at number six on the world scale. Less than 10% of the land mass has been explored using the detailed methods of modern mineralogy, so there is still a lot of ground to be covered.

Visitors to the Philippines are allowed to search for gold, the only drawback being that they are not allowed to keep or take out of the country any gold that they might find, as all wealth belongs to the state. In practice this is not always adhered to very strictly.

The best way to go fossicking is to get in touch with small-claim holders and make yourself known to local gold panners. If you want to follow a hot tip absolutely legally then you must find a Filipino partner for the business and use their name to contract mining rights with the Bureau of Mines & Geo-Sciences.

Sailing

Every two years Manila is the destination of the China Sea Race, a classic 1200 km regatta which starts in Hong Kong. This event not only serves to guide the participants through some exotic islands, but also brings with it thousands of spectators from the international yachting scene.

The monsoon which blows steadily from September to May in the north-east guarantees good sailing conditions and many natural harbours invite sailors to rest. It is not uncommon for a crew to decide to spend the winter in one of the beautiful bays of Puerto Galera or Balanacan.

Favourite spots for yachts include the anchorages in the Visayas. For sailing enthusiasts there is also the opportunity to take part in a round trip. You can ask about this at the Manila Yacht Club (MYC) on Roxas Blvd. The MYC is helpful to foreign yachts as well, and will organise guides or an escort from the coastguard when sailing through pirate-infested waters.

Trekking

There is always an alternative route available in the Philippines. Not just on the freeways and asphalt-covered streets, but along the paths and byways which crisscross the entire archipelago. It's possible to go from the far north to the deep south with minimum contact with motorised transport. On some islands in fact, it is practically impossible to see a car. Batan Island is an example. You can go around the island on a wonderful semi-surfaced coast road. Alternatively, there is Lubang where high-wheeled horse carts still dominate the traffic in spite of the introduction of a few jeeps. It is the same in Busuanga. There, once a day, a rattling old bus travels along the dirt road from Coron to Salvacion. The centre and the north of this island are practically free from cars.

There are wonderful opportunities for trekking along the Pacific coast in Bikol

Province and Quezon Province in Luzon. If you want to get to know the primeval landscape of Palawan, then you can try some of the many first-class treks there.

It is also tempting to read the recollections of the treks undertaken by European travellers in the last century, recorded in books which are witness to their love of the Philippines. Two of these are Fedor Jagor's *Travels in the Philippines* (London, 1873) and Paul de la Gironnière's *Adventures of a Frenchman in the Philippines* originally published in 1853 and republished in 1972 by Rarebook Enterprises, Caloocan City.

ACCOMMODATION

Have a look at the hotel room before you book in; inspect the showers and toilets and only then pay for the room. There are often cheaper rooms without windows in the inner part of the building. Hotels in the top category charge 25% for service and tax on top of the price of the room.

Throughout the Philippines you will find that prices for single and double rooms are sometimes the same. This is because single rooms sometimes have a double bed and can therefore be used by two people; to the Filipinos this is the same as a double room. Double rooms usually have two beds.

As there are frequently fires in the Philippines, you should check the exits. Having lived through a fire with useless fire equipment, been left hanging between floors in a lift several times due to power blackouts and having had to evacuate from a hotel because of an earthquake in Baguio, I've developed a preference for rooms on the ground floor. That may be somewhat overcautious.

The lighting in hotel rooms is often rather dim. If you want to read or write in the evenings you should get a light bulb of at least 60 watts beforehand.

It might be advisable to deposit any valuables in the hotel safe. If a simple drawer is used as a locker, don't entrust your things to the hotel. It is also inadvisable to leave large amounts of cash with the hotel reception.

If you do deposit your valuables in the hotel safe, get a receipt with an exact account of the details. Also ask whether you can get them back at any time. The night shift is not always entrusted with a key. When you do get your valuables back, check your cash and travellers' cheques carefully.

If you intend staying anywhere for some time ask about weekly and monthly rents. For a long stay it is worth taking a furnished apartment. This greatly reduces the expense.

In the provinces you may often be invited into private homes. It is the custom in the Philippines to offer guests the best food and lodging, but this can be very expensive for the family. Don't take advantage of this custom, but don't offer money directly for your board and keep either – say it's to educate their children, for example.

Should you have accommodation difficulties in smaller towns, go to the mayor or barrio captain. He will quickly arrange some shelter for you and may even find a place for you in the government resthouse.

Baths & Toilets

The term 'bath' has generally been used throughout the book to mean a bathroom that is equipped with a toilet and shower. It is only in 1st-class international hotels that you can expect a bathtub. Private Filipino homes normally have a shower and not a bathtub.

The toilets are known as comfort rooms or CRs – *lalake* means 'gentlemen' and *babae* 'ladies' in Filipino. The toilets in restaurants and bars are usually dirty and there is seldom toilet paper, but you will always find clean toilets in the lobbies of the larger hotels. Although Shakey's Pizza Parlours have expensive pizzas they do have clean toilets!

FOOD

Many Western travellers regard the Philippine diet as monotonous. Many dairy products are lacking and the daily fare consists of rice and fish, but if you are flexible you can add some variety. There are dairy products like milk, yoghurt, cheese and ice cream in most supermarkets, and meals can be varied by checking out the contents of the cooking pots in restaurants. In a turo-turo restaurant (turo means 'point') there is no menu: the food is displayed and customers point to what they would like to eat.

Of course the choice is more restricted in the country than in the city. In larger towns there are usually a number of Western and Chinese restaurants.

Filipino cuisine – with its Chinese, Malay and Spanish influences – is a mixture of Eastern and Western cuisine. The different dishes in a meal are all served at the same time with the result that certain dishes end up being eaten cold, something which Filipinos normally don't mind. Cold fried eggs for breakfast is a typically less-than-appetising possibility.

Apart from the regular meals, in the mornings and afternoons a more or less extensive snack called *merienda* is taken. Besides this, *pulutan* (small morsels) appear on the table when alcoholic drinks are served.

Westernised Filipinos usually eat with a spoon and fork; knives are not often used. However, the original *kamayan* mode, namely eating with the fingers off a banana leaf, has come back into fashion, so there is no cutlery laid on the table in a kamayan restaurant. Such restaurants are flourishing throughout the land.

It's worthwhile when travelling around to ask for the speciality of the province, which can be surprisingly good.

Eating & Drinking

As a rule of thumb, it is cheap and worthwhile eating where the locals eat, but even Western food is not that expensive. In some restaurants you can get a complete meal for around P100.

At the eateries in the larger towns, grills are very popular in the evenings. You can get liver, pork, chicken and seafood in the form of barbecue sticks. In the warm summer months of April and May, when selecting your choice of fresh meat for grilling, check it out with your nose first.

Water in the Philippines is always clean and drinkable, at least in the towns. In the country it pays to be a bit more careful. I would advise against ice cream in open containers from a travelling vendor. It would be better to buy the packaged Magnolia Dairy Bars.

The Filipino Menu

Rice is the staple food and will be served with most meals. A particular addition to the make-up of the dish requires skilful preparation.

The following description of Philippine foods and drinks may make it a little easier to choose when confronted with a menu.

Adobo – A national standard dish made from chicken *(chicken adobo)*, pork *(pork adobo)*, squid *(pusit adobo)* and/or vegetables and cooked with vinegar, pepper, garlic and salt.

Adobong Pusit – Cleaned cuttlefish is prepared with coconut milk, vinegar and garlic. The ink is used as a special seasoning.

Ampalaya con Carne – Beef with bitter melon, prepared with onions, garlic, soy sauce and some sesame oil. Served with rice.

Arroz Caldo – Thick rice soup with chicken cooked with onions, garlic and ginger, and black pepper added afterwards.

Asado – Seasonal smoked meat, served with sour *atsara* (papaya strips).

Aso – Dog! Stray mongrel in a piquant sauce. This is a special dish in central and North Luzon. Because of many protests from dog-loving countries, this practice is now forbidden. The Ifugao have lodged an appeal with the government for exemption, stating that aso is a fundamental part of their culture and tradition.

Atsara – This is a very healthy and vitamin rich side dish, the Philippine sauerkraut – unripe papayas.

Bagoong – Pungent smelling, fermented, salty fish or shrimp sauce or pasta. It is often prepared according to traditional folk-recipes. Bagoong is a popular accompaniment to dishes such as green mango, for example.

Balut – A popular Filipino snack for between meals, said to make you fit. Before a Filipino suitor invites a woman to see his stamp collection, he'll usually partake in a couple of baluts washed down with beer. Baluts can be purchased from street sellers and markets. A balut is a half-boiled, ready-to-hatch duck egg. You can distinguish the beak and feathers! Some baluts still contain some liquid so don't break open the whole egg: make a small hole first.

Bangus (Milkfish) – This is a herring-size fish that is lightly grilled, stuffed and baked.

Batchoy – This consists of beef, pork and liver in noodle soup. A speciality of the western Visayas.

Bulalo – A substantial soup of boiled beef (kneecap), marrow and vegetables.

Calamares Fritos – Fried squid.

Caldereta – A stew of goat's meat or beef, peas and paprika.

Crispy Pata – Pig skin first cooked then seasoned with garlic, salt, pepper and vinegar, and then baked in oil till crispy. There are many ways of seasoning and preparing it. Crispy pata is often served cut into small pieces. There is usually more crackling than meat – which is how the Filipinos like it!

Dinuguan – Finely chopped offal (pork or chicken) roasted in fresh blood and usually seasoned with whole green pepper corns. This dish is also called chocolate meat on account of its dark colour.

Gambas al Ajillo – Shelled raw shrimps prepared with olive oil, pepper, salt, some paprika and a lot of garlic. Served with white bread.

Ginataan – Dishes cooked in coconut milk.

Halo-Halo – Dessert made from crushed ice mixed with coloured sweets and fruits, smothered in evaporated milk and mixed together (halo-halo means 'all mixed together'). It tastes noticeably better with a little rum.

Inihaw – Grilled fish or meat.

Kare-Kare – A stew of oxtail, beef shank, vegetables, onions and garlic. The stock can be enriched with peanuts and lightly fried rice, both finely ground.

Kilawin – Small cuts of raw meat lightly roasted, then marinated in vinegar and other spices (ginger, onion, salt).

Kinilaw – Small cuts of raw fish or cuttlefish marinated with spices (ginger, onion, chilli) in vinegar or lemon.

Lapu-Lapu Inihaw – Grilled grouper, seasoned with salt, pepper, garlic and soy sauce. Lapu-Lapu is the most popular fish dish in the country, but is expensive. It was named after the Filipino chief who killed Ferdinand Magellan in battle.

Lechon – Suckling pig served with a thick liver sauce. Lechon *(litson)* is an important dish at fiestas.

Lechon Kawali – Pork leg, baked and seasoned with green papaya, ginger, vinegar and sugar.

Lumpia – Spring rolls filled with vegetables or meat. They are served with soy sauce, vinegar or a slightly sweet sauce.

Lumpia Shangai – These are fried spring rolls filled with meat, whereas the bigger *lumpia sariwa* are filled with vegetables and served uncooked.

Mami – Noodle soup; when made with chicken it's chicken mami, with beef it's *beef mami* etc.

Menudo – Stew made from either small liver pieces or chopped pork, with diced potatoes, tomatoes, paprika and onions.

Misua Soup – Soup made from rice noodles, beef, garlic and onions.

Nilaga – Soup with cabbage, potatoes and meat. With beef its *nilaga baka*.

Pancit Canton – This is a noodle dish made with thick noodles which are baked, then combined with pork, shrimps and vegetables. The pork is cooked in soy sauce beforehand.

Pancit Guisado – This is a noodle dish like pancit canton but thin Chinese noodles are used.

Pork Apritada – Pork is cut into small pieces and baked. The sauce includes pieces of tomato, onions, potatoes, pepperoni and garlic.

Shrimp Rebosado – Shrimps are baked in butter then cooked in a roux.

Sinigang – This is sour vegetable soup with fish *(sinigang na isda)* or pork *(sininang na baboy)*. It can be served with rice.

Siopao – A white, steam heated dough ball with a filling such as chicken or pork. A quick snack.

Tahong – Large green mussels are cooked or baked in sauce.

Talaba – Raw oysters are soaked in vinegar and garlic.

Tapa – This is baked dried beef served with raw onion rings. Tapa is also available as a vacuum-packed preserved food but this tastes dreadful – remarkably like plastic.

Tinola – A stew of chicken, vegetables, ginger, onions and garlic.

Atis (Custard Apple)

Tropical Fruit

In a tropical country like the Philippines you would expect to find many colourful fruit stalls, but you would be looking in vain. Naturally, fruits like pineapple, bananas, papaya and mangoes are available, but not on every street corner.

Atis (Custard Apple) – Also known as 'sugar apple' or 'cinnamon apple', this fruit has a scaly, grey-green skin and looks rather like a hand grenade. To get at its soft white flesh it's best to cut the custard apple in half and remove its kernel with a knife. The skin is not palatable. The fruit is in season from August to October.

Chico (Sapodilla) – This roughly egg-shaped fruit with a brown skin contains a soft, sweet, brownish coloured flesh that looks like wet sand. The skin is normally peeled off but you can also eat it. It's in season from November to February.

Durian (Durian) – This is the name of a thick, prickly fruit, about which opinions are sharply divided: either you're crazy about it or you can't stand it. There's no in-between. Cutting open the outer shell reveals four segments with several large seeds surrounded by the flesh of the fruit. Depending on your tastes, the creamy, yellowish-white flesh either has a very pleasant aroma or stinks terribly. This fruit, with its 'hellish stench and heavenly taste', is in season from August to October.

Chico (Sapodilla)

Durian (Durian)

Gayabas (Guava) – An egg-sized to apple-sized fruit with light, crispy, faintly acidic flesh and numerous small, hard seeds. Rich in Vitamin C. It's in season from July to January.

Gayabas (Guava)

Guayabano (Sour Sop) – The fibrous, juicy flesh of this thorny fruit, which can weigh up to two kg, has a tart, tangy taste and is ideal for making tasty juices and mixed drinks. It's in season from August to November.

Guayabano (Sour Sop)

Kaimito (Star Apple) – Slicing a star apple reveals an arrangement of several star shaped segments, hence its name. Soft and very juicy, it is best eaten with a spoon. There are green and violet kinds of star apple, both of which are ripe and edible. The violet ones are sweeter. It's in season from January to March.

Kaimito (Star Apple)

Kalamansi (Kalamansi) – This juicy, green lemon-like fruit is about the size of a pinball. It goes beautifully with black tea and is indispensable in the Filipino kitchen for the preparation of 'happy hour' drinks at sunset or whenever.

Kalamansi (Kalamansi)

Langka (Jackfruit) – This is a colossus among fruit. Greenish yellow with coarse skin, it can weigh up to 20 kg and may be as big as a blown-up balloon. The pale yellow flesh is split into portions and eaten as a salad or vegetable; the seeds should be cooked before being eaten. The jackfruit season is from February to July.

Langka (Jackfruit)

Lanzones (Lanson) – This looks like a little potato. Under its easily peeled, yellow-brown skin is a delicious, translucent flesh. But be careful: occasionally one of the flesh segments will contain small, very bitter inedible seeds. It's in season from August to November.

Lanzones (Lanson)

Mangga (Mango) – This oval shaped fruit can be up to 20 cm long and has a large, flat stone. When the skin is green it is unripe, hard and very sour, but tastes marvellous with salt or a bitter, salty shrimp-paste called bagoong. The flesh of a ripe mango is yellow, juicy and vaguely reminiscent of the peach in taste. The mango is split into three by cutting the fruit lengthwise along the flat stone. The two side sections are eaten with a spoon, the centre piece should be speared with a pointed knife and the flesh gnawed off. The skin is inedible. It's in season between April and June.

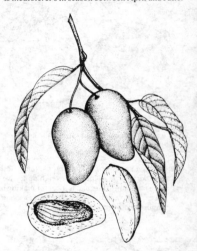

Mangga (Mango)

Mangostan (Mangosteen) – This dark purple fruit is about the size of an apple and has a tough skin. To get to the sweet-sour, white flesh you break it open or use a knife. It's in season from May to October.

Pakwan (Watermelon) – The size of a football, the flesh of this dark-green melon is red and watery. For a wonderfully refreshing dessert, pour a small glass of Cointreau over a chilled slice of watermelon. Watermelons are available all year-round, but especially from April to November.

Papaya (Papaya) – This is a species of melon which, when ripe, reveals a delicious, orange-red flesh under a shiny green to orange-coloured skin. It's best to cut one lengthways, remove the black seeds, sprinkle a little kalamansi juice over the halves and spoon out the pulp. Papaya are in season right through the year.

Pasionaryo (Passion Fruit) – The passion fruit is also known as *maracuja*. Under its skin you'll find a surprisingly sweet, liquid pulp which is best spooned out. The abundant seeds can be eaten too. The passion fruit is mostly available from March to October.

Piña (Pineapple) – Pineapples can be bought the whole year-round. They're at their juiciest and sweetest during the main season from March to May.

Rambutan (Rambutan) – This is a funny-looking fruit, shaped rather like an egg with a reddish, hairy skin. Under the cute packaging you'll find a delicious translucent sweet pulp. Rambutans are sold in bunches and are picked from August to October.

Saging (Banana) – There are over 20 known varieties. Bananas are available all year-round. You can have them not only as freshly picked fruit, but also cooked, grilled, baked or roasted.

Suha (Giant Orange) – This fruit also goes by the name of *pomelo* and resembles a huge grapefruit. It tastes rather like a grapefruit too, except that it's somewhat sweeter. You'll have to peel away a very thick skin to get at the flesh, which is usually fairly dry. You can get giant oranges right through the year.

DRINKS
Nonalcoholic Drinks

Most of the drinks in the Philippines are safe as they are bottled, including milk and chocolate drinks. Fruit juices served with water are also quite safe. However, it's best to avoid unbottled drinks or drinks with ice cubes.

Mineral water is called soda or soda water in the Philippines and is available in many tourists resorts.

Coconut Juice Only very young *buko* (coconuts) with their soft, nutritious flesh are considered edible in the Philippines. The hard flesh of older coconuts is dried in the sun and processed as copra. If you want to enjoy the delicious, refreshing juice of a young nut, get the fruit seller to open it for you to drink.

Here's a small tip for a taste sensation: pour out some of the coconut juice, insert small pieces of papaya, pineapple and, if possible, mango, top up the contents with rum and let it stand for about 12 hours in the refrigerator.

Alcohol

Tuba is a palm wine made from the juice of coconut palms. It is tapped from the crown of the tree. Tuba is drunk fresh or after a fermentation process. When distilled it is called *lambanog*.

An alcoholic drink made from fermented sugar cane juice is *basi*, an ice-cooled sweet variant of which has a taste reminiscent of sherry or port. *Tapuy (tapey)* is a rice wine and the end of its six-month fermentation process is eagerly anticipated. Only after this period can you discover whether the aimed-for taste has been achieved or if the wine has become sour and undrinkable.

There are several brands of beer. Apart from the strong Red Horse beer, they are all light and, with a few exceptions, are very good to drink. San Miguel is the most well-known beer and, with over a 90% share of the market, is also the most successful. Relatively new on the market from Denmark is Carlsberg, which is brewed and bottled in the Philippines, but whether it's 'probably the best beer in the world' or not is a matter of taste.

Hard drinks – rum, whisky, gin and brandy – of local manufacture are very good value. The well-aged rums of particularly fine quality are Tanduay, Anejo and Tondeña. Spirits are often called wine in the Philippines. If it is literally red or white wine you want, then grapes wine is what you should order.

ENTERTAINMENT
Cinemas

Cinemas are good value – for a few pesos (P15 and up) you frequently get a double feature. There are particular starting times but no fixed entry times, which means there is a constant coming and going during the programmes. Disaster movies, murders and vampires are the preferred themes. Watch out for the national anthem – sometimes they play it at the end, sometimes at the beginning, usually not at all. If they do play it, all the Filipinos will stand up. It's best to join them. Cameras are not allowed in cinemas.

Nightclubs

The Filipinos are very keen on their nightlife – it certainly does not depend solely on tourists. There are bars, clubs and massage parlours in the provinces where foreigners seldom go, but in the big cities tourism has certainly contributed to the booming nightlife.

Although they are more enticing after dark, you can, of course, frequent the bars during the day. However, serious drinkers will hang on to their money until the happy hour when the price of drinks is reduced. Most nightclubs demand a cover charge and/or a table charge. It's justifiable if there's a good programme, but it's also advisable to enquire beforehand how much you are likely to be up for in the end. The bars and clubs of the big hotels can be excellent places for meeting people.

There are many bars with 'hospitality girls' always ready for a 'chat' and happy to let men buy them a 'lady's drink' – which is usually little more than cola and two to three times more expensive than beer! The bar and the girls both profit from this. In an expensive club, conversation with one of the hostesses can cost P200 an hour – not bad for the conversational skills of the young 'student'. Women from overseas should not be misled by notices saying 'unescorted ladies not allowed': this only refers to the local professionals.

The private operators are called streetwalkers or, more picturesquely, 'hunting girls' – parks and open-air restaurants are their hunting grounds and they work around the clock. Some of these 'short timers' have made a lot of money in a short period of time. Giving in to temptation brings with it the risk of catching a sexually transmitted disease. Places where there is a high rate of change of partner do wonders for increased turnover in antibiotics.

THINGS TO BUY

There are many souvenirs you can buy in the Philippines, particularly in the handicrafts line. Cane work, woodcarving, clothes and articles made of shells are all popular. You can find many items in Manila, particularly around Ermita, in the Ilalim ng Tulay Market at the Quezon Bridge in Quiapo or the Shoemart department store in the Makati Commercial Center, but there is also a wide variety in Cebu, Davao and Zamboanga.

Clothing

The Philippines has become a major manufacturing centre for cheap Western-style clothing, but many men come away from the Philippines with the shirt which is the Filipino national dress – the long-sleeved barong tagalog or its short-sleeved version, the polo barong.

Woodwork

Much of the woodcarving is of the tourist-kitsch variety but you can also find some useful articles such as salad bowls. The Ifugao people in North Luzon's Ifugao Province also produce some high-quality woodcarving.

Cane Work & Basketry

In South Luzon abaca products are the main craft. Abaca is a fibre produced from a relative of the banana tree. Its best known end product was the rope known as Manila hemp but today it's made into bags, placemats and other woven products. There's some interesting basket work from Mountain Province and the island of Bohol. Mats and cane furniture are also good buys.

Other Items

Shell jewellery, wind chimes and plain shells are all popular purchases. Zamboanga and Cebu are shell centres. The usual caveat emptor – where the buyer bears the risks of purchase unless the seller provides a warranty – applies to Philippine antiques. Brass ware is a speciality in Mindanao. Hand-woven cottons from Mountain Province are produced in such limited quantities they don't even reach Manila – they're much cheaper in Bontoc or Banaue than in Baguio.

Baskets

Baskets of various shapes, patterns and colours of bamboo, rattan, buri and pandanus are made by the cultural minorities of Mountain Province (North Luzon) and the island of Bohol.

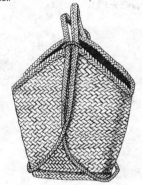

Carry basket

Snake basket

Hand basket

Grain container

Backpack

Grain container

Marble eggs and other marble items come from Romblon. Apart from the *piña* (pineapple-fibre) fabrics, Iloilo is also noted for *santos* (statues of saints). Cebu is the guitar centre of the Philippines, but note that cheap guitars are unlikely to be able to withstand drier, nontropical climates. Lilang's Guitar Factory on Mactan Island is a good place to buy one – you'll find pleasant people, and guitars for P250 to P3000.

Getting There & Away

AIR

Basically, the only way to get to the Philippines is by plane, and there are only a couple of entry points – Manila and Cebu. There are no regular shipping services into the Philippines.

There are flights to Manila from most of the Philippines' Asian neighbours, including Japan, Hong Kong, Singapore and Malaysia, as well as from Australia, New Zealand, the USA and Europe.

Officially, you must have an onward or return ticket before you're allowed to board a flight to the Philippines. This is even more necessary if you arrive without a visa. It has recently been reported that immigration officials in Manila have been denying entry to travellers who are unable to produce a departure ticket, especially when they don't have a visa stamped in their passport. If this happens, you can only hope to find some friendly person nearby who can quickly arrange the necessary ticket for you. You will find the airline offices upstairs in the airport building.

Other possible entry points are in Mindanao. From time to time there have been flights between Zamboanga (on Mindanao) and either Kota Kinabalu, Sandakan or Tawau in Sabah (the Malaysian state occupying the north-eastern corner of Borneo). At present none of these irregular flights seems to be operating. It's a drag because the idea of making your way through Borneo and then making the short hop across to Mindanao in the Philippines has a lot of appeal. Instead you have to backtrack to Kota Kinabalu and make the much longer and more expensive flight from there to Manila.

However, there are now regular flights operating twice a week with the Indonesian airline Bouraq Airlines between Davao in the south of Mindanao and Manado in the north Sulawesi of Indonesia. Apparently, there is also a ship, MV *Sonic*, belonging to the Sariphil-Indo Corporation, which makes the trip between the two cities twice a month. The tourist office or the Indonesian Consulate in Davao will probably be able to give you up-to-date information.

Round-the-World Tickets

RTW fares, as Round-the-World tickets are known, have become all the rage of late. Basically, two or more airlines get together and offer a ticket which gets you around the world using only their services. You're allowed stopovers (sometimes unlimited) and you have to complete the circuit within a certain period of time.

Philippine Airlines (PAL) offers a RTW ticket in combination with Canadian Airlines and Brazilian Airlines which will take you from Australia to the Philippines, Asia, Europe, the USA and back to Australia for A\$3199. The usual Apex booking conditions apply and you have 120 days to complete the circuit. From London, RTW tickets typically cost around UK£1000 to UK£1400, depending on the airlines and routes used.

Circle Pacific Tickets

Circle Pacific fares are a variation on the RTW idea and once again there's an option that includes the Philippines. PAL, American Airlines and Quantas have a ticket that lets you combine the USA, New Zealand, Australia, Asia and the Philippines in a loop around the Pacific. You can make as many stopovers as the two airlines' routes will permit and have up to six months to complete the loop. The ticket must be purchased at least 30 days before departure, after which the usual cancellation penalties apply.

Although you must make all reservations before the 30 day cut-off point, you can alter flight dates after departure at no cost as long as you have a revalidation sticker on your ticket. If you want to change your route, requiring your ticket to be rewritten, there's a US\$50 charge. Economy class Circle

---

Air Travel Glossary

Apex *A*-dvance *P*-urchase *Ex*-cursion is a discounted ticket which must be paid for in advance. You pay big penalties for changes or cancellations. Insurance can sometimes be taken out against these penalties.

Baggage Allowance This is written on your ticket: usually one or two items totalling 20 kg per person to go in the hold, plus one item of hand luggage.

Bucket Shop An unbonded travel agency specialising in discounted airline tickets. Not all are honest.

Bumped Just because you have a confirmed seat doesn't mean you're going to get on the plane; see Overbooking.

Cancellation Penalties If you have to cancel or change an Apex ticket there are often heavy penalties involved, insurance can sometimes be taken out against these penalties. Some airlines impose penalties on regular tickets as well, particularly against 'no show' passengers.

Charter Flights Group-tour charters can be cheaper than scheduled flights in the low season. Some tour operators will book you on a seat-only basis, though usually not very far in advance. Prices for unfilled seats may plummet as departure day nears, and 'bucket shops' do a thriving business in these last-minute bargains (though you may not have a wide choice of flight dates).

Check In Airlines ask you to check in a certain time ahead of the flight departure, typically 1½ to 2½ hours for international flights. If you fail to do so and the flight is overbooked, the airline may cancel your booking and give your seat to somebody else.

Confirmation Having a ticket written out with the flight and date you want doesn't mean you have a seat until the agent has checked with the airline that your status is 'OK' or confirmed. Meanwhile you could just be 'on request'.

Discounted Tickets There are two types of discounted fares – officially discounted (see Promotional Fares) and unofficially discounted. The lowest prices often impose drawbacks like flying with unpopular airlines, inconvenient schedules, or unpleasant routes and connections. A discounted ticket can save you other things than money – you may be able to pay Apex prices without the associated Apex advance booking and other requirements. Discounted tickets only exist where there is fierce competition.

Full Fares Airlines traditionally offer first class (coded F), business class (J) and economy class (Y) tickets. Thanks to discounts, few passengers pay full economy fare nowadays.

Lost Tickets If you lose your ticket an airline will usually treat it like a travellers' cheque and, after enquiries, issue you with another one. Legally, however, an airline is entitled to treat it like cash and if you lose it then it's gone forever. Take good care of your tickets.

No Shows No shows are passengers who fail to show up for their flight, sometimes due to unexpected delays or disasters, sometimes due to simply forgetting, sometimes because they made more than one booking and didn't bother to cancel the one they didn't want. Full fare

---

Pacific fares are US$2449 from the USA, A$2990 from Australia or NZ$3849 from New Zealand.

To/From the USA

From the west coast, Los Angeles or San Francisco, the nonstop economy fare is US$480/800 one way/return with Japan Air-lines and Cathay Pacific, and you can tag two stopovers on to this fare at US$50 a time.

You can fly with Continental Airlines and PAL from Tampa, Florida, for US$745/1200 one way/return, and from Honolulu, Hawaii with Korean Airlines for US$570/876 one way/return.

passengers who fail to turn up are sometimes entitled to travel on a later flight. The rest of us are penalised (see Cancellation Penalties).

On Request An unconfirmed booking for a flight, see Confirmation.

Open Jaws A return ticket where you fly out to one place but return from somewhere else; if available this can save you backtracking to your arrival point.

Overbooking Airlines hate to fly empty seats and since every flight has some passengers who fail to show up, airlines often book more passengers than they have seats. Usually the excess passengers balance those who fail to show up but occasionally somebody gets bumped – most likely those who fail to reconfirm and/or who check in late.

Promotional Fares Officially discounted fares like Apex fares which are available from travel agents or direct from the airline.

Reconfirmation At least 72 hours prior of an onward or return flight you must contact the airline and reconfirm your intention to be on the flight. If you don't, you could lose your seat. You don't have to reconfirm the first flight on your itinerary or if your stopover is less than 72 hours, but it can't hurt. It also doesn't hurt to reconfirm more than once.

Restrictions Discounted tickets often have restrictions attached to them. Advance purchase is the most usual one (see Apex). Another is the minimum and/or maximum period between departure and return.

Standby A discounted ticket where you only fly if there is a seat free at the last moment. Standby fares are normally available only on domestic routes.

Tickets Out An entry requirement for many countries is that you have an onward or return ticket, in other words, a ticket out of the country. If you're not sure what you intend to do next, the easiest solution is to buy the cheapest onward ticket to a neighbouring country or a ticket from a reliable airline which can later be refunded if you do not use it.

Transferred Tickets Tickets cannot legally be transferred from one person to another. Travellers sometimes try to sell the return half of a ticket, but officials can ask you to prove that you're the person named on the ticket. This is rare with domestic flights, but on international flights tickets may be compared with passports.

Travel Agencies These vary widely and you should pick one that suits your needs. Full-service agencies do everything from tours and tickets to car rental and hotel bookings and some simply handle tours. A good one can save you a lot of money and headaches, but if all you want is the cheapest possible ticket, then find an agency specialising in this.

Travel Periods (Seasons) Some discounts – on Apex fares in particular – vary with the time of year and sometimes the direction of travel. Certain journeys have a high or peak season (when everyone wants to fly) and a low or off-peak season, and sometimes an intermediate or 'shoulder' season as well. At peak times official and unofficial discounts will be lower or nonexistent. Usually the fare depends on when your outward flight is – ie, if you depart in the high season but return in the low season, you pay the high-season fare. ■

To/From Canada

From Vancouver, Canada, the cost of a flight to Manila is C$720/998 one way/return with Japan Airlines and C$760/1100 one way/return with Cathay Pacific.

To/From Australia

You can fly from Australia to the Philippines with PAL or Qantas. There are two fare seasons – high and low – but the high season level only applies during the school summer break in December and January.

On PAL the one-way economy fares are A$809/949 in the low/high season; return fares are A$1049/1249 in the low/high season. These fares are valid for a stay of 28 days only. With Qantas, one-way economy-class fares to Manila from Sydney,

Melbourne, Adelaide or Brisbane are A$809/949 in the low/high season. Return fares are A$1149/1349 in the low/high season.

To/From New Zealand

There are no direct flights between New Zealand and Manila so there are no real bargains. The cheapest fare available is on Thai International via Sydney and Bangkok for around NZ$1349 in the low season and NZ$1648 in the high season.

To/From Asia

There are lots of flights to the Philippines from its Asian neighbours. Cheap deals tend to vary these days – one day one country is cheaper, the next day another. Currently it appears that Bangkok is no longer the bargain basement and that Hong Kong is the place for good deals.

From Hong Kong the regular economy one-way/return fare to Manila is HK$1250/1800. From Japan the one-way fare is Y65,400 and the return Y106,820. From Korea it costs US$293 one-way or US$495 return, and from Taipei, Taiwan, flights costs US$230/380 one way/return.

Out of Malaysia, the regular one-way fare from Kuala Lumpur is US$281and US$490 return, and from Kota Kinabalu M$492 one way and M$986 return. In Thailand the regular one-way/return fare from Bangkok is 3600/5995B. You can fly to Manila from Singapore for S$465/665 one way/return, and from Siagon, Vietnam, for US$240 one way and US$480 return. From Jakarta, Indonesia, the cost of a one-way fare is US$250 and US$440 return and from Denpasar (Bali) the cost is US$275 one way and US$540 return.

To Cebu City, flights from Singapore cost S$464 one way and S$475 return. To Davao a one-way fare from Manado, Sulawesi, Indonesia, is US$150 and US$262 return.

To/From Europe

PAL and a number of European airlines, including British Airways, connect London and other major European capitals with Manila. The regular economy one-way/return fare from London to Manila is UK£400/640 and 90-day excursion return fares cost UK£865. You can get to Manila from London for much less by shopping around London's numerous bucket shops.

Bucket shops are travel agents who specialise in discounting airline tickets – a practice for which London is probably the world headquarters. To find out what fares are available, scan the weekly what's on magazine *Time Out* or the *News & Travel Magazine*, which is free. Two excellent places to look for cheap tickets are Trailfinders, on Earls Court Rd, or STA Travel, on Old Brompton Rd. Typical discount fares between London and Manila are around UK£259 one-way or UK£455 return.

Another way to get to the Philippines cheaply from London is to fly to Hong Kong and continue from there. Competition on the London to Hong Kong route is cut-throat. There are also attractively priced tickets available from London to Australia with the Philippines as a stopover.

Alternatively, the cost of a one-way/return fare from Frankfurt, Germany, to Manila is DM1000/1600 (US$610/920) and from Zurich, Switzerland, the cost is Sfr910/1380 (US$620/940). You can also find good ticket deals to the Philippines in Belgium and the Netherlands.

SEA

Although there are many excellent connections by ship around the Philippine islands, the possibilities of getting to the Philippines from overseas are very limited. You might find a passenger-carrying freight ship out of Hong Kong or Singapore, but, in these containerised days, it is increasingly unlikely. There are regular sea connections between Borneo and Mindanao, but, since smugglers and pirates mainly operate there, you're unlikely to be too popular on arrival.

LEAVING THE PHILIPPINES
Airfares

The Philippines is no place to look for cheap airline tickets. Although Manila has over 300 travel agents, the lack of competition is astounding. Discounts are available but you have to be persistent and shop around. There are lots of agents around the Ermita area, particularly off Roxas Blvd and in T M Kalaw St, by Rizal Park. Check out Mr Ticket Travel (☎ 5224835-38; fax 5224840) in the Hotel Swiss Inn, at 1030 Belen St, Paco; Interisland Travel & Tours (☎ 5222434; fax 5224795) at 1322 Roxas Blvd, Ermita; and Broadway Travel (☎ 591924; fax 5224795), 1322 Roxas Blvd, Ermita. You can also try the Youth & Student Travel Association of the Philippines (YSTAPHIL) (☎ 8320680; fax 8187948) at 4227 Tomas Claudio St, Parañaque.

Typical one-way fares from Manila include Bangkok US$180, Hong Kong US$120, Tokyo US$210, Taipei US$120 and Singapore US$230. Northwest, PAL, Korean Airlines and China Airlines have budget fares to the US. To go to the US west coast it costs US$370 in the low season and US$430 in the high. To the east coast it costs US$490 in the low season and US$545 in the high.

To reach European destinations, you can fly to Amsterdam, Frankfurt or London for around US$550, to Paris it costs US$600, to Stockholm US$660 and to Zurich US$610.

Departure

Make absolutely certain you confirm your onward flight with the airline at least 72 hours before departure. It's even better to confirm your outward flight when you arrive. That way you can be fairly certain that your booking has been registered on the computer. Don't check in at the last minute; flights are often overbooked and, in spite of a confirmed ticket, you can find yourself bumped from the flight! If you have excess baggage, it's worth giving the baggage hand-

lers a generous tip and letting them take care of the problem.

Departure Tax When you depart from NAIA you have to pay a P500 airport tax. You can take up to P1000 out with you, and have unused pesos reconverted, but only if you have receipts from official moneychangers or banks. The bank counter is in the exit hall.

One traveller advised keeping enough pesos for taxi fares and departure tax, but not arriving at the airport with too much money. In his case, when a PAL and a Qantas flight both left for Australia on a Sunday night, the bank did not have enough Australian dollars to meet demand. In that situation, it's probably better to change your money into US dollars or another hard currency, rather than trying to change pesos overseas at a bad rate.

WARNING

The information in this chapter is especially vulnerable to change – prices for international air travel are volatile, routes are introduced and cancelled, schedules change, rules are amended and special deals come and go. Airlines and governments seem to take a perverse pleasure in making price structures and regulations as complicated as possible; you should check directly with the airline or a travel agent to make sure you understand how a fare works. In addition, the travel industry is highly competitive and there are many lurks and perks. The upshot of this is that you should get opinions, quotes and advice from as many airlines and travel agents as possible before you part with your hard-earned cash.

The details given in this chapter should be regarded as pointers and not as a substitute for your own careful, up-to-the-minute research.

Getting Around

AIR

After practically monopolising the air traffic scene for many years, PAL (the state airline) is now facing a bit of competition from smaller companies like Aerolift and Pacific Airways. Though modest enterprises, these other airlines offer valid alternatives for people travelling in the region. Ever since the catastrophic shipping disasters of the 1980s, there's been a dramatic increase in the use of domestic airlines – the packed-out local commuter planes are proof enough of this. So these days it's very important to book a seat well in advance.

(The Aerolift & Pacific Airways Routes map on the facing page shows the routes covered by these airlines and the cost of one-way fares at the time of publication; you will find details of their flight schedules in the Getting There & Away section in the Manila chapter later in this book. Note: Pacific Airways flights are especially unreliable and should not be depended on when planning an itinerary.)

Philippine Airlines (PAL)

PAL flies between nearly all the larger cities. Over the Christmas period, between 15 December and 4 January, all flights are usually fully booked.

The flight schedule changes two to four times a year, but only in minor details, so you'll have a reasonable idea of what's available in local flights by consulting the information in the Getting There & Away section in the Manila chapter and allowing for slight variations. When available, a current 'Domestic Flight Schedule' can be obtained at the PAL office on Roxas Blvd, Manila. (If there are none printed, you can make your own copy of the table displayed on the 1st floor.) You'll find at least part of the flight schedule reproduced in the tourist magazine *What's on in Manila*, which is available free in the main hotels. The PAL

fleet contains jets (A-300, Boeing 737) and turboprops (Fokker 50). Smoking is not permitted on board.

PAL customers are attended to in numerical order in the city offices; even to obtain a small piece of information, you have to take a number and wait your turn. It's always best to ring up if you want quick information. The Manila office has set up a round-the-clock Info-Service on ☎ 8166691.

Students under 26 years of age taking round-trip flights (eg, Manila-Cebu-Manila or Manila-Zamboanga-Davao-Cebu-Manila) are entitled to a 15% reduction. As well as your student card, you may be asked to produce your passport (and a photocopy, including the photo) when purchasing the ticket.

PAL also offers a Golden Age Discount of 15% for passengers over 60 years of age. To be eligible for this, you have to pay P50 for an application form which you must fill out and hand in to the Discount counter, together with two photocopies of your passport. You will then receive an identification card which has to be produced when you buy a ticket.

Bookings can be changed free of charge only if made before noon on the day before the flight. After that, you'll have to pay a processing fee of about P50. Any airport tax payable on domestic flights is included in the price of the ticket. The airport tax for international flights is P500 at present.

Passengers on domestic flights are officially allowed only 18 kg of luggage free of charge. This limit is not strictly enforced in the case of tourists, so it's handy to be able to produce your passport or a copy of it as proof. Extra baggage costs about P15 per kg (depending on the route).

The PAL Airlines Routes map in this chapter shows regular PAL airfares on some of the main routes. PAL flight frequencies vary considerably. On some main sectors there are several flights daily (around 10 from Manila to Cebu), while on lesser routes

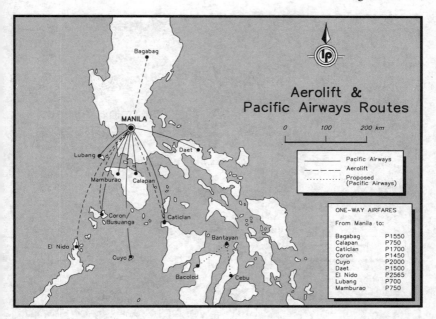

Aerolift &
Pacific Airways Routes

	Pacific Airways
	Aerolift
	Proposed (Pacific Airways)

ONE-WAY AIRFARES

From Manila to:

Bagabag	P1550
Calapan	P750
Caticlan	P1700
Coron	P1450
Cuyo	P2000
Daet	P1500
El Nido	P2565
Lubang	P700
Mamburao	P750

there may be just a few flights a week. Sample prices of one-way fares from Manila are: to Baguio P560 ($US20); to Cebu P1400 ($US50); to Puerto Princesa P1425 ($US50); and to Davao P2515 ($US90).

BUS
Long Distance Bus

There are large buses with or without air-con (described as air-con and ordinary or regular buses) as well as minibuses, also called 'baby buses'. If you have long legs, you will find the most comfortable seats in the minibuses are those beside the driver. In the large overland buses, the back seats may be your best choice, mainly because you get to sit close to your luggage – an important consideration as it might disappear otherwise. Like most Asians, Filipinos are often travel sick so being at the back has the further advantage of having no-one behind you. Of course, the weak stomachs may be the result of drivers from competing companies trying

to race each other off the roads, which are often bumpy and not at all suited to Le Mans-type speeds.

Street vendors flock to the buses with all kinds of edibles at each stop, so it's not necessary to carry food on long trips. Buses often set off before the scheduled departure time if they are full – if there is only one bus a day, it's wise to get there early! In country areas, even when the buses are full, they may go round the town several times, picking up freight or making purchases, which may take up to an hour. For shorter trips of up to 20 km, it's quicker to take a jeepney if you are in a hurry.

The fare is reckoned by the number of km travelled but it costs more to travel on gravel road than on surfaced road. On long stretches, fares are always collected fairly late. First the conductors ask passengers their destinations, then they dispense tickets; these will be inspected several times by different chief conductors. Finally they get

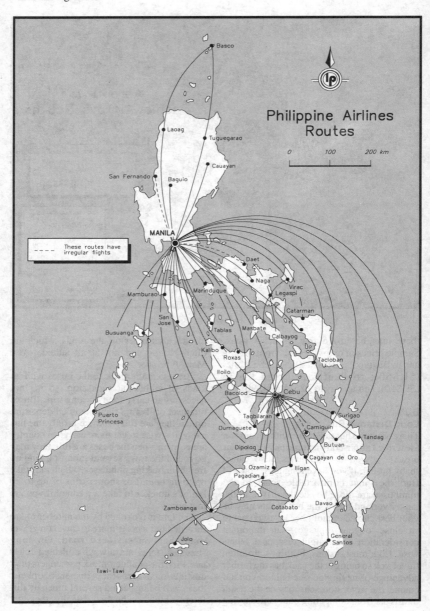

Philippine Airlines One–way Airfares

From Manila to:		From Cebu to:	
Bacolod	P1204	Bacolod	P590
Baguio	P560	Butuan	P578
Basco	P1358	Cagayan de Oro	P816
Busuanga	P1167	Cotabato	P746
Butuan	P1852	Davao	P1036
Cagayan de Oro	P1840	Dipolog	P540
Calbayog	P974	Dipolog	P540
Catarman	P944	Dumaguete	P402
Cauayan	P614	General Santos	P1003
Cebu	P1400	Iloilo	P680
Cotabato	P2062	Kalibo	P592
Daet	P561	Legaspi	P688
Davao	P2515	Ozamiz	P603
Dipolog	P1419	Pagadian	P615
Dumaguete	P1515	Puerto Princesa	P1179
Iloilo	P1145	Surigao	P483
Kalibo	P931	Tacloban	P657
Laoag	P858	Tagbilaran	P293
Legaspi	P889	Tandag	P614
Mamburao	P442	Zamboanga	P900
Marinduque	P445		
Masbate	P784	**From Zamboanga to:**	
Naga	P589	Cotabato	P611
Puerto Princesa	P1425	Davao	P1028
Roxas	P986	Dipolog	P599
San Jose	P835	Jolo	P445
Tablas	P589	Pagadian	P508
Tacloban	P1387	Tawi-Tawi	P722
Tagbilaran	P1257		
Tuguegarao	P948		
Virac	P764		

around to collecting the fares. If you have an international student card, show it when you state your destination. Discounts are not available during school holidays or on Sunday and public holidays.

One-hundred km by ordinary bus should cost around P40 (US$1.50), by air-con bus around P50 (US$1.80).

Ordinary bus/air-con bus fares from Manila are: to Alaminos (237 km) P100/110; to Baguio (250 km) P95/125; to Batangas (110 km) P40/50; to Olongapo (126 km) P50/70; and to Legaspi (544 km) P220/260.

See the Getting There & Away section of the Manila chapter for details of where the bus terminals are and for information about local buses.

TRAIN
The railway line from Manila (Paco Station) to Naga in South Luzon is now the only one operating. Typhoons damage bridges almost every year so journeys on this stretch can either be frequently interrupted or only partly completed. The trains are slow (it takes 12 hours or more from Manila to Naga) and cost about the same as buses.

CAR RENTAL
Apart from various local firms, the internationally known, reputable companies Avis, Budget and Hertz have good, reliable vehicles. You can rent cars by the day, week or month. The cheaper cars are usually booked, so it's worth reserving one if you

want a particular model. A Toyota Corolla with air-con and a radio costs US$65 a day, or US$390 a week, including unlimited km. Special rates apply from Monday to Friday (Biz Week) and from Friday to Monday (Weekender). Petrol costs about P10 a litre. Avis has several offices in Metro Manila (eg, in the Peninsula Hotel and on Roxas Blvd, between Padre Faura and Santa Monica Sts), Angeles, Baguio, Bacolod, Cagayan de Oro, Cebu City and Olongapo.

MOTORBIKE

Unlike Thailand or Indonesia, there is no organised set up to hire motorbikes. If you want to rent a motorbike, you have to ask around. For a Honda 125 cc, expect to pay P500 to P650 a day. In Manila you can hire motorbikes from Marisol-Rent a Motorbike (☎ 502795) at München Grill Pub, 1316 Mabini St, Ermita. You will find motorbikes for sale in the advertisements under 'Classified Ads-For Sale' in the *Manila Bulletin*, especially in the Sunday edition. The most common bike is a 125 cc, but it's better though dearer to buy a 350 cc, as you can overtake faster and more safely. However, outside Manila, parts are hard to come by. A new Honda 125 cc costs about P65,000.

If you buy a bike, make sure you obtain the originals of the following documents:

1 Contract of Sale – have it drawn up by a lawyer.
2 Registration Certificate – pink paper, endorsed by the Land Transportation Commission. A number-plate marked 'Ready for Registration' will do.
3 Official Receipt – you need this for the finance office. Get it at the Bureau of Land Transportation.

If you want to sell your motorbike before leaving the country, you'll be paid in pesos. You can only exchange these (with difficulty) for foreign currency on the black market. It is recommended that you change dollars into pesos before you buy. You can do this officially at the Central Bank, which will give you a receipt for the transaction. With this receipt you can then change the pesos back into dollars without problems.

It's useful to have the owner's manual with you. A tool set, including screwdriver and spark plug key is essential for both types of bike; for the 350 cc it is impera... ...e a spare tube, patching ki... ...l chain with you fro... Police insist upon

If you are islan... a shipment clearanc... from the police before y... You will also need a photo... Contract or Registration Cer...

BICYCLE

Although it's dangerous on busy r... elling by bicycle can be another in... way to explore the Philippines.

BOAT

Wherever you go there's always a boat ready to take you to the next island. For short trips, outrigger boats or pumpboats are used. The motor is at the back – a very noisy arrangement. A 16 hp pumpboat uses five litres of fuel for an hour's speedy motoring, so you can work out the cost of chartering.

The quality of the passenger ships of the inter-island operators varies greatly. The flagships of several companies run on the prestigious Manila, Cebu, Zamboanga, Davao route. They are punctual and fast and the service is relatively good.

Third class (deck-class or sun deck) is quite acceptable. Bunks or camp beds (depending on the quality of the vessel) are under cover and protected from sun and rain, whereas the air-con cabins and dormitories below deck are often cramped and sticky.

The quality of the large passenger ships varies widely also. Some of the boats may once have been top quality but as with all Asian inter-island boats you must expect:

1 As many people as possible crammed into the smallest possible space.
2 Bunks welded to every available bit of floor space.
3 Absolutely disgusting toilets, often overflowing because of overuse and the lack of water.
4 Lousy food, very few beverages and the boat arriving several hours late.
5 Everyone throwing up everywhere if it is slightly rough.

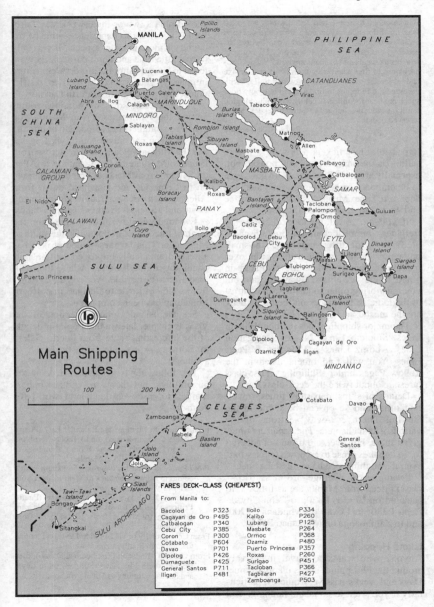

Main Shipping Routes

0   100   200 km

FARES DECK-CLASS (CHEAPEST)

From Manila to:

Bacolod	P323	Iloilo	P334
Cagayan de Oro	P495	Kalibo	P260
Catbalogan	P340	Lubang	P125
Cebu City	P385	Masbate	P264
Coron	P300	Ormoc	P368
Cotabato	P604	Ozamiz	P480
Davao	P701	Puerto Princesa	P357
Dipolog	P426	Roxas	P260
Dumaguete	P425	Surigao	P451
General Santos	P711	Tacloban	P366
Iligan	P481	Tagbilaran	P427
		Zamboanga	P503

Beware when there are two 3rd classes – we asked what the difference was between 3rd class deluxe and 3rd class ordinary and the answer was, 'Deluxe has bedding, ordinary doesn't'. It was only P5 extra but who needs sheets and blankets anyhow? We got ordinary only to find when we got on board that deluxe had reserved beds. In ordinary you had to fight with thousands of Filipinos to find a sq cm of empty floor space not near the toilets. Luckily a friendly Filipino family saved us, but make sure to check about reserved beds!

Piers & Jill Beagley

If possible, buy tickets a few days before sailing as the ships are quickly booked out, especially around Christmas. It's a good idea to be on board an hour before the scheduled departure time. Meals (fish and rice, coffee and water) are included in the fare.

If you are travelling long distances by freighter, you must count on long, unscheduled stops in the different ports. On the small passenger boats, which usually run over medium distances, tickets are also sold on board. Drinks are almost always for sale, but you must bring other foodstuffs. In contrast to the large ships, places on the upper deck are the most expensive.

The major shipping lines include William Lines, Sulpicio Lines, Negros Navigation Lines, Aboitiz Lines and George & Peter Lines. You will find others listed in the Yellow Pages under 'Shipping'. First-class fares are about twice the deck-class fares.

Details of ships, departure times, travelling times and so on can be found in the Getting There & Away sections of the various island chapters. The departure times given there, however, are often not adhered to, so it makes sense to go down to the wharf even if you think you have missed a boat.

Examples of average 3rd-class (deck-class) prices from Manila are as follows: to Bacolod on Negros P320; to Cebu City on Cebu P380; to Davao on Mindanao P700; and to Zamboanga on Mindanao P500.

Island Hopping

Anyone who wants to travel intensively around the Philippines needs plenty of time. Days and weeks pass very quickly, particularly if you want to go island hopping. You should plan a two or three week stay fairly well if you want to experience some of the country's more unusual aspects. If you only have a little time and don't particularly want to get to know Philippine airport architecture intimately, you would do well to restrict yourself to a round trip of north Luzon.

There are all sorts of possible routes around the Philippines. From Manila you can head straight off to Mindanao or into the Visayas. You can travel south, via Legaspi and the Mayon Volcano, and go across from Bulan to Masbate or from Matnog to Allen on Samar. From Masbate you can continue on to Cebu. Or you can head down from Allen, in northern Samar, through Samar and Leyte and go across to other Visayan islands.

Eventually there will be a road from the north of Luzon to Zamboanga in the south of Mindanao. This Japanese-aided project has already dramatically improved the transport conditions through Samar, where the main road used to be terrible. Work on the crossing from southern Leyte to Surigao in northern Mindanao has been completed.

See the Island Hopping section of the Visayas chapter later in this book for details of the interesting route from Puerto Galera to Boracay – it's one fantastic beach to another!

The following is a list of a few of the possibilities, but there are endless opportunities to discover the island world for yourself.

From Manila to Mindoro via Batangas City (Puerto Galera-Calapan-Roxas), on to Tablas/Romblon, then to Panay via Boracay. From Kalibo back to Manila or from Iloilo to Manila.

From Panay to Cebu via Negros going south with a detour to Bohol, then back to Manila direct from Cebu City.

From Panay (Iloilo) or Cebu to Palawan (Puerto Princesa), then travel to northern Palawan, returning to Manila from El Nido or from Busuanga.

From Cebu directly or via Bohol to Leyte and Samar, then through South Luzon to Manila.

From Cebu to Mindanao (Zamboanga, Davao), then from northern Mindanao (Surigao) on to Leyte and Samar, returning to Manila via South Luzon.

LOCAL TRANSPORT
To/From the Airport

For information regarding transport to/from Manila's NAIA see To/From the Airport in the Getting Around section of the Manila chapter later in this book.

Jeepney

These are the most popular form of transport for short journeys. Originally they were reconstructed Jeeps which were left in the Philippines by the US army after WW II. Few of these old models are left. The new jeepneys, which may be Ford Fieras, are brightly painted in traditional designs and the bonnets are decorated with a multitude of mirrors and figures of horses. They are part of any typical Philippine street scene. Much to the relief of many, the ubiquitous cassette players have now been banned in jeepneys. The jeepneys' route is indicated and the official charge is P1.50 centavos for the first four km, and 25 centavos for each extra km. When you want to get out, just bang on the roof, hiss or yell 'pára' (stop).

In the provinces, it is important to negotiate a price before setting out on a long trip over unfamiliar territory. Before you start, ask other passengers about the price or check in a nearby shop, and then confirm the price with the driver. This may save you an unpleasant situation when you reach your destination. Jeepneys usually only leave when full (or overflowing) with passengers, so you must allow for long waiting periods, especially if you are in a hurry. If you are prepared to pay for the empty 'seats' you can get the driver to leave immediately.

If you climb into an empty jeepney and the driver takes off straight away, it usually means you'll be charged for a Special Ride. If you don't want this, you must make it clear that you are only prepared to pay for a regular ride. You might need to get the driver to stop straight away, especially if no more passengers are getting on. It costs about P1200 to rent a jeepney for a day and more if the roads are in bad condition; petrol is extra.

Safety Tip If several men get into the jeepney straight after you and try to sit near you or get you to change seats under some pretext, they may be intent on relieving you of your valuables. Get out immediately.

Taxi

Under no circumstances should taximeters be switched off. Flat fare arrangements always favour the driver. It doesn't hurt to show taxi drivers that you know more than they think, so that they won't take round-about routes. Ordinary taxis (those not equipped with air-conditioning) have a flag-down charge of P10 which includes the first 500 metres, thereafter they charge P1 for every further 250 metres. However, almost all of the metres still show the old flag-down charge of P2.50, so there will be a surcharge of P7.50. Air-con taxis begin with P16 (the old flag-down charge of P3.50 plus P12.50 surcharge). If possible, have small change handy as it is difficult to get change for anything over P20. If a taximeter has obviously been rigged and is running too fast, the only sensible thing is to stop and take another taxi.

In spite of fines of up to P5000, countless taxis still have rigged meters. Pay particular attention to the price display if the driver honks the horn every few seconds. Sometimes horn and meter are linked up and the meter adds a unit every time the horn is sounded! Make sure the meter is turned on when you start. The taxis that wait outside the big hotels, bus stations, wharves and air terminals almost always have meters that run fast. It usually pays to walk to the next street. New taxis are fitted with a digital indicator that cannot (yet!) be interfered with.

PU-Cab

These are small taxis without meters; their minimum price is P10 for a short town journey of about three km. For longer journeys you pay correspondingly more and need to negotiate the fee beforehand. You will find PU-Cabs in Cagayan de Oro, Bacolod, Davao, Zamboanga and some other places, but not Manila.

Trishaw

These are bicycles with sidecars for passengers. As transport becomes increasingly motorised, trishaws are becoming rarer, even in the provinces. Prices start at about P2 per person for a short trip.

Tricycle

These are small motorcycles or mopeds with sidecars for passengers and go much better than you might think. The fare must be nego-

tiated, and is usually around P2 for a short ride.

Calesa

These two-wheeled horse-cabs are found in Manila's Chinatown, in Vigan, where they fit the local scene very well, and in Cebu City, where they are called *tartanillas*. In Manila, Filipinos pay about P10 for short trips; tourists are usually charged more. Establish beforehand if the price is per person or per calesa.

Manila

In 1975, 17 towns and communities were combined to form Metropolitan Manila. Known as Metro Manila, this conglomeration had at the last count a population of 10 million. San Nicolas, Binondo, Santa Cruz, Quiapo and San Miguel form the nucleus of the city, where you will find the markets (Divisoria Market, Quinta Market), the churches (Quiapo Church, Santa Cruz Church), the shopping streets ('Avenida' Rizal Ave, Escolta St), Chinatown (Binondo, Ongpin St), the official home of the president (Malacañang Palace in San Miguel) and many, many people.

The name Manila was originally two words: *may* and *nilad*. *May* means 'there is' and *nilad* is a mangrove plant which used to grow on the banks of the Pasig River. The bark of the mangroves gave a natural soap which the locals used for washing their clothes.

Three years after he founded the colony, King Philip II of Spain called the town '*Isigne y Siempre Leal Ciudad*', meaning 'Distinguished and Ever Loyal City'. This charming name could not, however, replace the name Maynilad. If you want to know what Maynilad looked like in the middle of the last century, read Fedor Jagor's classic book *Travels in the Philippines*, published in 1873.

Rizal Park, better known as Luneta Park, is the centre of Manila and is the city's most important meeting place. The two most popular areas for tourists flank Rizal Park. To the north is Intramuros, the Spanish walled city which was badly damaged during fierce fighting in WW II. To the south of Rizal Park is the area where the more peaceful modern invaders are drawn – Ermita and Malate. Here you will find most of Manila's hotels and international restaurants. It is known as the 'tourist belt', and its main street is the waterfront Roxas Blvd. Ermita is about 10 km north-west of NAIA.

Manila's business centre is Makati, where the banks, insurance companies and other businesses have their head offices. The embassies of many countries and many airline offices are also here. At the edge of Makati, along E de los Santos Ave (almost always called Edsa), lies Forbes Park, a millionaires' ghetto with palatial mansions and its own police force.

At the other extreme is Tondo, Manila's main slum. It's estimated that 1½ million Filipinos live in slums in Metro Manila, and Tondo has 180,000 living in 17,000 huts in just 1½ sq km. Other areas of Manila which may be of interest to the traveller include Caloocan City, a light-industrial engineering and foodstuff preparation centre, and Quezon City, the government centre, where you'll also find the Philippine Heart Center for Asia, the 25,000 seat Araneta Coliseum and the four-sq-km campus of the University of the Philippines (UP).

ORIENTATION

Although Manila is a fairly sprawling town, it's quite easy to find your way around. Like Bangkok, however, Manila has a number of 'centres'. Makati, for example, is the business centre, while Ermita is the tourist centre. The area of most interest to visitors can be defined by the Pasig River, Manila Bay and Taft Ave. The river forms the northern boundary of this rectangular area, while the bay and Taft Ave form the western and eastern boundaries.

Immediately south of the river is the oldest area of Manila, which includes Intramuros and is where you'll find most of the places of historic interest in Manila. The General Post Office (GPO) and the Immigration Office are also in this area. Farther south is the open expanse of Rizal Park (Luneta Park) which extends from Taft Ave to the bayside Roxas Blvd. This is the central meeting and wandering place in Manila. (Beware of pickpockets here and in areas like Santa Cruz.) South of the park is Ermita, the tourist centre,

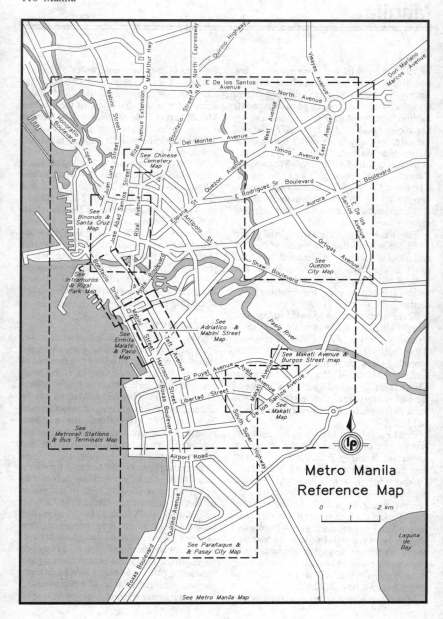

Metro Manila
Reference Map

0   1   2 km

Laguna
de
Bay

See Metro Manila Map

which has cheaper (and some more expensive) accommodation, restaurants, airline offices, and pretty much everything else you'll need.

Farther south again are Malate and Pasay City, where there are many up-market hotels, particularly along the bay, on Roxas Blvd. The modern Cultural Center is built on reclaimed land jutting into the bay. Continue down Taft Ave to the airport or travel southeast from Taft Ave to Makati. North of the river is the crowded and interesting Chinatown area and the sprawling slums of Tondo.

INFORMATION
Tourist Office

There are two Department of Tourism information centres in Manila: a reception unit at NAIA and the main Tourist Information Center (☎ 599031) on the ground floor of the Tourism Building, Agrifina Circle, Rizal Park. It is open daily from 8 am to 5 pm. An information service is available around the clock by telephone: call ☎ 501728 or ☎ 501660.

Visas

The Immigration Office (Commission on Immigration and Deportation – CID) (☎ 407651) in Magallanes Drive, Intramuros, is open Monday to Friday from 8.30 am to 5.30 pm.

Money

The following banks and their branches will change cash and travellers' cheques as well as arrange money transfers:

Bank of America
    Lepanto Building, Paseo de Roxas, Makati (☎ 8155000)
Bank of the Philippine Islands
    BPI Building, Ayala Ave, Makati (☎ 8185541)
City Bank, City Bank Building
    Paseo de Roxas, Makati (☎ 8172122, 8139333)
Deutsche Bank Asia
    Filinvest Financial Center, Paseo de Roxas, Makati (☎ 8172961)
Hongkong & Shanghai Banking Corporation
    6740 Ayala Ave, Makati (☎ 8101661, 8145200)

PCI Bank
    Makati Ave, on the corner of Dela Costa St, Makati (☎ 8171021)
Philippine National Bank
    Escolta St, Binondo (☎ 402051)

Addresses for credit cards & travellers' cheques:

American Express
    Philam Life Building, United Nations Ave, on the corner of Maria Orosa St, Ermita (☎ 509601, 5219492) (open Monday to Friday from 8.30 am to 4 pm and Saturday from 9 am to noon)
    ACE Building, Rada St, Legaspi Village, Makati (☎ 8159311) (open Monday to Friday from 9 am to 3 pm); 24-Hour Emergency Assistance (☎ 8154159, 856911)
    Interbank, 111 Paseo de Roxas, Legaspi Village, Makati (☎ 8186941, 8154598)
    Interbank, 1300 Mabini St, on the corner of Padre Faura, Ermita (☎ 582589)
Bank of America
    Lepanto Building, Paseo de Roxas, Makati (☎ 8155000)
Diners Club International
    Oppen Building, 349 Gil Puyat Ave, Makati (☎ 8104521)
Thomas Cook Travel
    Skyland Plaza Building, Gil Puyat Ave, Makati (☎ 8163701-10)
Visa card & MasterCard
    Equitable Bank, United Nations Ave, on the corner of Bocobo St, Ermita (☎ 509661)
    Equitable Bank, Paseo de Roxas, on the corner of Gil Puyat Ave, Makati (☎ 851726, 852971-75)
    Equitable Bank, 203 Salcedo St, Legaspi Village, Makati (☎ 8125871)
    Equitable Bank, ground floor Lai-Lai Hotel, Gandara St, on the corner of Ongpin St, Chinatown, Santa Cruz (☎ 496068)

Post

The quickest way to send mail from the Philippines is to take it to the Air Mail Distribution Center near the Domestic Airport or the office in the arrivals area at NAIA. Particularly at Christmas, make sure you see your mail being stamped so that the stamps can't be removed and resold. There are a lot of complaints about the small post office in Mabini St. The Rizal Post Office near the Manila Hotel is not as busy as the GPO or the Mabini St office.

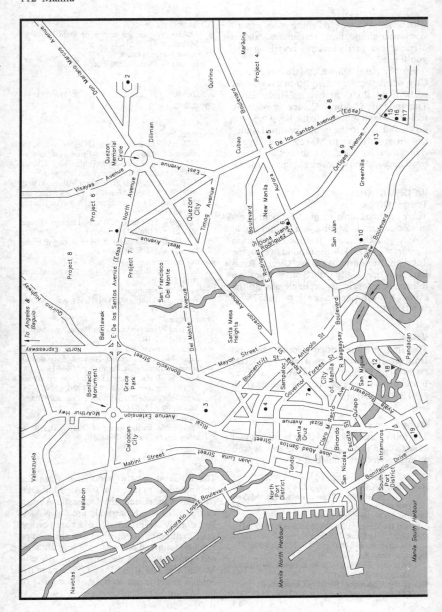

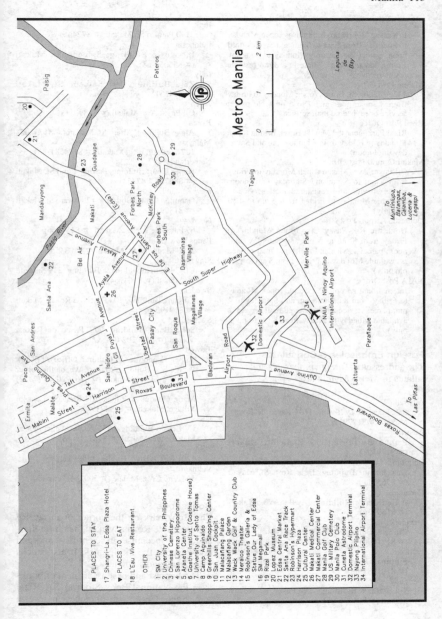

Metro Manila

PLACES TO STAY
- 17 Shangri-La Edsa Plaza Hotel

▼ PLACES TO EAT
- 18 L'Eau Vive Restaurant

OTHER
- 1 SM City
- 2 University of the Philippines
- 3 Chinese Cemetery
- 4 San Lorenzo Hippodrome
- 5 Araneta Center
- 6 Goethe Institut (Goethe House)
- 7 University of Santo Tomas
- 8 Camp Aguinaldo
- 9 Greenhills Shopping Center
- 10 San Juan Cockpit
- 11 Malacañang Palace
- 12 Malacañang Garden
- 13 Wack Wack Golf & Country Club
- 14 Meralco Theater
- 15 Statue Our Lady of Edsa
- 16 Robinson's Galleria &
    SM Megamall
- 19 Rizal Park
- 20 Lopez Museum
- 21 Edsa Central Market
- 22 Santa Ana Race Track
- 23 Robinson's Hypermart
- 24 Harrison Plaza
- 25 Cultural Center
- 26 Makati Medical Center
- 27 Makati Commercial Center
- 28 Manila Golf Club
- 29 US Military Cemetery
- 30 Manila Polo Club
- 31 Cuneta Astrodome
- 32 Domestic Airport Terminal
- 33 Nayong Pilipino
- 34 International Airport Terminal

GPO
Liwasang Bonifacio, Intramuros (open Monday to Saturday from 8 am to 5 pm and Sunday until noon; parcel service only Monday to Saturday from 8 am to 4 pm). There is a poste restante counter.

Mabini Post Office
1335 Mabini St, Ermita (open Monday to Friday from 8 am to noon and 1 to 5 pm). No parcel service or registered mail service.

Rizal Post Office
Rizal Park, near the Manila Hotel, Ermita (open Monday to Friday from 8 am to 6 pm and Saturday until noon)

Makati Central Post Office
Gil Puyat Ave, Makati (open Monday to Friday from 8 am to 5 pm and Saturday until noon; parcel service and registered mail service is available Monday to Friday from 8 am to 4.30 pm only)

Domestic Airport Post Office
Domestic Rd, Pasay City (open Monday to Friday from 8 am to 5 pm and Saturday until noon; parcel service and registered mail service is available Monday to Friday from 8 am to 4.30 pm only)

NAIA Post Office
International Airport, Parañaque (open Monday to Friday from 8 am to 5 pm and Saturday to 4 pm; parcel service and registered mail service is available Monday to Friday from 8 am to noon only)

Foreign Embassies & Consulates

The addresses of foreign embassies and consulates in Metro Manila are:

Australia
Salustiana D Ty Tower, 1104 Paseo de Roxas, Makati (☎ 8177911)

Austria
Prince Building, 117 Rada St, Makati (☎ 8179191)

Belgium
Don Jacinto Building, Dela Rosa St, Makati (☎ 876571)

Canada
Allied Bank Building, Ayala Ave, Makati (☎ 8159536)

Denmark
Citibank Building, 104 Paseo de Roxas, Makati (☎ 8191906)

France
Filipinas Life Building, Ayala Ave, Makati (☎ 8101981-88)

Germany
Solid Bank Building, 777 Paseo de Roxas, Makati (☎ 864906-09)

India
2190 Paraiso St, Makati (☎ 872445)

Indonesia
Indonesia Building, Salcedo St, Makati (☎ 856061-68)

Italy
Zeta Building, 191 Salcedo St, Makati (☎ 874531)

Japan
Gil Puyat Ave, Makati (☎ 8189011)

Korea
Alpap Building, Alfaro St, Makati (☎ 8175705)

Malaysia
107 Tordesillas St, Makati (☎ 8174581-85)

Netherlands
King's Court Building, Pasong Tamo St, Makati (☎ 886768, 887753)

New Zealand
Gammon Center Building, 126 Alfaro St, Makati (☎ 8180916)

Norway
69 Paseo de Roxas, Makati (☎ 8159866)

Papua New Guinea
2280 Magnolia St, Makati (☎ 8108456)

Singapore
ODC International Plaza Building, 219 Salcedo St, Makati (☎ 8161764)

Sweden
Citibank Building, 104 Paseo de Roxas, Makati (☎ 8191951)

Switzerland
Solid Bank Building, 777 Paseo de Roxas, Makati (☎ 8190202-05)

Taiwan
Taipei Economic & Cultural Office (TECO), Pacific Star Building, Makati Ave, on the corner of Gil Puyat Ave, Makati (☎ 8161920, 8177322)

Thailand
Marie Cristine Building, 107 Rada St, Legaspi Village, Makati (☎ 8154219)

UK
LV Locsin Building, 6752 Ayala Ave, corner of Makati Ave, Makati (☎ 8167116-18)

USA
1201 Roxas Blvd, Ermita (☎ 5217116)

Vietnam
554 Vito Cruz, Malate (☎ 500364)

Bookshops

The Bookmark on the corner of Pasay Rd and Paseo de Roxas, Makati, has little literature, as it specialises in scientific works and books about the Philippines. It also stocks magazines and stationery.

The biggest and best assortment of books is in the National Book Store at 701 Rizal Ave, Santa Cruz, with branches in several parts of Metro Manila. The National Book Store in the Araneta Center in Cubao is very good.

In Padre Faura, between Mabini and J Bocobo Sts, Ermita, is the Solidaridad Book Shop – 'an intellectual's delight' – with excellent sections on religion, philosophy, politics, poetry and fiction. This small, well-stocked bookshop specialises in scholarly publications, with an emphasis on Asia and the Philippines. Economics subjects and yearbooks are also available.

The Tradewinds Bookshop in the El Amenecer Building, General Luna St, Intramuros, specializes in Philippine literature, history, art and general culture, in addition to old and new maps.

Maps

Namria (formerly the Bureau of Coast & Geodetic Survey) on Barraca St, San Nicolas, is an excellently stocked shop which sells mainly nautical maps but also detailed maps. There is a Namria branch in Fort Bonifacio in Makati.

Medical Services

The addresses of reliable doctors and hospitals in Metro Manila include:

Makati Medical Center (☎ 8159911), 2 Amorsolo St, on the corner of Dela Rosa St, Makati.
Manila Doctors Hospital (☎ 503011), 667 United Nations Ave, Ermita.
Medical Center Manila (☎ 591661), 1122 General Luna St, Ermita.
General Practitioner (GP): Dr Heinz Varwig (☎ 8172632, 8100820), Royal Match Building (Hongkong & Shanghai Bank Building), 6780 Ayala Ave, Makati, speaks German and English and consults Monday to Friday from 8 am to noon. Two English-speaking doctors consult in the afternoons from 2 to 4 pm.
Dentist: Shafa Medical Clinic (☎ 573911), Midtown Arcade, Adriatico St, Ermita. Clinic hours are Monday to Saturday from 8 am to 9 pm and Sunday from 10 am to 7 pm.

Laundry

There's a quick, cheap laundromat on R Salas St, Ermita, between Mabini and Adriatico Sts. Washing handed in before 11 am will be washed, ironed and ready by 8 pm the same day. Minimum charge is 70p (for up to three kg), thereafter 15p per kg. The Laundryette Britania on Santa Monica St, Ermita, can also be recommended. It is open daily from 7.30 am to 10 pm.

Diving Equipment

Two of the best diving equipment shops in Manila are Aquaventure Philippines and Dive Mate, both on Pasong Tamo St, Makati. Both sell mainly US products, but also some Japanese.

Tourist Police

The Tourist Assistance Unit (☎ 501728, 501660) in the Tourism Building, Agrifina Circle, Rizal Park, Ermita, is open 24 hours.

RIZAL PARK

This is a real oasis in the centre of the city and is popularly known as Luneta Park. There are flowers, fountains, wide lawns and, of course, plenty of music attracting thousands of strolling Filipinos every day in the late afternoon and evening. If you're there at 5 am, you can see the first eager Chinese doing their t'ai chi. Sunday is a family day, with a chance to listen to the free concert at 5 pm, the Concert at the Park. On New Year's Day there are great celebrations here.

It is interesting to watch the changing of the guard at the Rizal Memorial, which is close to where the national hero Dr Jose Rizal was executed by the Spaniards on 30 December 1896. His farewell poem, *Mi Ultimo Adios* (My Last Farewell), is inscribed on a brass plaque in many languages. The dramatic scene of the execution squad pointing their weapons at Rizal is the theme of a group of statues at the site and forms the centrepiece of a lightshow based on the execution. It can be seen every evening in Tagalog at 6.30 pm and in English at 7.30 pm, except on rainy days and during power outages. Admission costs P30.

Tucked away between the monument and the fishpond (towards Kalaw St) is Rizal's Fountain – a well from Wilhelmsfeld, a

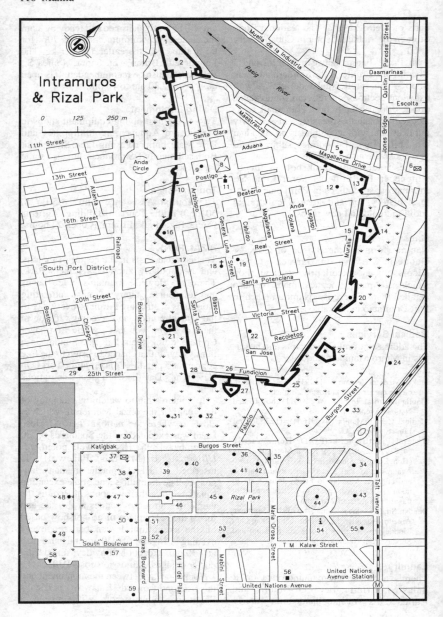

Intramuros & Rizal Park

0   125   250 m

■ PLACES TO STAY

30 Manila Hotel
56 Manila Pavilion Hotel

▼ PLACES TO EAT

58 Harbor View

OTHER

1 Rizal Shrine
2 Fort Santiago
3 Revellin de San Francisco
4 Seamen's Club
5 Immigration Office
6 General Post Office
7 Puerta Isabel II
8 Plaza de Roma
9 Palacio del Gobernador
10 Puerta del Postigo
11 Manila Cathedral
12 Letran College
13 Bastion de San Gabriel
14 Revellin del Parian
15 Puerta del Parian
16 Bastion de Santa Lucia
17 Puerta de Santa Lucia
18 San Agustin Church
19 Casa Manila Museum &
   San Luis Complex
20 Bastion de Dilao
21 Fortin San Pedro
22 El Amanecer Building &
   Tradewinds Bookshop
23 Revellin de Recoletos
24 Manila City Hall

25 Bastion de San Andres
26 Puerta Real
27 Aquarium
28 Bastion de San Diego
29 Bureau of Quarantine
31 Legaspi & Urdaneta Monument
32 Golf Course
33 National Museum
34 Department of Finance
35 Artificial Waterfall
36 Planetarium
37 Rizal Park Post Office
38 Carabao Statue
39 Rizal's Execution Spot
40 Chinese Garden
41 Concerts in the Park &
   Open-Air Stage
42 Japanese Garden
43 Philippines Model
44 Agrifina Circle &
   Skating Rink
45 Central Lagoon
46 Rizal Monument
47 Parade Ground
48 Quirino Grandstand
49 Children's Playground
50 Tamaraw Statue
51 Sightseeing Tours in
   Double-Decker Buses
52 Rizal's Fountain
53 National Library
54 Department of Tourism (DOT),
   Tourist Office & Tourist Police
55 Children's Playground
57 Army & Navy Club
58 Harbour Trips
59 US Embassy

village near Heidelberg in Germany. They say that Rizal used to drink from this well during his Heidelberg student days.

At the side of the park nearest the water is a children's playground, where you can enjoy the colourful Manila Bay sunsets. On the opposite side, near the Tourism Building, the roller-skating rink with its big globe and the topographical model of the Philippines, there is another playground, with wonderful large stone statues of dinosaurs and monsters.

On either side of the open-air auditorium are the Chinese and Japanese gardens, which are popular meeting places for couples.

INTRAMUROS
Literally the city 'in walls', Intramuros is the Manila of the past. This is where Legaspi erected a fortress in 1571 after his victory over the Muslims. Following attacks by the Chinese fleet and a fire, the Filipinos were forced to build the wall. A wide moat all around made the bulwark complete. Within the walls, the most important buildings were the numerous feudal lords' houses, 12

churches and several hospitals. Only Spaniards and Mestizos were allowed to live within the walls; Filipinos were settled on what is now the site of Rizal Park. Likewise, the Chinese were housed within the range of the cannons, about where the City Hall stands today. Neither the Dutch nor the Portuguese managed to storm this fortress and the attacks of the Sulu pirates were also unsuccessful.

Intramuros was almost totally destroyed by bomb attacks in WW II. The San Agustin Church remained relatively undamaged and the Manila Cathedral was rebuilt after the war. During the restoration, Puerta Isabel II and Puerta Real, two of the original seven gates of the city, were also restored.

A few houses are also well worth seeing, like the Casa Manila in the San Luis Complex and the El Amanecer, both in General Luna St.

Fort Santiango

The most important defence location of the Intramuros fortress-city was Fort Santiago. From this strategic location, at the mouth of the Pasig River, all activity in Manila Bay could be observed. During the Japanese occupation in WW II, innumerable Filipino prisoners lost their lives in the infamous dungeon cells which lay below sea level – at high tide there was no escape. Dr Jose Rizal also spent his last days in a cell at this fort before his execution by the Spaniards in 1896.

Today Fort Santiago is a memorial. There is an open-air theatre, the Rizal Shrine and a display of old cars which used to belong to important Filipino personalities.

In early 1988, Fort Santiago was turned inside out, with government permission, by US goldseekers who, by excavating, hoped to uncover the legendary war treasure of the Japanese general Yamashita, which was rumoured to have been hidden in the Philippines. All excavations were in vain, of course.

The fort is open daily between 8 am and 10 pm, and admission is P10.

San Agustin Church

The first constructions of the San Agustin Church were destroyed by fires in 1574 and 1583. In 1599 the foundation stone for the present construction was laid. The massive church was not damaged by the earthquakes of 1645, 1754, 1852, 1863, 1880, 1968 and 1970, nor by the bombardment in the fighting around Manila in February 1945. San Agustin is the oldest existing stone church in the Philippines. From 1879 to 1880, the crystal chandeliers came from Paris, the walls and roofs were masterfully painted by two Italian artists and the choir stalls were carved by the Augustinian monks themselves. In a small chapel to the left of the high altar lie the mortal remains of Legaspi. There is a museum and a contemplative inner courtyard adjoining the church.

Manila Cathedral

This cathedral, with its great cupola, is the Philippines' most significant Catholic church. It is in the Plaza Roma at Intramuros. With the help of the Vatican, the building, which was destroyed in WW II, was rebuilt from 1954 to 1958; some old walls were restored and integrated into the new construction. The large organ with its 4500 pipes came from the Netherlands and is the largest in Asia.

QUIAPO CHURCH

This church became famous because of its large crucifix of black wood. The Black Nazarene was carved in Mexico and brought to the Philippines by the Spaniards in the 17th century. Each day, especially on Friday, thousands of Catholics come to the church to pay homage to the crucifix. The climax of the adoration is the procession on 9 January and in Passion Week (the week between Passion Sunday and Palm Sunday, before Easter) on Monday and Friday.

CHINESE CEMETERY

It may seem irreverent to recommend a cemetery as a tourist attraction but this one should not be missed. It contains some of the most ostentatious tombs in the world. There are actual houses with mailboxes and toilets – some even have an air conditioner. It's probably only a matter of time before the first enterprising slum dwellers hit on the idea of leaving their hopelessly overcrowded hovels for the better life in the Chinese Cemetery. They would at least be exchanging their miserable slum houses for a well-built crypt – don't laugh, it's possible!

Things get lively on All Saints' Day (1 November), when the descendants of the dead come to visit their ancestors, just as Catholic Filipinos do. Most Sundays, in fact, it's a fascinating place to visit. One of the attendants who live there will take you round if you settle on a fee first; they have some amazing stories to tell. It's also just as well to have their company for safety reasons if it is a quiet day and you are going around the outside of the area, which is crossed by several streets and is about as big as Rizal Park.

The Chinese Cemetery is in the north of the suburb of Santa Cruz, just where Rizal Ave becomes Rizal Ave Extension. It has two entrances: the North Gate, which is almost always closed, and the South Gate, which is

tucked away and can be reached from Aurora Ave via Pampanga St and F Huertas St. Apart from taxis, the best way to get there from Ermita is by Metrorail to Abad Santos Station. From there it is about 600 metres. A tricycle from the station costs about P5; taking one saves asking the way. Otherwise you can get a jeepney at Mabini St or Taft Ave going towards Caloocan City; they carry the sign 'Monumento'. Get off at Rizal Ave, on the corner of Aurora Ave. It will cost you P50 to drive through the cemetery.

CHINATOWN

Chinatown is not a clearly defined suburb but a cultural and business district that takes in parts of Santa Cruz and Binondo, roughly the area between the three Chinese-Philippine friendship stores called the Welcome Gates. From Ermita you cross the Pasig River over the Jones Bridge, between the Immigration Office and the GPO, to the First Welcome Gate, also known as the 'Arch of Goodwill'. The southern part of Chinatown begins here. From Quintin Paredes St, which runs through the gate, several little streets seem to wind crazily towards the big east-west curve of Ongpin St that stretches between the other two Welcome Gates.

Ongpin St is the main business street of Chinatown, but in the next streets you can also find exotic shops like herb-scented drug stalls, well-stocked Chinese groceries, small teahouses and spacious restaurants. In contrast with the Chinatowns of other Asian cities, this one is very busy on Sunday.

MALACAÑANG PALACE

The Malacañang Palace is the single most noteworthy attraction in the suburb of San Miguel. It is in Jose P Laurel St, on the banks of the Pasig River. Malacañang is a derivation of the old Filipino description '*may lakan diyan*'meaning 'here lives a nobleman' and referring to the Spanish aristocrat Luis Rocha, who built the palace. In 1802 he sold it to an important Spanish soldier. From 1863 the nobleman's house was used as the domicile of the Spanish

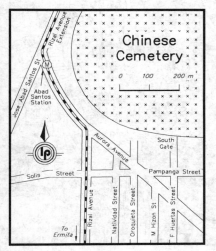

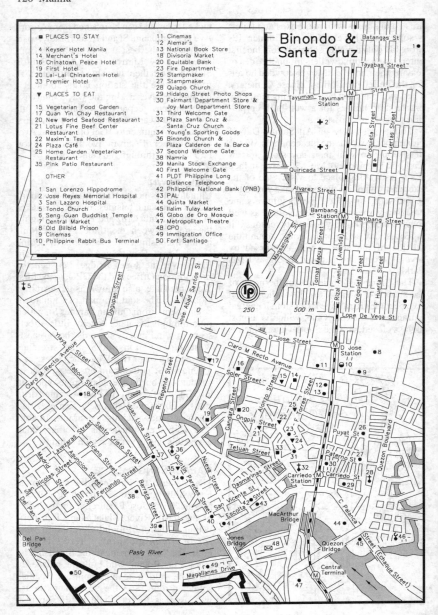

Binondo & Santa Cruz

■ PLACES TO STAY
4 Keyser Hotel Manila
14 Merchant's Hotel
16 Chinatown Peace Hotel
19 First Hotel
20 Lai-Lai Chinatown Hotel
33 Premier Hotel

▼ PLACES TO EAT
15 Vegetarian Food Garden
17 Quan Yin Chay Restaurant
20 New World Seafood Restaurant
21 Lotus Fine Beef Center Restaurant
22 Maxim's Tea House
24 Plaza Café
25 Home Garden Vegetarian Restaurant
35 Pink Patio Restaurant

OTHER
1 San Lorenzo Hippodrome
2 Jose Reyes Memorial Hospital
3 San Lazaro Hospital
5 Tondo Church
6 Seng Guan Buddhist Temple
7 Central Market
8 Old Bilibid Prison
9 Cinemas
10 Philippine Rabbit Bus Terminal
11 Cinemas
12 Alemar's
13 National Book Store
18 Divisoria Market
20 Equitable Bank
23 Fire Department
26 Stampmaker
27 Stampmaker
28 Quiapo Church
29 Hidalgo Street Photo Shops
30 Fairmart Department Store & Joy Mart Department Store
31 Third Welcome Gate
32 Plaza Santa Cruz & Santa Cruz Church
34 Young's Sporting Goods
36 Binondo Church & Plaza Calderon de la Barca
37 Second Welcome Gate
38 Namria
39 Manila Stock Exchange
40 First Welcome Gate
41 PLDT Philippine Long Distance Telephone
42 Philippine National Bank (PNB)
43 PAL
44 Quinta Market
45 Ilalim Tulay Market
46 Globo de Oro Mosque
47 Metropolitan Theatre
48 GPO
49 Immigration Office
50 Fort Santiago

heads of government. Later, the Americans also used the palace as their residence.

The first Philippine head of state, Manuel Quezon, occupied the palace. It was used as the seat of office by President Marcos until his reign ended in February 1986. The palace was then opened to the public. It has since been renovated, redecorated and partly reopened as a museum of 'historical, art and heritage values'. (For more information about the museum, see the Museums section later in this chapter.)

CULTURAL CENTER

The Cultural Center of the Philippines (CCP) was built under the umbrella administration of the ex-first lady Imelda Marcos. The P40 million project was opened in September 1969. It was designed by Leandro Locsin, a leading Filipino architect. The CCP includes a theatre, art gallery and museum. It was designed as a symbol of national cultural development and is open for public viewing daily between 9 am and 5 pm.

In the vicinity of the CCP are the Folk Arts Theater, the Philippine International Convention Center, the Film Theater, the Coconut Palace and the Philippine Plaza Hotel. The Folk Arts Theater was built in the record time of only 70 days. Anyone interested in seeing the conference rooms of the Convention Center can take a tour. It is also worth entering the splendid Philippine Plaza Hotel to see the elaborate modern interior decoration. It has what is probably one of the finest swimming pools in all of South-East Asia.

NAYONG PILIPINO

Nayong Pilipino means 'Philippine Village' and it is a miniature version of the whole country – a concept which has become popular in a number of countries in the region. Typical houses and distinctive landscapes have been built on the 45-hectare site, which represents the archipelago's various regions and its diverse cultural minorities. Unfortunately, almost all of the houses turn out to be souvenir shops and are not traditionally furnished as you might expect.

Jeepneys take you through the sites for free. There is the Museum of Philippine Dolls, the Nayong Pilipino Aquarium, the Aviary of Philippine Birds, the Garden of Philippine Plants and more.

A visit to the Philippine Museum of Ethnology can be highly recommended (see the Museums section later in this chapter). On Sunday afternoons between 3 and 4 pm you can watch folk dancing in the Mindanao section.

The Nayong Pilipino is open Monday to Friday from 9 am to 6 pm and Saturday and Sunday to 7 pm. Admission for Filipinos is P15, foreigners must pay P85 (or US$3). Buses go from Taft Ave to the NAIA, which is right beside the Nayong Pilipino. Jeepneys ply between Nayong Pilipino and Baclaran, from where you can carry on to Ermita by jeepney or Metrorail.

FORBES PARK

Such a cluster of opulent mansions as you can see in Forbes Park and its neighbouring Dasmariñas Village is almost unique. There is even a special police unit to guard this luxury neighbourhood.

Forbes Park is located in the south-east part of Makati. Buses marked 'Ayala (Ave)' go from Taft Ave or M H del Pilar St in Ermita to the Makati Commercial Center. You then do the remaining km by taxi as visitors on foot wouldn't stand much chance of getting in. However, even taxis are known to have been turned away if their passengers could not give a definite destination which could be verified. No photos are allowed and you may have to hand in your camera as you go in.

US MILITARY CEMETERY

The US Military Cemetery is directly east of Forbes Park. Here, in rank and file, are the bodies of 17,000 US soldiers who died in the Philippines during WW II. In the circular memorial built on a rise are numerous good pictures of the battles of the Pacific. It's worth seeing.

It's about two km from where Ayala Ave meets Edsa. The extension of Ayala Ave is called McKinley Rd and leads through Forbes Park, past San Antonio Church, the Manila Golf Club and the Manila Polo Club directly to the cemetery.

FAITH HEALERS

The unorthodox methods of the infamous Filipino faith healers are now world famous. Clearly some of these 'doctors' are no more than money-grubbing charlatans, but others are so skilful that even sceptics gape in awe.

Many patients travel to Baguio, some to Pangasinan Province, but there are also healers in Metro Manila. Anyone can watch after obtaining the consent of the patient.

For further information, get in touch with the Philippine Spiritual Help Foundation Inc (☎ 5210771), Manila Midtown Hotel, on the corner of Adriatico St and Pedro Gil, Ermita. The founder of this organisation is the famous and businesslike faith healer Alex Orbito, who also owns the travel bureau Orbit Tours.

MUSEUMS

You will find many interesting museums in Manila; they are listed here in alphabetical order.

The **Ayala Museum** on Makati Ave, Makati, specialises in high points of Philippine history, chronologically presented in over 60 showcase dioramas. There is also an ethnographic section which features artefacts, weapons and ships. Behind the museum is an aviary and tropical garden under a gigantic net. The museum is open from 9 am to 7.30 pm Tuesday to Sunday, and the charge is P20 (P5 for students).

The **Carfel Seashell Museum** at 1786 Mabini St, Malate, was originally a small private collection of the shells found in Philippine waters. The display room is on the 1st floor, and below is a shop selling shells, coral and shell ornaments; a Carfel Seaventure Dive Shop is also there. It is open from 9 am to 6 pm Monday to Saturday and admission is P10 (P5 for students).

The **Casa Manila Museum** on General Luna St, Intramuros, is one of the first examples of the restoration which Intramuros is undergoing. With its beautiful inner courtyards and antique furnishings, it is a faithful reproduction of a typical Spanish residence. Downstairs is a model of Fort Santiago and the bulwarks of Intramuros as well as a photographic display. Attached to the museum is the Restaurant Muralla. The museum is open daily from 9 am to noon and 1 to 6 pm except Monday, and admission is P10.

The **Metropolitan Museum of Manila** is on Roxas Blvd, Malate, near the Cultural Center. It has changing displays of various art forms, including some 'old masters'. It is open Tuesday to Sunday from 9 am to 6 pm. Admission is free.

The **Coconut Palace** is in the Cultural Center Complex, which is in Roxas Blvd, Malate. This former guesthouse of the Marcos regime, made of the best tropical timbers, was erected in 1981 especially for the visit of the Pope. It is open daily except Monday from 9 am to 4 pm and admission costs P100, including a guided tour which takes just under an hour.

The **Cultural Center Museum** on Roxas Blvd, Malate, has Oriental and Islamic art on permanent display on the 4th floor. The art displays in the main gallery are changed from time to time. It is open Tuesday to Sunday from 9 am to 6 pm; admission is P2.

The **Lopez Memorial Museum** is in the Chronicle Building (ground floor), Neralco Ave, Pasig. This is a private museum with a valuable collection of more than 13,000 Filipino books. The collection of historical travel literature is remarkable and includes one of three existing copies of *De Moluccis Insulis* (The Moluccan Islands) by Maximillianus Transylvanus. The work dates back to 1524 and is the first printed account of Magellan's voyage to the Philippines. Also on display are some important oil paintings, some of them award-winning works by the well-known classical Filipino artists Felix Resurreccion Hidalgo and Juan Luna. It is open Monday to Friday from 8.30 am to noon and 1 to 4 pm. Admission is P15.

The **Museo ng Malacañang** is on Jose P Laurel St, San Miguel. When you visit the

Malacañang Palace, it seems as if the family of former president Marcos has just left its 'modest residence'. Here you can see Imelda's famous shoes, Ferdinand's bedroom, their grandson's mini-Mercedes and many more of the extravagant luxuries which their successor Cory Aquino firmly renounced. It is open Monday and Tuesday from 9 am to noon and 1 to 3 pm, and Thursday and Friday until noon for guided groups. Admission is P200. There is a public viewing on Wednesday from 9 am to noon and 1 to 3 pm, and on Thursday and Friday from 1 to 3 pm, at a cost of P20. Tickets can be bought at the palace gate 3, where you also have to go through a security check. On certain official occasions the palace and museum are closed to the public. For information about these ring ☎ 588946 and ☎ 621321. There are jeepneys from Quiapo Market at Quezon Bridge to the palace.

The University of Santo Tomas, on Espano St, Sampaloc, the oldest university in the Philippines, houses the **Museum of Arts & Sciences**. It has an extensive collection of historic documents and a noteworthy library with more than 180,000 volumes. It is open Monday to Saturday from 8 am to noon and 2 to 4.30 pm. Admission is free.

The **National Museum** on Burgos St, Rizal Park, has many prehistoric finds, including a piece of the skull of 'Tabon Man' found in Tabon Cave, Palawan. There are also displays of pottery, weapons, costumes and ornaments. The museum is open Monday to Saturday from 8.30 am to noon and 1.30 to 5 pm. Admission is free.

The **Philippine Museum of Ethnology**, Nayong Pilipino, Pasay City, offers comprehensive information on the lifestyles of the so-called cultural minority groups. Tools, weapons, musical instruments and everyday utensils are on display. Written explanations and photos illustrate the differences between the various Filipino tribes. It is open Tuesday to Sunday from 9 am to 6 pm. Admission costs P20 (P10 for students).

Puerta Isabel II on Magallanes Drive, Intramuros, displays liturgical objects, *carrosas* (processional carriages) and some old

bells. It is open daily from 9 am to noon and 1 to 6 pm, except Monday. Admission is free.

The **Rizal Shrine** at Fort Santiago, Intramuros, is a memorial to the national hero, Dr Jose Rizal. You can see some personal effects and his death cell. The shrine is open Tuesday to Sunday from 9 am to noon and 1 to 5 pm, but closed on public holidays. Entrance is P5.

The **San Agustin Museum**, San Agustin Church on General Luna St, Intramuros, has been established since 1973 in the Augustinian monastery. You can see frescoes, oil paintings, antique choir stalls, precious robes and other liturgical items. It is open daily from 8 am to noon and 1 to 5 pm. Admission is P20.

MARKETS

The **Baclaran Flea Market**, one of the biggest markets in Manila, is on Roxas Blvd, Baclaran, near the Baclaran Church. Every day, from Roxas Blvd up as far as Harrison St (the Metrorail South Terminal), good-value clothing, food, flowers and household goods are on sale. The busiest time is on Wednesday, when the many churchgoers come looking for bargains after mass.

The **Cartimar Market** on the corner of Gil Puyat Ave and Taft Ave, Pasay City, could be compared to the Divisoria Market mentioned below, although it's quite a bit smaller and easier to find your way around. This is just the place for you if you're looking for a pet.

The **Central Market** on Quezon Blvd, Santa Cruz, is a big market hall full of clothing and accessories such as T-shirts, bags and shoes.

The **Divisoria Market**, San Nicolas, is on Santo Cristo St and the side streets nearby. It is a bright, lively market where examples of almost everything produced in the Philippines are sold at reasonable prices. There is a good vegetables and fruit section. Look out for pickpockets here!

The **Fiesta Filipino** is on Pedro Gil, between M H del Pilar and Mabini Sts, Malate. It is a fairly lifeless market, mainly for tourists. Still, it's a good place to find out about the country's handicrafts, and if you're a clever shopper you could do extremely well.

The **Quinta Market** on Carlos Palanca St, Quiapo, is also called the Santa Cruz or Quiapo Market. It is by Quezon Bridge, near Quiapo Church, and sells textiles, household goods and many other things. Handicrafts are sold in the **Ilalim ng Tulay Market** under the bridge.

The **San Andres Market**, San Andres St, Malate, has a wide range of top-quality tropical fruit. Perhaps the best and certainly the dearest fruit market in Manila, it is also open at night.

SWIMMING

If you feel like a swim several first-class hotels allow non-residents to use their swimming pools for an admission fee. Most of them are open from about 8 am to 7 pm.

Holiday Inn, Roxas Blvd, Pasay City. Admission is P110.

Manila Midtown Hotel, Adriatico St, on the corner of Pedro Gil, Ermita. Admission is P120.

Park Hotel, Belen St, Paco. Admission is P50.

The Westin Philippine Plaza Hotel, Cultural Center Complex, Roxas Blvd, Malate. Admission is P310.

Century Park Sheraton Hotel, Vito Cruz, Malate. Admission is P150.

Pool Bar, Guerrero St, Ermita. Admission is P50.

Seamen's Club, Bonifacio Drive, Port Area, South Harbour. The official name for this complex, which comprises a large swimming pool, table tennis, billiards, library and restaurant, is the Manila International Seamen's Center. Admission is P75, free for sailors whose ship is anchored in the harbour. A monthly ticket costs P300, or P100 for sailors on shore leave.

PLACES TO STAY

Manila has a very wide range of accommodation and it shouldn't be too hard to find something to suit you. The tourist centre is in Ermita, where you will find most of the government offices, while the business centre is in Makati. Most of the cheaper places to stay at are in, or very close to, Ermita. There are a few top-end hotels in Ermita, but quite a few more are strung out along the bay, fairly close to Ermita, in

Malate and Pasay City. Some of the top-end places can also be found in Makati.

Places to Stay – bottom end

Binondo & Santa Cruz There are only a few good and cheap hotels in the area north of the Pasig River.

The *First Hotel* (☎ 498811) on Ongpin St, Binondo, has fairly clean rooms with air-con and bath for P460/580, and there is a coffee shop. TV is P60 extra.

The *Merchants Hotel* (☎ 401071) at 711 San Bernardo St, on the corner of Soler St, Santa Cruz, has reasonable rooms with air-con and bath for P420/485, and there is a restaurant and a disco. The *Chinatown Peace Hotel* (☎ 215521-29; fax 215520) at 1283 Soler St, Binondo, has passable, clean rooms with air-con and bath from P450 to P600. The dearer rooms have TVs, and there is a restaurant.

Ermita, Malate & Paco The 'tourist belt' area is where numerous cheap hotels and pension houses can be found.

Lucen's Pension House (☎ 52112055, 5222389) at 2158 Carolina St, Malate, has basic, clean rooms with fan for P200/230, with fan and bath for P230/280 and with air-con and bath for P400. It's next to the big Victoria Court Motel and has a small restaurant. *Joward's Pension House* (☎ 5214845) is at 1726 Adriatico St, Malate. It has a restaurant and the rooms are clean but very small. Singles/doubles with fan cost P160/250 and with air-con and bath P480.

The *Richmond Pension* (☎ 585277) is at 1165 Grey St, Ermita, in a quiet little side street. It has small but clean singles/doubles with fan for P185/315 and with air-con for P435/465. *Pension Filipina* (☎ 5211488) at 542 Arkansas St, on the corner of Maria Orosa St, Ermita, is pleasant and has singles/doubles with fan for P225/280 and with air-con for P340/395. The *Santos Pension House* (☎ 595628) is at 1540 Mabini St, Ermita. It has rooms with fan for P275, with fan and bath for P335 and with air-con and bath for P485. The rooms vary in quality but are all clean, and there is a restaurant.

The *Malate Pensionne* (☎ 596671-73; fax 597119) at 1771 Adriatico St, Malate, has dorm beds with fan for P105 and with air-con for P120, and rooms with fan for P315/350, with fan and bath for P400 and P550 and with air-con and bath from P550 to P700. A suite with TV and kitchen costs P950, and there is a restaurant. It is relatively pleasant, although the rooms on the street side are somewhat noisy. Lockers can be rented and luggage left without charge for up to one week. Airport service costs P120. Prostitutes are not encouraged.

The *White House Tourist Inn* (☎ 5221535; fax 5224451) at 465 Pedro Gil, Ermita, has rooms with fan from P280 to P370 and with air-con for P490/530. It is quite a reasonable house and has a restaurant.

The *Mabini Pension* (☎ 594853, 505404; fax 595219) is at 1337 Mabini St, Ermita. It has rooms with fan for P320/350, with fan and bath for P400/550 and with air-con and bath for P650 and P700. The rooms are tidy and are all differently furnished. This is a popular meeting place. Urs, the owner, is Swiss and the people there are friendly and helpful. They will take care of tickets for Aerolift flights, visa extensions and will look after left luggage.

The *Birdwatchers Inn* (☎ 572292; fax 2585471) is a pleasant, comfortable place with a pub of the same name on the corner of A Flores and Mabini Sts, Ermita. It has really good rooms with fan for P400, with air-con for P560 and with air-con and bath for P800.

The *Tadel Pension House* (☎ 586895) at 453 Arquiza St, Ermita, has quite small singles/doubles with fan for P250 and fairly good singles/doubles with air-con and bath for P550 and P600.

The *Yasmin Pension* (☎ 505134; fax 5217225), next door to the Tadel Pension House on Arquiza St, Ermita, is a quiet place with comfortable rooms with air-con and bath for P450 and P600.

The *Midtown Inn* (☎ 582882) at 551 Padre Faura, Ermita, has passable, clean rooms with fan and bath from P400 to P500 and with TV, air-con and bath for P635/675.

The *Alexandria Pension Inn* (☎ 536 1336), directly next to the Las Palmas Hotel across from Pistang Pilipino, has unpretentious rooms with fan for P185 and fairly small but pleasant and clean rooms with TV, air-con and bath for P595. Unfortunately, the air-con is centrally controlled and cannot be regulated in the room. There is a coffee shop.

The *Pension Natividad* (☎ 5210524; fax 5223759) at 1601 M H del Pilar St, Malate, has dorm beds with fan for P120, rooms with fan for P350 and P400, with fan and bath for P500, and with air-con and bath for P700. There's a pleasant atmosphere in this well-run place. There is a coffee shop and staff will look after left luggage.

The *Sandico Apartel* (☎ 592036) in M H del Pilar St, Ermita, has rooms with air-con and bath for P495/530. The rooms are fairly pleasant, with fridges and TVs.

The *Ermita Tourist Inn* (☎ 5218770-72; fax 5218773) is at 1549 Mabini St, on the corner of Soldado St. Rooms with air-con and bath cost from P540 to P600, and there is a restaurant. It is a pleasant and fairly clean place but rooms overlooking Mabini St are more than a bit loud.

The *Manila Tourist Inn* (☎ 597721) at 487 Santa Monica St, Ermita, has quiet and fairly clean rooms with air-con and bath for P650. Another quiet, clean place but with rather small rooms is the *PM Inn* (☎ 584686) at 430 Plaza Ferguson, Ermita, where singles/ doubles with air-con and bath cost P600 and P700.

The *Iseya Hotel* (☎ 592016-18; fax 5224451) at 1241 M H del Pilar St, on the corner of Padre Faura, Ermita, has a restaurant, and quite comfortable singles/doubles with TV, fridge, air-con and bath for P770. The rooms facing M H del Pilar St are, however, quite noisy.

The *Villa Ermita Travel Lodge* (☎ 521 8665) at 1403 M H del Pilar St, Ermita, has clean and passable singles with air-con and bath from P780 and doubles with air-con and bath from P900.

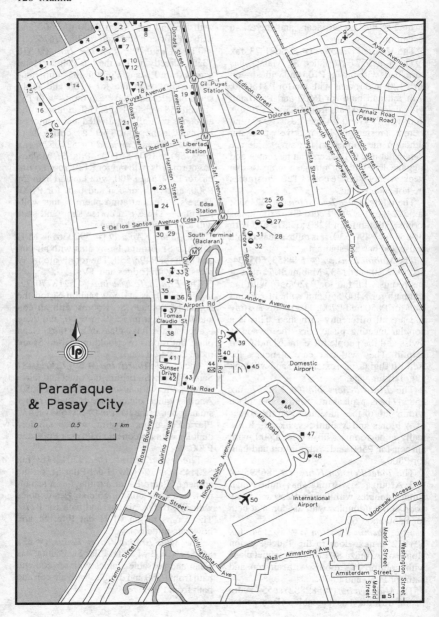

Parañaque
& Pasay City

0   0.5   1 km

■ PLACES TO STAY

1	Century Park Sheraton Hotel
7	Holiday Inn
8	Bohemia
16	The Westin Philippine Plaza Hotel
24	Hyatt Regency
29	Copacabana Apartment Hotel
30	Manila Clarion Hotel
35	Chateau de Baie
36	Hotel Carlston
38	Manila International Youth Hostel
41	The Townhouse
42	Bayview Towers
47	Philippine Village Hotel
51	La Petite Auberge

▼ PLACES TO EAT

12	Josephine's
17	Nandau Restaurant
18	Leo's Restaurant

OTHER

1	Harrison Plaza
2	Central Bank & Metropolitan Museum of Manila
3	Manila Yacht Club
4	Corregidor Ferry Terminal
5	Cultural Center
6	Legaspi Towers & Malaysia Airlines
9	Makati Medical Center
10	International Karaoke Complex
11	Folk Arts Theatre
13	Philcite Trade Center
14	International Convention Center
15	Coconut Palace
19	Cartimar Market
20	Libertad Cockpit
21	Philtrade Exhibits
22	Manila Film Center
23	Cuneta Astrodome
25	Victory Liner Bus Terminal
26	BLTB Bus Terminal
27	Inland Trailways Bus Terminal
28	Philtranco Bus Terminal
31	Pangasinan Five Star Bus Terminal
32	J B Bicol Express Line Bus Terminal
33	Baclaran Church
34	Seaside Market
37	Hertz Rent-a-Car
39	Domestic Airport
40	Air Link & Pacific Airways
43	Bouraq Airlines
44	Domestic Airport Post Office
45	Aerolift
46	Nayong Pilipino
48	Old MIA
49	Duty Free Shop
50	Ninoy Aquino International Airport (NAIA)

Parañaque & Pasay City In the area between the 'tourist belt' and airport there are a couple of hostel-style places.

The *Manila International Youth Hostel* (☎ 8320680; fax 8187948) at 4227 Tomas Claudio St, Parañaque, has dorm beds for P95 (YHA members P70). It is a good, tidy hostel with a garden. This is the office of the Youth & Student Travel Association of the Philippines (YSTAPHIL). It is next to the Excelsior Building, on the corner of Roxas Blvd.

The *Townhouse* (☎ 8331939; fax 804 0161) at the Villa Carolina Townhouse, 201 Roxas Blvd, Unit 31, Parañaque, has dorm beds with fan for P80, singles/doubles with fan for P200 and P250, with fan and bath for P300 and P350 and with air-con and bath for P500 and P550. Weekly rates can be arranged. There is also a good and inexpensive restaurant. It is a pleasant place, with a friendly atmosphere created by Bill and Laura, who like travelling themselves. It's in a small side street called Sunset Drive and is only about five minutes away by taxi from the Domestic Airport and NAIA. Airport service can be arranged for P50 (one or two persons).

Makati A relatively inexpensive place to stay is the *Pensionne Virginia* (☎ 885228, 877436) at 816 Pasay Rd. It has singles with air-con and bath for P750 and P1050 and doubles with air-con and bath for P1050 and P1400. The more expensive rooms have a fridge and TV. This place has a pleasant atmosphere and is clean and quiet.

Quezon City The *West Avenue Hotel* (☎ 982929) at 119 West Ave, Quezon City, has fairly good rooms with air-con and bath for P500/700, and there is a restaurant.

Places to Stay – middle

Binondo & Santa Cruz In this area, a couple of mid-range hotels can be recommended. The *Premier Hotel* (☎ 406061-72; fax 403794) on the corner of T Mapua and Tetuan Sts, Santa Cruz, has fairly comfortable rooms with air-con and bath for P740/860 and suites for P1170. There is a restaurant.

The *Lai-Lai International Hotel* (☎ 482061; fax 496110) on Gandara St, on the corner of Ongpin St, Santa Cruz, has comfortable rooms with TV, air-con and bath for P880/990. Suites are P1980. It's the best hotel in Chinatown, and also has a restaurant and a coffee shop.

Ermita, Malate & Paco The majority of the hotels in the 'tourist belt' area are in the middle price range.

The *True Home* (☎ & fax 5360351) at 2139 Adriatico St, Malate, is a beautiful house which you might not expect in this poor part of Adriatico. There is no proper name advertised, so look for the name written on the iron gate. Rooms with fan and bath are P580 and with TV, air-con and bath P1000 to P1300. All rooms have a different decor, and there is a restaurant and a swimming pool.

The *Hotel Roma* (☎ 5219431; fax 5215843) at 1407 Santa Monica St, on the corner of M H del Pilar St, Ermita, has clean rooms with fan and bath for P475, and comfortable rooms with air-con and bath from P675 to P1275.

The *Hotel Soriente* (☎ 599133), directly above the International Supermarket, on the corner of A Flores and J Bocobo Sts, Ermita, has well-kept rooms with air-con and bath for P730.

The *APP Mayfair Hotel* (☎ 503850, 504440; fax 52133039) at 1767 Mabini St, Malate, has quite comfortable rooms with TV, air-con and bath for P720 and P800. A

fridge is P50 extra. The rooms in the back building are bigger and quieter than on the Mabini St side.

The *Royal Palm Hotel* (☎ 5221515; fax 5220768) is good quality and has a restaurant. It is at 1227 Mabini St, Ermita, and has rooms with fridge, TV, air-con and bath from P830 to P1250. The rooms are all different sizes, the new ones on the Mabini St side are fairly loud. The dearer rooms are more spacious.

The *Cherry Lodge Apartelle* (☎ 507631-34; fax 5224172) at 550 J Bocobo St, Ermita, has comfortable rooms with TV, air-con and bath from P920 to P1830, and also has weekly and monthly rates. The dearer rooms have round beds and fridges, and there is a coffee shop. It is also a short-time hotel (three-hour rate is P250).

The *Rothman Inn Hotel* (☎ 5219251-60; fax 52222606) at 1633-35 Adriatico St, Malate, has rooms with TVs. Singles/doubles with air-con and bath cost P785 and P850; the more expensive rooms have fridges, and there is a restaurant.

The *Swagman Hotel* (☎ 599881-85; fax 5219731) at 411 A Flores St, Ermita, is pleasant. Rooms with fridge, TV, air-con and bath are from P1300. There is a 24-hour restaurant and airport service.

The *Hotel Swiss* (☎ 5224835; fax 522840) at 1030 Belen St, Paco, has comfortable rooms with TV, air-con and bath from P1175 to P1400. The more expensive rooms have fridges and cooking facilities. Check-out time is 2 pm. There is a restaurant also.

The *New Solanie Hotel* (☎ 508641-45) at 1811 Leon Guinto St, Malate, has good singles/doubles with air-con and bath from P1230 to P1520. The rooms have TVs, and the dearer ones have fridges and cooking facilities. It is quiet with a friendly atmosphere and has a coffee shop.

Las Palmas Hotel (☎ 506661-69; fax 5221699) is at 1616 Mabini St, Malate. It's an old favourite with pleasant rooms with air-con and bath from P1300. There is a restaurant and a swimming pool.

The *City Garden Hotel* (☎ 5218841; fax 504844) at 1158 Mabini St, Ermita, has rooms with TV, fridge, air-con and bath from P1200, and there is a restaurant. The rooms in this immaculately run hotel are nice and in good shape; they are often fully booked.

The *Sundowner Hotel* (☎ 5212751-61; fax 5215331) at 1430 Mabini St, Malate, has a newspaper stand with international papers and a restaurant. Singles/doubles with TV, air-con and bath cost P1640 and P2000. The dearer ones have fridges. The rooms are OK but less attractively decorated than you might think from the lobby.

The *Aurelio Hotel* (☎ 509061; fax 5867702) is on the corner of Padre Faura and Roxas Blvd, Ermita. It has singles with air-con and bath from P1300, and doubles with air-con and bath from P1450. Suites are P2650. The rooms have TVs, and there is also a restaurant.

The *Hotel Royal Co-Co* (☎ 5213911-18; fax 5213919) at 2120 Mabini St, Malate, is an attractive place that offers tastefully furnished rooms with TV, air-con and bath from P1175 to P2285, and there is a restaurant. The more expensive rooms have a fridge and jacuzzi.

The *Adriatico Arms* (☎ 5210736-40; fax 489256) at 561 J Nakpil St, on the corner of Adriatico St, has pleasant rooms with TV, air-con and bath for P1360/1560. A fridge is P50 extra, and there is a restaurant.

The *Palm Plaza Hotel* (☎ 582095-96; fax 508384) has clean and comfortable rooms with TV, fridge, air-con and bath from P1700/2100. Weekly and monthly rates are available, and there is also a restaurant.

The *Aloha Hotel* (☎ 599061-69; fax 5215328) at 2150 Roxas Blvd, Malate, is a comfortable place with rooms with air-con and bath for P1400, and suites with terraces overlooking the bay for P2400. There is a restaurant.

The *Park Hotel* (☎ 5212371-75; fax 5212393) at 1032-34 Belen St, Paco, has singles/doubles with air-con and bath for P1200/2050 and suites for P3415. The rooms are quiet and comfortable and have a TV and fridge, the suites also have a jacuzzi. There is a restaurant, a swimming pool and airport service.

Galleon's Hotel (formerly Friday's Manila Hotel) (☎ 5212283, 5210088; fax 5211072) at 1607 J C Bocobo St, Malate, is a beautiful old bourgeois house with very tastefully decorated rooms with TV, air-con and bath from P1500 to P2350, including breakfast. There is a restaurant, a bar and airport service.

The *Bohemia* (☎ 582751; fax 5218393) at 640 Vito Cruz St, Malate, is a small well-kept hotel opposite the Century Park Sheraton. The spacious and tastefully decorated rooms with TV, fridge, air-con and bath cost P1900, suites are P2250. There is a restaurant.

The *Ambassador Hotel* (☎ 506011-19; fax 5215557) at 2021 Mabini St, Malate, has good rooms with air-con and bath for P2100/2600 and suites for P4200. There is a restaurant, a disco and swimming pool.

The *Hotel La Corona* (☎ 502631-38; fax 5213909) at 1166 M H del Pilar St, on the corner of Arquiza St, Ermita, has well-looked after singles/doubles with TV, fridge, air-con and bath from P2400/P2600, including breakfast. Suites with a jacuzzi cost from P3600, and there is a restaurant. The M H del Pilar St side is pretty noisy.

The *Admiral Hotel* (☎ 572081-94; fax 5222018) at 2138 Roxas Blvd, Malate, has singles with air-con and bath for P3500 and P4000 and doubles with air-con and bath for P4000 and P4300. The rooms are comfortable and have a fridge and TV, and there is a restaurant and a swimming pool. This hotel is rich in tradition and has real character.

Makati In this area some attractive mid-range hotels can be found in or close to the 'food streets' Pasay Rd and Makati Ave.

The *El Cielito Tourist Inn* (☎ 8158951-54; fax 8179610) at 804 Pasay Rd, Makati, is a pleasant place with a restaurant and a coffee shop. It has singles with air-con and bath for P895 and P1010, doubles with air-con and bath for P985 and P1235, and suites from P1680.

The *Oka Hotel* (☎ 8944408-11; fax 8944395) at 8459 Kalayaan Ave, Makati, has pleasant rooms with TV, fridge, air-con and bath from P1145 to P1740. The cost inlcudes

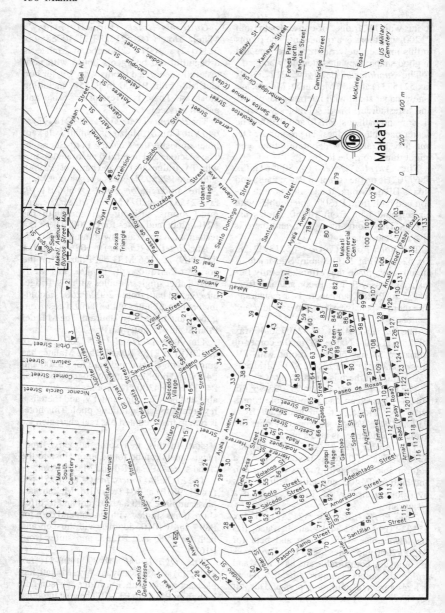

Makati

■ PLACES TO STAY

1	Traveler's Inn
18	Mandarin Oriental Hotel
40	Manila Peninsula Hotel
41	Shangri-La Hotel
63	Charter House Apartelle
79	Hotel Intercontinental
92	Amorsolo Mansion
95	Makati International Inn
103	Hotel Nikko Manila Garden
117	El Cielito Tourist Inn
119	Pensionne Virginia
126	Vacation Hotel

▼ PLACES TO EAT

2	Kusia Ni Maria Restaurant
3	Treffpunkt Jedermann Restaurant
27	Mother Sachi Restaurant
36	Bistro RJ
37	Nielson Tower Club & Restaurant
50	Maxim's Tea House
59	Café Adriatico
60	Nandau Restaurant & Truffles Restaurant
61	New Orleans Restaurant
62	La Tasca Restaurant
71	Taste of Thailand Restaurant
73	Café Rizal
75	Boccalino Pizza Restaurant
76	Flavours & Spices Restaurant & Beverly Hills Deli
77	Schwarzwälder Restaurant
80	Kimpura Restaurant
84	Tia Maria's Restaurant
85	Shakey's Greenbelt
86	Le Soufflé Restaurant
87	Josephine's
89	Max's Fried Chicken
90	Aling Asiang Restaurant, Aristocrat Restaurant & Prince of Wales Pub & Restaurant
91	Via Mare Restaurant
93	Thai Room Restaurant
95	Lalawigan sa Makati Restaurant & Siam Cuisine Restaurant
96	Kentucky Fried Chicken & McDonald's
97	McDonald's
98	Pizza Hut
104	Jollibee, Pizza Hut & Wendy's
105	Coney Island Ice Cream & Dunkin Donuts
106	Kowloon House
108	Saisaki Japanese Restaurant & Sushi Bar

114	Kamayan Restaurant
115	Hard Rock Café
116	Racks Bistro
117	Probinsiya Restaurant
118	Schatzie Bar & Grill & Pinausukan Seafood Restaurant
119	Chez Coppel Restaurant, Goldilocks Cake Shop & Kashmir Restaurant
120	The Gold Ranch Restaurant
122	Joni's Coffee Shop
123	Azumaya Noodle House & Milky Way Restaurant
124	Angelino's Pizza
125	Mey Lin Restaurant
126	Melo's Steak Restaurant
127	Foo Yiu Chinese Restaurant & Pep's Mexican Restaurant
128	Tian Tian Seafood Restaurant
130	Max's Fried Chicken
132	Sakura Restaurant & St Peters Terrace Bar & Restaurant

OTHER

4	Emirates Airlines, Swissair Airlines, Thai Airways International & Country Space I Building
5	United Airlines, Taiwanese Embassy (Teco Office) & Pacific Star Building
6	Japanese Embassy
7	Equitable Bank
8	Royal Brunei Airlines &. Saville Building
9	Philippine National Bank (PNB)
10	KLM Royal Dutch Airlines, Northwest Airlines & Athenaeum Building
11	Singapore Airlines
12	Air France & Century Tower Building
13	Zuellig Wine & Spirits
14	Makati Central Post Office
15	Saudi Arabian Airlines & Cougar Building
16	Air India, Korean Air, Canadian Pacific Airways, Cathay Pacific, Gammon Center & LPL Plaza
17	Korean Embassy & Alpap Building
19	Norwegian Embassy
20	Danish Embassy, Swedish Embassy, City Bank Center & City Bank

21	Qantas & China Bank Building	57	Thai Embassy
22	Lepanto Building & Bank of America	58	Australian Embassy
		62	San Mig Pub
23	Filinvest Financial Center & Deutsche Bank Asia	64	PAL
		65	Interbank
24	Pakistan International Airways (PIA) & ADC Building	66	Lufthansa German Airlines
		67	Austrian Embassy
25	Philippine Savings Bank Building, Philippine Savings Bank & Israeli Embassy	68	Equitable Bank
		69	Dive Mate
		70	Aquaventure Philippines
26	Skyland Plaza Building & Thomas Cook Travel	71	Mile Long Arcade
		72	Northwest Airlines
28	Makati Medical Centre	74	Greenbelt Mall
29	Oledan Building	76	New Garden Square
30	Filipinas Life Building & French Embassy	77	Faces Disco
		78	Rustan's Department Store
31	Dr Varwig, GP & Hongkong & Shanghai Banking Corp	81	Fairmart Department Store
		82	The Landmark Department Store
32	Finnair & Pacific Bank Building	83	Ayala Museum
		88	United Supermarket
33	Insular Life Building & Insular Life Theatre	91	Greenbelt Square
		94	Alitalia & Gallery Building
34	Solid Bank Building, German Embassy & Swiss Embassy	95	Creekside Building
		98	Bookmark
		99	Ayala Center Terminal, Love Bus Station & Park Square II
35	Atrium of Makati & Makati Atrium (Atrium Shopping Mall)	100	Quad Theatre (Cinemas)
36	Olympia Building	101	National Book Store
37	Nielson Tower Building	102	SM Shoemart Department Store
38	Ninoy Aquino Monument	103	Japan Airlines
39	Makati Stock Exchange	105	Park Square
40	Eastern Airlines, Garuda Indonesian Airlines & Blue Horizon Travel & Tours	107	Anson's Department Store
		109	Vietnam Airlines, Anson Arcade & Coronado Bowling Lanes
42	Locsin Building & UK Embassy	110	Bookmark
		111	Aeroflot Airlines
44	Continental Air Micronesia & SGV Building	112	Aerolift
		113	Makati Cinema Square
47	British Airways	115	Sunvar Plaza
48	Royal Jordanian Airlines & Golden Rock Building	118	Kiss Club
		121	Gecko's Bar, Kabooze Music Bar & Restaurant & Equinox Disco
49	Don Jacinto Building & Belgian Embassy	127	National Book Store & Hit Wave Disco
51	Dutch Embassy & King's Court Building	128	Bobby Magees Pub & Mars Disco
52	Indonesian Embassy	129	La O'Centre
53	Italian Embassy & Zeta Building	130	Illusion Entertainment Club
		131	Balikbayan Handicrafts
54	Egypt Air, Gulf Air & Windsor Tower Building	133	Pulse Disco
55	Air Nuigini & Fortune Building		
56	Scandinavian Airlines System & F & L Lopez Building		

breakfast. It's very conveniently located to Burgos St.

The *Makati International Inn* (☎ 8161187; fax 8195722) at 21178 Pasong Tamo Ave, Makati, has nicely furnished rooms with TV, air-con and bath for P1040/1235. Some rooms also have fridges and cooking facilities. There is a restaurant and a coffee shop.

The *Vacation Hotel* (☎ 867936; fax 8187756) at 914 Pasay Rd, Makati, has quiet and comfortable rooms with air-con and bath from P1370/1710, including breakfast, and there is a restaurant. The standard rooms are, however, a bit small.

The *Robelle House* (☎ 881931-35; fax 8180008) is good value for Makati. It is at 4402 Valdez St, opposite the International School. Singles with air-con and bath cost from P1100, doubles with air-con and bath cost P1225, and suites cost P1500. There is a restaurant and a swimming pool in a pleasant local atmosphere. The service is very friendly.

Parañaque & Pasay City *La Petite Auberge* (☎ & fax 8286311) is at 77 Madrid St, Parañaque. This pleasant little place is a bit hidden away in the Merville Park Subdivision south of the airport. It has only five singles/doubles with air-con and bath for P800, including breakfast, and there is a restaurant and a swimming pool. A free airport service is available for international flights. It's best to call and arrange for staff to pick you up if possible.

Quezon City Several medium-sized hotels in this category can be found in Quezon City. The establishments in this range are usually frequented by up-market Filipinos.

The *Villa Estela Hometel* (☎ 9229136, 961160) at 33 Scout Santiango St, on the corner of Scout Dr Lazcano St, Quezon City, has clean, comfortable rooms with TV, fridge, air-con and bath for P840. There is a restaurant, a disco and a swimming pool.

The *Metropolitan Apartment Hotel* (☎ 9214241, 9214498; fax 9214642) is in a quiet area in Quezon City near the Philippine

Heart Center for Asia. It is at 131 Malakas St, Diliman, and spacious singles/doubles with TV, air-con and bath are from P975 to P1325. Two-room apartments cost P1950. There is a coffee shop.

The *Hotel Danarra & Resort* (☎ 985161-68; fax 9242503) at 121 Mother Ignacia St, Diliman, Quezon City, has comfortable rooms with air-con and bath for P1000. There is also a restaurant and a swimming pool.

Places to Stay – top end

Manila has plenty of first-class hotels. Many of them, like the Philippine Plaza and the Sheraton, offer reductions of 40% in the off season from June to September. Others, like the Manila Midtown Hotel, cut their price by 50% for a stay of four weeks. The elegant Manila Hotel can be ranked with the Raffles in Singapore, the Oriental in Bangkok and the Peninsula in Hong Kong as among the oldest and most reputable hotels in South-East Asia. The new Philippine Plaza, with its 700 rooms, seems by contrast modern and elaborate. For a real extravagance, the Imperial Suite is available – a penthouse with 10 rooms and your own butler for US$2000 a night. Those who will settle for a mere five super rooms but who still need their own butler, swimming pool and garden, can book the Mandarin Suite at the Mandarin Oriental Hotel in Makati. It only costs US$1800.

Fifteen of the best luxury hotels in Manila are listed immediately below. All contain numerous bars, restaurants and nightclubs. The guests have the use of swimming pools, saunas and tennis courts. The rooms are of excellent international standard, and, of course, with TV, fridge, air-con and bath. To the price given in US dollars, you have to add a 10% service charge and a 13.7% government tax.

Ermita, Malate & Paco The *Century Park Sheraton* (☎ 5221011; fax 5213413) is on Vito Cruz in Malate. Singles cost from US$170, doubles from US$190 and suites from US$260. The *Manila Diamond Hotel* (☎ 5362211; fax 5362255), on the corner of

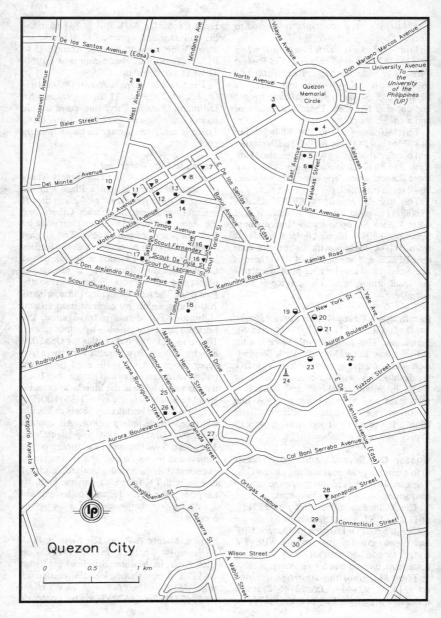

Quezon City

0   0.5   1 km

■ PLACES TO STAY

2   West Avenue Hotel
6   Metropolitan Apartment Hotel
13 Hotel Danarra & Resort
14 Camelot Hotel
17 Villa Estela Hometel & Clubhouse
26 Broadway Court

▼ PLACES TO EAT

7   Aristocrat Restaurant
8   Restaurants & Nightclubs
9   Bistro R J
10 Alavar's House of Seafood
11 Café de Chine
16 Restaurants
27 Josephine's
28 Restaurants

    OTHER

1   SM City
3   National Parks & Wildlife Center
4   Quezon City Hall
5   Philippine Heart Center for Asia
12 National Book Store
15 Thunderdome Cabaret
18 Kamuning Market
19 Dapupan Bus Terminal
20 Baliwag Transit Bus Terminal
21 Superlines Bus Terminal
22 Araneta Center
23 Dangwa Tranco Bus Terminal
24 Buddhist Temple
25 Goethe Institute (Goethe House)
29 Greenhills Shopping Center
30 Cardinal Santos Hospital

Ermita, has singles from US$140 and doubles from US$160. Suites are from US$280.

The *Silahis International Hotel* (☎ 521 0004; fax 5360112) at 1910 Roxas Blvd, Malate, has singles from US$120 and doubles from US$130. The *Westin Philippine Plaza Hotel* (☎ 8320701; fax 8323485) at the Cultural Center Complex, Malate, has singles from US$165, doubles from US$185 and suites from US$350.

Makati The *Hotel Inter-Continental* (☎ 815 9711; fax 8171330) on Ayala Ave, Makati, has singles from US$195 and doubles from US$230. The *Mandarin Oriental* (☎ 816 3601; fax 8172472) on Makati Ave, Makati, has singles from US$185 and doubles from US$230. Suites are from US$320.

The *Hotel Nikko Manila Garden* (☎ 8104101; fax 8171862) is on Fourth Quadrant, Makati Commercial Center, Makati. It has singles from US$140, doubles from US$170 and suites from US$240.

The *Manila Peninsula* (☎ 8193456; fax 815 4825) on Makati Ave, on the corner of Ayala Ave, Makati, has singles from US$195 and doubles from US$250 and suites from US$400.

The *Shangri-La Hotel* (☎ 8138888; fax 8135499) on Ayala Ave, on the corner of Makati Ave, Makati, has singles from US$210 and doubles from US$230. Suites are from US$330.

Roxas Blvd and J Quintos St, Malate, has singles from US$160 and doubles from US$180. Suites are from US$350.

The *Manila Hotel* (☎ 470011; fax 471124) at Rizal Park, Ermita, has singles from US$120, doubles from US$150, suites from US$250 and a penthouse for US$2000.

The *Manila Midtown Hotel* (☎ 5217001; fax 5222629) on Pedro Gil, Ermita, has singles from US$110 and doubles from US$125. Suites are from US$200.

The *Manila Pavilion Hotel* (☎ 5222911; fax 5223531) on United Nations Ave,

Parañaque & Pasay City The *Holiday Inn* (☎ 597961-80; fax 5223985) at 3001 Roxas Blvd, Pasay City, has singles from US$120, doubles from US$140 and suites from US$200.

The *Hyatt Regency* (☎ 8331234, 831 2611; fax 8335913) at 2702 Roxas Blvd, Pasay City, has rooms from US$115.

The *Philippine Village Hotel* (☎ 8314484; fax 8338248) on Mia Rd, near the airport, Pasay City, has singles from US$90 and doubles from US$110, and suites from US$220.

Apartments

If you're going to stay in Manila for a while it may be worth considering apartments instead of hotel rooms. It is possible to find apartments with cooking facilities, air-con, a fridge, TV and so on for a monthly rent of around P8000 to P20,000, depending on what is provided. A month's rent must be paid in advance, and a deposit is required for the electricity. Rentals are available on a monthly, weekly, and sometimes even daily basis. The daily rates include electricity and are around P500 to P1000. Apartments in Makati are often very dear, while those in Ermita and Malate are seldom available, especially the cheaper ones, so it's a good idea to book early.

Ermita, Malate & Paco The *Victoria Mansion* (☎ 575851; fax 5210193), 600 J M Nakpil St, Malate, has one-room apartments for P400 daily and P11,400 monthly.

The *Jetset Executive Mansion* (☎ 5214029-30; fax 344430) is at 1205 General Luna St, Ermita. It has rooms with air-con and bath for P600, and one-room apartments for P750 daily (monthly by arrangement), and there is a restaurant. At the *Doña Petronila Mall* (☎ 595355, 587550) at 1184 Mabini St, Ermita, you can get a one-room apartment for P600 to P650 daily, P3500 to P4000 weekly (including electricity) and P8000 to P8500 monthly.

The *Casa Blanca I* (☎ 596011-18) at 1447 Adriatico St, Ermita, has one-room apartments for P750 daily and P9000 monthly. Two-room apartments cost P1200 daily and P12,000 monthly. The *San Carlos Mansion* (☎ 590981-89) at 777 San Carlos St, Ermita, has one-room apartments for P600 and P700 daily and P13,500 and P16,500 monthly. Two-room apartments cost P800 daily and P19,000 monthly.

The *Mabini Mansion* (☎ 5214776) is at 1011 Mabini St, Ermita. A one-room apartment costs P1170 and P1630 daily and P15,000 and P22,000 monthly. A two-room apartment costs P2000 and P2920 daily and P23,000 and P29,000 monthly. It has a coffee shop.

The *Dakota Mansion* (☎ 5210701; fax 5218841), on the corner of Adriatico and General Miguel Malvar Sts, Malate, has one-room apartments for P1170 daily and P15,000 monthly. Two-room apartments cost P2000 daily and P23,000 monthly, and there is a restaurant and swimming pool.

The *Boulevard Mansion* (☎ 5218888; fax 5215829), 1440 Roxas Blvd, Ermita, has studios for P890 daily and P15,000 monthly; standard one-room apartments for P960 daily and P13,000 monthly; suites for P1125 daily and P22,000 monthly; and a penthouse for P4200 daily and P60,000 monthly. It also has a coffee shop.

The *Pearl Garden Apartel* (☎ 575911) at 1700 Adriatico St, Malate, has one-room apartments for P970 to P1260 daily and P23,000 to P30,000 monthly. Two-room apartments cost P1700 daily and P41,500 monthly. There is also a restaurant.

The *Ralph Anthony Suites* (☎ 5211107; fax 5210203), on the corner of Maria Orosa and Arkansas Sts, Ermita, has one-room apartments for P1200 to P1750 daily and P27,500 to P37,600 monthly. Two-room apartments cost P2100 to P2900 daily and P48,000 to P65,000 monthly.

The *Euro-Nippon Mansion* (☎ 5213921-25; fax 5213868) at 2090 Roxas Blvd, Malate, has studios for P835 daily and P16,000 monthly; one-room apartments for P985 daily and P18,000 monthly; and suites for P1650 daily and P25,000 monthly. There is a restaurant and a disco.

Robinson's Apartelle (☎ 52205581; fax 5219152) on Maria Orosa St, Ermita, has studios for P1150 daily and P20,500 monthly; one-room apartments for P1700 daily and P31,500 monthly; and two-room apartments for P2250 daily and P42,000 monthly.

The *Tropicana Apartment Hotel* (☎ 590061-76; fax 5223208) at 1630 Luis M Guerrero St, Malate, has standard one-room apartments for P1400 daily, P8500 weekly and P30,200 monthly. Deluxe one-room apartments are P1520 daily, P9700 weekly and P35,000 monthly. Standard two-room apartments are P3300 daily, P14,200 weekly and P48,500 monthly. Deluxe two-room apartments are P2500 daily, P15,200 weekly and P55,000 monthly. It has a restaurant and a swimming pool.

Makati The *Amorsolo Mansion* (☎ 8186811-19; fax 8172620) at 130 Amorsolo St, on the corner of Herrera St, has one-room apartments for P1200 daily and P17,000 monthly, and two-room apartments for P2000 daily and P24,000 monthly.

The *Charter House Apartelle* (☎ 8176001-16; fax 8177071) at 114 Legaspi St, Makati, has one-room apartments for P1600 and P1750 daily and P40,000 and P44,250 monthly. There is a coffee shop and a small swimming pool.

Regine's Apartelle (☎ 8126509; fax 8126778) at 8429 Kalayaan Ave, on the corner of Makati Ave, Makati, has studios for P1700 daily and P42,000 monthly; one-room apartments for P2400 daily and P59,000 monthly; and two-room apartments for P3400 daily and P83,000 monthly.

The *Robelle Mansion* (☎ 8163581-96; fax 8180008) at 877 J P Rizal St, Makati, has one-room apartments from P825 to P1100 daily and for P16,200 and P18,800 monthly.

The *Traveler's Inn* (☎ 857061-70; fax 872144) at 7880 Makati Ave, Makati, has one-room apartments from P1000 daily and P11,000 monthly.

Parañaque & Pasay City The *Copacabana Apartment Hotel* (☎ 8318711; fax 8314344) at 264 Edsa Extension, Pasay City, has one-room apartments for P1200 daily and P26,800 monthly; two-room apartments for P1600 daily and P30,000 monthly; and three-room apartments for P2800 daily and P35,000 monthly. There is a restaurant, coffee shop, sauna and a swimming pool.

Quezon City The *Broadway Court* (☎ 7227411; fax 7217795) is at 16 Dona Juana Rodriguez St, New Manila (Quezon City). It has one-room apartments costing P800 daily, P5600 weekly and P12,000 monthly. There is also a coffee shop and tennis court.

PLACES TO EAT

Manila's restaurants have an impressive diversity of cuisines and prices. Connoisseurs have the opportunity to try the local fare as well as the pleasures of other Asian cooking and European and American dishes. Fast food is available, or you can enjoy the generous fixed-price buffets provided by the top-class hotel restaurants at your leisure.

In most restaurants in Ermita you can get a decent meal for roughly P75 to P100. In Adriatico St, where there is a wide range of Asian places, prices are a bit higher. For a meal of several courses you can expect to pay from P150 to P250.

The top restaurants in Makati and in the luxury hotels are expensive, but a real gourmet would probably be prepared to pay the P250 to P350 or more charged for the excellent food, service and atmosphere. Sometimes these meals are accompanied by cultural entertainment or a fashion show. A lunch buffet costs about P200 to P250.

Good wine in a good restaurant will cost at least P500 a bottle. Wine is imported and transport costs and import duties make it very expensive. Maybe San Miguel beer is a better choice.

Only a few top restaurants insist on formal dress such as ties, jackets or barongs. Otherwise casual clothes are quite all right. However, even in a middle-range restaurant, thongs (flip-flops), shorts or singlets would be pushing tolerance a bit far.

The prices given for the following restaurants are the approximate current costs of dinner for one person. Drinks are not included, nor are extra helpings or expensive items like lobster tails by the dozen or caviar by the kg. With buffets in top hotels, about 25% is added for government tax and the service charge.

Filipino Food

Ermita is a good place to explore for Filipino food, especially along M H del Pilar St. There are also some good places in Makati.

Aida's on M H del Pilar St, Ermita, is a reasonably priced 'turo-turo' restaurant,

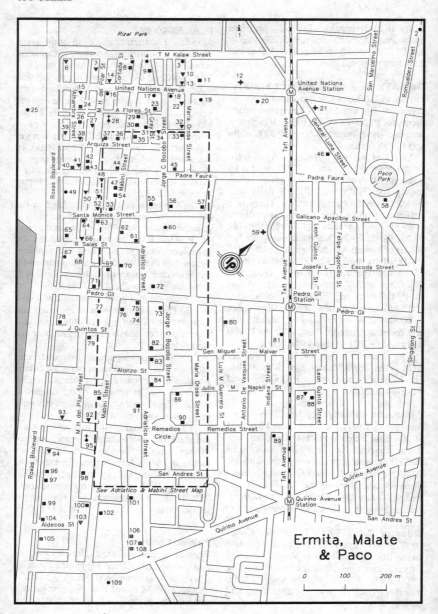

Ermita, Malate
& Paco

0   100   200 m

■ PLACES TO STAY

8	Mabini Mansion
9	San Carlos Mansion
11	Manila Pavilion Hotel
23	Hotel Soriente
24	Swagman Hotel
26	P M Inn
29	Birdwatcher's Inn
30	City Garden Hotel
31	Richmond Pension
33	Pension Filipina & Ralph Anthony Suites
35	Doña Petronila Mall
36	Tadel Pension House & Yasmin Pension
37	Hotel La Corona
40	Aurelio Hotel
42	Sandico Apartel
43	Iseya Hotel
44	Royal Palm Hotel
45	Midtown Inn
46	Jetset Executive Mansion
47	Tower Hotel
53	Manila Tourist Inn
54	Mabini Pension
55	Midland Plaza
56	Cherry Lodge Apartelle
57	Robinson's Apartelle
58	Hotel Swiss & Park Hotel
61	Casa Blanca I
62	Sundowner Hotel
63	Hotel Roma
64	Villa Ermita Travel Lodge
65	Boulevard Mansion
69	Ermita Tourist Inn
70	Santos Pension House
71	White House Tourist Inn
72	Manila Midtown Hotel
73	Galleon's Hotel
74	Rothman Inn Hotel
75	Palm Plaza Hotel
76	Alexandria Pension Inn & Las Palmas Hotel
78	Manila Diamond Hotel
79	Pension Natividad
80	Tropicana Apartment Hotel
82	Dakota Mansion
83	Pearl Garden Apartel
84	Adriatico Arms Hotel
85	APP Mayfair Hotel
86	Victoria Mansion
88	New Solanie Hotel
90	Remedios Pension House
91	Malate Pensionne & Shoshana Pension House
96	Silahis International Hotel
97	Euro-Nippon Mansion
98	Winner Lodge
99	Marabella Apartments
100	Ambassador Hotel
101	Carolina Pension
102	Hotel Royal Co-Co
104	Admiral Hotel
105	Aloha Hotel
106	Lucen's Pension House
107	True Home
108	Victoria Court Motel

▼ PLACES TO EAT

6	Maxim's Tea House
7	Hong Kong Tea House
10	Kentucky Fried Chicken
13	McDonald's
14	Diamond Tea House
15	Yakiniku Sakura Restaurant
22	Max's
27	Myrna's
32	Bulwagang Pilipino
34	Barrio Fiesta
38	Hang's 'N'
39	Emerald Garden Restaurant
41	The Pool
43	Iseya Restaurant & Rooftop Restaurant
48	Mrs Wong Tea House
50	Lili Marleen
51	Guernica's & Swiss Hut
52	Aida's
58	Old Swiss Inn Restaurant
66	Rosie's Diner
68	Fischfang
87	Sala-Thai
92	Erieze Seafood Restaurant
93	Shakey's Malate
94	Aristocrat
103	My Father's Moustache

OTHER

1	Tourist Office
2	Tabacalera
3	Avis Rent-a-Car
4	Singapore Airlines
5	Pakistan International Airways
11	Budget Rent-a-Car
12	Manila Doctors Hospital
16	Hidden Valley Springs Office & Grande Island Office
17	Alemar's
18	Equitable Bank
19	American Express
20	Western Police Station

21	Manila Medical Centre	59	Philippine General Hospital
22	Hertz Rent-a-Car	60	Robinson's
23	International Supermarket	67	PAL
25	US Embassy	69	Scenic View Travel Inc
28	Ermita Church	71	Sunshine Run Office
29	Birdwatcher's Bar	77	Fiesta Filiipino
33	Sabena Belgian Airlines	81	P L D T Philippine Long
41	The Pool		Distance Telephone Company
47	P T & T Telegram	89	Sarkies Tours
49	Avis Rent-a-Car,	95	Màlate Church
	Broadway Travel &	102	Interbank
	Interisland Travel & Tours	109	Manila Zoological &
54	Mabini Post Office		Botanical Gardens
58	Mr Ticket		

partly open air, which sometimes has good munggo (bean) soup. It is open 24-hours daily; a meal costs about P75.

Myrna's, also on M H del Pilar St, Ermita, is a typical simple Filipino restaurant. It serves good bangus (milkfish) and is crowded at meal times. It is open Monday to Saturday from 7 am to 11.30 pm, and a meal costs about P75.

The *Harbor View* on South Blvd, at the end of Rizal Park, right where the harbour trip starts, is a very pleasant place by the waterfront to watch the sunset and catch a fresh breeze while having a beer and enjoying good Filipino food like sinigang (vegetable soup) or bangus. It's open Monday to Saturday from 10 to 2 am and Sunday until midnight. Thongs (flip-flops) are not allowed. Meals cost about P150.

The *Patio Mequeni* on Remedios St, Malate, is a pleasant, simply furnished restaurant that specialises in dishes from Pampanga Province. It is open Monday to Saturday from 11 am to 3 pm and 6 pm to midnight. A meal costs about P150.

The *Aristocrat*, on the corner of Roxas Blvd and San Andres St, Malate, is a big, medium-priced restaurant. It is very popular with local people and the most popular of the six Aristocrat restaurants in Metro Manila. It is open daily all hours and charges about P150.

Josephine's on Roxas Blvd, Pasay City, is a well-known and popular seafood restaurant

with an extensive menu and live combo music in the evenings. It is open daily from 9 am to midnight; a meal costs about P150. There is another *Josephine's* restaurant in Greenbelt Park, Makati.

The *Bulwagang Pilipino* on the corner of Arkansas St and Maria Orosa St, Ermita, is another good Filipino restaurant. It is open daily from 9 am to 11 pm, and charges about P200 for a meal.

The *Aling Asiang* on Greenbelt Center, Makati, is a well-run speciality restaurant with authentic dishes from various provinces. It is open from 11 am to 11 pm daily, with meals for about P175.

Calle 5 on Mabini St, Ermita, has an open-air section as well as seating inside. In the evenings they have live music. Their sizzling plates (eg, squid) are outstanding. It is open daily from 8 am to 3 am and a meal costs about P175.

At the *Palais daan* on Adriatico St, Malate, you can get good Filipino dishes and seafood. It is open daily from 10 am to 1 am, and charges about P200 for a meal.

The *Tito Rey* at Sunvar Plaza on Amorsolo St, Makati, features finger-food specialties from different provinces. It is open daily from 11 am to 5 pm and 6 pm to 2 am. A meal costs about P175.

The *Barrio Fiesta* on J C Bocobo St, Ermita, is a good, medium-priced restaurant with branches all over the country. It has an extensive menu with specialities like crispy pata and kare-kare (stew). It is open daily from 8 am to 1 am, and a meal costs about P200. There is another *Barrio Fiesta* in Makati Ave, Makati.

The *Ang Bistro sa Remedios*, on the corner of Adriatico and Remedios Sts, Malate, is an elegant restaurant serving special dishes from Pampanga Province. It is open from 11 am to 2 pm and 6 pm to midnight daily, and a meal costs about P200.

At the *Kamayan Restaurant* on Padre Faura, Ermita, you can eat with your fingers in true Filipino style. There is a wide range of dishes from all over the Philippines. It is open daily from 11 am to 2 pm and 5 to 10 pm. A meal costs about P200.

The *Nandau* on the corner of Roxas Blvd and Lourdes St, Pasay City, is a well-known seafood restaurant which specialises in food from the province of Zamboanga del Norte in Mindanao – blue marlin, for example. It is open daily from 11 am to 11 pm and a meal costs about P250.

The *Seaside Market* on Roxas Blvd, Baclaran (near Baclaran Church), is a real market where you can buy freshly caught fish and have it prepared cheaply at the little adjoining restaurants. It is open all hours and a meal costs about P100. At *Leo's*, on the corner of Roxas Blvd and Dapitan St, Pasay City, you can eat á la carte or choose your fish and have it prepared as you wish. It is open 24-hours daily and a meal costs about P200.

The *Seafood Market* on J Bocobo St, Ermita, is relatively dear, but is a good seafood restaurant. It's almost like a real market, guests do their own selecting and then take their filled baskets to the cooks to be prepared as they wish. It is especially busy at night but the waiting time is usually short. You can round off the menu with coffee and cakes at the *Café Alps* next door. There is another *Seafood Market* on Makati Ave, Makati. It is open daily from 10 am to midnight and a meal costs about P300.

At *The Islands Fisherman* on Arquiza St, Ermita, guests also select their food which can be cooked in Chinese, Japanese, Filipino or Thai style, or according to their own recipes. Unlike, for example, the ever-popular Seafood Market, they do not charge extra for the preparation of the seafood and side-orders you choose, or for service. It is open daily from 10 am to midnight. A meal costs about P250.

Other Non-Western Cuisine

Chinese *Mrs Wong Tea House* on the corner of Padre Faura and M H del Pilar St, Ermita, is well patronised. It is open daily from 10 am to 7 am and a meal costs from P75 to P100.

The *Hong Kong Tea House* on M H del Pilar St, Ermita, is a long-established typical Chinese restaurant with good noodle soup. It is open daily from 10 am to 4 am and a meal costs from P75 to P100.

Maxim's Tea House on Roxas Blvd, on the corner of T M Kalaw St, Ermita, offers good, inexpensive food. There is also a *Maxim's Tea House* on M H del Pilar St, Ermita (opposite the Hong Kong Tea Room), on the corner of Pasong Tamo and Urban Sts, Makati, and in Ongpin St, Chinatown. It is open daily all hours and meals cost from P75 to P100.

The *Pink Patio* on Quintin Paredes St, Chinatown, is a pleasant café-cum-restaurant with inexpensive food and several kinds of coffee. It is open Monday to Saturday from 9 am to 6 pm. A meal costs P100.

The *Sea Palace* on Mabini St, Malate, is a good and relatively cheap Chinese restaurant which also serves Filipino food. It is open from 11 am to 2.30 pm and 6 to 11.30 pm daily, with meals for about P150. There is another Sea Palace on nearby Adriatico St, Malate.

Eva's Garden on Adriatico St, Ermita, is pleasant and reasonably priced. It is open Monday to Saturday from 11.30 am to 2 pm and 5 to 10 pm, and Sunday from 5 to 10 pm. A meal costs about P175.

The *Taipekey Restaurant* on Adriatico St, Malate, is also good but dear. It is open from 11 am to 2 pm and 5 to 9 pm daily; a meal costs about P200.

The *Shin Shin Garden* on Mabini St,

Malate, is good but somewhat dear. It is open from 11 am to 2 pm and 6 to 10 pm daily, and a meal costs about P200.

Indian & Middle Eastern *Al Sham's* on Makati Ave, Makati, has Arabian, Indian and Pakistani food, with mutton, lamb and goat meat dishes, and curries. It is open daily from 11.30 am to 10.30 pm; a meal costs about P150.

A good Indian restaurant on Padre Faura, Ermita, is the *Kashmir*, which serves mainly north Indian and Pakistani dishes, hot or mild as required. It is open from 10 am to 11 pm daily and meals cost about P200. There is another *Kashmir* restaurant on the corner of Makati Ave and Guerrero St, Makati.

Japanese The *Iseya Restaurant* on Padre Faura, Ermita, serves a business lunch that, at P100, is very good value. It is open daily from 11 am to 2 pm and 5 to 11 pm, and its usual meals are about P175.

The *Yamato* on Adriatico St, Ermita, is good for sushi and tempura. It is open daily from 11 am to 2 pm and 5.30 to 10.30 pm. Meals cost about P150.

The *Kimpura* on Ayala Ave, Makati, is a very popular, fairly inexpensive Japanese restaurant in the Makati Commercial Center. It is open daily from 10.30 am to 3 pm and 5.30 to 11 pm; meals cost about P250.

The *Tempura-Misono* is a very popular Japanese restaurant in the Hyatt Regency Hotel, Roxas Blvd, Pasay City. It is open daily from noon to 5 pm and 6 to 11 pm. Meals cost about P500.

Korean The *Korean Village* on Adriatico St, Malate, is supposed to be the biggest Korean restaurant in Manila. Its specialities are spare ribs and beef stew. It is open Monday to Saturday from 11 am to 2 pm and from 5 to 10 pm. Meals cost about P200.

The *Korean Palace* is also on Adriatico St, Malate, and competes with the Korean Village. It is open from 11 am to 2 pm and 5 to 10 pm daily, and meals cost about P200.

The *Korean Garden* on Burgos St, Makati, is one of a group of ten roughly comparable

Korean restaurants in Makati. It is open daily from 11.30 am to 2.30 pm and 5.30 to 10.30 pm. Meals cost about P250.

Thai The *Sala Thai* on J M Nakpil St, Malate, is a popular, fairly inexpensive restaurant. Amongst the dishes most ordered here are Thai curries, tom yum (a spicy, sour soup) and egg rolls. It is open daily from 10 am to 10 pm and meals cost about P175.

The *Sukhothai* on Makati Ave, Makati, is an unpretentious place with good, reasonably priced food. It is open Monday to Saturday from 11 am to 2 pm and 5 to 10 pm, with meals for about P150.

Flavours & Spices on New Garden Square, on the corner of Legaspi St and Greenbelt Drive, Makati, is a good restaurant where you can also buy Thai spices. It is open from 10 am to 10 pm and meals cost about P175.

Another good restaurant is *Taste of Thailand* in the Mile Long Arcade, Amorsolo St, Makati, which is open daily from 11.30 am to 2 pm and 6.30 to 10 pm. Meals cost about P175.

The Rama on Kalayaan Ave, Makati, is a restaurant and coffee shop with an atmosphere of efficiency. The house specialty is pat thai (fried noodles with vegetables, eggs and peanuts). The restaurant is open daily from 11.30 am to 2.30 pm and 6 to 10 pm, and the coffee shop from 6 am to midnight. Meals cost about P200.

Western Food
US Mainland The *Steak Town* on Adriatico St, Malate, has good steaks and seafood, soup, salad, bread, dessert and coffee. It is open from 8 am to 2 am daily and meals cost about P250. There is another *Steak Town Restaurant* in Makati Ave, Makati.

The Gold Ranch on Pasay Rd, Makati, serves excellent barbecued steaks. It is open daily (except holidays) from 11.30 am to 2.30 pm and 6.30 to 10.30 pm. Meals cost about P300.

The *New Orleans* on Legaspi St, Makati, specialises in US and Creole dishes, especially steaks and barbecued ribs, along with pretty good New Orleans jazz. It is open from 11 am to 2.00 pm and 6 pm to midnight daily. Meals cost about P400.

At the *Café Adriatico*, on the corner of Adriatico St and Remedios Circle, Malate, the usual menu features steaks, salads, seafood and fondue, topped off with various kinds of coffee and a good choice of cocktails. It's a place where trendy people go, especially at night after the cinema, disco or a party. It is open Monday to Friday from 10 am to 6 am and Sunday from 2.30 pm to 6 am. Meals cost about P250.

Max's on Maria Orosa St, Ermita, is one of the 10 branches of Max's in Manila. It serves chicken roasted in various ways as well as standard Filipino dishes. It is open daily from 8 am to 11 pm and meals cost about P150.

Australian & UK From the *Rooftop Restaurant*, on the corner of Padre Faura and M H del Pilar St, Ermita, you can enjoy a good view over Manila Bay. It is an Australian restaurant and beer garden on top of the Iseya Hotel and is open daily all hours; on Sunday there's an Aussie barbecue for P100. Normally, meals cost about P150.

The *Prince of Wales* in Greenbelt Center, Makati, is a pub with its own restaurant where they serve typically British food like roast beef and Yorkshire pudding. They also offer a lunchtime buffet from Monday to Saturday. It is open Monday to Saturday from 11 am to midnight and meals are about P175.

German, Austrian & Swiss The *München Grill Pub* on Mabini St, Ermita, has Bavarian dishes and is open Monday to Saturday from 10 am to 2 am. Meals cost about P100.

Old Heidelberg on J Nakpil St, on the corner of Bocobo St, Malate, serves German and international cuisine in a sophisticated setting. It is open daily from 10 am to midnight and meals cost about P200.

The *Schwarzwälder* on Makati Ave, Makati, has German dishes like bratwurst and eisbein (knuckle of pork) with sauerkraut, plus a salad bar and different sorts of coffee. It is open daily from 11.30 am to 2.30 pm and 5.30 pm to 3 am. Meals cost about P250.

The *Treffpunkt Jedermann* on Jupiter St, Makati, has found its own niche, offering Austrian cooking in a warm and friendly alpine atmosphere. It is open daily from 7 am to 2 am and a meal costs about P175.

The *Swiss Hut* on M H del Pilar St, Ermita, is the place to go for Swiss specialities. It also serves good, inexpensive meals of the day. It is open from 11 am to 3 am and meals cost about P100.

The *Old Swiss Inn Restaurant* is located in the Hotel Swiss on Belen St, Paco. This restaurant serves excellent Swiss food. It is open 24-hours daily and a meal costs about P200.

French The *L'Eau Vive* on Paz Mendoza Guazon Ave, Paco, is an out-of-the-ordinary restaurant, run by nuns and missionaries, which serves international and French cuisine. It is open Monday to Saturday from noon to 3 pm and 7 to 11 pm; meals cost about P300.

L'Orangerie on Zodiac St, Makati, is a very up-market French restaurant with some original dishes. It is open Monday to Friday from 11 am to 3 pm and 6 to 11 pm. Meals cost about P400.

Dutch The *Holandia* on Arquiza St, Ermita, is a small restaurant with Dutch specialties. It is open Monday to Saturday from 10 am to 1 am and Sunday from 4 pm to 1 am. Meals cost about P150.

Italian *Alda's Pizza Kitchen* on Adriatico St, Ermita, is a pleasant, friendly restaurant with a wide selection of good, inexpensive pizzas. It is open Monday to Saturday from 11 am to midnight, and Sunday from 3 pm to midnight. Meals cost about P100.

The well-run *La Taverna* on Adriatico St, on the corner of Pedro Gil, Malate, has been around for a long time. It offers a lunch special which changes daily. It is open Monday to Friday from noon to 2 pm and 6 pm to midnight, and Saturday and Sunday

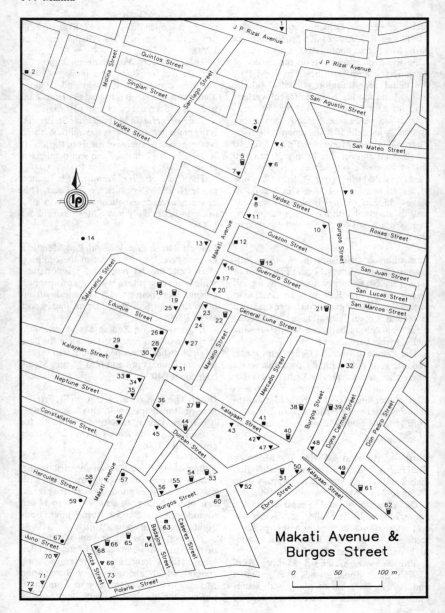

Makati Avenue &
Burgos Street

0   50   100 m

■ PLACES TO STAY

2	Robelle House
12	Aberdeen Court
26	Millennium Plaza Condominium
33	Regine's Apartelle
41	Makati Prime Tower Condominium
49	Oka Hotel
57	Traveler's Inn
60	The Bel-Air Place
63	Makati Prime Citadel Condominium

▼ PLACES TO EAT

1	Ihaw Ihaw at Kalde-Kaldero
4	Andok's Dine-in
6	Ulam Ni San Pedro Restaurant
7	Barrio Fiesta
9	The Flight Music Bar & Restaurant
10	Friend's & Neighbour Restaurant
11	Steak Town Restaurant
12	Café de Chine
13	Seafood Market Restaurant
16	Kashmir Restaurant
20	Sukhothai Restaurant
23	Wendy's
24	Pastry Shop & Café & Rhythm & Booze Jazz Bistro
25	Kentucky Fried Chicken
27	Café Oceanic
28	Di' Marks Pizzeria
30	Bun's Café
31	Jin Go Gae Korean Restaurant
33	The Rama Restaurant
34	Arnold's Diner
35	Shakey's Makati
42	Max's
43	Bakahan at Manukan Restaurant
45	Makati Café
46	La Gondola Italian Restaurant
47	Seki Tei Restaurant
48	La Tienda Supermarket & Coffee Shop
50	BG's Bar & Restaurant
52	Korean Garden Restaurant
55	Dean Street Café & Dooles Bar & Restaurant
56	Shiroi Hana Japanese Restaurant
57	Al Sham's Restaurant

58	Shinjuku Ramen House
62	Galleon Club & Restaurant & Nightwatch Club & Restaurant
64	Bar Café Mogambo
68	Pizza Hut
69	Dona Nena's
70	A&W Restaurant
71	Tsui Hang Seafood Restaurant
72	Nina's Papagayo Restaurant
73	Pancake House

OTHER

3	The Finals Disco
5	Planet Beer Bar
6	Carlsberg Beer Garden
8	Top of the World Disco
14	International School
15	Julian's Cocktail Bar & Music Lounge
17	Imperial Health Club
18	Tribu Music Lounge
19	After All (Paul Geneve)
21	Heiwa Karaoke
22	St Elsewhere
23	7-Eleven
29	New Roxy
32	Insular Bakery
36	Red Ribbon Bake Shop
37	John Z Disco Bar
38	Fridays
39	Jools Bar & Billard
40	Playhouse, Ritzy's & Fillies Disco
44	Durban Disco Bar
45	Sunette Tower
51	Rascal's Bar, Ivory Music Lounge & Cest la vie Bar
53	Dimples Bar
54	Danish Connection Pub & Papillion
57	The Grand Prix Bar
59	Arellano's Wine & Liquor
61	JJ's Bar
62	Louis de Vennis Club
65	Bar Hollywood
66	Roques
67	Karl's Mart

from 6 pm to midnight. Meals costs about P300.

The *La Gondola Italian Restaurant* on Makati Ave, Makati, serves good pasta. Apart from making any pizza you could think of, staff offer Italian ham and their own home-made ice-cream. It opens Monday to Saturday from noon to 2 pm and 7 to 11 pm daily. Meals costs about P400.

Mexican *Tia Maria's* on Remedios St, on the corner of Carolina St, Malate, serves cocktails and good Mexican food. It is open Monday to Saturday from 11 am to midnight and Sunday from 5 pm to midnight. Meals cost about P200. There is another *Tia Maria's* restaurant on Makati Ave, near Greenbelt Park, Makati.

Spanish *Guernica's* on M H del Pilar St, Ermita, offers typical dishes like paella, but also serves steaks. Guitar music provides atmosphere. It is open Monday to Saturday from 11 am to 2 pm and 6 pm to midnight, and Sunday from 6 pm to midnight. Meals cost about P250.

The *Patio Guernica* on J Bocobo St, near Remedios Circle, Malate, serves common Spanish dishes, as well as steaks. It is busy but not as lively as the older Guernica's in M H del Pilar St. It is open Monday to Saturday from 11 am to 2 pm and 6 pm to midnight, and Sunday from 6 pm to midnight. Meals cost about P250.

El Comedor, on the corner of Adriatico St and Pedro Gil, Ermita, serves traditional Spanish food plus some specialities and a relatively cheap lunch special. It is open daily from 11 am to 3 pm and 6.30 to 10.30 pm. Meals cost about P250.

The *Muralla* in the San Luis Complex, General Luna St, Intramuros, serves Spanish and Filipino food. It is open daily from 11 am to 2 pm and 6 to 11 pm. Meals cost about P300.

Vegetarian Food

Restaurants that serve only vegetarian meals are a rarity in Manila. However, there are a number of places which have vegetarian fare on their menu as well as fish and meat dishes. You have to watch though: some Filipino restaurants are fairly liberal with their use of the word 'vegetarian' and might serve, for example, 'vegetable soup' with both vegetables and meat. To be on the safe side, every restaurant that serves Japanese food, specifically tempura, will prepare you a guaranteed meatless yasaii tempura (deep fried vegetables in batter).

The *Quan Yin Chay* on Soler St, Chinatown, is a small restaurant which has good-value vegetarian dishes and fruit juices. It is open daily from 8 am to 9 pm and meals cost about P75.

The *Kim Wan Garden* on General Malvar St, Malate, serves Chinese and vegetarian food with separate menus for both. The staff are friendly and give helpful advice on what to order. It is open daily all hours; a meal costs about P100.

Mother Sachi on Gil Puyat Ave, between Pasong Tamo St and Ayala Ave, Makati, is self-service, with good, reasonably priced vegetarian dishes. Its specialities are Bhagavad fruit pie and soya fish. It is open Monday to Saturday from 11 am to 9 pm, with meals for about P150.

Tia Maria's on Remedios St, on the corner of Carolina St, Malate, features good Mexican food which they can prepare in a vegetarian manner if requested (eg, by substituting beans for meat in an enchilada). There is another *Tia Maria's* restaurant on Makati Ave, near Greenbelt Park, Makati. It is open Monday to Saturday from 11 am to midnight, and Sunday from 5 pm to midnight. Meals cost about P200.

The *Patio Guernica* on J Bocobo St, near Remedios Circle, Malate, is an excellent restaurant which serves mainly Spanish food, as well as some vegetarian dishes. It is open Monday to Saturday from 11 am to 2 pm and 6 pm to midnight, and Sunday from 6 pm to midnight. A meal costs about P250.

Al Sham's in Makati Ave, Makati, serves Arabic, Pakistani and Indian food, with a wide selection of vegetarian dishes. It is open daily from 11.30 am to 10.30 pm; a meal costs about P200.

The *Kashmir* on Padre Faura, Ermita, serves mainly north Indian and Pakistani dishes as well as vegetarian foods. It is open from 10 am to 11 pm daily and meals cost about P200. There is another *Kashmir* restaurant on the corner of Makati Ave and Guerrero St, Makati.

Fast Food

There are lots of reasonably priced small food stalls on J C Bocobo St, between Padre Faura and Robinson's, that sell Filipino snacks and meals for around P50. They open daily from 8 am to 10 pm.

Rosie's Diner on M H del Pilar St, Ermita, is comfortable and always fairly full, in the style of a US snackbar of the 1950s – all that's missing is the Wurlitzer. It is open all day every day and a meal costs around P100.

Shakey's Mabini on Mabini St, Ermita, sells pizzas with thick or thin dough, but their spaghetti is a bit dear. There is loud live music in the evenings. It is open daily from 11 am to 5 am and a meal costs around P100. There is also *Shakey's Malate* on Remedios St, open from 11 am to 5 am, *Shakey's Makati* on Makati Ave, open from 9 am to midnight, and *Shakey's Greenhills* on Padilla Ave, open from 10 am to 2 am.

The *Pizza Hut* on Harrison Plaza, Malate, is one of eight in Metro Manila. It specialises in pan pizzas and is a popular place in a busy shopping centre. It is open daily from 10 am to midnight; a meal costs around P100.

If you're really dying for a hamburger, *McDonald's* on United Nations Ave, Ermita, sells the 'real thing'. It is open daily from 7 am to midnight and a hamburger usually costs about P75. There are several branches of McDonald's in Manila.

The *Jollibee* on Padre Faura, Ermita, is one of a Filipino burger chain with lots of outlets. Its specialities are 'chickenjoy' and 'champ with cheese'; a full breakfast may also be offered. It is open Monday to Saturday from 7 am to 10 pm and Sunday from 7.30 am to 9.30 pm. A meal costs about P75.

Kentucky Fried Chicken in Harrison Plaza, Malate, has the traditional crispy chicken. It is open daily from 10 am to midnight and costs about P100. There are Kentucky Frieds all over Manila. Another is on Maria Orosa St, opposite the Manila Pavilion Hotel.

Mister Donut on Mabini St, Ermita, has a good choice of excellent doughnuts and good coffee – not a bad breakfast alternative. It is open 24-hours a day and costs about P25.

Buffets

You can get breakfast buffets daily from 6 to 10 am at the *Sundowner Hotel* on Mabini St, Ermita, for about P170; *The Brasserie* in the Mandarin Oriental Hotel, Makati Ave, Makati, for about P180; the *Café Coquilla* in the Manila Pavilion Hotel, United Nations Ave, Ermita, for about P200; and the *Café Ilang-Ilang* and *Lobby Lounge*, Manila Hotel, Rizal Park, Ermita, for about P200.

The *Café Vienna* in the Holiday Inn, Roxas Blvd, Pasay City, has breakfast buffets Monday to Friday from 6 to 10 am for P150; lunch buffets Monday to Friday from noon to 2 pm for P250; and dinner buffets Tuesday to Saturday from 7 to 10 pm for P300. It serves Continental and international cuisines.

The *Concourse* in the Hotel Nikko Manila Garden, Fourth Quadrant, Makati Commercial Center, Makati, serves an international cuisine breakfast buffet daily from 6 to 10 am for P180 and a lunch buffet daily from 11.30 am to 2 pm for P280.

The *1930's Banquet Hall*, Admiral Hotel, Roxas Blvd, Malate, has a Filipino lunch buffet Monday to Saturday from 11.30 am to 2 pm for about P200. The *Champagne Room* in the Manila Hotel, Rizal Park, Ermita, has a lunch buffet with international cuisine Monday to Friday from noon to 3 pm for about P280, and on Sunday at the same times for about P300. For Italian food, the *Roma* in the same hotel has a lunch buffet Monday to Friday from noon to 3 pm for P280.

The *Lobby Bar* in the Manila Pavilion Hotel, United Nations Ave, Ermita, has a daily lunch buffet from 11 am to 2 pm for P280, and *Pier 7* in the Philippine Plaza Hotel, Cultural Center Complex, Malate, has a daily lunch buffet that serves steaks and seafood (a speciality) for P350 from 11.30 am to 2.30 pm daily.

The *Sabungan Coffee Shop* in the Manila Midtown Hotel, Adriatico Street, on the corner of Pedro Gil, Ermita, has breakfast buffets daily from 8 to 10 am for P180; and dinner buffets daily from 7 to 10 pm for P230. It serves Filipino and international cuisines.

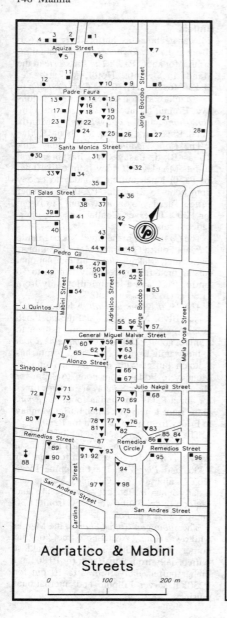

Adriatico & Mabini Streets

0	100	200 m

■ PLACES TO STAY

1 Doña Petronila Mall
3 Yasmin Pension
4 Tadel Pension House
8 Midtown Inn
11 Royal Palm Hotel
17 Tower Hotel
23 Mabini Pension
26 The Midland Plaza
27 Cherry Lodge Apartelle
28 Robinson's Apartelle
29 Manila Tourist Inn
34 Sundowner Hotel
35 Casa Blanca I
39 La Soledad Pension House
40 Ermita Tourist Inn
41 Santos Pension House
45 Manila Midtown Hotel
47 Palm Plaza Hotel
48 Alexandria Pension Inn &
   Las Palmas Hotel
51 Rothman Inn Hotel
52 Galleon's Hotel
53 Manila Manor Hotel
54 Bayfront Tower Condominium
55 Dakota Mansion
58 Pearl Garden Apartel
66 Joward's Pension House
67 Adriatico Arms Hotel
68 Victoria Mansion
72 APP Mayfair Hotel
74 Malate Pensionne &
   Shoshana Pension House
86 Remedios Pension House
90 Casa Dalco
95 Circle Pension
96 Royal Plaza Condominium

▼ PLACES TO EAT

2 Shakey's Mabini
5 Holandia
6 The Islands Fisherman
7 Café Alps & Sea Food Market
10 Jollibee, Kamayan Restaurant &
   Kashmir Restaurant
16 Mister Donut
18 München Grill Pub
19 Alda's Pizza Kitchen
20 Top Brass Restaurant &
   Zebrina Restaurant
21 Food Stalls
22 Calle 5
25 Eva's Garden Restaurant
31 Yamato Japanese Restaurant
33 Palace Avenue & Food Street

42	Lotus Garden Restaurant	91	Tia Maria's Mexican Restaurant
44	El Comedor	92	Patio Mequeni
46	La Taverna	93	Ang Bistro sa Remedios
50	Zamboanga Restaurant	94	1900 Restaurant
55	Green Park Restaurant	95	Penguin Café Gallery &
56	Kim Wan Garden Restaurant		Saloniki Restaurant
57	Hot Pot Garden Restaurant	97	Ducky's Restaurant
59	Dragon Express Tea House	98	Dinner Dance Restaurant
60	Blue Hill Korean Restaurant		
61	Estasia Music Lounge &		OTHER
	Restaurant		
62	Seoul Plaza Restaurant	9	Solidaridad Book Shop
63	Kopa Restaurant	12	Mercury Drugstore
64	Alberdoni Restaurant &	13	Philippine National Bank (PNB)
	Palais daan Restaurant	14	Interbank
65	Rose Villa Restaurant	15	7-Eleven
66	Joward's Hot Pot Restaurant	23	Mabini Post Office
67	Steak Town Restaurant &	24	T'Boli Arts & Crafts
	The Chronicle Café	30	Laundryette Britania
69	Old Heidelberg	32	Robinson's
70	Sea Palace Restaurant	34	Si-Kat Ferry Office
73	Sea Palace Restaurant	36	Shafa Medical Clinic,
74	Chateau 1771 Restaurant		Midtown Arcade ,
75	Rhythm of the Night		China Airlines & Egypt Air
76	Racks Bistro	37	Copy Shop
77	Hard Rock Café	38	Laundromat
78	The Library	40	Scenic VIew Travel Inc
80	Hobbit House &	43	Cathay Pacific
	Remember When?	49	Fiesta Filipino
81	Korean Village Restaurant	71	Metropolitan Tower &
82	Café Adriatico		Philippine National Bank (PNB)
83	Patio Guernica	79	Carfel Seashell Museum
84	Camp Gourmet Restaurant	88	Malate Church
85	Empress Garden Restaurant	93	Jazz Box
87	Korean Palace Restaurant	94	In The Mood Dance Bar &
89	Korean Village Restaurant		Limelight Theatre

Self-Catering

The *7-Eleven*, on the corner of Padre Faura and Adriatico St, Ermita, is one of the many branches of these small supermarkets found all over Manila which offer quick shopping and are open 24 hours a day.

The *La Tienda Supermarket* on Burgos St, Makati, is the place for Spanish specialties like olives, sardines, brandy and wine.

The *Saentis Delicatessen* (☎ 851154) at 7431 Yakal St, Makati, offers a wide range of European delicacies such as cheeses, cold meats, ham, smoked goods, olives and much more.

At the *Sheraton Delicatessen Shop*, Vito Cruz, Malate, you can buy, among other things, European specialities like bread and sausages. The entrance is on the Harrison Plaza side of the hotel.

The *Treffpunkt Jedermann* at 140 Jupiter St, bel Air II, Makati, has all sorts of Austrian specialties from bakery items and meat, to red and white wines.

Zuellig Wine & Spirits (☎ 868624) on Gil Puyat St, Makati, carries German, French and Spanish wines, champagne, cognac, sherry, whisky etc; they only stock up-market brands.

ENTERTAINMENT
Basketball

Games of the professional basketball league, the Philippine Basketball Association (PBA), are played in Manila at the Cuneta Astrodome on Roxas Blvd, Pasay City, on Tuesday, Friday and Sunday at 5 and 7.30 pm. Admission costs from P15 to P150. To find out which teams are playing, call ☎ 8337313 or ☎ 8337323.

Casinos

Soon after the Marcos era, the big casino on the renamed Ninoy Aquino Ave at the NAIA was closed, as were all other casinos in the area, by the Commission on Good Government set up by the Aquino government. But Marcos' successors weren't prepared to do without the chance of making quick money for long. Soon, the extremely profitable Casino Filipina company established local casinos all over the country and has been raking in the money ever since. In Manila you can play at the *Silahis Hotel*, Roxas Blvd, Malate, and at the *Manila Pavilion Hotel*, United Nations Ave, Ermita. Entry is free and players in casual clothes or even beachwear are admitted.

Cockfights

There are several cockpits in Manila – the Philippine Cockers Club in Santa Ana; the Olympic Stadium at Grace Park, Caloocan City; Libertad on Dolores St, Pasay City; Elorde on Santos Ave, Parañaque; and La Loma on Calavite St, Quezon City. Fights are staged on Sunday and feast days. Admission is from P20 to P200.

Cinemas

Amongst other places, there are cinemas in the large shopping centres such as Araneta Center, Harrison Plaza, Makati Commercial Center and Robinson's, as well as on Rizal Ave and Claro M Recto Ave, both in Santa Cruz. Films are advertised in the daily papers. Beware of pickpockets and bag snatchers in the cinemas.

Concerts

In idyllic Paco Park, San Marcelino St, Paco Park Presents puts on free chamber music at 6 pm on Friday.

The Puerta Real Evenings, which take place every Saturday night at 6 pm in Intramuros, offer free musical entertainment in the greenery near the aquarium by the old fortress wall.

The free Concert at the Park takes place every Sunday at 5 pm in Rizal Park.

Horse Racing

Races are held on Saturday and Sunday afternoon and Wednesday evening. Check the daily papers for more information, or contact the Philippine Racing Club (☎ 879951, 863442) or the Manila Jockey Club (☎ 7111251). The courses are at the Santa Ana Race Track, A P Reyes Ave, Santa Ana, and in the San Lazaro Hippodrome, Felix Huertas St, Santa Cruz.

Planetarium

The Planetarium is in the grounds of Rizal Park; you go in from Burgos St. There are audiovisual demonstrations daily at 10.30 am and 1.30 and 3.30 pm. Admission is P5.

Folk Dances

There is folk dancing on Sunday afternoon between 3 and 4 pm in the Mindanao section of Nayong Pilipino near the NAIA on Mia Rd, Pasay City.

Pistahan in the Philippine Plaza Hotel, Cultural Center Complex, Malate, has a dinner and cultural show every evening from 7 pm featuring Filipino food, songs and dancing. At 6 pm a torch light ceremony is held. Without drinks it costs about P450 per person.

Fiesta Filipino, on the corner of M H del Pilar St, Pedro Gil and Mabini St, Malate, has a cultural performance each afternoon and evening. Admission is free. For the special variety show at 11 pm, you pay a P50 cover charge or P180 for the the show and a buffet meal. At midnight there is a disco.

The Josephine's restaurant on Roxas Blvd, Pasay City, features Philippine folk dances daily from 8 to 9 pm, sometimes in Josephine's Annex, a few buildings farther down the street.

The Zamboanga Restaurant in Adriatico St, Malate, has Filipino and Polynesian dancing with dinner from 7 to 8.30 pm. Seafood dishes like fisherman's delight are a speciality. It is open daily from 8 am to midnight and costs about P200.

Theatre

Performances are irregular, so check the arts section of the daily papers or enquire at the tourist office (☎ 599031, 501703), or at the theatre itself.

The Cultural Center of the Philippines (CCP) is on Roxas Blvd, Malate (☎ 8321125).

The Folk Arts Theater is in the Cultural Center Complex, Roxas Blvd, Malate (☎ 8321120).

The Insular Life Theater (Repertory Philippines) is in the Insular Life Building, Ayala Ave, Makati (☎ 8173051).

The Meralco Theater is in the Meralco Building, Ortigas Ave, Pasig (☎ 7219777).

The Metropolitan Theater is in Lawisang Bonifacio, Lawton Plaza, Ermita (☎ 484721).

The Rajah Sulayman Theater is an open-air theatre in Fort Santiago, Intramuros.

Zoo

You will find the Manila Zoological & Botanical Gardens at the southern end of Mabini St, at the beginning of Harrison St, in Malate. The Philippine eagle which you can see there and the tamaraw, a dwarf buffalo from Mindoro, are of great interest, but otherwise the miserable accommodation (small enclosures, no shade, no plants) and the obvious neglect suffered by most of the creatures on display illustrate the usual Asian, and especially Filipino, attitude to animals. Animal lovers are advised to give it a miss. If you do want to visit the zoo, it is open daily from 7 am to 6 pm. Admission is P6.

Nightlife

Bars & Nightclubs Manila's mayor, General Lim, kept his election promise to rule with an iron fist and lead the battle against corruption, crime, prostitution and dirt in the city. Within one year of taking office he succeeded in putting an end to nightlife in the tourist district of Ermita. All bars and nightclubs had to close down by mid 1993. Not content with that, he introduced draconian fines on foreigners if they were caught with a Filipina woman and couldn't prove on the spot that they were married to her. Anyone caught smoking in public was also quickly relieved of a quantity of local currency in aid of the policeman's ball. The measures soon started to take grip, and Mayor Lim is already well on the way to achieving his goal of cleaning up Manila and restoring it to its former glory.

As Metro Manila comprises several different cities, including Makati, Pasay City and Quezon City, their own mayors rule the roost locally. They, of course, don't always agree with what Mayor Lim is trying to push through in his City of Manila. Most of them want to retain as much of the nightlife unchanged as is possible.

If you want to go out and not be hassled, then you can still find many discos, pubs and nightclubs in and around Burgos St in Makati, *Rascal's*, *Dimples*, *Ritzy's*, *Bar Hollywood* and *Jool's*, for example, where a professional dance show is on the programme.

In Pasay City, the nightlife has taken root in the International Karaoke Complex on Roxas Blvd, across and along from the Cultural Center. You will find a few bars which were uprooted from Ermita, such as *Australian Club*, *Firehouse* and *Visions*.

Filipinos like clubs which have stimulating entertainment – say, a model show. These so-called disco/theatres are mainly in Quezon City – *Bigwig* on Quezon Ave, for example.

Apart from these places, all of the bigger hotels have their own bars and nightclubs. The south end of Roxas Blvd is also home to exclusive nightclubs which feature first-class live music.

Bistros & Music Lounges Bistros are enjoying growing popularity in Manila. All the trendy people go there to be with the 'in' crowd. The classic watering holes are constantly being joined by new ones, others disappear after a short interval from the scene, leaving the stage for others to strut on. The ones given here are well established and should survive for some time. It's considered important for guests to be properly attired, for example, the Café Adriatico and the Hard Rock Café will not allow anyone in wearing shorts and thongs (flip-flops).

The *Bistro RJ* in the Olympia Building, Makati Ave, Makati, has live 1950's and '60s music, including Beatles and Beach Boys titles. The atmosphere here is good. It is open nightly from 6 pm to 3 am. Admission costs P50 on Sunday and Monday, P75 on Tuesday and Thursday and P100 on Wednesday, Friday and Saturday. There is another *Bistro RJ* on Quezon Ave in Quezon City.

The *Café Adriatico* on Adriatico St near Remedios Circle, Malate, started Manila's craze for bistros and is still a favourite. It is open Monday to Saturday from 10 am to 6 am and Sunday from 2 pm to 6 am. There is another *Café Adriatico* on Legaspi St, Makati, which is, however, less popular than its stablemate.

The *Calesa Bar* in the Hyatt Regency, Roxas Blvd, Pasay City, has good show bands. It is open Monday to Saturday from 7.30 pm to 2 am.

The *Hard Rock Café* on Adriatico St, Malate, has half a small plane protruding outside as if crashed; inside you can watch rock videos. It is open Monday to Saturday from 5 pm to 3 or 4 am in the morning. There is another *Hard Rock Café* in the Sunvar Plaza on Pasay Rd, on the corner of Amorsolo St, Makati.

Moviola in Remedios Circle, Malate, is a piano bar and restaurant open Monday to Saturday from 11 am to 4 am and Sunday from 6 pm to 4 am.

The *Penguin Café* on Remedios St near Remedios Circle, Malate, can be quite a lively place. It's open Tuesday to Sunday from noon to 2 pm and 6 pm to 2 am.

The *Remember When?* on Mabini St, Malate, is a pleasant, nostalgic bistro which plays popular oldies. It's next to the well-known Hobbit House, and is open daily from 4 pm to 3 am.

The *Siete Pecados* in the Philippine Plaza Hotel in the Cultural Center Complex, Malate, has show bands from 7.30 or 8 pm and is open daily from 5 pm to 1.30 or 2 am. Admission is P150.

Discos 'Let's go disco' is as much a part of the local lifestyle as reading comics or smoking menthol cigarettes, so naturally these modern dance-palaces abound. Among the best is *Euphoria* in the Hotel Inter-Continental, Ayala Ave, Makati, a modern disco that's very popular with the Filipino trendies. It is open daily from 9 am to 5 am. Admission is P125 (Friday and Saturday P200).

Lost Horizon in the Philippine Plaza Hotel, Cultural Center Complex, Malate, has good sound with live music and a DJ. It is open nightly from 7 pm to 2 or 3 am and admission is free.

Faces on Makati Ave, Makati, seems to be the one preferred by the local film and show stars. It is open nightly from 7 pm to 5 am and admission is P150 (Friday and Saturday P200).

Equinox on Pasay Rd, Makati, is so far the newest disco in Manila. It is open nightly, except Sunday, from 7 pm to 4 am and admission is P100 (Friday and Saturday P150). Also on Pasay Rd, *Mars* is fitted out with the latest high-tech equipment. It is open nightly from 7 pm to 6 am and admission is P150 (Friday to Sunday P200).

At the *Stargazer* in Silahis Hotel, Roxas Blvd, Malate, you use an outside lift to go up to the laser disco, which has a panoramic view over Manila. It is open nightly from 9 pm to 4 am and admission is P100.

The *Valentino* is in the Manila Midtown Hotel, on the corner of Pedro Gil and Adriatico St, Ermita. It is open nightly from 10 pm to 4 am. There's a floorshow on Saturday and admission is free.

Folk Clubs The *Hobbit House* at 1801 Mabini St, Malate, has a good international atmosphere and the dubious attraction of waiters who are all dwarfs. The minimum order after 8.30 pm is P60. Mexican dishes are a speciality. It is open nightly from 7 pm to 2 am. Admission is P50, except when Freddie Aguilar is performing, when it is P120. The most popular singer in the Philippines, he performs his songs of social criticism here about twice a week, usually Tuesday and Saturday.

My Father's Moustache, on M H del Pilar St, Malate, is a small rustic folk pub that is very relaxed. It has a special Mongolian barbecue, and is open nightly from 5 pm to 2 am.

The popular *Galleon Club & Restaurant* on Kalayaan Ave, Makati, features country & western music from Monday to Saturday.

Jazz Jazz is also enjoying an increase in popularity. So it is safe to assume that there will soon be more places than those listed here.

At present you can hear jazz nightly from 6 to 11 pm in the *Lobby Court* of the Philippine Plaza Hotel, Cultural Center Complex, Malate. There are also regular Sunday evening performances in the *Clipper Lounge* of the Mandarin Oriental Hotel, Makati Ave, Makati, and in the *Concourse Lounge* of the Manila Garden Hotel, Makati Commercial Center, Makati. Every Sunday from 10 am to 1 pm well-known musicians play at the Jazz Brunch in *The Lobby* of the Manila Peninsula Hotel, Ayala Ave, on the corner of Makati Ave, Makati.

Pubs Mayor Lim's campaign of closing down places meant the end for scores of pubs and bars in Ermita. The following survivors are still open until further notice: *Lili Marleen*, *Guernica's*, *Swiss Hut* , all on M H del Pilar St; *Holandia* and *Roy's Place* on Arquiza St; and the *Birdwatcher's Bar* on the corner of A Flores and Mabini Sts.

Amongst the best-known pubs in Makati are the *Danish Connection* and the *Playhouse* both on and around Burgos St, the *San Mig Pub* on Legaspi St, and the *Prince of Wales* in the Greenbelt Center.

You can also spend some pleasant afternoons and evenings in the restaurant bars with swimming pools, thus making a stay in noisy Manila's polluted air a little more bearable. Among these open-air oases are the *Pool Bar*, tucked away on Guerrero St, a small side street off Padre Faura, by the Aurelio Hotel, and *Treasure Island*, a nice little place among the lagoon-like swimming pools of the Philippine Plaza Hotel, where you can have a tropical cocktail while enjoying the magnificent display of the sunset over Manila Bay.

THINGS TO BUY

The full name of Philtrade Exhibits is the Philippine Center for International Trade and Exhibition. It is on Roxas Blvd, Pasay City, and here you can see goods that are manufactured in the Philippines for export. Prices are relatively high, but it's all right to bargain.

Silahis on General Luna St, Intramuros, has a wide range of handicrafts from the whole country. It's in the basement of the restored El Amanecer, and above are the Chang Rong Antique Gallery and the Galeria de las Islas.

On Paterno and Puyat Sts (side streets off Rizal Ave), Santa Cruz, stampmakers with the skill of surgeons will cut cheap rubber stamps like signatures, for P30 in 15 minutes.

At the La Flor de la Isabela cigar factory (☎ 508026), Tabacalera, on Romualdez St, Ermita, single visitors or groups can be shown how the world-famous Coronas are made. You can also buy cigars and, if you like, have the boxes engraved with initials. They prefer you to book.

T'boli Arts & Crafts on Mabini St, Ermita, sells the handicrafts of the T'boli, who are one of the ethnic minorities on Mindanao. This small shop is up some steps, opposite the post office, between Santa Monica St and Padre Faura.

Brocherie (☎ 7213683; fax 7213014) in the Virra Mall, Greenhills Shopping Center, Ortigas Ave, San Juan, is one of over 20 computer technology shops in the Virra Mall. It has a wide selection of hardware and software.

Shopping Centres

The Araneta Center on Edsa, at the corner of Aurora Blvd, Cubao, is a moderately priced shopping centre around the Araneta Coliseum with nearly 2000 speciality stores. These shops include lots of shoe shops (Marikina Shoe Expo etc), 12 department stores (SM Shoe-mart, Rustan's Superstore etc), 200 restaurants (McDonald's, Shakey's etc), 21 cinemas (Ali Mall Theaters, the New Frontier Cinema etc), 38 banks and the Farmers' Market, with its wide palettes heaped with farm produce and seafoods that are always fresh.

The Greenhills Shopping Center on Ortigas Ave, San Juan, has a large selection of restaurants ranging from the Aristocrat to a Shakey's Pizza, a supermarket, several cinemas and banks, as well as spotless arcades with small, elegant boutiques. All of this is housed in a pleasant complex which most people wouldn't expect to find in Manila.

The Harrison Plaza on Harrison St, Malate, has many different shops under one roof. It is air-conditioned and has theatres and restaurants. Rustan's has a good bakery department. Robinson's in Ermita is similar but smaller, with three cinemas.

The Makati Commercial Center (MCC), Makati, is a modern shopping district between Ayala Ave, Makati Ave, Pasay Rd and Edsa. There is plenty to choose from, including imported goods, and some good bookshops. Restaurants and rest areas are interspersed among the shops, the best of which are probably SM Shoemart, The Landmark and Rustan's. Other shopping centres in Makati are the Makati Atrium (Atrium Shopping Mall) in Makati Ave, Makati Cinema Square between Pasong Tamo and Amorsolo Sts and Greenbelt Square between Makati Ave and Paseo de Roxas.

Robinson's Galleria, Ortigas Ave, on the corner of Edsa, Mandaluyong, features several fully air-conditioned floors of shops and a wide selection of restaurants.

SM City on Edsa, on the corner of North Ave, Quezon City, is a big, air-conditioned shopping centre – a popular place to 'see and be seen at'. It's elegant and fashionable, and the expensive boutiques there attract many shoppers. The Shoemart will change travellers' cheques if you have your passport for ID. Right next door is the SM City Annex. The SM group of companies also includes the SM Centrepoint on Aurora Blvd, Santa Mesa, and the more extensive SM Megamall, Edsa, Mandaluyong, which offers a wide variety of shops and facilities, including an ice-skating rink; rental skates are available.

GETTING THERE & AWAY
Air

Manila has two airports. For flights within the Philippines you use the Domestic Airport. Small airlines like Aerolift and Pacific Airways have a small terminal building each, while PAL uses the main building; flights to Cebu and Davao go from the Cebu Terminal (Terminal 2), which is slightly to the side. You have to tell the taxi driver well in advance which terminal you want as well as the name of the airline and the destination you are travelling to.

When you depart from NAIA, you will have to pay a departure tax of P500. (For further information see the section called Leaving The Philippines in the Getting There & Away chapter earlier in this book.)

The PAL offices are, with very few exceptions, open Monday to Saturday from 8.30 am to 5 pm and closed on Sunday and holidays. PAL has a 24-hour telephone information & reservation service (☎ 8166691). Destinations, flight times, arrival and departure times of Aerolift, Pacific Airways and PAL are given in the Getting Around chapter. (See the Getting There & Away and Getting Around chapters earlier in this book for details of international and domestic flights to and from Manila, and the Getting Around section later in this chapter for information about transport from NAIA to the city and to the Domestic Airport.)

Airline Offices Following is a list of the airline offices in Manila:

Aeroflot Soviet Airlines
United Life Building, 835 Pasay Rd, Makati (☎ 867756)

Aerolift
Chemphil Building, 851 Pasay Rd, Makati (☎ 8172361, 8172369)
West Maintenance Area, Domestic Airport, Pasay City (☎ 8331694)
Tickets also available from:
Blue Horizon Travel & Tours, Manila Peninsula Hotel, Ayala Ave, Makati (☎ 876071-76)
Broadway Travel, Chateau Marie Building, Roxas Blvd, Ermita (☎ 591924, 5212903)
Interisland Travel & Tours, 1322 Roxas Blvd, Ermita (☎ 5222434)
Mabini Pension, 1337 Mabini St, Ermita (☎ 594853, 505404)
Sunshine Run, 451 Pedro Gil, on the corner of M H del Pilar St, Ermita (☎ 506601-06)

Air Canada
Cityland Condominium II, Esteban St, on the corner of Herrera St, Makati (☎ 8104461)

Air France
Century Tower Building, 100 Tordesillas St, Makati (☎ 8156970)

Air India
Gammon Center Building, Alfaro St, Makati (☎ 8151280, 8152441)

Air Nauru
Pacific Star Building, Makati Ave, on the corner of Gil Puyat Ave, Makati (☎ 8183580)

Air Nuigini
Fortune Building, Legaspi St, Legaspi Village, Makati (☎ 8101846, 81902206)

Alitalia
The Gallery Building, Amorsolo St, Makati (☎ 850265, 8123351)

American Airlines
Olympia Condominium, Makati Ave, on the corner of Santo Tomas St, Makati (☎ 8178645, 8103228)

Bourag Airlines
Quirino Ave, on the corner of Mia Rd, Parañaque (☎ 8332902)

British Airways
Filipino Merchants Building, Legaspi St, on the corner of Dela Rosa St, Legaspi Village, Makati (☎ 8170361, 8156556)

Canadian Airlines International
Allied Bank Center, Ayala Ave, Makati (☎ 8102656)

Canadian Pacific Airways
Gammon Center Building, Alfaro St, Makati (☎ 8159401)

Cathay Pacific
Gammon Center Building, Alfaro St, Makati (☎ 8159417)
1555 Adriatico St, Ermita (☎ 575691-94)

China Airlines
Midtown Arcade, Adriatico St, Ermita (☎ 590086)

Continental Air Micronesia
SGV Building, Ayala Ave, Makati (☎ 8188701)

Eastern Airlines
Manila Peninsula Hotel, Ayala Ave, Makati (☎ 872971)

Egyptair
Windsor Tower Building, Legaspi St, Makati (☎ 8158476)
Midtown Arcade, Adriatico St, Ermita (☎ 598929)

Emirates Airlines
Country Space I Building, Gil Puyat Ave, Salcedo Village, Makati (☎ 8160809, 8160744)

Finnair
Pacific Bank Building, Ayala Ave, Makati (☎ 8182601, 8182621)

Garuda Indonesian Airlines
Manila Peninsula Hotel, Ayala Ave, Makati (☎ 862458, 862205)

Gulf Air
Windsor Tower Building, Legaspi St, Makati (☎ 8176909)

Japan Airlines
Hotel Nikko Manila Garden, Edsa, on the corner of Pasay Rd, Makati (☎ 8121591, 8109352)

KLM Royal Dutch Airlines
Athenaeum Building, Alfaro St, Makati (☎ 8154790)

Korean Air
LPL Plaza, Alfaro St, Makati (☎ 8158911, 8159261)

Kuwait Airways
Jaka II Building, Legaspi St, Makati (☎ 8172778)

Lufthansa German Airlines
Legaspi Park View Condominium, Legaspi St, Makati (☎ 8105018, 8104596)

Malaysian Airlines
Legaspi Towers, Vito Cruz, on the corner of Roxas Blvd, Malate (☎ 575761)

Northwest Airlines
Athenaeum Building, Alfaro St, Makati (☎ 8197341)
Gedisco Building, Roxas Blvd, Ermita (☎ 5211911)

Pacific Airways
Domestic Airport Rd, Pasay City (☎ 8322731-32, 8332390-91)

Pakistan International Airways (PIA)
ADC Building, Ayala Ave, Makati (☎ 8180502)
Plywood Industries Building, T M Kalaw St, Ermita (☎ 505728)

PAL
  PAL Building, Legaspi St, Makati (☎ 8171509) (domestic), 8171479) (open Monday to Saturday from 8.30 am to 5 pm)
  Hotel Inter-Continental, Ayala Ave, Makati (☎ 8160238, 884178) (open Monday to Saturday from 8.30 am to 5 pm)
  NAIA, Pasay City (☎ 8310622) (open daily from 6 am to the time of the last PAL flight)
  Domestic Airport, Pasay City (☎ 8320991) (open daily from 4 am to 8 pm)
  Botica Boie Building, Escolta St, Binondo (☎ 492003) (open Monday to Saturday from 8.30 am to 5 pm)
  S & L Building, 1500 Roxas Blvd, Ermita (☎ 5218821-30) (open Monday to Friday from 8.30 am to 5 pm, and Saturday and holidays until noon)
  PWU Building, Taft Ave, Malate (☎ 598401) (open Monday to Saturday from 8.30 am to 5 pm)
  Central Bank Building, Mabini St, Malate (☎ 598422) (open Monday to Saturday from 8.30 am to 5 pm)
  Belson House, Edsa, Mandaluyong (☎ 771615) (open Monday to Saturday from 8.30 am to 5 pm)
  BPI Arcade, Aurora Blvd, Cubao, Quezon City (☎ 972731) (open Monday to Saturday from 8.30 am to 5 pm)
  Quezon City Office, Quezon Ave, on the corner of Borromeo St (☎ 9225334) (open Monday to Saturday from 8.30 am to 5 pm)
Qantas Airways
  China Bank Building, Paseo de Roxas, Makati (☎ 8159491, 8159431)
Royal Brunei Airlines
  Saville Building, Gil Puyat Ave, on the corner of Paseo de Roxas, Makati (☎ 8171631-34)
Royal Jordanian Airlines
  Golden Rock Building, Salcedo St, Legaspi Village, Makati (☎ 8185901)
Sabena Belgian Airlines
  Ralph Anthony Suite, Arkansas St, on the corner of Maria Orosa St, Ermita (☎ 508636)
Saudi Arabian Airlines
  Cougar Building, Valero St, Makati (☎ 8187866)
Scandinavian Airlines System
  F & M Lopez Building, Legaspi St, Makati (☎ 8105050)
Singapore Airlines
  138 Dela Costa St, Makati (☎ 8104951, 8104960)
  Magsaysay Building, T M Kalaw St, Ermita (☎ 593880)
Swiss Air
  Country Space I Building, Gil Puyat Ave, Salcedo Village, Makati (☎ 8188351)
Thai Airways International
  Country Space I Building, Gil Puyat Ave, Salcedo Village, Makati (☎ 8158421)

United Airlines
  Pacific Star Building, Makati Ave, on the corner of Gil Puyat Ave, Makati (☎ 8185421)
Vietnam Airlines
  Anson Arcade, Pasay Rd, on the corner of Paseo de Roxas, Makati (☎ 874878)

To/From the Batanes Islands From Manila to Basco via Laoag there is a PAL flight on Monday and Wednesday. On the same days flights go also from Tuguegarao to Basco.

To/From Bohol PAL flies daily from Manila to Tagbilaran.

To/From Catanduanes PAL flies daily from Manila to Virac and on Monday, Wednesday and Friday from Legaspi to Virac.

To/From Cebu PAL has daily flights from Manila to Cebu City; and on Monday, Wednesday, Thursday and Friday from Legaspi to Cebu City.

To/From Leyte PAL has daily flights from Manila to Tacloban.

To/From Lubang Pacific Airways has daily flights from Manila to Lubang.

To/From Marinduque PAL has daily flights from Manila to Boac.

To/From Masbate PAL has daily flights from Manila to Masbate and from Legaspi to Masbate on Monday, Wednesday and Saturday.

To/From Mindanao From Manila, PAL has daily flights to Cagayan de Oro, Cotabato, Davao, Dipolog and Zamboanga, and flights on Monday, Wednesday and Friday to Butuan.

To/From Mindoro Pacific Airways has flights from Manila to Calapan and from Manila to Mamburao on Monday, Wednesday and Friday. PAL has flights from Manila to Mamburao on Friday and Sunday, and daily except Wednesday and Friday from Manila to San Jose.

To/From Negros PAL flies daily from Manila to Bacolod and Dumaguete.

To/From Palawan From Manila to Busuanga, Pacific Airways flies daily, PAL flies on Friday and Sunday, Aerolift flies on Monday, Friday and Saturday, and Air Link flies on Monday, Thursday and Saturday.

Pacific Airways flies from Manila to Cuyo on Monday, Wednesday and Friday.

Aerolift flies daily from Manila to El Nido.

PAL flies daily from Manila to Puerto Princesa.

To/From Panay Aerolift, Boracay Air and Pacific Airways fly daily from Manila to Caticlan.

On peak days during the high season, Interisland Travel & Tours offer a Manila-Caticlan flight of their own at the fare of P1950. Their Manila office is in 1322 Roxas Blvd, Ermita (☎ 5221405).

PAL flies daily from Manila to Iloilo, Kalibo and Roxas.

To/From Romblon PAL has flights on Tuesday, Thursday and Saturday from Manila to Tugdan on Tablas.

To/From Samar PAL flies daily except Wednesday and Saturday from Manila to Calbayog, and daily except Monday and Friday from Manila to Catarman.

Bus

All bus companies use a combination of ordinary buses and air-con buses, but there aren't too many of the latter. You can ring and enquire about exact departure times and possibly reserve a seat.

Both Sarkies' Tours (☎ 508959, 8176615), Remedios St, on the corner of Indiana St, Malate, and Sunshine Run (☎ 506601-06, 584787), Pedro Gil, on the corner of M H del Pilar St, Ermita, specialise

in tours to North and South Luzon using air-con buses. It is advisable to book.

There is no central bus terminal in Manila. The terminals of the individual companies are scattered all over the city. Most of them are easy to reach by Metrorail.

Following is a list of the addresses and major routes of the principal bus companies in Manila (the number beside the bus company name refers to its number in the Bus Destinations From Manila map key and to its numbers in the Metrorail Stations & Bus Terminals map key):

5 Baliwag Transit (☎ 990132) at 33 Edsa, Cubao, Quezon City, has buses going north to Aparri, Bulacan Province, Baliwag, San Jose and Tuguegarao. Get to its terminal by taking a Cubao jeepney from Taft Ave or a Makati Love Bus from M H del Pilar St to the Ayala Commercial Center; then catch another Love Bus to Cubao.

2 Baliwag Transit (☎ 350778, 350860) at 199 Rizal Ave Extension, on the corner of 2nd Ave, Grace Park, Caloocan City, has buses going north to Aparri, Bulacan Province, Baliwag, San Jose and Tuguegarao. Get to its terminal by Monumento jeepney from Mabini St. The nearest Metrorail station is R Papa Station.

13 BLTB (☎ 8335501) is on Edsa, Pasay City. It has buses going south to Batangas, Calamba, Legaspi, Lucena, Naga, Nasugbu, Santa Cruz and Sorsogon. Get to its terminal by Baclaran jeepney or bus from Taft Ave or M H del Pilar St and change in or before Baclaran. The nearest Metrorail station is Edsa Station.

6 Dagupan Bus (☎ 976123, 995639) on New York St, Cubao, Quezon City, has buses going north to Alaminos, Baguio, Dagupan and Lingayen. Get to its terminal by taking a Cubao jeepney from Taft Ave or a Makati Love Bus from M H del Pilar St to the Ayala Commercial Center; then catch another Love Bus to Cubao.

10 Dangwa Tranco (☎ 705718) at 832 Aurora Blvd, on the corner of Driod St, has buses going north to Baguio and Banaue. Get to its terminal by taking a Cubao jeepney from Taft Ave or a Makati Love Bus from M H del Pilar St to the Ayala Commercial Center; then catch another Love Bus to Cubao.

8 Dangwa Tranco (☎ 7312859) at 1600 Dimasalang St, Sampaloc, has buses going north to Baguio. Get to its terminal by Blumentritt jeepney from Taft Ave. The nearest Metrorail station is Tayuman Station.

Bus Destinations
From Manila

0   75   150 km

9 Farinas Trans (☎ 7314507, 7314375) on M dela
Fuente St, on the corner of Laong Laan,
Sampaloc, has buses going north to Vigan and
Laoag. Get to its terminal by Blumentritt jeepney
from Taft Ave. The nearest Metrorail station is
Tayuman Station.

15 Inland Trailways (☎ 8336280) on Edsa, Pasay
City, has buses going south to Legaspi, Lucena,
Naga and Sorsogon. Get to its terminal by Bac-
laran jeepney or bus from Taft Ave or M H del
Pilar St and change in or before Baclaran. The
nearest Metrorail station is Edsa Station.

18 J B Bicol Express Line (☎ 8332949-50) on Aurora
Blvd (Tramo), Pasay City, has buses going south
to Legaspi, Lucena and Naga. Get to its terminal
by Baclaran jeepney or bus from Taft Ave or M

H del Pilar St and change in or before Baclaran.
The nearest Metrorail station is Edsa Station.

11 Maria de Leon (☎ 7314907) on Gelinos St, on the
corner of Dapitan St, Sampaloc, has buses going
north to Vigan and Laoag. Get to its terminal by
Blumentritt jeepney from Taft Ave. The nearest
Metrorail station is Bambang Station.

17 Pangasinan Five Star (☎ 3612781, 345544) on
Aurora Blvd (Tramo), Pasay City, has buses
going north to Bolinao, Cabanatuan and
Dagupan. Get to its terminal by Baclaran jeepney
or bus from Taft Ave or M H del Pilar St and
change in or before Baclaran. The nearest
Metrorail station is Edsa Station.

3 Pantranco North (☎ 997091-98, 951081) at 325
Quezon Blvd, Quezon City, has buses going

Destination (Town)	Km	Departure Time	Bus Company
Alaminos (Laguna)	78	1.30	7, 13, 15, 18
Alaminos (Pangasinan)	254	5.00	3, 6
Angeles/Dau	83	1.30	3, 4, 6, 8, 9, 10, 11, 12 ,14, 17
Aparri	596	11.00	2, 3, 5
Baguio	246	6.00	6, 10, 12, 14
Balanga	123	2.30	12
Baler	231	7.00	3
Banaue	348	9.00	10
Bangued	400	8.00	4
Batangas	111	2.30	13
Bauang	259	5.30	4, 9, 11, 12
Bolinao	283	6.00	3, 6, 17
Bulan	653	15.00	13, 18
Cabanatuan	115	2.30	2, 3, 5, 10, 17
Daet	350	7.00	7, 13, 15, 16, 18
Dagupan	216	5.00	3, 6, 17
Iba	210	5.30	1
Iriga	487	9.00	13, 15, 16, 18
Laoag	487	10.00	4, 9, 11, 12
Lingayen	227	4.30	3, 6
Legaspi	550	11.00	13, 15, 16, 18
Lucena	136	2.30	7, 13, 15, 16, 18
Matnog	670	14.00	13, 16, 18
Naga	449	8.30	13,15, 16, 18
Nasugbu	102	2.30	13
Olongapo	126	3.00	1
San Fernando (La Union)	269	6.00	4, 9, 11, 12
San Fernando (Pampanga)	66	1.00	1
San Pablo	87	2.00	7, 13, 15, 16, 18
Santa Cruz/Pagsanjan	101	2.00	13
Sorsogon	604	12.30	13, 15, 16, 18
Tabaco	580	11.00	15, 16
Tagaytay	56	1.30	13
Tuguegarao	483	9.00	2, 3, 5
Vigan	407	7.30	4, 9, 11, 12

north to Alaminos, Aparri, Baguio, Baler, Bolinao, Lingayen and Tuguegarao. Get to its terminal by Philcoa or Project 8 jeepney from Taft Ave or Mabini St, though these are not frequent.

12 Philippine Rabbit (☎ 7115819) is in Santa Cruz at 819 Oroquieta St, with another entrance on Rizal Ave. It has buses going north to Angeles, Baguio, Balanga, Laoag, Mariveles, San Fernando (La Union), Tarlac and Virac. Get to its terminal by Monumento jeepney from Mabini St. The nearest Metrorail station is D Jose Station.

16 Philtranco (☎ 8335061-64) in Edsa, Pasay City, has buses going south to Calbayog, Catbalogan, Daet, Davao, Legaspi, Lucena, Naga, Tacloban, Sorsogon and Surigao. Get to its terminal by Baclaran jeepney or bus from Taft Ave or M H del Pilar St and change in or before Baclaran. The nearest Metrorail station is Edsa Station.

7 Superlines (☎ 984910) at 670 Edsa in Quezon City has buses going south to Daet and Lucena. Get to its terminal by Cubao jeepney from Taft Ave.

4 Times Transit (☎ 7414146) at 79 Halcon St, Quezon City, has buses going north to Bangued, Laoag, San Fernando (La Union) and Vigan. Get to its terminal by Blumentritt jeepney from Taft Ave. The nearest Metrorail station is Tayuman Station.

1 Victory Liner (☎ 3611506, 3611514) at 713 Rizal Ave Extension, Caloocan City, has buses going north to Alaminos, Dagupan, Iba, Olongapo and Mariveles. Get to its terminal by Monumento

jeepney from Mabini St. The nearest Metrorail station is North Terminal (Monumento).

14 Victory Liner (☎ 8335019) at 561 Edsa, Pasay City, has buses going north to Baguio, Dagupan, Iba and Olongapo. Get to this terminal by Baclaran jeepney or bus from Taft Ave or M H del Pilar St and change in or before Baclaran. The nearest Metrorail station is Edsa Station.

To/From Leyte Air-con Philtranco buses leave Manila daily at 10 am and 2 pm for Tacloban. The travelling time, including the ferry trip from Matnog to San Isidro, is 28 hours.

To/From Mindanao Air-con Philtranco buses run daily from Manila to Davao, leaving at 2 pm. Travelling time, including the ferry from Matnog to San Isidro and from Liloan to Surigao, is 45 hours.

To/From Mindoro A through trip from Manila to Puerto Galera starts at the Sundowner Hotel in Mabini St, Ermita, daily at 9 am. The air-con bus goes to Batangas and the MB *Sikat II*, which leaves at noon and arrives in Puerto Galera at around 2.30 pm. Bookings and tickets (P260) are arranged at the Sundowner Hotel. Buses from Manila to' Batangas leave the BLTB bus terminal regularly; see the Batangas section of the Around Manila chapter later in this book.

To/From Samar Air-con Philtranco buses leave Manila daily at 10 am and 2 pm for Calbayog and Catbalogan, taking 25 and 26 hours respectively, including the ferry from Matnog to San Isidro.

Air-con Philtranco buses and Inland Trailways buses (the better of the two, because it has less stops) go from Manila to Catarman. This trip takes about 24 hours.

Train

See the Getting Around section later in this chapter for details.

Boat

Nearly all inter-island boats leave Manila from North Harbor. If you have trouble finding it ask a coastguard opposite Pier 8.

Next to the North Harbor piers are the docking facilities of the Del Pan Bridge (coming from the sea it is the first bridge over the Pasig River). Various small vessels to neighbouring islands depart from here but they don't have any schedule.

To get to North Harbor from Ermita by taxi costs about P40. There is a rather roundabout way of getting there by jeepney, although it goes through inner suburbs with heavy traffic and can take up to an hour. From Mabini St or Taft Ave get a jeepney to Divisoria; there you change for a jeepney to North Harbor.

It is extremely difficult to get a taxi with a properly adjusted meter when travelling from North Harbor to Ermita or other suburbs after a ship has docked. The 'fixed price' is between P70 and P100.

The travel bureau Scenic View Travel Inc (☎ 5223495, 5218770-72; fax 5218773), Mabini St, on the corner of Soldado St, sells tickets for the Aboitiz Lines shipping company. Just across the street (Mabini St) there is a Negros Navigation Lines ticket office, so you don't always have to go to the offices on the wharves.

The following companies have offices in Manila:

Aboitiz Lines
    Pier 4, North Harbor, Tondo (☎ 217581, 276332, 501816)
    Destinations: Panay, Romblon
Asuncion Shipping Lines, 3038 J A Santos St, Sampaloc; Santa Mesa (☎ 7113743)
    Pier 2, North Harbor, Tondo (☎ 204024)
    Destinations: Lubang/Mindoro, Palawan (Coron, Culion, Dumaran, El Nido)
Carlos Gothong Lines
    Pier 10, North Harbor, Tondo (☎ 214121, 213611)
    Destinations: Cebu, Mindanao, Panay
Negros Navigation Lines
    Negros Navigation Building, 849 Pasay Rd, Makati (☎ 8183804, 8163481)
    Pier 2, North Harbor, Tondo (☎ 215741, 212691)
    Destinations: Negros, Panay, Romblon
Sulpicio Lines
    415 San Fernando St, San Nicolas (☎ 479621, 475346)
    Pier 12, North Harbor, Tondo (☎ 201781, 201634)

A harbour tour boat at sunset, Manila Bay (JPk)

Top: Dawn at Lake Taal, Batangas (JPk)
Bottom: Rice terraces at Banaue, North Luzon (KD)

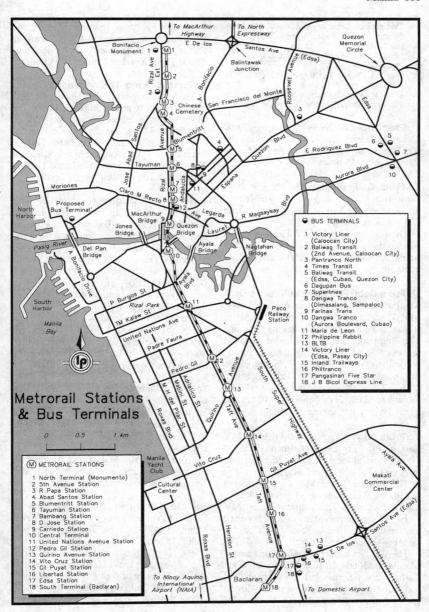

Metrorail Stations & Bus Terminals

0   0.5   1 km

● BUS TERMINALS
1 Victory Liner (Caloocan City)
2 Baliwag Transit (2nd Avenue, Caloocan City)
3 Pantranco North
4 Times Transit
5 Baliwag Transit (Edsa, Cubao, Quezon City)
6 Dagupan Bus
7 Superlines
8 Dangwa Tranco (Dimasalang, Sampaloc)
9 Farinas Trans
10 Dangwa Tranco (Aurora Boulevard, Cubao)
11 Maria de Leon
12 Philippine Rabbit
13 BLTB
14 Victory Liner (Edsa, Pasay City)
15 Inland Trailways
16 Philtranco
17 Pangasinan Five Star
18 J B Bicol Express Line

Ⓜ METRORAIL STATIONS
1 North Terminal (Monumento)
2 5th Avenue Station
3 R Papa Station
4 Abad Santos Station
5 Blumentritt Station
6 Tayuman Station
7 Bambang Station
8 D Jose Station
9 Carriedo Station
10 Central Terminal
11 United Nations Avenue Station
12 Pedro Gil Station
13 Quirino Avenue Station
14 Vito Cruz Station
15 Gil Puyat Station
16 Libertad Station
17 Edsa Station
18 South Terminal (Baclaran)

Destinations: Cebu, Leyte, Masbate, Mindanao, Negros, Palawan, Panay, Samar

William Lines

1508 Rizal Ave Extension, Caloocan City (☎ 3610764)

Pier 14, North Harbor, Tondo (☎ 219821, 405458)

Destinations: Cebu, Leyte, Mindanao, Negros, Palawan, Panay, Romblon, Samar

To/From Bohol The William Lines' MV *Cebu City* leaves Manila on Tuesday at 2 pm for Tagbilaran via Dumaguit and Batan on Panay, taking 36 hours.

To/From Catanduanes The Regina Shipping Lines' MV *Regina Calixta* leaves Tabaco daily for San Andres at 8 am, taking 2½ hours.

The Bicolano Lines' MV *Eugenia* leaves Tabaco daily for Virac at 8 am, taking four hours. An additional small boat leaves daily at 10 am.

To/From Cebu Several vessels run between Manila and Cebu City. The William Lines' MV *Wilines Mabuhay I* leaves on Sunday at 9 am and Thursday at 2 pm, taking 22 hours. The Sulpicio Lines' MV *Manila Princess* leaves on Sunday at 10 am, taking 23 hours, while their MV *Philippine Princess* leaves on Tuesday at 10 am and Friday at 8 pm, taking 21 hours. The Aboitiz Lines' MV *Superferry 2* leaves on Monday at 10 am and Thursday at 7 pm, taking 22 hours.

To/From Leyte The Sulpicio Lines' MV *Surigao Princess* leaves Manila on Friday at 10 pm for Calubian. It takes 36 hours and goes on to Palompon and Maasin.

The Aboitiz Lines MV *Legaspi* leaves Manila on Wednesday at 11 pm for Ormoc, taking 20 hours. The Sulpicio Lines' MV *Cebu Princess* leaves Manila on Friday at 10 am for Ormoc, via Masbate and Calbayog, taking 44 hours.

The William Lines' MV *Masbate I* leaves Manila on Monday at 10 am for Tacloban via Catbalogan on Samar and on Friday at 7 am for Tacloban direct. The time taken (direct) is 28 hours. The Sulpicio Lines MV

Tacloban Princess leaves Manila on Wednesday at noon via Catbalogan on Samar and on Sunday at 10 am for Tacloban direct. The time taken (direct) is 24 hours.

To/From Lubang The Asuncion Shipping Lines' MV *Catalyn A* leaves Manila for Tilik on Tuesday at 10 pm, taking eight hours. The MV *Catalyn B* leaves Manila for Tilik on Tuesday at 11 pm, taking seven hours, the MV *Asuncion XI* leaves Manila for Tilik on Thursday at 8 pm, taking eight hours, and the MV *Asuncion X* leaves Manila for Tilik on Saturday at 10 pm, taking eight hours.

To/From Marinduque There is one Viva Shipping Lines' ship a day from Lucena (Dalahican Pier) to Balanacan. Departure time varies as it is dependent upon the tides, but is usually around 10 am. The trip takes 3½ hours. There is a BLTB bus from Manila to Lucena which goes directly to the wharf. BLTB (☎ 8335501) can give you the departure time of the bus and probably the sailing time of the ship as well.

The MV *Antipolo* leaves Lucena (Cotto Pier) daily between 8 and 10 am for Buyabod, the port for Santa Cruz, which takes 4½ hours. The sailing times are the same as for the ship going to Balanacan.

To/From Masbate The Sulpicio Lines' MV *Cebu Princess* leaves Manila for Masbate at 10 am on Friday, taking 22 hours. The William Lines' MV *Cebu City* leaves Manila for Masbate on Saturday at 7 pm, taking 16 hours.

From Bulan the MV *Matea I* leaves for Masbate daily at noon, taking 3½ hours. There may be a second boat.

To/From Mindanao The Carlos Gothong Lines' MV *Our Lady of Lourdes* leaves Manila for Butuan on Tuesday at 6 pm, taking 35 hours.

The Negros Navigation Lines' MV *Princess of Negros* leaves Manila for Cagayan de Oro on Monday at 4 pm. It takes 42 hours and goes via Iloilo on Panay.

The William Lines' *Doña Virginia* leaves

Manila for Cagayan de Oro on Tuesday at 7 am. It takes 31 hours and goes via Dumaguete on Negros. The MV *Sugbu* leaves on Wednesday at 9 pm and takes 31 hours.

The Aboitiz Lines' *Superferry 2* leaves Manila for Cagayan de Oro on Thursday at 7 pm. It takes 38 hours and goes via Cebu City.

The Negros Navigation Lines' MV *Santa Ana* leaves Manila for Cagayan de Oro on Friday at noon. It takes 40 hours and goes via Iloilo on Panay.

The Sulpicio Lines' MV *Manila Princess* leaves Manila for Davao on Sunday at 10 am. It takes 53 hours and goes via Cebu City.

The William Lines' MV *Misamis Occidental* leaves Manila for Dipolog on Tuesday at 7 pm. It takes 31 hours and goes on to Iligan.

The William Lines' MV *Tacloban City* leaves Manila for Ozamiz on Friday at 9 pm, taking 37 hours.

The Aboitiz Lines' MV *Legaspi* leaves Manila for Surigao on Wednesday at 11 pm. It takes 41 hours and goes via Ormoc on Leyte.

The Sulpicio Lines' MV *Surigao Princess* leaves Manila for Surigao on Friday at 10 pm. It takes 54 hours and goes via Calubian, Palompon and Maasin on Leyte.

The William Lines' MV *Maynilad* leaves Manila on Thursday at 7 pm for Zamboanga. It takes 36 hours and goes on to Davao.

The Sulpicio Lines' MV *Cotabato Princess* leaves Manila on Saturday at 3 pm for Zamboanga, taking 45 hours and going via Estancia and Iloilo on Panay. From Zamboanga it continues on to Cotabato.

To/From Mindoro There are at least three boats daily from Batangas to Puerto Galera. There are possible additional departures at the weekend. The Viva Shipping Lines' MV *San Miguel de Ilijan* (car ferry) leaves at 11.30 am and 4 pm, taking one hour or more. Arrival is at Balateros, two km west of Puerto Galera. The MV *Batangas Express*, the MV *Princess* and the MV *Queen* of AC Shipping Lines cost from P40 to P65,

leaving at 12.30 pm and possibly at 1.30 pm. The trip takes two hours. The MV *Sikat II* of Si-Kat Ferry Inc leaves at noon and takes 2½ hours.

The MV *Marian Queen*, the MV *San Lorenzo Ruiz* and the MV *Santa Maria* of Santo Domingo Lines sail from Batangas to Calapan daily at 6 and 10 pm and 2 and 6 pm, taking two hours. The MV *Emerald I* and the MV *Ruby I* of Manila International Shipping Lines sail from Batangas to Calapan daily at 6.30 and 10.30 am and 2.30 and 6.30 pm, taking two hours. You can catch a jeepney from Calapan to Puerto Galera the next morning, taking 2½ hours.

A big outrigger boat or a ferry leaves Batangas daily at 9 am for Abra de Ilog, taking three hours.

The MV *Santa Anna* and the MV *Socorro* of Viva Shipping Lines sail from Batangas to Sablayan on Tuesday and Friday at 7 pm, taking 12 hours.

. The Asuncion Lines' MV *Asuncion XII* leaves Manila for San Jose on Tuesday at 5 pm, taking 18 hours and possibly going via Tilik on Lubang.

To/From Negros There are several Negros Navigation Lines' ships each week from Manila to Bacolod. The MV *Don Claudio* sails on Sunday at 9 am, taking 22 hours. The MV *Don Julio* leaves on Tuesday at 10 am and Friday at noon, taking 21 hours. The MV *Santa Florentina* leaves on Thursday at 8 am and takes 24 hours. The MV *Princess of Negros* leaves Friday at 5 pm and takes 23 hours.

From Manila to Dumaguete, the William Lines' MV *Doña Virginia* sails on Tuesday at 7 am, taking 23 hours.

To/From Palawan The William Lines' MV *Sugbu* leaves Manila for Puerto Princesa on Sunday at 1 pm, taking 19 hours.

The Asuncion Shipping Lines has several ships going from Manila to various towns on Palawan. The MV *Catalyn A* leaves Manila for Coron on Tuesday at 10 pm, via Tilik on Lubang. It takes 26 hours and continues on to Culion. The MV *Asuncion XI* leaves

Manila for Coron on Thursday at 10 pm, via Tilik on Lubang. It takes 30 hours and continues on to Culion. The MV *Asuncion X* leaves Manila for Coron on Saturday at 10 pm, via Tilik on Lubang. It takes 26 hours and continues on to Culion.

The MV *Asuncion IV* leaves Manila for El Nido on Wednesday at 11 pm. It takes 30 hours and continues on to Liminangcong.

The MV *Asuncion VI* leaves Manila for Dumaran on Monday at 10 pm. It takes 38 hours and continues on to Roxas, Caramay, Puerto Princesa Aborlan, Narra, Panacan and Brooke's Point.

The Viva Shipping Lines MV *Love Boat* leaves Batangas for Coron on Thursday at 6 pm, taking 15 hours.

To/From Panay The Aboitiz Lines' MV *Legaspi* leaves Manila for Dumaguit (near Kalibo) on Monday at noon, taking 19 hours. The William Lines' MV *Cebu City* leaves Manila for Dumaguit on Tuesday at 2 pm, takes 15 hours and continues on to Batan. The Carlos Gothong Lines' MV *Our Lady of Fatima* leaves Manila for Dumaguit on Tuesday at 6 pm, taking 17 hours.

There are several ships from Manila to Iloilo. The Sulpicio Lines MV *Dipolog Princess* leaves on Tuesday at 10 am and takes 22 hours. The Aboitiz Lines' MV *Superferry 1* leaves on Thursday at 3 pm and Sunday at 4 pm, taking 20 hours. The Negros Navigation Lines' MV *Santa Ana* leaves on Tuesday and Friday at 2 pm, taking 21 hours, the MV *Don Claudio* leaves on Wednesday at noon, taking 22 hours and the MV *Santa Florentina* leaves on Sunday at 12.30 pm, taking 24 hours.

From Manila to Roxas, the Carlos Gothong Lines' MV *Our Lady of the Sacred Heart* leaves on Saturday at 6 pm and takes 19 hours.

To/From Romblon From Batangas boats leave at 8 pm to San Agustin on Tablas on Monday, to Odiongan on Tablas on Wednesday and Saturday, and to Romblon on Romblon on Thursday. The trip takes 10 hours.

There are also several boats weekly from Lucena which go to Romblon on Romblon or to Magdiwang on Sibuyan.

To/From Samar The Sulpicio Lines' MV *Cebu Princess* leaves Manila for Calbayog on Friday at 10 am, taking 32 hours and going via Masbate.

The William Lines' MV *Masbate I* leaves Manila for Catbalogan on Monday at 10 am, taking 26 hours. The Sulpicio Lines' MV *Tacloban Princess* leaves Manila for Catbalogan on Wednesday at noon, taking 23 hours.

The ferries MV *Michelangelo* and MV *Northern Samar* sail daily at 10 am and 3 pm from Matnog to Allen. The crossing takes 1½ hours. The ferry MV *Marhalika I* of St Bernard Services leaves Matnog for San Isidro daily at 6 am and 12.30 pm, taking two hours. The Matnog terminal fee is P7 per passenger.

GETTING AROUND
To/From the Airport
NAIA Near the luggage collection point, you will find telephones provided for you to make free local (Manila) calls. These give you the opportunity of booking a hotel room while you wait for your luggage to appear. It costs P30 or US$1 to use a luggage trolley; the charge includes the service of a porter, but, unlike the trolleys, porters can be hard to locate.

If you want to confirm a connecting flight or your return flight before leaving the airport, you'll find the counters of all the major airlines two floors up; take the staircase in front of the arrival hall exit.

International Airport to the City Unfortunately, Filipinos don't seem to have heard of the saying 'You never get a second chance to make a first impression' in Manila. Since 1975 I've been arriving at the international airport at least twice a year, and almost each time my arrival has been marred by some inconvenience. Comparing Manila with other Asian cities, like Bangkok or Hong Kong, you can't help wondering why this place seems unable to provide a smooth arrival for visitors. And why on earth can't airport staff manage to arrange efficient transport to a hotel for visitors who are tired and worn out after many hours in a plane? For years the airport managers have been experimenting with various changes, none of which ever seems to benefit incoming travellers.

For instance, the reliable and inexpensive airport buses that once serviced a large number of hotels in different suburbs disappeared overnight.

Then the Golden Cabs (now history), which were equipped with meters that actually worked properly, were ousted from the arrival platform. With these gone, there were only the highly suspect yellow taxis to ferry tourists to the city – some of the fares charged would make your hair stand on end. For a trip from the airport to Ermita/Rizal Park, which normally should cost no more than P60 (US$2.30), up to US$50 has been demanded! If you get off with paying P100, you should consider yourself lucky.

Taxi At present, only air-con taxis with set fares are allowed to service the airport, for example, P220 to Pasay, P300 to Ermita and Makati, and P380 to Quezon City. If you don't want to put up with the hassle, then you can take the stairs up to the departure level. You'll find the nearest staircase before you come to the main exit from the arrival level, and there's another one outside about 50 metres to the left of the main exit. You can wait for a taxi at the departure level that has just dropped off passengers and would otherwise have to head back to town empty. Mind you, lots of sneaky taxi drivers have hit on this trick and now wait for victims at the departure level with bargain 'deals'.

If there are regular taxis to be found at the departure level again these days, they'll probably be standing some 100 metres to the right of the exit. The taximeter is supposed to be switched on just before the taxi starts off. If the driver tells you that the counter is out of order, you're quite entitled to get out again. However, ordering the driver to stop and let you out after you've gone 500 metres can be awkward, especially at night.

For standard taxi fares, see the general Taxi section later in this chapter. Certain taxi drivers, however, while switching off the meter at the end of the trip, nimbly turn it forward P20 or so! Other taxi drivers will proudly hand you typed 'official' fare lists, often impressively set in a leather binder with gold lettering. Be aware that these have no legal validity whatsoever and are simply another crude attempt to defraud unsuspecting tourists.

Keep your cool and don't allow yourself to be provoked if you encounter problems with a driver on the way to the hotel. You're in a much better position to win a fight when you and your luggage are already out of the taxi and you can call on the hotel staff for support.

Hotel Transport If instead of a fairly expensive taxi fare you'd rather spend your money on a decent hotel room, you can book a room for the first night at one of the accommodation counters near the main exit in the arrival hall. Most of the hotels represented offer a free limousine service for patrons arriving at the airport. Although the best way to get in from the airport would be to book a room well in advance and meet a car arranged with your hotel.

If you haven't booked ahead, and the hotel of your choice is booked out, you can (during the daytime) wait in the hotel lobby until a room becomes vacant. But remember that few guests tend to check out after midday. A polite request at the reception counter will usually find a member of staff willing to ring other hotels for a vacant room for you.

Metrorail A taxi from NAIA to the Metrorail South Terminal in Baclaran is unlikely to cost you more than P30 (providing, that is, a taxi will take you for this short distance). From there it's P6 to Pedro Gil Station or United Nations Ave Station in Ermita.

International Airport to the Domestic Airport Travellers landing in Manila and proceeding to another destination within the Philippines have to transfer to the nearby domestic airport. PAL provides passengers with a free bus service. As this shuttle bus is mostly underbooked, a friendly smile will normally get passengers of other airlines on it too. The bus only departs, however, when it has at least one PAL passenger on board. The shuttle bus counter is at the arrival platform exit.

A taxi ride from the international airport to the domestic airport generally costs no more than P15, but you can be charged up to P150.

Domestic Airport to the City Almost all of the taxi drivers waiting at the Domestic Airport will refuse to switch their meter on and will stubbornly demand a ridiculously inflated set price for the journey. Rather than giving in to these latter-day highwaymen, go through the car park until you come to the road which runs from the airport, Domestic Terminal Drive, and flag down a passing taxi there. At the time of this book's publication the normal fare to Ermita was around P50.

However, you're not obliged to take a taxi from the Domestic Airport to Ermita. An inexpensive alternative is to go right and walk to the crossing 200 metres away, then go left and walk 250 metres, crossing the river, until you come to Harrison St where buses and jeepneys leave for Mabini St and Taft Ave. If you go right at Harrison St and carry on for about 800 metres, you'll come to the South Terminal (Baclaran) of the Metrorail, which starts here and ends up at the North Terminal (Monumento) in Caloocan City. The two stops in Ermita are Pedro Gil Station and United Nations Ave Station, both on Taft Ave. A word of warning: passengers with extra-large baggage will be turned away.

Bus
Around Manila, city buses only display their final destination on the front of the buses.

That can be a large complex like the NAIA, a street name like Ayala (for Ayala Ave in Makati) or a whole suburb like Quiapo (north of Pasig River). The fare is P1.50 centavos for the first four km and 25 centavos for every km after that. At the end of Rizal Ave Extension there is a statue of Andres Bonifacio, known as the 'Monumento', a very popular destination and stop for jeepneys and buses.

The air-con Love Buses are very popular in Manila. They are blue (with red hearts), operate on several main routes and charge a flat rate of P10. Have small change available, as bus drivers usually cannot change large notes. The Escolta-Ayala/Medical Center bus is a useful one for tourists – the Love Bus goes from the Escolta St (Binondo/Santa Cruz) through Ermita (M H del Pilar St) to Makati (the embassies) and the Makati Commercial Center. It returns through Mabini St in Ermita. There are no fixed stops on the way. Don't throw your ticket away, as there are frequent inspections.

Train
The Metrorail Light Rail Transit (LRT) is an overhead railway which runs on concrete pylons several metres high, linking the suburbs of Caloocan City and Pasay City. The line runs from North Terminal (Monumento) in Caloocan City, over Rizal Ave to Central Terminal near the Manila City Hall and on over Taft Ave to South Terminal in Baclaran, Pasay City.

The Metrorail runs from 5.30 am until 10.30 pm, except on Good Friday. During rush hour the trains can be completely overcrowded. The fare is a flat rate of P6, irrespective of the number of stations you travel to. Instead of tickets, you have to buy tokens that open the barriers to the platforms. Smoking, eating and drinking are all forbidden both on the platforms and in the trains. Bulky objects which may cause obstruction will not be carried.

Following are the railway stations from north to south, and some of the prominent city features nearby:

North Terminal (Monumento)
　　Andres Bonifacio Monument, Edsa, Victory
　　Liner Bus Terminal
5th Ave Station
　　Caloocan City
R Papa Station
　　Baliwag Transit Bus Terminal
Abad Santos Station
　　Chinese Cemetery
Blumentritt Station
　　Chinese Hospital, San Lazaro Hippodrome
Tayuman Station
　　Dangwa Tranco Bus Terminal, Farinas Trans Bus
　　Terminal, San Lazaro Hippodrome
Bambang Station
　　Maria de Leon Bus Terminal, Times Transit Bus
　　Terminal, University of Santo Tomas
D Jose Station
　　Claro M Recto St (cinemas), Philippine Rabbit
　　Bus Terminal (Santa Cruz)
Carriedo Station
　　Chinatown, Escolta, Ilalim ng Tulay Market,
　　Quinta Market, Quiapo Church, Santa Cruz
　　Church
Central Terminal
　　GPO, Immigration Office, Intramuros, Manila
　　City Hall, Metropolitan Theater
United Nations Ave Station
　　Manila Doctor's Hospital, Manila Medical
　　Center, Manila Pavilion Hotel, Paco Park, Rizal
　　Park, tourist office, Western Police District
Pedro Gil Station
　　Manila Midtown Hotel, Philippine Long Dis-
　　tance Telephone Company (PLDT)
Quirino Ave Station
　　Malate Church, San Andres Market
Vito Cruz Station
　　Central Bank, Cultural Center, De la Salle Uni-
　　versity, Harrison Plaza, Sheraton Hotel
Gil Puyat Station
　　Cartimar Market, Philtrade Exhibits
Libertad Station
　　Libertad Cockpit, Pasay Market
Edsa Station
　　BLTB Bus Terminal, Philtranco Bus Terminal,
　　Victory Liner Bus Terminal, Inland Trailways
　　Bus Terminal, J B Bicol Express Line Bus Ter-
　　minal, Pangasinan Five Star Bus Terminal
South Terminal (Baclaran)
　　Baclaran Church, Baclaran Flea Market, Seaside
　　Market

Taxi

Manila is crawling with taxis, unless you
want one, that is, in which case there are none
around or they all have passengers. It's not
unusual to come across meters which have
been tampered with, so it's best to check the
speed of the counter now and again. I have
always been happy with the Fil-Nipon taxis
and City taxis. They have fairly new air-con
taxis which can be recognised by their white
finish. Always have some change ready
when you board a taxi in Manila, as there's
no guarantee the driver will have any. Ordinary taxis (those not equipped with
air-conditioning) have a flag-down charge of
P10 which includes the first 500 metres,
thereafter they charge P1 for every further
250 metres. However, almost all of the
meters still show the old flag-down charge
of P2.50, so there will be a surcharge of
P7.50. Air-con taxis begin with P16 (the old
flag-down charge of P3.50 plus P12.50 surcharge).

Examples of fares: ordinary taxi from
Ermita (corner of Mabini St and Padre
Faura) to Domestic Airport P50; Inter-
national Airport P60; Intramuros (GPO)
P20; Makati P40; North Harbour P40; Pasay
City (Edsa bus terminals) P35; and Santa
Cruz (Philippine Rabbit bus terminal) P30.

For further information see also the Taxi
section of the Getting Around chapter earlier
in this book.

Jeepney

You need to get to know Manila a bit before
you can travel through the city by jeepney
without problems. Crowding and the limited
view make it hard to see where you are
going, so a seat by the driver is desirable.
Jeepney routes are fixed. Their main streets
and stops are shown on the side of the vehicle
and mostly on the windscreen as well. For
example, jeepneys with the sign 'Baclaran,
Harrison, Santa Cruz, Rizal, Monumento'
will go from Baclaran in Pasay City, through
Harrison St to Harrison Plaza, then down
Mabini St, back down M H del Pilar St – both
one-way streets – past the City Hall
(Lawton), to the suburb of Santa Cruz, then
down Rizal Ave and Rizal Ave Extension to
Monumento in Caloocan City.

Jeepneys on the north-south route are
almost always marked 'Baclaran' or
'Libertad' to show the southern end of their
route, both in Pasay City. The northern end

could be Monumento (Caloocan City, at the end of the Rizal Ave Extension); Blumentritt (a street in northern Santa Cruz, by the Chinese Hospital and near the Chinese Cemetery); or Divisoria (the Divisoria Market in the suburb of San Nicolas). Jeepneys in Ermita run along M H del Pilar St and Mabini St (those marked 'Harrison') or Taft Ave (those marked 'Taft'). Jeepneys whose north-eastern destination is shown as 'Project 2', 'Project 3' or 'Project 4' are going to Cubao, while those marked 'Project 6' and 'Project 8' are heading for Quezon City. The fare is P1.50 for the first four km.

For further information see also the Jeepney section of the Getting Around chapter earlier in this book.

Car & Motorbike

To rent a car the following international companies are recommended:

Avis Rent-a-Car
    1322 Roxas Blvd, on the corner of Padre Faura, Ermita (☎ 5210062, 5222082)
    Kalaw St, on the corner of Maria Orosa St, Ermita (☎ 586228)
    Manila Hotel, Ermita (☎ 470071)
    Manila Peninsula Hotel, Makati (☎ 878497)
    NAIA, Arrival Area, (☎ 8322088)
Budget Rent-a-Car
    Manila Pavilion Hotel, Ermita (☎ 5222911)
    Hotel Inter-Continental, Makati (☎ 8162211)
    Manila Peninsula Hotel, Makati (☎ 8187363)
    Nikko Manila Garden, Makati (☎ 8177720)

If you want to hire a motorcycle probably the best place to go is:

Marisol Rent-a-Motorcycle
    temporarily (at the time of publication) in München Grill Pub, Mabini St, Ermita (☎ 502795)

Driving Traffic in Manila is chaotic and noisy, especially to someone who is used to fairly strict traffic controls. There are few bus stops and these are not always used. Buses and jeepneys stop wherever they see a fare to pick up and then taxis of various companies try to get in ahead of them. Horns and hand signals are used most often, brake lights and blinkers rarely, and traffic-lane markings seem to be thought a waste of paint. However, the Filipinos are used to these conditions and there are few accidents – the battered vehicles usually last longer than their appearance would lead you to believe. If you want a cheap and pleasant form of innercity public transport, try the Metrorail.

City Tour

For a quick and relatively cheap overview of Manila you should organise something for yourself, but preferably not during the rush hour in late afternoon, when traffic is heavily congested.

Try using the air-con Love Buses for transport. Get on a Love Bus in M H del Pilar St in Ermita which is going in the direction of Ayala/Medical Center and travel to the Ayala Center Terminal near the Makati Commercial Center, where you can sightsee, shop or visit the Ayala Museum. Then get another Love Bus from the Ayala Center Terminal to Cubao in Quezon City. In the Araneta Center in Cubao are numerous restaurants and cinemas as well as excellent opportunities for shopping and window shopping. From there, catch another Love Bus to Quiapo/Escolta, which will take you past numerous ministries and other official establishments, and the central part of the city. From Escolta St, head in the direction of Ayala/Medical Center and get off at Ermita.

The west end of Escolta St is, however, also a good starting point for a stroll through Chinatown. First you go though the First Welcome Gate into Quintin Paredes St which takes you to the Binondo Church. This is the beginning of Ongpin St, a busy street which ends at the Santa Cruz Church. All along Ongpin St and in the side streets leading off it there are plenty of opportunities to take a quick breather in one of the many restaurants.

One suggestion would be Maxim's Tea House near the Plaza Santa Cruz, or even before that in the Pink Patio Café near the

Binondo Church. (Opposite the café is the entrance to Carvajal St, an unassuming, but interesting little alley with small shops, which leads from Quintin Paredes St to Ongpin St.)

From Carriedo Station you can get the Metrorail to Pedro Gil Station, Taft Ave, and and finish your tour of the city there.

An extension of the walk from Carriedo Station is to go along Carriedo St to Quiapo Church, or along Carlos Palanca St (Echague St) past Quinta Market to Quezon Bridge, with its cheap craft shops in the Ilalim ng Tulay Market. From there, you can go to Quiapo Church or to the Globo de Oro Mosque with its shining gold dome.

Around Manila

All the trips described in this chapter can be done as day trips from Manila. The map shows towns that can be reached by bus within three hours. Olongapo, Pagsanjan and Matabungkay, however, deserve an overnight stay.

Some destinations can be combined – the volcano at Tagaytay and the beach at Matabungkay, for example. Some towns can be visited on the way to other destinations: Olongapo is on the way to the Hundred Islands and Pagsanjan is on the way to South Luzon.

In July 1991, 80 km north-west of Manila, in the eastern Zambales Mountains, the volcano Pinatubo erupted into life after six centuries of slumber. Violent eruptions continued unabated for several weeks after, making this without a doubt the worst volcanic outburst the world has seen this century. Volcanologists agree that it could be quite some time before the roughly 1700-metre- high mountain finally settles down again.

There is an expressway from Metro Manila north to Dau and Mabalacat, a little beyond Angeles, and another south to about Calamba. Buses using expressways rather than the ordinary roads carry the sign 'Expressway'.

BATAAN PENINSULA

It's not possible to do a round trip of the Bataan Peninsula. The stretch from Bagac to Olongapo is blocked for military reasons by the Philippines Navy. At Morong, about a thousand Vietnamese boat people live in a place known as the 'Refugee Processing Center'.

On Mt Samat, a little to the south of Balanga, the provincial capital, is Dambana ng Kagitingan, a national monument to the victims of the Battle of Bataan. There is a cross over 90 metres high from which you get a good view over the former battlefield and Manila Bay.

A large part of the south of the peninsula is industrialised. Most of the almost 650 manufacturing plants in the province, including the biggest, are in the Export Processing Zone in Mariveles, where textiles, clocks, electrical appliances and automobile parts are made.

Getting There & Away

Lots of Philippine Rabbit Company buses leave Manila daily for Balanga, Mariveles and Morong. Most go to Balanga. The travelling time to Mariveles is three hours.

Several Victory Liner buses run daily from Olongapo to Balanga, taking an hour or more.

SAN FERNANDO (PAMPANGA)

Don't confuse San Fernando (Pampanga), the capital of Pampanga Province, between Manila and Angeles, with the San Fernando that is the capital of La Union Province on the coast, north-west of Baguio. This town is notorious at Easter because on Good Friday at noon you can see at least one 'believer' being nailed to a cross in a rice field outside the gates of the city (in 1993 there were nine 'believers'). And on 24 December a spectacular parade of oversized lanterns mounted on trucks is driven through the town. (See also the Fiestas & Festivals section in the Facts about the Country chapter.)

Paskuhan Village, the 'Christmas Village', is just outside San Fernando. It was built in the late 1980s in the shape of an oversize Christmas star and houses the tourist office, the Pinatubo Museum, a big duty-free shop and several souvenir shops.

Information

The tourist office (☎ 2665; fax 3361) is at the Paskuhan Village on the Expressway. The

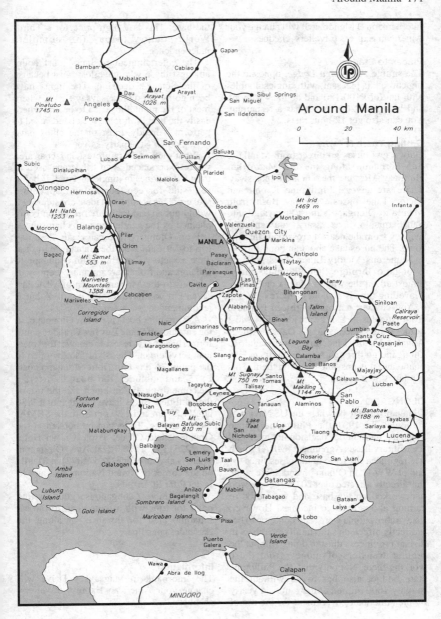

Around Manila

0   20   40 km

Interbank on B Mendoza St will change your American Express travellers' cheques.

Places to Stay

The simple *Pampanga Lodge*, opposite the big church, is pleasant, with singles/doubles with fan for P100/180 and doubles with fan and bath for P200, and it has a restaurant. You can also get 12-hour rates.

Getting There & Away

Only a few buses go direct from Manila to San Fernando along the old MacArthur Highway. Most use the quicker Expressway. There are several Philippine Rabbit and Victory Liner buses every day. Buses from Manila to Olongapo almost always go into San Fernando; if necessary, you can get a jeepney from the nearest crossroads into the town. The buses take about an hour.

Numerous Victory Liner buses go from Olongapo through San Fernando daily, almost all on the way to Manila or Baguio. Travelling time is an hour or more.

You can get reasonably priced jeepneys from Angeles to San Fernando daily. Most come from Mabalacat or Dau, north of Angeles. Victory Liner buses from Baguio to Olongapo go through Angeles and San Fernando and it is possible to get on them. This trip takes 30 minutes.

OLONGAPO

Olongapo used to be where the US Navy was stationed. In 1991 the Philippine Senate made the momentous decision not to extend the Military Bases Agreement (MBA) which had regulated the lease of the bases since the end of WW II. In Olongapo and Subic alone this directly affected over 20,000 people who had worked on the base and were used to earning above average incomes. However, many more people were (and continue to be) indirectly affected as the family members in distant provinces adjust to doing without the regular transfers of money from those working there. Not only that, the Philippine state budget also has to do without the roughly 1000 million dollar rent paid yearly by the American government for the use of the base. This is a high price for a Third-World country to pay for 'complete independence'.

The entertainment business must count amongst those who have lost most because of the Senate's decision. The lights have been going out on Magsaysay Drive, where most of the nightclubs used to be and where easily the best Philippine rock bands used to perform. Already, most of the clubs have closed down – the party's over.

What's left of the rainforest, in fact an area where experienced Ayta tribesmen used to train US marines in jungle survival, is being set aside for eco-tourists and adventure seekers. This is not a bad idea, considering it would put an end to the deforestation being planned by the gentlemen with chainsaws.

From Olongapo you can easily do a day trip to Mt Samat on the Bataan Peninsula. Take a Victory Liner bus from Olongapo to Balanga and from there go on by jeepney or minibus to the Mt Samat turn-off. The last seven km you have to hike uphill. A hat is recommended.

A 40-minute boat ride from Olongapo, at the entrance of Subic Bay lies Grande Island, formerly a R & R resort exclusive to American serviceman. The island is now open to the public. A day tour from Olongapo costs P875 and includes the boat transfer, a welcome drink, buffet lunch and the use of the facilities. Boats leave Olongapo at 9.30 am, 11.30 am and 2.30 pm from the SBMA, Fleet Landing. Tours can be booked at the Grande Island Office, Triple Crown Hotel (☎ 2225139), 1270 Rizal Ave, Olongapo. There is also an office (☎ 571872) in Manila on the corner of United Nations Ave and M H del Pilar St, Ermita.

What's more, Olongapo is a good starting point for trips with a rented car, to the Mt Pinatubo area for instance, or along the Zambales coastline.

Information

The Interbank in Magsaysay Drive will change your American Express travellers' cheques.

Places to Stay

The *Ram's Inn* at 765 Rizal Ave has reasonable rooms with fan for P150 and with air-con for P175.

The *Moonstone Apartments* (☎ 5301) at 2132-2148 Rizal Ave is probably the best hotel in the town. It has doubles with air-con and bath from P580 to P650. TV costs P40 extra. Apartments cost from P750. Monthly rates are available. All rates are payable daily in advance. It has a restaurant, coffee shop and swimming pool. It is near the big market, a few minutes on foot from the Victory Liner bus terminal in the direction of Manila.

Getting There & Away

Bus From Manila, several Victory Liner buses leave the bus terminal in Caloocan City (the Rizal Ave Extension) for Olongapo daily, and also from Pasay City (Edsa). The trip takes 2½ to three hours. There are also several Victory Liner buses from Alaminos to Olongapo daily, taking about five hours. You may have to change at Santa Cruz.

Victory Liner buses run roughly every hour from 5.30 am to 5.30 pm daily between Baguio and Olongapo, and it is possible to board them at Angeles. In Angeles you can also catch a San Fernando jeepney, get out at the turn-off to Olongapo and wait for the next bus. Travelling time from Baguio is six hours; from Angeles, it takes two hours. Victory Liner buses also run several times a day from San Fernando to Olongapo, taking 1½ hours.

Car Avis Rent-a-Car (☎ 3873, 5486) has an office in Perimeter Rd.

BARRIO BARRETTO & SUBIC

The withdrawal of the US Navy didn't just mean the end of an era in Olongapo, but also in Barrio Barretto and Subic, both of which were almost completely economically dependent on the American base. Attempts are now being made to attract tourists and investors to the facilities left behind on the former base.

While Subic will probably end up concentrating on industry and shipbuilding, Barrio Barretto with its various hotels and modest entertainment facilities could well have a future of sorts in tourism.

There are several resorts along the 12 km stretch of coast between Olongapo and Subic, but the beaches themselves are not particularly good. They are better north of Subic Bay, near San Miguel and beyond. (See Zambales Coast in the West Coast section of the North Luzon chapter later in this book.)

Places to Stay

Barrio Barretto The hotel *By the Sea Inn* has comfortable rooms with air-con and bath for P600 to P1200. The rooms in the new wing are better than those in the older one. It has a good restaurant.

The *Marmont Resort Hotel* (☎ 5571, 3791) has rooms with air-con and bath for P650 and suites for P1200. It also has monthly rates. It's attractive and comfortable, and has a restaurant, nightclub, gym and swimming pool.

The *Halfmoon Hotel* has rooms with TV, air-con and bath from P500 to P700. It has a restaurant and a swimming pool in beautiful grounds. The rooms near the pool are the quietest.

Subic The *Bamboo Inn* has good rooms with fan and bath for P300 and with TV, air-con and bath for P400, and it has a restaurant. Weekly and monthly rates available.

The *White Rock Resort Hotel* (☎ 5555, 2398) has singles with air-con and bath from P1400 and doubles with air-con and bath from P1800, apartments from P2000 and suites from P2500. It is pleasant in well-kept grounds with a restaurant and swimming pool. Admission for day visitors is P30.

Getting There & Away

Several Blue Jeepneys run daily from Olongapo to Barrio Barretto and Subic. But look out – this is a happy hunting ground for pickpockets. You can also use the Victory Liner buses which go to Iba. The trip takes 15 minutes.

AROUND BARRIO BARRETTO & SUBIC
Pinatubo Lake

The so-called Pinatubo Lake or New Lake at Buhawen was formed when avalanches of mud flowing down the valley in an un-stoppable stream dammed the Marbella River. All that remains to see of the little town of Buhawen are a bell tower, the school and the rooftops of various houses sticking forlornly out of the waters. Above the lake a dam, which was built by the local Benguet-Dizon Mining Company before the volcano erupted, can be made out. If this dam was to burst, it would mean disaster for all of the valley communities the whole way down to the coast. An employee of the company will accompany visitors from the checkpoint to the lake and show them around.

Getting There & Away Occasionally, the hotel By the Sea Inn in Barrio Barretto organises trips to the Pinatubo Lake for P450 per person. It is possible to make the trip by hire car, for example from Avis in Olongapo. From Barrio Barretto via Subic, head for San Marcelino. When there, turn right for San Rafael then go up the road towards Buhawen along the wide riverbed of the Marbella River to the lake. On the way, there is a signpost at a fork in the road indicating the way to 'Barangay Macarang'. The road from San Marcelino to Buhawen has a fairly good surface, although it is quite dusty, so it would be better to drive in an enclosed vehicle rather than an open jeep.

ANGELES

Angeles used to be home to the US Air Force's Clark Air Base. Just as in Olongapo, the base provided the impetus for a lively nightlife in the area, with loads of bars, night-clubs, discos, hotels and restaurants. And, similar to Olongapo, the withdrawal of the Americans had serious economic conse-quences for the town.

To make matters worse, the eruption of Pinatubo didn't just destroy the air base, it made a mess of Angeles itself and the sur-rounding area. Even considering how much has already been cleaned up and how well

life has returned to normal here, it will take years before townspeople have fully recov-ered from the devastation.

Almost all the local hotels have reduced their prices and now offer Pinatubo tours, a combination which has led to surprisingly high occupation rates. The tourists have also meant more business for the bars, restaurants and nightclubs that did manage to survive the fateful year of 1991 or have been rebuilt in the meantime. No doubt, Manila's mayor Lim contributed to Angeles' surge in busi-ness with his fortunately timed campaign against vice in the capital city.

Unfortunately, the upsurge in business encouraged the con men to try their luck in the town. With their familiar greeting 'Hello, my friend...' they could be witnessed round the clock doing their level best to relieve unsuspecting tourists of their money, and not taking no for an answer. However, it seems that the efforts of the alert local mayor and the chief of police have been successful in getting rid of petty criminals and gangsters alike.

Information

Visas The Immigration Office is on 7th St in Dau. You can get your visa extended here but your application and passport will probably be sent to Manila for processing and will not be available for a few days. Some travel agencies and hotels run by foreigners will also offer to take care of your extension application for a reasonable sum; ask at the Sunset Garden Inn or the Swagman Narra Hotel.

Money The Interbank on Miranda St, Angeles, will change your American Express travellers' cheques.

The money changers at the checkpoint, the Flamingo Hotel and the Norma Money Changer in a small side street near the Folk House Restaurant will all exchange US dollars.

Telephone International calls can be made at very reasonable rates from the Faxtel Center at the hotel Marlim Mansions, from the Angeles Business Center behind the Manhattan Transfer Restaurant and from the Bluestar Communication Center near the Oasis Hotel.

Places to Stay

The *Liberty Inn* (☎ 4588) on the MacArthur Highway is a good place to stay, with a restaurant, a swimming pool and lots of big old trees. Singles/doubles with fan and bath cost P150 and with air-con and bath cost P200/400.

The *Southern Star Hotel* (cellular ☎ 097-3779447) at 1934 Sampaguita St, Clarkview, has rooms with TV, fan and bath for P250 and with air-con and bath for P350. It is under Australian management and is well kept, has a restaurant and swimming pool, and is on a dusty lane (Pinatubo ash) behind the Clarkton Hotel.

The *Bonanza Hotel* (☎ 51082) on San Pablo St, Mountain View, has clean and quite comfortable rooms with TV, air-con and bath from P310 to P350, and offers favourable monthly rates. The hotel has a restaurant, swimming pool and fitness room.

The *Premiere Hotel* (☎ 22664, 24714) on Malabanas Rd, Clarkview, has clean and spacious rooms with TV, air-con and bath for P320. There is a restaurant and a swimming pool.

The *Endeavour Lord Hotel* (☎ 4578-51210) on Malabanas Rd, Plaridel I, has tidy rooms with TV, air-con and bath for P340. It is under Australian management and has a restaurant and a small swimming pool.

The *Capt Cook Hotel* (☎ 4578-24522) on Plaridel St, Plaridel I, has nice rooms with fan and bath for P280 and with TV, air-con and bath for P340. It has a restaurant and a swimming pool.

The *Sunset Garden Inn* (cellular ☎ 097-3781109) on Malabanas Rd, Clarkview, has rooms with fan and bath for P285 and with TV, air-con and bath for P375, with weekly and monthly rates available. This place, which is pleasant, clean and comfortable, has a restaurant, swimming pool, fitness room, and is under Swiss management.

The *Clarkton Hotel* (cellular ☎ 51231-33,

☎ & fax 912-3050614) is at 620 Don Juico Ave, Clarkview. It has rooms with fan and bath for P200 and with TV, air-con and bath from P325 to P1500. The place is clean and the rooms are immaculate. It has a restaurant, swimming pool, fitness room and is under German management.

The *Orchid Inn* (☎ 6020370; fax 8882708) on 109 Raymond St, Balibago, has nice, well-kept rooms with TV, fridge, air-con and bath from P400 to P450. There is a restaurant and a small swimming pool.

The *Woodland Park Resort* (☎ & fax 912-3010900), off MacArthur Highway, Dau, is a pleasant, generously appointed resort with a restaurant, a nightclub and a large swimming pool. Rooms with TV, air-con and bath are P450, with weekly and monthly rates available.

The *Maharajah Hotel* (☎ 2028806) on Texas St, Villa Sol, has fairly good rooms with air-con and bath for P400/500. It is a fairly large hotel with a restaurant and a swimming pool.

The *Oasis Hotel* (cellular ☎ 2025847) at Clarkville Compound has comfortable and tastefully furnished singles with air-con and bath for P450 and P500, and doubles with air-con and bath for P650. This is a peaceful, pleasant establishment. There is a restaurant and a swimming pool.

The *Swagman Narra Hotel* (☎ 25231, 912-30157) on Orosa St, Diamond, is under Australian management. It is clean and tidy, with a restaurant and swimming pool. It has rooms with air-con and bath from P500 to P760.

The *America Hotel* (☎ 4578-51023; fax 4578-51022) on Don Juico Ave, Clarkview, has rooms with TV, air-con and bath for P400, with TV and fridge for P500 to P650 and suites for P1200 with jacuzzi, fridge and TV. The place is well looked after and comfortable (especially the suites). There is a restaurant and a swimming pool, and massage is available.

The *Marlim Mansions* (☎ 22002, 51036) on MacArthur Highway, Balibago, has spacious and well appointed rooms with TV, air-con and bath from P600 to P800. Suites

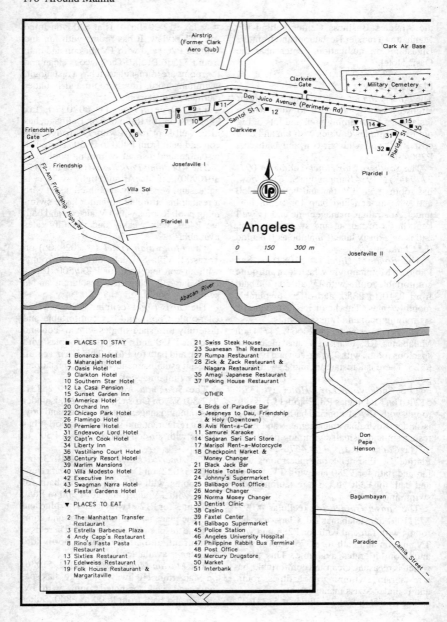

Angeles

0   150   300 m

■ PLACES TO STAY

1 Bonanza Hotel
6 Maharajah Hotel
7 Oasis Hotel
9 Clarkton Hotel
10 Southern Star Hotel
12 La Casa Pension
15 Sunset Garden Inn
16 America Hotel
20 Orchard Inn
22 Chicago Park Hotel
26 Flamingo Hotel
30 Premiere Hotel
31 Endeavour Lord Hotel
32 Capt'n Cook Hotel
34 Liberty Inn
36 Vastilliano Court Hotel
38 Century Resort Hotel
39 Marlim Mansions
40 Villa Modesto Hotel
42 Executive Inn
43 Swagman Narra Hotel
44 Fiesta Gardens Hotel

▼ PLACES TO EAT

2 The Manhattan Transfer
  Restaurant
3 Estrella Barbecue Plaza
4 Andy Capp's Restaurant
8 Rino's Fasta Pasta
  Restaurant
13 Sixties Restaurant
17 Edelweiss Restaurant
19 Folk House Restaurant &
  Margaritaville

21 Swiss Steak House
23 Suanesan Thai Restaurant
27 Rumpa Restaurant
28 Zick & Zack Restaurant &
  Niagara Restaurant
35 Amagi Japanese Restaurant
37 Peking House Restaurant

OTHER

4 Birds of Paradise Bar
5 Jeepneys to Dau, Friendship
  & Holy (Downtown)
8 Avis Rent-a-Car
11 Samurei Karaoke
14 Sagaran Sari Sari Store
17 Marisol Rent-a-Motorcycle
18 Checkpoint Market &
  Money Changer
21 Black Jack Bar
22 Hotsie Totsie Disco
24 Johnny's Supermarket
25 Balibago Post Office
26 Money Changer
29 Norma Money Changer
33 Dentist Clinic
38 Casino
39 Faxtel Center
41 Balibago Supermarket
45 Police Station
46 Angeles University Hospital
47 Philippine Rabbit Bus Terminal
48 Post Office
49 Mercury Drugstore
50 Market
51 Interbank

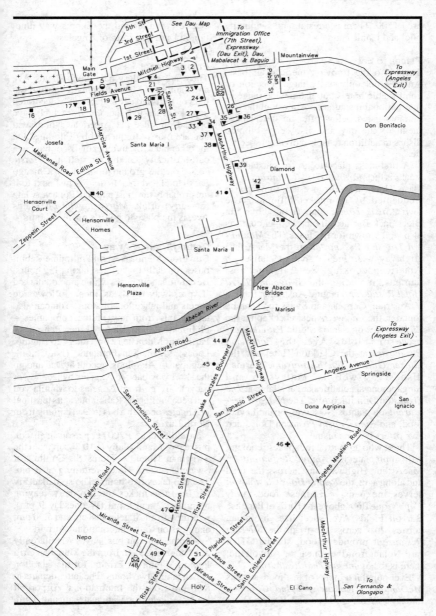

are P1500. There is a restaurant, swimming pool and tennis court.

Places to Eat

Thanks to the former American air base, Angeles not only has a large selection of comfortable hotels but also a wide range of international restaurants. Almost all the restaurants listed below offer an inexpensive menu of the day and also serve Filipino dishes in addition to their individual specialties.

A first-class place to go for outstanding steaks is the *Maranao Grill Restaurant* in the Oasis Hotel, a well-run establishment also frequented by up-market Filipinos. The *Swiss Steak House*, one floor above the Black Jack Bar near the basketball court, is also well known for its steaks. The *Manhattan Transfer Restaurant* on the MacArthur Highway near Fields Ave specialises in American cooking. Several hotel restaurants, including the *Swagman Narra Hotel Restaurant*, feature Australian food.

Austrian, German and Swiss food can be found at the *Edelweiss* near checkpoint, the *Zick & Zack* on Santos St, the *Estrella Barbecue* on Fields Ave, the *Panorama Restaurant* at the Clarkton Hotel and the *Sunset Garden Inn Restaurant*. German dishes, as well as Malaysian and Singaporean specialities are available at *The Sixties* on Don Juico Ave. The *Niagara Restaurant* on Santos St serves Scandinavian food, and *Rino's Fasta Pasta* on Don Juico Ave offers Italian cuisine.

Those who are partial to Japanese cooking will appreciate the *Amagi Restaurant* on MacArthur Highway. Just across the road and along a bit, the *Peking House Restaurant* serves inexpensive Chinese food. *Andy Capp's*, one floor above the Birds of Paradise Bar on Fields Ave, specializes in Indian curries. Just across the road, the *Fil-Thai Restaurant* provides good, standard Thai fare. Not far from there, near the Airwolf Inn, there is the *Suanesan Thai Restaurant*.

Ever popular temples of fast food, such as *McDonald's*, *Kentucky Fried Chicken*, *Shakey's Pizza*, *Jollibee* and *Rosie's Diner*

can be found around the Expressway junction in Dau, just north of Angeles.

Entertainment

There are countless bars along Fields Ave and Santos St. Most of them are fairly basic but you will find a few elaborately decorated karaoke clubs like the *Samurei* which have opened up since the American withdrawal and are mostly frequented by Filipinos. On the other hand, the number of discos has been cut drastically. Of the few left, the *Hotsie Totsie* on the ground floor in the Chicago Park Hotel and the *Music Box* just next to it are probably the most popular. For a very late (or early) drink, *Margaritaville* on Fields Ave, is the place to go. It's open 24 hours.

Getting There & Away

Bus From Manila, several Philippine Rabbit buses run daily to Angeles, taking 1½ hours. Be careful about buses which are not marked 'Expressway/Dau', as these follow side streets and make lots of stops. You can also take a bus from any of the companies – Philippine Rabbit, Victory Liner, Pantranco, Farinas or Maria de Leon Trans – to Baguio, Laoag, Vigan, San Fernando (La Union), Dagupan or Alaminos, get out at Dau and go the short way back to Angeles by jeepney or tricycle. To go from Angeles to Manila you can get a Philippine Rabbit bus at its terminal in Angeles or catch a bus in Dau coming from North Luzon.

In addition, for P200 per person an air-con bus leaves Manila daily at 10.30 am from the Swagman Hotel, A Flores St, Ermita, for Swagman Narra Hotel, returning at 3 pm. The trip takes two hours. The so-called Fly the Bus also makes the trip daily, leaving Manila at 2 and 8 pm (Wednesday 9 pm), returning from Angeles at 8 am and 5.30 pm, and goes on to the International Airport.

Another air-con bus leaves Manila daily at 12 noon and 9 pm from the München Grill Pub on Mabini St, Ermita, for the Clarkton Hotel, taking two hours. The latter departs at 8.30 pm from the International Airport. It leaves Angeles for Manila at 9 am and 3 pm,

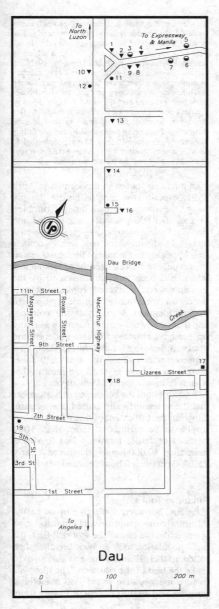

1 Jollibee & Jenra Market
2 Dunkin Donut
3 Buses To North Luzon
4 Michael's Fast Food &
   Coffee Shop
5 City Trams Bus Stop
6 Philippine Rabbit Bus Stop
7 Victory Liner Bus Stop
8 Shakey's Pizza
9 Kentucky Fried Chicken &
   Buses to Manila
10 Barrio Fiesta Restaurant
11 Caltex Petrol Station
12 Plaza Romana &
    Northwest Airlines
13 McDonald's
14 Nangking Chinese Restaurant &
    Philippine National Bank (PNB)
15 Nita's Handicraft
16 Rosie's Diner
17 Woodland Park Hotel
18 American Legion Restaurant
19 Immigration Office

the latter carries on to the International Airport, taking four hours.

An air-con bus leaves Manila daily at 10.30 am and 7.30 pm from the Sundowner Hotel, Mabini St, Ermita, for the Endeavour Lord Hotel, returning at 8 am and 3 pm. The trip takes two hours.

Another air-con bus leaves Manila daily at 1 pm from the Birdwatchers Inn, Mabini St, Ermita for the Southern Star Hotel, returning from Angeles at 3 pm. The trip takes two hours.

From Subic to Angeles, an air-con bus leaves daily at 9 am for the Endeavour Lord Hotel and Southern Star Hotel, returning at noon. The trip takes two hours. Another air-con bus leaves Subic daily at 12.30 pm for the Swagman Narra Hotel, returning at 10 am, taking two hours.

Hourly Victory Liner buses run from Olongapo to Angeles daily, they take two hours. In Olongapo you can also get a Manila bus; get off before San Fernando (Pampanga) and wait for a bus or jeepney to Angeles.

Victory Liner buses run from Baguio to Angeles hourly every day from 5.30 am to 5 pm. They are the ones marked 'Olongapo'. The trip takes four hours. Buses from other companies such as Philippine Rabbit and Pantranco travel from Baguio to Manila via Dau; it is just a short way from Dau to Angeles by jeepney or tricycle. Similarly, to go from Angeles to Baguio it's best to go to Dau and get on one of the buses from Manila.

Numerous buses of various companies travel daily from Laoag, Vigan and San Fernando (La Union) to Dau on the way to Manila. If you get out in Dau, it's only a short way by jeepney or tricycle to Angeles. To go from Angeles to San Fernando (La Union), Vigan or Laoag, it's best to go to Dau and get on the buses coming through from Manila.

Car & Motorbike Avis-Rent-a-Car (cellular ☎ 3011085) has an office on Don Juico Ave, Clarkview, between Clarkton and Oasis hotels.

Marisol Rent-a-Motorcycle can be found at Edelweiss Restaurant on Fields Ave, Balibago, near checkpoint.

Getting Around

Bus Apart from hotel buses, all buses stop in Dau, roughly two km north of Angeles. A tricycle from Dau to one of the Angeles hotels listed here will cost P20 to P30, depending on the distance.

Jeepneys & Tricycles It's a waste of time looking for taxis in Angeles. Jeepneys charge normal fares, but beware of Special Rides: they can turn out costly! Tricycles are comparatively expensive: P10 to P30. Filipinos do pay less than this.

MT PINATUBO

For many of those involved, the unprecedentedly violent eruption of Mt Pinatubo on 15 June 1991 was like a bad dream.

The clouds of steam and detritus produced by the eruption shot up to 40 km into the stratosphere, darkening the sky. Brilliant flashes of lightning rent the daytime darkness eerily, accompanied by rolling thunder and frightening, seemingly endless, earthquakes. Unbelievable amounts of ash and sand settled in wide areas around the volcano, stones the size of fists flew through the air and, to top it all off, a powerful typhoon chose this of all times to lash North Luzon violently. As a result of the heavy rainfall, awe-inspiring avalanches of lahar (mud) raced down the hillsides, demolishing bridges, shoving houses aside like toys, and burying entire villages. Most of the Aeta people living on Pinatubo managed to flee down the slopes of the mountain in time to save themselves from being suffocated by the ash falling relentlessly all around them. Many people fled to Manila, unsure whether the volcano would also start to exude deadly, red-hot poisonous gases.

And it had all started so innocently. In April 1991, exactly two months before the big bang, the mountain had quietly rumbled awake, after 600 years of peace nestled into the Zambales Mountains, emitting white clouds of steam which rose gently from a small opening to the side of the actual crater.

Yet only one week later the seismometers which had been hurriedly installed by the volcanologists delivered convincing evidence that pressure was building up in a magma chamber deep inside the volcano, and that slowly but surely magma was rising up through a chimney from the underground reservoir, heading for the crater. As the first major eruptions shook the area on 9 June, no-one could have guessed the inferno that was to follow in the next few days.

It wasn't until the beginning of September that the volcano finally settled down again, allowing the full extent of this natural catastrophe to be estimated: more than 1000 hectares of fertile farmland laid to waste, more than 40,000 houses destroyed, nearly 250,000 people left homeless and nearly 900 fatalities.

Pinatubo Tours

Filipinos, however, don't give up so easily. Although the eruption of Pinatubo had seemed like the end of the world at first, the local population took a quick breather then rolled up their shirt sleeves and got down to make the best of the situation. The idea was to turn the negative event into something positive, and so the concept of having tours to Pinatubo was born. Some said the idea was absurd, but they later had to eat their words. For, as far as tourism is concerned, the eruption of the volcano has not just brought calamity to the Philippines, but has provided the island state with a new attraction. The ash and sand deposited by the eruption in a wide area around Pinatubo has created a magnificent landscape. To the west of Angeles the grey mass of coagulated material can reach heights of up to 20 metres. The impressive terrain is criss-crossed with bizarre ravines, through which you can wander for hours. Other areas can be better explored with a vehicle, and for those who want to have the big picture, an aircraft will provide the perfect vantage point – it can all be arranged.

Half-Day Hikes It's a good idea to start early, for the heat starts to build up in the ravines from about midday onwards. Ideally you should do this in a small group, under no circumstances should you set out on your own.

Getting to the starting point: take a jeepney from Friendship Gate to the village of Sapang Bato. For P50 charter a jeepney from there to the Pinatubo trail; don't forget to arrange the pick-up time for the return journey. Four hours in the area should be enough to get a first-hand impression of the immense power of nature. Only the most adventurous with mountaineering experience should attempt the eight-km trek to the volcano itself.

Whole-Day Tours The following round trip is no problem with a normal car; you can hire a car from Avis. Heading south-west from Angeles towards Porac the first section is a drive of 100 km in all. This stretch takes you through a broad plain once covered by productive sugar cane plantations and now an uneconomic desert, stretching as far as the eye can see. The sight of half-submerged communities can only begin to convey an understanding of what unbelievable quantities of material were spewed out by Pinatubo. The exhibition of photographs in

Paskuhan Village near San Fernando, the next stop, gives a good visual impression of what happened. The Expressway comes to an end in Mabalacat, about 25 km north of there. From there it's a short drive to Bamban, where the new tourist attraction of Sacabia Lake Resort is located. The lake was formed in 1992 as a result of the avalanches of mud damming up the Sacabia River. Before heading back to Angeles it is worth making a short detour to Dolores, where enterprising Filipinos sell souvenirs made from volcanic rock at the roadside.

Basic round trips are available at Island Tours, c/o Capt Cook Hotel, Plaridel Rd, Plaridel I.

Off-road tours with 4WD all-terrain vehicles and basic tours combined with guided hikes can be arranged by the Clarkton Hotel, Don Juico Ave, also in Clarkview.

Sightseeing Flights It's a pity the airstrip of the former Clark Aero Club hasn't been brought up to scratch for small aircraft again. However, until this happens, pilots are continuing to use the Domestic Airport at Manila. The only exceptions are the ultra-light aircraft of the Angeles City Flying Club (ACFC), which can be flown directly from the Flight Park of the club itself. There are 20 two-seaters available in all. A flight to Pinatubo and back takes about one hour without pushing it. For solo flights a pilot's licence and health certificate are necessary, both of which can be obtained from the ACFC.

For flights with ultra-lights contact the Angeles City Flying Club, c/o Woodland Park Hotel, Lizares St, Dau. The charter price is P500 for 30 minutes, with one passenger only. Solo flights cost US$50 for one hour.

For flights with Cessnas and Pipers contact Interisland Travel & Tours (☎ 5224748; fax 5225795) at 1322 Roxas Blvd, Ermita, Manila. The charter price is US$440 for 1¼ hours, with up to five passengers.

· **When to Go** For safety reasons, car tours and hikes should only be attempted in the dry season, the best months being February, March and April. Theoretically, sightseeing flights are possible year-round, except during a typhoon. However, rainy days with lots of low clouds could also ruin any plans you may have had.

Equipment Those sensitive to the sun should wear long-sleeved clothing and preferably some head protection. When hiking, water is absolutely essential (two litres per person for four hours). Please do not leave empty bottles and rubbish in the area.

If going by car, in addition to tools remember to take a tow rope and shovel, as well as a board for supporting the jack in case of a flat tyre.

CORREGIDOR ISLAND

The fortified island of Corregidor was important in WW II. Even earlier, in 1898, Corregidor was used by the USA in its war against Spain because of its strategic position at the entrance to Manila Bay. Construction of the Malinta Tunnel began 25 years later and it served as General Douglas MacArthur's headquarters from December 1941 to March 1942, as Filipinos and Americans struggled in vain against the Japanese invaders. Quezon left by submarine and eventually MacArthur was smuggled out on a PT boat. Today ruins of the military installations and ordnance can be inspected, and there are elaborate plans for restoration. On the highest point of the island stands the Pacific War Memorial.

Organised Tours

For P750 per person (P500 at weekends) daytrips are available from Manila to Corregidor. The price includes the boat trip to the island, sightseeing tour by bus, and a guided tour of the island. Another P100 can be paid for a light & sound show in the shaft of the Malinta Tunnel, which is largely based on the history of the island, as well as P150 for lunch in the restaurant of the Corregidor Inn (it is also possible to eat à la carte if no advance booking was made). Tickets are available at any travel agency or directly at the pier.

Places to Stay

The *Corregidor Inn* has rooms with air-con and bath for P1700/2000, and suites for P3700. From the Visitor's Bar to MacArthur's Suite, this elegant hotel is furnished throughout with traditional Philippine furniture. The modern plastic chairs and tables on the restaurant terrace are even more noticeably out of a place because of this. There is a swimming pool. Reservations can be made through the tourist office in Manila (☎ 599031).

Getting There & Away

The MV *Island Cruiser* leaves the ferry terminal next to the Cultural Center Monday to Friday at 9 am, return trip at 3 pm; and Saturday and Sunday at 7.30 am and 1.30 pm, return trip 12.30 pm and 5.30 pm. The trip takes 1¼ hours.

The time and number of departures are seasonally variable, so you would be well advised to check for up to date information at the tourist office in Manila (☎ 599031). There is an alternative departure point, the Clipper Landing next to the Manila Hotel, so make sure you find out where your boat is leaving from.

An alternative to the organised tour is to go under your own steam via Mariveles on the Bataan Peninsula. Take one of the many daily Philippine Rabbit buses to Mariveles; the first leaves at 4.30 am. It is a three-hour trip. Get out just before Mariveles at the covered bus stop shortly after Cabcaban. From there, for P5, you can get a trishaw or tricycle down the old National Highway to the former Villa Carmen Beach Resort, where the owner of the Villa Carmen arranges round trips by boat to Corregidor for about P500.

You could also get a bus to Balanga and then do the last bit in a minibus or jeepney going to Mariveles down the old National Highway, as this goes past the gate of the Villa Carmen. Returning to Manila, the last

Philippine Rabbit bus leaves Balanga at about 6 pm. There is a landing fee of P10 per person at Corregidor.

LAS PIÑAS
This town is famous for its unique bamboo organ in the San Jose Church. Started in 1816 by the Spanish Father Diego Cerra, the organ was made from bamboo to save money and was finally completed in 1824. Standing over five metres high, it has 832 pipes of bamboo and 122 of metal. From 1973 to 1975 it was overhauled in Germany and now sounds as good as new. A small shop on the church porch sells records and cassettes of bamboo-organ music. The real thing can be heard on Sunday or during the Bamboo Organ Festival which lasts for a week every February. It's a social occasion, with internationally famous organists, choirs and ensembles. On normal weekdays the organ can be seen from 2 to 4 pm only.

By the way, Las Piñas is the place where the jeepneys are built, piece by piece in painstaking individual production. The people in the workshops have no objection to visitors watching them at work. They finish work for the day at 4 pm, and they have Sundays off. As you leave the church, the Sarao Motors jeepney factory is about three km farther south on the main street.

Getting There & Away
In Manila there are plenty of buses to Las Piñas that you can stop in Taft Ave. Destinations shown will be either Zapote or Cavite. The trip takes half an hour. Another possibility is to get a jeepney to Baclaran (you can get one from M H del Pilar St in Ermita), then go on with a Zapote jeepney to Las Piñas.

If you want to continue from Las Piñas to Tagaytay or Matabungkay, you can go to the main street and board any of the many buses coming through from Manila on the way to Nasugbu.

CAVITE
This town on the southern side of Manila Bay has no real tourist attractions to offer, and its beaches, like Lido Beach, are not particularly good. It does, however, make a pleasant day trip from the city, and the fair and leisure park known as **Covelandia** is nearby. The Philippines Navy is stationed at Cavite. The **Aquinaldo House Museum** in Kawit, Cavite, is worth seeing.

Places to Stay
The spacious *Puerto Azul Beach Resort* (☎ 574731-40) in Ternate, 40 km south-west of Cavite, has rooms with fan and bath from P1500 and suites from P5000. It is well kept, with a restaurant and coffee shop. There are facilities which belong to a local country club but for a small charge may be used by hotel guests. These include a swimming pool for P50, a tennis court from P100, squash courts for P100 an hour, a golf course for P500, Hobie Cats for P250 and windsurfing equipment for P200.

The *Caylabne Bay Resort* (☎ 8188385), also in Ternate, has rooms with air-con and bath from P1900/2400. It is attractive and comfortable, with a restaurant, tennis court, golf course and swimming pool. It also offers Hobie Cats and windsurfing. Reservations can be made in Manila (☎ 8148800).

Getting There & Away
Numerous buses leave Manila daily from Taft Ave, either on the corner of Vito Cruz or on the corner of Edsa, Baclaran. Travelling time is half an hour.

TAGAYTAY (TAAL VOLCANO)
Due to its high altitude (600 metres) and cool climate, Tagaytay was once proposed as an alternative summer resort to Baguio. However, in the end nothing came of it, although the idea was brought up again after the serious earthquake that rattled Baguio in mid 1990, and shares in the exclusive apartment buildings which had been built in the meantime were offered.

The sprawling town offers visitors superb views of the volcanic island with its crater lake, but only if the weather is clear. The volcano is one of the smallest and most dangerous in the world. Anyone who wants to climb it can arrange to be taken over to the volcanic island from Talisay, 17 km east of Tagaytay. An attractive alternative route is to go on to Batangas and then to San Nicolas.

About 10 km east of Tagaytay, on Mt Sungay (710 metres), are the ruins of the Palace in the Sky, the villa built by Ferdinand Marcos for the state visit of Ronald Reagan. From here you have a marvellous view of Lake Taal to the south, Laguna de Bay to the east and almost as far as Manila to the north. Admission is P3. You come from Tagaytay in a jeepney bound for Villa Adelaida, get out at the last stop and do the last few metres up to the mountain top on foot; the fare is P6. It's best to arrange a pick-up time with the driver for the return trip as, most often, people don't carry on as far as the terminus.

There is a magnificent view from Tagaytay Picnic Grove Park, between Villa Adelaida and the Palace in the Sky; admission is P10.

Places to Stay

The *Villa Adelaida* (☎ 267), Foggy Heights, has rooms with fan and bath for P850. At weekends it can be 20% dearer. It is pleasant, with a restaurant and swimming pool. Coming from Manila, you turn to the left instead of the right at the crossroads before Tagaytay. The Villa is by the road that runs down to the lake. You can make reservations in Manila (☎ 876031-39).

The *Taal Vista Hotel* (☎ 224, 226; fax 225) on National Rd (Aguinaldo Highway) is tidy and comfortable. It has rooms with air-con and bath for P1860. At the lookout in front of the lodge, folk dances with native music often take place at noon; the entrance fee is P15 and is deducted from the bill if you consume something in the restaurant. You can make reservations in Manila (☎ 8102016-19, 8172710).

Getting There & Away

Several BLTB buses run daily from Manila to Tagaytay, marked 'Nasugbu'. There are also others that pass through. The trip takes 1½ hours.

From Talisay to Tagaytay there are three to eight jeepneys a day on the 17 km of dusty, narrow road. It costs P10 per person and a Special Ride costs P200.

To get to Tagaytay from Pagsanjan you go by jeepney to Santa Cruz. There you get a Manila bus and get out at the junction at Calamba. From Calamba you go by jeepney through Binan to Palapala and from there you get a bus to Tagaytay. It takes about three hours. Or, instead of getting out at Calamba, you can continue to Alabang and there change to a jeepney to Zapote, where you can catch a bus from Manila heading for Tagaytay.

TALISAY

Talisay is right down on Lake Taal and is a good starting point for trips to the volcanic island. These trips are on offer from various local lodging houses in the Banga and Leynes districts. A boat to the volcano and back costs around P500, including guide; without guide P350. It makes sense to have a guide if you go to the lake in the old crater (last eruption 1911), whereas you don't really need one for the new crater (last eruption 1965). You should allow for at least half a day's stay on the island. Warnings made by basically lazy guides about hordes of dangerous snakes at the crater lake should be ignored with a benign smile! You might have to cope with heavy swells and may occasionally get sopping wet, so a plastic bag for your camera is a good precaution.

About five km west of Talisay in Buco, on the edge of Lake Taal, is an old seismological station of the Philippine Institute of Volcanology & Seismology (PHIVOLC). Its scope has been extended to that of a 'Science House', with staff always on duty and information available on the work of vulcanologists, the instruments and the geological history of Lake Taal.

Places to Stay

The *Taal Lake Guest House*, Leynes (halfway between Tagaytay and Talisay), has basic, comfortable rooms with fan for P150/300, and there is a restaurant. The place is, in fact, the former Natalia's Guest House.

Gloria de Castro's Store, Leynes, is a friendly little place with rooms with fan and bath for P200, and there is a good restaurant.

Rosalina's Place, Banga, has rooms for P70/120 and with fan and bath for P100/150. It is simple and fairly pleasant, and has a restaurant. It is located just outside of Talisay, across from the *International Resort* where rooms with fan and bath are P500.

Getting There & Away

From Manila the trip to Talisay is in two stages. First you get one of the numerous daily BLTB buses marked 'Lemery' or 'Batangas' and go as far as Tanauan. From there you can get a jeepney at the public market going to Talisay. Total travelling time is two hours.

From Tagaytay, the 17 km road to Talisay drops down to the lake and is dusty, narrow and little used, except by the three to eight jeepneys that run daily. The fare is P10 per person; a Special Ride is about P200. The last one leaves from the Aquino Monument, about two km from the Taal Vista Lodge, at 5 pm.

To reach Talisay from Pagsanjan you begin by catching a jeepney to Santa Cruz. Then catch a Manila bus and get out at the junction at Calamba. From there, catch a jeepney to Tanauan, where you can pick up a jeepney to Talisay. Total travelling time is about two hours. Instead of going through Calamba, you can use jeepneys from Pagsanjan and Santa Cruz via San Pablo to Tanauan and Talisay.

From Batangas, it's best to use the many daily Manila buses to get to Tanauan. This route is also served by jeepneys, but buses are more comfortable. In the public market in Tanauan you can get a jeepney to Talisay. The total travelling time is two hours.

NASUGBU & MATABUNGKAY

Matabungkay has the most popular beach in the neighbourhood of Manila, so on weekends there are lots of day trippers. Although the sand is not dazzlingly white, it's not bad and the water is clean. Among the main attractions are thatched-roof rafts with tables and chairs which can be hired for around P400 per day and anchored over the reef to act as platforms from which to swim and snorkel. The hirer also brings out food and ice-cold drinks to order. Day trips to nearby Fortune Island can be arranged for P600 to P800.

The beaches at Nasugbu are worth noting. The one at White Sands is three to four km to the north and can be reached by tricycle or outrigger boat. Out of Nasugbu, in the direction of the beach, is a good seafood restaurant, the Dalam Pasigan and, about 20 km east of Nasugbu, at the foot of Mt Batulao, is the exclusive Batulao Resort Hotel, with swimming pool and facilities for sports like riding, golf, tennis, squash, bowling, billiards and table tennis.

Places to Stay

The *Swiss House Hotel*, Matabungkay, has pleasant, clean rooms with fan and bath for P400 and with air-con and bath for P800. It is well kept and has a restaurant.

The *Twins Beach Club*, Ligtasin/Matabungkay, is under German management. It is good quality and all in all a comfortable establishment. Rooms with fan and bath cost P600 and with air-con and bath cost P800. It has a restaurant, and offers windsurfing.

The *Coral Beach Club*, Matabungkay, is also under Australian management. It has rooms with fan and bath for P600 and with air-con and bath for P900. This place has been well maintained, the cottages are pleasant, and there is a restaurant.

The *White Sands Beach Resort* in Muntingbuhangin Cove, Natipuan, Nasugbu, has cottages with bath for P750 and P1000. There is no electricity but it is pleasant and has a restaurant. Reservations can be made in Manila (☎ 8335608).

The *Maryland Resort*, Nasugbu, has rooms with fan and bath for P600 and with air-con and bath for P1420. It has a restaurant and a swimming pool.

The *Maya-Maya Reef Club* (☎ 233), Nasugbu, has cottages with fan and bath for P1250/1400 and cottages with air-con and bath for P1800/1950. It is popular, with a restaurant, swimming pool and tennis court in attractive grounds. There is also a diving shop. Reservations can be made in Manila (☎ 8108118; fax 8159288).

The *Punta Baluarte Inter-Continental Resort*, Calatagan, about 20 km south of Matabungkay, has rooms with air-con and bath from P1800/2200. It has a restaurant, swimming pool, golf course and tennis courts. You can make reservations in Manila (☎ 894011, 8159711).

Getting There & Away

BLTB buses leave Manila almost hourly every day for Nasugbu. An air-con bus leaves at 11.30 am and takes about two hours. To get to Matabungkay, it's best to get out at Lian and do the last few km by jeepney. These leave about 100 metres from the bus stop in the direction of the town centre. Special Rides in a tricycle cost about P50. There are also jeepneys that run from Nasugbu to Matabungkay via Lian.

At 12.30 pm a BLTB bus goes from Manila to Matabungkay and on to Calatagan, which saves changing at Lian.

From Batangas to Matabungkay and Nasugbu is a three or four-stage trip by jeepney: jeepney from Batangas to Lemery, jeepney from Lemery to Balayan, jeepney from Balayan to Nasugbu or from Balayan to Balibago and jeepney or tricycle (P30) from Balibago.

BATANGAS

There is talk of developing an industrial zone in and around Batangas, the provincial capital, which would provide a convenient location for foreign investors. The South Super Highway is to be extended to Batangas and the possible reopening of the old Manila-to-Batangas railway is being considered. The depth of Batangas Bay and the ease with which harbour facilities could be constructed are also being put forward as advantages Batangas has over other regions.

Tourists mainly use Batangas as a transit point on the way to Puerto Galera on Mindoro. However, it is also a good point

from which to make day trips to Lake Taal, to the hot springs at Calamba and Los Baños, to Banuan Beach and to Gerthel Beach near Lobo. Tabangao, on the farther part of the rocky coast, is just seven km from Batangas and offers good diving and snorkelling.

Places to Stay

JC's Pension House (☎ 3318) at 110 Del Pilar St has rooms with fan and bath for P300 and with air-con and bath for P350. Its reputation is fairly good, although there have been complaints about too many cockroaches.

The *Guesthaus* (☎ 1609), 224 Diego Silan St, on the corner of M H del Pilar St, has clean and quite comfortable rooms with fan and bath for P200/250.

The *Macsor Hotel* (☎ 3063) on Rizal Ave Extension has fairly clean, although a little too expensive, rooms with fan and bath for P350 and with air-con and bath for P500/600, and there is a restaurant and a disco. It is on the outskirts, towards the harbour.

The *Alpa Hotel* (☎ 2213), Kumintang Ibana, has rooms with fan for P100/200, with fan and bath for P220/290, with air-con for P260/300 and with air-con and bath from P400 to P600. The rooms are clean and acceptable, although those near the swimming pool can be quite loud (it's the scene of frequent sing-alongs until midnight). There is a restaurant, and it is on the outskirts in the direction of Manila.

Getting There & Away

Always ask for Batangas City when enquiring about transport, otherwise there will be confusion as to where in the Batangas Province you wish to visit.

Several buses leave the BLTB Terminal in Manila daily for Batangas. If you want the harbour in Batangas, look for the buses for Batangas Pier. Not all go through to the pier, in which case you have to get a jeepney down to the dock. The trip takes two hours or more. Beware of pickpockets on these buses – they often operate in teams of three.

If you arrive in Batangas from Mindoro,

you can take one of the Manila buses waiting at the pier and go directly to Manila, or go into town by jeepney and get a bus there – either the regular bus or a BLTB air-con bus to Pasay City/Manila.

If you are going from Manila to Batangas and on towards Puerto Galera, there is a daily combined bus and ship service from the Sundowner Hotel on Mabini St, Ermita, leaving at 9 am.

There is an interesting back-roads route from Batangas to Manila via Lemery which allows for a detour to Lake Taal. Go by jeepney from Batangas to Lemery; the road is dusty and not very good, so the best seat is that next to the driver. Then take a jeepney to San Nicolas on the south-western edge of the lake. The last jeepney back to Lemery leaves at 5 pm, which gives you ample time to catch the last BLTB bus in Lemery for Pasay City/Manila. If instead of Manila you are heading for Santa Cruz or Pagsanjan, then change at Calamba.

To go to Batangas from Pagsanjan quickly, take a jeepney to Santa Cruz; from there, catch a Manila-bound bus as far as Calamba. From Calamba, either take a jeepney directly to Batangas or take a jeepney to Tanauan and then can catch a Batangas-bound bus travelling from Manila.

ANILAO

In Anilao there are various diving centres where you can arrange trips to diving spots in Balayan Bay near Cape Bagalangit and near Sombrero and Maricaban islands. Boat hire for a day trip to Sombrero Island is around P800.

The beach at Anilao is not recommended. You can, however, hire thatched bamboo rafts with tables and chairs for P400 at places like the Anilao Beach Resort. These are anchored some distance out from the beach and are good platforms for swimming and snorkelling.

Places to Stay

Because Anilao is a tourist haunt, accommodation is relatively expensive. The San Jose Lodge on the edge of town has rooms for P150/200. The Anilao Seasport Centre, about two km out of town, has well appointed rooms with fan and bath for P800. You can also arrange full board for P1500 per person. It is pleasant, has a restaurant, and Hobie Cats, windsurfing and diving are offered. You can make reservations in Manila (☎ 8011850; fax 8054660).

The Aqua Tropical Resort has a Manila address: c/o Aqua Tropical Sports (☎ 587908, 5216407; fax 8189720), Manila Midtown Hotel, Pedro Gil, Ermita. It has rooms with fan for P750, with fan and bath for P1100 and with air-con and bath for P1900 and P2500. It is attractive and comfortable and has a restaurant and swimming pool. It also has diving equipment and organises diving trips. It is near Bagalangit, a few km south-west of Anilao. You can also reach it from Anilao by boat.

Getting There & Away

From Batangas, there are several buses and jeepneys daily, although it may be necessary to change at Mabini. The trip takes 1½ hours.

LEMERY

From Lemery you can get to Ligpo Point, eight km to the south, with the small Ligpo Island just offshore. It is a favourite place for divers, even though the underwater setting is fairly ordinary. The beach here is better than the one at Anilao.

Places to Stay

The only possible accommodation seems to be at the Vila Lobos Lodge, which is a simple, rather noisy place with small rooms and a disco. Rooms with fan and bath are P150 and with air-con and bath are P300.

In San Luis the Ligpo Beach Resort has rooms with fan and bath for P450/750, and the Ligpo Island Hotel & Resort has rooms with fan and bath for P500/900. Both have a restaurant and offer diving.

Getting There & Away

Several BLTB buses do the three-hour trip to and from Manila daily. From Batangas several jeepneys run daily. The road is poor and dusty and the trip takes 1½ hours.

SAN NICOLAS

You can cross fairly cheaply from San Nicolas to the volcanic island in Lake Taal. The round trip costs about P500. If you set out very early, you may see a magnificent sunrise. For a few pesos extra the boatman may guide his passengers up to the old crater with the lake inside it. It is easy to get lost on the way down to the lake, so it is advisable to have a guide. On the edge of the old crater a few shepherds live who know the island well and can act as guides.

There are four craters on the island. If you are climbing to the new crater, which last erupted in 1965, you don't need a guide. It doesn't take long and there is no need to stay overnight in San Nicolas.

Boats also go to the island from Subic, a little north of San Nicolas. The road along the lake's edge between Subic and San Nicolas is practically impassable for ordinary vehicles.

Places to Stay

You can ask for a room at the store, where you can sit outside on the corner of the plaza. It is also where you arrange boat trips.

The *Lake View Park & Resort* has basic cottages with bath from P400 to P600.

Getting There & Away

Several jeepneys run daily from Lemery to San Nicolas. The trip takes half an hour. The last jeepney from San Nicolas to Lemery leaves at 5 pm. See also details for getting to and from Batangas earlier in this chapter.

CALAMBA

The national hero Jose Rizal was born in Calamba. Rizal House, with its garden, is now a memorial and museum. It is located across from the Municipal Hall and is open Tuesday to Sunday from 8 am to noon and 1 to 5 pm.

There is a whole row of resorts along the highway in the Los Baños direction, a few km south of Calamba. These resorts take advantage of the local hot springs and are a popular source of relaxation for stressed-out inhabitants of Metro Manila. Almost all of them offer overnight accommodation, although the facilities can be used by non-residents for an admission fee.

Places to Stay

The *Cora Villa* (☎ 5451277), Bagong Kalsaga, has acceptable rooms with fan for P250/350 and with fan and bath for P300/450. This place has a restaurant and a swimming pool in peaceful grounds with a garden. It is located opposite *Crystal Springs* (☎ 5452496), which has singles/doubles with air-con and bath for P950. The rooms are spacious, each with their own private mini-pool, and there is a restaurant. This is a generously laid-out establishment with eight differently sized swimming pools.

Getting There & Away

In Manila, the buses marked 'Santa Cruz' leaving the BLTB Terminal daily frequently go through Calamba. The trip takes an hour.

In Batangas, the buses marked 'Manila' leaving the pier and market daily also frequently go through Calamba. The trip takes about an hour.

Similarly, in Santa Cruz and Pagsanjan, numerous Manila-bound buses go through Calamba daily, taking an hour.

LOS BAÑOS

The University of the Philippines (UP) has a forestry institute with a botanical garden in Los Baños. The garden is not so botanical but it has a big swimming pool. Not far from the UP is the International Rice Research Institute (IRRI). Look for the sign 'UP Los Baños' on the main road.

Los Baños is noted for its hot springs in which you can bathe. Most resorts are outside the town, along the highways as far as Calamba. About two km along the road to Calamba, between the highway and Laguna de Bay, you will find Alligator Lake, a deep crater lake which has none of the reptiles you would expect to find in it.

Not far from Los Baños is the Philippine

Art Center, from where you get a good view over Laguna de Bay. A Special Ride there in a jeepney costs P30. At nearby Mt Makiling there is a nice park with a zoo and pool, and good views. Jeepneys to the Scout Jamboree Park go there. Mt Makiling is a 1144 metre high volcanic massif, the upper slopes of which are covered with jungles with a vast variety of flora.

Places to Stay

The *Los Baños Lodge & Hot Springs* has rooms with fan for P250/430 and with air-con and bath for P550/700, and there is a swimming pool. Take a jeepney in Los Baños towards the City of Springs; the Los Baños Lodge is about 100 metres from the City of Springs Resort.

The *City of Springs Resort Hotel* (☎ 50137; fax 50731) on N Villegas St has attractive rooms with fan and bath for P300 and with air-con and bath from P450 to P970. Some of the rooms have a Roman bath and whirlpool. It has a restaurant and several swimming pools.

The *Lakeview Resort Hotel* (☎ 50101) at 728 Lopez St has comfortable rooms with fan and bath for P450 and with air-con and bath for P550. It is pleasant, with a restaurant and several swimming pools.

Getting There & Away

In Manila, the buses marked 'Santa Cruz' leaving the BLTB Terminal every day frequently go through Los Baños. The trip takes 1½ hours.

From Santa Cruz and Pagsanjan, the numerous buses marked 'Manila' go through Los Baños. The trip takes an hour.

ALAMINOS

Alaminos is known for **Hidden Valley**, a fascinating private property and resort with lush tropical vegetation and several springs. This wonderful natural area is a paradise for botanists and a popular subject for film and photography. It is part of Alaminos but is five km from the town centre. Tricycles firmly demand P100 for the short stretch from Alaminos to the gates. Here visitors are again hit hard. The admission fee gets more expensive by the year and in the meantime costs a whopping P1140 on normal weekdays, and P1425 on Sunday and public holidays. This includes a drink on arrival, buffet lunch, snacks in the afternoon and use of the facilities such as the swimming pool, showers, changing rooms etc.

Places to Stay

Hidden Valley Springs has singles with air-con and bath for P2565 and doubles with air-con and bath for P4700 and P5000, including a breakfast buffet. Cottages are from P5130 and tent accommodation costs P1000 per person. Filipinos pay 30% less. The rooms are pleasant enough, although they would cost quite a bit less in other surroundings. The price for overnight accommodation includes the admission fee for the resort, but does not include the lunch buffet, which will set you back P500. Reservations are made in Manila at the Hidden Valley Spring Office (☎ 509903), United Nations Ave, on the corner of M H del Pilar St, Ermita.

Getting There & Away

Several BLTB, Philtranco and Superlines buses leave Manila daily and go through Alaminos, for example, those marked 'San Pablo', 'Lucena', 'Daet', 'Naga' and 'Legaspi'. The trip takes 1½ hours.

Mt Makiling lies between Los Baños and Alaminos, so the route from Los Baños is a bit roundabout. Go by jeepney from Los Baños to San Pablo, then take either a Manila-bound bus or a Tanauan-bound jeepney to Alaminos. The trip takes an hour.

SAN PABLO

San Pablo is known as the City of the Seven Lakes. It's a good centre for walks. There's one to Sampaloc Lake, which has restaurants standing on piles along the lakeside, and others to Pandin and Yambo lakes. The remaining four lakes are Calibato, Mohicap, Palakpakin and Bunot.

Climbers may like to tackle the nearby **Mt Makiling**, a volcanic mass of 1144 metres with three peaks. This is best reached from Alaminos or Los Baños. However, if you are starting from San Pablo, the best climb is the 2188-metre **Mt Banahaw**. This dormant volcano, with its springs and waterfalls, is credited with mystical powers, and, especially at Easter, many Filipinos come to meditate and pray in the ravines and to drink or bathe in the 'holy water' of the splashing streams. The climb usually begins at Kinabuhayan, which is reached by jeepney from San Pablo. Three days are needed for the climb.

About 10 km south of San Pablo, just before Tiaong, is the **Villa Escudero**, a coconut plantation and resort combined. Admission is P80. In this complex, reminiscent of the Spanish colonial era, it is worth seeing the museum, which has many valuable historical and cultural artefacts.

Places to Stay

The *City Inn Agahan*, 126 Colago Ave, is very simple, with rooms for P50/100.

The *Sampaloc Lake Youth Hostel* (☎ 4448) is in Efarca Village, Schetelig Ave. Here dorm beds cost P90 and singles with fan and bath cost P120. Get there by tricycle from the church or plaza in San Pablo for P2.

The *San Rafael Swimming Pool Resort* has cottages for P300/450, and has two swimming pools.

The *Villa Escudero* (☎ 2379), Tiaong, has comfortable cottages with bath from P700, and there is a restaurant. Reservations can be made in Manila (☎ 593698, 5210830).

Getting There & Away

Several BLTB, Philtranco and Superlines buses leave Manila daily marked 'Lucena', 'Daet', 'Naga' and 'Legaspi'. All of these go through San Pablo. The trip takes two hours.

From Pagsanjan you get to San Pablo in two stages. First take a jeepney from Pagsanjan to Santa Cruz, then catch another jeepney to San Pablo. It takes an hour or more.

Numerous jeepneys run daily from Los Baños to San Pablo. It takes half an hour.

PAGSANJAN

A trip to Pagsanjan (pronounced pag-san-han) is a must on every Philippine tour itinerary. The last section of Francis Ford Coppola's Vietnam War film *Apocalypse Now* was filmed here. The Magdapio Waterfalls are only part of Pagsanjan's attractions; it's the river trip through the picturesque tropical gorge which is the real drawing card.

Two 'banqueros' will paddle you upstream against the strong current in a *banca* (canoe). It's a feat of strength which taxes even two men paddling together. At the last major waterfall you can ride on a bamboo raft for an extra P30. You come downstream at a thrilling speed. Shooting the rapids is most exciting in August and September, when the river is high. Don't hold too tightly to the sides of the boat and keep your hands inside or your fingers may be crushed. Use a plastic bag to keep your camera dry.

All things included, the officially fixed price of this harmless bit of fun is P200 plus P7 admission to the falls. (Up to three people can ride in a banca, so if you go alone, it costs P400.) However, tips may be requested, even demanded vehemently. Readers' letters have told of boat operators making most aggressive demands at times – sums of from P500 to P1000 were mentioned. Anyone who, halfway to the waterfall, is not prepared to promise an extra payment is not, according to most reports, going to enjoy the rest of the trip. So pay up or suffer. You can, of course, skip the trip, save your money and let others be annoyed. The banqueros, who are arranged through the youth hostel, Pagsanjan Falls Lodge and Willy Flores Lodge, apparently will not cause an unpleasant scene if challenged. However, there is no guarantee against unpleasant surprises.

Don't go on weekends, when there are so many tourists that it's like an anthill. If you stay overnight in Pagsanjan and leave for the falls at sunrise, you'll be on the river long before the hordes arrive. As sunlight comes late in the deep valleys, photographers will have difficulty taking pictures with normal equipment in the very early morning.

You get a good view over Pagsanjan and its surroundings from the watertanks on the hill above the school. Steps go up to the school from Mabini St – which runs parallel to Rizal St, the main street – and the path to the hill starts at the school.

Organised day tours from Manila can be arranged for about US$45 at the various travel agencies and the tourist office. This way all costs are covered and you may avoid hassles with banqueros.

The Pagsanjan Town Fiesta is on 12 December.

Places to Stay

A good rule for most places in Pagsanjan is to find your own way there. The place is not too big and guides are not needed, especially since the host is expected to pay them a commission and your room will end up costing more! An overnight stay in nearby Santa Cruz can provide temporary respite from tourist traps.

The *Traveller's Inn* in Santa Cruz has tidy rooms with fan and bath for P150 and P200 and with air-con and bath for P320. The rooms can also be rented for only 12 hours, in which case they cost 30% less.

In Pagsanjan, the basic *Pagsanjan Youth Hostel* (☎ 2124), 237 General Luna St, has dorm beds with fan for P50, singles/doubles for P90/100 and doubles with fan for P125. Go through the city gate to the end of Rizal St, turn right over the river, then right again. The hostel is a fair way down on the left. Look for the sign.

Willy Flores Lodge, 821 Garcia St, has rooms for P60 and with fan for P90/120. It is simple, with a family-style atmosphere, and staff will help to organise boat trips.

La Tour de Pagsanjan Lodging House (☎ 1231), F de San Juan St, has dorm beds for P100, rooms for P120/180 and with fan for P120/200. Two rooms share a bath. There is a motorbike for hire at P350 a day.

Miss Estella y Umale's *Riverside Bungalow* (☎ 2465) at 792 Garcia St has two bungalows with rooms with fan and bath for P220/380 and with air-con and bath for P500/600. It's not far from Willy Flores and Miss Estella is a good cook.

The *Camino Real Hotel* (☎ 2086), 39 Rizal St, has rooms with fan for P300/400, with fan and bath for P350/450, with air-con for P700 and with air-con and bath for P750. It is attractive and comfortable, with large rooms and a restaurant.

The *Pagsanjan Falls Lodge* (☎ 1251) has rooms with fan and bath for P450 and with air-con and bath for P550/700, and there is a restaurant. It is poorly maintained, however, and is a popular pick-up joint for elderly gays looking for young boys, so male guests need to make it clear if they're not interested or they'll be continually pestered. Try to get room No 10, 11 or 12 in the coconut grove as these have verandas looking straight out on to the river. There is also a beautiful pool.

The *Pagsanjan Village Hotel* (☎ 2116), Garcia St, has pleasant singles/doubles with fan for P550, singles/doubles with air-con for P600 and doubles with air-con and bath for P700.

Places to Eat

The *Dura-Fe Restaurant* on General Jaina St has very good food. It closes at 8.30 pm. Also recommended is the *D & C Luncheonette* on National Rd near Pagsanjan Falls Lodge. The small restaurant opposite is good and the staff will cook almost anything for you if you order in advance.

Getting There & Away

Several BLTB buses leave Manila daily for Santa Cruz. This takes two hours. The last few km from Santa Cruz are done by jeepney (P2). Special Rides by tricycle are not necessary, even when the driver tries to persuade the innocent foreigner to the contrary.

There are two shortcuts when travelling from Tagaytay to Pagsanjan which save you going right back to Manila. One involves travelling by bus to Zapote, then by jeepney to Alabang, by bus to Santa Cruz and by jeepney to Pagsanjan. Alternatively, take a bus from Tagaytay to Palapala, then a jeepney through Binan to Calamba, then a bus to Santa Cruz and a jeepney to Pagsanjan.

To get to Pagsanjan from Batangas, it's quickest to get a Manila-bound bus as far as Calamba. There, get a bus coming from Manila to Santa Cruz and go on to Pagsanjan by jeepney.

If you are going to South Luzon from Pagsanjan, there are several Supreme Lines buses running daily from Santa Cruz to Lucena, taking about three hours. If you don't want to wait for a bus, you can go by jeepney from Santa Cruz to Lucban and then get another jeepney to Lucena. All buses from Manila marked 'Daet', 'Naga', 'Legaspi' etc, go through Lucena, so you don't have to go right back to Manila.

AROUND PAGSANJAN

Visits to the following destinations make good day trips from Pagsanjan. **Paete** is the best known Philippine centre for wood carving in ebony. The **Japanese Garden** is a memorial to the Japanese soldiers who died in WW II in and around Pagsanjan. **Caliraya Reservoir** is a massive artificial lake with resorts like Sierra Lakes and Lake Caliraya Country Club featuring water skiing and windsurfing. The village of **Lucban**, halfway along the road to Lucena, is a good example of what villages must have looked like during the era of Spanish rule. Lucban has its harvest festival on 15 May (see the Fiestas & Festivals section in the earlier Facts for the Visitor chapter).

Top: Puraran Beach on Catanduanes (JP)
Bottom: A church built in 'earthquake baroque' style in Paoay, North Luzon (JP)

Top Left: A typical example of colonial church architecture (JP)
Top Right: Pounding rice (JP)
Bottom Left: Approaching the Mayon Volcano's symmetrical cone (TW)
Bottom Right: Ati-Atihan Festival in Kalibo, Panay (JP)

North Luzon

With over 100,000 sq km, Luzon is the largest island in the Philippines. About half of all Filipinos live there. It plays a leading role in the Philippines' economic and cultural affairs and the number of its tourist attractions is second to none. (For central Luzon see the Around Manila chapter.)

Most impressive in North Luzon are the Mountain and Ifugao provinces, with their rice terraces and numerous ethnic minorities, but many travellers are attracted to the Hundred Islands National Park and the beaches on Lingayen Gulf. The cultivated provinces of Ilocos Norte and Ilocos Sur with its old Spanish churches, extensive sand dunes and the historic town of Vigan are less frequently visited.

The West Coast

THE ZAMBALES COAST
The mountainous province of Zambales borders on the South China Sea to the west. Along the coast between San Antonio and Iba there are several beaches, some of which are over several km long, and some of which have places where you can stay the night. You will find beaches that have not been visited much up to now about 80 km north of Iba, on Dasol Bay. One of these is Tambobong White Beach, 15 km outside Dasol. Also remarkable are the extensive salt works north of Santa Cruz.

Pundaquit & San Miguel
After an hour's travel from Olongapo, you get to San Antonio, a pleasant little town with a clean market. At least twice a day a jeepney travels over the five-km trip from the plaza south-west to Pundaquit.

Pundaquit is a small fishing village on an attractive bay with a long beach. Using that as a base, you can explore the bays cutting deeply into the south coast of Zambales with

a boat for about P400 a day. You could also make a day trip from there to **Camera Island** or **Capones Island**. Both islands have white beaches and are rocky, but parts of Capones Island are covered with palms and bushes. There is a lighthouse at the western end of the island which juts out from the sea like a cathedral. Occasionally a few tourists come here to go diving.

From Pundaquit you can walk along the wide beach to San Miguel and beyond, after crossing a fairly shallow river.

Places to Stay
The *San Miguel Hotel* in San Miguel has simple rooms with fan and bath for P140 and with air-con and bath for P240. The *Big Foot Resthouse* in San Miguel has rooms with fan and bath for P150 and with air-con and bath for P280 (with TV P300). It is pleasant and quite a lot better than the San Miguel Hotel. Both places are not on the beach but on the street just north of San Antonio.

The *Capones Beach Resort* (☎ 6327495; fax 6317989) in Pundaquit has clean and comfortable rooms with fan and bath for P450 and with fridge, air-con and bath for P650. It offers a 40% discount from July until October. There is a restaurant, and billiards and diving are available. This is a quiet little place on the beach.

Places to Eat
The *Meathouse Carlsberg Garden Restaurant* in San Miguel serves both Filipino and German dishes. The *San Miguel Restaurant* offers good Filipino cuisine with live music.

In San Antonio you can eat cheaply at the market.

Getting There & Away
Several Victory Liner buses travel daily from Manila to San Antonio via Olongapo and go on to Iba and Santa Cruz. This takes four hours.

There are several Victory Liner buses from Olongapo to San Antonio which go on

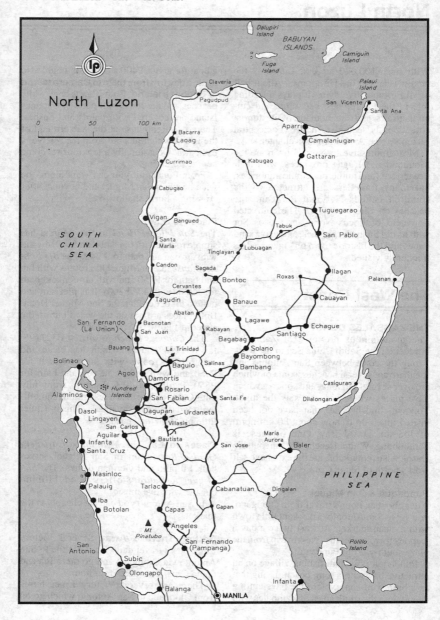

North Luzon

0   50   100 km

to Iba, Santa Cruz and Alaminos. The trip takes 45 minutes.

You can travel between San Antonio and San Miguel by tricycle.

Several Victory Liner buses also travel daily from Alaminos to San Antonio, headed for Olongapo. They take five hours.

Botolan

Until the last eruption of Pinatubo, Botolan was a good base to visit the Negrito of the Zambales Mountains. Former weapon carriers (old lorries) used to leave this little place about seven km south of Iba to go inland to Maguisguis or Villar – maybe they have started doing that again. However, the Ayta-Negrito have lost their ancestral living area, some of them having been evacuated to other islands, like Mindoro.

Places to Stay The *Fil-Aussie Lodge* at Binoclutan is about seven km south of Botolan. It has dorm beds for P75, rooms with fan and bath for P350 and with air-con and bath for P500, but the price is reduced for longer stays. It is nice and tidy and has a restaurant.

Getting There & Away There are several Victory Liner buses from Manila to Botolan daily which travel via Olongapo and continue on to Iba and Santa Cruz. This takes five hours.

Several Victory Liner buses travel daily from Olongapo to Botolan, headed for Iba, Santa Cruz and Alaminos. The trip takes two hours.

There are also several Victory Liner buses travelling daily from Alaminos to Botolan, headed for Olongapo. This takes four hours.

Iba

Iba is the capital of the mountainous Zambales Province, which is bordered on its west flank by the South China Sea. There are several beach resorts a little outside the town but some of these, unfortunately, have gone a bit downhill – except for the prices. Probably the best beach around Iba is the one slightly north of the centre, just behind the

airstrip. The Kalighawan Festival is celebrated here in March of each year with parades, games, beauty contests and agricultural exhibitions.

Places to Stay The *Vicar Beach Resort* (☎ 7114252) has cottages with fan and bath for P350/500. This place is attractively located on a palm-lined, gently curving bay.

The *Sand Valley Beach Resort* (☎ 9111739), about one km north of Iba, has rooms with fan and bath for P280 and with air-con and bath for P770. This place has seen better days.

The *Rama International Beach Resort* is in Bangantalinga, about four km north of Iba, on National Rd. It has rooms with fan and bath for P500/750 and with air-con and bath for P750/1065. It is well kept with a restaurant and offers diving trips.

Getting There & Away From Manila to Iba and Santa Cruz there are several Victory Liner buses daily, going via Olongapo. The trip takes 5½ hours. There are also several Victory Liner buses daily from Olongapo to Iba. The buses to Santa Cruz and Alaminos also go via Iba and take over two hours.

From Alaminos to Iba, you have the choice of several Victory Liner buses travelling daily to Olongapo, taking 3½ hours.

Masinloc

Masinloc is a small place about halfway between Iba and Santa Cruz, however it does offer six discos and beer houses! Offshore there are three small islands. On the island of **San Salvador**, there is a wide beach which is good for snorkelling and diving. You can stay overnight but the accommodation is basic and is without electricity. The crossing costs P10 per person, with special trips for P50.

A transmitting station of the Catholic radio Veritas is on a peninsula near Masinloc. This setup includes a beautiful guesthouse for invited guests only, with a swimming pool and other amenities, such as speedboats for water skiing.

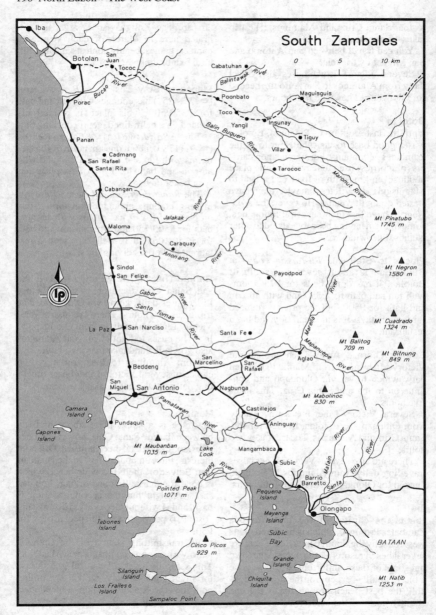

South Zambales

0   5   10 km

Places to Stay The *Little Hamburg* (☎ 9311089) at the southern edge of town has rooms for P100/150, with fan and bath for P200/250 and with air-con and bath for P350/450. There is a restaurant which serves German and Filipino cuisine and there is also a disco. The construction of the cottages at the beach, called *Little Hamburg Seaside*, should be finished by the time of this book's publication.

The *Puerto Asinan Lodge* lies about three km north of Masinloc at Kahawangan. It has rooms with fan for P150 and with fan and bath for P200. There is also a three-bedroom cottage built on stilts over the water for P500. This is a cosy place with a restaurant. You could have transport problems at night but there are tricycles for about P5 in the daytime.

Getting There & Away Victory Liner buses go from Manila to Masinloc several times a day, via Olongapo on to Santa Cruz. The trip takes six hours.

From Olongapo to Masinloc, there are several Victory Liner buses daily going on to Santa Cruz and Alaminos. This trip takes three hours.

There are also several Victory Liner buses daily from Alaminos to Masinloc which go on to Olongapo. The trip takes three hours.

LUCAP & ALAMINOS

A small place, Lucap is the starting point for the **Hundred Islands National Park**. Lots of local tourists come here during Easter week and the hotels could be booked out. There is not much happening here for night owls, as the few restaurants close at 10 pm.

Entertainment in nearby Alaminos is limited to bowling and discos. On Sunday there are cockfights a little outside of town. You can do trips from Alaminos to Agno, Sabangan Beach, with its Umbrella Rocks, or Bani, where there is a subterranean river in the **Nalsoc Caves**. To get there, take a jeepney to Bani, then go on to Tiep and continue by tricycle (for about P30) to Colaya.

Places to Stay
The following prices are valid during the off season. For the high season, which is Easter week and the weekends in April and May, some hotels raise their tariffs by about 50% to 100%.

Most of the accommodation is in Lucap. The *Kilometre One Tourist Lodge* has dorm beds for P85 and singles/doubles with fan for P130/180. It is simple and clean and has a restaurant. It also serves as a youth hostel. *Gloria's Cottages* have clean and spacious rooms with fan and bath for P150. The *Hundred Islands View Lodge* (☎ 5527203) has rooms with fan and bath for P350 and with air-con and bath for P450, and it has a restaurant.

Maxine by the Sea has rooms with fan for P250, with fan and bath from P395 and with air-con and bath for P495. It is pleasant and comfortable, and has a restaurant and a beautiful terrace. The *Last Resort* has rooms with fan and bath for P350 and with air-con and bath for P450. It is fairly pleasant and has a restaurant and boating facilities. You can make reservations in Manila (☎ 5214073).

The *Ocean View Lodge* has rooms with fan for P150, with fan and bath for P200 and with air-con and bath for P450/550. It is well kept and has a restaurant. You can make reservations in Manila (☎ 7324668).

The *Paradise Island Resort* has rooms with fan and bath for P400. The place is clean and has a family-style atmosphere. It has a restaurant, and offers diving and boat trips to Hundred Islands National Park. You can see the resort from Lucap in the south of Cabarruyan Island (Anda Island). The boat trip over there takes about 15 minutes and costs P100; the Rosing Store in Lucap will make the arrangements for you.

The *Alaminos Hotel* (☎ 5527241) on Quezon Ave, Alaminos, has singles with fan for P100, doubles with fan and bath for P150 and with air-con and bath for P400. This place is clean and pleasant and also has a restaurant.

Places to Eat

You can eat cheaply in Lucap at the small *Canteens* by the wharf. Some lodges have restaurants, such as the *Ocean View Restaurant*, which also offer quite inexpensive and good meals. Apart from *The Last Resort Restaurant*, restaurants close quite early on most days, sometimes even by 8 pm.

At Alaminos, the *Plaza Restaurant* is worth a visit; sometimes there are folk singers. You could also try the *Imperial Restaurant*.

Getting There & Away

Tricycles make the trip between Alaminos and Lucap costing from P20 to P25, regardless of whether you are on your own or are a party of up to four people.

Dagupan Bus and Pantranco North buses go hourly every day from Manila to Alaminos, and take five hours. You may have to change at Lingayen. These buses go via Dau/Angeles, where you can also board them. It is also possible to take a bus from Manila to Dagupan and change there. The advantages are frequent departures and air-conditioning.

Several Victory Liner buses travel daily between Olongapo and Alaminos, and take five hours.

A few Pantranco North buses travel daily from Baguio to Alaminos. The last bus leaves at about 11.20 am. The trip takes four hours and you may have to change at Dagupan.

To travel from Banaue to Alaminos you will have to take the first Baguio bus early in the morning then get off at Rosario and board a Dagupan, Lingayen or Alaminos bus coming from Baguio.

HUNDRED ISLANDS

The Hundred Islands aren't palm-fringed dream islands, but coral formations of varying sizes with scrub and occasionally small, white beaches. They are of limited appeal for snorkelling as the water isn't always crystal clear, often obscuring the reputedly colourful underwater world, which has also been damaged by the long-standing use of dynamite for fishing.

Places to Stay & Eat

Take adequate food supplies with you if you want to spend a night or several days on an island. The cheapest place for food is the market at Alaminos and you should be able to get a can of water from the hotel at Lucap. The fee for putting up your own tent is P10 a day on Quezon, Governor's and Children's islands. You can rent a so-called pavilion on Quezon Island for P200 or a two-roomed cottage for six people on Governor's Island for P600. On Children's Island there are tents of various sizes for between P50 and P150. Water is provided and there are toilets and fireplaces.

Getting There & Away

To get to Hundred Islands National Park you first have to go to Alaminos. There is a direct connection to Alaminos from Manila. You can also go via Olongapo and along the Zambales coast (see the Around Manila chapter).

The fare from Lucap to the Hundred Islands National Park by outrigger boat, which can take up to six persons, has been fixed officially at P250 plus P5 entry fee per person. It is wise to agree upon the duration of the trip or the driver might return after only 30 minutes. You can also go on an island round trip which will cost you between P100 and P200, depending on the duration and extent of the trip. This makes it possible to choose your 'own' island and be dropped off there, but don't forget to fix a time to be picked up for the return trip. Four or five hours of island life will probably be quite enough, especially when there is no shade. Most day trippers go to Quezon Island, particularly on weekends. You can get drinks at the kiosk there.

BOLINAO

Bolinao is a little town which hasn't yet been overrun by tourists. Unfortunately, there are no acceptable beaches in the area, so you have to drive a few km to get to them. For a bit of variety, you could arrange to cross to one of the offshore islands. Take your own snorkelling equipment as it is next to impossible to find even a pair of goggles in Bolinao.

The **Bolinao Museum** on the outskirts of town has a collection of Philippine flora and fauna which is worth a look, but, because of the lack of money, it has only a few historical items. In the town centre is the church, which dates back to 1609. It used to double as a fortress during attacks by pirates and by the English, Japanese and Americans. If you can catch the priest when he is not too busy, he might tell you more about those times.

Places to Stay

The *A & E Garden Inn* in the centre of town, next to the Pantranco Bus Terminal, has rooms with fan for P80/150, with fan and bath for P150/200 and with air-con and bath for P300/350. A tree house with bath costs P200. The inn is simple but reasonable and has a good restaurant (a tree-house dining room). It's next to the Pangasinan Five Star bus terminal.

The *Celeste Seabreeze Resort* by the sea has rooms with fan and bath for P200/250 and with air-con for P375. It is simple but comfortable and has a restaurant which specialises in seafood. You can hire outrigger sailing boats there.

The *Cascante Beach Resort* is just outside the town centre on the sea and has recently changed owners. After being thoroughly renovated, it is due to reopen soon under a new name with Philippine-Italian management.

Getting There & Away

Several jeepneys and minibuses leave the market at Alaminos for Bolinao daily. You can also catch a Pantranco North bus, which takes one hour. The last jeepney from Bolinao to Alaminos leaves at about 5 pm.

An outrigger boat leaves Bauang for Bolinao daily at 4 am. The trip takes two hours and costs P100. Information can be obtained from the Gatchalian family at the entrance to the China Sea Resort. The departure from Bolinao is at 9 am. A Special Ride costs around P500.

Dagupan Bus, Pangasinan Five Star and Pantranco North buses run several times daily from Manila to Bolinao. The trip takes six hours and you may have to change at Lingayen or Alaminos.

LINGAYEN

Lingayen is the capital of Pangasinan Province, which dates back to about 1611. Lingayen Beach is outside the town. As on other well-known beaches at the southern end of the Lingayen Gulf, none of them particularly impressive, you will find many Filipinos from polluted Manila in search of recreation.

Places to Stay

The *Viscount Hotel* (☎ 137) on Maramba Blvd has rooms with fan and bath for P200 and with air-con and bath for P350. It is clean and has a restaurant.

The Lion's Den Resort (☎ 198) on Lingayen Beach has rooms with fan and bath for P350. It has a restaurant, but if you want to buy fresh fish and vegetables in the nearby market, where you can go by tricycle for P2, the hotel restaurant staff will prepare them for you for about P20. *Letty & Betty Cottages*, also on Lingayen Beach, has rooms or cottages for P200/300.

Getting There & Away

Pantranco North and Dagupan Bus run many buses daily from Manila to Lingayen. The trip takes over four hours and goes via Dau/Angeles, where you can also board the bus. You can also board buses bound for Alaminos or Dagupan, which usually pass through Lingayen.

DAGUPAN

Dagupan was founded and named by Augustinian monks in 1590 and became an important trading and educational centre, eclipsing the provincial capital, Lingayen. Only three km away in Bonuan is Blue Beach; the trip there by jeepney costs P3.

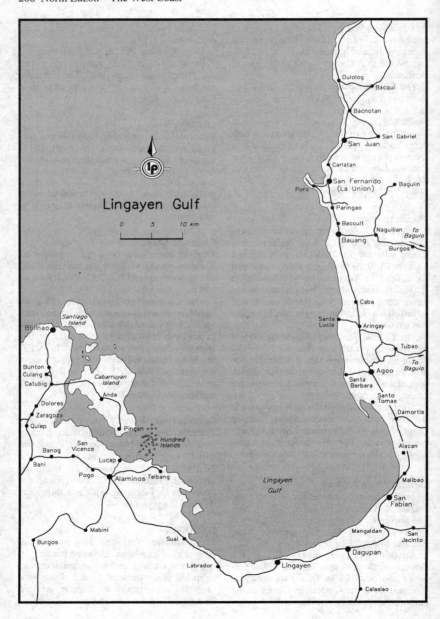

Information

The Interbank on A B Fernandez Ave will change your American Express travellers' cheques.

Places to Stay

The *Vicar Hotel* (☎ 2616) on A B Fernandez Ave has rooms with fan for P100/150, with fan and bath for P180/240 and with air-con and bath for P320, and it has a restaurant. The *Hotel Mil Exel* (☎ 4463) also on A B Fernandez Ave has rooms with fan and bath for P270 and with air-con and bath for P360. This place is simple and comfortable, and has a restaurant.

The *Hotel Boulevard* on Arellano St has clean and pleasantly furnished rooms with fan and bath for P200/250 and with air-con and bath for P450. It also has a restaurant.

The *Victoria Hotel* (☎ 2081) on A B Fernandez Ave has rooms with fan and bath for P280/325 and with air-con and bath from P345/395, and there is a restaurant.

The *Tondaligan Fiesta Cottages* (☎ 2593, 2595) in Bonuan has rooms with air-con and bath for P540/720. It is on Blue Beach, about three km outside Dagupan, and has a seafood restaurant.

Places to Eat

The *Dagupena Restaurant* on A B Fernandez Ave (near the Vicar Hotel) has a large selection of tasty food.

Getting There & Away

From Manila to Dagupan, many Pantranco North, Dagupan Bus, Pangasinan Five Star and Victory Liner buses travel daily via Dau/Angeles, where you can also board them. The trip takes five hours.

From Bolinao to Dagupan, there are many Dagupan Bus buses a day. They take two hours and go via Alaminos, where you can also board them.

Minibuses leave Alaminos for Dagupan practically every hour. The trip takes one hour.

From Baguio to Dagupan there are a few Pantranco North buses daily. The last bus goes at about 11.20 am and the trip takes 2½ hours.

SAN FABIAN

San Fabian is a friendly little place, lying a few km north-east of Dagupan. Slightly outside the town, from Nibaliw West to Bolasi, stretches **White Beach**, although the old name of Center Beach was more accurate. Like almost all beaches in the Lingayen Gulf, the sand is not dazzling white but brownish-grey. There are a few more resorts four or five km north-east of San Fabian, on the beach at Bolasi and Alacan, which have not been developed much for tourism yet.

Places to Stay

Nibaliw West The *Holiday Village & Beach Resort* has rooms with fan for P120/180, double rooms with air-con and bath for P350 and cottages with fan and bath for P250. Monthly rates also apply. It is not very clean, but there is a restaurant. The *Center Beach Resort* has cottages with fan and bath for P350. This place, which also has a restaurant, is now rather run down.

The *Lazy 'A' Resort* (☎ 4726) has rooms with air-con and bath from P700 to P1650 and cottages with fan and bath from P600 to P2800. The more expensive cottages have two bedrooms and cooking facilities. It has a restaurant and a swimming pool. The *Sierra Vista Beach Resort* (☎ 7668; fax 7532) is a nice little hotel with pleasantly furnished rooms with air-con and bath for P1120/1900. There is a restaurant and a swimming pool, and windsurfing and diving are available.

Alacan & Bolasi The *Windsurf Beach Resort* (☎ & fax 3055101) in Alacan has spacious cottages with fan and bath for P430. There is a restaurant with European and Filipino cuisine. The manager, Frederic, is Swiss.

The *San Fabian Resort* in Bolasi has clean and quite comfortable rooms with air-con for P500/550 and with air-con and bath for P650/700; including breakfast. There is a restaurant and a swimming pool.

The *San Fabian Presidential Resthouse* (☎ 2052) in Bolasi has dorm beds with fan for P185, tastefully furnished rooms with air-con and bath from P530 to P900 and a suite for P2350, and there is a restaurant. The late president Marcos used to stay here when he was travelling through northern Luzon.

Getting There & Away
A few Pantranco North buses go south from Baguio to San Fabian daily. Take any headed for Dagupan or Alaminos. The last bus leaves at about 11.20 am and takes two hours.

From San Fernando (La Union) to San Fabian there are many minibuses daily, going on to Dagupan. The trip takes two hours.

From Dagupan to San Fabian there are also many buses daily. Take either a minibus going to San Fernando or one of a few Pantranco North buses going to Baguio. It will take 30 minutes. Some of these buses may be coming from Lingayen or Alaminos.

The best way to get from Manila and Angeles to San Fabian is to take a bus heading for San Fernando, Vigan or Laoag. Get out at Damortis and cover the remaining 15 km south to San Fabian via Alacan and Bolasi by minibus (see the Getting There & Away section under San Fernando later in this chapter).

It is also possible to travel from Manila and Angeles via Dagupan.

ARINGAY & AGOO
Agoo and Aringay lie between San Fabian and Bauang. In Aringay, the small **Don Lorenzo Museum** is opposite the old church.

Worth seeing in Agoo is the **basilica**, which was rebuilt in 1892 after a severe earthquake. It has a Shrine of Our Lady and is the most important place of pilgrimage of La Union Province during Holy Week. The climax of the Semana Santa (Holy Week) activities is the procession on Good Friday.

Next to the Agoo Municipal Hall is the **Museo Iloko**. This is a small museum with liturgical objects, antique furniture and

china. Next door, in **Imelda Park**, visitors can pass the time in a beautiful tree house. On the northern outskirts of Agoo is a large stone statue of an eagle, marking the start of the Marcos Highway, which leads to Baguio. On the way there, near Pugo, is the former **Marcos Park** with golf course, swimming pool, hostel and cottages. Towering over it all is a huge bust of Marcos which has been partly carved into the rock.

Several hundred thousand Filipinos congregated on **Apparition Hill** near Agoo at the beginning of March 1993, to witness the appearance of the Blessed Virgin Mother which had been prophesied. The miracle didn't happen, bet even serious newspapers reported that the air there had been filled with a miraculous fragrance and that thousands of pilgrims had seen the sun dancing.

Places to Stay
The *Agoo Playa Resort* has rooms with air-con and bath from P1200/1500. It is attractive, comfortable and beautifully laid out. There is a restaurant and a swimming pool.

Getting There & Away
There are numerous Philippine Rabbit, Times Transit, Farinas Trans and Maria de Leon buses from San Fernando to Agoo, all going to Manila. The trip takes one hour.

From Manila, take any bus heading for San Fernando, Vigan or Laoag; the trip takes five hours.

BAUANG
Bauang has developed into the most popular beach resort in North Luzon. The places to stay mentioned here are only a small cross section, as there are many others. Nearly all of them are on the long, grey beach between Baccuit and Paringao, a little to the north of Bauang proper and about five km south of San Fernando. You can't see much from the road except a few signposts. If you are arriving by bus or jeepney, it is best to warn the driver or conductor that you want to be dropped off at the hotel of your choice. If it is booked out, walk along the beach and you

will find plenty of alternative accommodation.

The small White Beach near Poro Point, offers snorkelling and is a good alternative to the beach at Bauang.

In **Naguilian**, 10 km east of Bauang, *basi* (an alcoholic drink made from fermented sugar-cane juice) is manufactured, which is reputed to be the best in the country and is especially popular with Ilokanos. The sweet variant of basi tastes a bit like sherry or port.

Information

Swagman Travel (☎ 415512) on the National Highway will take care of the reservation and confirmation of inland and international flights and visa extensions. They are agents for a few different resorts.

Places to Stay

The following prices apply during the high season from December to May. They are about 25% cheaper in the off season from June to November, so it is worth haggling a bit.

The *Lourdes Beach Homes* at Baccuit have rooms with fan and bath for P200. These are large cottages which have, unfortunately, seen better days.

There are plain but cosy rooms with fan and bath for P350/400 at *Leo Mar Beach Resort* at Baccuit. It also has a restaurant.

The *Jac Corpuz Cottages*, also at Baccuit, has rooms with bath for P200 to P300. They are basic cottages between the resorts of Lourdes and Leo Mar. At this southern end of the beach, you will also find the pleasant *Hide Away Beach Resort*, a large house with rooms with fan and bath from P280 to P600. It has a restaurant and Hobie Cats are available.

The *Sunset Palms Beach Resort* (☎ 413708) at Paringao has rooms with fan and bath for P250/350. It has a restaurant and offers favourable monthly rates.

The *Mark Teresa Apartel* (☎ 3022) on the highway at Paringao has apartments with two bedrooms for P350. It has favourable monthly rates (P2700, including electricity) but is often booked out.

The *Umay Kay Homes* at Pagdalagan Norte has rooms with fan and bath for P500 and with a kitchen for P750. Monthly rates are possible. The rooms are spacious, comfortable, and tastefully furnished. This is a pleasant establishment, built in a mediterranean style, but unfortunately situated in a residential area near the beach.

The *Cesmin Beach Cottages* (☎ 412884) at Pagdalagan Sur has cottages with a fridge, cooking facilities, air-con and bath from P600 to P800. The monthly rates are favourable. The *Southern Palms Beach Resort* (☎ 415384; fax 415448) also at Pagdalagan Sur has comfortable rooms with TV, air-con and bath from P550 to P995. It has a restaurant, nightclub and a swimming pool.

The *Fisherman's Wharf Beach Club* (☎ 415384; fax 415448) at Paringao Sur has rooms with TV, fridge, air-con and bath for P650 and P750. The rooms, which are in attractive stone-built bungalows, are pleasant and spacious, and there is a restaurant and a night club.

The *China Sea Beach Resort* (☎ 414821; fax 413708) at Paringao has rooms with fan and bath for P650 and with air-con and bath for P750. It is pleasant and has a restaurant and a swimming pool. The *Coconut Grove Resort* (☎ 414276; fax 415381) at Paringao has comfortable and spacious rooms with air-con and bath from P850 to P1200. This is a sophisticated establishment with a large outdoor lawn bowl complex. There is also a restaurant and a swimming pool.

The *Bali Hai Resort* (☎ 412504; fax 414496) at Paringao has rooms with fan and bath for P790 and with air-con and bath for P890. It is attractive and comfortable, and has nice duplex cottages. Monthly rates can be arranged. It has a restaurant and a swimming pool, and offers windsurfing and Hobie Cats. The *Cabana Beach Resort* (☎ 412824; fax 414496) at Paringao has rooms with air-con and bath for P850. It has a restaurant and beautiful swimming pool with a bar, and you can also go windsurfing or take a course in diving.

The *Villa Estrella Beach Resort* (☎ 413794; fax 413793) at Paringao has comfortable rooms with TV, air-con and bath for P1400. This is a well-looked after hotel, built in the Spanish colonial style. There is a restaurant, and windsurfing and Hobie Cats are available.

The *Cresta del Mar* (☎ 413197; fax 414496) at Paringao has rooms with air-con and bath from P1800. This large, attractive place is well looked after. It has a restaurant and a swimming pool.

Places to Eat
Try one of the resort restaurants along the beach for a change, though their prices are slightly higher than most places. The cuisine at the *Villa Estrella* is good, as it is at the *Fisherman's Wharf* and *Bali Hai*. Also worth trying is the Mongolian barbecue at the *Cabana* on Saturday night.

The *Ihaw-Ihaw Restaurant*, next to the Sir William Disco on the National Highway, serves barbecued food.

Entertainment
Although it was true until recently that the only entertainment available at Bauang was billiards, videos and a few resort restaurants, there is now some sign of nightlife at the *Captain's Club* at Fisherman's Wharf and *Stiletto's* at Southern Palms. More than likely, other resorts will follow their example soon. Not far from these two resorts, right on the National Highway, the clubs *Genesis* and *Fire Cat* are already open for business in the afternoon. The *Bayside Disco*, which looks like it could do with some redecorating soon, next to the Leo-Mar Beach Resort, has showtime at 11 pm. At the *Tradewinds Disco Club* at the Villa Estrella Beach Resort the nightly show begins one hour earlier, at 10 pm. There are more discos and a few bars in Poro Point junction near San Fernando. You can get there by tricycle from Bauang Beach for P30.

Getting There & Away
Air PAL flies at irregular intervals from Manila to San Fernando and back. They usually fly when the highway is blocked because of typhoon damage or suchlike, or

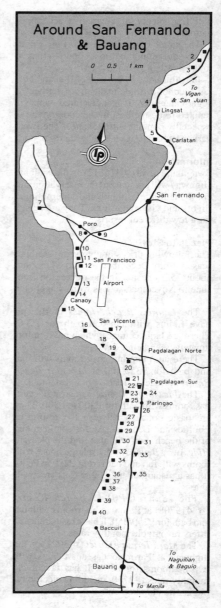

Around San Fernando & Bauang

■ PLACES TO STAY

1	Hacienda Beach Resort		Sunset Palms Beach Resort
2	Surf Camp &	31	Mark Teresa Apartel
	Mona Liza Cottages	32	Long Beach Hotel &
3	Williams Residence Beach Resort		North Palm Beach Resort
4	Shalom Beach Cottages	34	Nalinac Beach Resort
5	Oceana Apartments	37	Jac Corpuz Cottages,
6	Golden Heaven Beach Resort		Leo-Mar Beach Resort &
7	Miramonte Beach Resort		Leo-Mar R & L Cottages
10	Driftwood Resort &	38	Lourdes Beach Homes
	Shipside Housing Area	39	Bauang Beach Resort &
11	Acapulco Beach Resort		Mendoza Beach Resort
12	Ocean Deep	40	Hide Away Beach Resort
13	Blue Lagoon Resort		
14	Sunset Bay Swiss Beach Resort	▼	PLACES TO EAT
15	Coral Point Beach Resort		
16	Lorenza Beach House	18	Patio del Sol Restaurant
17	Meridian Beach Cottages	33	Jasmin Restaurant
19	California Resort	34	Cogon Hut Restaurant
20	Umay Kay Homes	35	Ihaw-Ihaw Restaurant
21	Southern Palms Beach Resort		
23	Cesmin Beach Cottages &		OTHER
	Fisherman's Wharf Beach Resort		
25	Bali Hai Beach Resort,	8	Nightclub District
	Sea Breeze &	9	Mascotte Disco
	South Pacific Resort	21	Stiletto's Nightclub
27	Cabana Beach Resort	22	Fire Cat Club &
28	China Sea Beach Resort &		Genesis Club
	Coconut Grove Resort	24	Swagman Travel Office
29	Villa Estrella Beach Resort	26	Half Moon Bar
30	Cresta del Mar Hotel &	35	Sir William Disco
		36	Bayside Disco

the flight connection between Manila and Baguio has been temporarily discontinued. The airport is between San Fernando and Bauang.

Bus There are plenty of Philippine Rabbit, Times Transit, Farinas Trans and Maria de Leon buses travelling between Manila and Bauang. Take any going to San Fernando, Vigan and Laoag. The trip takes 5½ hours. These buses go via Dau/Angeles and you can board them there.

The best way to catch a bus on the highway from Bauang to Manila is to stop every bus until you get one that suits you. At Christmas time, when a lot of buses are full, the best idea is to take a jeepney to the bus companies' terminals in San Fernando and try to get a decent seat there.

To go from Baguio to Bauang you have a choice of several Philippine Rabbit and Marcitas Liner buses bound for San Fernando. The trip takes 1½ hour. The trip along the winding Naguilian Rd down to the coast is especially attractive in the late afternoon. For the best view, sit on the same side as the driver. You can also go by jeepney, which is a bit faster than the bus.

There are many jeepneys daily from San Fernando to Bauang. You can get off on the highway near the beach resorts. The jeepneys take 30 minutes.

From Laoag and Vigan there are several Philippine Rabbit, Times Transit, Farinas Trans and Maria de Leon buses daily, all going to Manila. The trip to Bauang takes five hours from Laoag and three hours from Vigan.

Boat An outrigger boat leaves Bolinao for Bauang daily at 9 am. The trip takes two hours and costs P100. Information can be obtained at the TV-repair shop The Islander, Arosan St, Bolinao. Departure from Bauang is at 4 am. A Special Ride costs around P500.

SAN FERNANDO (LA UNION)

Also called the city of the seven hills, San Fernando is the capital of La Union Province. There is a beautiful view over the South China Sea from **Freedom Park**, also known as Heroes' Hill. You can also get good views from the Bayview Hotel on the Gapuz Zigzag Rd, near the Provincial Capitol Building. The **Museo de La Union**, next to the Provincial Capitol Building, gives a cultural overview of the province. It's closed on weekends. The **Fil-Chinese Pagoda** and the **Ma-Cho Temple**, which is at the northern edge of town, bear witness to the Chinese influence in San Fernando. From 12 to 16 September, the Chinese-Filipino religious community holds an annual celebration of the Virgin of Caysasay at the Ma-Cho Temple.

About three km south-west of San Fernando, on the bay south of Poro, there is a beach with a reasonable stretch around about the Acapulco Beach Resort. The rest of the beach is fairly stony and not really suitable for swimming. Most of the hotels are isolated and not well situated for getting anywhere, apart from the airport.

Information

The tourist office is in the Matanang Hall on General Luna St in the town plaza.

The rate of exchange at the Central Bank (☎ 412631-35) is sometimes better than at

■ PLACES TO STAY		OTHER	
1	Sea & Sky Hotel	2	Ma-Cho Temple
16	Fel Flor Lodge	3	Partas Bus Terminal
17	Casa Blanca Hotel	6	Fiesta Supermart
18	Mandarin House Hotel	9	New Market
32	Plaza Hotel	10	Market
34	Bayview Hotel	12	Mercury Drug Store
		19	Police Station
▼ PLACES TO EAT		20	La Union Trade Center
		21	Town Hall
4	Cindy's	22	Buses to Baguio &
5	Town & Country Hut Restaurant		Marcites Liner Bus Terminal
7	New United Food Palace	23	Philippine National Bank (PNB)
8	New Society Restaurant	24	Post Office
11	Midtown Food Palace	25	Christ the King College
12	Crown Food Center	26	Town Plaza
13	Mr Donut & Mac Machine	27	PAL
14	The Danish Baker	28	PCI Bank
15	Nuval's Carinderia	29	St William Cathedral
18	Mandarin Restaurant	33	Tourist Office
30	Café Esperanza	35	Fil-Chinese Pagoda
31	Bamboo Grill Restaurant	36	Bethany Hospital
		37	Museo de La Union &
			Provincial Capitol Building
		38	Freedom Park (Heroes Hill)
		39	Bank of the Philippine Islands
		40	Central Bank
		41	Times Transit Bus Terminal

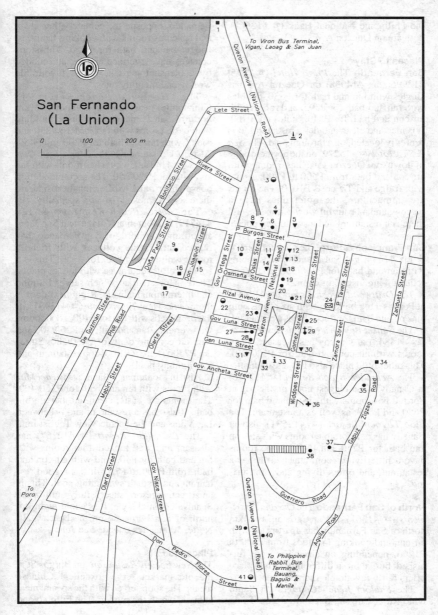

San Fernando
(La Union)

0   100   200 m

the Philippine National Bank (☎ 412561), both are on Quezon Ave.

Places to Stay

San Fernando The *Plaza Hotel* (☎ 2515, 412996; fax 414938) on Quezon Ave has singles with fan and bath for P330, doubles with fan and bath for P395, and rooms with air-con and bath for P540. Suites are P760. It is nice and clean and has a restaurant. It is centrally located, on a through road. The *Sea & Sky Hotel* (☎ 415279) on the northern edge of town on Quezon Ave has rooms with air-con and bath from P500 to P700; a suite with fridge and TV costs P1000. The rooms are immaculate, the quiet ones have a balcony and a beautiful view of the sea, and there is a restaurant and a swimming pool.

San Francisco & Poro The *Ocean Deep* (☎ & fax 414440) at San Francisco has rooms with fan and bath for P200/300, and offers scuba diving instructor courses.

The *Driftwood Beach Resort* (☎ 413411) at Poro is a big building with six rooms with air-con and bath for P600. It has a restaurant.

The *Sunset Bay Swiss Beach Resort* (☎ & fax 414843) at Canaoy has pleasant, clean rooms with air-con and bath for P550/650. This quiet little place also has a restaurant.

The *Acapulco Beach Resort* (☎ 412696) at Canaoy is the biggest hotel on the bay at Poro. It has rooms with air-con and bath for P650 and P800, as well as a restaurant. The *Blue Lagoon Resort* (☎ 412531) also at Canaoy has comfortable rooms with air-con and bath for P750 and P850. Some rooms have a little living room attached. It has a restaurant, and offers diving and windsurfing.

North of San Fernando The *Oceana Apartments* (☎ 413611-13) at Carlatan, two km north of San Fernando, has apartments with air-con and cooking facilities from P600 to P1200, depending on size. They are furnished but a bit indifferently. This place offers fairly favourable monthly rates.

The *Shalom Beach Cottages* on Santo Niño Rd at Lingsat, three km north of San Fernando, opposite the cemetery, has clean and spacious rooms with cooking facilities, fridge, fan and bath for P350. The stone cottages have a terrace and are surrounded by a pleasant garden. It has favourable weekly and monthly rates.

The *Hacienda Beach Resort* in Urbiztondo, near San Juan, about five km north of San Fernando, is a rustic building with basic rooms with fan for P160/230 and rooms with fan and bath for P300 and P450. Also in Urbiztondo is the *Mona Liza Cottages* (☎ 414892), which has rooms with fan and bath for P220/250. The accommodation doesn't have much to offer, but the restaurant there serves smoked fish as a speciality.

The *Sunset Beach Resort* (☎ & fax 414719) in Montemar Village near San Juan, about nine km north of San Fernando, has rugged little stone cottages with friendly rooms with fan and bath for P350. This is a small, well-tended place with lots of plants. There is a restaurant which serves Filipino and international cuisine. Right next door is the *Scenic View Tourist Inn* (☎ 413901). It has dorm beds with fan for P100, good rooms with veranda, fan and bath for P250/300 and with air-con and bath for P450/500. Suites are P750. There is a roof-top restaurant and a swimming pool.

Also in Montemar Village is *Casa del Mar* with rooms with fan and bath for P350/400. The rooms are basic, clean and have a big bath. It also has a restaurant and is between Las Villas and the Scenic View Tourist Inn.

The *Las Villas Resort* (☎ 412267) has pleasant and well-looked after rooms with fan and bath for P400 and with air-con and bath from P500 to P700. It has a good restaurant and a small swimming pool. This is an attractive resort, successfully built in the Spanish colonial style. It is about eight km north of San Fernando on the beach at Ili Norte, 500 metres outside San Juan.

Places to Eat

The *New Society Restaurant* on Burgos St at the old market serves excellent Chinese meals. The soup served with the special meal alone is worth the money. The Filipino and

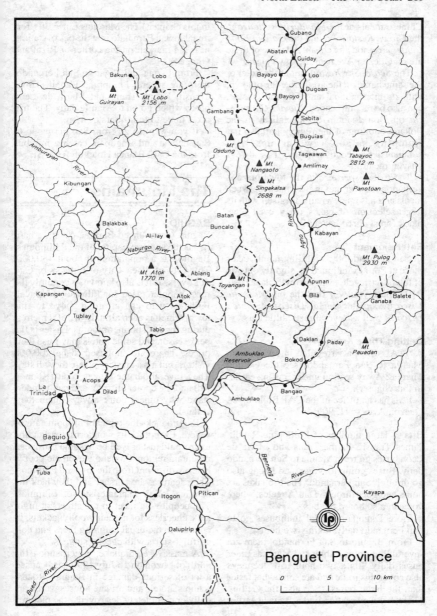

Benguet Province

0   5   10 km

Chinese meals at the *Mandarin Restaurant*, the *Crown Restaurant* and the *Garden Food Center* are good and cheap. All three of these are on Quezon Ave near the town plaza.

The *Sea & Sky Restaurant* at the hotel of the same name on the northern edge of town, with its international and Filipino cuisine, can also be recommended. *Nuval's Caranderia* on Don Joaquin St specialises in the Ilokano cooking of the region and also has 'jumping salad', raw shrimps with kalamansi poured over them. It is always busy at mealtimes.

The *Café Esperanza* in the town plaza is very popular for having a snack between meals and has made a name for itself with its large selection of cakes (they even have black forest cherry gateau!).

Entertainment

In San Fernando, the nightlife mainly takes place at Poro Point junction, slightly outside of town. A tricycle from the town plaza costs P10. There you will find the big *Mascotte Disco*, the smaller *Mama's Disco* and *Annie's Disco* as well as several rustic little bars.

Getting There & Away

Air PAL flies at irregular intervals from Manila to San Fernando (see the Getting There & Away section under Bauang earlier in this chapter).

PAL has an office in the CAP Building on Quezon Ave (☎ 412909).

Bus A large number of Philippine Rabbit, Times Transit, Farina Trans and Maria de Leon buses go from Manila to San Fernando daily. Buses going to Vigan and Laoag also go through San Fernando. The trip takes six hours and goes through Dau/Angeles, where you can also board the bus.

From Dagupan several minibuses go to San Fernando daily, taking two hours.

From Baguio to San Fernando, there are several Philippine Rabbit and Marcitas Liner buses daily. It's a two-hour trip. Jeepneys also cover this route and are somewhat faster than the large buses. (See also the Getting There & Away section under Bauang earlier

in this chapter.) The Marcitas Liner Bus Terminal in San Fernando is at the petrol station, near the market, on the corner of Rizal and Ortega Sts.

From Laoag and Vigan to San Fernando, there are several Philippine Rabbit, Times Transit, Farina Trans and Maria de Leon buses which go on to Manila daily. The trip takes three to four hours or more.

If you want to go from San Fernando to San Fabian and Dagupan, catch a minibus from the Casa Blanca Hotel on Rizal St.

The Mountains

BAGUIO

Baguio (pronounced Barg-ee-o with a hard 'g') is the summer capital of the Philippines. Baguio has a population of about 180,000. This City of Pines, City of Flowers or City of Lovers, as it is also known, is certainly the most popular place for Filipinos to travel. Filipinos who can afford it move to this town, which is at an altitude of 1500 metres, during the hot summer months. Easter is the peak season and some hotels may raise their prices. There are supposed to be 200,000 visitors, but it's a mystery where they all stay. They rave about the zigzag road (Kennon Rd) and the cooler climate, and can't understand why others don't always share their enthusiasm.

Baguio lacks the typical Philippine atmosphere. Except for its wonderful market, the town could just as well be in some European mountain region. Somehow even the people here are different from the lowland Filipinos. Their features are harsher and they lack the carefree jollity characteristic of Filipinos. The people you meet in the streets at night are a cheerless lot in their woolly jackets, in contrast to the usual laughing faces and colourful T-shirts with cheeky slogans.

A massive earthquake, which shook the north of Luzon on 16 July 1990, also caused a lot of serious damage in Baguio. Roads, schools, hotels and private houses were partially or completely destroyed – the pictures went around the world. Since then most places have either been repaired or demolished and rebuilt, so that visitors will hardly notice any of the damage caused by this natural catastrophe.

Warning Keep in mind that Baguio is a favourite hunting ground of various tricksters who will claim acquaintance with you at the airport or immigration office for ulterior motives. Others may pretend that their sister is working in the same country you come from and invite you for a drink (to drug and rob you). Stay clear of them.

Information
The tourist office (☎ 6708) is on Governor Pack Rd. It is open daily from 8 am to noon and 1 to 5 pm.

An American Express office can be found at 28 Governor Pack Rd, next to the Baden Powell Inn.

City Market
The things on sale here are mostly local products made or grown in Benguet Province, which is the area around Baguio. You will find basket ware, textiles, silver jewellery and woodcarvings as well as vegetables, fruit, honey and so on. Look out for the strawberries and the sweet, heavy strawberry wine. In the meat section, the grinning dog heads are no longer sold. After strong international criticism, this highland delicacy was forbidden by the government, so dog meat is no longer prominently displayed at markets where Westerners go. The traditional arts & crafts of the mountain dwellers are sold in the adjoining Maharlika Livelihood Center, a large complex with numerous shops. You can buy woodcarvings at more reasonable prices there, direct from the makers in the so-called Woodcarver's Village. You will find it on Asin Rd, about four or five km west of Baguio.

Burnham Park
Burnham Park is a green reserve with a small artificial lake in the middle of town. It is named after Daniel H Burnham, the town planner of Baguio. There are boats for hire, a children's playground and other attractions. Be careful at night, as people have been attacked here.

Mountain Provinces Museum
This small museum at Camp John Hay gives a vivid picture of the life of the cultural minorities in the Central Cordillera (a mountain chain). Ethnographic artefacts like wood carvings, baskets, jewellery, pottery and weaving work are on display here. The opening hours are Tuesday to Sunday from 9 am to noon and 1.30 to 5 pm. Admission costs P10.

A jeepney from the main gate of Camp John Hay to the museum costs P2.

St Louis Filigree
Young silversmiths are trained at the St Louis University trade school. You can watch them make the finest filigree. Their work is sold in the St Louis Filigree Shop at fixed prices, but not all have a hallmark. If you want one, arrange to get it while you are there. The opening hours for both the workshop and the shop are Monday to Saturday from 8 am to noon and 1 to 5 pm.

Easter School of Weaving
The Easter School of Weaving is on the north-western outskirts of Baguio. The weavers make tablecloths and clothing, and you can watch them at work.

Jeepneys leave from Kayang St or from Chugum St, on the corner of Otek St.

Lourdes Grotto
There is a statue of Our Lady of Lourdes here and if you climb the 225 steps, you will get a beautiful view of the surrounding countryside. Jeepneys leave from Kayang St.

Camp John Hay
Camp John Hay, in the south-east suburbs of town, was a recreation base of the US Army, and has been run by the Bases Conversion Development Authority (BCDA) as a 'Resort & Recreation Area' since it was given back to the Philippines in July 1991.

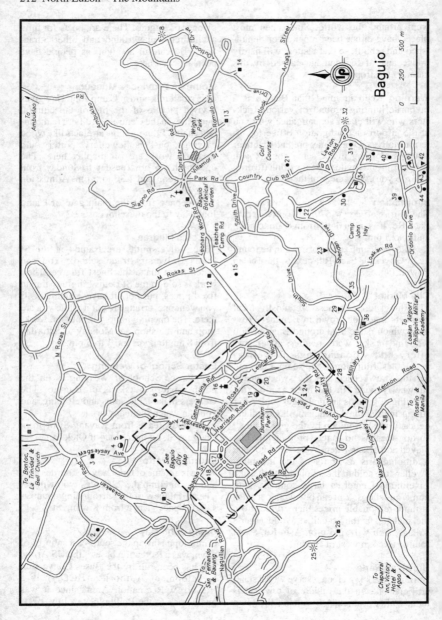

Baguio

■ PLACES TO STAY

1   Hotel Supreme
3   Baguio Village Inn
9   Vacation Hotel Baguio
10   Skyview Lodge
12   Mountain Lodge
13   Mansion House
14   Villa La Maya Inn
26   Diplomat Hotel &
     Dominican Hill
34   Igorot Lodge
36   Woods Place Inn

▼ PLACES TO EAT

5   Slaughterhouse Restaurant
23   Halfway House
29   Uncle's Music Lounge & Restaurant,
     Session Bistro Music Lounge &
     Restaurant
42   Lone Star Steak House &
     Mexican Restaurant

     OTHER

2   Easter School of Weaving
4   Times Transit Bus Terminal
6   St Louis University
7   St Joseph Church

8   Mines View Park
11   City Market
15   Teacher's Camp
16   Cathedral
17   Marcitas Liner Bus Terminal
18   City Hall
19   Dagupan Bus Terminal,
     Pantranco Bus Terminal &
     Philippine Rabbit Bus Terminal
20   Victory Liner Bus Terminal
21   Baguio Country Club
22   Mile-Hi Recreational Center
24   Tourist Office
25   Lourdes Grotto
27   University of the Philippines (UP)
28   Convention Center
30   Snider Hall
31   Tennis Courts
32   MacArthur Park View Point
33   19th Tee Patio
35   Camp John Hay Main Gate
37   Baguio Medical Center
38   Baguio General Hospital
39   Swimming Pool &
     Tennis Courts
40   Main Club
41   Cemetery of Negativism &
     Liberty Park
43   Tennis Courts
44   Mountain Provinces Museum

Open to the public is a golf course, swimming pool and tennis courts, as well as the restaurants, the Half Way House, the 19th Tee Patio and the Lone Star Steak House. The Americans also left behind the 'Cemetery of Negativism', where bad habits are buried – a glimpse into the homespun American philosophy of living.

Camp John Hay (now also known as Club John Hay) can be reached from the city centre by jeepney from Kayang St or by taxi to the main gate. Jeepneys and taxis also drive on the camp grounds themselves.

Baguio Botanical Gardens, Wright Park & Mines View Park

The botanical gardens, about one km out of town, were for a time named after the then first lady Imelda Marcos but are now known again by their original name. Unfortunately, all that is left of the different types of houses of the Central Cordillera, which used to be on view, is a broken-down Ifugao hut. There is also a handicrafts centre with a souvenir shop – a rather touristy affair. You can combine a trip to the botanical gardens with an excursion to Wright Park, where you can go horseback riding, and to the Mines View Park, 2½ km out of town, behind the Baguio Botanical Gardens, from where you can get a beautiful panoramic view of the valley and the mountains.

To get there, take a jeepney from Magsaysay Ave, opposite the city market, or from Harrison Rd, on the corner of Perfecto St.

Bell Church

There is a Chinese temple a little to the north of town in the direction of La Trinidad. This place is run by the Bell Church Sect, which believes in a mixture of Buddhist, Taoist, Confucian and Christian doctrines. You can,

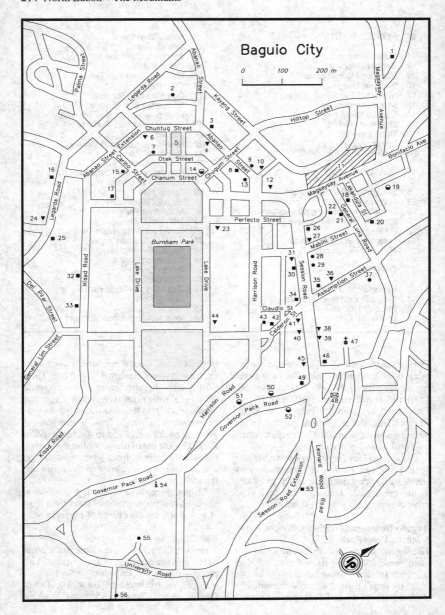

■ PLACES TO STAY

1   Leisure Lodge
3   Swagman Attic Inn
8   Cypress Inn
16 Holiday Villa Court
17 Benguet Pine Tourist Inn
18 New Belfranlt Hotel
20 Travelers Inn
21 Highland Lodge
22 Diamond Inn
25 Baguio Palace Hotel
26 Mido Hotel
30 Baguio Goodwill Lodge
32 Venus Parkview Hotel
33 Kisad Pension Inn
34 Benguet Prime Hotel
35 New Plaza Hotel
42 Burnham Hotel
46 Patrio de Baguio
49 Baden Powell Inn
53 Casa Vallejo

▼ PLACES TO EAT

4   Manila Café
6   Café by the Ruins
10 Music Box Pizza House
12 Café Teria &
    Fast Food Center
23 Ganza Steak & Chicken House
24 Golden Hot Pot Seafood
    Restaurant
25 Mr Ching Cuisine Restaurant
26 Sunshine Restaurant
27 Star Café
30 456 Restaurant
31 McDonald's
34 Jollibee
36 Cozy Nook Restaurant
38 Mr Donut & Swiss Baker

39 Bread of Life
40 Sizzling Plate Restaurant
41 Shakey's Pizza
42 Cook's Inn Restaurant
44 The Solibao Restaurant
45 Mario's Restaurant &
    Barrio Fiesta

OTHER

2   City Hall
5   Rizal Park
7   New York Disco
9   Peak a Boo Disco
11 City Market
12 Maharlika Livelihood Center
13 Orange County
14 Marcitas Liner Bus Terminal
15 Spirits Disco
16 Joey's Place
18 Fast Food Shopping Arcade
19 Dangwa Tranco Bus Terminal &
    Skyland Express Bus Terminal
28 Philippine National Bank (PNB)
29 Rumors Disco
34 Benguet Supermarket
37 St Louis Filigree Shop
38 Bookmark
43 PAL
46 Songs Music Gallery
47 Cathedral
48 Post Office
49 American Express
50 Dagupan Bus Terminal &
    Pantranco Bus Terminal
51 Philippine Rabbit Bus Terminal
52 Victory Liner Bus Terminal
54 Tourist Office
55 University of the Philippines (UP)
56 Convention Center

on request, get your fortune told by one of the priests.

To get to Bell Church, catch a jeepney from Magsaysay Ave, on the corner of Bonifacio St.

Faith Healers
The mass media have given much coverage to the practices of the Filipino faith healers, who 'open' the skin of the patient with their fingers and 'operate' with their bare hands –

a dubious business. But as faith can move mountains, there are always sufferers who come from all over the world to Baguio to be saved. If you aren't put off by blood or bad smells, you can always watch one of these miracles. According to critical reports in some Western mass media, however, most of these healers don't like to be watched too closely. If they do let you, then it is only for a pretty good fee. Taxi drivers can usually organise a visit.

Places to Stay – bottom end

The *Highland Lodge* (☎ 7086) on General Luna Rd has rooms for P100/150 and with bath for P230/250. The rooms are fairly small, but the staff is friendly. There is no restaurant, but there is room service.

The *Travelers Inn* (☎ 5444) at 60 Lakandula Rd has rooms for P120/240. This place is basic, with quite small rooms. The *Baguio Goodwill Lodge* (☎ 6634) at 58 Session Rd has rooms for P140/220 and with bath from P270/340. It is basic but pleasant. The *Benguet Pine Tourist Inn* (☎ 7325) at 82 Chanum St, on the corner of Otek St, has dorm beds for P100, singles/doubles from P200 to P300 and with bath for P450. It is clean, comfortable and quiet, and has a restaurant.

The *Casa Vallejo* (☎ 3045, 4601) at 111 Session Rd Extension has fairly good rooms for P200/300 and with bath for P300/400. It is a rustic building with a friendly atmosphere.

Places to Stay – middle

The *Kisad Pension House* (☎ 3507) at 24 Kisad Rd has clean, comfortable rooms with bath for P650/900. Rooms for four people cost P1450. Some rooms have a view of Burnham Park. There is a coffee shop.

The *Cypress Inn* (☎ 2416) at 29 Abanao St has rooms with bath for P320/450. Rooms for three to five people cost between P550 and P700. This place is quite comfortable and has a restaurant.

The *Mountain Lodge* (☎ 4544) at 27 Leonard Wood Rd has singles/doubles with bath for P600/650 and doubles with a fireplace for P900. This pleasant, friendly hotel is good value, cosy and comfortable, and there is a restaurant.

The *Baden Powell Inn* (☎ 5836, 8177) at 26 Governor Pack Rd has dorm beds for P120, singles with bath for P400 and P500 and doubles with bath for P600 and P800. It also has spacious, comfortable suites with two bedrooms, kitchen and open fireplace for P2500. The rooms are clean and quiet, as they are at the back, looking downhill and away from the noise of the street. This place is conveniently located for some of the bus terminals.

The *Burnham Hotel* (☎ 2331, 5117; fax 4428415) at 21 Calderon St has rooms with bath for P550/650, the more expensive rooms have TV. This is a fine, tastefully decorated house which also has a good Chinese restaurant.

The *Benguet Prime Hotel* (☎ 7066) on the corner of Calderon St and Session Rd has comfortable rooms with TV, fridge and bath from P600 to P950, although those facing the street are a bit on the loud side.

The *New Belfranlt Hotel* (☎ 4298, 5012) on General Luna St has clean, spacious and comfortable rooms with TV and bath for P785, and it has a restaurant.

The *Swagman Attic Inn* (☎ 5139) at 90 Abanao St has nicely furnished rooms with TV and bath for P770 and P870. This pleasant place is managed by Australians and has a restaurant.

Places to Stay – top end

The *Hotel Supreme* (☎ 2855) at 113 Magsaysay Ave, just outside town, has singles with bath for P900 and doubles with bath for P1035. Suites are P1250. It is clean and quiet and has a restaurant.

The *Woods Place Inn* (☎ 4642) at 38 Military Cut-Off Rd, on the corner of Wagner Rd, has tidy, comfortable rooms for P750 and pleasantly furnished rooms with balcony, TV and bath for P1500. A suite with a jacuzzi costs P1950. This is a cosy little hotel with a restaurant.

The *Vacation Hotel Baguio* (☎ 3144, 4545) at 45 Leonard Wood Rd has comfortable rooms with TV and bath from P1220 to P1900. It's a well-looked after hotel, opposite the Baguio Botanical Gardens, and there is a restaurant and disco.

The *Baguio Palace Hotel* (☎ 7734) on Legarda Rd has rooms with bath for P1300 and suites for P2200. This place is clean and comfortable, though maybe a bit expensive, and it has a Chinese restaurant.

Places to Eat

The simple restaurant in the Dangwa Tranco Bus Terminal serves good and cheap Filipino cuisine. The so-called *Slaughterhouse Restaurants*, next to the slaughterhouse near the Times Transit Bus Terminal on Balajadia St, are also simply furnished. However, they offer excellent meat dishes at reasonable prices, so the locals have every reason to frequent them as often as they do.

The *Cook's Inn* at the Burnham Hotel, Calderon St and *Mr Ching Cuisine* at the Baguio Palace Hotel, Legarda Rd, are two of the best Chinese restaurants in town.

Both *The Solibao* and the *Ganza Steak & Chicken House* are in Burnham Park and have tables outside. There are other restaurants of varying quality and price on Session Rd. One of these is the *Sizzling Plate*, where you can have a proper breakfast. *Mario's*, which has been around for a long time, is well known for its steaks and pizzas. At the *Bread of Life* coffee shop, you can enjoy imported cheeses and European sausages as well as coffee and bread.

The *Swagman Attic Inn Restaurant* on Abanao St serves passable international cuisine and is open 24 hours. Friends of fast food can choose between *McDonald's*, *Jollibee* and *Shakey's Pizza*, all on Session Rd.

If you would like to try traditional Cordillera cooking and drinks, then the unconventional *Café by the Ruins* opposite the town hall is the place to go. This bamboo restaurant is tastefully decorated with plants and traditional artwork, and its menu consists mainly of seasonal specialities, served with tapuy (rice wine), basi or salabat (ginger tea).

Entertainment

For years folk pubs were all the rage in Baguio, but with the demand for a more modern sound, sing-along and karaoke have established themselves here in the mountains, with *Joey's Place* on Legarda Rd and the *Cosy Nook* on Assumption Rd the most popular venues. The *Music Box Pizza House* on Zandueta St still has folk music.

Jazz freaks meet in the evening at the *Songs Music Gallery* next to the Patria de Baguio, located appropriately enough on Session Rd, although sometimes classical music is played there. The guests in the *Café Teria* at the Marhalika Livelihood Center are entertained with jazz and oldies, whereas the *Orange County* on Abanao St specialises in country & western and rock music. The *Peak a Boo Disco*, diagonally across the road, has go-go dancers.

By far the most popular disco, however, is *Spirits*, in a magnificent building on Otek St. *Rumors* on Session Rd and the *Crystal Den* at the Victory Hotel, Marcos Highway, are also popular. The *Chaparral Inn* is also on Marcos Highway and is a hotel complex with several nightclubs.

Getting There & Away

Air PAL has return flights daily between Manila and Baguio. Flying time is 50 minutes.

PAL has an office at Loakan Airport (☎ 2734, 6753) and on Harrison Rd (☎ 2628, 2695).

Bus From Manila to Baguio, there are plenty of Philippine Rabbit, Pantranco North, Victory Liner, Dagupan Bus and Dangwa Tranco buses daily, taking six hours. Buses go via Dau/Angeles, where you can also board the bus. The trip from Baguio to Manila takes 30 minutes less than in the reverse direction, as the first part is downhill.

From Olongapo, you can get to Baguio by Victory Liner bus. These leave hourly and take six hours. They pass through Angeles, where you can also board the bus.

From Dagupan to Baguio, there are several Pantranco North buses a day, taking two hours.

From San Fernando, several Philippine Rabbit and Marcitas Liner buses travel daily to Baguio. It takes two hours and the last bus leaves at about 5.30 pm. They travel via Bauang, where you can also board the bus. You can also go by jeepney.

From Banaue, the Dangwa Tranco buses run a daily service to Baguio, leaving at 6.45

and 7.30 am, and sometimes at 5 am. They follow the southern route via Bayombong, San Jose and Villasis, taking nine hours.

From Bontoc, Dangwa Tranco buses run daily to Baguio, leaving at 6, 7, 8 and 9.15 am. The trip takes eight hours.

From Sagada, there are Dangwa Tranco, Lizardo Trans and Skyland Express buses which run daily to Baguio, leaving between 5.30 and 6.30 am, sometimes also at 9 am. The trips takes 6½ hours.

Look out for buses from Sagada and other places in Mountain Province, which have sometimes been stopped by military and Narcotic Commission (NARCOM) officials searching passenger luggage for marijuana.

Getting Around

To/From the Airport Loakan Airport is about eight km south of Baguio. If you're catching a flight to Manila, you can get a jeepney from Baguio to the airport which leaves from Mabini Rd, between Session and Harrison Rds.

Car Avis Rent-a-Car (☎ 4018) can be found in the Padilla Building on Harrison Rd.

KABAYAN

Kabayan is well known for the many burial caves of the local Ibaloy tribe. There are mummies with their legs hunched up against their bodies lying in hollow tree trunks which serve as coffins. Some are said to be at least 500 years old. Because some of the caves were plundered in the 1970s, the nearest and best known of them have since been sealed. Those that are still open can only be reached with guides after long hikes. You can also see some mummies in a small museum in the town hall.

Getting There & Away

There is a daily Dangwa Tranco bus from Baguio to Kabayan, leaving at about 9.30 am. The trip takes 6½ hours. There is no connection for Abatan to the north. To get there, you have to walk or take the daily bus back to Baguio.

SAGADA

Sagada is a pleasant little place in the mountains, known for its caves and so-called 'hanging coffins'.

Information

The Rural Bank of Sagada will only change US dollars.

You can get a detailed map of the Sagada area for P5 at the Masferré Inn and various other places in town.

Caves

If you are a climber and are curious to see the caves, you would be well advised to get one of the locals to guide you through them. A well-known and experienced guide is Jacinto Degay, who lives next to St Theodores Hospital, and whose sons have also followed in his footsteps. Any guesthouse can arrange other good guides. The usual price is around P200 for four people, plus P35 for a lamp. You need a kerosene lamp, as a torch won't offer enough light. Careful guides will put up ropes for safety at dangerous spots. Good footwear is also important for a visit to the caves.

A guide is not essential for most of the burial caves. They are not very far from the centre of town – at most a 30-minute walk away. Among these are the **Matangkib**, **Sugong** and **Lumiang** caves. **Sumaging Cave** (Big Cave) does not contain any coffins. You need a guide to go into this cave, as a thorough exploration can take up to six hours. Mind you, the water is almost waist high in places and there are a few narrow places to negotiate. A guide is also recommended if you want to visit **Crystal Cave**.

Places to Stay

The *Sagada Guesthouse* has rooms for P55/100. It is clean and comfortable with warm water (P10 extra), and has good and reasonably priced meals. The *St Joseph Resthouse* has rooms for P55/100, is tidy and pleasant and has a restaurant. The *Masferré Inn* is comfortable and has spacious rooms for P55/100.

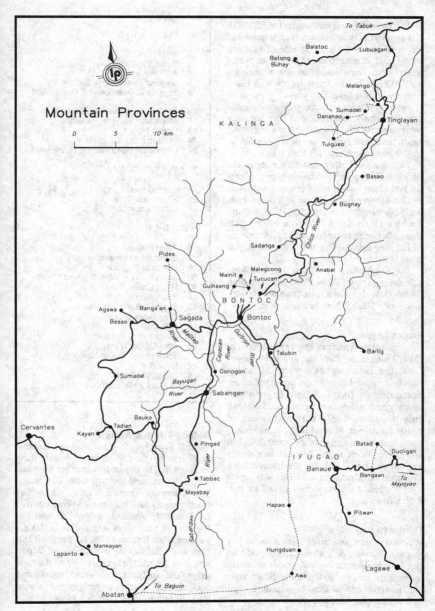

Mountain Provinces

0   5   10 km

The *Green House* has rooms for P50/100. It is an older private house which is quiet and has four rooms to let, with use of kitchen, living and dining rooms. There is warm water. The *Traveller's Inn* has rooms for P50/100 and is in a quiet location. It has a friendly atmosphere.

Also very quiet is the cosy *Pines View Inn* with its family atmosphere. There are only two rooms for P50/100 as well as a big living room and kitchen. The nearby *A-Seven House* has rooms also for P50/100.

The *Rocky Valley Inn* has rooms for P55/110. The accommodation here is pleasant and clean, and it has a good restaurant.

The *Mapiyaaw Pensione* has dorm beds for P60, singles/doubles for P70/140 and doubles with bath for P150 (one bathroom is shared between two rooms). This is a clean, welcoming establishment in a quiet area just outside the town centre.

The *Olahbinan Resthouse* has comfortable rooms from P75 to P200 and with bath for P400. It also has a suite (two rooms with bath) for P1000. There is a restaurant.

Places to Eat
You can eat well and cheaply at the *Masferré Café*, *Moonhouse Café* and at the *Shamrock Café*; the latter serves several Mountain Province specialities. At the popular *Cabine Restaurant* the food is extremely good, and an early reservation is recommended as it can only accommodate a certain number of guests for dinner. Several of the guesthouses serve large evening meals and breakfasts, but you should book ahead. Most restaurants in Sagada close at 9 pm, but the unique *Rock Café* near the Underground River stays open a bit longer. It's a very cosy cave-like pub with a fire place.

Things to Buy
Weavers make beautiful materials at the Sagada Weaving & Souvenir Shop, and you can buy traditional woven goods at fairly reasonable prices. Josephine's Store sells handicrafts made by local highlanders, such as jewellery, baskets and woodcarvings.

■ PLACES TO STAY

1	Billi Haus
2	Pines View Inn
3	A-Seven House
5	Sagada Guesthouse & Café
9	St Joseph Resthouse & Restaurant
11	Traveller's Inn
12	Rocky Valley Inn & Restaurant
16	Mapiyaaw Sagada Pensione
23	Green House
24	Masferré Inn & Café
27	Olahbinan Resthouse & Restaurant

▼ PLACES TO EAT

4	Cabine Restaurant
22	Shamrock Café
26	Moonhouse Café

OTHER

6	Town Bakery
7	Ganduyan Museum
8	Buses to Baguio
10	Sagada Weaving & Souvenir Shop
13	Rock Café
14	Josephine's Store
15	Studio Eduardo Masferré
17	Cangbay's Store
18	Hospital
19	Jeepneys to Bontoc
20	Post Office, Bank, Town Hall & Police Station
21	Market
25	St Mary's Church
28	St Mary's High School

Getting There & Away
Several Dangwa Tranco, Skyland Express and Lizardo Trans buses leave Baguio daily for Sagada. The departure times are 6 am and 7 or 7.30 am, and the trip takes 6½ hours. The Dangwa Tranco buses, which are usually pretty full, may come to Baguio from La Trinidad, which is a few km north of Baguio. If you want a good seat, take a jeepney from Baguio to the La Trinidad Bus Terminal well before the scheduled departure time. Sit next to the driver or on the right side of the bus for the best view. It gets fairly cool, so take a jacket or jumper out of your luggage before it gets stowed away.

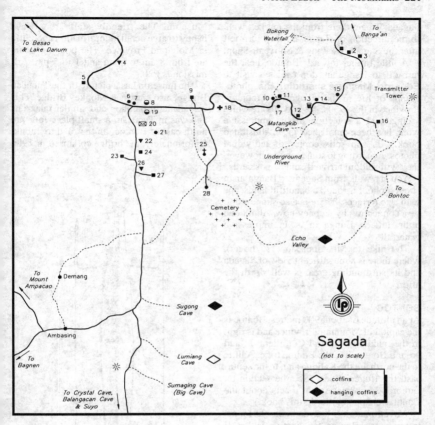

Sagada
(not to scale)

◇ coffins
◆ hanging coffins

The buses leave Sagada for Baguio between 5.30 and 6.30 am, and possibly at 9 am.

From Bontoc to Sagada, there are at least three jeepneys daily, usually leaving at 8 am, 9.30 am and 1.30 pm from the Caltex petrol station. The trip takes one hour.

If you want to go from Sagada to Banaue via Bontoc on the same day, then the best thing is to take the first jeepney at 6 am from Sagada to Bontoc, and catch the jeepney to Banaue there, which leaves at about 7.30 am from the Mountain Hotel.

An unusual way to go to Sagada is from Vigan via Bangued, right across Abra Province (see also Vigan to Bangued & Sagada in the Vigan section later in this chapter).

AROUND SAGADA

Although the flow is reduced almost to a trickle in April and May, a visit to **Bokong Waterfall** with its natural swimming pool is worthwhile and very refreshing after touring the caves in Sagada. It's a little hard to find, so you may have to ask for directions. It takes about 30 minutes to get there on foot from

Sagada. To get there from the market, walk in the direction of Banga'an, then turn left after the Sagada Weaving & Souvenir Shop.

A little farther towards Bontoc, near the turn-off to Banga'an, don't miss a visit to **Eduardo Masferré's studio**. His photographs of life in the villages of Mountain Province in the 1930s, 40s and 50s are worth seeing, and a selection of his impressive work has been published in an illustrated book. His son sells copies of individual photos. According to some reports, however, they will seldom arrive if sent as postcards.

You can walk from Sagada to Banga'an in about an hour through a beautiful landscape with rice terraces. There is also supposed to be a connection by jeepney now. About one hour outside Banga'an is an impressive waterfall.

The hike to Mt Ampacao (1½ hours), where there is a magnificent view of Sagada and its surrounding area, is well worth the effort.

BONTOC
At an altitude of about 900 metres, Bontoc is the capital of Mountain Province and is right in the middle of Central Cordillera. In and around Bontoc live the Bontoc tribe. A little to the north are the Kalinga and, to the south-east, the Ifugao tribes. (See the section on Cultural Minorities in the Facts about the Country chapter earlier in this book.)

Woven materials are made on old looms in and around Bontoc, for example, in the All Saints Elementary School and in Barangay Samoki, a village on the other side of the river. As well as woven materials, locals also make simple utensils. It takes about 30 minutes to walk from Bontoc to Samoki.

Information
There is a branch of the Philippine National Bank in Bontoc if you want to change travellers' cheques.

Bontoc Museum
You can get a good overview of the differences and similarities between the mountain tribes in the small but excellent Bontoc

Museum. The friendly staff are always happy to give detailed information about life in Mountain Province. The opening hours are from 8 am to noon and 1 to 5 pm. Admission is P20.

The museum has a picture of the Tucucan Bridge, also known as Monkey Bridge. This was made of bamboo and similar materials and was in Tucucan, a small place four km north-east of Bontoc, on the road to Tabuk. Unfortunately, the bridge collapsed in 1986

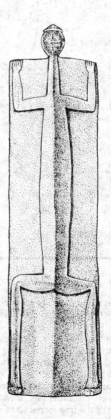

Bontoc Shield – Filipinos used shields made of engraved buffalo leather or carved out of wood to protect themselves in battle

and was replaced by an uninteresting modern construction.

Trekking

The Pines Kitchenette & Inn will arrange three to four-day treks through the area of the Kalinga, based in Tinglayan. These cost P500.

Massage

If you feel like a soothing massage after your strenuous walks up and down mountains, go to the Massage Centre of Bontoc. There are two blind masseurs who, for P60, will give a professional massage lasting one hour.

Places to Stay

The *Mountain Hotel* (☎ 3018) has small, basic rooms for P50/90 and has a restaurant. The *Bontoc Hotel* has rooms for P50/100. It is comfortable, and there is a restaurant. The *Chico Terrace* (☎ 3099) has rooms with bath for P60/110. It is basic but well kept and has some rooms with three or five beds.

The *Happy Home Inn* (☎ 3021) has singles/doubles for P50/100 and double rooms with bath for P160. It is simple but habitable and has hot showers for an extra P10. You can also get a good walking map of Bontoc and its surroundings.

The *Village Inn* has singles for P60 and doubles for P110. The rooms are cosy and clean. Two double rooms share a bath; this is ideal for small groups of people. Breakfast can be arranged on request.

The *Pines Kitchenette & Inn* has rooms for P70/140 and with bath for P250/300, and there is a restaurant. It is fairly good, although not all of the sanitary facilities work properly.

The *Vista Pension*, behind the town hall, has rooms for P70/140 and doubles with bath for P420. The rooms are attractive, clean and quiet. This is a small hotel with a pleasant atmosphere; it has a coffee shop.

Between Baguio and Bontoc, the only possible overnight stop is at the *Mount Data Lodge* north of Abatan, which has double rooms with bath for about P350.

Places to Eat

You can get good cheap meals in the restaurants at the Bontoc and Mountain hotels. There is also the *Pines Kitchenette & Inn* where you can get a good cheap breakfast as well as other meals.

Getting There & Away

Bus & Jeepney There are five Dangwa Tranco buses from Baguio to Bontoc a day. Departure times are at 6, 7, 8, 9 and 10 am. The trip takes eight hours. Some buses start in La Trinidad, a few km north of Baguio, and are generally pretty full when they get to Baguio. If you want a good seat, it is worth going the short distance from Baguio to La Trinidad by jeepney.

From Banaue to Bontoc there is one jeepney which leaves at about 6.30 to 7.30 am and sometimes earlier. There is also a daily bus, except on Sunday, which leaves between 10 and 11 am and takes three hours.

The bus connection between Tuguegarao and Bontoc via Tabuk and Lubuagan is probably still suspended. It is a bad stretch which takes 10 hours. The bus then carries on via Roxas, Santiago and Banaue, leaving at 4 am.

There are at least three jeepneys a day from Sagada to Bontoc. They leave at 6 and 10 am and noon or early afternoon. The trip takes one hour.

There is a cross trip from San Fernando to Bontoc and Sagada, leaving from Tagudin (50 km north of San Fernando) and going as far as Cervantes. Two jeepneys leave at 6 to 6.30 am from Bitalag Rd junction, about five km north of Tagudin. There is nothing after that time along this stretch. The road is bad and it's a very time-consuming trip. If your jeepney gets to Cervantes too late, you won't get an onward connection until 5 am the next morning, when you can catch a bus going to Baguio via Abatan. There are jeepneys during the day on this stretch. At Abatan you can take a bus coming from Baguio which goes to Bontoc or Sagada.

To go from Abatan to Cervantes there is a Dangwa Tranco bus coming from Baguio which leaves between 10 and 11 am. You can also get a jeepney from Abatan to Mankayan and from there go on by minibus to Cervantes. In the afternoon, this connection may not be available. From Cervantes to Tagudin there is at least a daily jeepney at 1 and 3 pm. On Thursday, which is market day, there is an additional jeepney at 11 am. There is no problem getting connecting buses at Tagudin and at Bitalag Rd junction heading either north or south.

Car & Motorbike The trip from Baguio to Bontoc is very beautiful and interesting, but strenuous too as some sections of the road are very bad. The surfacing of this so-called mountain highway is, however, progressing.

AROUND BONTOC
Bugnay
Bugnay is a Kalinga village that expects visiting tourists to pay as much as possible for the pleasure of their visit. You will be asked P20 or more for a local guide or for the 'new bridge construction'. They also charge an extra few pesos for taking photographs. There are other charges as well as the obligatory gifts. It is advisable to take no more valuables than necessary, as several attacks have been reported in this area.

Fighting is now going on between the Cordillera People's Liberation Army (CPAL) and the New People's Army (NPA), so travelling through this area could be dangerous.

Getting There & Away You can get a bus from Bontoc to Tabuk via Banaue, Santiago and Roxas which leaves between 7.30 and 8 am. Buses between Bontoc and Tabuk via Bugnay, Tinglayan and Lubuagan are probably still suspended.

From Bontoc to Tinglayan going via Bugnay there is a daily jeepney, which leaves after the arrival of the bus from Baguio between 1 and 2 pm. There are several checkpoints on this stretch and the soldiers may check baggage thoroughly. They will also want to see identity documents, but are usually satisfied with a photocopy of your passport.

The jeepney returning from Tinglayan to Bontoc does not leave until 6 am the following morning. A day trip from Bontoc to Bugnay is therefore impossible. To charter a jeepney would cost at least P800, and then only if you can find one. You can add to this the cost of presents and of a guide, whom you should have for safety reasons alone. All in all, it would be an relatively expensive business.

Malegcong
You can get the best view of the rice terraces from this village. They are even better here than in Bauang. It may be possible to obtain up-to-date information on life in Malegcong and in the mountains from the English-speaking teacher there.

You should carry some provisions, particularly water, and gifts for the locals. Whatever you do, don't take alcohol for a general drinking session. A small gift is not just recommended, it's compulsory unless you want to be muttered about and sworn at by all the villagers.

Getting There & Away As there is not supposed to be any connection by jeepney from Bontoc to Malegcong any more, the trip will take three hours on foot, which is quite a walk. It can get very hot; take some kind of headcover as well as provisions, including water.

There may be a jeepney from Bontoc to Guinaang at 6.30 to 7 am. Just before the village of Guinaang, on the right, there is a track to Malegcong which goes past rice terraces to a mountain summit where you have to turn right to get to Malegcong. The walk from Guinaang to Malegcong takes two hours. From Malegcong you can walk back to Bontoc, which takes another two hours. You will first pass rice terraces and then the track runs downhill, until you reach a road which vehicles can use.

Mainit
Mainit means hot. Even the springs in this little place where people pan for gold are hot.

Getting There & Away There may be a jeepney which leaves Bontoc daily for Guinaang at about 6.30 to 7 am. From there it is about 45 minutes on foot downhill to Mainit.

There may be a jeepney in the afternoon from Guinaang back to Bontoc. There is also a track from Mainit to Malegcong. It is hard to find, so a guide may be useful. The track starts before you get into Mainit, at a sulphur spring, which you can smell a long way off. If you are coming from Guinaang, you have to turn right at the sulphur spring and follow the track past the rice terraces to Malegcong.

Tinglayan & Kalinga Villages
Tinglayan is a good starting point from which to visit Kalinga villages. From there you can try to get to the villages with Kalinga who have been to see their relatives in hospital. Still, the area must be regarded as dangerous because of several ambushes and numerous fights between the politically distinct units of the Armed Forces of the Philippines (AFP), the NPA and the CPLA. You should check the situation before you go there.

The following round trip will take at least three days on foot, including stopovers in the villages. You can count on three hours from Tinglayan to Tulgueo, one hour or more from Tulgueo to Dananao, two hours from Dananao to Sumadel and one hour from Sumadel to Malango. From Malango you get on to the main road and go back to Tinglayan.

Always get a guide to take you from one village to the next to reduce the likelihood of an attack. Women are normally honoured and treated with respect by the Kalinga, as a Kalinga who attacks a woman loses face for good, yet women should also have a guide. Unfortunately, generous travellers have caused expectations of handouts. There have been reports of emphatic demands for hundreds of pesos for the construction of a (non-existent) school.

Lubuagan
In and around Lubuagan, the former government of president Marcos came into direct

Ifugao God – Bulnl, the protector of rice

Woodcarving
Woodcarving is part of the culture of the Ifuagao who live in the Central Cordillera. They like making sacred figures that represent humans in different positions. The most famous wooden figures are the Bulul, male and female gods who, after harvest, are placed at the entrance of the storehouse to protect the rice. The rice gods, attracted by the ceremony, are supposed to inhabit these figures and ensure that the rice not only lasts until the next harvest, but also increases miraculously. ■

conflict with the Kalinga because of the Chico Valley dam project, which was to comprise four single dams and produce 1000 megawatts of electricity.

The Chico Valley dam would have been the largest in South-East Asia and would have flooded the Kalinga's valleys, forcing them to resettle. The Kalinga were opposed to the move as it would have meant the end of their centuries-old culture, which has developed in isolation of the colonised lowlands. The Kalinga's religion was another reason for their opposition to the move. They live in a world of gods and spirits and show great respect to the dead, so their ancestors' resting places must be left undisturbed.

At first there was only scattered fighting against the surveying for the dam. In 1980, however, following the murder of Bugnay's Chief Macliing Dulag, who had been sabotaging the works of the national energy company, the 20 or so groups of Kalinga, comprising about 100,000 members, formed a united front. Macliing was shot by several volleys of machine-gun fire through the thin walls of his hut and it is said that the murderers were wearing military uniforms. The conflict widened and soldiers and construction workers were beheaded and rebellious Kalinga shot. Members of the communist NPA joined the Kalinga and instructed them in the use of modern M-16 rifles.

Today, relations between the mountain dwellers and the NPA, as well as the government, are anything but harmonious. The Kalinga now distrust any power which tries to intrude on them. They continue to be vigilant and regard any stranger as a threat – do not venture into the mountains alone.

BANAUE
Banaue is at an altitude of about 1200 metres. The rice terraces around Banaue have been called the eighth wonder of the world. It took the Ifugao tribespeople, with their primitive implements, over 2000 years to create this imposing landscape.

The Ifugao plant rice according to the following calendar: in the second half of December, they begin to sow the seed; from the beginning of February to the middle of March, they transplant the first seedlings; from the middle of April until the middle of June, they weed the fields; in July, the harvest takes place; and from the beginning of August until the middle of December, they work on improvements to the rice terraces and preparing the fields for the next seeding.

Information
A Tourist Information Center can be found next to the market. You can buy a useful map of Banaue's surroundings there for P6. It shows the way to various interesting sights and describes them in detail on the back.

There is an authorised foreign exchange counter at the Banaue Hotel. However, the exchange rate is poor and there is a fee of P50 for each travellers' cheque.

Things to See & Do
There are a number of things to do around Banaue. You can visit several Ifugao villages, take some of the paths through the rice terraces, enjoy the panorama from **Banaue View Point** or take a refreshing dip in the clear water of **Guihon Natural Pool**. On the way there you can make a detour to the bronzesmiths of **Matanglag**, or visit Josef Blas, who makes artistic woodcarvings.

A tricycle to Banaue View Point costs P50 to P70; jeepneys to Bontoc also use this route. Colourfully dressed Ifugao wait at the view point for photographers, and expect them to pay a few pesos for a photo.

Trekking Peter Gatik is a good guide and can offer excellent information. He lives in Bayongong and carries out trekking tours, from Batad to Bontoc for example. However, other guides such as Simon Rufino and Johnny Ambojnon, who can both be contacted via jeepney drivers at the market, are also more than happy to guide small groups through the mountains.

Places to Stay
The *Jericho Guest House* is a reasonable place which has rooms for P40/80. The *Brookside Inn* and *Traveler's Inn* (☎ 4020) both have simple but clean rooms for P45/90. The *Wonder Lodge* (☎ 4017) has basic but good quality rooms for P60/100 and with bath for P250/350. The *Halfway Lodge* (☎ 4082) has basic, clean and cosy rooms

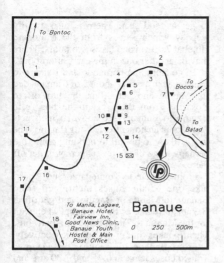

1 Terrace Ville Inn
2 Traveler's Inn
3 Brookside Inn
4 Cozy Nook
5 Halfway Lodge
6 Stairway Lodge
7 Las Vegas Restaurant
8 Green View Lodge
9 People's Lodge & Bakery
10 Wonder Lodge
11 Banaue View Inn
12 Cool Winds Restaurant, Market &
  Tourist Information Center
13 Valgreg Lodge
14 Sanafe Lodge
15 Post Office &
  Town Hall
16 Jericho Guest House
17 Spring Village Inn
18 J & L Pension

for P60/120 and with bath for P200/3050. It also has a restaurant.

The *Stairway Lodge* (☎ 4053) has singles/doubles for P75/150 and double rooms with bath for P250. It is pleasant and has a restaurant.

The *Banaue View Inn* (☎ 4078) has dorm beds for P75 and rooms with bath for P350/450. It is a pleasant, quiet place with a beautiful view of Banaue. The *J & L Pension* (☎ 4035, 4057) has rooms for P150/250. An Ifugao house costs P300. It is a cosily decorated place slightly outside Banaue, on the way to the Banaue Hotel. The *People's Lodge* (☎ 4014) is a friendly place with a bakery and restaurant. The rooms are basic, clean and comfortable, and cost P75/100 and with bath P350. There is warm water.

The *Spring Village Inn* (☎ 4037) has passable rooms for P150/250 and with bath for P400. The *Terrace Ville Inn* (☎ 4069) has clean and comfortable rooms with bath for P350, and it has warm water. The *Fairview Inn* (☎ 4002) has rooms with bath for P250/350. It is quiet, attractive and cosy. Meals can be arranged on request.

The *Green View Lodge* (☎ 4021) is a good place with dorm beds for P75 and clean and neat rooms with bath for P300/400. The single rooms are OK for two people. The *Sanafe Lodge* (☎ 4085) has dorm beds for P75, singles with bath for P470 and doubles with bath for P600. The rooms are really comfortable. There is also a restaurant. The *Banaue Youth Hostel* has dorm beds for P150. It is administered by the Banaue Hotel, whose swimming pool is available for use.

The exclusive *Banaue Hotel* (☎ 4087, 4088; fax 4048) has singles with bath for P1700 and doubles with bath for P1850. It has a restaurant and swimming pool. This tastefully decorated hotel is the best place to stay in Banaue. Nonresidents can use the swimming pool for P15.

Places to Eat
Most hotels have a small restaurant or else the staff will cook meals for guests. The *Cool Winds Restaurant* next to the market, the *People's Restaurant*, *Halfway Restaurant*, *Stairway Restaurant* and the *Las Vegas Restaurant* near the Catholic church are good and cheap. The latter restaurant entertains guests in the evening with folk music.

The restaurant at the *Banaue Hotel* is excellent and, if there are enough guests,

Ifugao dances are held at night. Although these performances are in contrast to the setting and are perhaps out of place, they do seem to be relatively authentic. Admission is P10. On the return to the village at night it is likely to be very dark, so don't forget to take a torch.

There is also live music at the *Patina Bar Folkden*, where you can get beer and snacks quite late.

Getting There & Away
Air Aerolift has flights on Wednesday, Friday and Sunday from Manila to Bagabag and return (most probably only between October and May). The flight takes about one hour. A shuttle bus runs from Bagabag (between Solano and Lagawe) to Banaue, taking two hours.

Bus From Manila to Banaue, there is a Dangwa Tranco bus daily which leaves between 7 and 7.30 am and takes nine hours. You can also take a Pantranco North bus from Manila which goes almost as far as Banaue. Take one bound for Ilagan, Tuguegarao and Aparri. Get off in Solano, just before the turn-off to Banaue, take a jeepney to Lagawe and then go on by jeepney to Banaue. From late afternoon onwards there are unlikely to be jeepneys from Lagawe to Banaue, so make sure you don't arrive too late. There is no accommodation in Lagawe.

There are two Dangwa Tranco buses from Baguio to Banaue a day, taking the southern route via Villasis, San Jose and Bayombong. They leave at 6.45 and 7.30 am and take nine hours. It is necessary to be at the bus terminal early, as the bus will leave up to an hour early if it is full, especially at Easter. The departure times are often altered, so it's a good idea to check the day before leaving.

If you want to go from Baguio to Banaue via Bontoc, you will have to stay the night in Bontoc, as there is no direct connection. From Bontoc to Banaue, there is a bus daily, except on Sunday, which leaves between 7.30 and 8 am, going on to Tabuk. The trip takes three hours. Be very early if you want

to get a good seat. There is also a daily jeepney which leaves from the Mountain Hotel at 7.30 am and takes two hours. There may be another one in the early afternoon.

To go from San Fernando and Bauang to Banaue, take a bus at about 5 or 6 am headed for Manila and get off at the turn-off to Rosario. From there catch the bus from Baguio to Banaue (see above) which gets there about an hour after leaving Baguio. The bus is likely to be full to bursting point, but perhaps some of the passengers will get off there.

From Banaue to Tuguegarao and Aparri take one of the buses mentioned from Banaue to Manila or Baguio, and get off at Bagabag, Solano or Bayombong. Then wait for the Manila to Tuguegarao or Aparri bus. The trip takes four or six hours respectively.

From Banaue to Baguio, the Dangwa Tranco buses leave at 6.45 and 7.30 am, and sometimes even at 5 am.

From Banaue to Manila, a Dangwa Tranco bus leaves daily between 7 and 7.30 am, taking eight hours.

Warning Because of attacks on private vehicles it is advisable to drive in front of a bus or jeepney.

AROUND BANAUE
Batad & Cambulo
Batad is about 16 km north-east of Banaue. The rice terraces in Batad are in the shape of an amphitheatre. Many Ifugao houses now have corrugated iron roofs, but luckily these have not yet been generally accepted. There is a beautiful waterfall with a natural swimming pool. It's only about an hour's walk away in Batad, but it would be better to stay overnight rather than include it in a day's visit to Banaue.

If you want to photograph villagers in Batad, you should ask them first as they either don't want any photos to be taken, or else will demand payment.

About two hours on foot from Batad is Cambulo, a typical little Ifugao village, in the midst of rice terraces. It is advisable to

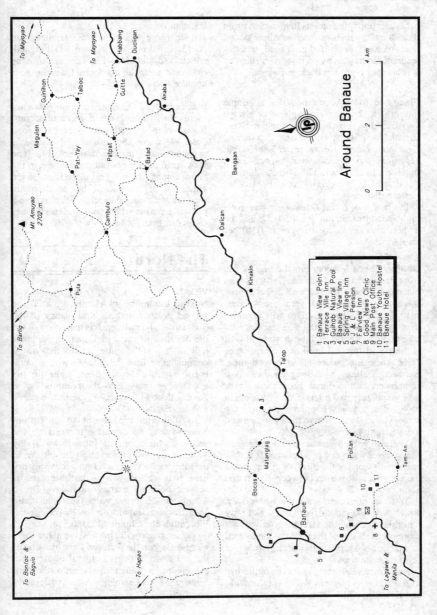

Around Banaue

1 Banaue View Point
2 Terrace Ville Inn
3 Guihob Natural Pool
4 Banaue View Inn
5 Spring Village Inn
6 J & L Pension
7 Fairview Inn
8 Good News Clinic
9 Main Post Office
10 Banaue Youth Hostel
11 Banaue Hotel

use water purifying tablets in this area. From there a trail, which takes about three hours, leads to Kinakin on the main road, where a jeepney might pass by on its way to Banaue. It is another eight km back to Banaue.

Places to Stay Accommodation is simple throughout, but the atmosphere is always very friendly. You can stay the night in Batad for about P50 at the *Batad Pensionne*, *Cristina's Guest House*, *Foreigner's Inn*, *Mountain View Inn*, *Summer Inn*, or *Simon's Inn* and *Hillside Inn*. The Hillside Inn has good meals, especially Israeli/Middle-Eastern dishes.

In Cambulo, *Lydia Domanglig* has overnight accommodation for P30. Lydia, the owner, also cooks for her guests (P40 per meal).

Getting There & Away For the first 12 km from Banaue to Batad you can go by vehicle, but the rest you have to walk. The Tourist Information Center and several guesthouses, such as the Halfway Lodge, will organise trips by jeepney for P500. The jeepney will take up to 14 people and the driver will wait at the Batad turn-off until late afternoon or come back for guests at an agreed time. Between Dalican and Bangaan there is a signposted path to Batad. From there it will take you barely two hours. Don't be taken in by 'guides' who just happen to be going the same way to Batad, where they will demand a pretty high price.

There may be a jeepney from Banaue to Mayoyao at 8 am or a bus between 9 and 11 am, which stops at the turn-off to Batad. On the way back, it passes between 10 am and noon.

You can of course walk the whole way, which will take about five hours. Not only will this save you the fare, but you will get more pleasure out of the countryside as well as meeting a surprisingly large number of people on the way.

An attractive alternative for the return trip to Banaue is to go from Batad via Cambulo and Kinakin, which takes seven hours.

Bangaan

To see more beautiful rice terraces, you could also visit the village of Bangaan, which is south of Batad. It's not far from the road and is easier to reach than the now popular Batad.

Places to Stay The *Bangaan Family Inn* has rooms for P40/60. It offers pleasant accommodation in a family atmosphere. There's even hot water for showers. The food is excellent, and full board is possible. The view from the big roofed terrace next to the house is magnificent. This place is not in the village of Bangaan itself, but on the main road before it goes downhill. There is also a path near the inn which leads to Batad (takes about one hour).

The North

VIGAN

Next to Intramuros in Manila, Vigan is the second greatest architectural legacy of the Spaniards. The difference is that many of the old houses still stand in Vigan. In the latter half of the 16th century, after the young conquistador Juan de Salcedo won a naval battle against the Chinese, Legaspi, his grandfather, gave him the commission to govern Ilocos Province. Vigan thus became a Spanish base.

In planning the layout of the town, Salcedo was no doubt influenced by the secure fortifications of Intramuros. Today Vigan is the best preserved Spanish town in the Philippines. You can almost sense history here. It is well known as the birthplace of several national heroes, including Diego Silang and his brave wife, Gabriela, Padre Jose Burgos, Isabelo de los Reyes, Leona Florentina and Elipido Quirino.

Vigan is especially impressive in the early morning, when the diffused light transforms the old town with its colonial houses and calesas into a scene reminiscent of the 17th century. Mena Crisologo St is particularly beautiful.

Things to See & Do

The partially restored old town is the birthplace of Padre Jose Burgos, who was executed by the Spaniards in 1872. The house in which he was born has housed the **Ayala Museum** since 1975. It is open Tuesday to Sunday from 9 am to noon and 2 to 5 pm. Admission is P10. You can also get information there about the Tingguian, who live east of Vigan.

The **National Museum** is on Liberation Blvd, between Quezon Ave and Governor A Reyes St. Although it is also obviously intended to be a memorial to the ex-governor Crisologo and the 'good old Marcos days' (Marcos was born in this region), it offers a fairly good idea of life in Vigan under Spanish rule. The colonial furniture on the 2nd floor is interesting. The museum is meant to be open daily from 8.30 to 11.30 am and 1.30 to 4.30 pm but is usually closed. Admission is free. The **Cathedral of St Paul** near Plaza Burgos, built in 1641, is one of the oldest and biggest churches in the country.

Along Rizal St where it crosses Liberation Blvd there are **potteries** where you can observe the traditional production of water containers. The fat-bellied pots with the small lid are called *burnay*, a pottery is called *pagburnayan*.

Mindoro Beach, about four km southwest of Vigan, is grey and not particularly recommended for swimming, although it is quite suitable for a lonely walk along the ocean. On the way, there is a **tobacco factory** and a small **pottery**. It's a good idea to make this short trip (in a way fitting for Vigan) by calesa, which should be possible for around P100.

Places to Stay

Grandpa's Inn (☎ 2118) at 1 Bonifacio St has rooms with fan for P130, with fan and bath for P200 and with air-con and bath for P350. The place is basic and not all the rooms are clean enough to pass muster.

The *Vigan Hotel* (☎ 2588) on Burgos St has rooms with fan for P200/300 and with air-con and bath for P400/500. It is clean and fairly good, although some of the rooms appear to be a bit stuffy. It has a restaurant.

The Cordillera Inn (☎ 2526; fax 2840) at 29 Mena Crisologo St is a good place with comfortable, tastefully furnished rooms with fan for P340, with fan and bath for P550 and with air-con and bath from P730 to P840. There is a restaurant. The owners have also opened the *Teppeng Cove Beach Resort*, about 40 km north of Vigan, which has rooms from P300 to P650.

The *Aniceto Mansion* on Mena Crisologo St is the best hotel in town. It has clean and comfortable rooms with air-con and bath for P700/900. It also has a restaurant.

Places to Eat

The *Vigan Plaza Restaurant* on Florentino St has good sandwiches and Magnolia ice creams. The *Tower Café* and the *Unique Café*, both on Burgos St, have reduced their range to barbecues and beer. At the *Victory Restaurant* on Quezon Ave different menus are offered each day. The *Cool Spot Restaurant* is an attractive half open-air establishment, not far from the Vigan Hotel, and is known for its good Ilokano cooking. You can get coffee and cake at *Mr Donut* on Quezon Ave.

If you want a beer after 9 pm, when most places close, you should try the beer garden *PNB Snack*, near the Philippine National Bank, and several little pubs near the Philippine Rabbit Bus Terminal.

Getting There & Away

Bus From Manila to Vigan, there are several Philippine Rabbit, Times Transit, Farina Trans and Maria de Leon buses daily. The trip takes over seven hours. Not all Laoag buses go right into town, so you have to go the rest of the way, from the highway to Vigan, by tricycle.

From San Fernando several Philippine Rabbit buses go to Vigan daily, leaving from the plaza. You can also board a bus from Manila to Vigan or Laoag there. This takes over two hours.

From Aparri to Vigan via Claveria, buses go daily, leaving at 5.30 and 11.30 pm from

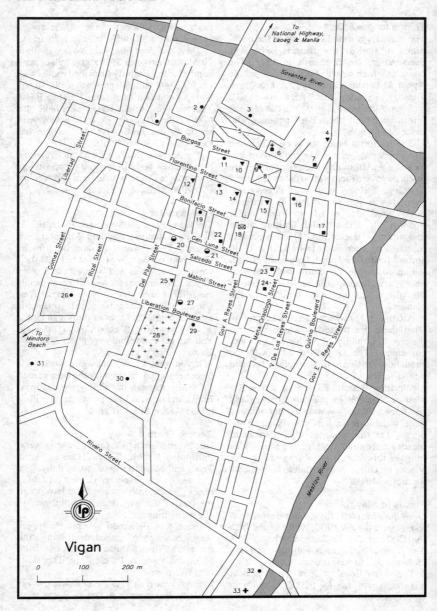

To
National Highway,
Laoag & Manila

Sovantes River

Burgos Street

Liberdad Street

Florentino Street

Bonifacio Street

Gen Luna Street

Salcedo Street

Mabini Street

Liberation Boulevard

Gomez Street

Rizal Street

Del Pilar Street

Gov A Reyes Street

Mena Crisologo Street

V De Los Reyes Street

Quirino Boulevard

Gov E Reyes Street

To
Mindoro
Beach

Rivero Street

Mestizo River

Vigan

0   100   200 m

■ PLACES TO STAY		3	St Paul's College
		5	Plaza Salcedo
7	Vigan Hotel	6	Cathedral of St Paul
17	Grandpa's Inn	8	Plaza Burgos
22	New Luzon Inn	9	Tower
23	The Cordillera Inn	11	Municipal Hall
24	Aniceto Mansion	13	Philippine National Bank (PNB)
		16	Leona Florentina Building
▼ PLACES TO EAT		18	Post Office
		19	Metrobank
4	Cool Spot Restaurant	20	Minibuses to Laoag & Bangued
10	Tower Café & Unique Café	21	Philippine Rabbit Bus Terminal
12	Victory Restaurant	26	Pottery
14	PNB Snack	27	Times Transit Bus Terminal
15	Vigan Plaza Restaurant	28	Church
25	Mr Donut	29	National Museum
		30	Market
	OTHER	31	Mira Hill Park
		32	University of Northern Philippines
1	Ayala Museum	33	Provincial Hospital
2	Provincial Capitol Building		

the Shell petrol station. The trip takes nine hours. One bus goes from Tuguegarao to Vigan via Aparri, everyday at 5 pm, taking 11 hours. It is possible to board the bus either in Aparri or at the new bridge, seven km south.

From Laoag to Vigan, there are many minibuses daily as well as Philippine Rabbit, Times Transit, Farina Trans and Maria de Leon buses bound for Manila or San Fernando. The trip takes two hours. You may have to get off the bus on the highway outside the town and complete the last stretch to Vigan by tricycle (this costs P2).

Vigan to Bangued & Sagada

An unusual way of getting to Sagada is by crossing Abra Province. At the time of writing, there was sporadic fighting between the military and the NPA in the south of the province so it is best to check with local authorities in Vigan first before undertaking this route.

A good stopover is the little town of **Manabo**, about halfway to Sagada. Nearby are several villages of the Tingguian tribe that you can visit by walking through Boliney, Bucloc and Sallapadan. In Boliney

are the **Bani Hot Springs** and the **Nani Waterfalls**. Bucloc has rice terraces, and, if you are lucky, you may be able to see the Grand Tingguian Festival at Sallapadan. This is the most important cultural event in Abra Province and is usually held in March or April each year. The exact date is fixed only shortly beforehand.

Getting There & Away Several minibuses travel from Vigan to Bangued daily, leaving from the bus terminal on Quezon Ave. They take three hours. There is also an irregular connection between Bangued and Tubo several times a week. A jeep leaves Bangued at about 6 am. If you ask the driver the day before, you will be picked up at your hotel and you might get to sit at the front. It takes eight hours to travel this stretch of barely 50 km.

The jeep does not go beyond Tubo. The mountains of the Central Cordillera would make the direct walk to Sagada difficult if not impossible. The best way to go is probably via Dilong, Quirino and Besao, and there could possibly be a shortcut from Dilong. As an alternative route to Sagada, you may be able to get a bus or at least a

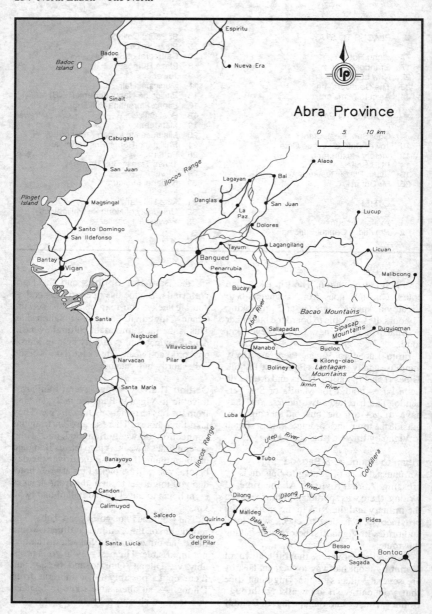

Abra Province

jeepney connection from Candon, on the main west coast road, to Quirino.

BANGUED

Bangued was founded in 1598 by Augustinian monks and is the capital of Abra, which has been a province since 1917. From little Victoria Park, on Casmata Hill, you can get a good view of the town and of the Abra River flowing through the wide valley.

Places to Stay

The *Marysol Pension House* (☎ 8260) on Taft St has rooms with fan for P200/250 and with air-con and bath for P400/500. Though simple, it is the best hotel in town. It also has a restaurant. At the Marysol Pension, meals are only served if ordered in advance.

The *Bangued Inn* also on Taft St has simple rooms with fan for P100/200 and with air-con for P300.

The *Tingguian Lodge* at Calaba has rooms with fan for P100/160, with fan and bath for P200 and with air-con for P300. A simple place, it is a bit outside town, so you may have trouble getting transport there.

The *Diocesan Pastoral Center* has rooms with fan and bath for P150/200 and with air-con and bath for P300. Make enquiries at the convent near the church, as it is not a hotel but accommodation run by the church.

Places to Eat

Reasonably good restaurants are hard to come by in Bangued. Worth mentioning perhaps are *Jade's Restaurant* and the *Yan Yan Mami House*.

Getting There & Away

From Manila to Bangued there are only a few Times Transit buses daily, taking eight hours for the trip.

From Vigan to Bangued there are several minibuses daily from the terminal on Quezon Ave. The trip takes three hours. Large Times Transit buses are also likely to be there.

CURRIMAO

Currimao, with the D'Coral Beach Resort, is about 75 km north of Vigan and 25 km south of Laoag. Slightly farther north is a long bay with a fine beach. Unfortunately, it is not fringed appropriately by palm trees but by mixed vegetation. This is where you'll find the Playa Blanca Resort.

Places to Stay

The *Playa Blanca Resort* (☎ 220784) has rooms with fan and bath for P700/850. It is pleasant and has a restaurant and windsurfing is available. To get there, get off at the Currimao Outpost; it is another five minutes' walk away.

The *D' Coral Beach Resort* (☎ 221133) has rooms and cottages with fan and bath for P300 and with air-con and bath for P600. It is fairly comfortable and has a restaurant. Get off near Port Currimao and walk just 500 metres to reach it.

Getting There & Away

From Vigan to Currimao, there are many minibuses daily as well as several big Times Transit and Philippine Rabbit buses bound for Laoag. The trip takes 1½ hours.

From Laoag to Currimao, there are also many minibuses daily as well as several big Philippine Rabbit, Times Transit, Farinas Trans and Maria de Leon buses, all going on to Vigan and Manila. The trip takes 30 minutes.

LAOAG

In 1818, when Ilocos Province was divided in two, Laoag, on the Laoag River, became the capital of Ilocos Norte, one of Luzon's most beautiful provinces. Worth seeing is **St Williams Cathedral**, which was built between 1650 and 1700, and is one of the many old Spanish churches in this province. Also interesting is the mighty sinking belfry, which stands a little apart from the cathedral.

You get a good view over this city of 100,000 inhabitants from **Ermita Hill**. Day trips into the nearby countryside are recommended. (See the Around Laoag section later in this chapter.)

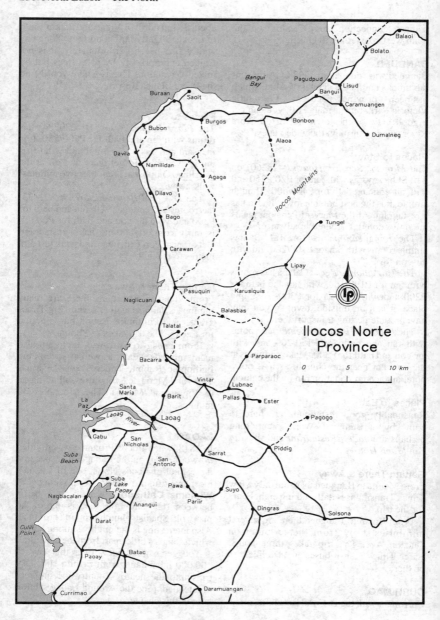

Ilocos Norte Province

Places to Stay

The *City Lodging House* is on General Antonio Luna St and has rooms with fan for P80/160. It is unadorned and the rooms are small, but it is often booked out. There is a restaurant. The *Modern Hotel* on M Nolasco St has simple rooms with fan for P80/160 and with fan and bath for P260.

The *Texicano Hotel* (☎ 220606, 220290) on Rizal St has rooms with fan for P100/140, with fan and bath for P130/150 and with air-con and bath for P330/400. These prices are for rooms in the old building. You can get rooms with air-con in the new building from P420/520. It has been well maintained and there is a restaurant. The hotel entrance is on General Hizon St.

The *Casa Llanes Pension* (☎ 221125) on Primo Lazaro Ave is nice and tidy, and has a restaurant. It has spacious rooms with fan and bath for P140 and with air-con and bath for P240. The rooms can also be rented for three and 12 hours.

The *Pichay Lodging House* (☎ 221267) on Primo Lazaro Ave has rooms with fan and bath for P120/180 and with air-con and bath for P270/300. It is pleasant and well appointed, and is probably the best hotel in town.

The *Fort Ilocandia Resort Hotel* (☎ 221166-70; fax 415170) has rooms with air-con and bath for P2000 and P2200. Suites are P3000. It's an exclusive hotel on Suba Beach, south of the airport, and has a restaurant, disco, casino, swimming pool and tennis court. Dune buggies, Hobie Cats and windsurfing are also available. You can take a jeepney going from Laoag to Calayab there.

Places to Eat

You can get good and cheap Chinese and Filipino dishes at the *City Lunch & Snack Bar*, on the corner of General Antonio Luna and Nolasco Sts. It also serves very reasonably priced breakfasts.

Worth mentioning is the *Magic Bunny* on Rizal St. In the same street is the good and cheap *Dohan Food & Bake Shop*. The *McBurgee* is a small fast-food restaurant on

F R Castro Ave. The following restaurants belong to the mid-price range: the *Airways Restaurant* on Paco Roman St, the *Barrio Fiesta* on Manuel Nalasco St and the *Hot Stuff House* on General Fidel Segundo Ave.

The Ilokano cooking is good at the *Peppermint Brickside Café* on Don Severo Hernando Ave, where they sometimes have singers in the evenings, as does *Colonial Fast Food*, a good restaurant on F R Castro Ave.

Entertainment

To the relief of Chinese tourists, the introduction of flights to and from Taiwan brought about the re-opening of the Casino in the Fort Ilocandia Resort Hotel. Cock-fighting takes place on the edge of town on Sunday and public holidays from 2 pm onwards.

Next door, you will find Laoag's nightlife at *Discoland*, consisting of about 10 discos.

Getting There & Away

Air PAL has return flights on Monday, Wednesday and Friday between Manila and Laoag. Flying time is one hour.

PAL has an office at Laoag International Airport (☎ 220537) and on Jose Rizal St (☎ 220135).

Bus From Manila to Laoag, there are many Philippine Rabbit, Farina Trans and Maria de Leon buses daily, taking 10 hours. The buses go via San Fernando and Vigan. Vigan is off the highway and not all buses make the detour into town. If you are in a hurry, get a tricycle for P2 to the highway and stop one of the buses there.

There are also many minibuses travelling from Vigan to Laoag daily, which take three hours.

From Aparri to Laoag, there are only a few buses, going via Claveria and Pagudpud. Of the ones that do go, some are bound for Vigan. You can also go by jeepney to the new bridge and catch a bus there coming from Tuguegarao and going to Laoag or Vigan.

From Baguio to Laoag via San Fernando, Philippine Rabbit buses go every hour,

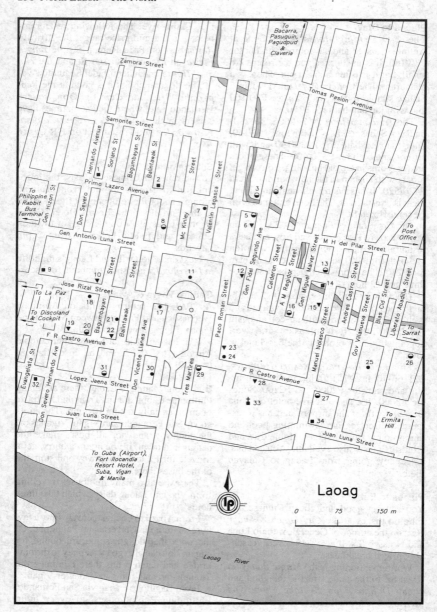

Laoag

0   75   150 m

■ PLACES TO STAY

1	Pichay Lodging House
2	Casa Llanes Pension
9	Texicano Hotel
14	City Lodging House
32	Golden Dragon Hotel
34	Modern Hotel

▼ PLACES TO EAT

6	Hot Stuff House
10	Magic Bunny Restaurant
12	Kookee House
14	City Lunch & Snack Bar
15	Barrio Fiesta Restaurant
19	Peppermint Brickside Café
22	Colonial Fast Food
23	Airways Restaurant
28	McBurgee Restaurant

OTHER

3	Ordinary Buses to Manila
4	Florida Liner Bus Terminal
5	Jeepneys & Minibuses to Bacarra & Pasuquin
7	Fire & Ash Disco
8	Minibuses to Pagudpud
11	Provincial Capitol Building
13	Jeepneys to La Paz
16	Jeepneys to San Nicolas
17	Philippine National Bank (PNB)
18	PAL
20	Farinas Trans Bus Terminal
21	Cinemas
24	Sinking Belltower
25	Market
26	Jeepneys to Sarrat & Dingras
27	Jeepneys to Suba & Jeepneys to Fort Ilocandia Resort Hotel
29	Jeepneys to Batac & Paoay
30	Town Hall
31	Maria de Leon Bus Terminal
33	St Williams Cathedral

unfortunately seldom with air-conditioning. The trip takes six hours.

From Laoag to Manila, Philippine Rabbit buses go hourly via Vigan, leaving on the hour between 7 am and 11 pm. The Maria de Leon buses are better. They leave at about 7.30 and 8.30 am, and 8.30, 9 and 9.30 pm. The air-con Farina Trans buses are very good, but it is advisable to book. Several buses leave between 6.30 am and 12.30 pm. Another air-con bus leaves at 8.15 pm. The regular buses leave at 7 am and every half hour between 5.30 and 9 pm. The trip takes 10 hours.

From Laoag to Aparri via Pagudpud and Claveria, there are few daytime buses, leaving from the corner of Primo Lazaro and General Fidel Segundo Aves. There are night buses to Aparri at 10 pm (Florida bus) and 2.30 am (Pantranco bus). Go by day so that you can see the spectacular landscape and the beautiful views over the South China Sea. You can also get a minibus to Pagudpud and then go by jeepney to Claveria. The road

from Pagudpud to Claveria is in bad condition, but the views are especially worth seeing. About halfway is the so-called Riviera of the North, at Banua, where there is also a government resthouse. It takes over four hours to reach Claveria and eight hours to reach Aparri.

AROUND LAOAG
North

North of Laoag, **Bacarra** has a massive belfry which stands next to the town's church. It dates back to 1783 and was partly destroyed in the severe earthquake of 1930. The top of the spire was crooked and, until 1984, was held in place solely by 'the hand of God'. Another earthquake then caused its complete collapse.

Ten km farther north is Pasuquin; from there you can go to **Seksi Beach**, which is four km outside the town and can be reached by tricycle. There you can see women strenuously at work harvesting salt in the late afternoon.

At low tide, the top layer of salt, mixed with sand, is scraped together and put in a light hanging basket. Water is then poured in and runs out through the bottom of the basket into an earthenware pot, now with a very high salt content. This water is taken to the village and boiled in a large pot until it has almost completely evaporated. The remaining slurry is then ladled out of the pot into a hanging basket, which the remaining water seeps through to form a long, hanging white cone of the finest salt.

West

The nearest good beach to Laoag is in **La Paz**, an unhurried, long drawn-out place at the mouth of the Laoag River. Hardly any vegetation exists on the wide beach, but there are very extensive sand dunes.

South-East

A fine country road leads to Sarrat, the birthplace of former president Marcos. In the centre of town is the restored **Sarrat Church & Convent**, built in 1779 by Augustinian monks.

Only ruins remain of the church in Dingras, which was destroyed by fire in 1838.

South

There is a **church** in San Nicolas which was built in the latter part of the 17th century and restored in the 19th century. In Batac is the so-called **Malacanang del Norte**, formerly the vast domain of Marcos and today a public museum.

A few km to the south-west is the fortress-like church of **Paoay**, which is worth a stop. Its side walls are supported by strong posts. Styled in 'earthquake baroque', this church is probably the most famous in Ilocos Norte. You can also see the scenically attractive Lake Paoay. Going from Paoay through bamboo forests, along the western shore of the lake to Suba, you could make a detour to **Suba Beach**. The road there is hilly and winding and there are high, extensive sand dunes, more imposing than those at La Paz, where many Philippine films have been shot. It is usually windy on this wide beach and there is good surf.

If you have come up from Paoay by tri-cycle and want to return to Laoag by jeepney, ask the driver to drop you off at the Fort Ilocandia Resort Hotel or at the Suba Golf Course. The last regular jeepney leaves the hotel at about 4 pm and passes the golf course on the way back to Laoag. The exclusive hotel is about five km south of Gabu, where Laoag Airport is located. Marcos had it built especially for guests on the occasion of the wedding of his daughter Irene to Greggy Araneta in 1983. The tables and seats under cover on the beach belong to the hotel and may be used free of charge.

PAGUDPUD

Pagudpud lies on Bangui Bay, about 60 km north of Laoag, and could become a tourist destination in the near future. The beautiful **Saud White Beach** at Pagudpud is probably the best and most attractive in North Luzon.

The *Villa del Mar* has simple rooms for P80 to P200 and spacious cottages with two rooms and a kitchen for P350 to P600. The *Ivory Beach Resort*, with similar rates, should be open for business at the time of this book's publication. Both places are about four km out of town.

Getting There & Away

Buses from Vigan and Laoag to Aparri and Tuguegarao go via Pagudpud. The trip to Pagudpud takes two hours from Laoag and seven hours from Aparri. From Laoag there are several minibuses which travel to Pagudpud daily and leave from Don Vicente Llanes Ave.

CLAVERIA

If you want to sunbathe at Waikiki Beach, you don't have to fly to Hawaii. Claveria too has a **Waikiki Beach**. It has the same name because of its supposed similarity to the world-famous beach of Honolulu, but that is hardly justified. The NPA is also very active in the surroundings of Claveria.

South of Claveria live the Ita tribespeople. They are Negrito who still go hunting with bows and arrows. If you want to visit them, you have to go about eight km by tricycle and then walk another four km. On the way there you will pass the village of Santa Filomena.

You can make side trips from Claveria to the **Babuyan Islands**. There is a passenger boat once a week to Calayan Island, north-east of Dalupiri, which takes five hours. From Calayan Island, there are boats going to Babuyan Island, farther north-east, taking four hours. The people there live in almost total seclusion from modern civilisation. It is suggested that visitors take a few presents or objects for barter even though the value of money is known there. You can sleep and eat at the priest's or the mayor's house.

The 837-metre-high Babuyan Claro Volcano, with its two craters, on Babuyan Island is worth seeing. **Fuga Island** is supposed to be the most beautiful of the Babuyan Islands. As it is the private property of Mr Lim, you need a visitor's permit, which you can get at his timber yard in Claveria. However, the manager or other person authorised to issue a permit is seldom there.

Places to Stay
The cottages on the beach at Claveria were destroyed by a severe typhoon, but you can stay in the house of the former owner of Sun Beach Cottages who now runs the Grass-roots Restaurant in Claveria.

There is supposed to be accommodation at Taggat, a few km west of Claveria, in the *Company House* and the *Public House* for about P50/100. Both houses are adjoining, but they are not designated as hotels. They are about a one-km walk from the bus stop.

Between Claveria and Taggat, next to the Shell petrol station, is the *Traveller's Inn*. This is an old house without electricity, where you can stay for P40.

Getting There & Away
From Aparri to Claveria, there are a few buses headed for Laoag or Vigan daily. The trip takes four hours.

From Tuguegarao to Claveria, there is a daily bus going on to Vigan, which takes five hours.

From Claveria to Aparri, there is a daily

AML bus at about 10 am. Additional buses come from Laoag, but the seats are mostly booked out. You can stop the buses in the main street. They take four hours.

There is a daily Pantranco North bus from Claveria to Tuguegarao and Manila at 10 am. This bus also goes close to Aparri. If you want to stop there, get off at the new bridge and continue by jeepney. It takes five hours to get to Tuguegarao and 14 hours to get to Manila.

From Vigan and Laoag to Claveria there are few buses. It takes between four and six hours or more (see the Getting There & Away sections under Vigan and Laoag earlier in this chapter).

APARRI
It's not worth staying in Aparri, unless you want to do some deep-sea fishing. Big-game fishing is popular in the **Babuyan Channel**, north of Luzon. The waters around **Point Escarpada**, near San Vicente, are well known as the best Philippine fishing grounds for marlin. If you want to explore this north-eastern corner of Luzon, you should take the bus from Aparri to Santa Ana. You will have to continue by tricycle to San Vicente if there is no bus or jeepney. From there you can get somebody to take you across to Palaui Island by outrigger boat.

Places to Stay & Eat
The *Pipo Hotel* (☎ 22122) at 37 Macanaya St has simple rooms with fan for P100/200 and with fan and bath for P200/350. It has a restaurant. It is before Aparri, on the right hand side. Bus drivers will halt if requested.

The *Ryan Mall Hotel* (☎ 22369) on Rizal St has good rooms with fan and bath for P250 and with air-con and bath from P375 to P550. Apart from the *Magnolia Restaurant*, down near the river, this hotel's restaurant is probably the only decent one in town.

Getting There & Away
From Manila to Aparri, there are daily Pantranco North buses more or less every hour. They go via Ilagan, Tuguegarao and Gattaran, and take 11 hours.

Trees of the Philippines

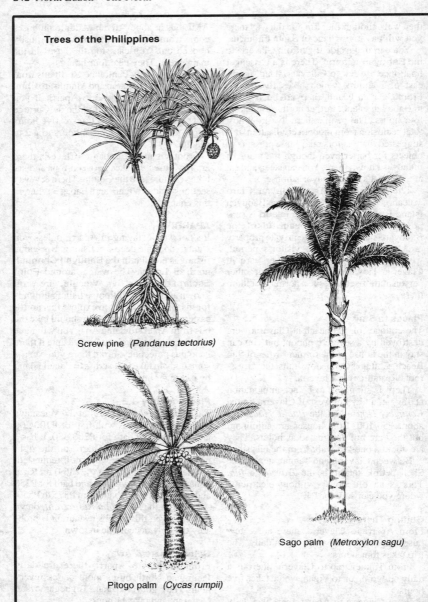

Screw pine *(Pandanus tectorius)*

Sago palm *(Metroxylon sagu)*

Pitogo palm *(Cycas rumpii)*

Coconut palm
(*Cocos nucifera*)

Nipa palm (*Nypa fruticans*)

Fan palm
(*Corypha elata*)

Royal palm (*Roystonea regia*)

From Vigan and Laoag, there are few buses to Aparri. The trip takes 11 and nine hours respectively (see the Getting There & Away sections under Vigan and Laoag earlier in this chapter).

From Claveria to Aparri, there is a daily AML bus, which leaves at 10 am and takes over three hours. There are also buses coming from Vigan and Laoag, but the seats are usually booked out.

From Aparri to Manila via Gattaran (one hour) and Tuguegarao (two hours), there are Pantranco North buses daily, taking 11 hours. The minibuses from Aparri to Tuguegarao stop frequently and leave from opposite the Victoria Hotel; the first leaves at 7 am.

GATTARAN

If you are coming from Manila or Tuguegarao, you can break the journey to Aparri in Gattaran and make a lengthy detour to the **Tanlagan Waterfalls**, which have a drop of over 100 metres. You would have to be a dedicated lover of waterfalls, however, to make the trip, as this natural spectacle is almost 40 km to the east, beyond Cumao, which you can only reach by jeepney from Gattaran. The last part of the trip can only be done by vehicle in the dry season, as there are several rivers to be crossed.

TUGUEGARAO

Tuguegarao is the capital of Cagayan Province. The **Cagayan Museum & Historical Research Center**, next to the Provincial Capitol Building, exhibits archaeological finds, historical and cultural artefacts, liturgical items and ethnographic objects of the province.

Tuguegarao is also the starting point for the **Callao Caves** near Peñablanca, about 25 km east of Tuguegarao. You can go there by jeepney or tricycle. If you want to make more than a day trip of it, you can stay the night at the Callao Caves Resort.

Apart from speleology, this cave country also offers very interesting treks to the distant villages of the **Sierra Madre**. Some villages can only be reached by boat on the Pinacanauan River or on foot. If you want to experience real Philippine country life, you ought to stay a few days longer.

In **Iguig**, slightly north of Tuguegarao, there are 14 large statues which represent the Stations of the Cross to Calvary. It is an important place of pilgrimage, especially during Easter week.

Places to Stay

The *LB Lodging House* on Luna St is a simple place with rooms for P60 per person, and there is a restaurant. The *Hotel Leonor* (☎ 1806) (previously called the Casa Lavadia) on Rizal St has rooms for P80/150, with fan for P100/180 and with air-con for P200/250. This place is simple, clean and comfortable, and has a restaurant. All in all, it's fairly comfortable accommodation.

The *Olympia Hotel* (☎ 1805) on Washington St has rooms with fan and bath for P130/180 and with air-con and bath for P220/300. It is basic but quite good and has a restaurant.

Georgie's Inn (☎ 1434) on Aguinaldo St has rooms with fan and bath for P140/180 and with air-con and bath for P240/280. It is pleasant and has a restaurant. It is better than the *Pensione Abraham* (☎ 1793) which is on Bonifacio St. It has rooms with fan for P120/160, with fan and bath for P160/200 and with air-con and bath for P250/280.

The *Hotel Delfino* (☎ 1952, 1953) on Gonzaga St has rooms with air-con and bath from P280 to P400 and suites for P500. It is fairly clean and has a restaurant and disco.

The *Pension Lorita* (☎ 1390) on Rizal St has passable rooms with air-con and bath for P400/450, and it has a coffee shop.

The *Pensione Roma* (☎ 1057, 1282) on the corner of Luna and Bonifacio Sts has rooms with fan and bath for P200 and with air-con and bath for P500/550. This is a pleasant, friendly hotel and there is a small restaurant.

The *Callao Caves Resort* (☎ 1801, 1087) in Peñablanca has rooms from P120 to P260, with fan and bath for P300 and cottages from P400 to P600.

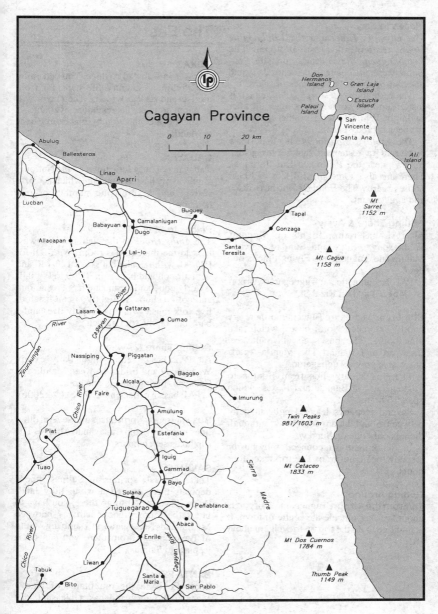

Cagayan Province

Places to Eat

The *Olympia Hotel* and the *LB Lodging House* restaurants close at 9 pm. The *Pampanguena Restaurant*, opposite Pensione Abraham, changes its menus daily and has a surprisingly large choice of cakes.

The restaurant at *Georgie's Inn*, which is just around the corner, stays open till after midnight. While the food is rather expensive, the beer is pretty cheap.

The *Apollo Restaurant* is a big Ihaw-Ihaw restaurant (a restaurant that serves grilled inihaw) near the Pantranco Bus Terminal. There are also some small discos and beer houses nearby. The *Hotel Delfino* has a disco and a restaurant.

Getting There & Away

Air PAL has return flights on Monday, Wednesday, Friday and Sunday between Manila and Tuguegarao. Flying time is one hour.

PAL has an office at Tuguegarao Airport (☎ 446120) and on Rizal St.

Bus From Manila to Tuguegarao there are hourly Pantranco North buses, which take nine hours. The buses go via Santa Fe, Cauayan and Ilagan. The Manila-Aparri buses also go via Tuguegarao.

There is a daily bus from Bontoc to Tuguegarao via Banaue and Roxas, which takes 10 hours.

Several jeepneys leave Tinglayan daily between 6 and 11 am for Tabuk, although there is only one on Sunday.

In Tabuk there is a connection by bus or jeepney to Tuguegarao. The trip takes four hours.

Getting Around

To/From the Airport Tuguegarao's airport is about four km outside the centre of town. It is possible to do the trip by tricycle for about P15.

The East

ROXAS

Roxas is in Isabela Province. You can enjoy real Philippine country life here, far from tourists and rucksack roads. The mayor will be happy to make his resthouse available.

There is a connection by bus from Roxas to Manila.

CAUAYAN

Cauayan is a busy little town on the National Highway with a large market which is worth seeing, and a surprising number of restaurants.

Places to Stay

The *Amity Hotel* on the National Highway, next to the market, has rooms with fan for P75/90, with fan and bath for P120/140 and with air-con and bath from P200 to P300. It is fairly good and clean, and has a restaurant and coffee shop. At night you can listen to live folk music while you enjoy beer and a barbecue on the roof garden.

Getting There & Away

Air PAL has a return flight daily except Wednesday and Friday between Manila and Cauayan. Flying time is one hour.

PAL has an office on F L Dy St (☎ 22006).

Bus Pantranco North buses and several other lines run daily from Cauayan to Manila. The trip takes seven hours.

SALINAS

There are salt springs in Salinas whose deposits have created a white hilly landscape. If you want to go there, you have to break the journey about halfway between Manila and Tuguegarao in Bambang, south of Bayombong. From there you can get a jeepney to Salinas.

SANTA FE

Santa Fe is in the mountains of Nueva Vizcaya Province and has a pleasant, dry

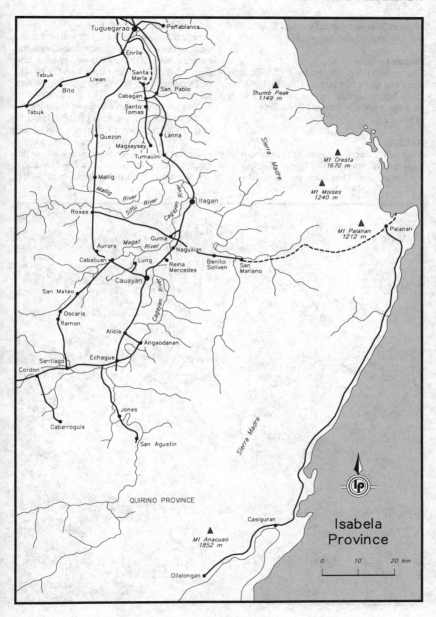

climate. You can buy all sorts of handicrafts there, especially basket ware.

Places to Stay

Tony's Hotel has rooms for P75/140. It is basic but has a restaurant. The *Golden Rose Hotel* has reasonable rooms for P100/180. It also has a good restaurant that offers plenty of choice.

BALER

Baler is the capital of Aurora Province. The main part of Francis Ford Coppola's *Apocalypse Now* was shot there on the wild east coast of North Luzon. The town itself is not very interesting, but you can go on excursions to the surrounding mountains, visit the Negrito tribes (Dumagat), or spend a few days snorkelling or just lazing on the beach. In December the strong surf should attract surfers.

You may also be able to go on fishing trips in the open Pacific in small fishing boats if you can talk the Baler fishermen into taking you. If you want to, you can hire a fully equipped boat. On the way from Baler to the radar weather station on Cape Encanto there are several refreshing springs, such as the

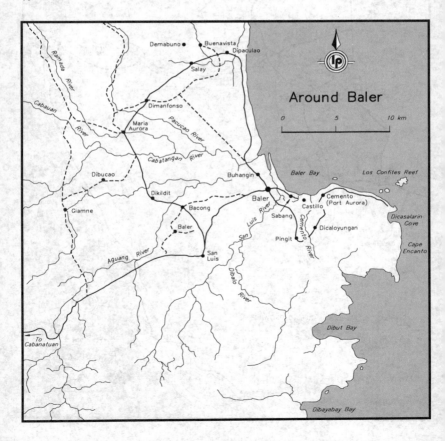

Around Baler

Digisit Springs. In **Dibut Bay**, a bit farther south, you can find beautiful coral. You can get there by boat, or on foot across the mountains. **Dipaculao**, north of Baler, is a starting point for mountain treks; some Ilongot tribes live in the mountains.

Places to Stay

The *Amihan Hotel* on Bitong St has rooms with fan for P120/140 and with fan and bath for P150/200. It is basic and clean and has a restaurant, but the cocks next door crow pretty early in the morning.

There are various places along the beach in Sabang. The *Baler Guest House* has rooms with fan for P120 and with fan and bath for P200. The *Ocean View Lodge* has rooms with fan and bath for P170/220 and also has a restaurant. The *MIA Surf & Sports Resort* has rooms with fan for P120/180 and with fan and bath for P220/280. You can hire surfboards there and take surfing lessons.

If you want bigger surf than that at Sabang Beach, you can get a surf guide to take you to another beach.

Getting There & Away

There are several Pantranco North Buses from Manila to Cabanatuan daily, some of which also go through to Baler. You can either take a direct bus or one labelled San Jose, Ilagan, Tuguegarao or Aparri. They take 2½ hours. If you are coming from the north, you have to change at Cabanatuan for Baler.

The last bus from Cabanatuan to Baler leaves at 3 pm. The road across the Sierra Madre is bumpy but the views are beautiful. If you are going towards Baler, you will get the best view sitting on the left-hand side of the bus. The trip will take you four hours or more.

There are several Baliwag Trans and E Jose Trans buses daily from Olongapo to Cabanatuan which also stop in San Fernando (Pampanga). From San Fernando to Cabanatuan, Arayat Express buses run several trips daily, leaving from the bus terminal next to the Philippine National Bank.

Baler to Cabanatuan

Roughly halfway, you will come to the entrance to the **Aurora Memorial Park**, where there are a few restaurants. The bus stops there for half an hour, long enough for a scrumptious eggcaldo soup in *Lorelyn's Restaurant*.

South Luzon

The convoluted peninsula stretching south from Manila has an impressive, volcano-studded landscape which includes the Mayon Volcano. Mayon's symmetrical cone is said to be the most perfect in the world. It's one of the symbols of the Philippines and the most imposing feature of South Luzon. North of Mayon, hot springs dot the active geothermal area around Tiwi, while the slopes of Mt Isarog, near Naga, and Mt Iriga, near Iriga, are home to several Negrito tribes. Between Sorsogon and Matnog, Mt Bulusan, with its long spurs, has earned the area the name 'Switzerland of the Orient'.

Between Lucena City and Lamon Bay is the mountainous, in places heavily wooded, Quezon National Park. Forget the little-known beach resorts from Atimonan to Gumaca: those at Daet and San Miguel Bay are better. Good beach weather is rarer here than in other parts of the islands, as the Pacific climate is usually rough. The best time to travel is in April and May.

South Luzon also makes a good departure point for travels to the islands of the Visayas.

GETTING THERE & AWAY

Most transport from Luzon to other islands goes through Manila. See Getting There & Away in the Manila chapter earlier in this book.

Bus

Several buses go south from Manila through Lucena, Daet, Naga, Iriga and Legaspi daily. To travel right through to Legaspi takes between 10 and 12 hours. There are air-con buses at 8 am and 7 pm.

The road to Legaspi, the main town in the south, is long and winding – particularly the stretch to Daet. If you want to, you can take one of the large Philtranco buses and follow the Philippine Highway all the way to Matnog at the southern tip.

Train

The journey by train from Manila to South Luzon is quite an experience. Starting at Paco terminal, the Philippine National Railways (PNR) runs two trains everyday bound for Bikol: the rickety economy-class train for Polangui (40 km before Legaspi) leaves at 4 pm (P138) and the only a little bit better (air-con) tourist-class train for Naga leaves at 9 pm (P170). It takes two hours to San Pablo, 4½ hours to Lucena, 14 hours to Naga and 17 hours to Polangui. Don't expect a smooth and comfortable journey – the coaches were imported from India, Japan and Romania over 20 years ago, and the tracks they travel on are over 100 years old!

LUCENA

Depending on the tide, boats leave either from Dalahican or from the river harbour of Cotta Port, just outside of Lucena, to Marinduque and Romblon. A few km north of Lucena, on the road to Pagsanjan, is the little town of Lucban, where you can get a fairly accurate idea of how towns looked during the Spanish rule.

If you don't get to Dalahican Beach, six km from Lucena, you won't have missed anything – it's dirty and swampy. On the other hand, a trip to **Quezon National Park** between Lucena and Atimonan would be worth the trouble, especially if you are the kind of birdwatcher who likes adventure. The reason for this comment is not the numerous birds who have their home in the park, but the fact the military have set up a camp here, which means the NPA turn up regularly.

The Maharlika Highway crosses the park and is used by all the large buses, so it is better to take a minibus. These take the old zigzag road and stop at the picnic ground in the middle of the park. There are interesting walks through the jungle-like vegetation, with lovely flowers, monkeys and so on, but it's not so enjoyable if it's raining. If you want to continue south, you can take a minibus to Atimonan and change to a larger bus there.

Places to Stay

The *Tourist Hotel* (☎ 714456) in Iyam District has rooms with fan for P100/110, with fan and bath for P140/160 and with air-con and bath for P280/380. It is simple but fairly clean and has a small restaurant.

The *Hotel Halina* (☎ 712902) at 104 P Gomez St has rooms with fan and bath for P160/220 and with air-con and bath for P320/390. Suites are P630. The rooms facing the back yard are quiet.

The *Lucena Fresh Air Hotel & Resort* (☎ 712424, 713031) is in the Isabang District, just outside town on the left hand side, coming from Manila. Singles/doubles with fan cost P135/155, with fan and bath P200 to P265 and with air-con and bath P385/440. This place is clean and comfortable. The rooms at the back are large and quiet, and there is a restaurant and a swimming pool.

The *Travel Lodge Chain Motel* (☎ 714489) also in the Isabang District has singles/doubles with fan and bath for P180/230, with air-con for P380/450 and suites for P650. It has a restaurant and a swimming pool.

Getting There & Away

Plenty of Philtranco, Superlines and BLTB buses go from Manila to Lucena every day. They may be going only as far as Lucena or be on their way to Daet, Naga, Legaspi or Matnog. The trip takes about three hours.

Several Supreme Lines buses go from Santa Cruz/Pagsanjan to Lucena daily and take three hours. To save waiting, you can take a jeepney from Santa Cruz to Lucban and change there for another to Lucena. The other, more complicated, way is to take a bus from Santa Cruz to Los Baños, then a jeepney to San Pablo, and from there another bus to Lucena.

ATIMONAN & GUMACA

If you travel by motorcycle or car along the Maharlika Highway, note that the only places to stay between Lucena and Daet are at Atimonan and Gumaca, where there are a couple of reasonable beach resorts.

Places to Stay

The *Victoria Beach Resort* (☎ 965, 975) on the Maharlika Highway at Atimonan has rooms for P100, with fan and bath for P200/300 and doubles with air-con and bath for P400.

In Gumaca, 25 km east of Atimonan, *Pinky's Lodge & Restaurant* has rooms with fan for P50/80, with fan and bath for P100/120 and with air-con and bath for P150/300. It is outside the centre of town and is comfortable and well maintained.

DAET & APUAO GRANDE ISLAND

Daet is a good overnight stop if you're heading to San Miguel Bay for a few days on the beach. **Bagasbas Beach** is the best in the vicinity of Daet. It is 4½ km away and is simpler and cheaper to get to than the beaches on San Miguel Bay. You can also visit the gold fields of **Paracale** and **Mambulao**. In **Caplonga**, farther west, the Black Nazarene Festival takes place every year on 12 and 13 May.

Early risers should catch the remarkable fish market in **Mercedes** from 6 to 8 am. Mercedes is a small coastal village about 10 km north-east of Daet from where you can reach Apuao Grande Island in San Miguel Bay, where the beach is white and the Australian company Swagman Travel has a beach resort.

Places to Stay

The *Mines Hotel* (☎ 2483) on the outskirts on Vinzons Ave has rooms with fan and bath for P60/90 and with air-con and bath for P125/160. It's a basic, clean place.

On Moreno St, the *Karilagan Hotel* (☎ 2265) has rooms with fan and bath for P130/165 and with air-con and bath for P295/350. Suites are P410 and P485, and there is a restaurant. This place is tidy and very pleasant. It is centrally located, which also means it is quite loud.

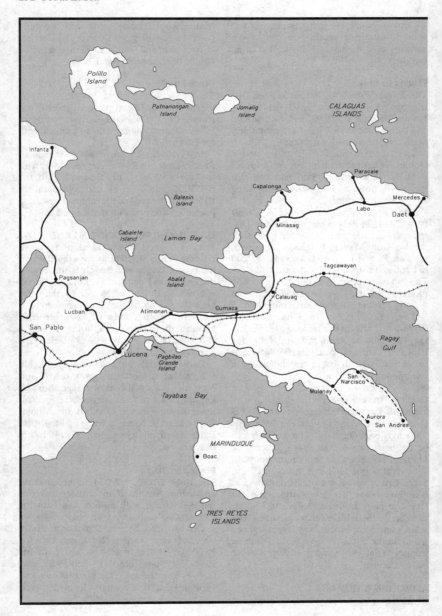

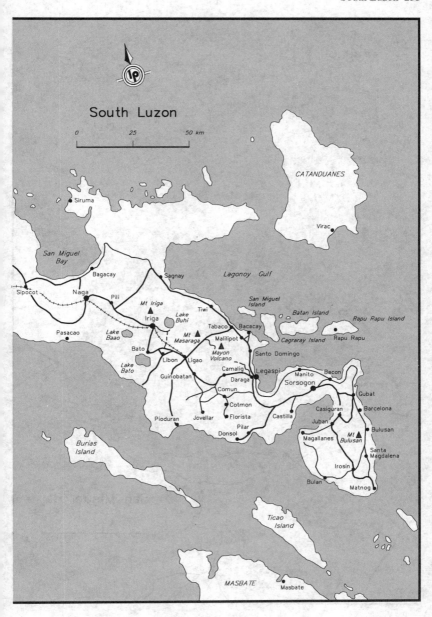

South Luzon

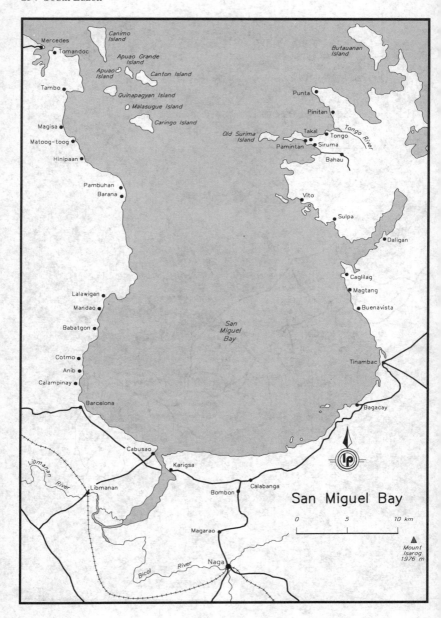

San Miguel Bay

The *Apuao Grande Island Resort Hotel* has cottages with fan and bath for P600. The resort has a tennis court, golf course and swimming pool as well as a restaurant, and you can go water skiing, windsurfing and diving or sail Hobie Cats. Complete tours, including return travel, can be booked and reservations made at the Swagman Hotel in Manila.

Places to Eat

The *Golden House Restaurant* has good food, as does the *Sampaguita Restaurant* upstairs in the Sampaguita Department Store.

Getting There & Away

Air Pacific Airways has return flights on Monday and Friday from Manila to Daet. Flying time is about one hour.

Bus Several buses run from Manila either to Daet only or through Daet to Naga, Legaspi or Matnog daily. Superlines buses leave every two hours; BLTB, J B Bicol Express Line and Philtranco are less frequent. It is advisable to book. The trip takes about seven hours.

Several Philtranco and J B Bicol Express Line buses go from Legaspi to Daet via Naga daily, some going through to Manila, taking three hours. You can get minibuses from Naga.

It's only a short jeepney ride from Daet to Mercedes, which is the departure point for islands in San Miguel Bay.

NAGA

Naga is a friendly, noticeably clean town, which is famous for its late-September Peñafrancia Festival on the river. (See also the Fiestas & Festivals section in the Facts for the Visitor chapter earlier in this book.) The parade of boats usually takes place on Saturday afternoon. Some years have seen the wooden bridge collapse under the weight of spectators.

You can make day trips from Naga to the **Inarihan Dam**, the **Malabsay Falls** at Mt Isarog and the **Nabontalan Falls**. There is a

shop in the market at Naga which sells all varieties of pili nuts – a speciality of the region.

Places to Stay

Naga draws in loads of visitors during the Peñafrancia Festival and the hotels are booked solid in spite of the increased prices (twice to three times as much as usual). Rooms should be booked by the middle of August at the latest, if possible.

The *Fiesta Hotel* (☎ 212760) on Padian St has good, clean rooms with fan for P90/120, with fan and bath for P180/220 and with air-con and bath for P280/350. Suites are P425 and P545, and there is a restaurant and a disco.

The *Sampaguita Tourist Inn* (☎ 214810, 212712) on Panganiban Drive has singles with fan and bath for P145 (good value), singles with air-con and bath for P235 and doubles with air-con and bath for P325 and P450. This is a friendly hotel with clean, although small, rooms, and it has a restaurant and a disco.

At the *Crown Hotel* (☎ 212585) on Burgos St a single room with fan costs P130 and with fan and bath P175. Singles/doubles with air-con and bath cost P340 to P590 and suites are P650. It is a well-kept place, though the beds in the fan-cooled rooms are rather narrow.

The *Midtown Traveller's Pension* (☎ 212474) at 31 General Luna St is pleasant and has rooms with fan and bath for P260/460 and with air-con and bath for P360/520.

The *Aristocrat Hotel* (☎ 215230, 213422) on Elias Angeles St has reasonably comfortable rooms with fan for P245, with fan and bath for P310 and P365 and with air-con and bath for P430 and P555. Suites are P1050, and there is a restaurant and a disco.

The *Moraville Hotel* (☎ 33584, 213513) on Dinaga St has singles with air-con and bath for P350 and doubles with air-con and bath for P400 and P800. This place is clean and is good value. The rooms are quiet, comfortably furnished and have TV. The

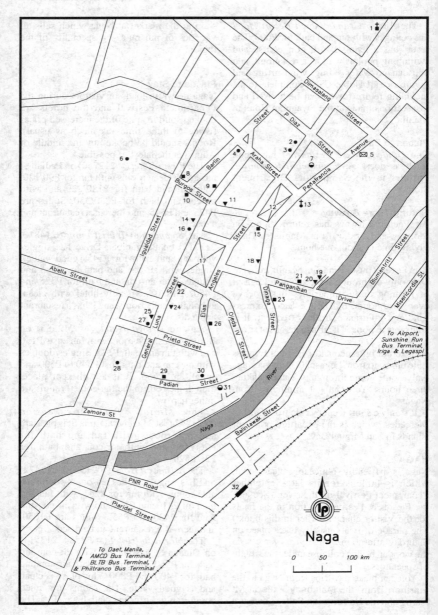

Naga

0   50   100 km

■ PLACES TO STAY

8	Rodson Garden Hotel
9	Midtown Traveller's Pension
10	Grand Imperial Plaza Hotel
15	Crown Hotel
21	Sampaguita Tourist Inn
23	Moraville Hotel
26	Aristocrat Hotel
29	Fiesta Hotel

▼ PLACES TO EAT

10	Karihan Restaurant
11	Graceland Bakeshop
14	Graceland Fast Food
18	Ming Chun Foodhouse
19	Pawlene Foodstreet Restaurant
20	Wok Food Garden Restaurant
22	Carl's Diner
24	Café Candice
25	New China Restaurant
26	Shakey's Pizza
29	Fiesta House Restaurant

OTHER

1	Naga Cathedral
2	Flower's Disco
3	PAL
4	Police Station
5	Post Office
6	University of Nueva Careres
7	Jeepney Terminal
12	Plaza Martinez
13	San Francisco Church
16	PCI Bank & Philippine National Bank (PNB)
17	Plaza Rizal
21	Ball Room Disco
27	Shopper's Mall
28	Market
30	Peñafrancia Tours & Travel
31	Aircon buses to Manila
32	Railway Station

more expensive double rooms have a fridge. There is a restaurant and a nightclub.

The *Grand Imperial Plaza* (☎ 211965, 214193) on Burgos St has comfortable and cosily furnished rooms with air-con and bath for P550 and P650. Suites are P1600. The suites are spacious and have a fridge and TV,

otherwise the TV costs P50 extra. There is a restaurant and a coffee shop.

Places to Eat

The clean *Ming Chun Foodhouse* on Peñafrancia Ave serves good Filipino and Chinese dishes, dim sum among them. The *New China Restaurant* on General Luna St offers a fresh menu every day. The Chinese food in the pleasant *Wok Food Garden*, by the river next to the bridge, is outstanding. You can get Bikolano food in the *Karihan Restaurant* on the ground floor of the Grand Imperial Plaza.

Carl's Diner at Plaza Rizal is a 1950s-style fast-food restaurant and is clean, inexpensive and popular. It serves a wide choice of sandwiches, Korean spare ribs with kimchi, chili con carne, filet mignon and various dishes of the day. You can find hamburgers and ice cream at *Graceland Fast Food*, also at Plaza Rizal. And if you feel like a pizza, the place to go is *Shakey's Pizza* on the ground floor of the Aristocrat Hotel on the south end of Elias Angeles St.

Getting There & Away

Air PAL has return flights daily between Manila and Naga. Flying time is one hour. PAL has an office at Pili Airport and on Elias Angeles St (☎ 2574).

Bus From Manila, several BLTB, J B Bicol Express Line and Philtranco buses run to Naga daily. The trip takes 8½ hours, and it is wise to book. An air-con Sarkies Tours bus leaves Manila daily at 8 am from the corner of Remedios and Indiana Sts, Ermita, heading for Naga. The trip takes 9½ hours. It is advisable to book (☎ 508959, 8176615). Sunshine Run air-con buses leave Manila from Tramo St, Pasay City, for Naga daily at 8 am and 7.15 pm, taking 9½ hours. It is advisable to book. There is an office on the corner of M H del Pilar and Pedro Gil Sts, Ermita (☎ 506601-06, 584787).

From Daet, several BLTB, Philtranco and J B Bicol Express Line buses leave daily, either for Naga only or for Legaspi or

Matnog via Naga. The trip takes 1½ hours. There are also minibuses.

Similarly, from Legaspi, BLTB, Philtranco and J B Bicol Express Line buses go daily to Naga or through Naga on the way to Daet or Manila. It is a two-hour trip. Also from Legaspi to Naga every hour from 6 am to 4 pm and at 7.30 pm an AMDG air-con bus leaves from the Shell petrol station in Peñaranda St, taking 2½ hours (many stops!).

Several air-con buses leave Naga daily (Padian St, diagonally across from the office of Peñafrancia Tours & Travel) for Manila. The trip takes 9½ hours.

Getting Around

To/From the Airport Pili Airport is about 12 km south-east of Naga, just off the road to Pili. For P200 you can arrange airport service with the Aristocrat Hotel, even as a non-resident of the hotel. Otherwise jeepneys (Naga-Pili) are an alternative, although they don't go directly to the airport but stop at the turn-off to the airport on the main road.

Bus The bus terminals of the bigger companies are all on the bypass at the southern edge of town. A tricycle to the town centre costs P10. The Sunshine Run bus terminal is on Panganiban Drive, about 500 metres east of the town centre.

PILI

Pili, to the east of Naga, is noted for its nuts and is an access point to Mt Isarog National Park.

The *El-Alma Hotel*, Old San Roque, has rooms with fan for P70/100, with fan and bath for P150 and with air-con and bath for P300.

IRIGA & LAKE BUHI

Iriga is the turn-off point for visits to Lake Buhi, the 16½ sq km lake where, thanks to intervention by the Bureau of Fisheries and Aquatic Resources (BFAR), the smallest edible fish in the world has at least a chance of survival. Called sinarapan, they, like the tabios in Lake Bato, were previously threat-

ened with extinction. The short-sighted fishing methods of the *parasarap*, as the locals call the fishermen, were to blame for this. They were overfishing the lake with their *sakags* (large fine-mesh V-shaped nets) often destroying the spawn as well. You can see this interesting species close up at the aquarium in the Municipal Building.

Boat trips on Lake Buhi are rather expensive if you hire a boat at the market right on the lake. The ferry which leaves from there and runs to the other side of the lake is much cheaper.

A tribe of Negrito, the Agta, live on Mt Iriga – also called Mt Asog – between Iriga and Lake Buhi.

Places to Stay

Lemar's Lodge (☎ 594) on San Nicolas St has rooms with fan for P70/90, with fan and bath for P120/140 and with air-con and bath for P200. It's a simple but pleasant place, and the air-con rooms have wide beds.

The *Bayanihan Hotel* (☎ 556, 558) on Governor Felix Alfelor St, close to the railway station, has singles with fan for P75 and singles/doubles with air-con and bath for P160/195. It's a reasonably comfortable place with air-con singles that are big enough for two.

The small and elegant *Ibalon Hotel* (☎ 352, 353) on San Francisco St has rooms from P360/420. It's the best hotel in town and probably one of the finest in South Luzon.

Getting There & Away

Jeepneys to Lake Buhi leave from Governor Felix Alfelor St, where the Bayanihan Hotel is. The last jeepney back to Iriga leaves at 7 pm.

LEGASPI

Legaspi is the capital of Albay Province. There are no sights worth talking about in the town itself. The only ones worth mentioning are the bustling port area and the headless statue in front of the post office, a monument to the unknown heroes who died at the hands of the Japanese in WW II. St Rafael Church,

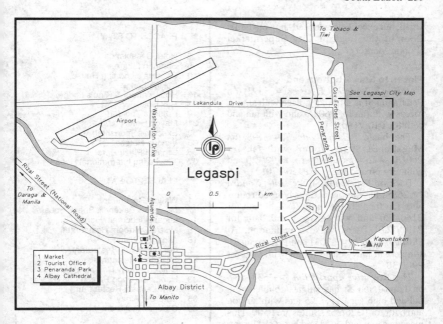

Map legend:
1 Market
2 Tourist Office
3 Penaranda Park
4 Albay Cathedral

opposite the Plaza Rizal, has a 10-tonne chunk of volcanic rock from Mayon as the altar.

However, there are many interesting attractions to see in the Legaspi area, including the ruins of **Cagsawa**, the **Hoyop-Hoyopan Cave** in Camalig, and of course the mighty **Mayon Volcano**. In the rainy season the volcano is unfortunately often draped with clouds; however, even on such days a full, clear view of it can be obtained at sunrise.

From the top of the Kapuntukan Hill you can get a fascinating panoramic view of the port area, with the impressive Mayon in all its glory in the background. The best time to view the volcano is in the early morning hours and at sunset, which is also the best time for taking photographs.

A tricycle from the centre of town to the hill costs P10; negotiate the fare beforehand. On foot, the following route should be taken.

Go down Quezon Ave in the direction of the wharf and cross over the little bridge opposite the beginning of Elizondo St; this takes you to the idyllic fishing village of Victory Village. At the south end of the village next to the barangay toilet turn left, then after about 50 metres at the sari sari store, turn left again and up the unassuming steps. A few metres before the concrete path at the top leads down to the water, you will see an almost hidden, fairly overgrown path on the right, which will take you to the top of the hill.

Information

The tourist office (☎ 44492, 44026) is in Peñaranda Park (Plaza) in the Albay District of town. Jeepneys go there from downtown Legaspi. A tricycle from the tourist office to the airport costs around P10.

At the Namria Sales Office on Rizal St maps and nautical charts are sold. It's a small, but excellently stocked shop on the 1st floor of the Legaspi City Supermarket (Public Market).

Places to Stay – bottom end

Catalina's Lodging House (☎ 3593) on Peñaranda St is a friendly place with simple rooms with fan for P60/90 and with fan and bath for P100/130.

The basic *Peking Lodge* (☎ 3198) on Magallanes St has rooms with fan for P50/70, with fan and bath for P100/120 and with air-con and bath for P150/170.

Back on Peñaranda St, the *Hotel Xandra* (☎ 2688) has simple and fairly good rooms with fan for P80/100, with fan and bath for P160/180 and with air-con and bath for P190/260. There's also a restaurant. At *Shirman Lodge* (☎ 23031) on Peñaranda St, simple and fairly clean rooms with fan cost P90/130.

The *Executive Tourist Inn* (☎ 3533) also on Lapu-Lapu St has singles/doubles with fan and bath for P195/225 and with air-con and bath for P325/365. Suites are P500. This place is clean and good and has a restaurant. It is in the J & O Building (3rd floor) opposite the post office.

The rooms at *Tanchuling International House* (☎ 2788, 23494) on Jasmin St, Imperial Subdivision, are simple, clean and spacious, and there is a pleasant roof garden. Singles/doubles with fan cost P190 and with air-con and bath P450. The atmosphere is friendly and it is in a quiet, unfortunately not too easily accessible, area south of the town centre. However, it is good value for money.

Places to Stay – top end

On Lapu-Lapu St, the *Legaspi Plaza Hotel* (☎ 3344, 3345) has passable, clean singles/doubles with fan and bath for P355/340 and with air-con and bath for P490/590, and it has a restaurant and a disco.

The *Hotel Casablanca* (☎ 3130, 3131) on Peñaranda St has clean rooms with air-con and bath for P625 and P700, the more expensive rooms have a big balcony and TV. It also has a restaurant and a disco.

■   PLACES TO STAY

5	Hotel Casablanca
6	Shirman Lodge
10	Catalina's Lodging House
15	Peking Lodge
16	Hotel Xandra & King's Lodge
17	Rex Hotel
19	Hotel La Trinidad
21	Mayon Hotel
30	Executive Tourist Inn
35	Victoria Hotel
36	Legaspi Plaza Hotel
37	Tanchuling International House

▼   PLACES TO EAT

1	Waway Restaurant
11	Mamalola Bakery & Snack House
14	Legaspi Icecream House
16	Mike's Oakroom Restaurant
18	Alibar Foodland
22	Peking House Restaurant
27	Shangrila Restaurant
28	Quick'n Hearty Restaurant
33	Hangzhou Food Palace
34	New Legaspi Restaurant
35	Café Old Albay
38	Garden Reasurant

OTHER

2	Caltex Petrol Station
3	Paayahayan Beer Garden
4	BLTB Bus Terminal
6	Melon Patch Nightclub
7	Small Bars
8	AMDG - Bus To Naga & Shell Petrol Station
9	Vejor's Disco
12	St Rafael Church
13	Plaza Rizal
19	Sunshine Run Bus Stop
20	Philippine National Bank (PNB)
23	Jeepneys To Santo Domingo & Tabaco
24	City Bus Terminal, Buses to Tabaco, Iriga & Naga & Jeepneys to Daraga
25	Legaspi City Supermarket (Market) & Namria Sales Office
26	LCC Department Store
29	J B Bicol Express Line Bus Terminal
31	Post Office & Headless Monument
32	Philtranco Bus Terminal

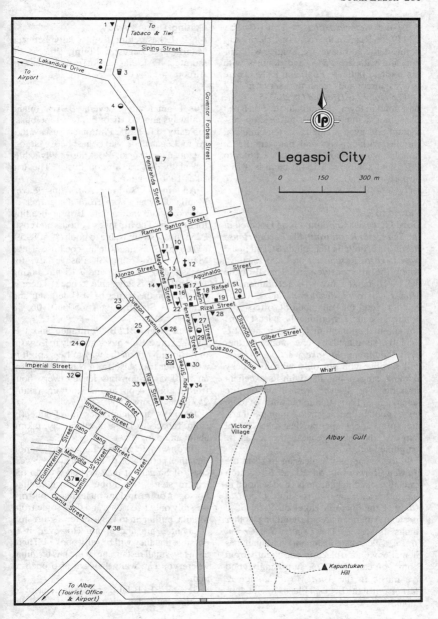

Legaspi City

0   150   300 m

At the *Victoria Hotel* (☎ 22101-04; fax 23439) on Rizal St the rooms are clean, very comfortable and have TV. Singles with air-con and bath are P545, and doubles with air-con and bath are P640 and P715. There is a restaurant and free airport service.

The *Hotel La Trinidad* (☎ 2951-55) is the best hotel in town, centrally located on Rizal St, with a swimming pool, coffee shop, restaurant and even a cinema in the complex. Singles with air-con and bath are P595, doubles with air-con and bath are P685 to P875 and suites are P1345; there is a free airport service.

Places to Eat

Good Chinese and Filipino food is served in the *Shangrila Restaurant*, the *Peking House Restaurant*, both on Peñaranda St, and in the *New Legaspi Restaurant* on Lapu-Lapu St, where the inexpensive special meal of the day – changed daily – is recommended. *Mike's Oakroom Restaurant*, next to the Xandra Hotel on Peñaranda St, offers economical menus. Unfortunately, at least in the hot summer months this place is not sufficiently ventilated. A few metres farther north the *Mamalola Bakery & Snack House* will surprise you not only with its plucky Karaoke singers but also with its excellent cooking. The *Waway Restaurant* on the Peñaranda St Extension in the north of town serves good Filipino dishes. Amongst others, the spicy local specialities à la 'Bikol Express' and the vegetarian meals can be recommended.

In the evenings it's pleasant to sit in the *Garden Restaurant* on Rizal St, which specializes in chicken, steaks and seafood in the mid-price range. In the little *Café Old Albay* at the Victoria Hotel on Rizal St, a passable American breakfast, amongst other things, is served. The *Legaspi Ice Cream House*, a clean establishment on Magallanes St, makes wonderful ice cream. Nightly from 8 pm, you can often hear surprisingly good live music in the *Aura Music Lounge & Restaurant* at the Legaspi Plaza Hotel, Lapu-Lapu St.

Getting There & Away

Air PAL has return flights daily between Manila and Legaspi. Flying time is 50 minutes. PAL has an office at Legaspi Airport (☎ 5247).

Bus From Manila, several BLTB, Inland Trailways and J B Bicol Express Line buses run daily to Legaspi. Philtranco buses either go to Legaspi or via Legaspi to Matnog, Tacloban or Davao. Booking is advisable, especially for the air-con buses. The trip takes 10 to 12 hours.

An air-con Sarkies Tours bus leaves Manila daily at 7 pm from the corner of Remedios and Indiana Sts, Ermita, heading for Legaspi. The trip takes 11 hours and costs P255. It is also advisable to book (☎ 508959, 8176615). Sunshine Run air-con buses leave Manila from Tramo St, Pasay City, for Legaspi daily at 8 am and 7.15 pm, taking 11½ hours. It is advisable to book. There is an office on the corner of M H del Pilar and Pedro Gil Sts, Ermita (☎ 506601-06, 58 4787).

From Naga, BLTB, Philtranco and J B Bicol Express Line buses go daily to Legaspi or through Naga on the way to Legaspi. It is a two-hour trip. Also from Naga to Legaspi an AMDG air-con bus leaves every hour from 6 am to 4 pm and at 7.30 pm, taking 2½ hours (many stops!).

Jeepneys and minibuses run frequently from Tabaco to Legaspi every day, taking about an hour.

If you want to go from Legaspi to Matnog (and then perhaps on to Tacloban via the west coast of Samar), it may be better to do the trip in stages, changing somewhere like Sorsogon or Irosin. Few buses make this trip, possibly only two a day, and they come from Manila, pulling in to Legaspi for a short stop at about 3 am and 5 pm. However, it is possible that they will be fully booked. There are a few small restaurants at the bus terminal where you can wait; they are also open at night.

Several BLTB buses go from Legaspi to Manila daily, departing between 2.15 and

7.40 pm; air-con buses leave at 5.20, 5.30, 6.20 and 6.30 pm.

Getting Around

To/From the Airport Legaspi Airport is about three km north-west of the town centre. A tricycle costs P20. For a short journey within the town you should pay P2 per person.

AROUND LEGASPI
Mayon Volcano

Mayon stands 2462 metres high and is famed for its perfectly symmetrical cone. The name Mayon is a derivation of the Bikolano word *magayon*, which means beautiful. Beauty can also become dangerous, as the clouds of smoke rising from the crater indicate.

The last serious eruption was at the beginning of February 1993 when, without any warning, the volcano spewed ash and steam five km into the atmosphere. Rivers of glowing hot mud, rocks and stones rushed down the south-east slope, totally destroying villages and farmland on the way. Seventy people died, a further 50,000 had to be evacuated. Only after a series of smaller eruptions lasting until late March did the volcano calm down again, but weeks later the glowing lava was still flowing, offering a fascinating spectacle at night. The most violent eruption to date took place on 1 February 1814 (see the following Daraga & Cagsawa section).

If you want to climb Mayon, the tourist office in the Albay District of town will supply detailed information and organise the climb. The usual cost for two people is US$50 for guide, porter and tent; each additional person costs US$20. To that P300 must be added per person for food and a second porter, who the guide brings along. Anyone thinking of saving a few pesos by carrying everything themselves would definitely regret the decision later.

To reach Mayon, you get a jeepney in the market to Buyuhan (this is not included in the price), from where it is a 2½ hour climb to Camp 1 (Camp Amporo) at about 800 metres. If you start late, you will have to spend the night at the simple hut there; there is a spring nearby.

It's another four hours to Camp 2 (Camp Pepito) at about 1800 metres. Here you have to use a tent, as there is no hut and the nights can be fairly cold. In the morning you have another four-hour climb to the summit. The last 250 metres is a scramble through loose stones and over steep rocks, and it is advisable for climbers to be roped.

Going down it takes about three hours from the crater to Camp 2, almost two hours from Camp 2 to Camp 1 and over two hours from Camp 1 to the road.

Take warm clothing, a sleeping bag and provisions for two days. On some days you'll need sunscreen lotion as well. You can try hiring a guide and porters in Buyuhan yourself. The standard daily rate is about P500. To try the ascent without a guide is reckless and irresponsible, as it's easy to get lost at the foot of Mayon. Many of the harmless-looking canyons turn out to be dead ends with sheer drops.

Getting There & Away To get from Legaspi to the Mayon Vista Lodge (formerly known as the Mayon Resthouse) on the northern slope, take a bus or jeepney to Tabaco, then a bus or jeepney to Ligao. Get off at the resthouse turn-off about halfway to Ligao. From there you've got about an eight-km walk up to the lodge. You can hire a jeepney in Tabaco but it's cheaper to persuade the regular Ligao jeepney drivers to make a small detour to the lodge and drop you there. The tourist office advises people not to climb the north slope of the volcano as it is apparently too dangerous.

Note: the Mayon Vista Lodge provides an excellent view point on the northern slope halfway to the top of the volcano, but it might not be open for overnight accommodation.

Daraga & Cagsawa

The magnificent baroque church in Daraga, built by Franciscan monks in 1773, offers an excellent view of Mayon from its vantage point on the top of a hill overlooking the town. On Sunday and public holidays

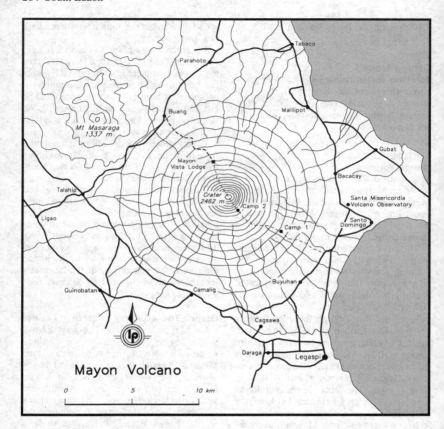

Mayon Volcano

0   5   10 km

Daraga is the scene of heated cockfights which take place in the cockpit at the edge of town, near the petrol station. The atmosphere at Daraga's night market is very pleasant with its sounds and smells of frying and cooking. Along the road between Daraga and Cagsawa you can find small workshops where they make whole furniture suites from used car tyres.

The catastrophic eruption of Mayon on 1 February 1814 totally destroyed the villages of Camalig, Cagsawa and Budiao on the southern side of Mayon. About 1200 people perished as ash fell as far away as the China coast. Many local residents took shelter in the church at Cagsawa, only to be smothered by falling ash. Today, only the church steeple stands as a reminder of 'Beautiful's' terrible powers. The rest of the village was buried under ash and lava. Today, plants, including orchids, are offered for sale near the church tower, and with the grandeur of Mayon in the background the scene is idyllic.

Getting There & Away From Legaspi, several jeepneys leave the market or the city bus terminal daily for Daraga. The turn-off to the Cagsawa ruins is on the right, two km west of Daraga. A tricycle from Daraga to the ruins shouldn't cost more than P10. Buses and jeepneys for Camalig, Guinobatan, Ligao, Polangui and Naga also drive through Daraga, directly past the turn-off to the Cagsawa ruins where you can get out. (Don't forget to tell the driver in good time!) From there, it is about 10 minutes to the ruins on foot.

Camalig

The town of Camalig is famous for the **Hoyop-Hoyopan** limestone caves which are in Cotmon, about eight km to the south. There is an admission fee of P40. The name Hoyop-Hoyopan means 'blow-blow' from the sound of the wind rushing through. Bones have been found in the caves as have potsherds, which are over 2000 years old. They are now on display in a small museum in the Camalig Catholic church.

Ask for Alfredo Nieva, who will guide you to the Calabidogan Cave, about two or three km (a 45-minute walk) away from the Hoyop-Hoyopan caves. It is best to have a word with Alfredo the day before, to work out times and prices. It is possible that he himself will not be the guide as he may give the job to one of his sons.

The **Pariaan Cave**, known as the 'Fountain of Youth', is near Pariaan. Eduardo (Eddie) Nalasco is an experienced guide – he lives opposite the Municipal Hall in Camalig but you can also catch him now and again in Mike's Oakroom Restaurant in Legaspi. To get there take a jeepney either from Legaspi or Camalig to Guinobatan, where you can get a jeepney for Pariaan. Ask the driver to drop you at the path for the cave and, after a 10-minute walk, you will come to a hut where the cave's 'owner' lives. For a few pesos he'll look after excess clothing – it's very hot and humid inside the cave. A strong torch or, even better, a kerosene lamp is necessary for exploring the cave. There's a natural pool in the cave with warm water, surrounded by beautiful stalactites. After staying in a cave, it's a pleasure to jump into the private swimming pool on the left side of the road towards Jovellar; admission is P2.

Getting There & Away Camalig is about 14 km north-west of Legaspi. Jeepneys and buses go there from the market or the bus terminal, either directly or en route to Guinobatan, Ligao, Polangui or Naga. From Camalig, you have to take a tricycle to the cave. Occasionally it is possible to find a jeepney in the market going to Cotmon. After 6 pm the only way to return to Camalig is to arrange a Special Ride.

Santo Domingo

About two km outside of Santo Domingo town, 15 km north-east of Legaspi, is a long, black, lava-sand beach which occasionally has quite high surf. The beach resorts on the so-called 'Mayon Reviera' vary considerably in size and price. The *Reyes Beach Resort* with its inexpensive restaurant is popular; the *Sirangen Beach Resort* is basic and nicely laid out. Local day trippers like to use the beach at Santo Domingo for long, drawn-out picnics, but the beach is not really suitable for bathing and is actually quite disappointing.

Getting There & Away To get to Santo Domingo, take a jeepney from Legaspi market or ask if there's a direct bus to Santo Domingo, as some of the Tabaco buses take the route around the outskirts. Tricycles go from Santo Domingo to the beach resorts.

Malilipot

For lovers of waterfalls in more or less unspoiled nature a day trip from Legaspi to Malilipot can be warmly recommended. From here, on the north-east foothills of Mayon, there is a path leading in the direction of the volcano to the Busay Falls, also known as the Malilipot Falls. These falls descend in stages from a height of 250 metres, flowing into seven pools on the way that tempt you to swim in them. If you don't want to jump straight into the first pool, then turn off onto the path on the right just before it. After about a 15-minute walk this will take you to the second pool.

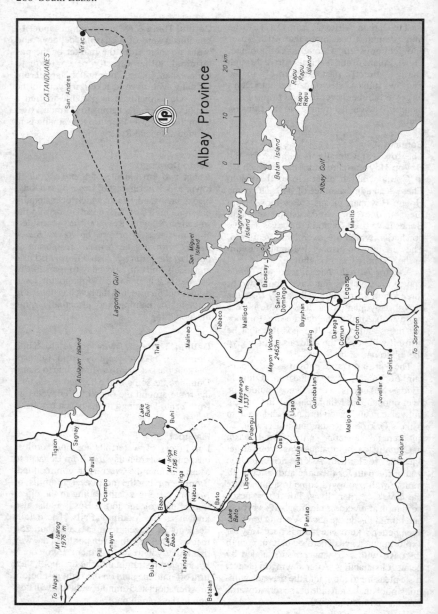

Getting There & Away Go from Legaspi to Malilipot by a jeepney or bus travelling to Tabaco. Then it's about another hour on foot.

TABACO

Tabaco is the main departure point for the boat to San Andres and Virac, both on Catanduanes Island. Probably the only thing worth seeing in Tabaco is the two-storey market, where some interesting knives are among the wares.

Places to Stay & Eat

Tony's Hotel on Riosa St near the market has simple, but fairly good rooms with fan and bath for P90/130 and with air-con and bath for P170/220. There's a disco, and the *EF-Palace Restaurant* is in the same building. Opposite the Municipal Hall is the *Royal Crown Canteen* – a very clean restaurant.

Getting There & Away

Several Philtranco buses go from Manila to Tabaco daily. A few go via Legaspi, and travelling time is 11 hours. From Tabaco to Manila, an air-con bus leaves at 4.50 pm; the last bus for Manila leaves Tabaco at about 7 pm.

Jeepneys run frequently between Tiwi and Tabaco in about half an hour, and plenty of buses and jeepneys from Legaspi to Tabaco leave from the city bus terminal. These take 45 minutes.

TIWI

North of Legaspi, Tiwi is noted for its hot springs, which were for many years a small health resort or spa. Some of the springs were so hot that the locals stood their pots in them to cook their dinners. Nowadays six geothermal power stations have reduced the underground water pressure and some of the springs have mostly dried up.

Two well-known but not particularly good beaches, with black sand, are **Sogod Beach** and **Putsan Beach**. If you walk to Putsan, take a look at the primitive potteries on the way.

Places to Stay

The *Baño Manantial de Tiwi Youth Hostel & Mendoza's Resort* has rooms with fan and bath for P350/400 and with air-con and bath for P500/600. There's an outside swimming pool and thermal baths in the basement, and a restaurant.

Getting There & Away

To get from Legaspi to Tiwi, take a minibus or a jeepney from the city bus terminal, and from Tabaco continue on by jeepney. Jeepneys also go regularly and directly to Tiwi from Peñaranda St in Legaspi. From Tiwi to the Tiwi Hot Springs Resort – a distance of about three km – take a tricycle. The whole trip takes about 1½ hours.

Leaving Tiwi, if you want to go beyond Legaspi to Matnog the same day, you must depart early in the morning or you'll have connection problems in Irosin.

For Manila, a Philtranco bus leaves Tiwi market daily at 9 am and 3 pm and takes 11 hours.

SORSOGON & GUBAT

Sorsogon is the capital of Sorsogon Province, an area at the eastern tip of South Luzon which is subject to frequent violent typhoons.

You can reach Rizal Beach at Gubat from Sorsogon or directly from Legaspi, but this highly praised beach is definitely not the best or most beautiful in the Philippines.

Places to Stay

The *Dalisay Lodge* (☎ 6926) at 182 V L Peralta St, Sorsogon, is a simple, but fairly clean place with a restaurant. It has rooms with fan for P60/100 and with fan and bath for P90/130.

The *Rizal Beach Resort Hotel*, Gubat, has dorm beds with fan for P75, rooms with fan and bath for P200/300 and with air-con and bath for P400. Weekly rates are possible and meals can be ordered in advance.

Getting There & Away

From Legaspi, J B Bicol Express Line buses run to Sorsogon roughly every half hour

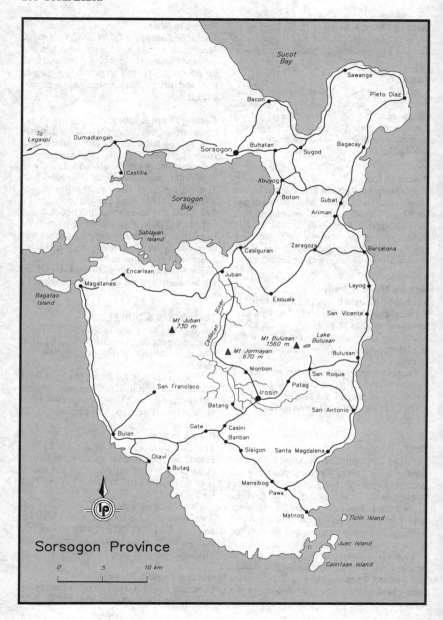

Sorsogon Province

0   5   10 km

throughout the day. It's a 1½ hour trip. There are also Philtranco buses, but they are not so frequent. They come from Manila, go through to Matnog and are usually full.

BULAN

Bulan, on the west coast, is simply a departure point for a daily boat to Masbate. (See under Boat in the Getting There & Away section in the Manila chapter earlier in this book).

Places to Stay

Mari-El's Lodging House (☎ 721), on the pier site, is a basic place with rooms for P35/70 and with fan for P50/100.

Getting There & Away

Philtranco and J B Bicol Express Line buses leave from Legaspi for Bulan about every hour between 4.30 am and 3 pm. Take a bus by 8 am if you want to be on time for the boat to Masbate. It takes 3½ hours.

BULUSAN & IROSIN

You can't help but see Mt Bulusan, the 1560-metre-high volcano at the centre of the Juban-Bulusan-Irosin triangle. Nearby, surrounded by lush vegetation, is a small crater lake of the same name, at a height of 600 metres with a three-km-long path around it called Lovers' Lane. For the walk around the lake, which in parts is fairly difficult and tiring, you will need 1½ hours, including rests.

From Bulusan to Lake Bulusan is about eight km. Only a few jeepneys make the trip between Bulusan and Irosin; the first one leaves at 7 am, the last one at 4 pm. They will stop at the turn-off for the crater lake if requested to. The walk up to it is very pleasant.

The refreshingly cool **Masacrot Springs**, complete with big swimming pool, are in the foothills of the volcano, near San Roque. Unfortunately, the way there is not signposted.

Apart from Bulusan, there is another good base for a stay in the so-called 'Switzerland of the Orient': the Mateo Hot & Cold Springs

Resort. This pleasant establishment is in a forest about four km north-east of Irosin (three km in the direction of Sorsogon and then one km north-east). There is a signpost at the point where the path leaves the road. The resort has three pools (cool, lukewarm and hot) and there is a small restaurant and a variety of cottages. It is easy to get from the resort to Irosin. Unlike in Bulusan there are more than enough tricycles in Irosin, so it should be easy to negotiate the fare for a Special Ride from there to the volcano. It's a good idea to have the tricycle wait for you, then you don't have to worry about the return trip to Irosin.

Places to Stay

In Bulusan you can stay at the *Bulusan Lodging House* belonging to the friendly teacher Mrs Nerissa Bartilet. It's directly behind the town hall. Rooms with fan are comfortable and cost P60/120.

The pleasant *Villa Luisa Celeste Resort* in Dancalan, Bulusan, has clean and spacious rooms with fan and bath for P250/300 and with air-con and bath for P450. A cottage with bath and kitchen costs P300, and there is a restaurant and a swimming pool.

At the *Mateo Hot & Cold Springs Resort*, San Benon, Monbon, Irosin, rooms with fan cost P100/200 and with fan and bath P200. Cottages with fan, bath and kitchen are P200. It's a nice, peaceful place with a restaurant. (See the introductory paragraph for this section for more information.)

Lena's Lodging House in Irosin is a friendly place with simple rooms for P50/100.

Getting There & Away

J B Bicol Express Line buses run from Legaspi daily to Irosin or to Bulan via Irosin. It takes 2½ hours. Philtranco buses also go from Manila through Irosin to Matnog and on to Tacloban or even to Mindanao, but these are usually full. Jeepneys go from Irosin to Bulusan in an hour, but there are only a few a day.

MATNOG

This little coastal town, on the south-eastern side of Sorsogon, is the departure point for boats to Allen and San Isidro on Samar. During bad typhoons all shipping is stopped, so you could be held up in Matnog for a few days – not a cheerful prospect. It's better to wait somewhere like Bulusan or Legaspi until the seas go down.

On sunny days, a trip to the little offshore island of **Ticlin**, with its palms and beautiful white sand beach, would be well worthwhile.

Places to Stay

The only place to stay is the basic *Mely's Snack House*, which charges around P30 per person. You could always do what many Filipinos do who have missed the last ferry: sleep on a bench in the big waiting room.

Getting There & Away

Several jeepneys run daily from Legaspi to Irosin, taking one hour. From Irosin to Matnog there are a few jeepneys daily. In Irosin you can also try to board a bus arriving from Legaspi and going through Matnog en route to Tacloban or Mindanao, but the seats are usually occupied so it's better to do the trip in stages using other means of transport. It takes three hours. For more details see Getting There & Away in the Legaspi section earlier in this chapter.

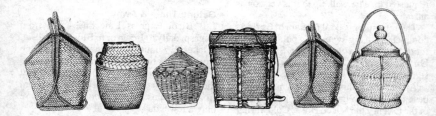

Around Luzon

Several islands around the main island of Luzon are also generally grouped with Luzon. They include the Batanes, which are scattered off the far northern coast of Luzon; Catanduanes, off the south-eastern coast near Legaspi; and the smaller islands of Lubang, Marinduque and Masbate and the larger island of Mindoro, all off the western coast.

Batanes

The Batanes Islands are the northernmost islands of the Philippines. Y'ami is only 100 km from Taiwan. The biggest and economically most important islands are Batan, Ibayat and Sabtang. Dinem Island is uninhabited. The climate of the Batanes Islands is harsh and changeable. Compared with other parts of the Philippines, all 10 of these islands are hit by typhoons relatively frequently between June and September. From October to February or March it is often wet and stormy. The best months to visit are April and May.

Geographically isolated from the big important islands and archipelagos of the country, the Batanes Islands are surprisingly unspoilt and different. Many houses are built of solid rock and have roofs thickly thatched with cogon grass to resist the weather. They are low, with few windows, and are usually found in small groups in niches protected from the wind. If you know your Asterix, sometimes you feel as if you had been transported back to a village populated by stubborn Gauls and would probably not be in the least surprised if around the next corner were a venerable druid brewing his potions.

People here protect themselves from sun and rain with a *suot*, a head-covering made from *voyavoy* leaves which reaches right down the back.

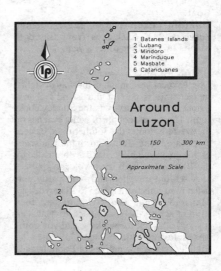

Goods which aren't produced on the islands are slightly more expensive here than they are in Luzon, as they have to be flown in or shipped on the occasional freighter. The main crops are garlic, onions, taro yams and camotes. The main occupations are cattle farming and fishing.

GETTING THERE & AWAY

You can get to the Batanes Islands from Laoag and Tuguegarao on Luzon (see the Getting There & Away section of the Manila chapter earlier in this book). Travel in and out depends first and foremost on the weather. On rainy days, if the partly concreted runway at Basco is wet, planes can neither land nor take off. Delays may also occur, even in the summer months of March, April and May.

Air

To/From Luzon PAL has flights from Basco to Laoag and Manila on Monday, Wednes-

271

day and Friday, and flights from Basco to Tuguegarao on Monday and Wednesday.

Boat

To/From Luzon The Avega Exchange Services' MV *LSD* goes from Basco to Manila two or three times a year.

BATAN ISLAND

Don't expect very much in the way of sights; in fact, this is part of the island's charm. About the only activity is the Sunday cockfight. There are a couple of white beaches on the western coast; the southern and eastern coasts are rocky. To the north the landscape of this green and hilly island is dominated by the 1008-metre-high Iraya Volcano.

A seldom-travelled and only partly surfaced road runs from Basco to Riacoyde (via Mahatao, Ivana and Uyugan) and then straight across the island back to Mahatao. It's a good track for walking and you come across lovely little villages inhabited by friendly Ivatan, the natives of Batan Island.

Basco

Basco is the capital of the province of Batanes, which is the smallest in the Philippines, both in area and population. Next to the big church, with its beautiful façade, are numerous governmental buildings which dominate this well-kept town at the foot of Mt Iraya. Roughly 5000 people live here. There is a Philippine National Bank which will cash travellers' cheques. In Basco you can hire private jeepneys, motorbikes and bicycles. Enquire at Mama Lily's Pension House.

Places to Stay *Mama Lily's Pension House* has rooms with fan for P400/700. It is basic but clean and the price includes full board. Guests can use the living room and terrace, and there is a restaurant. You can also stay at the *Iraya Lodge* which has rooms with fan for P125/250.

The *School Canteen* has rooms for around P50. Food in the School Canteen is inexpensive.

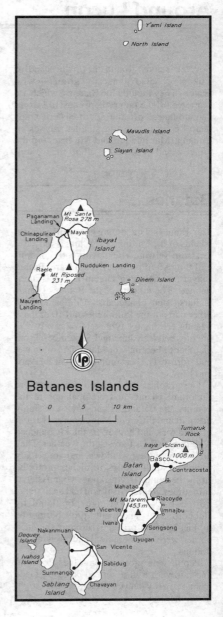

Batanes Islands

SABTANG ISLAND

In contrast to Batan Island, there are no cars on Sabtang. It is worth going around the island on foot and visiting the four villages. The mayor will place at your disposal a guide who knows the paths and the shortcuts. Through him you will find it easier to get to know the villagers and to see how things such as suots are made. On the eastern coast of the neighbouring island of Ivahos there is an extensive coral reef. You can get there by boat from Nakanmuan or Sumnanga.

There are no hotels on Sabtang, but it is possible to stay with the mayor or the director of the Fishery School. You can also get something to eat there, but since no-one will charge you money or accept it, it is rather nice to 'happen' to have a small gift on hand.

Getting There & Away

A boat goes once a week from Basco to Sabtang Island. If you don't want to wait, you will have to go to Ivana, but the jeepney to Ivana usually only goes when a plane lands. In good weather a boat goes daily from Ivana to San Vicente on Sabtang at about 8.30 am and takes about 30 minutes. It should return the next morning.

IBAYAT ISLAND

Ibayat is the largest island of the group. It has few beaches and a rocky coast. A feature of the island is the *tatus*, the coconut crab, which is so fond of coconuts that it will climb trees to get them. You can stay and eat with the mayor.

Getting There & Away

The boat service from Basco to Paganaman Landing or Mauyen Landing on Ibayat is irregular. Travel time is about four hours. The boats only go in good weather and are fairly unpredictable – not so good if you are on a tight schedule. East of Raele is a landing strip for small aircraft.

Catanduanes

Also known as the 'land of the howling winds', this kidney-shaped island lies in the Pacific Ocean, separated from South Luzon by the Maqueda Channel and the Gulf of Lagonoy. The province consists of the main island and a few smaller ones, the most important of which are Panay to the north-east and the Palumbanes Islands to the north-west. The Palumbanes Islands are made up of Palumbanes, Porongpong and Calabagio.

Catanduanes is mostly hilly. The only flat land is found east of the capital, Virac, and around Bato and Viga. The climate has shaped the landscape. As a result of typhoons, several coastal hills are barely covered with grass, many palms are uprooted or broken off, and steep cliffs and deeply indented bays are typical of the eastern and north-eastern coasts. The typhoons blast into this part of the Philippines straight off the Pacific. In Catanduanes you have to expect rain throughout the year, particularly from November to January, while not quite so much from April to June.

The main industries are fishing and farming. The most prolific fishing grounds are the Maqueda Channel, the Gulf of Lagonoy and Cabugao Bay. The main agricultural products are abaca (Manila hemp), rattan and coconuts, rice, sweet potatoes, cassava and fruits such as avocados, jackfruit, papaya and oranges. Mining has not been developed much, although there are deposits of coal, gold, silver, manganese and copper.

Many islanders have left Catanduanes in search of work, most settling in Manila. The greatest migrations take place after typhoons when houses and crops have been destroyed. People only come back then to visit on important occasions like festivals or family gatherings.

The people are friendly and very religious. They are Bikolano, and speak Bikolano, the language of South Luzon. English is also

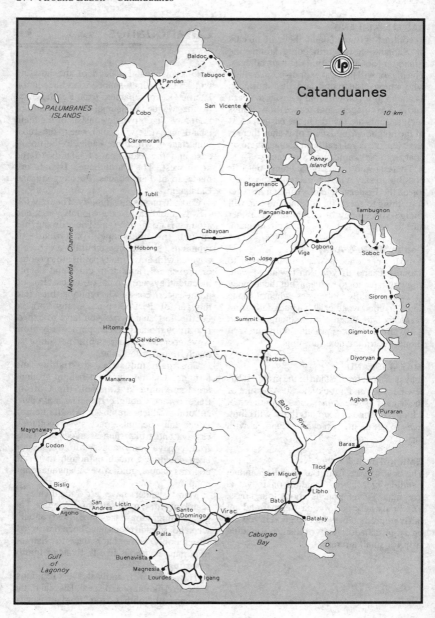

spoken and understood. Visitors are nearly always invited into homes, and you'll have to depend on this hospitality because, with few exceptions, there is no commercially run accommodation on the islands.

GETTING THERE & AWAY

You can travel to Catanduanes Island from Manila, Legaspi and Tabaco (see the Getting There & Away section of the Manila chapter earlier in this book).

Air

To/From Luzon PAL flies Monday, Wednesday and Friday from Virac to Legaspi and daily from Virac to Manila.

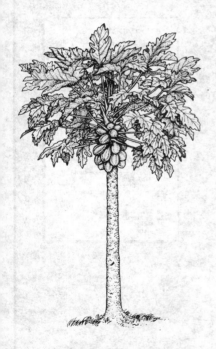

Papaya Tree – This short-lived melon tree is actually a giant herb. It is one of the commonest fruit trees in the Philippines

Boat

To/From Luzon The Bicolano Lines' MV *Eugenia* leaves Virac daily at 1 pm for Tabaco, taking four hours. An additional small boat leaves daily at 10 am.

The Regina Shipping Lines' MV *Regina Calixta* leaves San Andres daily at 1 pm for Tabaco, taking 2½ hours.

VIRAC

The cosy and clean little town of Virac is the capital of Catanduanes Province. Popular destinations for day trips from there are **Igang Beach**, eight km south-west, and the **Binanuahan Falls** in Cabugao, a little south of Bato; they are easily reached by tricycle and a short walk. A trip to the Balongbong Falls in Bato is, however, hardly worth the effort, especially because they are not easily accessible.

Places to Stay

Virac The *Cherry Don Resthouse* (☎ 516) on San Pedro St has basic rooms with fan for P60/100. *Sandy's Pension House* (☎ 617) near the pier has rooms with fan for P85/170. It is basic and has a restaurant with a small terrace. The *Catanduanes Hotel* (☎ 280) on San Jose St has rooms with fan and bath for P200/275. It is unpretentious but quite cosy and has a restaurant.

Around Virac The *Twin Rock Beach Resort* at Igang Beach, eight km south-west of Virac, has cottages with fan for P225 and with fan and bath for P340. Comfortable rooms with fan and bath costs P450 and nice rooms with air-con and bath are P680. Its a well-kept place and has a restaurant and a swimming pool.

The *Bosdok Beach Resort* at Magnesia has cottages with fan and bath for P250 and P350. This is a group of solidly built, roomy, clean cottages on the side of a hill. The resort covers an extensive area in an idyllic bay and has a sandy beach. There is also a big restaurant and a swimming pool. Bosdok Beach is a bit out of the way, 12 km south-west of Virac. A Special Ride by tricycle costs P200. A service jeep belonging to the resort leaves

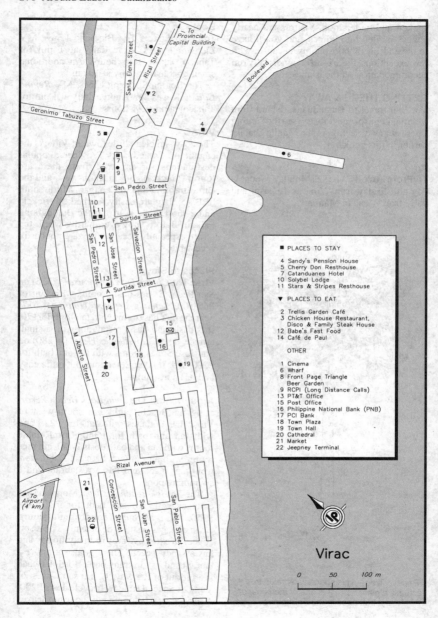

■ PLACES TO STAY

4 Sandy's Pension House
5 Cherry Don Resthouse
7 Catanduanes Hotel
10 Solybel Lodge
11 Stars & Stripes Resthouse

▼ PLACES TO EAT

2 Trellis Garden Café
3 Chicken House Restaurant, Disco & Family Steak House
12 Babe's Fast Food
14 Café de Paul

OTHER

1 Cinema
6 Wharf
8 Front Page Triangle Beer Garden
9 RCPI (Long Distance Calls)
13 PT&T Office
15 Post Office
16 Philippine National Bank (PNB)
17 PCI Bank
18 Town Plaza
19 Town Hall
20 Cathedral
21 Market
22 Jeepney Terminal

Virac

0   50   100 m

daily from Virac market and also meets the plane and the ferry boat.

Places to Eat

It is possible to eat good, inexpensive Filipino food at the *Catanduanes Hotel Restaurant* on the roof of the hotel. Also good value are the fine dishes served at the *Café de Paul* on the corner of A Surtida and San Jose Sts, worth trying are the sizzling blue marlin and the wanton soup. The *Trellis Garden Café* not only serves coffee, but also ice-cold beer and dishes like spaghetti and lasagne. *Sandy's Restaurant*, in the pension house of the same name at the pier, serves snacks and non-alcoholic drinks.

Getting There & Away

Jeepney Transport connections within Catanduanes are fairly limited. Three jeepneys run daily from Virac market to Pandan, north of the island, and back. One jeepney runs daily from Virac to Tambugnon via Viga, leaving there at 9 am and returning at midnight. Two jeepneys go from Virac to Gigmoto via Puraran, leaving between 9 and 10 am and returning between 2 and 3 am. A regular service of jeepneys and buses runs between Virac and Baras. The bumpy but scenic road from Virac to Gigmoto follows the coast and winds around one bay after another. The dirt road from Bato to Viga, goes through forest and little villages in the centre of the island. This and the Virac to Gigmoto coast road are good for hiking.

Car Rodino Molina, owner of the small Halik-Alon Restaurant opposite the Provincial Capitol Building, hires out his jeep for around P1000 per day, including driver and petrol.

Getting Around

To/From the Airport The airport is about four km south-west of Virac. The trip into town by tricycle should normally cost P2 per person. The least they will charge, however, is P10.

The PAL office (☎ 260) is at the airport, not in town, so you might as well confirm your return flight when you first arrive.

PURARAN

Puraran is a small place on the wild Pacific coast about 30 km north-east of Virac. It is a good stopover on a journey to the north of the island. However, many of the few foreigners who have visited Catanduanes up till now take one look at its long white beach and decide to finish the journey right there. Surfers especially like to stay in Puraran for the excellent breakers which usually start at the beginning of July. In September and October the surfing is good, while from November to January the particularly high breakers even provide a challenge for experts.

It is safe to swim at high tide in front of the reef, but be careful: there is a dangerously strong current near the beach, and especially over the reef itself – you have been warned! Even excellent swimmers have been known to get into serious trouble in this current. Only when the water is calm is it worth snorkelling. Typhoons can put an end to all thoughts of water sports. So, apart from surfers, the best time to stay would probably be from the middle of March until the middle to end of June.

Places to Stay

The *Puting Baybay Resort* has cottages for P250 per person, including two meals daily. Its a simple place directly on the beach and has a restaurant.

The *Pacific View Beach Resort* has very basic cottages for P250 per person, including two meals. This friendly place is situated at the northern end of the bay and has a restaurant and free surfboards.

The *Puraran Beach Resort* has nice cottages for P250/500. Three meals a day cost an extra P250. There is a restaurant with a beautiful view of the beach. This pleasant resort with a lawn at the south end of the bay is run by a Japanese-Philippine corporation.

Getting There & Away

Two jeepneys leave Virac market for Puraran between 9 and 10 am daily, going on to Gigmoto. Another may leave after the arrival of the boat from Tabaco. You can also go to Baras by jeepney and then travel the following five km by tricycle (about P30). A tricycle for the whole trip from Virac costs at least P250. There is a pathway leading from the street in Puraran down to the beach which takes about five minutes on foot.

From Puraran to Virac, there is a regular jeepney service at about 3.30 am (it can even be as late as 4.30 am). This jeepney comes from Gigmoto.

Lubang

The Lubang Islands are part of the province of Mindoro Occidental. They hit the world headlines in 1974 when the Japanese soldier Hiroo Onoda, who had been hiding in the mountains of Lubang for 30 years, finally decided it was time to give himself up as a WW II prisoner of war. Fumio Nakahura, a captain in the Japanese Imperial Army, held out for another six years before being discovered in April 1980 on Mt Halcon on Mindoro.

The people of Lubang earn their income mainly from the sale of garlic. They would like to share in the profits from tourism but seem at present most likely to inspire only one wish in visitors: to leave for Manila or Mindoro as soon as possible. I found people in Tilik and farther south-east to be less forthcoming than elsewhere. As you go from Tilik towards Lubang, attitudes become noticeably more relaxed.

Accommodation

There is no commercial accommodation

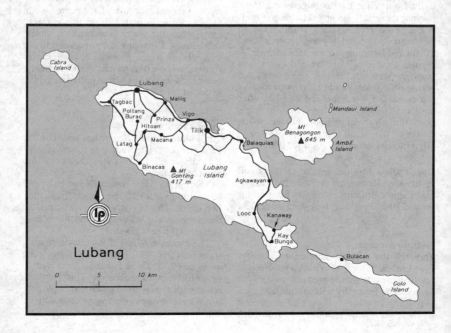

available in Lubang, so you will have to find a family who will rent you a room. Just ask at the church or one of the shops in Tilik.

GETTING THERE & AWAY
You can get here from Luzon, Mindoro and Palawan (see the Getting There & Away sections of the Manila and Palawan chapters and the Getting There & Away section for Mindoro later in this chapter).

Air
To/From Luzon Pacific Airways flies daily from Lubang to Manila.

Boat
To/From Luzon The Asuncion Shipping Lines' MV *Asuncion XI* leaves Tilik for Manila on Monday at noon. The MV *Asuncion X* leaves on Wednesday at 10 am, the MV *Catalyn B* leaves on Wednesday, Friday and Sunday at 1 pm and the MV *Catalyn A* leaves on Saturday at 10 am. The trip takes eight hours.

To/From Mindoro The Asuncion Shipping Lines MV *Asuncion XII* leaves Tilik for San Jose on Wednesday at 3 pm, taking eight hours. However, this route is not reliable. The ship goes from Manila to San Jose and may dock in Tilik.

To/From Palawan The Asuncion Shipping Lines' MV *Catalyn A* leaves Tilik for Coron on Wednesday at 8 am. The MV *Asuncion XI* leaves on Friday at 10 am and the MV *Asuncion X* leaves on Sunday at 8 am. The trip takes 16 hours and continues to Culion.

GETTING AROUND
Tilik is the port for this area. When a boat docks, a regular jeepney runs to Lubang and a truck takes freight and passengers to Looc. There is no other public transport. Once in a while there may be a *carretela* (a calesa or horse-drawn cab) from Tilik to Lubang. If you don't want to wait around, you could take a Special Ride, which costs about P60 and takes one hour. Transport costs on Lubang are at least twice those on other

islands. This applies also to the short trip by banca from Balaquias across to Ambil Island, for which they now ask P250. It's not worth it, especially if you are expecting to look for and find the jade which the Philippine technical literature claims is there.
The airport is along the road from Lubang to Tagbac.

TILIK
You can't travel around much here because of the lack of transport, but the country around Tilik is good for walks, such as the one to Como Beach near Vigo. It's no tropical paradise, but there's some real surf and it's not crowded. There's a beautiful sandy beach at Tagbac, west of Lubang, but the sea floor is muddy. If you go by paddle boat from Tilik to the other side of the bay, make sure there is at least a 15 cm clearance above the water line. The centre of the bay is exposed and even a light wind can blow water into the boat. It's easy to get thoroughly drenched.

Marinduque

Marinduque is the near-circular island between South Luzon and Mindoro. The Marinduquero are Tagalog and most of them come from Batangas and Quezon provinces.

Coconuts and rice are the main agricultural products. Two mining companies extract iron ore and copper; there are large copper deposits at Labo near Santa Cruz. The main tourist attraction is the Moriones Festival at Easter, which is great fun and which everyone joins in with good humour (see the Fiestas & Festivals section of the Facts for the Visitor chapter earlier in this book). This is when Marinduque gets most of its tourists. At other times there aren't many around, as the tourist industry here is just getting going.

GETTING THERE & AWAY
You can get to Marinduque from Luzon and Mindoro (see the Getting There & Away section of the Manila chapter earlier in this

book and under Getting There & Away in the Mindoro section later in this chapter).

Air
To/From Luzon PAL flies daily from Boac to Manila.

Boat
To/From Luzon There is one boat daily from Balanacan to Lucena at 5 am, taking four hours.

The MV *Antipolo* leaves from Buyabod, the harbour for Santa Cruz, for Lucena daily at 2 am, taking 4½ hours. Because of the demand for this ship it would not be a bad idea to be on board the evening before departure.

To/From Mindoro A boat leaves Gasan for Pinamalayan on Mindoro daily at 8.30 am, taking 3½ hours.

BOAC
Boac, on the Boac River, is the capital of Marinduque Province. It is a pretty little town towered over by a massive church with a richly decorated altar built on a hill. Of the passion plays performed all over the island

at Easter, each claiming to be the best, the star production of the Moriones Festival is the one staged in Boac from Easter Thursday to Easter Sunday.

Boac Airport is 12 km to the south near Masiga. On the way are a few beach resorts on the pebbly beaches.

Places to Stay
Boac *Cely's Lodging House* (☎ 1519) at 10 de Octobre St has rooms with fan for P150. It is simple and clean, and has a restaurant.

The basic *Boac Hotel* (☎ 1121) on Nepomuceno St has rooms with fan for P100/200, singles with fan and bath for P160 and doubles with air-con and bath for P200.

The *Susanna Inn* (☎ 1997) has quite comfortable rooms with fan for P200/250, with fan and bath for P250/350 and with air-con and bath for P400/600, and it has a restaurant.

Around Boac A short way out of Boac, towards Mogpog, is the *Swing Beach Resort* (☎ 1252) on Deogracias St. It has rooms (with four beds) for P200 per person or P400 per person for full board.

The *Cassandra Beach Resort* in Cag anhao, on the beach between Boac and Cawit, has rooms with fan for P150 and cottages with fan and bath for P175. There is a restaurant and the kitchen can be used by the guests.

Also in Caganhao is the *Aussie-Pom Guest House* with pleasant, spacious rooms with fan for P200. Weekly and monthly rates can be arranged. There is a restaurant and the kitchen can be used by the guests. You can hire snorkelling equipment for P30 a day (there is a fairly good coral reef not far from the pebbly beach).

The *Pyramid Beach Resort* (☎ 1493), also in Caganhao, has rooms for P150/200 and rooms with fan for P200/250, and is good value. Meals should be ordered in advance.

In Cawit, the *Sunraft Beach Hotel* has rooms for P120/180 and with fan and bath for P250. It is basic but relatively good. The *Seaview Hotel* has good, clean rooms with fan and bath for P240/300.

BALANACAN
This small town in north-west Marinduque has a little harbour in a sheltered bay which provides shipping services to and from Lucena on Luzon.

The *LTB Lodge* is a simple place near the wharf, where there are a few small restaurants. Rooms are P40/80 and with fan P70/100.

Getting There & Away
There aren't many jeepneys between Boac and Balanacan daily. It's safer to rely on those that meet the boats.

SANTA CRUZ
Although Boac is the capital of Marinduque, Santa Cruz has the most inhabitants. Its great church, built in 1714, is very impressive with its old paintings and sculpture.

Equipment for diving trips from Santa Cruz can be hired from Franco Preclaro, though it's a good idea to have your own regulator. He can also advise on good areas for diving and arrange trips there.

The **Bathala Caves**, about 10 km north-west of Santa Cruz, are a complex of seven caves in all, only four of which are accessible. They are on the private property of the Mendoza family, so before a visit you should ask for their permission. You may be able to swim in the natural pool behind the house – you'll find a swim very welcome after visiting the bats in the caves!

On the three Santa Cruz islands north-east of the town of Santa Cruz there are long beaches and good snorkelling, particularly on **Maniuayan Island**. A boat leaves Bitik, on the north-eastern coast of Marinduque, daily at about 7 or 8 am and makes the crossing in 45 minutes.

Places to Stay
The *Park View Lodge*, near the Santa Cruz Town Hall, has rooms for P200. This place is basic, perhaps a bit too expensive for what it is.

On Maniuayan Island, Lucita Perlada offers a room in a *cottage* on the beach for P200 per day, including meals.

Places to Eat

Probably the best place to eat is the *Tita Amie Restaurant*, on the corner of Palomares and Pag-asa Sts. Here the choice is limited but special dishes can be ordered in advance.

Getting There & Away

Several jeepneys run daily from Boac to Santa Cruz via Mogpog.

There is a connection by ship from Santa Cruz and Lucena on Luzon. Buyabod is the pier for Santa Cruz and is a few km to the east.

TORRIJOS

White Beach at Poctoy near Torrijos is probably the best beach on Marinduque. The outlying coral reef is good for snorkelling and the beach has a magnificent view of **Mt Malindig**.

Maranlig and **Sibuyao**, both north-west of Torrijos, make good day trips. Maranlig has cockfights on Sunday; Sibuyao is on a plateau with rice terraces. A jeepney runs daily to Maranlig. There is only one to Sibuyao and that is on Sunday, which is market day.

You can reach the white beach on **Salomague Island** by boat in an hour, but the Salomague Island Resort, opened a few years ago, is no longer regularly open to guests. It is suffering from a lack of customers and is usually closed.

Places to Stay

A typhoon destroyed the White Beach Cottages. But local people only 50 metres or so from the beach rent out rooms with cooking facilities for about P50. Try Leonard Pilar or Jose Roldan. In Torrijos the mayor, Ben Cordero Lim, has rooms for P50.

Getting There & Away

A few jeepneys run daily from Buenavista to Torrijos via the hill town of Malibago, but be careful, as from late afternoon they don't go beyond Malibago.

There aren't many jeepneys from Santa Cruz to Torrijos. It is safest to rely on those which meet the boat. Anybody wanting to go to the White Beach near Poctoy could ask the jeepney driver to make a short detour there.

BUENAVISTA

This town, on the southern coast of Marinduque, is the departure point for **Mt Malindig** at Marlanga Point, a 1157-metre-high dormant volcano on which a telegraph station has been built. About five km by road inland from Buenavista are the **Malbog Hot Springs** – sulphur springs which are claimed to heal certain skin complaints.

The **Buenavista Market** is especially worth seeing at weekends, when mountain people from all around bring their wares. Pigs and goats are sold, slaughtered and cut up on the spot.

Places to Stay

The *Three Kings Cottages* on the rugged beach at Buenavista is run by Manuel Sarmiento and his family, and has rooms with fan for P120 and a cottage with two bedrooms, cooking facilities, fan and bath for P300. All the rooms are comfortable. Trips in outrigger boats can be arranged.

The *Susanna Hot Spring Resort* at Malbog has rooms with bath for P500. There is a restaurant and a nice garden with a small swimming pool with water at least 40°C warm.

Getting There & Away

Several jeepneys run daily between Boac and Buenavista via Cawit and Gasan.

ELEFANTE ISLAND

High up on the little Elefante Island, to the south of Marinduque, Japanese investors have built a club with extensive facilities set in its own grounds. Jeeps belonging to the hotel run from the club to the beach, saving guests a walk. The place was designed originally to be only for club members, but ordinary guests are accepted when occupancy rates are low. It is definitely worth a day trip there, to get an impression of just what can be done for tourism with an island of that size and the right amount of money. The same company is building a similar establishment on Marinduque, just across from Elefante Island.

Places to Stay
The *Fantasy Elephant Club* has very comfortably furnished rooms with TV, air-con and bath from P3000 to P12,500 and cottages for P6000 and P7700. This is a well-looked after establishment with a beautiful view. There is a restaurant, swimming pool, whirlpool, Japanese garden, golf course and tennis court; diving and windsurfing are available.

Getting There & Away
A boat from Lipata to Elefante Island and back costs around P300. For security reasons guards of the Fantasy Elephant Club check visitors on arrival.

TRES REYES ISLANDS
It's a 30-minute trip in an outrigger boat from Buenavista to the outlying Tres Reyes (Three Kings) Islands. Although Balthazar and Melchor islands are rocky and uninhabited, the third, Gaspar, has a small village and a lovely coral beach that is good for snorkelling and diving. In 1980 the wreck of a Chinese junk that sank 200 years ago was discovered about 100 metres north of Gaspar Island in 38 metres of water. Although most of its rich cargo of porcelain has already been salvaged, from time to time local divers bring up a few more finds, so the treasure hunt goes on.

GASAN
Like Boac and Mogpog, Gasan is heavily involved in the Easter passion play. Handcrafted basket ware and ornaments are made here; in the UNI Store, for example, you can see how the carved wooden birds are painted.

Places to Stay
The *Amigo's Lodge* has simple rooms with fan for P100 and there is a restaurant. The *UNI Lodge* near the Municipal Building is basic but relatively good, with rooms with fan for P150/200. Tricycles, motorbikes and a jeep can be hired here.

The *Sunset Garden Resort* in Pangi is a well kept place about two km north of Gasan. Cottages with fan and bath are P400. Reservations can be made in Manila (☎ 8016369).

Places to Eat
The *Sunset Garden Restaurant* belonging to the resort of the same name has European and Filipino food.

Getting There & Away
There is a boat route connecting Gasan and Pinamalayan on Mindoro.

Masbate

The province of Masbate includes Masbate Island and the smaller Ticao and Burias islands. Although the island group is officially part of the Bicol region, the influence of the Visayas is unmistakable, so the Cebuano and Hiligaynon languages are also frequently spoken. Before WW II, Masbate was a leading gold field. Today it is noted for its meat production, having some herds of cattle as large as 4000 head. Fishing is also important economically. Tourism doesn't mean much here, as few foreigners come to these islands, which are off the main traffic routes, so visitors accustomed to rusticity will have a pleasant time here. Even basic commercial overnight accommodation is really only available in the towns of Masbate, Mobo, Aroroy and Mandaon. Lovers of tuba should try the white variety, which is a speciality of Masbate.

GETTING THERE & AWAY
You can get to Masbate from Cebu, Luzon, Romblon and Samar (see the Getting There & Away section of the Manila chapter earlier in this book and the Getting There & Away sections of the chapters on the other islands).

Air
To/From Luzon PAL has flights from Masbate to Legaspi on Monday, Wednesday

and Saturday, and daily flights from Masbate to Manila.

Boat

To/From Cebu The Sulpicio Lines' MV *Cebu Princess* leaves Masbate for Cebu City on Saturday at 2 pm. It takes 36 hours, going via Calbayog on Samar and Ormoc on Leyte. The boat comes from Manila.

The Lapu-Lapu Shipping Lines' MV *Rosalia* leaves Cataingan for Cebu City on Thursday and Sunday at 7 pm, taking 11 hours. The Georgia Shipping Lines' MV *Princess Joan* leaves Cataingan for Cebu City on Sunday at 10 pm, taking 10 hours.

Apparently, a boat goes from Cataingan to Hagnaya twice a week on Monday and Thursday, and from Cawayan to Hagnaya twice a week on Wednesday and Saturday.

To/From Luzon The MV *Matea* leaves Masbate daily for Bulan at 5 am, taking 3½ hours. There may be a second boat some other time during the day.

The Sulpicio Lines' MV *Cebu Princess*

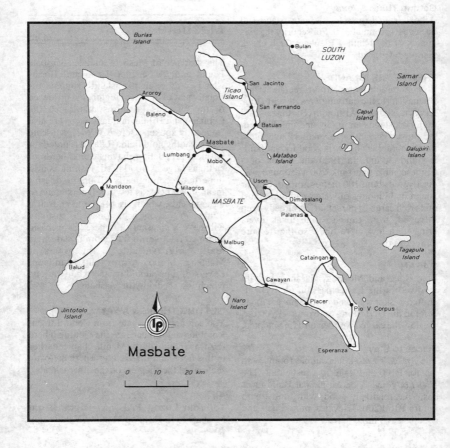

leaves Masbate for Manila on Wednesday at 10 pm, taking 22 hours. The William Lines' MV *Cebu City* leaves Masbate for Manila on Sunday at 10 pm, taking 16 hours.

To/From Romblon There is one ship a week from Mandaon to Sibuyan Island, leaving on Wednesday or Thursday at 7 pm. After a short trip, it anchors for a time in Maolingon Bay (about 15 to 30 minutes by boat from Mandaon), before leaving at about 1 am. The journey takes five hours. You can only find out the exact departure time in Mandaon. Information given in other places varies widely and is not reliable.

To/From Samar The Sulpicio Lines' MV *Cebu Princess* leaves Masbate for Calbayog on Saturday at 2 pm, taking four hours.

MASBATE

The town of Masbate is the capital of the province but hasn't a great deal of note beyond the harbour, the market and numerous stalls which line the streets. It is the base for air and sea travel to places like South Luzon. A few km south-east, in Mobo, is Bitu-on Beach, a popular place to visit, with a beach resort whose cottages are a good alternative to the hotels in the town.

Places to Stay

The *St Anthony Hotel* (☎ 180) on Quezon St has simple rooms with fan for P110/150, with fan and bath for P200/250 and with air-con and bath for P300/350. It's the only halfway decent hotel in town.

Places to Eat

For a good, reasonably priced meal try the *Peking House* in the port area or the *Petit Restaurant* opposite the St Anthony Hotel on Quezon St. The clean *Kapihan Restaurant* on Mabini St is known for good seafood.

CATAINGAN

Cataingan is a small harbour town at the head of a narrow bay which reaches quite a way inland, at the south-east of the island. Boats leave there for Cebu.

Getting There & Away

A few jeepneys run daily from Masbate to Cataingan. The trip takes five hours on the bad road.

MANDAON

Boats go from Mandaon to Sibuyan Island in Romblon Province. Near the town is Kalanay Cave, where numerous archaeological finds have been made.

Mesa's Lodging right on the beach has rooms for P30/60.

Getting There & Away

Several jeepneys and buses run daily from Masbate to Mandaon, taking two hours. Try to get a seat on the roof if you want a good view of some lovely countryside.

Mindoro

Mindoro is the next big island to the south of Manila. It is divided into the provinces of Mindoro Occidental, which is the western part, and Mindoro Oriental, the eastern part. Only the coastal strip is heavily populated. In the jungles and mountains inland there are various groups of the Mangyan tribes (see under Cultural Minorities in the People section of the Facts about the Country chapter earlier in this book).

Fishing and the cultivation of rice and coconuts are the main economic activities, with some cattle raising around San Jose. Although the name Mindoro is a contraction of the Spanish *Mina de Oro*, meaning 'gold mine', no major gold discovery has yet been made. The difficult terrain of the island has also limited Mindoro's potential for copper and iron-ore mining, and the main mining activity has been the quarrying of marble. There has, however, been some promising oil prospecting in the south-west.

The usual tourist route on Mindoro is from Puerto Galera to Roxas and Mansalay, via Calapan. In and around Puerto Galera there are popular beaches and still mostly intact coral reefs. Roxas is the starting point for boat trips to Tablas and Boracay islands, and from Mansalay you can get to the villages of the Mangyan tribes.

It's a fair bet that it will not be long before the northern stretch of coastline from Mamburao to Sablayan in Mindoro Occidental will have become an important centre of tourism. Unfortunately, there is still no regular shipping route from Sablayan or San Jose to Coron on Busuanga in the north of Palawan. Such a route would really add to the attractions of island hopping in the region.

GETTING THERE & AWAY

Several buses leave the BLTB bus terminal in Manila daily for Batangas. An air-con bus leaves the Sundowner Hotel in Ermita every day at 9 am. You can get combined bus and boat tickets to Mindoro from an office in the hotel.

There are boats daily from Batangas to Abra de Ilog, Calapan and Puerto Galera. For more information about getting to Mindoro from Luzon, see the Getting There & Away section of the Manila chapter earlier in this book.

You can also get to Mindoro from Marinduque, Panay and Romblon (see the Getting There & Away sections of the chapters on the other islands).

Air

To/From Luzon Pacific Airways has flights from Calapan to Manila on Monday, Wednesday and Friday; on the same days they also fly from Mamburao to Manila.

PAL has flights on Friday and Sunday from Mamburao to Manila, and daily except Wednesday and Friday from San Jose to Manila.

Bus

To/From Luzon Combined bus and boat tickets for the journey from Puerto Galera to Manila via Batangas can be bought, and reservations made, at the docks. If you want to buy your tickets separately, you can catch an ordinary public bus or air-con bus for Manila in Batangas (see the Batangas section

of the Around Manila chapter earlier in this book).

Beware! The buses between Manila and Batangas are especially popular with pickpockets.

Boat

To/From Luzon From Puerto Galera to Batangas, there are at least three boats daily. There are possible additional departures at the weekend. The MV *Batangas Express*, the MV *Princess* and the MV *Queen* of AC Shipping Lines cost from P40 to P65, leaving at 7.30 am and possibly at 1 pm. The trip takes two hours. The Viva Shipping Lines' MV *San Miguel de Ilijan* (car ferry) leaves at 9.15 am and 1.45 pm, taking one hour or more. Departure is at Balateros, 2½ km west of Puerto Galera. The MV *Sikat II* of Si-Kat Ferry Inc leaves at 9.30 am. Its air-con bus waits at the dock in Batangas for the boat to arrive, and goes direct to the Sundowner Hotel in Manila. The trip (boat and bus) takes five hours or more.

From Abra de Ilog to Batangas, a big outrigger boat or a ferry leaves daily at 8.30 am, taking three hours.

From Calapan to Batangas, the MV *Marian Queen*, the MV *San Lorenzo Ruiz* and the MV *Santa Maria* of Santo Domingo Lines leave daily at 6 and 9.30 pm and at 6 pm, taking two hours. The MV *Emerald I* and the MV *Ruby I* of Manila International Shipping Lines leave daily at 6.30 and 10.30 am and 2.30 and 6.30 pm, taking two hours.

From Sablayan to Batangas, the MV *Santa Anna* and the MV *Socorro* of Viva Shipping Lines sail on Wednesday and Sunday at 7 pm, taking 12 hours.

From San Jose to Manila, the Asuncion Lines' MV *Asuncion XII* leaves on Friday at 5 pm, taking 18 hours and going possibly via Tilik on Lubang.

To/From Marinduque One boat goes daily from Pinamalayan to Gasan, leaving at 5 am or 2 pm and taking 3½ hours.

To/From Panay A big outrigger boat goes from Roxas to Boracay on Monday and

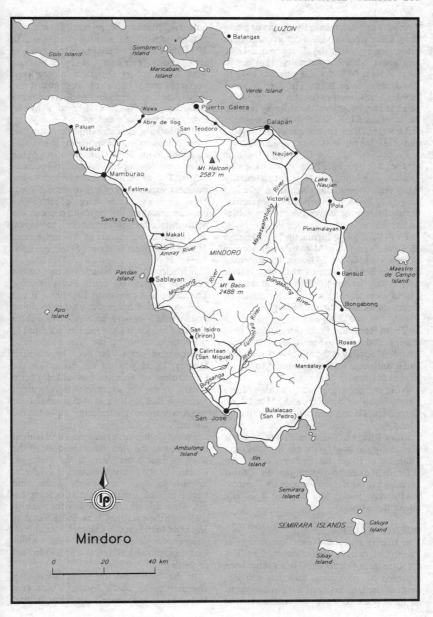

Mindoro

0   20   40 km

Thursday at 9 am, taking five hours or more. From December to May it can even leave as often as every other day. If it goes via Looc on Tablas Island in Romblon Province it takes at least 10 hours and you may have to stay overnight in Looc. The fare is about P200. In bad weather the sea in the Tablas Strait is very rough and the crossing is not to be recommended. Small boats sometimes sail over, but they are completely unsuitable and often dangerously overloaded.

From San Jose to Buruanga there is another big outrigger boat which leaves on Thursday and Sunday at 9 am. It usually takes eight hours, but sometimes takes as long as 12 hours. This trip is also not recommended when the waves are high in Tablas Strait.

From San Jose to Lipata, the MV *Princess Melanie Joy* and the MV *Aida* sail once or twice a week, taking 24 hours. The trip takes them via Semira Island and Caluya Island, where they lie up to 10 hours at anchor. Lipata is a small place five km north of Culasi on the west coast of Panay.

To/From Romblon From Bongabong, a big outrigger boat runs to San Agustin on Tablas Island on Sunday at 2 pm. It takes six hours and continues on to Romblon town on Romblon Island.

A big outrigger boat runs irregularly from Pinamalayan to Sibali Island (Maestro de Campo Island) and then continues to Banton Island.

From Roxas to Looc on Tablas Island, a big outrigger boat goes on Monday and Thursday at 10 am, taking 3½ hours.

From Roxas to Odiongan on Tablas Island, a big outrigger boat goes on Tuesday, Wednesday, Friday and Sunday at 10 am, taking three hours.

PUERTO GALERA

The fine beaches and excellent diving at Puerto Galera have been attracting travellers for some time. For about 60 years, it has been regarded by zoologists, botanists and students of the University of the Philippines as an ideal place to study the ecostructure of animals, plants and microorganisms in almost undisturbed natural conditions. In 1934, the UP Marine Biological Station was set up. Forty years later, the United Nations Man & Biosphere Program International declared Puerto Galera a nature centre. It was at this time that the media also discovered the attractions of Puerto Galera as a tourist resort, and the place took off.

The town's new wealth has attracted foreign interest and investment. It has also split the population into two opposing camps: the developers and the environmentalists. The developers see tourism as the business opportunity of a lifetime and advocate expansion at any price. The environmentalists are concerned about the detrimental effects development is having on the customs and morals of the inhabitants and on the natural features of their environment.

It is a trendy place which tourism, unless carefully supervised, could easily destroy. The adage that tourism is like fire – it can cook your food but it can also burn down your house – should be heeded in Puerto Galera. Considering the tourism potential of this little beauty spot, the disruption of the environment has so far been kept within bounds. Mind you, in the meantime the Department of Tourism has added Puerto Galera to the list of special development areas, so that will mean the go-ahead for projects designed for the more sophisticated tourist.

Puerto Galera has a most beautiful natural harbour, and the view from the deck of the ferry as you come through the Batangas Channel or the Manila Channel is a delight. Spanish galleons once sought shelter here from typhoons, and the name dates from that era, when this was the gateway for Spanish traders on their way to China, India, Sumatra and Java. In the small museum by the church you can see pieces of pottery from various Chinese dynasties as well as a fine collection of shells.

In the hinterland are some interesting alternatives to beach living. There is a Mangyan village barely one km behind

Top: Rainbow over the Chocolate Hills, Bohol (JPk)
Bottom: Filipino house and tropical flowers (JP)

Top: Panning for gold in Negros (JP)
Bottom: A steam-age dinosaur brings in the sugar cane in Negros (JP)

White Beach. Near Dulangan, about six km towards Calapan, villagers pan for gold in the river. The **Tamaraw Waterfalls** are about 15 km towards Calapan. You can visit a marble quarry or climb **Mt Malisimbo** and explore the nearby jungle.

The Ponderosa Golf & Country Club is run by members and has a nine-hole golf course. It is south-west of Puerto Galera at about 600 metres above sea level. There is a tremendous view, and guests are welcome. It's about five km from the village of Minolo up to the club. Transport can be requested at the Ponderosa waiting station in Minolo.

The journey from Manila to Puerto Galera by bus and boat is comfortable by Philippine standards and only lasts about five hours. Although it can be rainy and somewhat cool, most visitors come to Puerto Galera in December and January. Tourist numbers have usually declined by mid-March, but sunny and exceptionally calm weather can still be enjoyed between June and October.

Information

Money The Rural Bank in Puerto Galera changes cash and may also change travellers' cheques, albeit at a less favourable rate than

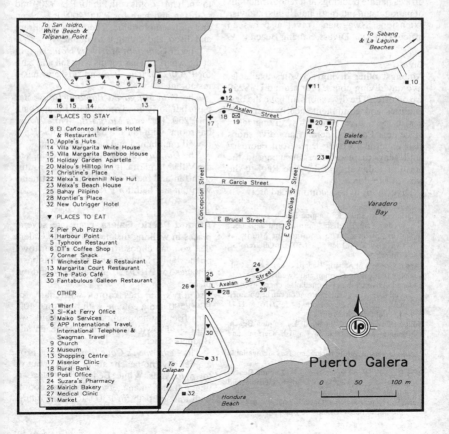

■ PLACES TO STAY

8 El Cañonero Marivelis Hotel
& Restaurant
10 Apple's Huts
14 Villa Margarita White House
15 Villa Margarita Bamboo House
16 Holiday Garden Apartelle
20 Malou's Hilltop Inn
21 Christine's Place
22 Melxa's Greenhill Nipa Hut
23 Melxa's Beach House
25 Bahay Pilipino
28 Montiel's Place
32 New Outrigger Hotel

▼ PLACES TO EAT

2 Pier Pub Pizza
4 Harbour Point
5 Typhoon Restaurant
6 DT's Coffee Shop
7 Corner Snack
11 Winchester Bar & Restaurant
13 Margarita Court Restaurant
29 The Patio Café
30 Fantabulous Galleon Restaurant

OTHER

1 Wharf
3 Si-Kat Ferry Office
5 Maiko Services
6 APP International Travel,
International Telephone &
Swagman Travel
9 Church
12 Museum
13 Shopping Centre
17 Miserior Clinic
18 Rural Bank
19 Post Office
24 Suzara's Pharmacy
26 Mairich Bakery
27 Medical Clinic
31 Market

Puerto Galera

the money changers and banks in Manila. It is sometimes possible to change both travellers' cheques and US dollars in cash at the Margarita Shopping Center.

Post & Telecommunications The small post office can be found diagonally across from the church on H Axalan St. There is a telephone for international calls at the pier.

Travel Agencies Both APP International Travel Corporation and Swagman Travel have an office at the Puerto Galera pier. Both offices handle bookings and reconfirmations of national and international flights, and visa extensions. Swagman Travel also has an office with Asia Divers, Sabang Beach.

Diving
Amongst other diving activities available, five-day diving courses for around US$250 are on offer. The dive shops all have the best facilities and equipment; nearly every one has its own dive boat. Most diving takes place near Puerto Galera. Many dive shops also undertake diving trips from February until May, to places like Busuanga in the north of Palawan and the Apo Reef to the west of Mindoro.

Dive shops to be recommended are:

Asia Divers at Small La Laguna Beach: courses are available in English, German and Japanese; information can be obtained in Manila at Swagman Travel (☎ 5223650) on Guerrero St, Ermita.
Capt'n Gregg's at Sabang Beach: courses are available in English, German and Swedish.
Encenada Dive Club at Encenada Beach: courses are available in English; information can be obtained in Manila at the Iseya Hotel (☎ 592016) at 1241 M H del Pilar St, Ermita.
Galleon Diving School at Small La Laguna Beach: courses are available in English, German and French.
Pacific Divers at White Beach: courses are available in English and French.
Reef Raiders Dive Center at Big La Laguna Beach: courses are available in English, German and Japanese.
South Sea Divers at Sabang Beach: courses are available in English, German and Spanish.

Places to Stay
Puerto Galera The *Bahay Pilipino* has basic rooms with fan for P100/150, and so does *Malou's Hilltop Inn*. Also basic is *Melxa's Greenhill Nipa Hut* which has rooms with fan for P60/120.

Christine's Place on the edge of town on the quiet Balete Beach has basic rooms with fan for P150/180. Also on Balete Beach, *Melxa's Beach House* has spacious rooms with kitchen, fan and bath from P250 to P450. Monthly rates are available.

The *Viva Outrigger Beach Resort* is on Hondura Beach on the southern edge of town. It has rooms with fan for P150/200 and with fan and bath for P300/400. It is clean and quite comfortable. There is a restaurant and disco, and diving is available.

The *El Cañonero Marivelis Hotel* is right at the wharf and has rooms with fan and bath for P200/250. It is nice and tidy and has a restaurant.

The *Villa Margarita Bamboo House* has basic but fairly good rooms with fan and bath for P250. The *Villa Margarita White House* has rooms with fan and bath for P250/350. It is well maintained and has a restaurant.

The *Holiday Garden Apartelle* belongs to the Villa Margarita. It has good, clean rooms with fan and bath for P350 and apartments with fan and bath for P750.

Around Puerto Galera There are several places in walking distance of Puerto Galera that you can choose from. Just out of town on the road to Sabang, *Apple's Huts* has basic cottages for P100/120. It's a nicely laid out place.

Cathy's Inn has rooms with bath for P300/500 and a cottage with bath for P400. This friendly accommodation is about two km out of town towards Halige Beach and Boquete Beach.

The *Fishermen's Cove Beach Resort* is on a quiet bay (no beach) about one km out of town towards White Beach. The place is under Italian management and has rooms with fan and bath for P300. It has an Italian restaurant.

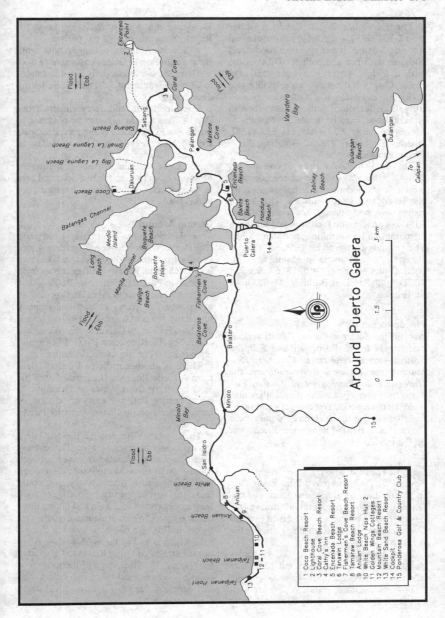

Around Puerto Galera

1 Coco Beach Resort
2 Lighthouse
3 Coral Cove Beach Resort
4 Cathy's Inn
5 Encenada Beach Resort
6 Fishermen's Cove Beach Resort
7 Tamaraw Beach Resort
8 Aniuan Lodge
9 White Beach Nipa Hut 2
10 Golden Wings Cottages
11 Mountain Beach Resort
12 White Sand Beach Resort
13 Cockpit
14 Ponderosa Golf & Country Club

3 km

0   1.5

Escarceo Point

Coral Cove

Sabang

Sabang Beach

Small La Laguna Beach

Big La Laguna Beach

Coco Beach

Daluruan

Batangas Channel

Medio Island

Long Beach

Manila Channel

Haligi Beach

Boquete Beach

Boquete Island

Fishermen's Cove

Balateros Cove

Palangan

Markoe Cove

Varadero Bay

Encenada Beach

Balete Beach

Hondura Beach

Puerto Galera

Tabinay Beach

Dulangan Beach

Dulangan

To Calapan

Balatero

Minolo

Minolo Bay

San Isidro

White Beach

Aniuan

Aniuan Beach

Talipanan Beach

Talipanan Point

Flood Ebb

Flood Ebb

Flood Ebb

The *Encenada Beach Resort* (cellular ☎ 912-3012289) is about 1½ km out of town towards Sabang. It has spacious rooms and cottages with fan and bath for P700, some with a fridge. There is a restaurant, and Hobie Cats, windsurfing, water skiing and diving are available. It is a pleasant, beautifully laid out place with its own beach. Reservations can be made in Manila at Moneytec Inc (☎ 522 4105; fax 522 4152), Room 221, Aurora Plaza 2 Building, Padre Faura, Ermita.

The *Tanawin Lodge* is about one km out of town on the way to Sabang, near Encenada Beach (a short descent). It has small fully furnished two-storey houses with living rooms and bedrooms. They cost P700 to P1800 depending on facilities, and there is a restaurant and a swimming pool with a bar. The grounds are the nicest in Puerto Galera. Bookings can be made in Manila at Afro-Asian Tours & Travel (☎ 5218167; fax 521 7622), 1006 San Luiz Building, Maria Orosa St, Ermita.

Places to Eat

Around the docks at Puerto Galera various restaurants serve European and Filipino dishes. Among these are *El Cañonero Restaurant*, the *Typhoon Restaurant* and the *Harbour Point Restaurant*. In the *Pier Pub Pizza* they don't just make pizzas, they also make tasty seafood. You can get good international cuisine in the *Bahay Pilipino*, near the market, and in the *Winchester Restaurant* on the road to Sabang.

Getting There & Away

Several BLTB buses leave from Pasay City in Manila daily for Batangas. An air-con bus leaves the Sundowner Hotel in Ermita every day at 9 am. You can get combined bus and ferry tickets at the Si-Kat Ferry Office in the hotel (☎ 521 3344).

From Batangas to Puerto Galera ferries depart daily at 11 am, noon and 12.30 pm. The trip takes two hours.

From Batangas to Balatero, 2½ km west of Puerto Galera, a car ferry departs daily at 11.30 am and 4 pm, taking 1½ hours. A jeepney to town costs P5 per person.

A Special Ride by outrigger boat from Batangas to Puerto Galera costs about P800.

There are two boats daily from Batangas to Calapan leaving at 7.30 and 9 am, taking three hours.

Combined bus and ferry tickets from Puerto Galera to Manila can be obtained in the Si-Kat Ferry Office at the pier. Bus seats should be reserved at least one day in advance.

For more information about getting to Mindoro from Luzon, see the Getting There & Away section of the Manila chapter earlier in this book.

Getting Around

Several jeepneys run from Calapan to Puerto Galera every day between 7 am and 4 pm, leaving from the market. The trip takes two hours. A Special Ride by outrigger boat from Calapan to Puerto Galera costs P600.

From Mamburao to Abra de Ilog and on to the wharf at Wawa at least one jeepney runs daily at about 6 am. It takes two hours. The boat for Puerto Galera leaves Wawa at 9 am. A Special Ride costs P400. The regular price is P50. The trip takes 2½ hours.

There is another route to Puerto Galera from Abra de Ilog, via Batangas. Catch the 8.30 am ferry from Wawa to Batangas (3 hours, costing P50) and carry on at noon, or in the afternoon, with the ferry to Puerto Galera.

The trip from San Jose to Puerto Galera has to be done in several stages. The jeepney from San Jose to Bulalacao leaves between 6 and 7 am from the Metro Bank; it's a rough trip of four hours. Alternatively, you could make this part of the trip by outrigger boat, leaving between 8 and 9 am and taking three hours or more. From Bulalacao, you travel by bus to Roxas, a one-hour journey along a road which is bad as far as Mansalay. A big bus then takes you from Roxas to Calapan in four hours. The final stage of the journey is done by jeepney and takes two hours. The last jeepney leaves Calapan for Puerto Galera at 4 or 5 pm.

Warning The buses between Manila and Batangas are especially popular with pickpockets.

The road between Abra de Ilog and Puerto Galera, shown on most maps of the Philippines, was never built.

PUERTO GALERA BEACHES

In almost every bay with a beach that's at all usable, you'll find cottages for local and foreign tourists. To the east, resorts have sprung up at Sabang Beach, Small La Laguna Beach and Big La Laguna Beach. To the south, they go as far as Tabinay Beach. To the west, Talipanan Beach is about the limit at the present. Besides Puerto Galera the main beaches also have had electricity connected. However, considering the number of power failures, it's a good idea to have a torch handy.

Beaches just outside Puerto Galera, such as Balete Beach and Hondura Beach, are rather undeveloped and may disappoint some pampered beachlovers. Most travellers prefer the ones a few km farther away.

There's more for the visitor to do and see in **Sabang**, especially after dark. It can get very loud at night around the discos and bars. Some restaurants have been built on sites close to the water and the remaining beach is almost completely blocked by outrigger boats. A hill path takes you through a palm grove and over a grassy meadow to Escarceo Point, two km east of Sabang. There you can visit the 14-metre-high lighthouse from where you can get a gorgeous view, especially at sunrise and sunset.

The **Small La Laguna Beach** is fairly quiet and cosy. Most people go there for the snorkelling and diving. Many travellers prefer to stay overnight at Small La Laguna Beach, or just spend the days there, and go out at night at the nearby Sabang Beach.

At **Big La Laguna Beach** some of the cottages are packed close together, but the coral reef is worth seeing and is good for snorkelling.

The reefs at **Balete Beach**, **Long Beach** and **Halige Beach** are also good for

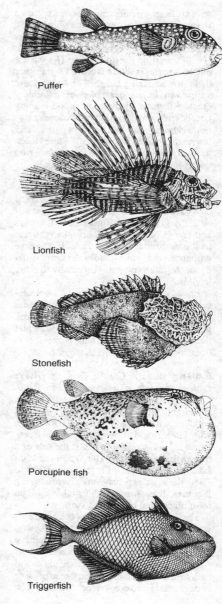

Puffer

Lionfish

Stonefish

Porcupine fish

Triggerfish

snorkelling. Strong currents can make Boquete Beach dangerous for swimmers.

There's not much action on the beaches between San Isidro and Talipanan Point, a few km west of Puerto Galera. The busiest one of them all is **White Beach**. On the other hand, the adjoining beaches of **Aniuan** and **Talipanan** in the next bay are extremely quiet. All three of them are good bathing beaches, although – unlike the beaches mentioned above – snorkelling is not particularly interesting there. The water at White Beach gets very deep a few metres from shore – too deep for children and non-swimmers.

Places to Stay

The following list of resorts is only a small cross section of the accommodation available. If you want to stay more than a few days and are willing to pay in advance, you can negotiate quite reasonable rates. But to save embarrassing your landlord, keep quiet about the rates you get – especially to other landlords!

Prices can vary, depending on how successful the season is. Especially around Christmas time and during the Easter week price hikes of up to 200% are possible, while the off-season from June until November is occasionally good for big discounts.

Sabang Beach *Capt'n Gregg's Divers Lodge* has rooms with fan and bath for P300. The atmosphere is pleasant and there is a restaurant. Divers prefer it. *Gigi's Inn* has cottages with fan and bath for P300, each with kitchen and fridge, and there is a restaurant. This is a quiet place on the side of a hill, with a good view. The *Seabreeze Vista Lodge* has cottages with fan from P200 to P350, the more expensive ones have cooking facilities. It is situated a bit higher up than most places and has a good view.

The *Traveller's Station* has cosy cottages with fan and bath from P250 to P400, and also has a restaurant. The more expensive cottages have a kitchen, fridge and TV. *At Can's Inn* has cottages with kitchen, fan and bath from P250 to P400. The more expensive cottages also have a fridge and TV. The

Seashore Lodge has cottages with fan and bath for P250 and P400. The more expensive cottages have a kitchen, fridge and TV. There is a restaurant. The *Big Apple Beach Resort* has cottages with fridge, TV, fan and bath for P400 and with kitchen for P650. There is a restaurant and billiards. The *Terraces Garden Resort* (cellular ☎ 912-3080136) has rooms with fan and bath for P400/450. It is clean and comfortable, and has a restaurant. The surroundings are pleasant – small houses among tropical plants on a slope above Sabang.

Coral Cove Beach The *Coral Cove Beach Resort* is under British management and has rooms with bath for P450. This is a big, tastefully designed house in a small, remote bay, about one km from Sabang. There is a restaurant and diving available, and staff can arrange day trips by boat. Reservations can be made in Manila at the Sundowner Hotel, Mabini St, and at the Iseya Hotel, M H del Pilar St, Ermita.

Small La Laguna Beach *Nick & Sonia's Cottages* is a friendly place with cottages with fan and bath for P250 and P450. The more expensive cottages have a kitchen and fridge. There is a restaurant. The *Full Moon* has plain but well-maintained cottages with fan and bath for P250/300, and also has a restaurant. The *Sunsplash* has spacious cottages with fan and bath for P350 and P600, and it has a restaurant and billiards. *El Galleon Beach Resort* has large rooms with fan and bath for P350 and P450. It is comfortable and has a restaurant, and diving is also available.

Carlo's Inn (cellular ☎ & fax 912-301 717) is on the slopes right at the beach. It has rooms with fan and bath from P250 to P350, and apartments with kitchen, fridge, fan and bath for P350 to P550. Well-appointed rooms with TV, fridge, air-con and bath cost P1500. It also has weekly and monthly rates, is clean and comfortable and has a restaurant with international cuisine, billiards and an international telephone.

Big La Laguna Beach *Rosita's* has rooms with fan and bath for P300/450. It is pleasant and has a restaurant. The *El Oro Resort* has cottages with fan and bath for P400, and there is a restaurant and billiards. The garden here is beautiful. The *La Laguna Beach Club* has rooms with fan and bath for P840 and with air-con and bath for P1120. There is a restaurant, floating bar, swimming pool, and diving and windsurfing are available. Reservations can be made in Manila at the Park Hotel (☎ 5212371; fax 5212393) on Belen St, Paco.

Coco Beach The *Coco Beach Resort* (cellular ☎ 912-3050476) has rooms with fan and bath from P1150 to P1950. It is well-looked after with a restaurant, swimming pool, and a quiet private beach with drop-off. Windsurfing, sailing, diving and tennis are available. Reservations can be made in Manila at the Coco Beach Booking Office (☎ 5215958; fax 5215260), Sundowner Hotel, Mabini St, Ermita.

White Beach The *White Beach Lodge* has several fairly roomy cottages with fan and bath for P250/300, and also has a good res-

taurant. This is a popular placen The *White Beach Nipa Hut* is a fairly large establishment with lots of little cottages with fan and bath for P250/300, and there is a restaurant. The *Lodger's Nook* (cellular ☎ 912-3057011) has several single and duplex cottages with fan and bath for P250/300, and also has a restaurant and a billiard hall.

The *Summer Connection*, at the western end of White Beach, has cottages with fan and bath for P400. It is a pleasant, quiet little place, with a restaurant. The *Majesty Lodge* has cottages with fan and bath for P200 and P350. The more expensive cottages are roomy and have a kitchen and a fridge. There is a restaurant. The *Crystal Garden Beach Resort* has rooms with fan and bath for P250/300, and it has a restaurant. *Lenly's Cottages* has spacious cottages with fan and bath for P300. There is also a restaurant.

Delgado's Cottages has fairly roomy cottages with fan and bath for P300. It's a good place with a restaurant. *Simon's Place* has cottages with fan and bath from P350 to P600. The cottages are all different sizes, one larger one has a kitchen and fridge. This is a pleasant little establishment. The *Arcobalono Apartelle & Beach Resort* has

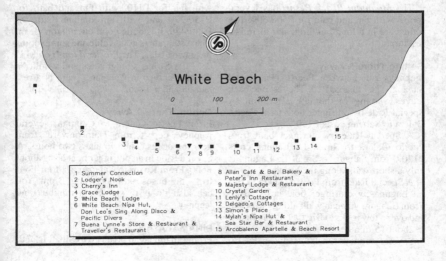

White Beach

0   100   200 m

1 Summer Connection
2 Lodger's Nook
3 Cherry's Inn
4 Grace Lodge
5 White Beach Lodge
6 White Beach Nipa Hut,
   Don Leo's Sing Along Disco &
   Pacific Divers
7 Buena Lynne's Store & Restaurant &
   Traveller's Restaurant
8 Allan Café & Bar, Bakery &
   Peter's Inn Restaurant
9 Majesty Lodge & Restaurant
10 Crystal Garden
11 Lenly's Cottage
12 Delgado's Cottages
13 Simon's Place
14 Mylah's Nipa Hut &
   Sea Star Bar & Restaurant
15 Arcobaleno Apartelle & Beach Resort

rooms with fan and bath for P200 and comfortable cottages with kitchen, fan and bath for P300/350. This is a pleasant and quiet place.

Aninuan Beach The *Aninuan Lodge* has cottages with bath for P250 and P350. It is a small, fairly quiet place directly on the beach, with a few cottages of different sizes and a restaurant.

The *Tamaraw Beach Resort* (cellular ☎ 912-3066388) has cottages with bath for P350 and P500, and there is a restaurant. This is a popular place shaded by trees and with several cottages of different sizes.

Talipanan Beach The *White Sand Beach Resort* has rooms with fan and bath for P250 and P300. A cottage with kitchen, fridge, fan and bath costs P600. It is a fairly large establishment with duplex cottages and rooms in terrace houses, and it has a restaurant. The *White Beach Nipa Hut 2* is a large place with lots of practical, basic cottages with fan and bath for P300 and P400. There is also a restaurant.

The *Golden Wings Cottages* has a restaurant and only a few cottages of different sizes with fan and bath for P300 and P600.

The *Mountain Beach Resort* has several rooms with fan and bath for P500/600. The rooms are in a long building, and there is a restaurant.

Getting There & Away
Jeepneys run between Puerto Galera and Sabang. They charge P10. The last one back leaves Sabang in the late afternoon. A Special Ride by outrigger boat from Puerto Galera to Sabang costs P150.

A Special Ride by outrigger boat from Puerto Galera to Small La Laguna costs P120. From Sabang to Small La Laguna is only a short walk along the beach.

A Special Ride from Puerto Galera to Big La Laguna by outrigger boat costs P100. From Sabang, you can walk along the beach and over a few rocks to Big La Laguna Beach in about 15 minutes.

Several jeepneys run daily between Puerto Galera and White Beach in San Isidro, and charge P10. Some of them go on to Talipanan Point. This costs P15. The last one back from San Isidro to Puerto Galera leaves at about 5 pm. The fare for a Special Ride is between P100 and P150. You can go from White Beach to Talipanan Beach along the beach in about 45 minutes.

A Special Ride by outrigger boat from Puerto Galera to White Beach costs P440, and to Talipanan Beach P500.

CALAPAN
Calapan is the capital of Mindoro Oriental Province. The Sanduguan Festival was held here for the first time from 18 to 21 May 1981. *Sanduguan* means friendship in the Mangyan language. At the festival the locals re-enacted the first meeting between seafaring Chinese traders and the indigenous Mangyan at Aroma Beach. It was such a success, it is now a yearly event in the middle of May or the middle of November.

Places to Stay
The *Travellers Inn* (☎ 1926) on Leuterio St has simple rooms with fan for P80/100 and with air-con and bath for P320.

The *Riceland Inn I* on Rizal St has rooms with fan for P110, with fan and bath for P150/270 and with air-con and bath for P340/440. It is quite good but not too clean. The restaurant is good value and some rooms have wide beds. The *Riceland Inn II* on M H del Pilar St has similar rates and would be the best choice in Calapan. There is a restaurant and a disco.

Getting There & Away
From Puerto Galera to Calapan, several jeepneys depart from 7 am onwards from near the docks. The trip takes two hours. A Special Ride in an outrigger boat costs about P600. From Roxas to Calapan is a four-hour trip – big buses run hourly until 3 pm. You can also do it in stages by minibus and jeepney.

PINAMALAYAN
From Pinamalayan boats go to Sibali Island,

the local name for Maestro de Campo Island, and to Banton Island, both in Romblon Province. You can also take a boat from here to Marinduque. You can ask about timetables at the coast-guard station, 200 metres beyond the market.

BONGABONG

Bongabong is a small, not very interesting place. Boats run from there to Tablas Island in Romblon Province (see the Getting There & Away section at the beginning of this chapter).

Mabuhay Lodging House near the market has basic rooms with fan for P50/100.

ROXAS

From Roxas, big outrigger boats run to Tablas Island in Romblon Province and Boracay north-west off Panay (see the Getting There & Away section at the beginning of this chapter). That's probably the only reason for staying here. Some of the waiting time can be spent at the nearby Melco Beach.

Places to Stay

The *Santo Nino Lodging House* has basic rooms for P50/100, and it has a restaurant. The *Catalina Beach Resort* at Lodpond, 1½ km from Roxas, has simple rooms for P50/100 and rooms with bath for P80/100.

The *Melco Beach Lodge* at Dangay has cottages for P65/110 and with fan for P150. It is simple but comfortable, and has a restaurant. It is a P20 tricycle ride from town and, although the beaches are not terribly good, it's a good place to stay while waiting for boats to Tablas or Boracay.

Getting There & Away

Big buses leave the market at Calapan every hour from early morning to 3 pm daily, bound for Roxas via Pinamalayan and Bongabong. It takes two hours to reach Pinamalayan, three hours to Bongabong and four hours to Roxas.

Minibuses in the market at Calapan go to Bongabong. From Bongabong to Roxas, the last jeepney or minibus goes at about 6 pm

from the market. The only reliable information about departure times comes from the drivers; information that the waiting passengers give you will usually be useless.

MANSALAY

This is a good starting point for visits to the Mangyan tribes, but be warned that rubbernecks or camera-happy tourists are not appreciated. Father Antoon Postma, a Dutch missionary who has published a number of books and articles on this peaceful tribe, took care of the Mangyan around Mansalay for many years. A visit without reason is intrusive and unnecessary. If, however, you are genuinely interested in the problems of these minority groups, the members of the mission are informative and cooperative.

Getting There & Away

Several jeepneys run daily from Roxas to Mansalay. If you want to go on into the mountains to visit the Mangyan, go early or you'll be walking in the noon heat.

SAN JOSE

Among other things, San Jose is one of the starting points for diving excursions to Apo Reef. It is in the south-western part of Mindoro Occidental and is handy for people with a bit of time to fit in a boat trip to Palawan. (Boats only leave occasionally for Coron on Busuanga and for islands of the Quiniluban Group, which is the northernmost part of the Cuyo Islands.) However, San Jose lacks the kind of appeal that could tempt you to stay longer; the amount of comfortable hotels to choose from is limited, and good restaurants are a rarity. To make up for it, there are an unbelievable amount of beauty parlours.

In Mindoro Occidental there are many cultural minorities, the most remote tribes having little contact with civilisation. Occasionally some come into town and with luck you may meet Mangyans who will guide you to their village.

Queen's Ranch is a good place for a day trip. It is two hours away by jeepney and you can stay there overnight for about P75 per

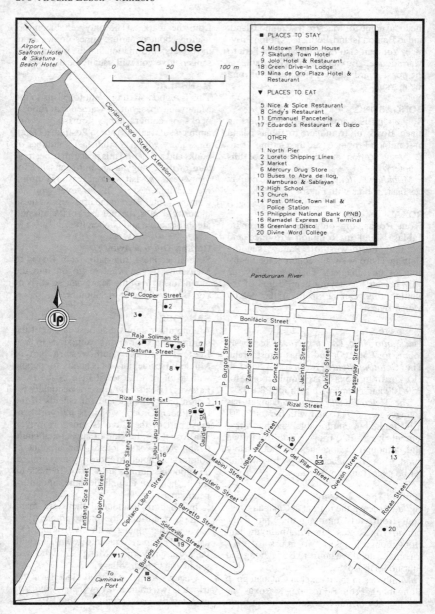

San Jose

0   50   100 m

To
Airport,
Seafront Hotel
& Sikatuna Beach
Hotel

■ PLACES TO STAY
4 Midtown Pension House
7 Sikatuna Town Hotel
9 Jolo Hotel & Restaurant
18 Green Drive-In Lodge
19 Mina de Oro Plaza Hotel &
   Restaurant

▼ PLACES TO EAT
5 Nice & Spice Restaurant
8 Cindy's Restaurant
11 Emmanuel Panceteria
17 Eduardo's Restaurant & Disco

   OTHER
1 North Pier
2 Loreto Shipping Lines
3 Market
6 Mercury Drug Store
10 Buses to Abra de Ilog,
   Mamburao & Sablayan
12 High School
13 Church
14 Post Office, Town Hall &
   Police Station
15 Philippine National Bank (PNB)
16 Ramadel Express Bus Terminal
18 Greenland Disco
20 Divine Word College

person. From there it takes about eight hours on foot to reach the Mt Iglit Tamaraw Reservation.

Boats can also be hired in San Jose for swimming and snorkelling on the nearby islands of Ilin and Ambulong. Both islands have white beaches. On Ilin Island is the Mina de Oro Beach Resort.

Places to Stay

The *Jolo Hotel* (☎ 618) on Rizal St has rooms for P60/80, with fan for P70/90 and with fan and bath for P100. It is simple and has a restaurant and a disco.

The *Midtown Pension House* on Raja Soliman St has rooms with fan for P55/110 and with fan and bath for P75/150. It's very basic and anything but inviting. As it is beside the market, you can be sure of waking early in the morning.

The *Sikatuna Town Hotel* (☎ 697) on Sikatuna St has rooms with fan for P70/100, with fan and bath for P145 and with air-con and bath for P410. This place is simple, clean and fairly good. A modest breakfast is included, however the restaurant doesn't open until 7 am, after the early buses have already left.

The *Sikatuna Beach Hotel* on Airport Rd, outside of town at the beach near the airport, has basic, clean accommodation. The rooms are from P70 to P130, with fan and bath from P130 to P175 and with air-con and bath from P415 to P450. The air-con rooms are overpriced, however. There is a restaurant.

The *Seafront Hotel* also on Airport Rd has modest rooms with fan and bath for P130/150 and with air-con and bath for P380, and there is a restaurant.

The *Mina de Oro Plaza Hotel* in Soldevilla St has basic, fairly small plain rooms, some of which are a bit stuffy. Singles with fan are P220 and singles/doubles with air-con and bath are P550/860. The air-con rooms are well on the pricey side. The most impressive thing about this hotel is its name.

The *Mina de Oro Beach Resort* at Inasakan on Ilin Island has pleasantly furnished rooms in a big bamboo house. Singles/doubles with bath are P1200 to P1600. The restaurant is rather expensive. Diving and windsurfing are available. This is a cosy resort in a small, palm-lined bay with a white sand beach.

Places to Eat

Cindy's Restaurant on Cipriano Liboro St offers a small selection of simple Filipino dishes, as does the spotless *Emmanuel Panciteria* on Rizal St – however, they ration their guests to two bottles of beer each! *Nice & Spice* on Sikatuna St serve pizzas, ice cream and cakes, starting in the late afternoon, but they don't have coffee.

Getting There & Away

Air PAL has an office at San Jose Airport (☎ 676).

Bus Few buses make a daily trip from Roxas to Bulalacao, so it's better to go by jeepney to Mansalay and then get another jeepney on to Bulalacao. This takes about two hours. Leave early if you don't want to stay in Bulalacao overnight. (See under Boat in this section for a connection to San Jose.)

Three rickety Ramadel Express buses travel daily from Mamburao to San Jose via Sablayan, taking six hours. From San Jose to Mamburao the buses leave at 5, 6.30 and 8.30 am from Gaudiel St near the Jolo Hotel. Further departure times are 1 and 3 am and 11 pm; these buses go to Abra de Ilog via Mamburao.

Jeepney In the dry season, from December to May, it is also possible to travel by jeepney from Bulalacao to San Jose, leaving at 4 am and taking four hours.

Boat A boat leaves Bulalacao for San Jose in the morning any time between 8 and 11 am, depending on the tides. The trip takes three hours or more, usually finishing at South Pier, Caminawit Port, four km out of San Jose.

APO ISLAND & APO REEF

Right in the middle of the busy Mindoro Strait, which separates Mindoro from the

Calamian Group in the north of Palawan, you will find the little flat island of Apo with the vast Apo Reef to the east of it. A 36-metre-high lighthouse warns passing ships against getting too close to the reef, where countless rocks and coral heads jut out of the water at low tide. What is for mariners a highly dangerous area, is for divers one of the most spectacular areas in the Philippines for underwater sights, in spite of the enormous number of coral reefs destroyed in recent years by dynamite fishing. In the summer months of March, April and May, several diving expeditions head for Apo Island and Apo Reef. However, this is a paradise not only for divers but also for snorkellers and latter-day Robinson Crusoes.

The only place to camp is at the south-eastern end, but make sure your tent is closed up before sunset or you will be tortured by sandflies. Take your own food and about five litres of water per day.

Don't confuse this island with the other Apo Island loved by divers, just off the south-east coast of Negros.

Getting There & Away

There is no regular connection to Apo Island so you will have to charter a boat. A return trip in a big outrigger boat from Sablayan, including a trip round the island, shouldn't cost more than P2500. Arrange a pick-up time beforehand.

SABLAYAN

This friendly, clean little town is at the mouth of the Bagong Sabang River in the south of Pandan Bay. There are several shops here and a lively market with a few simple local restaurants along the riverside, where boats are tied up which will take you to the islands of Pandan Bay. Larger boats dock at the Sablayan Pier, in a sheltered little bay near the lighthouse.

Places to Stay

The *Emely Hotel* on Rosario St has simple but clean rooms for P60/120. Meals can be arranged. The small restaurants at the market close at about 7 pm.

Getting There & Away

Buses and jeepneys pass through Sablayan on their way to and from San Jose, Abra de Ilog and Mamburao. The track along the west coast of Mindoro is very dusty in parts; you would be well advised to take along a rag over your mouth as a mask. The trip from Sablayan to Mamburao and San Jose takes three hours each.

NORTH PANDAN ISLAND

North Pandan would be near the top of my personal Top 10 Philippine islands. In the south this gorgeous spot has a beautiful white sand beach with palms and other tropical trees. The remaining northern part of this roughly triangular island is covered by dense jungle which comes right down to the beach. The animal population of this jungle still appears to be intact.

Places to Stay

The *Pandan Island Resort* has rooms for P200, cottages with fan and bath for P350 and a house for four people for P800. The cottages are extremely spacious and supplied with solar energy. This quiet, rambling establishment is managed by French people. There is a restaurant, a beach bar and diving available, and there are plans to introduce windsurfing.

Getting There & Away

The resort service boat leaves for North Pandan Island around 10 am from the river landing place at the market in Sablayan. A Special Ride costs P100. The trip takes 30 minutes.

Arrangements to be picked up by boat from Mamburao (P1500), and reservations, can be made in Manila at Asiaventure Services (☎ 5222911; fax 583323), Manila Pavilion, Room 501, United Nations Ave, Ermita.

MAMBURAO

The not very appealing community of Mamburao is the capital of Mindoro Occidental Province.

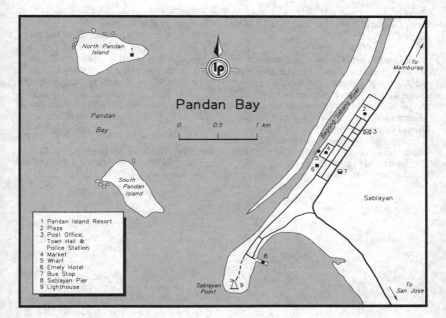

Pandan Bay

Pandan Bay

0   0.5   1 km

1 Pandan Island Resort
2 Plaza
3 Post Office,
   Town Hall &
   Police Station
4 Market
5 Wharf
6 Emely Hotel
7 Bus Stop
8 Sablayan Pier
9 Lighthouse

North Pandan Island

South Pandan Island

Bagong Sabang River

To Mamburao

Sablayan

Sablayan Point

To San Jose

Places to Stay

Mamburao The *Traveller's Lodge* has rooms with fan for P80/150, with fan and bath for P150/250 and with air-con and bath for P450/800. It is a passable place with a restaurant.

Around Mamburao The *Tayamaan Palm Beach Club*, about four km north-west of Mamburao, has cottages with fan and bath for P450; full board is available on request. The cottages are clean, well-built stone buildings standing under palm trees on a beautiful bay with a sandy beach suitable for bathing. There is also a restaurant. It costs P40 to get there by tricycle from the airport.

La Dolce Vita Garden Resort at Fatima, about 12 km south of Mamburao, has cottages with fan and bath from P250 to P450; full board is possible. There is a good restaurant serving European and Filipino cuisine. It also has a swimming pool, and Hobie Cats and windsurfing are available. You can hire a motorbike, and day trips by boat or jeep can be arranged on request. It costs P100 by tricycle from the airport.

The *Mamburao Beach Resort* also at Fatima has cottages with fan and bath for P2000 per person, including meals. It is pleasant and has a restaurant, and Hobie Cats and windsurfing are available. It is about 12 km south of Mamburao, near La Dolce Vita Garden Resort. Information and reservations can be made in Manila at Mamburao Resort Corporation (☎ 8152733), Cityland Condominium III, on the corner of Estaban and Herrera Sts, Makati.

Getting There & Away

Air There are flights to and from Manila at least two times a week.

PAL has an office at Mamburao Airport.

Bus From San Jose to Mamburao via Sablayan rickety Ramadel Express buses leave at 1, 3, 5, 6.30 and 8.30 am and 11 pm from Gaudiel St near the Jolo Hotel, taking six hours.

Boat From Puerto Galera, a boat leaves daily at about noon for Wawa – the landing place for Abra de Ilog – as long as there are enough passengers. It takes 2½ hours and costs P75. A Special Ride by outrigger boat from Puerto Galera to Wawa costs P400. From Wawa to Puerto Galera the boat leaves at 9 am.

Jeepneys ply between from Wawa to Mamburao via Abra de Ilog. The trip takes 2½ hours and costs P35.

If you are stranded in Wawa you can spend the night at the *Lodging House*, which is clean and about 500 metres before you get to the pier. Rooms are available for P120/150.

Another way to get from Puerto Galera to Abra de Ilog is to go via Batangas: take a ferry from Puerto Galera to Batangas, stay the night there, and the next morning at 8.30 or 9.30 am take the ferry from Batangas to Abra de Ilog. The trip takes three hours and costs P50.

Warning The road between Puerto Galera and Abra de Ilog, shown on most maps of the Philippines, was never built.

The Visayas

South of the island of Luzon is the main island group of the Philippines, the Visayas. The major islands in this group are Bohol, Cebu, Leyte, Negros, Panay, Romblon, Samar and Siquijor. The Visayas are bordered to the south by Mindanao and to the west by long, narrow Palawan.

ISLAND HOPPING

It's in the Visayas that possibilities for island hopping in the Philippines are at their best. A possible circuit of the Visayas could take you to most of the places of interest with minimal backtracking. Starting from Manila, you could travel down to the Bikol region and, from Matnog, at the southern tip of Luzon, there are ferries everyday across to Allen, at the northern end of Samar. The new road down the west coast of Samar means it is now a quick and relatively easy trip through Calbayog and Catbalogan across the bridge to Tacloban on the island of Leyte. This was where MacArthur returned towards the end of WW II. From Tacloban or Ormoc there are regular ships to Cebu City or less regularly from Maasin to Bohol.

Cebu was where Magellan arrived in the Philippines and you can still find a number of reminders of the Spanish period. From Cebu City there are daily ferries to the neighbouring island of Bohol, famous for its Chocolate Hills. Ferries also cross daily between Cebu and Negros, either in the south of the island to Dumaguete, or closer to Cebu City from Toledo to San Carlos. You can then continue by bus to Bacolod, where you can get a ferry across to Iloilo City on Panay.

Panay has the usual assortment of bus and jeepney routes. At the north-west tip you can make the short crossing by outrigger boat to the beautiful and laid-back island of Boracay. After a spell of lazing on the beach there, you can find another boat to cross to Tablas Island in the Romblon group, usually to Looc in the south. Take a jeepney to Odiongan and a boat from there to Roxas in

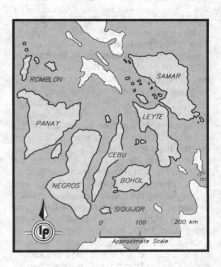

Mindoro. Another bus ride will take you to Puerto Galera, a popular travellers' beach centre. Finally, there are daily ferries to Batangas, only a few hours by bus from Manila – quite an interesting and adventurous trip.

If, however, you're looking for something a shade more adventurous yet still easy to manage, the following trip through the Visayas will fit the bill. Starting off in Manila, take a bus heading south to Batangas or Lucena, from where boats leave more or less regularly for Romblon on Romblon Island. Although this island is well known for its marble, travellers are still fairly thin on the ground. Boats leave from Romblon daily for the adjacent island of Tablas and on from there to the popular little island of Boracay. (If you are in a hurry and want to avoid some of the hassles of travel, you can fly direct from Manila to Tablas.)

After a few lazy days on the beach you can carry on by bus right across Panay to Iloilo

City and from there take the ferry to Bacolod on Negros, the sugar island of the Philippines. Take a bus or jeepney to Cadiz, a small harbour town on the north coast of Negros and from there a boat to Bantayan Island, which is already in Cebu Province. This friendly island in the centre of the Visayas can be best explored by bicycle. The ferry from Santa Fe to Hagnaya on Cebu is met on arrival by a bus or jeepney which will take you to Maya, the most northerly settlement on Cebu Island. From there, outrigger boats will take you to the offshore island of Malapascua. If you find Boracay a bit too overrun with tourists, you'll feel at home on this beautiful little island.

Next stop is the island of Leyte. From San Isidro in the north-west you can carry on in two or three stages by bus via Ormoc and Baybay along the scenic coastal route south to Bato or Maasin, where a boat will take you to Bohol. After you've visited the bizarre Chocolate Hills, the smaller islands of Cabilao, Balicasag and Panglao west of Bohol are good for a few days relaxation. From Cabilao Island you can have yourself taken over to Argao on the south-east coast of Cebu and take a bus from there to Bato, where several ferries leave daily for the big island of Negros. The pleasant provincial capital of Dumaguete is a departure point for trips over to Siquijor Island where, according to many Filipinos, witchcraft flourishes. If you can drag yourself away from the magic of the island, there is a ship to Cebu City three times weekly. From there you can carry on your journey, for example, to Mindanao or Palawan, or back to Manila.

Bohol

Situated between Leyte and Cebu, in the south of the Visayas, Bohol is the 10th largest island of the Philippines. Another 72 small islands belong to the province of the same name. Agriculture is the main source of income of the Boholano. The main crop is coconut, but maize and rice are also grown.

Visayas

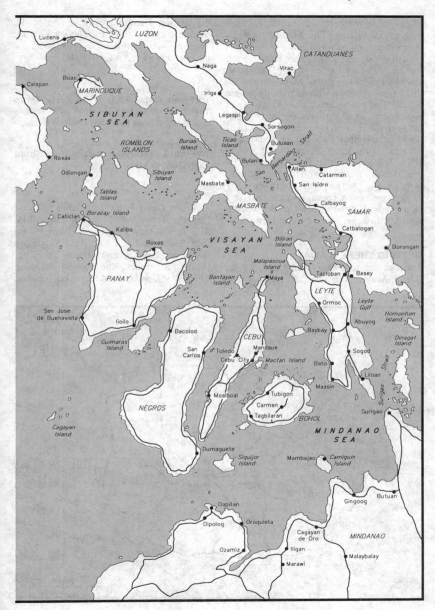

They even have rice terraces near Lila, 25 km east of Tagbilaran. The Manila souvenir shops are well stocked with woven and plaited goods and basket ware from Bohol, but the prices are much lower in Tagbilaran and other places on Bohol itself. Tourism on this attractive island with its friendly people is only just being developed. Its historical significance is due to the blood compact between the Spanish conqueror Legaspi and the Boholano chieftain Sikatuna. Today most visitors go to Bohol to see the Chocolate Hills. The Swiss author Erich von Däniken would have a field day with this strange hilly landscape. A few km north-east of Tagbilaran, near Corella, live the rare, shy tarsier monkeys, the smallest monkeys in the world, with large, round eyes and long tails.

GETTING THERE & AWAY

You can get to Bohol from Cebu, Leyte, Luzon, Mindanao, Panay and Siquijor (see the Getting There & Away section of the Manila chapter and the relevant Getting There & Away sections of this chapter and of the chapters on the other islands).

Air

To/From Cebu PAL flies daily from Tagbilaran to Cebu City. It is advisable to reconfirm at least three days before flying.

To/From Luzon PAL has daily flights from Tagbilaran to Manila.

Boat

To/From Cebu From Tagbilaran to Cebu City the Trans-Asia Shipping Lines' MV *Asia Taiwan* leaves daily at 8.30 am, taking four hours; and the MV *Asia Singapore* leaves on Tuesday and Sunday at 9 pm, taking four hours. The Palacio Shipping Lines' MV *Don Martin 6* leaves on Tuesday,

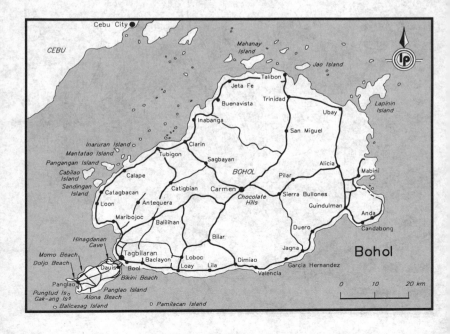

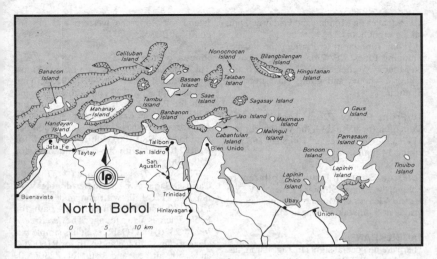

Thursday and Saturday at midnight and takes 5½ hours.

From Tubigon to Cebu City, the MV *Charing* leaves daily at 9 am, taking three hours; the MV *Rayjumar* leaves daily at 11 am, taking 2½ hours; the MV *Betchie* leaves daily at noon; the MV *Queen Leonora* or the MV *Queen Vicki* leaves daily at 4 pm, taking 2½ hours; and the MV *Harvey* leaves daily at midnight, taking three hours.

From Talibon to Cebu City MV *Krishia* leaves daily at 8 am, taking 3½ hours; the MV *Talibon Cruiser* leaves daily at 9 am, taking four hours; and the MV *Andy* leaves daily at 10 pm, taking four hours.

From Loon to Argao the MV *LCT Barge St Mark* (car ferry) of Lite Shipping Corporation leaves on Monday, Wednesday and Friday at 7 am and 1 pm; on Tuesday, Thursday and Saturday at 10 am; and on Sunday at 8.30 am. The crossing takes 2½ hours.

To/From Leyte To go from Ubay to Bato, you catch the big outrigger boat, which leaves daily at 10 am, sometimes going via Lapinin Island and taking three or four hours.

A big outrigger boat leaves Ubay for Maasin daily at 10 am, taking four hours.

From Jagna to Maasin, the Trans Asia-Shipping Lines' MV *Asia Brunei* leaves on Sunday at 3 am, taking four hours.

To/From Luzon From Tagbilaran to Manila via Dumaguit and Batan on Panay, the William Lines' MV *Cebu City* leaves on Thursday at 8 pm, taking 33 hours.

To/From Mindanao From Jagna to Butuan, the Carlos Gothong Lines' MV *Doña Lili* leaves on Sunday at noon, taking six hours. The Trans-Asia Shipping Lines' MV *Asia Brunei* leaves on Wednesday at 2 am and on Friday at midnight, taking seven hours. The Sulpicio Lines' MV *Nasipit Princess* leaves on Thursday at midnight, taking six hours.

From Jagna to Cagayan de Oro, Carlos Gothong Lines' MV *Our Lady of Guadalupe* leaves on Sunday at 10 pm, taking six hours. The Trans-Asia Shipping Lines' MV *Asia Brunei* leaves on Thursday at 10 pm, taking seven hours. The Sulpicio Lines' MV *Cagayan Princess* leaves on Saturday at midnight, taking five hours.

From Tagbilaran to Cagayan de Oro, the Trans-Asia Shipping Lines' MV *Asia Sing-*

apore leaves on Monday and Friday at 9 pm, taking eight hours.

From Tagbilaran to Plaridel the Palacio Shipping Lines' MV *Don Martin 6* leaves on Monday, Wednesday and Friday at 6 pm, taking 14 hours and going via Larena on Siquijor.

To/From Panay From Tagbilaran to Dumaguit (near Kalibo), the William Lines' MV *Cebu City* leaves on Thursday at 8 pm, taking 14 hours.

To/From Siquijor From Tagbilaran to Larena, the Palacio Shipping Lines' MV *Don Martin 6* leaves on Monday, Wednesday and Friday at 6 pm, taking four hours.

TAGBILARAN

There are no special sights in Tagbilaran, the capital of Bohol Province on the south-west coast of Bohol.

Orientation

The main street is Carlos P Garcia Ave, or CPG Ave for short. Every day there is a never-ending stream of noisy tricycles, and the dust and exhausts make for a really thick atmosphere. In this street you will find several hotels, restaurants and many shops, as well as the Agora Market and the Torralba Market where handicrafts and local made products are sold.

Information

The Philippine National Bank on A Clarin St near the plaza will change travellers' cheques.

In the Tagbilaran Friendly Bazaar on Carlos P Garcia Ave a moneychanger on the ground floor will give a good exchange rate. The post office is on J S Torralba St, near the town hall.

Things to See

The best beach near the city is **Caingit Beach**, behind the Hotel La Roca, but even it is nothing special. Some interesting trips are possible: from Tagbilaran to Panglao

Island, or along the western and eastern coasts of Bohol.

Places to Stay

The *Vista Lodge* (☎ 3072) on Lesage St has singles/doubles with fan for P75/95, with fan and bath for P100/120 and with air-con and bath for P250/275. It is unpretentious but fairly good. The *Executive Inn* (☎ 3254) on J S Torralba St has simple singles/doubles with fan for P80/100, with fan and bath for P130/240 and with air-con and bath for P290/390.

The *Nisa Travellers Inn* (☎ 3731) on Carlos P Garcia Ave has singles/doubles with fan for P120/150, with fan and bath for P160/180 and with air-con and bath for P350. There is also a lounge. The *Sea Breeze Inn* (☎ 2326) on C Gallares St has simple but clean rooms with fan and bath for P160/200 and with air-con and bath for P280/400. There is a restaurant.

The *Charisma Lodge* (☎ 3094) on Carlos P Garcia Ave has passable, clean rooms with fan for P100/150, with fan and bath for P175/200 and with air-con and bath for P330/350. The *LTS Lodge* (☎ 3082, 3310) on Carlos P Garcia Ave has clean, comfortable rooms with fan for P100/160, with air-con for P200/300 and with air-con and bath for P300/400. The rooms overlooking the street are quite loud. The *Gie Garden Hotel* (☎ 2021, 3182) on M H del Pilar St has rooms with air-con and bath for P330/480. It is friendly and well kept, and has a restaurant.

The *Hotel La Roca* (☎ 3179) on Graham Ave, on the northern edge of town near the airport, has rooms with air-con and bath from P400 to P740 and suites for P880. It's a comfortable place with a restaurant and a swimming pool. The *Bohol Tropics Resort Club* (☎ 2134, 3510-14; fax 3019) on Graham Ave, on the northern edge of town near Hotel La Roca, has pleasant, well-appointed rooms with TV, air-con and bath from P980 to P1450 and suites for P1450. The suites also have a fridge. There is a restaurant, swimming pool, fitness room and tennis court. This fairly large establishment

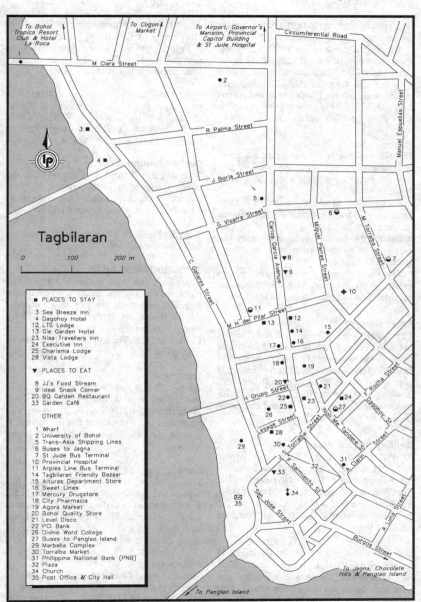

Tagbilaran

0   100   200 m

■ PLACES TO STAY

3   Sea Breeze Inn
4   Dagohoy Hotel
12 LTS Lodge
13 Gie Garden Hotel
23 Nisa Travellers Inn
24 Executive Inn
25 Charisma Lodge
28 Vista Lodge

▼ PLACES TO EAT

8   JJ's Food Stream
9   Ideal Snack Corner
20 BQ Garden Restaurant
33 Garden Café

    OTHER

1   Wharf
2   University of Bohol
5   Trans-Asia Shipping Lines
6   Buses to Jagna
7   St Jude Bus Terminal
10 Provincial Hospital
11 Arples Line Bus Terminal
14 Tagbilaran Friendly Bazaar
15 Alturas Department Store
16 Sweet Lines
17 Mercury Drugstore
18 City Pharmacia
19 Agora Market
20 Bohol Quality Store
21 Level Disco
22 PCI Bank
26 Divine Word College
27 Buses to Panglao Island
29 Marbella Complex
30 Torralba Market
31 Philippine National Bank (PNB)
32 Plaza
34 Church
35 Post Office & City Hall

with cottages directly along the waterfront is the best hotel in Tagbilaran.

The *Island Leisure Inn* (☎ 2482) in the Ilaw International Center at Bohol is about three km east of Tagbilaran. It has rooms with fan and bath for P230/280 and with air-con and bath for P340/400. Some rooms have a balcony. It is pleasant and tidy, and has a restaurant, bar and disco.

Places to Eat

The *Gie Garden Hotel* restaurant has good cheap meals. The food at the *seafood restaurants* to the right of the wharf can also be recommended.

An excellent breakfast can be had in the pleasant *Garden Café* next to the church, which is run by hearing-impaired people. Although the menu is not large, they are happy to do special orders such as mango and banana omelettes.

JJ's Food Stream has reasonably priced meals. In the evening, barbecue stands are put up in front of the Agora Market.

Entertainment

The *Ideal Snack Corner* not only serves snacks and cheap daily meals but also shows nonstop videos on a big screen. *JJ's Food Stream* offers videos as well as live music. If you want a late beer with billiards and bowling, try the *Marbella Complex*, the *Zoom Disco* on A Clarin St and the *Level Disco* near the Agora Market.

Getting There & Away

Air PAL has an office at Tagbilaran Airport (☎ 3102). Anyone wanting to leave Bohol by plane would be well advised to reconfirm the flight out immediately on arrival and have it put down on a list, as the system may not yet be computerised. PAL does not have an office in town.

Bus Most of the transport on the island is taken care of by the Arples Line and St Jude Bus companies. The Arples Line bus terminal can be found diagonally across from the Gie Garden Hotel on M H del Pilar St and the St Jude Bus terminal near the Provincial Hospital on M Torralba St.

Friday is market day in Tagbilaran and on that day there are bus and jeepney connections in practically every direction.

Boat Trans Asia Shipping Lines (☎ 3234) is on Carlos P Garcia Ave. Sulpicio Lines (☎ 3079) is on Grupo St, William Lines (☎ 3048) is on G Gallares St and Palacio Shipping Lines is on M Cara St.

Getting Around

To/From the Airport The airport is at the northern edge of the city. A tricycle from the airport to the city centre (Agora Market) costs P3 and to Alona Beach P100.

Tricycle From the wharf to the city centre is only one km and costs P2 by tricycle.

AROUND TAGBILARAN

There are some some historical sights to the north and east of Tagbilaran. It is best to hire a car and do a round trip, possibly starting at Alona Beach on Panglao Island. There would also be time to include a detour to the Chocolate Hills. The following places can be reached by public transport from Tagbilaran.

Maribojoc

About 15 km north of Tagbilaran near Maribojoc stands the old **Punta Cruz Watchtower**, built in the time of the Spaniards in 1796 to look out for pirates. It gives a good view over other islands of the Visayas.

Loon

Loon, a few km north-west of Maribojoc, has a beautiful old church dating back to 1753. It has noteworthy ceiling frescoes. There is a daily connection by car ferry between Loon and Argao on Cebu (see Getting There & Away earlier in this section).

Antequera

Various kinds of basket ware are for sale on Sunday in the market at Antequera, about 10 km north-east of Maribojoc. Little more than a km out of town and situated in a forest you will find the beautiful **Mag-Aso Falls** with a deep natural pool to swim in. Admission is P1. The last bus from Antequera to Tagbilaran departs at 3 pm.

Bool

A memorial at Bool, barely three km east of Tagbilaran, is a reminder of the blood compact between Legaspi and Sikatuna, who sealed their bond of friendship on 16 March 1565 by making a cut in their skin, letting the blood drip into a cup of wine and then emptying the cup together. At Bool there is also the Ilaw International Center, with its open-air restaurant, bar and disco. Big weddings are often held here on Saturday.

Baclayon

About four km to the east of Bool is Baclayon, the oldest town in Bohol. It has one of the oldest churches in the Philippines, built in 1595. A small **museum** adjoins it. The museum is open Monday to Saturday from 9 to 11 am and from 2 to 4 pm. Admission is P20.

There are a few cheap restaurants in the market, and boats go from Baclayon to nearby Pamilacan Island.

Loay & Loboc

At Loay, where you can visit an old church with an adjoining convent school, the Loboc River flows into the Mindanao Sea. You can take an exciting river trip in a chartered outrigger boat from the Loay bridge until just before the Tontonan Hydroelectric Power Station, about two km north of Loboc. In Loboc itself it's worth seeing the large old **San Pedro Church**, built in 1602, because of the remarkable naive painting on the ceiling.

JAGNA

Jagna is a busy, clean little town. Ships sail from here to various destinations in the Visayas. Departure times are usually late at night; the atmosphere at the wharf is best then. The old **church**, with its ceiling frescoes, is worth seeing. **Ilihan Hill**, four km north from Jagna, can be reached by a winding road and is frequently a place of pilgrimage.

Places to Stay

The *DQ Lodge* in the port area near the landing stage has rooms for P50/90, with fan for P60/120 and with air-con and bath for P350. It is basic but quite comfortable and has a restaurant.

Getting There & Away

There are buses from the Chocolate Hills area going to Jagna, leaving from Carmen. The route goes past the Chocolate Hills turnoff and then via Bilar and Dimiao. It is also possible to take the bus to Tagbilaran, get off in Loay and then wait for a bus or jeepney from Tagbilaran to Jagna.

Several buses leave the St Jude bus terminal in Tagbilaran daily for Jagna. The trip takes two hours.

From Tubigon, on the west coast, there are several buses a day going to Jagna via Talibon. They go along the coast instead of going through Carmen.

ANDA

Anda is a clean, somewhat sleepy little community on a peninsula in the south-east of Bohol. Right on the doorstep there is a long, wide beach with white sand that strangers seldom happen onto. With one exception there is no commercial accommodation available, a situation that could change quickly considering the attractions of this coastline.

The picturesque scenery begins just outside Guindulman, where lonely bays with little white beaches and crystal-clear water tempt the visitor to stay. The ideal way to explore here is by boat, as the untarred road which runs about 500 metres from the ocean has few paths offering access to the coast. One of these idyllic bays is **Bugnao Beach** near Candabong, which has little stretches of white sand sectioned off by rocky cliffs eaten away at their bases by the sea.

Places to Stay

The friendly *Dap Dap Beach Resort* is about three km west of Anda and has a few cottages with fan and bath for P300. It is best to bring your own food or buy it locally and have the resort cook it for you.

Getting There & Away

There are only a few jeepneys that go from Jagna to Anda, taking 1½ hours for the 40-km trip. The last trip back to Jagna is at about 5 pm. A Special Ride costs about P250 one way.

Coming from Tagbilaran, instead of stopping at Jagna, you can carry on in the direction of Ubay, get out at Guindulman and take a tricycle from there. A tricycle from Guindulman to Dap Dap Beach Resort costs about P100.

PANGLAO ISLAND

Several beach resorts have opened very recently on Panglao Island. From Bohol you can cross to this island over two bridges. The older bridge is near Tagbilaran City Hall. The newer one is almost two km south-east of Tagbilaran and joins the district of Bool on Bohol with Dauis on Panglao.

Information

There is neither a bank nor a money changer on Panglao Island, so bring enough pesos.

Things to See

The lake in **Hinagdanan Cave** at Bingag on the north-east of the island has refreshingly cool water. However, as all kinds of disease-spreading bacteria thrive in still waters, it is best to do without that tempting swim. For a few coins the caretaker will switch on the light in the cave.

The white sand **Alona Beach** is the most beautiful, most popular and touristically the most developed beach on the island. Spread along the beach for 1½ km there are small, individually designed resorts, cosy restaurants, rough-and-ready beach bars, several dive shops and even bicycle hire. The bathing, unfortunately, is spoilt a bit by the sea grass which grows knee deep and is inhabited by sea urchins, so you can't go in for more than a few metres without being careful. Still, this beach is good for snorkell-

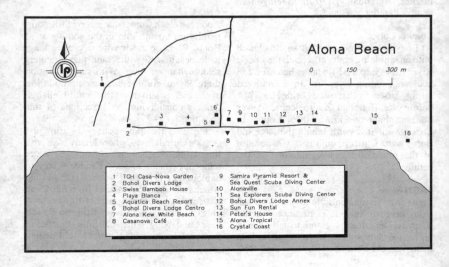

Alona Beach

0   150   300 m

1 TGH Casa-Nova Garden	9 Samira Pyramid Resort &
2 Bohol Divers Lodge	Sea Quest Scuba Diving Center
3 Swiss Bamboo House	10 Alonaville
4 Playa Blanca	11 Sea Explorers Scuba Diving Center
5 Aquatica Beach Resort	12 Bohol Divers Lodge Annex
6 Bohol Divers Lodge Centro	13 Sun Fun Rental
7 Alona Kew White Beach	14 Peter's House
8 Casanova Café	15 Alona Tropical
	16 Crystal Coast

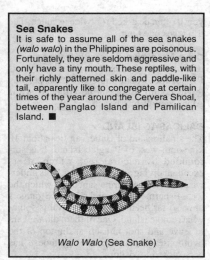

Sea Snakes
It is safe to assume all of the sea snakes (*walo walo*) in the Philippines are poisonous. Fortunately, they are seldom aggressive and only have a tiny mouth. These reptiles, with their richly patterned skin and paddle-like tail, apparently like to congregate at certain times of the year around the Cervera Shoal, between Panglao Island and Pamilican Island. ■

Walo Walo (Sea Snake)

ing and especially (with a bit of luck) for watching sea snakes. There are several variously priced places to stay at Alona Beach.

Doljo Beach is also good, but the water there is pretty shallow, however, it's largely clear of sea grass. It is a good departure point for Pontod or the other two nearby islands.

Momo Beach is another shallow beach, where the Gie Garden Hotel lets several large cottages, though only to groups. Only the name is left of Bikini Beach, after a very severe typhoon blew everything away.

Diving

A five-day diving course (PADI) at the Sea Quest Scuba Diving Center or at the Sea Explorers Scuba Diving Center at Alona Beach costs US$200. Further prices include one dive at the drop-off for US$15; a dive from a boat for US$20; and two dives from a boat for US$40, for example, to Balicasag Island.

Places to Stay

You can choose from several places at Alona Beach. The *Alonaville* belongs to the Executive Inn at Tagbilaran. It has rooms with fan for P100/150 and cottages with fan and bath for P250/300. Its restaurant has a good view of the beach and the ocean, and diving and diving courses are available.

The *Playa Blanca* has cottages with fan and bath for P300/380. There is a restaurant and staff will arrange day excursions by boat and jeep. The *Samira Pyramid Resort* has pleasantly decorated rooms with fan for P200 and spacious, two-storey cottages with a balcony, fan and bath for P350 and P400. *Peter's House* is a pleasant place with spacious, clean rooms for P250 and P300, the more expensive have a balcony. Motorbikes are available for hire.

The *Alona Kew White Beach* has rooms with fan for P250/300, cottages with fan and bath from P400 to P600 and with air-con and bath for P1000/1200. The grounds are quite large and there is a fine, big restaurant. You can hire a car or a motorbike, or try windsurfing (P150 per hour).

The *Aquatica Beach Resort* has rooms with fan and bath for P350, and there is a restaurant. The *Alona Tropical* has cottages with fan and bath for P250 as well as a very good, popular restaurant.

The *Swiss Bamboo House* has a few rooms with fan and bath for P350. It's a small, friendly place with a restaurant which serves good bread and pizzas. Diving equipment and boats are available for hire.

The *Bohol Divers Lodge* (☎ 61949; fax 216993) has cottage accommodation with fan and bath for P400 and P600 (the smaller A-frame cottages at the *Bohol Divers Lodge Annex* at the other end of the beach cost P250). There is a restaurant and a tennis court, and day trips by boat or jeep can be arranged. Motorbikes are also available for hire. You can go diving with the French proprietor Jacques, who also speaks English and German. He will organise day trips by boat or jeep on request.

The *Crystal Coast* has clean and comfortable two-level rooms with air-con and bath for P620/785, albeit in an unimaginatively designed building. It is situated on a flat clifftop at the east end of the beach and belongs to the La Roca Hotel in Tagbilaran.

The *TGH Casa-Nova Garden*, about 300 metres inland from Alona Beach, has rooms with fan and bath from P350 to P475, with air-con and bath for P650 and a cottage with two bedrooms, a living room and cooking facilities for P800. It is a well-kept place and there is a restaurant, disco and a swimming pool.

The *Bohol Beach Club* on the hotel's own beach, barely two km east of Alona Beach, has rooms with fan and bath for P1500/1700. It has a restaurant, swimming pool, tennis court and sauna. Diving and windsurfing are also available.

At Palm Island Beach along Doljo Beach Cove, about two km from Panglao town, the *Palm Island Beach Resort* has rooms with fan for P200. Though a simple set up, there is a restaurant. This resort has seen better days.

The *Momo Beach Resort* at Momo Beach has cottage accommodation with fan and bath for P1400 per person, including meals and transfer. Only groups of at least six people staying for three days or longer are accepted. You can book at the Gie Garden Hotel, Tagbilaran.

Getting There & Away
Bus Several JG Express buses go from Tagbilaran to Panglao Island daily, leaving from the corner of Noli Me Tangere and F Rocha Sts. Not all go to Alona Beach. Those marked 'Panglao' go right across the island to Panglao town near Doljo Beach. Those marked 'Panglao-Tauala' go along the southern coast and detour to Alona Beach. The first departure is at about 7 am, but it may be advisable to confirm. The trip as far as Alona Beach takes 1½ hours. The first bus from Alona Beach to Tagbilaran leaves between 6 and 6.30 am, while the last leaves at about 4.30 pm. This is important if you are just making a day trip as normally there are no tricycles waiting for passengers at the beach.

Tricycle From Tagbilaran to Doljo Beach or Alona Beach by tricycle costs P100, but you'll often be asked for twice as much. The trip takes one hour.

Car & Motorbike A car with driver for a day trip to Bohol (Chocolate Hills etc) costs P1200. Motorbike hire costs P500 per day (eight hours). Both can be arranged at the Alona Kew White Beach.

BALICASAG ISLAND
The small island of Balicasag lies about 10 km south-west of Panglao Island. It is surrounded by a coral reef which offers excellent diving and snorkelling. This underwater world is a marine sanctuary which the local fishermen know and respect. Strangers have so far been very scarce on this somewhat remote island. One of them didn't want to leave and shot himself at the top of the lighthouse. Since then, the lighthouse has been closed to visitors.

Places to Stay
The *Balicasag Island Dive Resort* has dorm beds for P160 and pleasantly designed duplex cottages with bath for P1000/1200, as well as a mediocre, but expensive restaurant. Diving costs US$40 for two dives, plus P150 for the boat. A diving course costs US$300 and diving equipment can be hired. Reservations can be made in Manila at the Philippine Tourism Authority (PTA) (☎ 599031) on Rizal Park; in Cebu City at the PTA (☎ 214430) in GMC Plaza Building on Plaza Indepencia; and in Tagbilaran at the PTA (☎ 3369) in the Governor's Mansion. Transfer to the resort from the airport or hotel in Tagbilaran costs P250 which is paid at the time of registration.

Getting There & Away
A proposal has been made to run boats regularly from Tagbilaran to Balicasag Island, which would take two hours. Please make enquiries. Otherwise the Alona Beach resort proprietors offer Special Rides for about P600.

Traders often travel between Balicasag Island and Panglao Island and take passengers with them to their island.

PAMILACAN ISLAND

The beautiful small island of Pamilacan is about 20 km south-east of Tagbilaran and is surrounded by an extensive coral reef which unfortunately has been severely damaged by dynamite fishing. Foreigners don't come here often. If you want to cross over for a few days, you should take provisions for the first day, as the locals are unlikely to be prepared for visitors. From the second day on, you should be able to arrange for supplies from the fishermen.

Places to Stay

In the northern part of the island, near the old Spanish watchtower, you can stay at *Nita's Nipa Hut* for P200, including meals.

Getting There & Away

There are boats almost daily from Baclayon to Pamilacan Island which take one hour. Your best chance of a cheap trip over is on Wednesday, which is market day, and Sunday when the fishermen and their families return home from church. That will cost you only a few pesos. Even on weekdays there are often people from Pamilacan in Baclayon. They always anchor their boats on the right-hand side of the landing stage looking towards Pamilacan and leave for home shortly before 3 pm. If you can wait for them, you won't have to pay the P350, which is about what a Special Ride (round trip) would cost.

A Special Ride from Alona Beach on Panglao Island to Pamilacan Island and back costs around P800.

CABILAO ISLAND

Cabilao Island is 30 km, as the crow flies, north-west of Tagbilaran in Cebu Strait between Bohol and Cebu. The nearby reef offers excellent snorkelling and diving. Several large beach resorts on Cebu prefer these diving grounds for their guests and send diving boats almost daily.

Places to Stay

The pleasant *La Estrella Beach Resort*, located under the palm trees on a white sand beach, has really good accommodation. Dorm beds are P100 and rooms with bath cost P250. There is a restaurant which serves Filipino and German cuisine, as Babie, the owner, spent several years in Germany. Their well-stocked Sea Explorers Dive Shop is run by Chris who's from Switzerland.

Getting There & Away

From Catagbacan, on Bohol, to Cabilao Island, there are several regular boats daily for P8 per person, going to the landing stage at Talisay or Cambaquis. From there it's about 30 minutes on foot to La Estrella Beach Resort adjoining the lighthouse in the north-west of the island. A Special Ride from Catagbacan directly to the resort costs about P150 to P200. There are buses between Tagbilaran and Catagbacan.

If you go by car ferry from Taloot near Argao on Cebu to Bohol, you can walk to the landing stage in Loon after you arrive (which should take about 10 minutes) to get an outrigger boat from Catagbacan to Cabilao Island. An outrigger boat even goes directly from Looc near Argao on Cebu to Cabilao Island on Tuesday and Saturday between noon and 3 pm. The trip costs P25 per person.

CHOCOLATE HILLS

Over a thousand in number, the Chocolate Hills are about 30 metres high and covered in grass. At the end of the dry season the grass is quite dry and chocolate coloured, hence the name. If you are not in a hurry, you should spend the night in the **Chocolate Hills Complex** to experience the strange effect of the sunrise in this mysterious landscape the following morning. Admission to the complex is P10.

There are two legends about the origin of the Chocolate Hills and two geological explanations. The first legend tells of a fight between two giants who threw stones and sand at each other for days, until they were so tired and exhausted they made friends and left the island. They didn't, however, tidy up the battlefield, leaving the Chocolate Hills. The second legend is a lot more romantic. Arogo, a young and unusually strong giant, fell in love with an ordinary mortal, Aloya. After Aloya's death, Arogo cried bitterly. The

Chocolate Hills are proof of his grief, for his tears turned into hills.

According to some geologists, Bohol lay under water in prehistoric times. Volcanic eruptions caused unevenness on the bottom of the sea which was gradually smoothed and rounded by the movement of the water. Most serious geologists, however, regard such an explanation as nonsense. Even though the geological origin of the hills has not yet been explained beyond doubt, the consensus is that they are weathered formations of a kind of marine limestone lying on top of impermeable clay soils. Comparisons have been made with the Hundred Islands of North Luzon.

Places to Stay
The *Hostel Chocolate Hills* has dorm beds for P80 and double rooms with bath and balcony (beautiful view) for P200. There is a restaurant and a swimming pool (which is unusable most of the time).

Getting There & Away
There are several St Jude Bus and Arples Line buses a day from Tagbilaran to Carmen. The trip takes two hours. As you have to get out four km before Carmen, don't forget to tell the driver. It is about a 500-metre walk from the main road to the Chocolate Hills Complex. The last bus leaves Carmen for Tagbilaran at about 4 pm.

From Tubigon to Carmen, there are several buses a day. They leave fairly reliably after the arrival of a ship from Cebu and take two hours. They may continue beyond Carmen and pass the turn-off to the Chocolate Hills Complex. Otherwise, take the next bus or jeepney going to Bilar, Loay or Tagbilaran to the turn-off. From there it is about a 500-metre walk. You can also take a tricycle from Carmen to the complex, for P30 to P40.

TUBIGON & INARURAN ISLAND
Tubigon is a small place with a wharf for ships to and from Cebu.

Just under 10 km west of Tubigon is the island of Inaruran with its white sand beach fringed by palm trees. There is a small resort there.

The *Inaruran Island Beach Resort* has spacious cottages with fan, bath and big verandah for P920. The restaurant serves Filipino and French dishes. The *Cosare Lodging House* has simple, clean rooms with fan for P60/120.

Getting There & Away
There are several buses from Carmen to Tubigon daily, taking two hours. The last bus leaves at about 2 pm. If there is no bus from Tagbilaran that you can take from the turn-off on the main road to Carmen, you can always hitchhike.

UBAY
Ubay is a little place on the eastern coast of Bohol from where boats leave daily for Maasin and Bato on Leyte.

The *Royal Orchid Pension House* has rooms with fan for P120/180. It's an unpretentious but comfortable place with a common room. The *Casa Besas Pension House* has fairly good rooms with fan and bath for P85/170 and with air-con and bath for P400.

Getting There & Away
From Carmen to Ubay via Sierra Bullones, there are several buses daily. They either come from Tagbilaran (you can board these at the turn-off on the main road) or from Carmen.

From Tagbilaran to Ubay, there are a few buses going via Jagna or via Carmen and Sierra Bullones daily. The trip takes four hours.

A few buses travel daily from Ubay to Tagbilaran via Sierra Bullones and Carmen or via Jagna. The last bus via Carmen departs at 2 pm.

TALIBON
Talibon is on the northern coast of Bohol and has a wharf for ships to and from Cebu. You can also cross to nearby Jao Island from here.

The *Lapyahan Lodge* (☎ 745) has rooms

with fan and bath for P50/100. It is basic with a pleasant, friendly family atmosphere.

Getting There & Away
Several buses coming from Tagbilaran leave daily from the Chocolate Hills Complex turn-off to Talibon between 8 am and 4 pm. The trip takes 2½ hours.

From Tagbilaran to Talibon via Carmen, there are several St Jude Bus and Arples Line buses (possibly also JG Express buses) daily between 6 am and 2 pm, taking 4½ hours.

JAO ISLAND
Jao (pronounced 'how') Island is one of the many small islands off the northern coast of Bohol. Unfortunately, a severe typhoon has destroyed the coral reef, so there is nothing for snorkellers to see. Even the swimming is not especially good. At the south-eastern corner of the island the German-Canadian Heinz Kunzemann and his Filipina wife operate a small resort on a lagoon near the beach. Yachts can moor here and you can hire outrigger boats. Heinz is a passionate sailor who decided to sell his ship after a long trip from Canada via the South Seas, so he dropped anchor at Jao. He is a radio ham and has contacts around the world.

Places to Stay
The *Laguna Escondido Resort & Yacht Haven* has dorm beds for P90 and cottages with bath for P260. There is a beer garden/disco and a restaurant which serves European-Filipino meals. You can also arrange full board.

Getting There & Away
From Talibon, boats leave regularly for Jao Island for P3 per person, taking 15 minutes. Special Rides are offered for P50. Every day at 9 am the 'service boat of Mr Heinz' usually comes to Talibon and returns to Jao Island after a short stop.

Cebu

This island, more than 200 km long and just 40 km across at its widest point, is at the centre of the Visayas, locked between Negros, Leyte and Bohol. It is the main island of Cebu Province and home to the capital, Cebu City. Of the smaller islands which are also part of the province, the most important are Mactan, Bantayan and Camotes. Cebu is a hilly island and flat areas are only to be found on the coast and in the north.

When the Spaniards arrived in Cebu, it was called Sugbu and trade was already being carried on with China. Today, many different industries contribute to the province's economic importance. There are large copper mines near Toledo, and coal, iron ore, gold and silver are also mined. Cement has been produced in Cebu for some years, but oil is the hope of the future. At the moment, Cebu supplies the West with fashionable shell and coral jewellery and also with rattan furniture.

The cultivation of maize is the dominant agricultural activity. However, there are also sizeable sugar plantations in the north and more are planned. The mangoes of Cebu are famous; they only cost a few pesos each during the harvest season, which is in March, April, May and June.

The people of Cebu are all very friendly. They speak Cebuano, the main dialect of the Visayas. Many Chinese live in Cebu City, and they speak Chinese among themselves. Visitors, though, can get by quite well with English.

Cebu has many expensive beach resorts which are always promoted in the island's tourist literature. Those who can do without luxury, however, will feel more comfortable on the less touristically developed beaches, such as those on Bantayan Island or Malapascua Island for example. The coral gardens at Pescador Island near Moalboal are worth seeing, as are the guitar factories on Mactan Island. Treks into the interior are

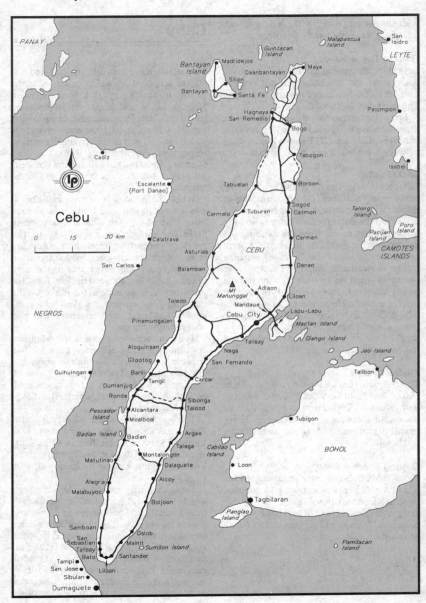

growing in popularity, as are lazy days near the refreshing waterfalls.

GETTING THERE & AWAY
You can get to Cebu from Bohol, Camiguin, Leyte, Luzon, Masbate, Mindanao, Negros, Palawan, Panay, Samar and Siquijor (see the Getting There & Away section of the Manila chapter and the relevant Getting There & Away sections of this chapter and of the chapters on the other islands).

Air
Airline Offices As a result of the opening of Mactan International Airport and of the boom in tourism and the economy in general, not only inland airlines but also foreign airlines have opened offices in Cebu City. More will inevitably follow soon.

The following are the addresses and telephone numbers of the major airline offices in Cebu City:

Cathay Pacific
    98 F Ramos St (☎ 91300, 220821)
China Airlines
    Dimerco Agency, F Ramos St (☎ 219435)
Continental Airlines
    Q C Pavilion, Gorordo Ave (☎ 71611, 211753)
Gulf Air
    Dimerco Agency, F Ramos St (☎ 219441, 219443)
KLM Royal Dutch Airlines
    Escario St (☎ 52888, 52080)
Northwest Orient Airlines
    Q C Pavilion, Gorordo Ave (☎ 73011-13)
Pacific Airways
    Mactan International Airport (☎ 88204, 92854)
PAL
    Escario St/East Capitol Site (☎ 52736, 53146)
    General Maxilom Ave (☎ 79154, 94664 domestic flights; 94249, 90602 international flights)
    Mactan International Airport (☎ 88435, 400181)
Qantas Airways
    Q C Pavilion, Gorordo Ave (☎ 73016)
Scandinavian Airlines System (SAS)
    Q C Pavilion, Gorordo Ave (☎ 311227, 73015)
Singapore Airlines
    Silkair Office, Royal Wings Inc, 424 Gorordo Ave (☎ 211343)
Thai Airways International
    Q C Pavilion, Gorordo Ave (☎ 311227, 73014)

To/From Bohol PAL flies daily from Cebu City to Tagbilaran.

To/From Camiguin PAL has flights from Cebu City to Mamburao on Monday and Saturday. However, these flights are not very reliable. They have often been cancelled because of lack of demand.

An alternative fast connection is from Cebu City via Cagayan de Oro or Butuan by air, then by bus to Balingoan and by ship to Benoni, where jeepneys wait at the wharf for passengers to Mambajao.

To/From Leyte PAL has flights from Cebu City to Tacloban on Monday, Wednesday, Friday and Saturday.

To/From Luzon PAL flies daily from Cebu City to Manila and on Monday, Wednesday, Thursday and Friday to Legaspi.

To/From Mindanao From Cebu City, PAL flies daily to Butuan, Davao, Dipolog, General Santos, Pagadian, Surigao and Zamboanga. It also has flights on Monday, Wednesday and Saturday to Cagayan de Oro; daily except Wednesday and Sunday to Cotabato; daily except Monday, Friday and Saturday to Ozamiz; and on Wednesday and Saturday to Tandag.

To/From Negros PAL flies daily from Cebu City to Bacolod and to Dumaguete.

Pacific Airways is planning a service from Bantayan Island to Bacolod.

To/From Palawan PAL flies on Wednesday, Thursday and Saturday from Cebu City via Iloilo on Panay to Puerto Princesa.

To/From Panay PAL flies daily from Cebu City to Iloilo and Kalibo.

To/From Siquijor PAL is planning a service from Siquijor to Cebu City.

Bus
To/From Negros Five Ceres Liner buses leave Cebu City daily for Bacolod between

5 and 6.30 am from the Southern Bus Terminal. They meet the ferry going from Carmelo/Tuburan to Escalante (Port Danao) and go on to Bacolod. The trip, including the ferry ride, takes eight hours.

Boat

The shipping lines in Cebu are pretty relaxed about keeping to the timetables. Ships are cancelled and others put on without any notice. Even the people on the ticket counters seem to be quite clueless. The announcements in the dailies *The Freeman* and *Sun Star* are more or less reliable. Information from the shipping lines is more accurate, but probably only if you phone and say you are a foreign tourist.

The following are the addresses and telephone numbers of the major shipping lines in Cebu City:

Aboitiz Lines
    Pier 4, Reclamation Area (☎ 77294)
Cokaliong Shipping Lines
    46 Jakosalem St (☎ 212262, 71220)
Escaño Lines
    Quezon Blvd, Reclamation Area (☎ 73225)
George & Peter Lines
    Jakosalem St (☎ 75914, 74098)
Georgia Shipping Lines
    V Sotto St (☎ 79276, 210680)
Carlos Gothong Lines
    Quezon Blvd, Reclamation Area (☎ 211196, 211181)
K & T Shipping Lines
    MacArthur Blvd (☎ 62359, 90633)
Palacio Shipping Lines
    Zulueta St (☎ 54538, 54540)
Roble Shipping Lines
    Pier 3, V Sotto St (☎ 97136, 79632)
Sulpicio Lines
    Reclamation Area (☎ 73839, 99723)
Trans-Asia Shipping Lines
    Cuenco Ave (☎ 226491-97)
Western Samar Shipping Lines
    V Sotto St (☎ 91229, 74050)
William Lines
    Briones St (☎ 73619, 71233)

To/From Bohol The journey from Cebu City to Tagbilaran takes four hours. The Trans-Asia Shipping Lines' MV *Asia Taiwan* leaves daily at 7.30 pm; and the MV *Asia Singapore* leaves Monday and Friday at noon. The Palacio Shipping Lines' MV *Don Martin 6* leaves on Monday, Wednesday and Friday at 1 pm.

From Cebu City to Talibon, the MV *Andy* leaves daily at noon, taking 3½ hours; the MV *Krishia* leaves daily at 7 pm, taking 3½ hours; and the MV *Talibon Cruiser* leaves daily at 9 pm, taking four hours. You can sleep on the boat until morning.

From Cebu City to Tubigon, the Anco Shipping Lines' MV *Tubigon* leaves daily at 9 am, noon and 4 and 10 pm, taking 2½ hours; and the Charisse Shipping Lines' MV *Charisse* leaves daily at noon, taking two hours; the Roble Shipping Lines' MV *Betchie* leaves daily at 7 pm, taking two hours.

From Argao to Loon the Lite Shipping Corporation's MV *LCT Barge St Mark* (car ferry) leaves on Monday, Wednesday and Friday at 10 am; on Tuesday, Thursday and Saturday at 7 am and 1 pm; and on Sunday at 11.30 am. The crossing takes 2½ hours.

A big outrigger boat goes from Argao to Cabilao Island on Tuesday and Saturday at 2 pm, taking 1½ hours.

To/From Camiguin There are ships from Cebu City to Cagayan de Oro and Butuan.

Both the Cokaliong Shipping Lines' MV *Filipinas Surigao* and the Georgia Shipping Lines' MV *Luzille* leave Cebu City for Mambajao on Tuesday at 7 pm and take 14 hours, going via Maasin on Leyte.

To/From Leyte A big outrigger boat leaves Carmen for Isabel daily at 8 am, taking four hours.

The K & T Shipping Lines' MV *Samar Queen* leaves Cebu City for Baybay on Tuesday, Thursday and Saturday at 10 pm, taking six hours.

From Cebu City to Hilongos the Roble Shipping Lines' MV *Guada Cristy* leaves on Monday, Wednesday, Friday and Saturday at 10 pm, taking six hours; and the MV *Queen Belinda* leaves on Tuesday, Thursday and Sunday at 10 pm and Saturday at 10 am, taking six hours.

The K & T Shipping Lines' MV *Guiuan*

Colourful costumes abound at the Ati-Atihan Festival in Kalibo, Panay (JP)

Top: Scene from the Ati-Atihan Festival in Kalibo, Panay (JP)
Bottom: The Miagao Fortress Church, south-east of Iloilo, Panay (JP)

leaves Cebu City for Liloan on Monday and Friday at 8 pm, taking six hours.

There are several ships from Cebu City to Maasin. The trip takes six to seven hours. The Escaño Lines' MV *Escaño* leaves on Monday at 10 am. The Trans-Asia Shipping Lines' MV *Asia Brunei* leaves on Monday at 10 pm; and the MV *Asia Singapore* leaves on Wednesday at 6 pm. The Cokaliong Shipping Lines MV *Filipinas Surigao* leaves on Monday at 7 pm and on Sunday at noon; the MV *Filipinas Siargao* leaves on Tuesday at 7 pm; and the MV *Filipinas Maasin* leaves on Thursday at 7 pm, which goes on to Sogod. The Georgia Shipping Lines' MV *Luzille* leaves on Tuesday and Thursday at 7 pm.

The Aboitiz Lines' MV *Elcano* leaves Cebu City for Ormoc daily at 1 pm. The Sulpicio Lines' MV *Cebu Princess* makes the same journey on Monday at 7 pm. Both take six hours.

The Carlos Gothong Lines' MV *Our Lady of the Sacred Heart* leaves Cebu City for Palompon on Tuesday at 7 pm; the MV *Doña Cristina* leaves on Wednesday at 7 pm; and the MV *Our Lady of Fatima* leaves on Friday at 7 pm. They all take five hours.

From Cebu City to Tacloban the Carlos Gothong Lines' MV *Don Calvino* leaves on Monday, Wednesday and Friday at 6 pm, taking 12 hours. The K & T Shipping Lines' MV *Leyte Queen* leaves on Tuesday, Thursday and Saturday at 6 pm, taking 12 hours.

A big outrigger boat leaves daily at 10.30 am from Maya in northern Cebu to San Isidro, taking two hours. After the arrival of the boat in San Isidro a bus leaves for Ormoc and Tacloban.

To/From Luzon From Cebu City to Manila, the William Lines' MV *Wilines Mabuhay I* leaves on Monday and Friday at 3 am, taking 22 hours; the Sulpicio Lines' MV *Philippine Princess* leaves on Wednesday at 8 pm and on Sunday at 10 am, taking 21 hours; and the Sulpicio Lines' MV *Manila Princess* leaves on Friday at 10 am, taking 23 hours. The Aboitis Lines' MV *Superferry 2* leaves on

Wednesday at noon and on Saturday at 8 pm, taking 22 hours.

To/From Masbate The Georgia Shipping Lines' MV *Princess Joan* leaves Cebu City for Cataingan on Monday at 10 pm, taking 10 hours. The Lapu-Lapu Shipping Lines' MV *Rosalia* leaves Cebu City for Cataingan on Tuesday and Friday at 7 pm, taking 11 hours.

The Sulpicio Lines' MV *Cebu Princess* leaves Cebu City for Masbate on Monday at 7 pm and takes 36 hours, going via Ormoc on Leyte and Calbayog on Samar.

Apparently, a boat goes from Hagnaya to Cataingan twice a week on Wednesday and Sunday, and from Hagnaya to Placer twice a week on Tuesday and Friday.

To/From Mindanao From Cebu City to Butuan, the Sulpicio Lines' MV *Nasipit Princess* leaves on Monday, Wednesday and Saturday at 8 pm, taking 12 hours and arriving at Nasipit; the Carlos Gothong Lines' MV *Doña Lili* leaves on Tuesday, Thursday and Saturday at 6 pm and takes 18 hours, going via Jagna on Bohol; and the Carlos Gothong Lines' MV *Our Lady of Lourdes* leaves on Friday at 6 pm, taking 10 hours.

From Cebu City to Cagayan de Oro, the Sulpicio Lines' MV *Cagayan Princess* leaves on Monday, Wednesday and Friday at 7 pm, taking 12 hours; the Trans-Asia Shipping Lines' MV *Asia Japan* leaves on Monday, Wednesday, Friday and Sunday at 7 pm, taking 10 hours; the Trans-Asia Shipping Lines' MV *Asia Thailand* leaves on Tuesday, Thursday and Saturday at 7 pm, taking 10 hours; and the Carlos Gothong Lines' MV *Our Lady of Guadalupe* leaves on Tuesday, Thursday and Saturday at 7 pm and takes 9 hours (11 hours on Saturday when it goes via Jagna on Bohol).

From Cebu City to Dapitan the MV *Dumaguete Ferry*, the MV *Georich*, the MV *Palauan Ferry* or the MV *Don Victorino* of George & Peter Lines leaves daily at 10 pm and takes 12 hours, going via Dumaguete on Negros. The Cokaliong Shipping Lines' MV *Filipinas Dumaguete* leaves Cebu City for

Dapitan on Monday, Wednesday and Friday at 7 pm and takes 16 hours, going via Dumaguete on Negros.

From Cebu City to Davao, the Sulpicio Lines' MV *Manila Princess* leaves on Monday at 2 pm, taking 25 hours.

From Cebu City to Iligan, the Carlos Gothong Lines' MV *Doña Cristina* leaves on Monday, Thursday and Saturday at 7 pm, taking 11 hours. The William Lines' MV *Iligan City*, the MV *Tacloban City* or the MV *Misamis Occidental* leaves on Monday, Wednesday and Friday at 7 pm, taking 12 hours.

From Cebu City to Ozamiz, the William Lines' MV *Tacloban City* leaves on Monday at 7 pm, taking 10 hours; and the MV *Iligan City* leaves on Wednesday and Friday at 7 pm, taking 10 hours. The Carlos Gothong Lines' MV *Our Lady of Mount Carmel* leaves on Tuesday, Thursday and Saturday at 7 pm, taking 10 hours.

From Cebu City to Surigao, the Cokaliong Shipping Lines' MV *Filipinas Maasin* leaves on Monday and Saturday at 7 pm, taking 11 hours; and the MV *Filipinas Surigao* leaves on Wednesday, Thursday and Friday at 7 pm, and takes 10 hours and goes on to Dapa on Siargao Island. The Trans-Asia Shipping Lines' MV *Asia Singapore* leaves on Wednesday at 6 pm, taking 11 hours and going via Maasin on Leyte.

From Cebu City to Zamboanga, the MV *Georich* or the MV *Don Victorino* of George & Peter Lines leaves on Monday at 10 pm and on Friday at 9 pm, taking 24 hours and going via Dumaguete on Negros and Dapitan.

To/From Negros Several ferries leave Bato for Tampi daily, taking 45 minutes. The last departure is at about 4.30 pm. A boat may go from San Sebastian and Talisay to San Jose, where jeepneys for Dumaguete wait at the wharf. ABC Liner air-con buses leaving daily at 6, 7, 8 and 11 am and 1.30, 2 and 3 pm from the ABC Liner Bus Terminal in Cebu City for Bato will meet the ferries for Tampi. The buses also stop at the Southern Bus Terminal (which is not so good, because

the best seats will probably already be taken). The trip takes three hours.

From Cebu City to Dumaguete, you can go by the George & Peter Lines' MV *Dumaguete Ferry*, MV *Georich*, MV *Palauan* ferry or MV *Don Victorino*. The boats leave daily at 10 pm and possibly at 9 pm on Monday, taking six hours. The Cokaliong Shipping Lines' MV *Filipinas Dumaguete* leaves on Monday, Wednesday and Friday at 7 pm and on Sunday at noon, taking six hours.

From Liloan to Sibulan, a big outrigger boat leaves daily about every 30 minutes. The last departure is at about 3 pm. The trip takes 20 minutes. A jeepney from Subulan to Dumaguete costs P5.

Boats leave Tangil daily for Guihulngan at 6.30 and 8 am, taking two hours.

A ferry from Toledo to San Carlos leaves daily at 9 am and 2 pm from Monday to Saturday, and at 1.30 pm on Sunday. There may be different departure times on holidays. Only one boat goes on Maundy Thursday and none on Good Friday. The timetable on this route changes frequently. Buy your ticket from the kiosk at the entrance to the pier and not from the shady men offering tickets. The trip takes 1¾ hours.

The last bus from San Carlos to Bacolod waits for the last boat from Toledo. A combined bus and boat ticket is cheaper than two single tickets.

From Bantayan town on Bantayan Island, a big outrigger boat leaves daily at 11 am for Cadiz on the northern coast of Negros, taking three hours or more.

To/From Panay The Trans-Asia Shipping Lines' MV *Asia Indonesia* leaves Cebu City for Iloilo on Tuesday, Thursday and Sunday at 6 pm, taking 12 hours; their MV *Asia Korea* leaves on Friday at 7 pm, taking 13 hours.

The Carlos Gothong Lines' MV *Our Lady of Fatima* leaves Cebu City for Dumaguit (near Kalibo) via Palompon on Leyte on Friday at 7 pm, and takes 22 hours.

The Carlos Gothong Lines' MV *Our Lady*

of the Sacred Heart leaves Cebu City for Roxas via Palompon on Leyte on Tuesday at 7 pm, taking 18 hours.

To/From Samar The Western Samar Shipping Lines' MV *Elizabeth Lilly* leaves Cebu City for Allen on Friday at 6 pm, taking 14 hours.

The Sulpicio Lines' MV *Cebu Princess* leaves Cebu City for Calbayog on Monday at 7 pm and takes 24 hours, going via Ormoc on Leyte. The Palacio Shipping Lines' MV *Don Martin Sr* leaves Cebu City for Calbayog every Monday, Wednesday and Friday at 8 pm, taking 12 hours.

The Western Samar Shipping Lines' MV *Elizabeth Lilly* leaves Cebu City for Catbalogan on Tuesday at 6 pm, taking 13 hours. The Carlos Gothong Lines' MV *Don Calvino* leaves Cebu City for Catbalogan on Friday at 6 pm and takes 18 hours, going via Tacloban on Leyte.

To/From Siquijor The Palacio Shipping Lines' MV *Don Martin 6* leaves Cebu City for Larena on Monday, Wednesday and Friday at 1 pm, going via Tagbilaran on Bohol and taking nine hours. The MV *Don Martin 7* leaves Cebu City for Larena on Tuesday, Thursday and Sunday at 10 pm, taking seven hours.

CEBU CITY

Cebu City is the third largest city in the Philippines, with a population of about 650,000. Even so, the so-called 'Queen City of the South' is easy to get to know. The busy city centre, called Downtown, includes Colon St, the oldest street in the Philippines. It has unfortunately lost some of its charm in recent years. The houses and streets are only just being maintained, and the easy and natural friendliness of many of the locals has obviously suffered because of their economic difficulties. The many beggars and homeless who camp in the streets and in doorways bear witness to their privations.

In contrast to the depressed Downtown, Uptown – the area north of the Rodriguez St, Fuente Osmeña, General Maxilom Ave axis

– has obviously gained in prosperity. Smart restaurants, varied places of entertainment and a well-cared-for townscape provide a marked contrast with the very busy Colon area, particularly in the late afternoon. The densely populated outer suburbs and adjoining barrios are gradually joining up with Cebu City. According to the projections of the city's progressive town planners, its appearance will change considerably in the near future. An imposing new city is being planned in the Reclamation Area in the harbour, with numerous skyscrapers, shopping centres, leisure and recreation centres and a new city hall.

Life in Cebu City is more leisurely than in Manila. There are, of course, many jeepneys and taxis and even a few *tartanillas* (horse-drawn carriages), but you can get almost anywhere in this city on foot. There are plenty of hotels, restaurants and cinemas, while beaches are great for leisure activities. Transport facilities to other islands are excellent.

The colourful and crowded Sinulog Festival takes place in Cebu City every January. (See also the section on Fiestas & Festivals in the Facts for the Visitor chapter.)

Orientation

Recently several streets in Cebu City were renamed, but people still use the following names in brackets: Osmeña Blvd (Jones Ave, Juan Luna St), General Maxilom Ave (Mango Ave), V Gullas St (Manalili St), Rizal Ave (South Expressway) and Fuente Osmeña (Osmeña Circle).

Information

Tourist Office The tourist office (☎ 91503, 96518) is in the GMC Building on Plaza Independcia near Fort San Pedro. It has a service counter at Mactan International Airport (☎ 88229), where room reservations and other travel arrangements can be made.

Money The Philippine National Bank, the Standard Chartered Bank and the Bank of the Philippine Islands, all near Cebu City Hall,

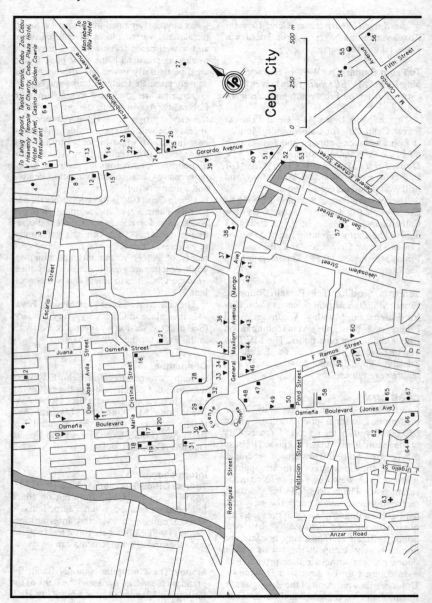

To Lahug Airport, Taoist Temple, Cebu Zoo, Cebu
Heavenly Temple of Charity, Cebu Plaza Hotel,
Hotel Nivel, Casino & Golden Cowrie
Restaurant

To Montebello
Villa Hotel

Cebu City

0   250   500 m

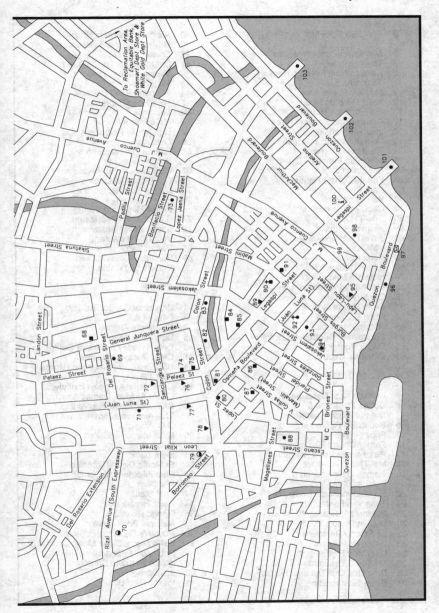

■ PLACES TO STAY

2	Mayflower Pension House
3	The Apartelle
5	Kukuk's Nest Pension House & Tonros Apartelle
7	Myrna's Pensionne
12	West Gorordo Hotel
16	Gali Pension House
17	Casa Loreto Pension House
18	Jasmine Pension
19	Verbena Pension House
21	C'est la vie Pension
23	Maanyag Pension House
26	St Moritz Hotel
28	Fuente Pension House
32	Park Place Hotel
47	Kan Irag Hotel
48	Cebu Midtown Hotel
50	Emsu Hotel
58	Jasmine Pension
64	Jovel Pension House
65	YMCA
66	Benz Pension
68	Elicon House
74	Hotel de Mercedes & McSherry Pension House
75	Century Hotel
81	Cebu Hallmark Hotel
84	Hotel Esperanza
85	Ruftan Pensione
86	Sundowner Centrepoint Hotel
87	Pacific Tourist Inn
91	Patria de Cebu

▼ PLACES TO EAT

5	Kukuk's Nest Restaurant
8	Coffee House 24 & Maiko Nippon Restaurant
9	Boulevard Restaurant
10	Food Street
12	Family Choice Restaurant
13	Pistahan Seafood Restaurant
14	Mai Thai Restaurant
15	Europa Delicatessen & Butcher Shop
22	Royal Concourse Restaurant
24	Tung Yan Restaurant
26	St Moritz Restaurant
30	Dunkin Donuts
32	La France Restaurant
33	Ginza Restaurant
34	Old Cebu Restaurant
35	Mikado Restaurant
36	Ding Qua Qua Dimsum House
37	Swiss Restaurant

39	Alavar's Seafoods House
40	Grand Majestic Restaurant
41	Shakey's Pizza
42	La Dolce Vita Restaurant & Vienna Kaffee-Haus
43	Mister Donut
44	Sunburst Fried Chicken
46	Ric's Food Express
49	Sammy's
50	McDonald's
52	Lighthouse Restaurant
60	Café Adriatico
61	Europa Delicatessen & Butcher Shop
62	Cosina sa Cebu Restaurant
72	Our Place Restaurant/Pub
74	Master Key Restaurant
76	Pete's Kitchen & Pete's Mini Food Center
77	Snow Sheen Restaurant
78	Snow Sheen Restaurant
84	Visayan Restaurant
85	Ruftan Café
89	Sunburst Fried Chicken
95	Eddie's Log Cabin

OTHER

1	Provincial Capitol Building
3	PAL
4	Singapore Airlines
5	Duty Free Shop
6	Cebu Holiday & Fitness Center
11	Cebu Doctors Hospital
14	US Consulate, American Express & PCI Bank
15	Continental Airlines, Northwest Orient Airlines, Qantas Airways, SAS – Scandinavian Airlines, Thai Airways International & Q C Pavilion
20	Rizal Memorial Library & Museum
25	Metrobank
26	St Moritz Disco-Nightclub
27	Club Filipino Golf Course
29	Interbank
31	Fruit Stalls
34	Hertz Rent-a-Car
35	Mango Plaza & National Book Store
36	Rustan's Department Store
37	Ball's Disco, Cities Music Lounge & Robinson's Foodorama
38	Iglesia Ni Kristo Church
40	Interbank
41	Puerto Rico Bar

45	Brown Bear Bar, Kentucky Pub & The Viking Bar	71	Central Bank
47	Bachelor's Too & Love City Disco	73	Casa Gorordo Museum
48	Robinson's Department Store	79	Minibuses to Argao
49	Silver Dollar Bar	80	Gaisano Metro Department Store
51	PAL	82	Gaw Department Store
52	Captain's Bar	83	Gaisano Main Department Store
53	Steve's Music Bar	88	Carbon Market
54	Caretta Cemetery	90	Cebu Cathedral
55	Northern Bus Terminal	92	Basilica Minore del Santo Niño
56	Chinese Cemetery	93	Magellan's Cross
57	ABC Liner Bus Terminal	94	City Hall & Philippine National Bank
59	Cathay Pacific	96	Immigration Office
60	China Airlines & Gulf Air	97	GPO
63	Sacred Heart Hospital	98	Fort San Pedro
67	PLDT Philippine Long Distance Telephone Company	99	Tourist Office
		100	Plaza Independencia
69	San Carlos University	101	Pier 1
70	Southern Bus Terminal	102	Pier 2
		103	Pier 3

will change travellers' cheques and foreign currency.

It is best to change American Express travellers' cheques at the Interbank, at both Fuente Osmeña and Gorordo Ave, and directly at American Express (☎ 73498) in the PCI Bank Building, 2nd floor. The entrance is at the US Consulate, Gorordo Ave. There you can also get an American Express cash advance. It is open Monday to Friday from 8.30 am to 4 pm and Saturday until 11 am.

Thomas Cook Travel (☎ 219229) has an office on the ground floor of the Metrobank Plaza on Osmeña Blvd, where you can change your Thomas Cook travellers' cheques.

The Equitable Bank on Juan Luna Ave will give you a cash advance on your Visa or Eurocard/MasterCard. This applies only to the branch in the Reclamation Area and not to the two Downtown branches.

Department stores like Gaisano and Rustan's will also change cash, sometimes even at a better rate than the banks will offer.

Post The GPO is on Plaza Independencia. The poste restante service is apparently not very reliable here. Branch offices are in the Cebu City Hall, at the University of the Visayas (UV), on Colon St, and at the University of San Carlos, Del Rosario St.

Visas The Immigration Office (☎ 77410) is in the Customs Building near Fort San Pedro. You can get your visa extended here from 21 to 59 days. If you want a visa for more than 59 days, your application and passport could be sent to Manila for processing and will not be available for at least two weeks. You should bring a pen to fill out the forms. It also wouldn't hurt to be dressed respectably and look as if you had spent the night asleep.

Bookshops & Magazines The monthly tourist bulletin *What's on in Cebu* has interesting articles and useful advertisements, and is handed out free at the airport and in various hotels and restaurants. The advertising pages of the Cebu City dailies *Sun Star* and *The Freeman* contain up-to-date information on entertainment and shipping connections.

There is a good branch of the National Book Store on General Maxilom Ave.

Dawn Subscriptions, downstairs in Robinson's Department Store, Fuente

Osmeña, has a small but good selection of PC literature (software and hardware).

Medical Services If you are seriously in need of medical attention go to the Cebu Doctors Hospital (☎ 93341, 72048) on Osmeña Blvd, near the Provincial Capitol Building.

A professionally administered shiatsu massage costs P300 at the Cebu Holiday & Fitness Center, Molave St. It is open daily from 1 pm until midnight.

Dangers & Annoyances Such a big city and traffic interchange, Cebu City is obviously a lucrative field for pickpockets. They usually work in the late afternoon and evening in the vicinity of Colon St and Osmeña Blvd, and in the harbour area during the arrival and departure of big passenger ships.

Even in Cebu City it is best not to take apparently friendly invitations at face value!

The 'well-loved' money changers, who always offer a seductively high rate of exchange but more or less never stick to it, are active at the Plaza Independencia in front of the tourist office.

Tourist Police The Tourist Assistance Unit can be reached at (☎ 91503, 96518).

Fort San Pedro

Legaspi himself turned the first sod of earth on 8 May 1565 for this fort, which was built as a defence against marauding pirates. He gave it the name of the ship in which he crossed the Pacific. At the end of the Spanish era, in 1898, it was taken over by the freedom fighters of Cebu. Later, it served as a base and barracks for the Americans, and from 1937 to 1941 it was used for training purposes. In WW II the fort was used as a prison camp by the Japanese. The bitter liberation struggle towards the end of the war took its toll, and much of Fort San Pedro was destroyed. Restoration work began in the late 1960s and a well-tended garden was laid out in the inner courtyard – a beautiful little place of refuge not too far from the hustle and bustle of the harbour. Admission in P7.50.

Magellan's Cross

The first Catholic Mass on Cebu was celebrated on 14 April 1521, when Rajah Humabon, his wife, sons and daughters and 800 islanders had themselves baptised by Father Pedro de Valderrama. Magellan marked this beginning of Christianity in the Philippines with the erection of a cross. The original cross is said to be inside the present cross, which stands in a pavilion near the Cebu City Hall.

Basilica Minore del Santo Niño

The present basilica – formerly San Agustin Church – was finished in 1740, three earlier wooden structures having been destroyed by fire. Undoubtedly, the focal point of the slightly weathered stone church is Santo Niño, a statue of the infant Jesus, but if you want to admire this valuable object on the left of the altar you either need a telescope or have to wait in a long queue. In 1565 this treasure, with its jewelled crown and gem-covered clothes, was found undamaged by Juan de Camus, one of Legaspi's soldiers, in a hut near the basilica. Since then Santo Niño has been the patron saint of the Cebuano.

Casa Gorordo Museum

The Parian district in today's Downtown area was the residential home of Cebu's wealthy at the turn of the century. Of the remaining four houses, the Gorordo residence has been restored and furnished in the style of the period. The Gorordo family produced the first Bishop of Cebu. Apart from furniture, you can see porcelain, liturgical items, clothes and old photographs of Cebu. New exhibits and written material on the same theme are being added all the time. The museum is open daily except Sunday from 9 am to noon and 2 to 6 pm. Admission including a friendly and informative guided tour costs P10; students P2.

University of San Carlos Museum

The museum of the University of San Carlos (founded 1595) was opened in 1967. Its divisions cover ethnography, archaeology, natural sciences and the Spanish colonial period. Filipino objects from different epochs and exhibits from other Asian countries are also displayed. The museum is open Monday to Friday from 9 am to noon and 2 to 5 pm, and Saturday until noon. It is closed during vacations.

Carbon Market
The agricultural produce and the many and varied handicrafts of Cebu Province are on offer at this big and colourful market. There are also products from other Visayan islands, such as basket ware from Bohol.

Caretta Cemetery
A visit to this large cemetery near the Northern Bus Terminal is probably only of significance on 1 November – All Saints Day – or perhaps the night before, when everyone is pretty wound up (see the Fiestas & Festivals section in the Facts for the Visitor chapter earlier in this book). Opposite is the Chinese Cemetery. To get there, catch a jeepney from Colon St going towards Mabolo.

Taoist Temple
Some six km from the city centre lies Beverly Hills, the millionaires' quarter of Cebu City. Here also is the temple of the Taoist religious sect. Its size and architecture indicate that a considerable part of the population of Cebu is Chinese. You can get a good view of the city from this temple.

The taxi fare to the temple from the Downtown area should be about P30, but fix the fare first. It is cheaper by Lahug jeepney, which will get you fairly close. Catch it on the corner of Jakosalem and Colon Sts and get off at the Doña M Gaisano Bridge in Lahug (don't forget to tell the driver in good time), cross the small bridge, turn right and walk for another km or so.

Cebu Heavenly Temple of Charity
On the way to the Taoist Temple you will see the Cebu Heavenly Temple of Charity on a hill to the left. There is a natural spring underneath it. The middle altar of this beautiful temple houses the statues of the Supreme Gods and of Milagrosa Rosa, the temple's patron saint.

To get there, take a jeepney from the Downtown area to the Taoist Temple, but when you get to the little bridge, don't turn right but go straight on. One hundred metres farther on you will see an iron gate with two guardian lions on the left. Walk through this gate and follow the path until you get to the road about 400 metres away, then turn off to the right. The entrance gate to the temple is 200 metres farther on. If it is closed you can go around the temple to the open main gate.

Tops
To enjoy probably the best panoramic view of Cebu City, with Mactan Island and Bohol in the background, you have to make the trip to Tops. This is a generously built viewpoint on Busay Hill, around four km north of the Cebu Plaza Hotel and 15 km from Downtown. The view is particularly impressive at sunset, when the lights of the city below come on. At this time of day, however, it can get cool, so you would be well advised to take a pullover or a jacket with you. But beware: there is no public transport back to Cebu City in the evening! The place is owned by the Lito Osmeña family, whose domed, glittering silver residence is not far away. Admission to Tops is P20.

You can get there by taking a Lahug jeepney as far as the La Nival Hotel, changing across the road from there at the turn-off for the Cebu Plaza Hotel to a jeepney heading in the Tops direction. Get out about five km farther at the top of the pass, and walk up the last stretch to the summit. The walk should take about 20 minutes on this rather steep, but well-maintained road.

The much easier trip by taxi from the Downtown area to Tops should cost around P50.

Places to Stay – bottom end
The *Patria de Cebu* (☎ 72084) on P Burgos St has very basic, unpretentious rooms with fan for P80/150. It's an old place and has a restaurant and offers billiards and bowls.

The *YMCA* (☎ 214057) at 61 Osmeña

Blvd has rooms with fan for P120/200, with fan and bath for P150/300 and with air-con and bath for P240/480. Couples may be accepted. It is simple but good and has a restaurant, swimming pool, billiards, table tennis and bowls. YMCA members get a discount and temporary membership is obtainable for P50.

The *Mayflower Pension House* (☎ 72948, 53687; fax 216647) on East Capitol Site has rooms with fan for P135/185 and with fan and bath for P215/265. Singles with air-con and bath are P340 to P395 and doubles with air-con and bath are P400 to P455, the more expensive ones with TV. It is quiet and clean, and is near the Provincial Capitol Building.

The *Elicon House* (☎ 73653, 210367; fax 73507) on General Junquera St has rooms with fan for P120/190, singles with air-con and bath for P260 and P320 and doubles with air-con and bath for P320 and P390. It is clean and comfortable and the service is friendly. Downstairs is the Elicon Café.

The *Ruftan Pensione* (☎ 79138) on Legaspi St has rooms with fan for P120/150 and with fan and bath for P200/300. It's simple but habitable and has a restaurant. The rooms looking out on to the courtyard are the quietest.

The *McSherry Pension House* (☎ 52749, 96772) has rooms with fan and bath for P210/280 and with air-con and bath for P320/430. Monthly rates are available. It's a pleasant central place in a quiet lane off Pelaez St, next to the Hotel de Mercedes.

The *Verbena Pension House* (☎ 210203, 214440) at 584-A Don Gil Garcia St has clean rooms of varying sizes. It has singles/doubles with fan and bath for P150/200, singles with air-con and bath for P240 and P280 and doubles with air-con and bath for P300 and P340. The rooms are not rented to unmarried couples. There is a restaurant.

The *Gali Pension House* (☎ 213626, 53698) on the corner of Juana Osmeña and Maria Cristina Sts has passable, tidy rooms with fan for P175 and with air-con and bath for P400. There is a restaurant which has a nightclub – The Blue Bar – in the evenings.

The *C'est la vie Pension* (☎ 215266) on Juana Osmeña St is clean and comfortable with fairly small rooms with fan and bath for P200/250 and with air-con and bath for P350/400, and there is a coffee shop.

The *Jovel Pension House* (☎ 215242) at 24-K Uytengsu Rd has quiet and comfortable rooms with fan for P245/300 and with air-con and bath for P375/425. The owner is friendly, and there is a coffee shop.

The *Maanyag Pension House* (☎ 95056, 75573) on 255 Archbishop Reyes Ave has rooms with fan for P200, singles with air-con and bath for P300 and doubles with air-con and bath for P350 and P450. It's reasonable but the rooms are small. There is a coffee shop. The *Kukuk's Nest Pension House* (☎ 312310) at 157 Gorordo Ave is a pleasant old bourgeois house with clean, cosily furnished rooms with fan for P300/350 and with fan and bath for P450, including breakfast. There is a restaurant.

The *Jasmine Pension* (☎ 54559) on the corner of Don Gil Garcia and Filimon Sotto Sts has rooms with fan and bath for P290/350 and with TV, air-con and bath for P350/410. The rooms are clean and of different sizes. The affiliated *Jasmine Pension* (☎ 213757) at 395 Osmeña Blvd is more centrally located.

The *Casa Loreto Pension House* (☎ 52 879, 79544) at 21 Don Gil Garcia St has rooms with air-con and bath for P300/380. This place is clean and quite good, with spacious rooms and a coffee shop.

The *Fuente Pension House* (☎ 214133; fax 224365) at 13 Don Julio Lloreno St has pleasant, clean rooms with air-con and bath for P560/680. There is a coffee shop on the roof top and a restaurant. This friendly little place is located in a quiet area near General Maxilom Ave and Fuente Osmeña.

Places to Stay – middle

The *Century Hotel* (☎ 97621) on Pelaez St has quite good, clean rooms with air-con and bath for P400. The single rooms on the 4th floor are good for two people. The rooms on the 5th floor, next door to the disco nightclub, are noisy.

The *Cebu Hallmark Hotel* (☎ 77671-75; fax 53733) on Osmeña Blvd has rooms with fan and bath for P200/260, singles with air-con and bath for P390 and P480 and doubles with air-con and bath for P485 and P620. It's fairly well kept with a restaurant. Not all rooms have windows.

The *Pacific Tourist Inn* (☎ 212151-59; fax 225674) on the corner of V Gullas and Balintawak Sts has singles with air-con and bath from P380 to P480 and doubles with air-con and bath from P450 to P870. Suites are P1100. The place is clean and fairly good. The rooms are of varying degrees of comfort, the more expensive ones have windows, fridge and TV.

The *Hotel Esperanza* (☎ 221331-35; fax 53733) on V Gullas St has singles with fan and bath for P270, singles with air-con and bath for P390 and P680 and doubles with air-con and bath for P490 and P750. Suites are P1500. This place is clean, good and has a restaurant. Unfortunately, it is in a street in the Downtown area which can get a bit rowdy at night.

The *Kan Irag Hotel* (☎ 211151; fax 216935) on F Ramos St has rooms with air-con and bath for P775/850. The rooms are clean and good enough, the ones overlooking the street are, however, a bit on the noisy side. It has a restaurant.

The *Hotel de Mercedes* (☎ 211105-10; fax 213880) on Pelaez St has rooms with air-con and bath for P635 and P715. Suites are P825 and P1030. The rooms are passable, perhaps a bit too expensive. There is a restaurant.

The *Sundowner Centrepoint Hotel* (☎ 21 1831-39; fax 210695) on Plaridel St, on the corner of Osmeña Blvd, has rooms with air-con and bath for P1130/1450. The rooms are clean and comfortable, and have a TV. There is a restaurant and a disco.

The *Park Place Hotel* (☎ 211131; fax 210118) on Fuente Osmeña has singles with air-con and bath from P1000 to P1600 and doubles with air-con and bath from P1850 to P2200. Suites are P2700, including breakfast. The rooms are pleasant and clean, but the cheaper ones have no windows. There is a coffee shop and a restaurant.

Places to Stay – top end

The *West Gorordo Hotel* (☎ 314347; fax 311158) on Gorordo Ave has rooms with TV, air-con and bath for P1210. Suites are P2500. The rooms are very comfortable and well looked after in this immaculately run hotel. There is a restaurant, fitness room and a sauna.

The *St Moritz Hotel* (☎ 74371-74; fax 312485) on Gorordo Ave has pleasant and tastefully furnished rooms with air-con and bath for P1345 and P1590; suites are P2075. It's very good quality and has a restaurant and a disco cum nightclub.

The *Montebello Villa Hotel* (☎ 313681; fax 314455) at Banilad has singles with air-con and bath for P1100 and P1625 and doubles with air-con and bath for P1250 and P1800. Suites are P1800 to P5300. It's an attractive establishment in the outskirts of town, with a restaurant, coffee shop, a swimming pool and a beautiful garden.

The *Cebu Midtown Hotel* (☎ 219711-40; fax 219765) on Fuente Osmeña has rooms with air-con and bath from P2700 to P3600. Suites are P3800 to P12,000. It is directly above the Robinson's Department Store and has a restaurant, swimming pool, jacuzzi, sauna and a fitness room.

The *Cebu Plaza Hotel* (☎ 311231; fax 312069) at Nivel Hills, Lahug, has rooms with air-con and bath from P2600 to P5200 and suites from P7000 to P30,000. It has a restaurant, coffee shop, disco, swimming pool and tennis court. It is on a rise a little out of town and is the best hotel in Cebu City. From Downtown, take a Lahug jeepney marked 'Plaza'.

Apartments It is possible to get apartments for a longer stay in Cebu City – look at the ads in the local dailies *Sun Star* and *The Freeman*. Usually what is being offered are furnished air-con apartments with kitchen or cooking facilities, a fridge and TV. Electricity has to be paid separately.

The *Apartelle* (☎ 76271, 61944) on Escario St has two-room apartments to let for P900 a day, P9000 a fortnight and P14,000 a month.

The *Tourists' Garden Lodge* (☎ 461676, 93770; fax 70518) at 27 Eagle St in Santo Niño Village, Banilad, has two-room apartments to let for P750 a day, P5300 a week and P18,200 a month.

Places to Eat

Filipino Food *Pete's Kitchen* on Pelaez St is a clean restaurant with amazingly inexpensive food. It is full from the early morning hours on.

Pete's Mini Food Center on Pelaez St is a big, semi-enclosed restaurant where the guests can choose their food at a long buffet and have it warmed up if they want. *Ric's Food Express* on F Ramos St has good, cheap meals, with mainly barbecue dishes.

Sammy's on Osmeña Blvd is open 24-hours daily. This unassuming restaurant next to the Silver Dollar Bar is very popular with the Cebuanos, especially in the evening. They are drawn here by excellent pochero, a strong tasting soup with leg of beef and bone marrow. There is seating both inside and out.

The *Boulevard Restaurant* on Osmeña Blvd is a popular café and garden restaurant, and at the same time a favourite meeting place for young people, especially in the evenings.

Food Street on Osmeña Blvd consists of several small, cheap restaurants opposite the Boulevard Restaurant.

The *Ruftan Café* on Legaspi St is good for breakfasts and also serves Filipino meals. The *Royal Concourse* on Gorordo Ave is a big, very clean self-service restaurant with inexpensive Filipino and Japanese dishes.

Cosina sa Cebu on Ascension St is a clean restaurant serving cheap Cebuano meals. It is popular with students.

The *Fuente O* on Fuente Osmeña is a coffee shop on the 1st floor of the Park Place Hotel. Here they serve Cebuano specialties, amongst other things a first-class green mango shake. It is open 24-hours daily.

Sunburst Fried Chicken on General Maxilom Ave serves different kinds of excellent roast chickens and also good Filipino meals. It is open daily from 9 am to 11 pm.

There is another *Sunburst Fried Chicken* on Legaspi St.

The *Golden Cowrie* on Salinas Drive, Lahug, has inexpensive seafood dishes which can be recommended. Popular orders are baked mussels and green mango shakes. This one-off, rough and ready bamboo restaurant is always well patronised. It is open from 11 am to 2 pm and 6 to 10 pm.

The *Pistahan Seafood Restaurant* on Gorordo Ave has Filipino seafood specialties in the medium price range, such as sizzling squid. It is open daily from 11 am to 2.30 pm and 6 to 10.30 pm.

The *Lighthouse Restaurant* on General Maxilom Ave is a pleasant, well-looked after restaurant with laid-back live music. Apart from Filipino dishes – mostly seafood – which are usually eaten with the fingers here, standard Japanese dishes such as tempura and sushi are also served. It is open daily from 10.30 am to 2 pm and 5.30 to 10.30 pm.

Alavar's Sea Foods House on Gorordo Ave is an excellent restaurant specialising in food from Zamboanga on Mindanao, such as blue marlin. It's open daily from 11 am to 2.30 pm and 5 to 10.30 pm.

Chinese Food The big *Snow Sheen Restaurant* on Osmeña Blvd has been popular for years for its good cooking. Another, somewhat smaller *Snow Sheen Restaurant* is round the corner on Colon St.

The *Visayan Restaurant* on V Gullas St is notable for its excellent, inexpensive food, big portions and friendly service.

Downstairs in Robinson's Department Store on Fuente Osmeña, there is a dim sum restaurant which is worth trying and really good value.

On the top floor of the Gaisano Metro Department Store on the corner of Colon and Lopez Sts there are several self-service restaurants that serve dim sum, but also serve cakes and ice cream etc.

The *Tung Yan Restaurant* on Gorordo Ave is relatively expensive and probably the best Chinese restaurant in Cebu. It is open daily from 11 am to 2 pm and 6 to 10 pm.

Japanese Food The *Ginza Restaurant* in Belvic Complex, General Maxilom Ave, is good with friendly service. Korean food is also served. It's open daily from 10 am to 2 pm and 6 to 11 pm.

The *Mikado Restaurant* in Mango Plaza, General Maxilom Ave, serves authentic Japanese dishes; favourites are sushi and sashami. It is open daily from 10 am to 2 pm and 4 to 10 pm.

Western Food *Shakey's Pizza* on General Maxilom Ave is a favourite local rendezvous for pizzas and live music.

McDonald's on Osmeña Blvd serves its well-known fast food on the ground floor in the new Emsu Hotel.

The *Europa Delicatessen* in the Q C Pavilion, Gorordo Ave, which sells meat, and gourmet cheese, caviar and smoked salmon also has a cosy restaurant on the premises. It also sells wine and champagne. There is another *Europa Delicatessen* on Ramos St. It's open Monday to Saturday from 9 am to 10 pm.

Eddie's Log Cabin on M C Briones St has good US and Filipino meals and cheap daily dishes. To be recommended are the American breakfast and steaks and salad. It is open daily from 7 am to 2 am.

The *Master Key Restaurant* is a charming old-fashioned restaurant at the Hotel de Mercedes, Pelaez St, which serves international cuisine and good American breakfasts.

Our Place on Pelaez St has relatively cheap European, US and Filipino meals. This pub/restaurant is on the 1st floor; a narrow staircase leads up to it. It's open Monday to Saturday from 9 am to 10 pm.

The *Café Adriatico* on F Ramos St serves steaks, seafood and salads as well as a selection of wines. This attractive restaurant with a pleasant atmosphere is definitely not cheap. It is open daily from noon to 2 am.

The *Kukuk's Nest* on the corner of Gorordo and Escario Sts serves good European and Filipino cuisine in a pleasant garden restaurant.

La France is a very good restaurant at the Park Place Hotel, Fuente Osmeña, that serves French cuisine and other European specialties. It is open 24-hours daily.

The *St Moritz Restaurant* on Gorordo Ave serves excellent European and Filipino meals, and is open daily between 8 am and 10.30 pm.

The *Swiss Restaurant* on General Maxilom Ave serves good Swiss and Filipino meals. It is well run and the atmosphere is civilised. It is open daily from 9 am to 11 pm.

Self-Catering The fruit stalls on Don Julio Llorente St, near Fuente Osmeña, have an excellent selection of tropical fruits.

Entertainment

There are nightclubs spread out all around the town, and more are being opened all the time. Nevertheless, a few pubs like *Our Place* on Pelaez St and *The Kentucky Pub* on General Maxilom Ave have managed to survive. The youth of Cebu City often meet at the *Boulevard* on Osmeña Blvd where the beer is cheap and new video clips are shown on a large screen. Also on Osmeña Blvd the go-go girls at the *Silver Dollar Bar* attract numerous guests.

There is a wide selection of entertainment available on General Maxilom Ave, including the simple go-go bars *The Viking* and *The Brown Bear*; the *Puerto Rico Bar*, which is a show disco; *Ball's*, which is a sports bar, theatre lounge and disco all in one; the *Cities Music Lounge*, which features good live music and wide-screen videos; and the big *Steve's Music Bar*.

The *Bai Disco* in the Cebu Plaza Hotel is the most popular in Cebu City. It is open from 9 pm and admission costs P100 (minimum consumption). It's a safe bet that gamblers would prefer the *Casino* opposite the Cebu Plaza Hotel, where there is a full house every evening until the wee small hours. On Sunday in the *Century Game Club* near the Capitol you can sometimes watch 'high rollers' place their bets. The first cockfights take place in the forenoon.

Things to Buy

Amongst the biggest and best department stores are Shoemart and White Gold, both in the Reclamation Area; Gaisano Main and Gaisano Metro, both Downtown on Colon St, Robinson's on Fuente Osmeña; and Rustan's on General Maxilom Ave.

Getting There & Away

Bus There are three important bus terminals in Cebu City: the Northern Bus Terminal on M J Cuenco Ave for trips in a northerly direction, the Southern Bus Terminal on Rizal Ave for trips in a southerly direction and the ABC Liner Bus Terminal on San Jose St for trips in a southerly direction to catch the ferry to Negros. Buses of the ABC Liner company also stop at the Southern Bus Terminal.

See also Getting There & Away at the beginning of this section.

Getting Around

To/From the Airport Pacific Airways and Aerolift flights using light aircraft use Lahug Airport. This small airport is on the northern edge of town. A taxi from Lahug Airport to the Downtown area shouldn't cost more than P30.

Mactan International Airport is on Mactan Island, about 15 km from Cebu City. The PAL inland flights use this airport, as do the few international flights from places such as Singapore and Japan.

From Mactan International Airport to Cebu City there are shuttle buses which cost P30 per person. They go to the Park Place Hotel at Fuente Osmeña.

From Cebu City to Mactan International Airport the shuttle buses leave from the Park Place Hotel at Fuente Osmeña every 30 minutes from 6 am to 5 pm. The trip can take up to an hour, as road blockages often create delays and have sometimes caused passengers to miss their plane. If you have an early plane to catch, it could pay to spend the night near the airport instead of in town (see Lapu-Lapu in the following Mactan Island section).

An air-con taxi or air-con limousine from Mactan International Airport to the city should cost P100 to P150, but make sure the price is agreed upon before departure. Hardly any taxis will switch on their meters, unless they have been fixed beforehand. If there are no traffic jams a taxi should take around 20 minutes for the journey.

Tricycles are prohibited in the airport area. You will find them in front of the nearby Silangan Hotel. They cost about P10 as far as the Mandaue-Mactan Bridge or the jeepney terminal, where you can board a jeepney to Cebu City for P4.50.

Taxi Taxis cost P10 and air-con taxis P16 for the first 500 metres, thereafter P1 for every farther 200 metres. Mind you, not every taxi driver switches on the meter if it is not pointed out to him! It is worthwhile trying to negotiate a fare in advance for longer trips.

Boat The piers are not far away from the city centre, so a taxi to a hotel in Downtown should cost P30. If you want to stay in Uptown a taxi should cost about P40. It is not unusual to be charged P100; after the arrival of a bigger ship you will scarcely find a taxi driver who will switch on his meter.

Jeepney Of the many jeepney routes available, the following ones are probably the most important for tourists: Capitol (Uptown at the end of Osmeña Blvd), Lahug (Lahug district in the north of the city), Carbon (Carbon Market, Downtown) and Colon (Colon St, Downtown). The charge is P1.50.

Car The most reliable car hire would be Hertz (☎ 91143) on General Maxilom Ave at the corner of Juana Osmeña St.

MT MANUNGGAL NATIONAL PARK

Each year on 17 March the Cebu City Tourist Office organises a big trek to nearby Mt Manunggal north-west of Cebu City. This is the anniversary of the death of President Magsaysay, who, in 1957, crashed to his death here in his private plane. This trek includes an overnight stay, so take a tent, provisions and water. Share of jeep transport to Adlaon costs about P50.

MACTAN ISLAND

When people talk about the boom in tourism on Cebu, they are usually talking about Mactan Island, which is connected with Cebu by the 864-metres-long Mandaue-Mactan Bridge. On the south-east coast of the island there is a row of exclusive beach hotels like nowhere else on the Philippines. But there is a catch. Although no expense was spared during the building of these resorts – they even constructed beaches with tons of imported sand – the authorities responsible for the areas outside of the development showed practically no interest in developing and improving the approach roads. So the road from Mactan International Airport to the beach hotels does not come anywhere near the standards to be expected from skilfully designed advertising brochures.

Lapu-Lapu

Lapu-Lapu was founded in 1730 by Augustinian monks. About 130,000 people live today in the former administrative centre of Opon. There is a memorial to Chief Lapu-Lapu, who killed Ferdinand Magellan in the battle of Mactan Island on 27 April 1521.

Places to Stay

The *Heidelberg Hotel* (☎ 88569) at the Mandaue-Mactan Bridge has rooms with fan for P400 and with air- con for P600/950. It's a simple and fairly good place, albeit a bit pricey. There is a restaurant and beer garden. A tricycle to the airport costs P10 (even early in the morning).

The *HR Tourist Hotel* (☎ 400048, 40 0158) at Pusok near the Mandaue-Mactan Bridge has singles/doubles with fan and bath for P400/500 and with air-con and bath for P600 to P850. The more expensive rooms have fridges and TV. It's a clean, comfortable place and the staff is friendly. There is a restaurant, swimming pool and free airport service.

The *Cesar's Mansion Hotel* (☎ 400211-13; fax 400615) at Pusok has very comfortable rooms with air-con and bath from P1500 to P2000. It also has a restaurant, and cars for rent.

Places to Eat

The *Heidelberg Restaurant* at the Mandaue-Mactan Bridge serves good European meals, although the prices will come as a nasty surprise to some of the guests. To be recommended is the *Café Cesario* in Cesar's Mansion Hotel, Pusok. It is clean and air-conditioned, and they serve good Filipino and international food. You can get various snacks at the little *1890* pub on the way from the centre of town to the jeepney terminal. Near the markets are two *Lechon* restaurants. Try them if you like pork.

The *Silangan Restaurant* in the hotel of the same name at the airport is rather expensive.

Entertainment

You can dance at the *Phoenix Disco* at the former Imperial Hotel, where the women workers from the TMX factory opposite now live. Other night spots are *Blitz Disco*, *Starfire* and *Lucky Five*.

Getting There & Away

A lot of jeepneys go from Cebu City to Lapu-Lapu daily – just listen for the 'opon-opon' call. All go through V Gullas St (Manalili St), where a few passengers get on. The seats next to the driver are best, as the ones behind get very crowded. The fare is P4.50.

At the Lapu-Lapu Market the tricycles wait for passengers going farther, perhaps to the beaches.

A taxi from Cebu City to Lapu-Lapu costs about P70, but if you want to go to the beach you have to pay another P20.

The last jeepney from Lapu-Lapu to Cebu City leaves at 11 pm, and the next does not go till about 4 am the following morning. The jeepney terminal is a bit outside of town, towards Cebu City.

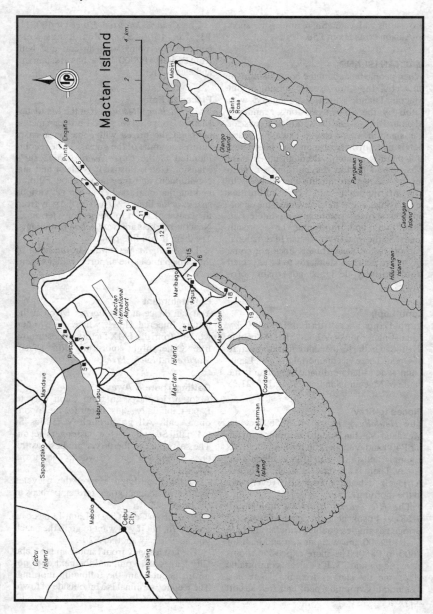

■   PLACES TO STAY

1   Hotel Clubhouse
2   HR Tourist Hotel
3   Cesar's Mansion Hotel
5   Heidelberg Hotel
6   Golden Views Beach Resort
8   Shangri-La's Mactan Island Resort
9   Mar Y Cielo Beach Resort
10 Tambuli Beach Resort
11 Costabella Tropical Beach Resort
12 Buyong Beach Resort &
    Maribago Bluewater Beach Resort
13 Cebu Beach Club
14 Hawaiin Village Inn
15 Hadsan Beach Resort
16 Club KonTiki Resort
17 Bahia Beach Club
18 Coral Reef Hotel &
    Golden Sunrise Beach Resort
19 Kalingaw Beach Resort
20 Southern Island Club Resort

    OTHER

4   Lapu-Lapu City Hall
7   Magellan Marker

MARIGONDON

The nearest good public beach beyond Cebu City is **Marigondon Beach**. It is a favourite with the locals and is especially popular at the weekend. There is ample roofed seating for P30 where day visitors can eat freshly grilled fish at low prices and drink beer and tuba. The beach itself is only just acceptable, but you can hire a boat and get out to Olango Island for a bit of snorkelling. Fix the price beforehand.

Places to Stay

The *Hawaiian Village Inn* has cottages with fan and bath for P400. This is a simple place on the road from Lapu-Lapu to Marigondon, therefore not directly on the beach. Diving is offered here.

The *Coral Reef Hotel* (☎ 211191; fax 211192) at Agus has rooms with air-con and bath from P3600 to P4600. Suites are P11,300 and P15,000. It is a luxurious but somewhat dreary establishment, with a res-

taurant, swimming pool, tennis court, Hobie Cats, diving, water skiing, windsurfing and a private beach only for hotel guests.

Getting There & Away

Lapu-Lapu to Marigondon Beach by tricycle usually costs no more than P3 per person, though sometimes you can't get the price down to that figure no matter how hard you bargain. A fair price per tricycle is P20. It may be advisable to agree on a pick-up time for the return.

MARIBAGO

At Maribago, between Marigondon and Punta Engaño, you can inspect some **guitar factories**. The biggest is probably Lilang's Guitar Factory, but the smaller factories also make quite good and well-priced guitars; it pays to compare them. If you want a guitar that will last, it is worth spending a few pesos more and buying an export guitar, as the ones that are made for the local market are dirt cheap but perish quickly once out of the tropics. You can get a good export guitar from P3000. Since PAL will not accept them as hand luggage, at least beyond Cebu, they have to go in the hold, so have them well packed. It is even better to invest in a strong guitar case.

Maribago has several fine hotels by the beach. Day visitors have to pay admission, a part of which is deducted from the bill later.

Places to Stay

The *Buyong Beach Resort* (☎ 217337) at Buyong has rooms with fan and bath for P400 and with air-con and bath for P750. It's a reasonable place and has a restaurant, but the name is a bit of a misnomer because the beach is missing.

The *Hadsan Beach Resort* (☎ 72679, 70247) at Buyong has rooms with fan and bath for P510/680, singles with air-con and bath from P750 to P2400 and doubles with air-con and bath from P900 to P2500. The cheaper rooms are of an older vintage. There is a restaurant, swimming pool and a small beach, and diving and windsurfing are offered here. Admission is P10.

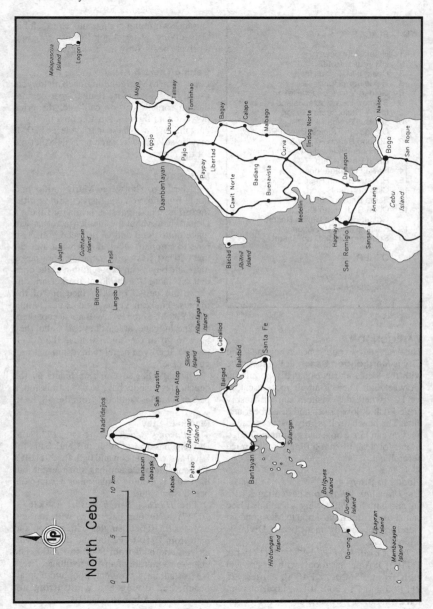

North Cebu

Club KonTiki Resort (☎ 400310; fax 400306) at Maribago has rooms with fan and bath from P650 to P1500, and it has a restaurant. It is a solidly built place with almost no vegetation or beach. Divers prefer it.

The *Costabella Tropical Beach Resort* (☎ 210828; fax 210838) at Buyong has singles with air-con and bath from P1600 to P2500, doubles with air-con and bath from P1900 to P2700 and suites for P3600 to P5000, and a rather expensive restaurant. There is also a swimming pool and tennis court, and windsurfing and diving are offered. This is a well kept, clubby establishment, with lots of different leisure time facilities (table tennis, darts, billiards etc). The hotel seems to be popular with Japanese tourists.

The *Tambuli Beach Resort* (☎ 211543; fax 211545) has rooms and cottages with air-con and bath from P1700 to P2000. It's a comfortable, well-designed place with a restaurant, swimming pool, jacuzzi and sauna, and Hobie Cats, windsurfing and diving are available. A few years ago this attractive resort was the first on Mactan Island to cater for the better-off tourist. Admission for day visitors is P150, of which P100 are later deducted from the bill.

The *Maribago Bluewater Beach Resort* (☎ 211620; fax 5010633) at Maribago has comfortable rooms with air-con and bath for P3000 and spacious cottages with a living room, bedroom, air-con and bath for P5500. There is a restaurant, a beautiful swimming pool and a tennis court, and they offer diving, water skiing and windsurfing. This is a pleasant, generously furnished establishment. The beach is noticeably clean. Admission for day visitors is P200.

Getting There & Away

A tricycle from Lapu-Lapu to Maribago costs P3 per person. A Special Ride costs P25, but you will have to do some bargaining as the drivers are used to higher fares from guests at the beach resorts.

PUNTA ENGAÑO

Punta Engaño is the north-eastern corner of Mactan Island. In 1866 the **Magellan Marker** was erected to commemorate the explorer Magellan who was killed here on 27 April 1521 by Chief Lapu-Lapu. This historic battle is re-enacted each year by amateur actors on the anniversary of his death.

Places to Stay

The *Mar Y Cielo Beach Resort* (☎ 212232-34; fax 5011268) has rooms with air-con and bath from P2500 to P3400. There is a restaurant, a swimming pool with a bar, and diving, water skiing and windsurfing are offered. This is a large, well-looked after establishment, a bit out of the way, with tastefully designed, spacious cottages and a small private beach. The admission for day visitors is P250, which includes one meal; at the weekends it's P350.

Shangri-La's Mactan Island Resort (☎ 310288; fax 311688) is a big first-class hotel, with around 350 well-equipped rooms from P4600 to P10,200; suites are P27,500. There are four restaurants, a swimming pool and a tennis court, and diving, water skiing, windsurfing and parasailing are offered.

Getting There & Away

A tricycle from Lapu-Lapu to Punta Engaño costs P3 per person. You should be able to get a Special Ride for P25 by bargaining skilfully.

OLANGO ISLAND

Olango Island is the long island visible from Maribago and Marigondon. It has small white beaches and beautiful stands of palms. The bungalow hotel Santa Rosa, which is closed at present, is in the south-western corner. This hotel has given Olango its other name of Santa Rosa.

The island is surrounded by a reef stretching another 10 km in a south-westerly direction towards the islands of Panganan, Caohagan, Lassuan (Kalassuan) and Hilutangan. Much of the coral has unfortunately been destroyed by dynamite fishing.

Getting There & Away

The trip from Maribago to Olango Island costs P10 per person by outrigger boat. A Special Ride should cost about P150.

LILOAN

The road from Cebu City along the east coast heading north takes you through several clean, inviting little provincial towns. It is about 20 km to Liloan. There is another Liloan at the southernmost tip of Cebu.

Places to Stay

Franziska's Beach Resort at Jubay, Liloan, has passable cottages with fan and bath for P850. It's a pleasant place with a swimming pool and a restaurant that serves Filipino and Swiss food.

Getting There & Away

There are several buses from Cebu City to Liloan daily, leaving the Northern Bus Terminal. The trip takes 30 minutes.

SOGOD

The Cebu Club Pacific Beach Hotel in Sogod was one of the few beach resort hotels on the north-east coast of Cebu for many years. It now has competition from Alegre Beach Resort.

Places to Stay

The *Cebu Club Pacific Beach Hotel* (☎ 21 2291, 79147; fax 314621) has cottages with air-con and bath for P1850. It's attractive, well maintained and has a restaurant and a tennis court. It also offers Hobie Cats, windsurfing, water skiing and diving. Day visitors must pay P100 admission, which goes towards their purchases.

The *Alegre Beach Resort* at Calumboyan has very comfortable rooms with TV, fridge, air-con and bath for P6000. Suites are P11,000. There is a restaurant and tennis court, and Hobie Cats, diving, water skiing and windsurfing are available. Information is available in Cebu City (☎ 311231-50; fax 214345).

Getting There & Away

There are several buses from Cebu City to Sogod daily, leaving the Northern Bus Terminal. The trip takes two hours.

BANTAYAN ISLAND

A little off the usual tourist routes is Bantayan Island, in the north-west of Cebu Province. It has beautiful beaches, particularly on the southern coast between Santa Fe and Maricaban, including Sugar Beach, Paradise Beach and the picturesque beach near Tingting-on. Near Paradise Beach you will find the small Ogtong Cave with its freshwater spring. Right next to it is a large swimming pool belonging to the Santa Fe Beach Club. Admission is P20.

Up until now only a few tourists have come to this pleasant island with its friendly locals. There are only two beach resorts, both of which can be comfortably reached on foot from Santa Fe, where the ferries from Hagnaya on Cebu arrive. A small airport was built about two km east of Santa Fe, which it is hoped will bring a boom in tourism for the island (there is talk of regular flights with Pacific Airways to and from Bacolod and Cebu City). Local fishermen supply squid to the Cebu mainland, while the farmers use their land for poultry raising and ship millions of eggs to other islands – no wonder all the roads are carefully asphalted.

Bantayan

With its 60,000 inhabitants Bantayan is the largest town on the island of the same name. It has a nice plaza, a clean and lively market, a picturesque port, a hospital, two lodges, some simple restaurants along the pier and a branch of the Rural Bank where you can cash travellers' cheques, albeit at an unfavourable rate. There is a boat service daily between this small harbour town and Cadiz on Negros, so you can include Bantayan Island in a round trip through the Visayas.

Places to Stay The *Saint Josef Lodge* on President Osmeña Sr St has simple but relatively good rooms with fan for P40/70. The *Admiral Lodging House* on Rizal Ave has

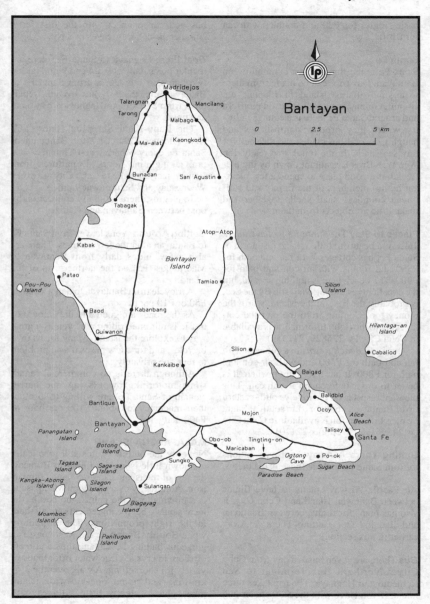

Bantayan

basic singles for P80 and doubles with fan for P140.

Santa Fe

Santa Fe is the third-largest community on Bantayan. Day trips can be made from there to the small offshore islands of Hilantaga-an, Jibitnil, Guintacan and other destinations. In and around Santa Fe there is a cottage industry where they produce lampshades and hanging decorations made from the shells of tiny sea snails. In the rough and ready Ten Wee Wee Bros Restaurant down by the pier (which is a good place to spend a few pleasant hours) members of the family and staff thread countless snail shells together and make little art objects from them.

Places to Stay The *Santa Fe Beach Club* in Talisay, a beautiful little village just north of Santa Fe, has cottages with fan and bath for P300 and rooms with air-con and bath for P900. The beach here is nothing special, but the excellent restaurant, Majestic By the Sea, is probably the best on the island, worth the money too. Coming from the pier the cottages are to the right. Information is available in Cebu City (☎ 225829, 211339).

The *Kota Beach Resort* has cottages with fan and bath for P500 and with air-con and bath for P800. It has a restaurant where it is better to order beforehand if you can. This pleasant resort is on the lonely south-eastern tip of Bantayan, about one km south of Santa Fe pier. Information is available in Cebu City (☎ 225661, 222726; fax 221701).

Getting There & Away Transport options to/from Sante Fe include those listed below.

Air Pacific Airways plans to have flights between Bantayan Island and Cebu City. It also has plans for flights between Bantayan and Bacolod (see Getting There & Away earlier in this section).

Bus There are seven buses a day from Cebu City's Northern Bus Terminal to San Remedio and Hagnaya. The trip takes three hours. If you leave with the 5.30 am air-con bus you can connect with the first ferry. Another air-con bus leaves at 2 pm.

Boat From Hagnaya to Santa Fe, there are regular boats daily at 9 am and 9 pm, taking two hours. A bus leaves from Santa Fe to Bantayan after the ferry has arrived. Departures from Santa Fe to Hagnaya are at 6 am and noon.

The Lapu-Lapu Shipping Lines' MV *Honey* leaves Cebu City for Bantayan or Santa Fe every Monday and Thursday at 9 pm, taking nine hours. Departures from Bantayan or Santa Fe to Cebu City are every Wednesday and Saturday at 9 pm.

To Negros, there is a daily connection by boat between Bantayan and Cadiz.

Getting Around A bus leaves from Santa Fe to Bantayan after the ferry arrives. There are also a few buses daily from Bantayan to Madridejos (P5) on the northern tip of the island.

A tricycle from Bantayan to Santa Fe costs P50 or P10 per person.

As the roads are good and the amount of traffic is minimal, riding a bicycle is a great way to explore the island. Many locals own bicycles, and for a few pesos it's no problem to rent one privately.

Although there is no commercial rental, some motorbike owners (eg, the barrio captain of Santa Fe) are willing to hire out their machines for about P100 per hour or P400 daily.

MALAPASCUA ISLAND

Not only the outline of this still practically unknown little island is similar to Boracay, the rest of the island can also stand comparison. Admittedly everything on Malapascua is a bit smaller – the palms, the beach, the local's huts – but the ingredients are all there in the right proportions. The blindingly white **Bounty Beach** on the west coast is a gorgeous bathing beach, and the coral reefs offshore in crystal clear water offer loads of variety for snorkelling. A walk over the 2½-km-long and about one-km-wide island takes you to sleepy little villages with friendly fishermen and deserted bays in idyllic locations. Malapascua Island is about eight km north-east of Cebu and 25 km west of Leyte. It is sometimes referred to as Logon, after Barangay Logon, the main community in the south of the island.

Places to Stay
At *Cocobana Beach Resort* a roomy cottage with bath costs P500, in the off season, from the beginning of May until the end of November, you will pay only P300. You can sleep in a tent for P200. This was the first establishment on Malapascua and belongs to the Swiss Freddy and his Filipina wife, Noravilla. It is likely that further resorts will open in the next few years.

Getting There & Away
Bus D'Rough Riders air-con buses leave from Cebu City's Northern Bus Terminal for Maya at 5 and 6 am, taking 3½ hours. If possible take a direct bus to Maya, because buses that make a detour to Hagnay allow for 30 minutes extra. The last D'Rough Riders and Cebu Autobus ordinary buses leave at noon, taking 4½ hours. Some buses only go to Daanbantayan. From there a Special Ride by tricycle (it's a murderous ride!) to Maya costs P50.

Boat Two outrigger boats leave Maya for Malapascua daily between 10.30 and 11.30 am. The MB *Brother's* goes directly to Bounty Beach. The trip takes 45 minutes. A Special Ride costs P300.

A big outrigger boat leaves Maya for San Isidro on Leyte daily at 10.30 am, taking two hours.

A bench outside the Mayami Restaurant at the wharf in Maya could be handy as a place to sleep if you miss a boat or bus.

TALISAY
This makes a nice day trip from Cebu City but not much more. The Talisay beaches, such as Tangque Beach and Canezares Beach, are anything but impressive.

The *Tourist Seaside Hotel* (☎ 97011) has rooms with fan and bath for P250 and P350 and with air-con and bath for P480 and P600, and there is a restaurant and a swimming pool. This hotel has seen better days.

The *Canezares Beach Cottages* is on Canezares Beach, about 100 metres from the Tourist Seaside Hotel. Simple cottages cost about P100.

Getting There & Away
There are many jeepneys from Cebu City to Talisay daily, taking 30 minutes.

TOLEDO
Toledo is on the west coast of Cebu and has a population of about 120,000. Many of the people are economically dependent on the Atlas Consolidated Mining & Development Corporation. This mine, which is one of the biggest in the world, often employs several members of one family.

You can go by ship from Toledo to San Carlos on Negros (see Getting There & Away earlier in this section).

Places to Stay
You can enquire at the Vizcayno Restaurant near the wharf whether the simple *Lodging House* has rooms available.

Getting There & Away
Several buses leave the Southern Bus Terminal in Cebu City for Toledo daily. The trip takes two hours.

MOALBOAL
A fierce typhoon severely damaged Moalboal in September 1984. Nothing but bare rock was left of **Panagsama Beach**, three km from the main road. The fabulous coral reef which had taken centuries to grow was almost totally destroyed within a few minutes. If you're after a beach, go to nearby **White Beach**, which is 15 minutes away by outrigger boat (P150 including pick-up service), or you can use the beach of the Moalboal Reef Club Diving Lodge for P20.

Luckily for the many divers who are the majority of the visitors to Moalboal, the colourful underwater world of nearby Pescador Island survived the fierce whirlwinds

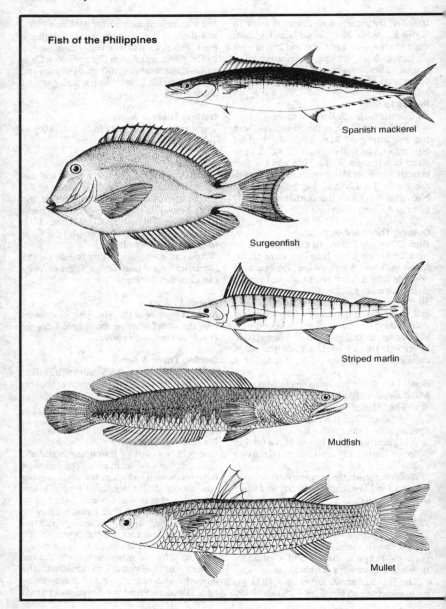

Fish of the Philippines

Spanish mackerel

Surgeonfish

Striped marlin

Mudfish

Mullet

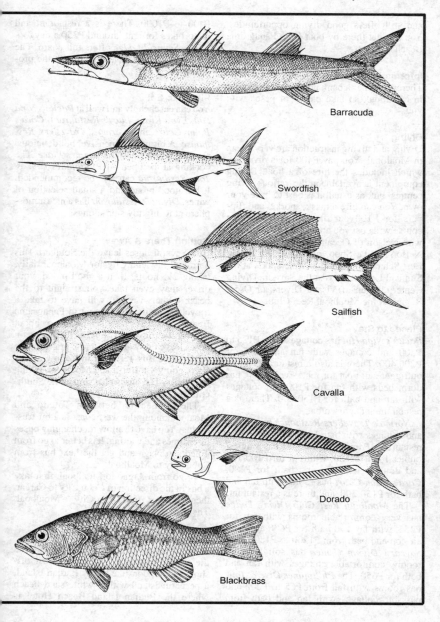

Barracuda

Swordfish

Sailfish

Cavalla

Dorado

Blackbrass

and still offers good diving opportunities. You can get there by boat from Panagsama Beach.

Information
There is neither a bank nor a money changer in Moalboal, so take plenty of pesos with you.

Diving
Diving and diving instruction are very cheap in Moalboal. You pay P400 for a dive trip, which includes the hire of a boat. Diving equipment is available at the various diving centres, but, as usual, it is best to have your own. You can hire a mask, snorkel and flippers for P100 per day. A week's diving course will cost you about US$220. Enquire with Nelson of Ocean Safari Philippines at Nelson's Dive Shop, next to Eve's Kiosk; Bert Schaap of Aquarius Watersports at the Sumisid Lodge; Hans at the Savedra Diving Center; Jürgen of Visaya Divers; or Oscar Regner at the Moalboal Reef Club.

Places to Stay
Pacita's Nipa Hut has cottages from P125 to P300 and cottages with fan and bath for P200/400. There is also a restaurant and an outrigger sail boat for rent. *Eve's Kiosk* has dorm beds with fan for P100 and cottages with fan and bath for P150/200. There is a restaurant and a disco/bar.

Norma's Travellers Resthouse has rooms and cottages with bath for P100 as well as a restaurant. *Pacifico's Cottages* has singles/oubles for P75/120, with fan for P100/150 and doubles with fan and bath for P180. *Cora's Palm Court* has rooms with fan and bath for P150/200, and there is a restaurant.

The *Moalboal Reef Club Diving Lodge* has very comfortable rooms with fan for P455, with fan and bath for P600 and with air-con and bath from P1200 to P1800. The *Savedra Diving Center* has solidly built, roomy, comfortable cottages with fan and bath for P650. The *Philippines Dive & Tour* has rooms with fan from P65 to P200 and passable cottages with fan and bath from

P400 to P1000. There is a restaurant and motorbikes for rent (around P350 a day).

The *Sumisid Lodge* offers full board. The fee charged must be arranged with the proprietor.

Places to Eat
You can eat cheaply and well at *Pacita's Nipa Hut*, *Eve's Kiosk*, *Lucy's Restaurant*, *Cora's Palm Court* and *Norma's Travellers Resthouse*. A bit more expensive, but delicious, are the garlic dishes at *Hannah's Place*. The cooking at the open-air *Philippines Dive & Tour Restaurant* can also be recommended. It has good bread and a small selection of wines. *Divina's Restaurant* has a nice atmosphere at its nightly sing-alongs.

Getting There & Away
Bus Several buses leave the Southern Bus Terminal in Cebu City for Moalboal daily, taking 2½ hours. If in a good mood, your driver may even take you straight to the beach. Otherwise you will have to take a tricycle from the main street to Panagsama Beach, at a cost of P5 per person or about P20 for the tricycle. The ABC Liner air-con buses leave daily at 7 am and 2 pm from the ABC Liner Bus Terminal in Cebu City for Bato, going via Barili and Moalboal, taking two hours. The buses also stop at the Southern Bus Terminal.

The connection between Toledo and Moalboal along the west coast is a bit frustrating. You have to allow for changing buses three times and waiting. It is better to go from Toledo to Naga and get the next bus from Cebu City to Moalboal.

To go from Argao to Moalboal, first take a bus in the direction of Cebu City to Carcar, then get a bus from Cebu City to Moalboal. The trip takes two hours.

BADIAN & BADIAN ISLAND
About 10 km south of Moalboal you will find the small community of Badian. Just offshore in a lagoon-like bay is Badian Island, a peaceful island with a white sand beach where the Badian Island Beach Hotel is

located. This hotel can be found in more and more tour catalogues these days.

Places to Stay

The *Lambug Beach Resort* at Lambug has cottages from P300 to P400, and there is a restaurant. This is a Philippine-American establishment where you can snorkel, go diving or try water skiing. It is about two km from the main road on a very quiet, white sand beach, next to the Green Island Golf & Beach Resort. It can be reached by tricycle from the main road.

The *Green Island Golf & Beach Resort*, also at Lambug, has spacious and comfortable rooms with air-con and bath for P2500. Suites are P5000. There is a restaurant and swimming pool, and water skiing and diving are offered. The grounds are quite extensive and there is an 18-hole golf course. The place is run by the Cebu Green Island Club (☎ 73980, 95935; fax 311269), Suarez Building, Gorordo Ave, Lahug.

The *Badian Island Beach Hotel* on Badian Island has tastefully furnished rooms with fan and bath for P2800. This is an attractive place under Philippine-German management. There is a restaurant and swimming pool, and windsurfing and diving are available.

MATUTINAO

In the midst of lush tropical vegetation in the mountains near Matutinao you can find the refreshingly cool, crystal-clear **Kawasan Falls**. They are probably the best waterfalls on Cebu, and the natural pools are great for swimming. This really idyllic place is a good starting point for mountain treks. There is a P5 entrance fee.

Places to Stay & Eat

There are a few cottages near the waterfalls which you can rent for P100 to P250. There is also a small restaurant which serves cold drinks as well as simple meals. As these cottages may be booked out, it is probably a good idea to organise a day trip first to check them out. Here the German, Heraldo, could possibly help you. He is a man who has found the secret of dedicating himself to the art of living by a waterfall in his own little paradise.

Getting There & Away

There are no problems getting from Moalboal to Matutinao by jeepney or bus during the day, but you could have trouble getting transport in the late afternoon. The trip takes 45 minutes. Get off at the church in Matutinao and follow the trail upriver on foot. This will take you about 20 minutes. Motorbikes can be parked at the church for P5.

SAN SEBASTIAN & BATO

Several ships go from San Sebastian and Bato to San Jose or Tampi on Negros daily (see Getting There & Away earlier in this section).

Contessas Restaurant at San Sebastian has rooms for P40/80. These are very simple rooms by the wharf.

Getting There & Away

ABC Liner air-con buses leave daily at 6, 7, 8 and 11 am and 1.30, 2 and 3 pm from the ABC Liner Bus Terminal in Cebu City for Bato. The buses also stop at the Southern Bus Terminal. The trip takes you along the east coast via Argao, Dalaguete, Mainit and Lilian to Bato, and there is a direct transfer to a boat heading to Tampi on Negros. Note: buses leaving at 7 am and 2 pm go along the west coast via Barili, Moalboal and San Sebastian to Bato.

LILOAN

There are several outrigger boats from Liloan to Sibulan on Negros daily for P15 per person and at least P200 for a Special Ride. If you don't want to go right through, you can spend the night at the Manureva Beach Resort. A 10-minute walk from Liloan pier, it is right on the white beach and is managed by Jean-Pierre Franck, who is French. Apart from jeepney trips into the surrounding country, he offers diving trips to Apo Island, Sumilon Island and Dako Island.

A day trip to Sumilon Island costs P600 by boat.

Places to Stay
The *Manureva Beach Resort* has rooms with fan and bath for P500 and with air-con and bath from P600 to P1200. It's a tastefully designed large house with a restaurant, and offers diving and windsurfing.

MAINIT
For about P300 you can get from Mainit to Sumilon Island by small outrigger boat and be picked up again. You pay almost twice that for a round trip from Liloan or Santander, although the boats are bigger and therefore safer.

SUMILON ISLAND
Sumilon Island, off Cebu's south-eastern coast, is a favourite with divers and snorkellers. On the western side of this little island south of the sandbank the water is only two to five metres deep and 200 metres wide, which makes it ideal for snorkelling, while drop-off plunges into the darkness are only about 100 metres off the south-west coast. Unfortunately, the contract with Silliman University at Dumaguete on Negros for the preservation of wildlife was not renewed by the authorities in Oslob. The Marine Research Center no longer exists, and the former Sumilon Marine Park is being fished day and night. That could mean the end of the coral reef: fishing with dynamite is so easy! But perhaps tourism will help to put a stop to this wanton destruction. The influential Green Island Club, which runs amongst other things the Green Island Golf & Beach Resort in Badian, has recently opened the Sumilan Island Resort on the north coast of Sumilon Island for its guests who are interested in diving.

MONTALONGON
Montalongon is a few km inland from Dalaguete, south of Argao. The road across the island from Sibonga to Dumanjug is probably no longer usable. There is now a new road from Talood to Ronda in the south of Cebu. Apart from the highway from Carcar to Barili, it is now the only connection from the eastern coast over the mountains to the western coast, as the road from Dalaguete to Badian was severely damaged by a typhoon and now ends at Montalongon.

Montalongon is at an altitude of about 700 metres and is also called 'Little Baguio of Cebu'. The **market** held here every Thursday has a remarkably wide range of vegetables. The extensive **chrysanthemum fields** a little outside Montalongon are beautiful.

Getting There & Away
Several jeepneys go from Dalaguete Market to Montalongon daily, taking an hour or more. The last jeepney for Montalongon leaves Dalaguete at 3 pm, though there is a very wobbly bus at about 4 pm. It's a pleasant 14 km walk from Montalongan down to Dalaguete, with good views and almost no sound of traffic.

ARGAO
Argao is a small provincial town on the southern coast of Cebu which became known when the exclusive Argao Beach Club opened at the beginning of the 1980s, a few km from the town centre. Nonresidents pay P50 admission, but this is credited towards anything consumed. Next door is **Dalaguete Public Beach**, which is free. Showers are available and the daily rent for sun shelters is P15, or P25 on Sunday and holidays. The meals are cheap here. There is a daily connection by car ferry between Argao (five km north of town) and Loon on Bohol (see Getting There & Away at the beginning of this section).

Places to Stay
The *Four Brothers & Sisters Inn* (☎ 280) has rooms for P50/100 and rooms with fan for P150/250. It is basic and a bit noisy and has a restaurant. *Luisa's Place* has cottages with fan and bath for P250. It's a pleasant place and has a restaurant.

The *Sunshine Beach Club* has rooms with fan and bath for P250/300, singles with air-con and bath for P500 and P740 and doubles with air-con and bath for P620 and P925, and there is a restaurant and a swimming pool. *Bamboo Paradise* (☎ 271) has rooms with fan and bath for P300/350. It has a family atmosphere, is good value and has an excellent restaurant. Diving costs US$15 per dive, and US$200 for a diving course. The owners, Carola, who is German, and Rey Rubia will organise island trips on request; they have their own boat.

The *Argao Beach Club* (☎ 74613) has singles with air-con and bath for P2000, doubles with air-con and bath for P2400 and suites for P5000. It's excellent and has a restaurant, swimming pool and tennis court, and offers Hobie Cats, windsurfing and diving.

Places to Eat
You can eat well and cheaply at Luisa's Place and at the Four Brothers Inn. At *Carmen's Kitchen* it's no problem to have fish you've brought from the market prepared for you. The *Bamboo Paradise* has German and Filipino cuisine. The *Tan-awan Restaurant* at the Argao Beach Club is mainly geared to international guests.

Getting There & Away
There are several ABC Liner buses daily from Cebu City going to Argao. They leave from the ABC Liner Bus Terminal bound for Bato. The buses stop also at the Southern Bus Terminal. The trip takes 1½ hours. The air-con buses are a bit faster, leaving at 6, 8 and 11 am and 1.30 and 3 pm.

Several minibuses also leave from the Argao bus terminal daily, but they are pretty uncomfortable.

Leyte

Leyte is one of the Visayan Islands and lies between Samar, Cebu, Bohol and Mindanao. The San Juanico Bridge, which is over two km long and joins the islands of Leyte and Samar across the San Juanico Strait, is prob-ably the most beautiful bridge in South-East Asia. Central and southern Leyte are somewhat mountainous with plains in the northern and western parts of the island. Administratively, it is divided into the province of Leyte, whose capital is Tacloban, Southern Leyte, whose capital is Maasin, and Biliran, whose capital is Naval.

Copra is Leyte's most important export product. More than 30% of cultivable land is planted with coconut palms. Other important agricultural exports are rice, maize, sugar cane and abaca. These are mostly shipped directly from Tacloban, making it unnecessary to send exports via Manila.

Leyte is particularly remembered as the place where General MacArthur fulfilled his 'I shall return' pledge. In October 1944, US troops landed at Red Beach in Palo, a little south of Tacloban, and started pushing the Japanese out of the Philippines. A little farther south is Tolosa, the birthplace of former first lady Imelda Marcos.

The main dialect in and around Tacloban is Waray-Waray, whereas in the north-west and the south it is Cebuano. You can get by quite well with English.

GETTING THERE & AWAY
To reach Leyte you can go from Bohol, Camiguin, Cebu, Luzon, Mindanao, Panay and Samar (see the Getting There & Away section of the Manila chapter and the relevant Getting There & Away sections of this and the Mindanao & Palawan chapter).

Air
To/From Cebu PAL flies from Tacloban to Cebu City on Monday, Wednesday, Friday and Sunday.

To/From Luzon PAL flies daily from Tacloban to Manila.

Bus
To/From Luzon Philtranco Company air-con buses leave Tacloban daily for Manila at 5.30 am and 4 pm. Travel time is 28 hours, including the ferry from San Isidro to Matnog. It is advisable to reserve a seat.

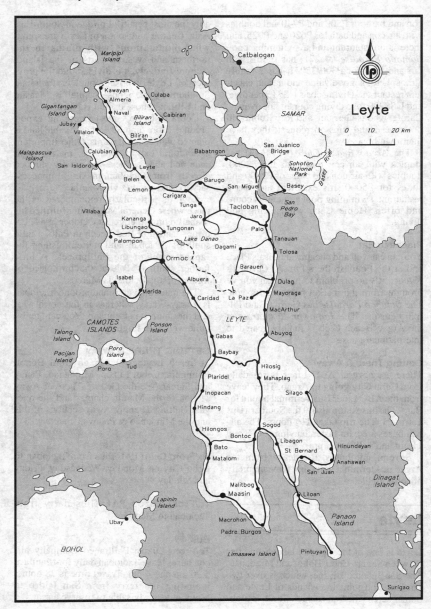

To/From Samar Air-con Philtranco buses leave Tacloban for Manila daily at 5.30 am and 4 pm, going through Catbalogan and Calbayog. Travel time to Catbalogan is three hours and four hours to Calbayog. It is advisable to book. Several buses leave daily from the wharf for Catbalogan, taking three hours.

Boat
To/From Bohol A big outrigger boat leaves Bato daily for Ubay at 10 am sometimes going via Lapinin Island, taking three or four hours.

The MV *Asia Brunei* of Trans-Asia Shipping Lines leaves Maasin for Jagna on Thursday at 8 pm, taking four hours.

A big outrigger boat leaves Maasin daily for Ubay at 10 am, taking four hours.

To/From Camiguin The Cokaliong Shipping Lines' MV *Filipinas Siargao* leaves Maasin for Mambajao on Wednesday at 5 am, taking five hours.

To/From Cebu There are numerous ships to Cebu City, leaving from various towns in Leyte.

From Hilongos, the MV *Queen Belinda* of Roble Shipping Lines leaves on Monday, Wednesday, Friday and Saturday at 10 pm, taking six hours. The MV *Guada Cristy* leaves on Tuesday, Thursday and Sunday at 10 pm and on Saturday at 10 am.

From Isabel, the MV *Our Lady of Fatima* of Carlos Gothong Lines leaves on Monday at 3 pm, taking five hours.

From Liloan, the MV *Guiuan* of K & T Shipping Lines leaves on Thursday and Sunday at 6 pm, taking six hours.

From Maasin, the MV *Asia Brunei* of Trans-Asia Shipping Lines leaves on Monday at 10 pm, taking six hours and the MV *Asia Singapore* leaves on Thursday at midnight, taking five hours. The MV *Filipinas Surigao* of Cokaliong Shipping Lines leaves on Wednesday at 2 am and Sunday at 10 pm, taking six hours; the MV *Filipinas Siargao* leaves Thursday at 1 am, taking seven hours; and the MV *Filipinas Maasin* leaves Friday at midnight, taking seven hours.

From Naval, the MV *Katarina* leaves twice a week, probably on Wednesday and Friday, taking 10 hours.

From Ormoc, the MV *Elcano* of Aboitiz Lines leaves daily at midnight, taking six hours. The MV *Cebu Princess* of Sulpicio Lines leaves on Sunday at 10 pm, taking six hours.

From Palompon, the MV *Our Lady of Mount Carmel* of Carlos Gothong Lines leaves on Tuesday at 8 am, and the MV *Our Lady of Fatima* leaves on Thursday at 8 am. Both take five hours.

From Tacloban, the MV *Don Calvino* of Carlos Gothong Lines leaves on Tuesday, Thursday and Sunday at 4 pm, taking 13 hours. The MV *Leyte Queen* of K & T Shipping Lines leaves on Wednesday, Friday and Sunday at 5 pm, taking 12 hours.

If you're not heading for Cebu City, there is a big outrigger boat that leaves Isabel daily at 4 pm for Carmen, taking four hours. Another big outrigger boat leaves San Isidro for Maya in northern Cebu daily at 8 am, taking two hours. For an additional payment of P200 the boat will make a stop at Bounty Beach on Malapascua Island. After the arrival of the boat in Maya a bus leaves for Cebu City.

To/From Luzon The Sulpicio Lines' MV *Surigao Princess* leaves Maasin on Wednesday at 8 am, Palompon at 4 pm and Calubian at midnight for Manila, taking 25 hours from Calubian.

The Aboitiz Lines' MV *Legaspi* leaves Ormoc for Manila on Saturday at noon, taking 28 hours.

The Sulpicio Lines' MV *Tacloban Princess* leaves Tacloban on Monday at 5 pm for Manila direct and on Friday at 10 am for Manila via Catbalogan on Samar. The time taken (direct) is 24 hours. The William Lines' MV *Masbate I* leaves Tacloban on Wednesday at noon for Manila via Catbalogan on Samar and on Saturday at 4 pm for Manila direct. The time taken (direct) is 24 hours.

To/From Mindanao The MV *Maharlika II* (car ferry) of Bernard Services leaves Liloan for Lipata, 10 km north-west of Surigao, at 8 am, taking three hours.

The MV *Filipinas Surigao* of Cokaliong Shipping Lines leaves Maasin for Surigao on Tuesday at 3 pm, taking four hours. The MV *Asia Singapore* of Trans-Asia Shipping Lines leaves Maasin for Surigao on Thursday at 2 am, taking three hours. The MV *Surigao Princess* of Sulpicio Lines leaves Maasin for Surigao on Sunday at midnight, taking four hours.

The MV *Legaspi* of Aboitiz Lines leaves Ormoc for Surigao on Friday at 8 am, taking nine hours.

To/From Panay The MV *Our Lady of Fatima* of Carlos Gothong Lines leaves Palompon for Dumaguit (near Kalibo) on Saturday at 8 am, taking nine hours.

The MV *Our Lady of the Sacret Heart* of Carlos Gothong Lines leaves Palompon for Roxas on Wednesday at 8 pm, taking 10 hours.

To/From Samar The MV *Cebu Princess* of Sulpicio Lines leaves Ormoc for Calbayog on Tuesday at 10 am, taking eight hours.

The MV *Masbate I* of William Lines leaves Tacloban for Catbalogan on Wednesday at noon, taking four hours. The MV *Tacloban Princess* of Sulpicio Lines leaves Tacloban for Catbalogan on Friday at 10 am, taking four hours. The MV *Don Calvino* of Carlos Gothong Lines leaves Tacloban for Catbalogan on Saturday at 4 pm, taking four hours.

The MV *Stacey* of K & T Shipping Lines leaves Tacloban for Guiuan in southern Samar every other day at 11 pm. The trip takes six hours.

TACLOBAN

The capital of Leyte is a port town with about 140,000 inhabitants. It has an excellent harbour with facilities for handling large ships and overseas trade. The colourful market at the western end of the wharf is full of life. A large relief on the wall of the Provincial Capitol Building depicts MacArthur's return to the Philippines. This historic event is celebrated each year on 19 and 20 October with cockfights and parades.

The **museum** in Tacloban's Divine Word University has rare and priceless artefacts from Leyte and Samar, which date from the early trade with China, and from the Sohoton Cave diggings. Another good museum is the colonial-style **Santo Niño Shrine & Heritage Museum**, that also gives an impression of the state of luxury the Marcos clan lived in. A guided tour for up to five persons costs P200. If you are on your own, there are usually other people to join in with. Tours start every hour form 8 to 11 am and 1 to 4 pm. Next door is the equally large People's Center, with a library for Samar and Leyte.

As a reward for climbing the many steps (decorated with 14 statues representing the Stations of the Cross) to the base of the statue of Christ, you will get a beautiful view over Tacloban and its busy port. You can get there from the market along Torres St.

If you are keen on history, you should visit **MacArthur Park** on Red Beach, where General MacArthur landed. Nature lovers will enjoy a day trip to **Sohoton National Park** near Basey on the island of Samar.

Information

The tourist office (☎ 2048) is in the Children's Park on Senator Enage St.

The Philippine National Bank on Justice Romualdez St changes travellers' cheques but you will need a photocopy of your passport.

The Equitable Bank on the corner of Rizal Ave and Gomez St will give you cash advances on your Visa and MasterCard.

Places to Stay – bottom end

The *San Juanico Travel Lodge* (☎ 3221) at 104 Justice Romualdez St is a simple but fairly good place with rooms with fan for P80/100 and with fan and bath for P100/120. *Cecilia's Lodge* (☎ 2815) at 178 Paterno St is a basic but comfortable place. It has rooms with fan for P100/160, with fan and bath for

P130/250 and with air-con and bath for P280/400.

The *Manabó Lodge* (☎ 3727) on Zamora St has reasonable rooms with fan for P160/250 and with fan and bath for P190/300. The *Leyte State College House* (☎ 3175), also known as LSC House, on Paterno St, has rooms with fan and bath for P180 and rooms with air-con and bath for P210/320. It's a reasonable place with a cafeteria and a tearoom.

Places to Stay – top end

The *Primerose Hotel* (☎ 2248), on the corner of Zamora and Salazar Sts, has clean rooms with fan and bath for P200/250 and with air-con and bath from P400 to P550, and there is a restaurant. The more expensive rooms have TVs.

The *Tacloban Plaza Hotel* (☎ 2444) on Justice Romualdez St has rooms with TV, air-con and bath for P300 to P470. The rooms are clean, pleasantly furnished and good value. Some of them are above the bowling alley and could be a bit noisy. There is a restaurant.

The *Tacloban Village Inn* (☎ 2926) on Veterano St has rooms with fan for P125/175, with fan and bath for P210/320, with air-con and bath for P285/410 and suites from P460 to P560. The more inexpensive rooms are actually in the annex *Village Townhouse* (☎ 4475), which is quite comfortable and has a restaurant.

The *Manhattan Inn* (☎ 4170, 4180) on Rizal Ave has clean, comfortable rooms with air-con and bath for P420/500 and suites for P600. This well-run hotel is often booked out, so it is advisable to make reservations in advance. There is a restaurant.

Places to Eat

The *Good Morning Restaurant* on Zamora St has an adjoining bakery where you can get a decent breakfast. There are two other restaurants quite closeby with the same name: *Good Morning Square*, an air-conditioned McDonald's look-alike, and the *Good Morning Complex*, which has a sing-along starting at 8 pm.

There is a good variety of chicken and Filipino dishes at the *Sunburst Fried Chicken* on Burgos St. The *Rovic Restaurant* on Zamora St serves more or less international cuisine; the daily special is to be recommended.

Good Chinese and Filipino meals can be had at the *Asiatic Restaurant* and the *Savory Steak House*, both on Zamora St. *Mandawe Fast Food* on Justice Romualdez St serves inexpensive Filipino food which, for a few pesos more, will be served to you in *Don's Cabin* on the 1st floor. This air-conditioned restaurant also prepares really good steaks. *Dahil Sa Iyo Fastfood* on the corner of Burgos and Real Sts is clean and popular, but closes at 8 pm. The house special is pakdol, a hearty dish similar to meat stew.

The best place to go for seafood is the rustic *Agus Restaurant* next to the fish market in Sagkahan in the south of town. You will have to get over your first impression of the outside, which is not its best side, and also the journey along the gradually narrowing Esperas Ave, which doesn't exactly raise your spirits. It is, however, well worth the visit, especially for little groups who can enjoy the excellent, yet inexpensive, food and the sea view. The restaurant closes at 10 pm.

Entertainment

The nightlife is fairly limited here. Two of the best places to dance are the *Stone Age Disco* at the Tacloban Village Inn and the *Spacer Disco* on Real St. Right next door, the *Satellite Cocktail Lounge* has a late show, as do the nightclubs *Schooner* and *Andres* nearly two km farther south on Real St.

Getting There and Away

Air PAL has an office at Romualdez Airport (☎ 601, 2212) and on Veterano St (☎ 2213).

Bus Philtranco air-con buses are often booked out when heading for Manila, so it is worthwhile booking a seat at least one day before leaving.

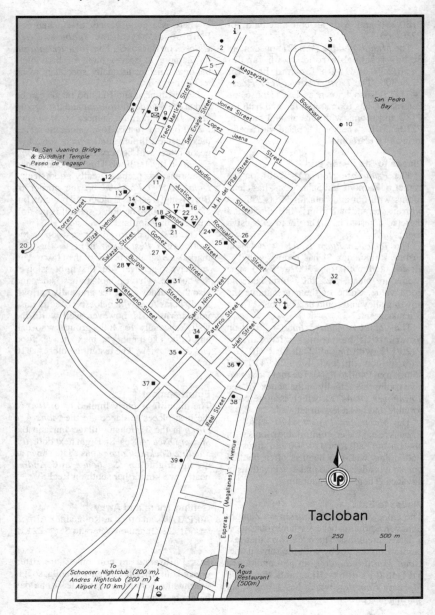

To San Juanico Bridge
& Buddhist Temple
Paseo de Legaspi

San Pedro Bay

To Schooner Nightclub (200 m),
Andres Nightclub (200 m) &
Airport (10 km)

To Agus
Restaurant
(500m)

Tacloban

0   250   500 m

■ PLACES TO STAY

3	Leyte Park Hotel
13	Manhattan Inn
15	Primerose Hotel
16	San Juanico Travel Lodge
18	Traveller's Lodge
21	Manabó Lodge
25	Tacloban Plaza Hotel
29	Tacloban Village Inn
31	Allee Lodge
34	Cecilia's Lodge
37	Leyte State College House

▼ PLACES TO EAT

17	Asiatic Restaurant & Good Morning Restaurant
19	Good Morning Square
21	Blueberry Restaurant
22	Chinatown Restaurant & Savory Steak House
23	Rovic Restaurant
24	Don's Cabin Restaurant & Mandawe Fast Food
27	Good Morning Complex
28	Sunburst Fried Chicken
36	Dahil Sa Iyo Fastfood

OTHER

1	Tourist Office
2	Children's Park
4	Provincial Capitol Building
5	Plaza Libertad
6	Wharf
7	K & T Shipping Lines
8	Post Office
9	William Lines
10	Botanical Garden
11	Sulpicio Lines
12	Market
14	Equitable Bank
20	Stations of the Cross
26	Philippine National Bank (PNB)
30	PAL
32	City Hall
33	Santo Niño Church
35	Divine Word University
38	Satellite Cocktail Lounge & Spacer Disco
39	Santo Niño Shrine & Heritage Museum, People's Center & Library
40	Philtranco Bus Terminal

Getting Around

To/From the Airport It is 11 km from Romualdez Airport to the centre of town. The trip should not cost more than P20 per person by jeepney; going back, the trip should cost a little less.

AROUND TACLOBAN
Sohoton National Park & Basey

Although Sohoton National Park is on the island of Samar, the simplest way to get there is from Tacloban via Basey. It has waterfalls, underground waterways and a labyrinth of **caves**, which are also called 'wonder caves' because of their glittering stone formations. The biggest and most beautiful are Panhulugan I, Bugasan III and Sohoton. A park ranger lives at the entrance to the park and will, on request, guide you through the caves with a kerosene lamp. You can stay overnight with the ranger, but you have to take your own provisions. The best time to see the caves is from March to July, as you can only visit them when the water level is low, not after prolonged rainfall.

Basey is well known for its colourful mats and other woven goods, which are sold in the markets in Tacloban.

Staff at the tourist office in Tacloban should be able to help you arrange some of these trips and they should also know about possible NPA activities in the national park.

Getting There & Away The first jeepney leaves Tacloban for Basey at about 7 am, the second not till 9.30 am, each taking over an hour. A day trip from Basey to the Sohoton National Park is only worthwhile if you arrive early in Basey, as the last jeepney leaves for Tacloban at about 3 pm and then only if there are enough passengers.

A necessary permit can be obtained from Francisco Corales or Arnulito Viojan in Basey, who will also arrange a boat. The permit, which has to be shown at the entrance to the national park, costs P2.50, the rental charge for a kerosene lamp P50, and a guide and boat P500. The guide also expects a small tip.

The beautiful trip upriver to the park takes about 1½ hours.

Palo

A monument and a plaque on Red Beach at Palo commemorate the return of General MacArthur to the Philippines on 20 October 1944 after a major naval battle. He liberated the country from Japanese occupation roughly 2½ years after fleeing from the island fortress of Corregidor in Manila Bay.

Palo Cathedral, built in 1596 with an altar covered in gold leaf, was temporarily converted to a hospital by the Americans in 1944.

Places to Stay The *City Lodge Pension* has rooms with air-con and bath for P350. It's comfortable, clean and you can rent rooms by the hour.

The *MacArthur Park Beach Resort* (☎ 3015, 3016) has rooms with fan and bath for P640/800, with air-con and bath for P920/1150 and suites for P1500. It is pleasant and has a restaurant. You may be able to negotiate the prices.

Getting There & Away Several jeepneys leave Tacloban wharf for Palo daily, but not all make the detour to MacArthur Park (formerly Imelda Park), about 1½ km from the main road.

BILIRAN & MARIPIPI ISLANDS

Until 1992 Biliran Island was a subprovince of Leyte but then became an independent province, with Naval as the capital. The island is connected by bridge with the main island of Leyte. Heading north on the road along the west coast, you can go from Biliran to Naval, Almeria and Kawayan. Another road leads from Biliran along the south coast and the east coast to Caibiran. The densely vegetated interior is mountainous and full of extinct volcanoes that are up to 1200 metres

high. If you want to climb **Biliran Volcano**, the barrio captain in Caibiran will help with the hire of a jeep to take you as high as the camp. It is a little more than an hour to go from the camp to the summit.

The little Agta Beach Resort of Clemencio Sabitsana is about three km north of Almeria on a bay with an average, but clean, palm-fringed beach. Jeepneys from Naval to Kawayan, which is in the north of the island, go through Almeria and pass the resort, taking about 20 minutes. There are only a few a day so you might have a long wait. A tricycle for this relatively short stretch will cost you about P70. It takes about an hour to walk from Almeria to the Agta Beach Resort. In Ca-ucap, near Agta Beach, there is a waterfall, which is unfortunately a bit hard to find.

Once you have made it to Biliran Island, you should make a detour to Maripipi Island. There is no closer point of departure. Because of its out-of-the-way location, about 10 km north of Biliran, this exceptionally beautiful island has so far not been affected very much by civilisation. There is no electricity or telephone, but the hospitable inhabitants seem to be happy with their simple and caring way of life.

This exotic island is dominated by an extinct volcano that is almost 1000 metres high and partly covered in dense jungle. You will find a beautiful white beach with palms and crystal clear water in **Napo Cove**, a relatively isolated beach on the north coast. On the south coast, the women in **Barrio Binalayan** make clay utensils, which are renowned for their good quality, to sell to other islands.

Places to Stay

The *Agta Beach Resort* at Almeria has basic rooms with fan for P75/150, with fan and bath for P100/200 and with air-con and bath for P350. You can eat well at the restaurant there and the cook will try to meet any special orders. Paddleboats for hire cost P20 a day. The resort is popular with day visitors at the weekends.

The *Rosevic Executive Lodge* on

Vicentillo St at Naval has rooms with fan for P100/175, with fan and bath for P200 and with air-con and bath for P300.

Getting There & Away

Bus Buses for Caibiran leave the Ormoc bus terminal by the wharf at 3 and 4 am. You may have to change at Lemon.

There is a daily bus leaving from the wharf at Tacloban for Caibiran between 9 and 11 am. The trip takes five hours.

From Ormoc to Naval there are daily JD buses at 4.30 and 5.30 am. The trip takes over two hours.

From Tacloban wharf there are daily EGV Lines and San Juan Lines buses to Naval or Almeria at 4 and 5 am, noon and 3 pm, taking five hours.

Boat A boat is said to leave daily at 9 am from Carigara, on Leyte, to Biliran. If you miss it, you can spend the night at the unpretentious but clean *Travellers House* on Real St. Singles/doubles cost P30/60 and with fan and bath P100.

SAN ISIDRO

San Isidro is a small community in the north of Leyte, connected by boat to northern Cebu. You can also go to the small island of **Malapascua** from San Isidro (see Getting There & Away at the beginning of this section).

Places to Stay

There are two small, basic places to stay at in San Isidro, as is the case with Calubian, 15 km away. In Calubian, you can also spend the night in the Jesom Bakery for P50.

Getting There & Away

A bus goes from Tacloban to Calubian four times a day, taking two hours. A Special Ride by motorbike from Calubian to San Isidro costs P100.

One bus and some jeepneys leave Ormoc in the early morning for San Isidro, taking 4½ hours.

PALOMPON

Palompon is a coastal town north-west of Ormoc and three hours away by jeepney. Ships go from Palompon to Cebu and Panay. If you follow the road from Palompon northwards along the coast, you will reach Jubay (pronounced 'hu-bye'), where you can get a boat to small Gigantangan Island, which is off the usual routes.

Places to Stay

The *Russell Lodging House* on Rizal St, not far from the pier, has rooms with fan for P90/120 and with air-con and bath for P270/380. This place is simple and fairly tidy.

Getting There & Away

There are several jeepneys from Ormoc to Palompon daily, taking 2½ hours.

ORMOC

This port town is connected to Cebu by ship. The wharf area is always lively, especially in the late afternoons and evenings, when a lot of people meet for a yarn on the wall of the wharf.

On 5 November 1991 Ormoc experienced the blackest day in its history, when the typhoon Uring stormed over Leyte, leaving in its wake massive quantities of water raging down into town from the mountains, taking everything with it that was in its way or couldn't make it to safety. Over 5000 people died from injuries or drowned, while almost 50,000 were made homeless. There is no doubt these floods were made possible by the activities of illegal logging operators who for many years got away scot-free with denuding the slopes, leaving them stony and barren as a result.

South-west of Ormoc are the **Camotes Islands**, which belong to Cebu Province and can be reached by outrigger boat in about three hours. If you want to go somewhere quiet, try **Tudela** and **Poro** on Poro Island.

In Tungonan, a little north of Ormoc, is a hot spring that is being developed to provide geothermal energy and make Leyte less dependent on energy imports. The steam from the spring has damaged the surrounding vegetation, making it look spooky. If you want to visit the geothermal project, you need a permit which you have to apply for in writing two weeks beforehand to the Project Manager at the following address: PNOC EDC Geothermal Project, Tungonan, Ormoc City.

North-east of Ormoc City is **Leyte National Park**, the northern beginning of the Leyte Nature Trail, which is about 50 km long, and leads through mountainous Central Leyte, connecting Danao and Mahagnao

lakes. Because of the chance of NPA activities in this area, the tourist office in Tacloban advises against a stay in the national park at present.

Places to Stay

The *Pongos Hotel* (☎ 2211, 2482) on Bonifacio St has rooms with fan and bath for P150/280, with air-con and bath for P250/360 and suites for P500. This hotel also runs *Pongos Lodging House* which has basic, clean rooms with fan for P80.

The best hotel in Ormoc is the *Don Felipe*

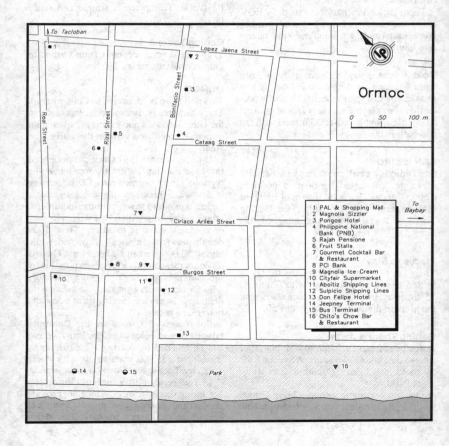

Ormoc

0   50   100 m

To Baybay

1 PAL & Shopping Mall
2 Magnolia Sizzler
3 Pongos Hotel
4 Philippine National Bank (PNB)
5 Rajah Pensione
6 Fruit Stalls
7 Gourmet Cocktail Bar & Restaurant
8 PCI Bank
9 Magnolia Ice Cream
10 Cityfair Supermarket
11 Aboitiz Shipping Lines
12 Sulpicio Shipping Lines
13 Don Felipe Hotel
14 Jeepney Terminal
15 Bus Terminal
16 Chito's Chow Bar & Restaurant

To Tacloban

Lopez Jaena Street

Bonifacio Street

Real Street

Rizal Street

Cataag Street

Ciriaco Ariles Street

Burgos Street

Park

Hotel (☎ 2460, 2007; fax 2160) on Bonifacio St, beside the wharf. It has rooms with fan and bath for P130/200, singles with air-con and bath from P320 to P675, doubles with air-con and bath from P385 to P795, and suites from P400 to P1230. The cheapest rooms are in the annex. This place is clean and good value, and there is a restaurant.

Places to Eat

Chito's Chow Bar & Restaurant on the harbour promenade is airy and open and a good place to sit. It offers a fine selection of inexpensive dishes. The *Don Felipe Hotel Restaurant* on Bonifacio St and the *Magnolia Sizzler* on the corner of Bonifacio and Lopez Jaena Sts can both be recommended. The *Gourmet Cocktail Bar & Restaurant* on Ciriaco Ariles St serves good seafood.

Getting There & Away

Buses for Ormoc leave Tacloban wharf daily from 4 am until the early afternoon. The trip takes three hours. A JD express bus leaves at 3 pm from the corner of Veterano and Santo Nino Sts, opposite the Divine Word University.

Buses for Ormoc leave Naval on Biliran Island at 8 am, noon and 3 pm, taking three hours.

After the arrival of the boat from Maya on Cebu, a bus leaves San Isidro around noon for Ormoc. The trip takes 4½ hours.

The first bus leaves Ormoc for Tacloban from the wharf immediately after the ship from Cebu arrives.

BAYBAY

Ships go from Baybay to Cebu and other islands. With mountains in the background and an old Spanish church dominating the town, it makes a most attractive picture seen at dawn from a ship just arriving in port.

About seven km north of Baybay is the modern Visayan State College of Agriculture (VISCA) which was financed by the World Bank. This is a surprisingly clean, well-looked after establishment. If they have rooms available, travellers can spend the night in the guesthouse called the Visca Hostel.

Places to Stay

Ellean's Lodge is an unpretentious place with rooms for P70/110 and with fan for P100/150. The *Vista Hostel* has comfortable rooms with fan and bath for P280/450.

The small *Enzian Beach Resort* is in Caridad, about 18 km north of Baybay. Rooms with fan and bath are P700. Full board is possible. There is a restaurant which serves Swiss and Filipino cuisine, and there is a swimming pool.

Getting There & Away

Several buses go from Tacloban wharf to Baybay daily, taking 2½ hours.

BATO & HILONGOS

Bato is a small port between Baybay and Maasin with sea links to Cebu and Bohol. Ships also leave for Cebu from Hilongos, a little north of Bato, where there is a tall belfry dating from the Spanish conquest. It costs P2 to go by tricycle from Bato to Hilongos.

Places to Stay

The *Green House Lodging* on Rizal St at Bato is a simple place with rooms for P50/100 and with fan for P70/140.

Getting There & Away

Several buses go from Tacloban wharf to Bato daily, taking three hours.

From Ormoc to Bato, the first bus leaves at 6 am. There are several buses daily, taking three hours.

MAASIN

Maasin is the capital of Southern Leyte Province. There are connections by ship from here to Bohol, Cebu and Mindanao.

Places to Stay

The *Sky View Lodging House* on Garces St has rooms with fan for P50/100. It is basic, clean and relatively good value.

The *Verano Pension House* at Matahan has tidy, pleasantly furnished rooms with fan for P120/150. There is a family-style atmosphere, and breakfast will be prepared on request. It is about 10 minutes by tricycle from Maasin.

Places to Eat
The *Valtenian Restaurant* and the *Avenue Restaurant* on Tunga-Tunga St, Maasin's main street, both have good Filipino food, the former with live music in the evenings.

Getting There & Away
Several buses leave the Tacloban wharf for Maasin, taking over three hours for the trip. The last bus leaves Maasin for Tacloban around 1 pm.

LILOAN & LIMASAWA ISLAND
Liloan is at the northern tip of Panaon Island in the south of Leyte. The waters there are good for diving and snorkelling. A ferry service operates between Liloan and Surigao in north-east Mindanao.

About 20 km west of Panaon Island you will find Limasawa Island, a somewhat remote island where motorised transport of any kind is banned and bicycles are the best means of getting around. On 29 March 1521 Ferdinand Magellan landed on Limasawa after setting foot for the first time on the Philippines on the island of Homonhon, to the east of Leyte.

Places to Stay
The *C & S Lodge* has good, simple rooms for P50/100. The comfortable *Liloan Hillside Lodge* behind the ferry terminal has rooms for P60/120.

Places to Eat
The *Annie & Boys Carenderia* on Quezon St offers tasty, cheap food.

Getting There & Away
There are several buses daily from Tacloban to Liloan, leaving from the wharf. The trip takes three hours and over four hours via Maasin.

Negros

Lying between Cebu and Panay in the south-west of the Visayas, Negros consists of the provinces of Negros Occidental and Negros Oriental, which are separated by mountain chains in the centre of the island. The south takes its character from the extended Tablas plateau and the wide plains west of an imaginary line from Ilog to Cadiz.

Negros is the sugar island of the Philippines. Around 450,000 hectares, or more than half of the total land area, is used for the production of sugar. About 60% of the total sugar production of the country comes from here. There are big sugar-cane plantations and refineries in Victorias and Binalbagan.

Sugar exportation began in the middle of the 19th century, when the production of the first plantations were shipped to Japan, China, Australia, the UK, Canada and the USA. From then on it brought great wealth and political power to the few sugar barons living on their haciendas. During the years of the sugar boom the seasonally employed field workers were at least able to earn enough to support their families. This irresponsible system of exploitation and social indifference existed until 1985, when the world market price of sugar fell so drastically that it wasn't even worth cutting the cane.

Negros, with its single product economy, was economically at rock bottom. About a quarter of a million Sacada (the name of the plantation workers) were out of work. Because of the absence of any government relief programme and the unwillingness of most *hacienderos* to make some land available for grain planting by their needy workers, many desperate Negrenses took to the mountains to join the antigovernment NPA in its underground fighting.

If government figures are to be believed, conditions on Negros have improved with rising sugar prices since 1988. An important part in this improvement is due to the new extensive prawn culture (Black Tiger Prawn, *Penaeus monodon*) and the successful

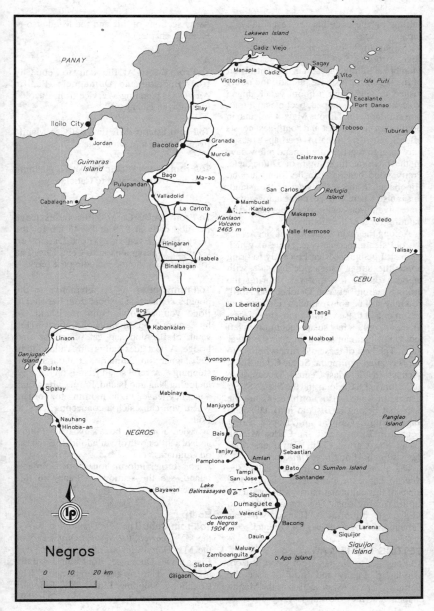

PANAY

Lakawan Island

Cadiz Viejo

Manapla Cadiz Sagay Vito

Victorias Isla Puti

Silay Escalante
Port Danao

Iloilo City Toboso Tuburan

Jordan Granada

Guimaras
Island Bacolod Murcia Calatrava

Bago Ma-ao

Pulupandan San Carlos Refugio
Island

Cabalagnan Valladolid Mambucal
Kanlaon

La Carlota Kanlaon Makapso
Volcano
2465 m Valle Hermoso Toledo

Hinigaran Talisay

Binalbagan Isabela CEBU

Guihulngan

Ilog La Libertad Tangil

Kabankalan Jimalalud Moalboal

Linaon

Ayongon

Danjugan
Island Bulata Bindoy Panglao
Island

Sipalay Mabinay

Manjuyod

Nauhang
Hinoba-an NEGROS

Bais

Tanjay San
Sebastian

Pamplona Amlan

Tampi Bato Sumilon Island

San Jose Santander

Bayawan Lake
Balinsasayao Sibulan

Dumaguete

Cuernos
de Negros Valencia
1904 m Bacong Larena

Dauin Siquijor

Maluay Siquijor
Island

Negros Zamboanguita Apo Island

Siaton

0 10 20 km Giligaon

selling of these delicacies, especially to Japan.

'Sugarland', of course, also aims to develop tourism, but leisure facilities like the Mambucal Summer Resort in the central part of the island for instance, are still too rarely visited to talk about a boom yet. Kanlaon Volcano may, it is hoped, become an attraction similar to the famous Mayon Volcano in South Luzon. The east and south-east coasts offer Spanish-style charm – perhaps a reason why foreign tourists often spend a few days in the pleasant little town of Dumaguete. Pretty good beaches can be found around Hinoba-an in the south-west of the island; this is also where you will come across inveterate adventurers seeking their pot of gold by panning for it in the mountains.

Among the main attractions of Negros are the old steam locomotives, some of which were still being used until recently to bring home the sugar cane, side by side with modern diesel locomotives. During the milling season between October and April, you may still be able to hitch a ride for a few km on one of these working museum pieces. There are only a few steam locomotives left today, but you can see them near the sugar mills. The best of these old-timers belong to the Hawaiian-Philippine Sugar Co in Silay; Vicmico in Victorias; Central Azucarera de la Carlota in La Carlota; and the Ma-ao Sugar Central in Bago. Also worth seeing are the ones that belong to Biscom in Binalbagan; Sagay Sugar Central and Lopez Sugar Central in Toboso; and San Carlos Milling Co in San Carlos. Colin Carraf describes them all in his book *Iron Dinosaurs*.

The aborigines of Negros are called the Negrito, hence the name of the island. Some tribes of this cultural minority still live in the mountain regions. The main dialect in Negros Occidental is Ilongo, whereas Cebuano is spoken in Negros Oriental.

GETTING THERE & AWAY

You can get to Negros from Cebu, Luzon, Mindanao, Panay and Siquijor (see the Getting There & Away section of the Manila chapter and the relevant Getting There &

Away sections of this and the Mindanao & Palawan chapter).

Air

To/From Cebu PAL flies daily to Cebu City from Bacolod and Dumaguete. Pacific Airways is planning a service from Bacolod to Bantayan Island.

To/From Luzon PAL flies daily to Manila from Bacolod and Dumaguete.

To/From Panay Pacific Airways is planning a service from Bacolod to Caticlan.

Bus

To/From Cebu Ceres Liner buses leave Bacolod daily at 8, 9 and 9.45 am for the ferry from Escalante (Port Danao) to Carmelo/Tuburan and on to Cebu City. The trip takes eight hours, including the ferry.

To/From Panay As an alternative to the popular connection by boat from Bacolod to Iloilo, you can go via Guimaras Island. Go by jeepney or bus to Valladolid, about 30 km south of Bacolod and get off at the first bridge. A boat goes daily from Valladolid to Cabalagnan, on Guimaras, at about 11 am, stopping at several small islands on the way, including Nagarao Island. From Cabalagnan a jeepney leaves in the morning for Jordan, where you can catch a connecting ferry to Iloilo.

Twice a week a boat sails from Pulupandan, a little north of Valladolid, to Suclaran on Guimaras.

For further information about Guimaras Island, see the section on Panay in this chapter.

Boat

To/From Cebu The MV *Dumaguete Ferry*, the MV *Georich*, the MV *Palauan Ferry* or the MV *Don Victorino* of George & Peter Lines leaves Dumaguete for Cebu City daily at 10 pm. The trip takes eight hours. The Cokaliong Shipping Lines' MV *Filipinas Dumaguete* leaves on Tuesday, Thursday,

Saturday and Sunday at midnight, taking six hours.

From Tampi to Bato, a ferry runs several times a day. The last departure is at about 3.30 pm and the trip takes 45 minutes. The boat from San Jose may also go to Talisay. Jeepneys and minibuses run from Real St, on the corner of Locsin St, in Dumaguete, to the wharf. ABC Liner air-con buses meet the 6, 8 and 10.30 am and 1.30 pm boats for Bato and leave immediately for Cebu City, taking three hours.

From Sibulan to Liloan, a big outrigger boat leaves daily approximately every 30 minutes. The last departure is at about 3 pm. The trip takes 20 minutes.

From Guihulngan for Tangil, a boat leaves daily at 6.30 and 8 am, taking two hours. The connection from Tangil to Moalboal is better than the one from Toledo to Moalboal.

From San Carlos to Toledo, a ferry leaves daily at 5.30 am and 1.30 pm, and on Sunday usually at 10.30 am, taking 1¾ hours. The departure times may be different on holidays. On Maundy Thursday there may only be one boat and on Good Friday there are none. The times of departure are liable to change. For reliable information ask at the wharf rather than the trishaw drivers in town.

From Cadiz on the north coast of Negros to Bantayan town on Bantayan Island in northern Cebu, a big outrigger boat leaves daily at 11 am, taking 3½ hours. The river port in Cadiz is several km long and the boat for Bantayan anchors in the Reclamation Area, near the Hitalon Bridge, where you have to get off the jeepney or bus.

To/From Luzon To go from Bacolod to Manila, you can take several Negros Navigation Lines' ships. The MV *Don Claudio* leaves on Monday at 4 pm, taking 22 hours; the MV *Don Julio* leaves on Wednesday at 4 pm, taking 21 hours; the MV *Princess of Negros* leaves on Thursday at 11 am and on Sunday at 9 pm, taking 23 hours; and the MV *Santa Florentina* leaves on Friday at 6 pm, taking 24 hours.

The MV *Doña Virginia* of William Lines leaves Dumaguete for Manila on Thursday at 8 am, taking 23 hours.

To/From Mindanao The MV *Doña Virginia* of William Lines leaves Dumaguete for Cagayan de Oro on Wednesday at 8 am, taking six hours.

The MV *Dumaguete Ferry*, the MV *Georich*, the MV *Palauan Ferry* or the MV *Don Victorino* of George & Peter Lines leaves Dumaguete for Dapitan daily at 8 am. The trip takes four hours and continues on to Zamboanga. The MV *Filipinas Dumaguete* of Cokaliong Shipping Lines leaves Dumaguete for Dapitan on Tuesday, Thursday and Saturday at 7 am, taking four hours.

To/From Panay The MV *Don Vicente* and the MV *Santa Maria* of Negros Navigation Lines sail from Bacolod to Iloilo from Monday to Thursday and Saturday at 7 and 10 am and 3 pm, and on Friday and Sunday at 8 and 11 am and 4 pm. The trip takes two hours. Warning: these times are subject to change. Tickets are on sale at the wharf; the queue can take up to 30 minutes.

Banago Wharf is about seven km north of Bacolod. To go there, a jeepney takes about 30 minutes and costs P7, and a PU-Cab costs about P40.

From Da-an Banwa, the port of Victorias, the MV *Queen Rose* or the MV *Princess Jo* leaves daily between 9 and 11 am for Culasi, and the MV *Seven Seas* or the MV *San Vicente* leaves daily between 9 and 11 am for Malayu-an, both near Ajuy on the east coast of Panay, taking two hours.

To/From Romblon The Negros Navigation Lines' MV *Santa Maria* leaves Bacolod for Romblon on Saturday at 6 pm, taking 11 hours.

To/From Siquijor A big outrigger boat leaves Dumaguete for Cangalwang or Larena daily at 6 and 10 am, taking 2½ hours. For safety reasons, this trip is not recommended in bad weather.

The MV *Catherine* leaves Dumaguete daily for Siquijor at 2 pm, taking three hours.

A tricycle from Siquijor to Larena costs about P5 per person.

BACOLOD

The capital of Negros Occidental province, Bacolod has about 300,000 inhabitants and is the sugar capital of the Philippines. The name Bacolod is derived from the word *buklod*, or hill, which refers to a rise on which the town's first church stood.

Information

The helpful tourist office (☎ 29021) is in the city plaza. The main office of the Philippine National Bank on Lacson St (near the Capitol Provincial Building) changes travellers' cheques. The Interbank on Lacson St changes American Express travellers' cheques.

Things to See

Next to the old **San Sebastian Cathedral** is the **Bacolod City Plaza**, with benches under shady trees, where cultural events are often held on Sunday afternoons and special occasions.

Bacolod is a leading producer of ceramics in the Philippines. Most of the workshops, such as **NLS Ceramics** and **Bilbao Ceramics**, are on the edge of town. Only **MDS Ceramics** at 26 Rosario St has a central location.

You can take quite a few interesting day trips from Bacolod. Lovers of old locomotives especially will not be disappointed.

Festivals

Every year in October or November Bacolod boisterously celebrates the MassKara Festival. (See also the section on Fiestas &

■ PLACES TO STAY		28	Mira's Café
		30	Ang Sinugba Restaurant
1	L'Fisher Hotel	36	Cactus Room Restaurant
2	Pension Bacolod	37	Sugbahan Restaurant
9	Las Rocas Hotel	38	Alavar's Sea Foods House
15	Downtown Lodge		
16	Bascon Hotel		OTHER
17	Hotel Best Inn		
21	Sea Breeze Hotel	3	Ceres Liner Bus Terminal
29	Halili Inn	4	Philippine National Bank (PNB)
31	Deja-vu Lodge	5	Interbank
35	Ester Pension	6	Northern Bus Terminal
36	The Family Pension House	7	Provincial Capital Building
		10	San Sebastian Cathedral
▼ PLACES TO EAT		14	Tourist Office & City Plaza
		17	Bakery
1	Café Marinero	18	Market
8	The Basement	19	Philippine National Bank (PNB)
11	Manokan Country	20	Shopping Center
12	Reming's & Sons Restaurant	21	Spectrum Disco
13	Tita's Food Center	24	Gaisano Department Store
17	Kong Kee Diner &	25	City Hall
	Batchoy Restaurants	27	Post Office
20	Fantasy Food	31	Deja-vu Disco
22	Coney Island Ice Cream	32	Jeepneys to Mambucal
23	Nena's Chicken Barbecue	33	Southern Bus Terminal
24	Gaisano Food Plaza	34	Sports Complex
26	Barrio Fiesta Restaurant		

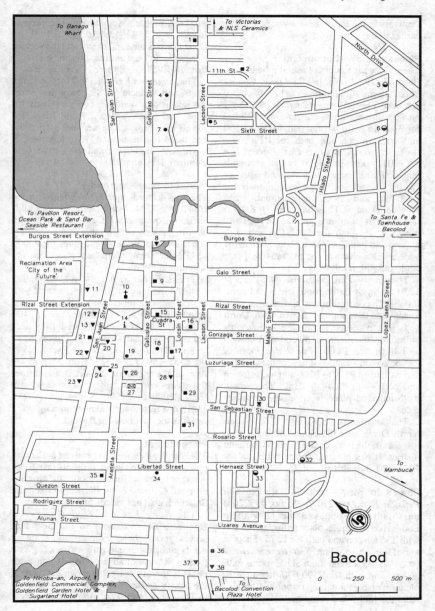

To Banago Wharf

To Victorias & NLS Ceramics

North Drive

San Juan Street

Galusao Street

1

11th St 2

Lacson Street

4

3

5

6

Sixth Street

Hilado Street

7

To Pavillon Resort, Ocean Park & Sand Bar Seaside Restaurant

To Santa Fe & Townhouse Bacolod

Burgos Street Extension

Burgos Street

8

Galo Street

Reclamation Area 'City of the Future'

9

Lopez Jaena Street

Rizal Street Extension

10

11

Rizal Street

Mabini Street

12

13

14

15

Cuadra St

Lacson Street

16

San Juan Street

Gonzaga Street

21

20

18

19

Galusao Street

Locsin Street

17

Luzuriaga Street

22

23

24

25

26

28

29

30

San Sebastian Street

27

31

Rosario Street

32

To Mambucal

35

Libertad Street

34

(Hernaez Street)

33

Quezon Street

Rodriguez Street

Alunan Street

Lizares Avenue

Bacolod

36

0   250   500 m

37

38

To Hinoba-an, Airport, Goldenfield Commercial Complex, Goldenfield Garden Hotel & Sugarland Hotel

To Bacolod Convention Plaza Hotel

Festivals in the Facts for the Visitor chapter earlier in this book.)

Places to Stay – bottom end

There is a wide variety of accommodation in Bacolod. The *Downtown Lodge* on Cuadra St has rooms with fan for P60/120. It's basic and fairly clean. *Pension Bacolod* (☎ 23883) on 11th St has simple, clean rooms with fan for P70/115, with fan and bath for P140/160 and with air-con and bath for P290, and there is a restaurant. *Las Rocas Inn* (☎ 27011) on Gatuslao St has singles with fan for P100, rooms with fan and bath for P180/240 and with air-con and bath for P330/390, and there is a restaurant. It has seen better days. The *Halili Inn* (☎ 81548) on Locsin St has rooms with fan for P75/100, with fan and bath for P120/170 and with air-con and bath for P340. There are narrow beds in the cheaper rooms and the place could do with renovating.

The *Family Pension House* (☎ 81211) at 123 Lacson St Extension is clean and comfortable, has a restaurant and is in a quiet location on the southern edge of town. Dorm beds in fan-cooled rooms are P75, rooms with fan and bath are P150 and with air-con and bath are P200. The *Ester Pension* (☎ 23526) on Araneta St has rooms with fan and bath from P120 to P200 and with air-con and bath from P220 to P350. This small, well-managed place is clean and comfortable.

The *Townhouse Bacolod* (☎ 81552) is on North Drive near the corner of Burgos St, just east of the town centre in the Villamonte district. It has pleasant rooms with fan for P120/170 and with air-con for P220/270.

Places to Stay – middle

The *Bacolod Pension Plaza* (☎ 27076-79; fax 4332203) on Cuadra St, opposite the Downtown Lodge, is a new, quiet place with clean rooms with TV, air-con and bath for P575. There is a coffee shop. The *Sea Breeze Hotel* (☎ 24571-75) on San Juan St has rooms with air-con and bath for P590/690. It's a clean, pleasant place, though you wouldn't think so from the lobby and restaurant. Warm water

can be a problem sometimes. The *Bascon Hotel* (☎ 23141-43; fax 4331393) on Gonzaga St is nice and clean, and the service is friendly. Rooms with air-con and bath cost from P450/540, and there is a restaurant.

The *Sugarland Hotel* (☎ 22462-69; fax 28367) on Araneta St, Singcang, has comfortable rooms with air-con and bath for P885, and suites with a TV and fridge for P1180 and P1320. The service is friendly, and there is a restaurant. It is just outside town, near the airport and the Goldenfield Commercial Complex.

Places to Stay – top end

The well-looked after *Goldenfield Garden Hotel* (☎ 83541; fax 22356), in the Goldenfield Commercial Complex, near the airport, has very comfortable rooms with air-con and bath for P1200 and suites for P2000 and P2400. There is a restaurant, a disco and a swimming pool.

The *L'Fisher Hotel* (☎ 82731-39; fax 4330951) on Lacson St, on the corner of 14th St, has pleasant rooms with TV, air-con and bath for P1650/2050 and suites from P3400 to P5450. This is an elegant, tastefully decorated hotel in the northern part of town.

The *Bacolod Convention Plaza Hotel* (☎ 83551-59; fax 83392) on Magsaysay Ave, on the corner of Lacson St, has attractive rooms with TV, fridge, air-con and bath from P2000 to P2500. Suites are P3600. There is a restaurant and a swimming pool, and it is the best hotel in Bacolod.

Places to Eat

The *Reming's & Sons Restaurant* in the city plaza serves very good Filipino fast food. Another favourite for fast food is the air-conditioned *Gaisano Food Plaza* on Luzuriaga St, which also has videos and live music.

The *Kong Kee Diners & Bakery* on Bonifacio St, next door to the Best Inn, serves good, cheap Filipino and Chinese meals and fresh bread rolls. *Mira's Café* on Locsin St serves native coffee. If you want cakes with your coffee, you can get them at the bakery on the corner.

The clean, well-kept *Ang Sinugba Res-*

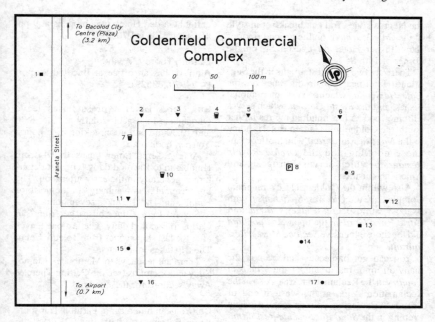

To Bacolod City Centre (Plaza) (3.2 km)

Goldenfield Commercial Complex

0   50   100 m

Araneta Street

To Airport (0.7 km)

■   PLACES TO STAY

1   Sugarland Hotel
13   Goldenfield Garden Hotel

▼   PLACES TO EAT

2   Alice Log Cabin &
     Popeye's Ice Cream Parlour
3   Nova Park Restaurant &
     Old West Steakhouse
5   Franky's Restaurant
6   Carlo Pizza Garden
11   Shakey's Pizza
12   Seafood Market Restaurant

13   Nagoya Restaurant &
      Orchid Royale Restaurant
16   Senyang Restaurant

      OTHER

4   Alfonso Pub & Disco 2000
7   Square Circle Pub
8   Car Park
9   Cinema
10   Negros Hot Spot
14   Foodland
15   Casino
17   Super Bowling Lanes

---

taurant on San Sebastian St is well known for its superb seafood. In the cosy *Cactus Room Restaurant*, at the Family Pension House on Lactos St Extension, you will find a wide choice of cheap steaks. Nearby is the Bacolod branch of the popular *Alavar's Sea*

Foods House with excellent dishes in the Zamboanga style.

The *Basement* on Gatuslao St at the corner of Burgos St is known for its pleasant atmosphere, its wide variety of good steaks and its expertly prepared Filipino dishes, cooked in the Negros style. You can breakfast in style at the *Café Marinero* on the ground floor of the L'Fisher Hotel on Lacson St, on the corner of 14th St.

There are two good restaurants in the Sugarland Hotel near the airport. They are the *Café Hacienda*, which serves international dishes, and the *Fiesta Garden*, which serves Filipino food. A few hundred metres farther south, the Goldenfield Garden Hotel is home to the *Nagoya Restaurant* which offers Japanese cooking and the *Orchid Royale Restaurant* which serves European and American cuisine.

Also within the Goldenfield Commercial Complex are the *Old West Steakhouse*, with its cosy atmosphere, *Shakey's Pizza* and *Carlo Pizza Garden*, the open-air *Foodland* and the more expensive *Seafood Market Restaurant*.

You can get barbecues and beer at the many all-night restaurants at the *Manokan Country* in the Reclamation Area. Also in the Reclamation Area, at the western end of Burgos St Extension, you can spend a breezy evening in the *Sand Bar Seaside Restaurant* and the *Pavillion Resort Restaurant*. Make sure a taxi will pick you up afterwards as there is almost no transport back to the city at night.

Entertainment

The pleasant *Ang Sinugba Restaurant* on San Sebastian St entertains its guests with folk music every evening until midnight. The *Spectrum Disco* downstairs on the Sea Breeze Hotel seems to have missed the boat on every trend going and is not very inviting. The *Deja-vu Disco* on Locsin St has live bands from 9 pm. Go-Go girls keep the audience interest level up during the breaks in the live music.

Among the most popular in the Goldenfield Commercial Complex are *Disco 2000* and the big *Negros Hot Spot* with live music nightly and a cheery atmosphere. Within the complex, there are also entertainment venues like the *Casino*, the 40-lane *Super Bowling Lanes*, the biggest in the Visayas, and the *Quorum Disco* in the Gold-

enfield Garden Hotel, which opens at 9 pm and admission is P70.

Getting There & Away

Air PAL has an office at Bacolod Airport (☎ 24929, 83529).

Bus Ceres Liner express buses leave Dumaguete for Bacolod daily at 6.45, 8.30 and 10.30 am and noon, taking nine hours. You can book seats.

A few Ceres Liner buses travel from Hinoba-an to Bacolod daily. The last departure is generally in the early afternoon. The bus terminal is in Nauhang, a little north of Hinoba-an. The trip takes seven hours.

Several Ceres Liner buses go from San Carlos to Bacolod daily. The last one leaves after the last ship arrives from Toledo, Cebu. The trip takes four hours.

There are jeepneys to Mambucal, Ma-ao, Silay and Victorias (see the Getting There & Away sections for these towns).

Car You can hire a car at Parmon Transportation & Tours (☎ 29593; fax 23222) at the USB Building on 6th St. They have branches at the Bacolod Convention Plaza Hotel, Goldenfield Garden Hotel and L'Fisher Hotel.

Getting Around

To/From the Airport Bacolod's airport is about five km south of the city. On leaving the terminal, turn left to go towards the city. You can stop a passing jeepney, as they all go to the city plaza.

A PU-Cab from the airport to the city centre should cost no more than P30, but it is best to agree on a price with the driver beforehand.

Bus Buses from Dumaguete and San Carlos arrive at the Northern Bus Terminal or in the Ceres Liner Bus Terminal about 200 metres farther on. Jeepneys marked 'Libertad' leave both bus terminals for the city centre and cost P2. In the other direction the destination is marked 'Shopping'. A PU-Cab from the bus terminal to the city centre should cost no more than P15.

Boat Banago Wharf is about seven km north of the city. A jeepney will cost you P7 and a PU-Cab about P40, but determine the price first.

MAMBUCAL

With its hot sulphur springs, Mambucal is the best known resort on Negros, yet it's not overcrowded. The **Summer Resort** has swimming pools, waterfalls and accommodation. You can't go from Mambucal across the island to the east coast as, in the central area of Negros, all roads end at the Kanlaon massif.

It's about five km from the edge of town to **Mt Kanlaon National Park**. If you want to climb Kanlaon, you need to allow three to four days for the round trip. Edwin Gatia of the tourist office in Bacolod can organise guides from the Negros Mountaineering Club (☎ 23807, 21839). An excellent guide, he advises those who intend to climb the volcano or visit the national park for birdwatching or other activities to inform the club for coordination and safety purposes. An organised tour for two people will cost P3500 (via Mambucal) or P2500 (via La Carlota).

You can also find knowledgeable guides on your own in Mambucal, such as Chris Garzon, who will also provide a tent and cooker.

Places to Stay

The *Pagoda Inn* has rooms for P70. It is simple and pleasant, even if the showers are on the other side of the road. The food is tasty, especially the chicken with vegetables, and grandma brews an excellent native coffee.

The *Mambucal Health Resort* has rooms from P50/80 and with bath from P80/140, and also has a swimming pool.

Getting There & Away

Several jeepneys go from Bacolod to Mambucal daily, leaving from Libertad St.

The trip takes one hour, but the morning trip from Mambucal to Bacolod can take up to two hours because of the many stops. The last jeepney back leaves at about 5 pm.

MA-AO

The sugar-cane fields of Ma-ao stretch to the foot of the Kanlaon Volcano, crisscrossed by about 280 km of railway tracks. Just as exciting as the bridges that cross the rivers and ravines are the old steam locomotives, which were used until recently for harvesting.

These old-timers were recently pensioned off and pushed on to the 'old-timer tracks' of the **Ma-ao Sugar Central (MSC)**, where they are open to inspection. There are two American Locomotive Company (Alco) 2-6-0s: one is the TS 1-3, dated 1921, and the other is the BM 5, dated 1924.

Getting There & Away

Several jeepneys go from Libertad St in Bacolod to Ma-ao daily, taking one hour. The last trip back is at 4 or 5 pm.

SILAY

A little outside Silay is the **Hawaiian-Philippine Sugar Company**, one of the largest plantations on Negros, which has a rail network that is about 180 km long.

Nicknamed 'Red Dragons', the steam engines used here are in excellent condition. The name goes back to the time when they were bright red, but today they are blueblack in colour. In WW II, most of them were hidden from the Japanese by being run on special rails into the wooded mountains. They include a 1920 Henschel 0-6-0 and six Baldwin 0-6-0s built in 1919, 1920 and 1928. Please check at the tourist office in Bacolod whether it is still possible to inspect the locomotive, and if so, at what times.

Getting There & Away

Several jeepneys leave from Lacson St, on the corner of Libertad St, in Bacolod for Silay daily, taking 30 minutes. Buses and jeepneys from the Northern Bus Terminal also go through Silay.

Jeepneys leave from the market in Silay to

go to the Hawaiian-Philippine Sugar Company.

VICTORIAS

The Victorias Milling Company, **Vicmico**, is open for inspection from Tuesday to Friday. It's part of a large industrial complex where sugar is processed in several stages for the consumer. Guided tours start at the porter's lodge, which is at the main entrance, where the jeepneys from Victorias stop. Men wearing shorts and women wearing shorts or miniskirts will be refused admission. Sandals and thongs (flip-flops) are not permitted for safety reasons.

Vicmico's 349-km railway track is the longest on Negros and possibly the longest two-foot gauge track in the world. As with the Hawaiian-Philippine Sugar Company on Silay, the diesel and steam locomotives are directed by radio remote control from a central point, but the dark-green old-timers are now used only during the peak season from January to February. The rolling stock includes eight Henschel 0-8-0Ts, dating back to 1926 to 1928, and two Bagnall 0-4-4Ts, which were built for the Kowloon (Hong Kong) to Canton Line in China.

Apart from the sugar mill, the **St Joseph the Worker Chapel** is worth seeing. The unusual coloured mural showing an angry Filipino Jesus, the 'Angry Christ' has received international attention after an article about it appeared in *Life* magazine.

Getting There & Away

Several jeepneys and buses run from the Bacolod Northern Bus Terminal to Victorias daily, taking one hour. Several jeepneys marked 'VMC' go daily from Victorias to the Vicmico sugar mill, taking 15 minutes.

LAKAWON ISLAND

Just over two nautical miles from the north coast of Negros lies the delightful little island of Lakawon. The actual name is Ilacaon, but it is pronounced Lakawon, and the locals only know it under this name. The island is in the shape of a banana and is just under one km long and 100 metres wide. It is only two metres high and forms the tip of an extensive reef which for a short time at full moon and new moon is almost completely exposed to the elements.

Nature has provided Lakawon with a gorgeous white beach consisting of coarse coral sand, and the island is covered with palm trees and in places dense bushes. There is a picturesque village on the west side of the island which is home to some friendly fishermen. Lakawon Island is popular at the weekends with day trippers.

Places to Stay

The *Lakawon Island Resort* has cottages with bath for P400. The huts are basic, but acceptable. Tents can be hired for P200. The restaurant's menu varies according to the local fishermen's catch for the day. The Sales & Booking Office, Casa de Amigo II (☎ 21641, 26029) on Libertad St, Bacolod, is the place to go to find out the availability of beds and their cost.

Getting There & Away

Take a bus from the Northern Bus Terminal in Bacolod in the direction of Cadiz or San Carlos. Get off at the Caltex petrol station in Cadua-an, a few km after Manapla (you definitely have to ask the bus driver to drop you there, because the place is hardly recognisable from the road). The trip takes one hour. Carry on from there by tricycle to the little coastal town of Cadiz Viejo. It takes about 15 minutes to get there, and the fare is P40, or P7 per person. The 15-minute trip over to the island by boat shouldn't cost more than P200.

SAN CARLOS

There is a shipping service between San Carlos and Toledo, Cebu. The offshore **Sipaway Island** (or Refugio Island) is supposed to have a few beautiful beaches and walking tracks. There are several Sari-Sari stores, but their stock is limited, so it's advisable to bring your own provisions from San Carlos.

Places to Stay
Van's Lodging House (☎ 2704) on Carmona St, near the wharf, is basic with rooms for P40/80.

The *Coco Grove Hotel* (☎ 2560) on Ylagan St, about 150 metres from the Ceres Liner Bus Terminal has rooms with fan for P150/250, with fan and bath for P280/380, and with air-con and bath for P680/750. The hotel has a restaurant and is quiet and fairly clean, although a bit on the shabby side.

Getting There & Away
Several Ceres Liner express buses leave the Northern Bus Terminal at Bacolod for San Carlos daily, some going on to Dumaguete, taking 3½ hours.

From Dumaguete there are Ceres Liner express buses going to Bacolod via San Carlos, leaving daily at 6.45, 8.30 and 10.30 am and at noon. The trip takes four hours.

DUMAGUETE
Dumaguete is a pleasant town with well-tended little park areas and what must be the cleanest market in the Philippines. It's the capital of Negros Oriental Province and also a university town. **Silliman University**, whose extensive campus is on the northern edge of town, is the only Protestant university in the Philippines and was named after its founder, Dr Horace B Silliman. It has a small anthropological museum and a post office. For further information about the university, ask at the administration building.

Silliman Beach is not good for swimming and is also in a flight path, but members of the nearby marine laboratory run diving courses there twice a year. They also use a boat that you can charter for diving excursions. Favourite destinations are South Cebu, Sumilon Island and Apo Island, south of Dumaguete.

About 150 metres from the Panorama House & Beach Resort (see Places to Stay in this section) you will find the International Dive Center (☎ & fax 87121), which offers diving courses and dive trips. There is also a golf course not far from Panorama House where you can have reasonably priced golf lessons.

Every year between 21 and 25 January, Dumaguete celebrates Negros Oriental Founder's Day. The folkloric dances in the Aquino Freedom Park are among the best of the many attractions of this important festival.

Information
The Equitable bank on the corner of Perdices and San Juan Sts will give you cash advances on your Visa and MasterCard.

Places to Stay
Dumaguete *Jo's Lodging* (☎ 2160) on Silliman Ave is unpretentious and has a restaurant. Singles/doubles with fan cost P40/80. The rooms overlooking the street are very loud and are above a place which grills chickens.

The *Casa Lona Hotel* (☎ 3384) on Real St has rooms with fan and bath for P140/190 and with air-con and bath for P450/600. It is basic, but has spacious rooms. The *OK Pensionne House* (☎ 2133, 2755) on Santa Rosa St has simple but clean rooms with fan and bath for P180/230 and with air-con and bath for P350/450. It also has a restaurant.

Opena's Hotel (☎ 3462) on Katada St has singles with fan for P150, rooms with fan and bath for P200/280 and with air-con and bath for P350/400. It's comfortable and has a restaurant. The rooms at the back are quiet.

The *Plaza Inn I* (☎ 3103, 3538) on 50 Dr V Locsin St has rooms with fan for P375 and with air-con and bath for P490. This place is good, with fairly small rooms, and there is a restaurant. The *Plaza Inn II* (☎ 3400, 4441) on Percides St (Alfonso III St) is also recommended. Same prices and rating apply.

The *Insular Flintlock Hotel* (☎ 3495, 4255) on 55 Silliman Ave, near the university, is clean and pleasant. It has rooms with fan and bath for P400/450 and with air-con and bath for P480/570. The rooms are actually better than you would think from the outside of the hotel, and there is a restaurant.

The *Hotel El Oriente* (☎ 3486, 2539) on Real St has singles with fan and bath for

P250, singles with air-con and bath from P450 to P680 and doubles with air-con and bath from P520 to P840. The rooms with fan are basic and small, while the air-conditioned rooms are tidy, comfortable and spacious. The more expensive rooms have a fridge and TV, and there is a restaurant.

The *Al Mar Hotel* (☎ 52567) on Rizal Blvd, on the corner of San Juan St, is a homey place. It has rooms with fan and bath for P190/280 and with air-con and bath for P280/450. There are both small and large rooms, and there is a restaurant.

The *Habitat Hotel* (☎ 3134, 42295) on Hibbard St has rooms with fan and bath for P400/550, singles with air-con and bath for

P700 and P900 and doubles with air-con and bath for P800 and P1100. It's a well-kept hotel with spacious, pleasant air-con rooms, some with a small balcony. Snacks are available in the restaurant. It's in a quiet area on the university campus.

Around Dumaguete The *South Sea Resort Hotel* (☎ 2857, 3683) in Bantayan has singles with fan and bath from P625 to P825, doubles with fan and bath from P725 to P940, singles with air-con and bath from P815 to P1960 and doubles with air-con and bath from P945 to P2200. The more expensive rooms have a fridge and TV, and there is a restaurant and a swimming pool. It's a

---

■ PLACES TO STAY

2	The Habitat Hotel
5	Opena's Hotel
12	Jo's Lodging
14	Insular Flintlock Hotel
16	Hotel El Oriente
23	Al Mar Hotel
31	Plaza Inn I
38	Casa Lona Hotel
47	Plaza Inn II
48	O K Pensionne House

▼ PLACES TO EAT

7	Silliman University Cafeteria
11	Ocean's Chicken House
12	Jo's Restaurant
16	Lé Manny's Restaurant
18	Rosante Restaurant
19	Etcetera Restaurant
21	Aldea Restaurant
22	N's Pizza Plaza
23	Don Atilano Restaurant, Café Fernando & Grill House
24	Angela's Cuisine
26	The City Burger
28	Chin Loong Restaurant
31	Cheer's Bar & Restaurant
32	Kamagong Restaurant
33	Hassaram's Restaurant
46	Century Restaurant & D'Cowboy's Restaurant

OTHER

1	New Silliman Medical Centre
3	Silliman University
4	Provincial Capitol Building
6	George & Peter Lines & Cokaliong Shipping Lines
8	Silliman Post Office
9	Silliman Cooperative Store
10	Administration Building & Museum
13	Immigration Office
15	Philippine National Bank (PNB)
17	Equitable Bank
20	The Office
25	Plaza Department Store
27	Smash (Billiard Hall)
29	Fortune Mart
30	The Tavern Disco & Sing-Along
34	Music Box
35	National History Museum
36	PCI Bank
37	Jeepneys & Minibuses to San Jose & Tampi
39	Bank of the Philippine Islands
40	Post Office
41	City Hall
42	Church
43	Market
44	Jeepneys to Valencia, Maluay & Zamboanguita
45	Sulpicio Lines
47	Royal Salut Bar
49	Ceres Liner Bus Terminal

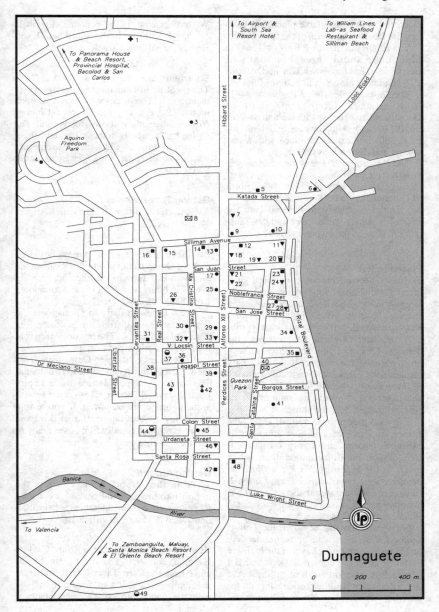

To Airport &
South Sea
Resort Hotel

To William Lines,
Lab-as Seafood
Restaurant &
Silliman Beach

To Panorama House
& Beach Resort,
Provincial Hospital,
Bacolod & San
Carlos

Aquino
Freedom
Park

Hibbard Street

Looc Road

Katada Street

Silliman Avenue

San Juan
Street

Ma. Cristina
Street

Cervantes Street

Real Street

Noblefranca Street

San Jose Street

(Alfonso XIII Street)

V Locsin Street

Dr Meciano Street

Libertad
Street

Legaspi Street

Perdices Street

Quezon
Park

Rizal Boulevard

Santa Catalina Street

Borgos Street

Colon Street

Urdaneta
Street

Santa Rosa Street

Banica

River

To Valencia

To Zamboanguita, Maluay,
Santa Monica Beach Resort
& El Oriente Beach Resort

Luke Wright Street

Dumaguete

0   200   400 m

clean and very comfortable place near Silliman Beach, two km north of the town centre.

The *El Oriente Beach Resort* (☎ 4264) in Mangnao, about three km south of Dumaguete, has rooms with fan and bath for P280 and with air-con and bath for P560.

The *Santa Monica Beach Resort* (☎ 3441) in Banilad, about four km south of Dumaguete, has rooms with fan and bath for P610/730 and with air-con and bath for P730/880. It's a pleasant place with a restaurant and diving is available.

The *Panorama House & Beach Resort* is an attractive, large house by the sea on Cangmating Beach at Sibulan, about six km north of Dumaguete – a P30 tricycle ride away. It has singles/doubles with fan and bath for P550. It's homey, good value and has a restaurant. Charly, the owner, is Swiss.

Places to Eat
The *Chin Loong Restaurant* on Rizal Blvd offers good Chinese food, the special menu is great value. The *Rosante Restaurant* on Percides St serves good Filipino dishes. *Jo's Restaurant* on Silliman Ave has what is probably the best chicken dish in town: the delicious Chicken Inato. The *Silliman Cooperative Store* at the entrance to the university campus sells snacks and fresh milk from the Silliman Farm. Cheap Filipino food is available in several small, clean restaurants in the covered market near the church.

The roof-garden restaurant *Aldea* on the corner of Percides and San Juan Sts is extremely pleasant and offers good, inexpensive Filipino and Chinese food; there is live music in the evenings. *N's Pizza Plaza* on Percides St is popular and always busy. It serves not only pizzas, but also several international dishes, a selection of cakes, and excellent fruit juices.

For those who like seafood, the *Lab-as Seafood Restaurant* can be recommended; on Friday evening they have an inexpensive buffet. It is on the corner of Looc and E J Blance Rds, two km north of Silliman Ave along the water. Another good restaurant for seafood, which also serves Filipino and Western cuisine, is the romantically rustic *Baybay Restaurant* in the South Sea Resort Hotel near Silliman Beach.

Entertainment
The nightlife in Dumaguete is hardly worth mentioning. The places which are still open in the late evening are *Ocean's Chicken House*, where they show videos, and *The Office* bar, which is nothing like an office. The disco *Music Box* is a favourite meeting place, also of expat Europeans. It is under Swiss management.

Getting There & Away
Air PAL has an office at Dumaguete Airport (☎ 2081, 3426).

Bus Several Ceres Liner express buses go daily to Dumaguete via San Carlos from the Northern Bus Terminal in Bacolod. The trip takes 7½ hours from Bacolod and four hours from San Carlos.

A few buses go daily to Dumaguete via Hinoba-an, leaving from the Southern Bus Terminal in Bacolod. The last departure is at 8 am and the trip takes 12 hours.

A few buses go daily to Dumaguete from the Nauhang bus terminal near Hinoba-an. The last bus is supposed to leave at 2.45 pm, possibly earlier. The trip takes six hours with a one-hour stop in Bayawan. If you're in a hurry, buy a ticket only as far as Bayawan because you will usually find buses ready to leave for Dumaguete.

Getting Around
To/From the Airport A tricycle from the airport into town should cost no more than P3 per person, but considerably more is often demanded (P15 to P20 will do).

Bus Buses heading north (San Carlos, Bacolod) and south (Bawayan, Hinoba-an) leave from the Ceres Liner Bus Terminal on the southern outskirts of town. A tricycle from the town centre costs P2 per person.

AROUND DUMAGUETE
Twin Lakes
About 25 km west of Dumaguete are two crater lakes surrounded by dense rainforest: Lake Balinsasayao and the smaller adjoining Lake Danao, at a height of about 800 metres. Environmentalists are demanding that these lakes (also known as Twin Lakes), located in what is for Negros rare forestland, be declared a national park. This would prevent the possible construction of a hydroelectric power station in this area. There is a basic nipa hut where you can stay overnight, but you have to bring your own provisions.

Getting There & Away You can get to Twin Lakes from Dumaguete by bus or jeepney going north. Get off about two km before San Jose, or travel back from San Jose by tricycle to the small track leading from the road up to Twin Lakes. You have to walk the remaining 15 km or so as it is impossible for jeepneys or tricycles. Motorcyclists without cross-country experience would have great difficulty too because of the steep slope and rough track.

San Jose & Tampi
Ships for Bato on Cebu leave from San Jose and Tampi, north of San Sebastian (see also Getting There & Away earlier in this section).

Getting There & Away Jeepneys and minibuses for San Jose and Tampi leave Dumaguete from the corner of Real and Locsin Sts.

Valencia
From Valencia you can take a tricycle to Camp Lookout at the extinct volcano Cuernos de Negros from where there is a beautiful view of Dumaguete, Cebu and Siquijor Island. This should cost about P60 but it's a hard trip by tricycle so you might find it better to walk. The trip is between eight to 12 km, according to different reports.

In Terejo, about two km out of Valencia, is the Banica Valley Resort, which has a small creek, a swimming pool and a few resthouses. It's popular with the locals, especially at weekends. If you want to go there on foot, ask for the swimming pool, which is near a shrine.

Getting There & Away Several jeepneys run daily to Valencia from Real St, on the corner of Colon St, in Dumaguete.

MALUAY & ZAMBOANGUITA
Probably the best beaches in the Dumaguete area are those near Maluay (Malatapay) and Zamboanguita. Although the sand is black, the water is clean and clear. You can get to offshore Apo Island from either place. The friendly and well-maintained Salawaki Beach Resort, about two km south-west of Zamboanguita, is an excellent place to stay in this area.

Quite close to the beach resort is a centre for the World Peace & Life's Survival organisation called Spaceship 2000. Its members are concerned with reafforestation and trying to restore the ecological balance. They are very forthcoming and happy to show visitors around Zoo Paradise World as they call this establishment.

Maluay has a large **market** on Wednesday which is worth seeing. Farmers come from the mountains, and fishermen from the coast and nearby islands tie their boats up there. The market trades in agricultural produce, livestock and seafood. Chickens and fish are grilled, and whole pigs roasted on the beach, amid much chattering, gossiping, laughing, eating and drinking.

Places to Stay
The *Salawaki Beach Resort*, two km beyond Zamboanguita coming from Dumaguete, has dorm beds for P150 and cottages with fan and bath for P300 and P500. The rooms are spacious and well furnished and there is a restaurant with good cheap meals and native coffee. The resort is on the beach, about 200 metres from the large sign on the road. A boat to Apo Island costs P300.

Getting There & Away
Several jeepneys leave for Maluay and

Zamboanguita daily, from the corner of Real and Colon Sts in Dumaguete. You can also take a Ceres Liner bus bound for Bayawan and Hinoba-an. The trip takes 40 minutes.

APO ISLAND

Little Apo island, about eight km south-east of Zamboanguita, is barely 120 metres high and has a five-metre-deep lagoon separated by a white beach from the sea. To protect some unusual coral formations and rare fish, part of the waters around Apo Island have been declared a sanctuary and placed under the protection of Silliman University in Dumaguete. As a result, the 'fish sanctuary' offers excellent diving and snorkelling conditions, although the strength of the currents and undertow should not be underestimated.

Places to Stay

The *Seaquest Beach Resort*, small and attractively situated, has dorm beds for P150 and comfortable cottages with bath for P300, and there is a good restaurant. From around the time of this book's publication diving will be offered.

Getting There & Away

A boat leaves Maluay daily at 4 pm to Apo Island. The fare is P20. Departure from Apo Island for Maluay is at 7.30 am.

You can hire boats in Zamboanguita and Maluay for about P300 to go to Apo Island. It's better to leave before 8 am and return after 4 pm because of the swell.

BINALBAGAN

Binalbagan is on the west coast of Negros, about 80 km south of Bacolod. This is where you will find the biggest sugar refinery and plantation in the world. It is called **Biscom**, which is short for Binalbagan Sugarmill Company. The two Baldwin locomotives 2-6-2T No 6, dated 1924, and Davenport 0-4-0T No 28, dated 1929, are no longer used, but you may have a look around them.

KABANKALAN

Kabankalan is about 40 km south of Binalbagan. This small town celebrates the Sinulog Festival on the third weekend (Friday, Saturday and Sunday) in January with parades, cultural events and horse fights. The Kabankalanons maintain that their Sinulog Festival is older and more authentic than the better known one in Cebu City.

Places to Stay

The *Friends Inn*, about two km north of Kabankalan, has double rooms with fan and bath for P100 and with air-con and bath for P160. It's basic but fairly comfortable.

HINOBA-AN

As an interesting alternative to the usual route from Bacolod to Cebu via San Carlos and Toledo, you can travel along the west and south coasts via Hinoba-an and Dumaguete. However, the roads are rather difficult, so you will need to take two days to do this route. The last section from Bayawan to Zamboanguita is particularly attractive, but the road is in poor condition.

Early in 1982 Hinoba-an experienced a real gold rush. Both the national and international press published daily reports about new finds which brought numerous adventurers and optimists. Gold fever broke out in earnest when it was reported that a Filipino had found gold to the value of P23,000 in a single day. Soon afterwards an estimated 20,000 people were trying their luck along a 17-km stretch of the Bacuyongan River and many did find gold. The average daily yield at the peak of the rush is said to have been one gram per person; this sold at P80.

Unfortunately, there were disastrous events, too. Within eight weeks one digger died in a landslide and another three in fighting over claims. Altogether, 17 victims were counted in two months. The most lucrative yields were those won by the buyers, merchants and traders, who soon made the sleepy village of Nauhang into a lively trading centre with a wild-west character. From the Crossing Golden Southbend (a junction near Nauhang), jeepneys run about seven km inland to Spar III at Sitio Sangke, where the well-trodden path to the promising river begins.

Government drilling to a depth of 300 metres was not completed until the end of 1982. The result surpassed all expectations, indicating a probable 10 million tonnes of rock with a content of three grams of gold per tonne. That could have been the discovery of the century. The government put an embargo on freelance gold prospecting, ending the adventurous wild times.

Places to Stay

The *Gloria Mata Lodging House* in Hinoba-an is reasonably good with rooms for P25/50. The *Mesajon Lodging House* on Gatuslao St, Hinoba-an, has simple but comfortable and clean rooms with fan for P50/100. Mrs Mesajon is very skilled in preparing an excellent Chicken Binakol. Made with onions and lemon grass in young coconut, this chicken dish is a speciality of south-west Negros.

About 25 km north of Hinoba-an is *Dalula's Lodging House* in San Jose/Sipalay. It's a simple but pleasant place; rooms with fan cost P50/90.

Getting There & Away

Several Ceres Liner buses go from Bacolod to Hinoba-an daily from the Southern Bus Terminal. They are either direct or continue on to Dumaguete. The road is good until Kabankalan, after which it deteriorates, but the views are much better. The trip takes six hours. Some buses only go to Nauhang, and a tricycle from there to Hinoba-an costs P2 per person. The last bus from Bacolod to Dumaguete via Hinoba-an leaves at 8 am, taking 12 hours.

A few Ceres Liner buses run daily from Dumaguete to Hinoba-an, taking six hours. The bus stops for an hour at Bayawan. The first bus leaves Dumaguete for Bayawan at about 4.30 am, and continues from there with an express bus at 10 am which goes to Bacolod via Hinoba-an.

BAYAWAN

Anyone who happens to get stuck in the little village of Bayawan because of transportation problems can spend the night in the basic, but clean *Sacred Heart Pharmacy & Lodging House* at the market, for about P50.

Panay

Panay is the large triangular island in the west of the Visayas. It is subdivided into the provinces of Iloilo, Capiz, Aklan and Antique. Iloilo City, with about 300,000 inhabitants is the biggest city on the island. The economy is predominantly agricultural, although there is also a textile industry in Iloilo City. Fabric made from piña, the fibres of the pineapple leaf, is used to make Filipino barong tagalog shirts.

Among the main tourist attractions in Panay are the Ati-Atihan Festival in Kalibo and the Dinagyang Festival in Iloilo. There are also several beautiful old churches along the south coast.

The little dream island of Boracay is extremely popular, not only with the 'international travel set' but also with quite 'normal' holidaymakers. In the meantime, travel agents can make bookings with several different resorts with above-average facilities. It still remains to be seen what will come of plans to develop the island into a fully fledged tourism centre. Before and after the Ati-Atihan Festival in Kalibo, Boracay is full!

GETTING THERE & AWAY

You can get to Panay from Bohol, Cebu, Leyte, Luzon, Mindanao, Mindoro, Negros, Palawan and Romblon (see the Getting There & Away section of the Manila chapter and the relevant Getting There & Away sections of this chapter and of the chapters on the other islands.)

Air

To/From Cebu PAL flies daily from Iloilo City and Kalibo to Cebu City.

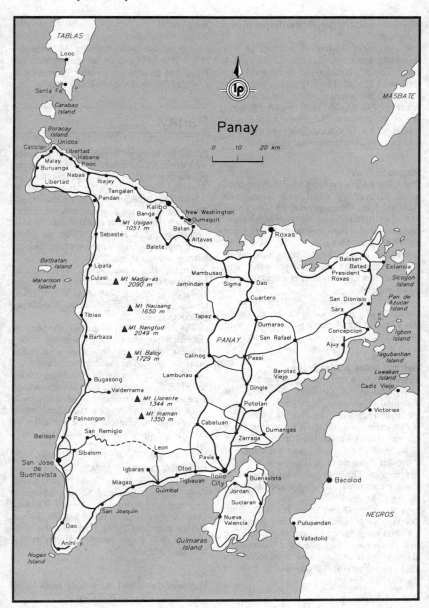

Panay

To/From Luzon Aerolift, Boracay Air and Pacific Airways fly daily from Caticlan to Manila. PAL flies daily to Manila, from Kalibo, Iloilo City and Roxas.

To/From Mindanao PAL has a flight on Sunday from Iloilo City to General Santos City.

To/From Palawan PAL flies on Monday, Wednesday, Thursday and Saturday from Iloilo City to Puerto Princesa.

Boat

To/From Bohol The William Lines' MV *Cebu City* leaves Batan on Wednesday at 7 am and Dumaguit (near Kalibo) on Wednesday at 10 am for Tagbilaran, taking 17 hours from Dumaguit.

To/From Cebu From Iloilo City to Cebu City, the Trans-Asia Shipping Lines' MV *Asia Indonesia* leaves on Monday, Wednesday and Friday at 6 pm, taking 12 hours; the MV *Asia Korea* leaves on Thursday at 4 pm, taking 13 hours.

To/From Leyte The MV *Our Lady of Fatima* of Carlos Gothong Lines leaves Dumaguit for Palompon on Wednesday at 6 pm, taking 11 hours. The MV *Our Lady of the Sacred Heart*, also of Carlos Gothong Lines, leaves Roxas for Palompon on Sunday at 6 pm and takes 10 hours.

To/From Luzon The Negros Navigation Lines has several ships going from Iloilo City to Manila. The MV *Santa Ana* leaves on Monday and Thursday at 10 am and takes 21 hours. The MV *Santa Florentina* leaves on Tuesday at 12.30 pm and takes 24 hours. The MV *Don Claudio* leaves on Friday at 12.30 pm and takes 14 hours. The MV *Don Julio* leaves on Sunday at 1 pm and takes 21 hours.

Also from Iloilo City to Manila, Aboitiz Lines' MV *Superferry 1* leaves on Wednesday at 10 am and on Friday at 7 pm, taking 22 hours. The Sulpicio Lines' MV *Philippine Princess* leaves on Sunday at 2 pm, taking 20 hours.

Various ships go to Manila from different towns in Panay. The MV *Cebu City* of William Lines leaves Dumaguit on Friday at noon and Batan at 2 pm, taking 15 hours from Batan. The MV *Legaspi* of Aboitiz Lines leaves Dumaguit on Tuesday at 2 pm, taking 19 hours. The MV *Our Lady of Fatima* of Carlos Gothong Lines leaves Dumaguit on Sunday at noon, taking 17 hours.

From Estancia, the MV *Cotabato Princess* of Sulpicio Lines leaves Thursday at 9 pm, taking 17 hours.

From Roxas, the MV *Our Lady of the Sacred Heart* of Carlos Gothong Lines leaves on Thursday at 6 pm and takes 13 hours.

To/From Mindanao From Iloilo City to Cagayan de Oro, the MV *Superferry 1* of Aboitiz Lines leaves on Monday at 4 pm, taking 16 hours. The MV *Santa Ana* of Negros Navigation Lines leaves on Saturday at 5 pm, taking 13 hours; the MV *Princess of Negros* leaves on Tuesday at 7 pm, taking 15 hours.

From Iloilo City to Zamboanga, the MV *Philippine Princess* of Sulpicio Lines leaves on Wednesday at 3 pm, taking 14 hours. The MV *Asia Korea* of Trans-Asia Shipping Lines leaves on Saturday at 5 pm, taking 18 hours. The MV *Cotabato Princess* of Sulpicio Lines leaves on Sunday at 7 pm. It takes 14 hours and continues on to Cotabato.

To/From Mindoro A big outrigger boat goes from Boracay to Roxas on Monday and Friday at 9 am, taking five hours or more. From December to May it can even leave as often as every other day. The fare is about P200. In bad weather the sea in the Tablas Strait is very rough and the crossing not to be recommended. Small boats sometimes sail over, but they are completely unsuitable and often dangerously overloaded.

From Buruanga to San Jose there is another big outrigger boat which leaves on Friday and Monday. It usually takes eight hours, but sometimes takes as long as 12 hours. This trip is also not recommended when the waves are high in Tablas Strait.

From Lipata to San Jose, the MV *Princess Melanie Joy* and the MV *Aida* leave once or twice a week, taking 24 hours. The trip takes them via Semira Island and Caluya Island, where they lie up to 10 hours at anchor. Lipata is a small place five km north of Culasi on the west coast of Panay.

To/From Negros The MV *Don Vicente* and the MV Santa Maria of Negros Navigation Lines go from Iloilo City to Bacolod on Monday, Tuesday, Wednesday, Thursday and Saturday at 7 and 10 am and 3 pm, and on Friday and Sunday at 7, 8 and 11 am and 4 pm. The trip takes two hours. Note that these times change frequently.

From Culasi, the MV *Queen Rose* or the MV *Princess Jo* leaves for Da-an Banwa, the port of Victorias, daily between 9 and 11 am, and the MV *Seven Seas* or MV *San Vicente* leaves from Malayu-an for the same destination daily between 9 and 11 am. Either trip takes two hours. Culasi and Malayu-an are two small places near Ajuy on the east coast of Panay.

To/From Palawan The Milagrosa Shipping Lines' MV *Milagrosa-J-Tres* leaves Iloilo City for Cuyo and Puerta Princesa on the 2nd, 12th and 22nd of each month at 6 pm. It takes 12 hours to reach Cuyo and 38 hours to reach Puerto Princesa (eight hours stopover in Cuyo). Their MV *Milagrosa-J-Dos* sails on the 6th, 16th and 26th of the month at 6 pm.

To/From Romblon A big outrigger boat leaves Boracay for Looc on Tablas about twice a week, taking two hours, and for Santa Fe on Tablas daily at 6.30 am, taking 1½ hours. At Santa Fe, you can get a jeepney to Tugdan, Tablas Island's airport.

ILOILO CITY

Apparently the name Iloilo stems from the expression 'Ilong-Ilong', which means 'like a nose'. This refers to the outline of the city centre, which lies between the mouths of the Iloilo and Batiano rivers. Iloilo is not very different from other Philippine port towns of a similar size, but its image has recently been improved. What attracts attention apart from some lovely old houses in the side streets are the modern jeepneys and those like the American street cruisers of the 1950s.

Information

The tourist office (☎ 75411) is in the Sarabia Building on General Luna St.

The Central Bank does not accept travellers' cheques. The Chartered Bank gives a good rate but charges a P33 handling fee per cheque. Your best bet is to go to the Philippine National Bank , on the corner of General Luna and Valeria Sts.

The Interbank branches on Delgado and Iznart Sts will change your American Express travellers' cheques.

PAL has an office at Iloilo Airport (☎ 70887, 70925) and on General Luna St (☎ 75925, 78471).

Things to See

The small 'Window on the Past' **Museo Iloilo** on Bonifacio Drive is worth a visit. On request, visitors are shown videos of the attractions of Panay and various Philippine festivals. It's open daily from 9 am to noon and 1 to 5 pm. Admission is P10.

Six km west of the city is the suburb of **Arevalo**. Until a few years ago, it was well known as a centre for the production of woven fabrics from *jusi* and piña. Today only one loom still exists at the Sinamay Dealer on Osmeña St. You can buy clothes and fabrics here. It is in a beautiful old house partly furnished with valuable carved furniture – something that only wealthy Filipinos can afford. On the way to Arevalo, you pass through **Molo**, which has a 19th-century church built of coral.

Festivals

Every year on the weekend after the Ati-Atihan Festival in Kalibo, the people of Iloilo City celebrate the city's greatest festival, the Dinagyang. The paraw regatta, a race between outrigger sail boats in the Iloilo

Strait, between Iloilo City and Guimaras Island, is held on the second Saturday or Sunday in February.

In Pavia, a little north of Iloilo City, water buffalo races take place each year on 3 May from 8 am. To get there, take a jeepney from the Shoemart.

Places to Stay – bottom end

The *Iloilo Lodging House* (☎ 72384) on the corner of Aldeguer and J M Basa Sts, has rooms with fan for P130/180, with fan and bath for P160/230 and with air-con and bath for P230/310. The basic and small rooms are anything but comfortable, and bathrooms are shared between two rooms. The *Eros Travellers Pensionne* (☎ 71359) on General Luna St has rooms with fan and bath for P160/200 and with air-con and bath for P220/290. It offers simple accommodation and has a restaurant.

The *Family Pension House* (☎ 27070, 79208) on General Luna St has rooms with fan and bath for P150/175 and with air-con and bath for P275 and P600. This popular place is clean and there is a restaurant.

Places to Stay – middle

Situated in a lane between J M Basa and Iznart Sts, the *Centercon Hotel* (☎ 73431-33) is very central; it has rooms with fan for P200 and with air-con and bath for P390/495. It's a quiet place, apart from the rooms with fans on the 6th floor, and it has a restaurant. The *Madia-as Hotel* (☎ 72756-59) on Aldeguer St has rooms with fan and bath for P270/300 and with air-con and bath from P395 to P485. It's clean and comfortable, and there is a restaurant. The standard is decidedly better than the modest entrance stuck in a hallway off Aldeguer St would lead you to expect.

The *Original River Queen Hotel* (☎ 76667, 270176; fax 200854) on Bonifacio Drive has rooms with fan and bath for P185/260 and with air-con and bath for P360/460, and there is a restaurant. Also on Bonifacio Drive, *The Castle House* (☎ 81021-23), with its imposing façade, has small but clean single rooms with fan and

bath for P250, with air-con and bath for P395 and double rooms with air-con and bath from P470 to P800. There is a restaurant.

The *Casa Plaza Pension* (☎ 73461-65; fax 72543) on General Luna St is reasonably good and has a restaurant. Rooms with air-con and bath cost P540/695, including breakfast. The tastefully decorated *Pension del Carmen* (☎ 81626) on General Luna St, on the Iloilo River, offers a pleasant family style atmosphere. Rooms with air-con and bath cost P495/550. Next to it is *Manfred's Inn* (☎ 73788) with decent rooms with air-con and bath from P555 to P790, and there is a restaurant. Also on General Luna St, *The Residence Hotel* (☎ 72454) has nice rooms overlooking the river, with TV, air-con and bath for P590/645. It has a restaurant and a coffee shop.

A pleasant hotel is the *Hotel Villa Rosa by the Sea* (☎ 76953) in Calaparan, Villa, about six km west of Iloilon Rooms with air-con and bath cost P340. It also has a restaurant and a swimming pool.

Places to Stay – top end

The best hotel in the centre of town is the *Amigo Terrace Hotel* (☎ 74811-19; fax 270610) on Iznart St. It has rooms with air-con and bath for P850/900 and suites from P1460 to P2800. Some parts of the hotel are a bit noisy. There is a restaurant and a swimming pool.

The *Hotel del Rio* (☎ 271171; fax 70736) on M H del Pilar St is a lovely place with a restaurant and swimming pool a little outside the centre of town on the Iloilo River. It has rooms with air-con and bath for P700/750 and suites for P1400 and P1680.

The *Sarabia Manor Hotel* (☎ 271021, 72731-35; fax 79127), General Luna St, has pleasantly furnished rooms with TV, air-con and bath from P700 to P900 and suites from P2500 to P3800. This is a well-run hotel, next to the tourist office. There is a restaurant, casino, disco and swimming pool.

Places to Eat

The most popular, and probably the best,

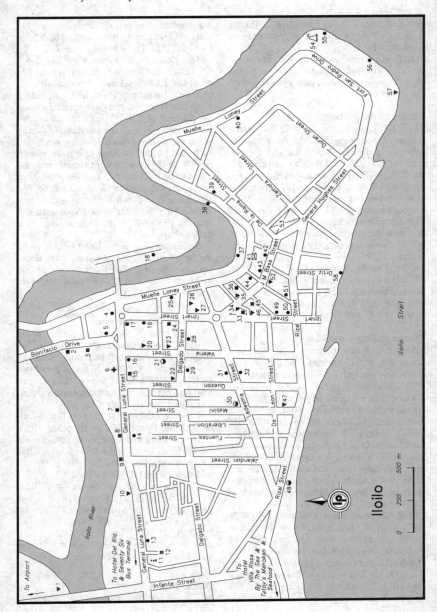

■ PLACES TO STAY

2	The Original River Queen Hotel
3	The Castle Hotel
7	Family Pension House
8	Del Carmen Pension & Manfred's Inn
9	The Residence Hotel
12	Sarabia Manor Hotel
15	Eros Travellers Pensionne
17	Casa Plaza Pension
24	Amigo Terrace Hotel
33	Centercon Hotel
36	Iloilo Lodging House
45	Madia-as Hotel

▼ PLACES TO EAT

1	Marina's Restaurant
7	Tree House Restaurant
10	Nena's Manokan
20	Bistro Valeria
22	The Tavern Pub
23	Oak Barrel
26	Ihawan Garden Restaurant
27	Magnolia Icecream & Pancake House & Dunkin Donut
34	The Summer House
35	Mansion House Restaurant
46	Aldous Snack Bar
47	Ted's Oldtimer Lapaz Batchoy
52	S'Table Restaurant & Snack Bar
57	Fort San Pedro Drive Inn

OTHER

4	Provincial Capitol Building
5	Museo Iloilo
6	St Paul's Hospital
11	Tourist Office
12	Base Disco
13	PAL
14	Universidad de San Agustin
16	Philippine National Bank (PNB)
18	William Lines
19	Bank of the Philippine Islands
21	Shoemart & Jeepneys to Pavia
24	Amigo Plaza Shopping Centre & Tivoli Disco
28	Interbank
29	Marymart Mall
30	Jeepneys to Miagao & San Joaquin
31	Fountain Head Disco
32	Kuweba Disco Theatre
37	Boats to Jordan
38	Ships to Bacolod
39	Negros Navigation Lines
40	Sulpicio Lines
41	Post Office & Immigration Office
42	Plaza
43	Springhead Disco Bar
44	Love City Disco
48	Tanza Bus Terminal (Buses to Kalibo, Caticlan, Estancia & Roxas)
49	Interbank
50	Central Market
51	Gaisano Department Store
53	Plaza Libertad
54	Lighthouse & Rotary Park
55	Boats to Buenavista
56	Wharf
58	Boats to Jordan

native restaurant is called *Tatoy's Manokan & Seafood*, at Villa Beach on the western edge of town, about eight km from the city centre. Especially if you know how to appreciate a relaxed atmosphere, the short drive there by jeepney or taxi will be well worth the effort. Hundreds of Filipinos make the trek there everyday, many of them only because of the tasty chicken, which gave Tatoy's its reputation in the first place. But the other items on the menu are also excel-

lent. First you go to the buffet and pick out your food, then you wash your hands and wait only a few minutes until the waitress serves the tasty morsels. Here the food is eaten with the fingers, a struggle the locals particularly enjoy watching from the neighbouring tables.

However, there are also some cosy little rustic restaurants to be found nearer the city centre, which serve Filipino food. These include *Nena's Manokan* restaurant on

General Luna St, where the food is also eaten with the fingers; the airy *Tree House Restaurant* (good steaks) belonging to the Family Pension House with its really pleasant atmosphere; and the popular *Marina's Restaurant*, a beautifully situated garden restaurant on the north bank of the river.

You can get good Chinese and Filipino meals on J M Basa St, upstairs in the *Mansion House Restaurant* and in *The Summer House*, which also serves a mean Western breakfast. Iloilo City has several Batchoy restaurants – two of the best are *Ted's Oldtimer Lapaz Batchoy* on Mabini St and the *Oak Barrel* on Valeria St. (Batchoy is a speciality of the western Visayas and consists of beef, pork and liver in noodle soup.)

The Tavern Pub, on the corner of Quezon and Delgado Sts, is air-conditioned, well kept and cosy. The prices are a bit steep, but the fish dishes are fairly inexpensive and the choice of cocktails impressive. The *Golden Salakot*, one of three good restaurants in the Hotel Del Rio, serves fairly cheap buffet lunches and dinners daily.

The *Aldous Snack Bar* keeps long hours, and is a popular night-time rendezvous. In good weather, the open-air restaurant *Fort San Pedro Drive Inn* is popular for beer and barbecues.

If you have a sweet tooth, don't miss the *S'Table Restaurant & Snack Bar* on J M Basa St, which probably has the best selection of cakes in Iloilo. For snacks and ice cream, try the *Magnolia Icecream & Pancake House* on Iznart St. Right next to it, the *Dunkin Donut* is open 24 hours.

Entertainment

The best and most popular discos in Iloilo are *Tivoli* in the Amigo Terrace Hotel and the *Base Disco* in the Sarabia Manor Hotel. Among the simplest discos are the rustic *Fountain Head* and *Love City Disco*. The *Ihawan Garden Restaurant* on Delgado St features live music and is packed every evening.

Getting There & Away

Bus Ceres Liner buses from Iloilo City to Estancia, Roxas, Kalibo and Caticlan leave from the Tanza bus terminal on Rizal St near the corner of Ledesma St. There is a daily bus at 3 and 9 am direct to Caticlan. As a rule, the 11 am bus to Kalibo is in time for the last connection from Kalibo to Caticlan and Boracay, but it could be dark when the boat from Caticlan reaches Boracay. The trip takes four hours to Kalibo, and six hours to Caticlan.

Getting Around

To/From the Airport It's about seven km from the airport to the centre of town. If you take a PU-Cab, it should cost P40.

GUIMARAS ISLAND

Until 1992 Guimaras was a subprovince of Iloilo Province but then became an independent province, with Jordan as the capital. Lying between Panay and Negros, the island makes a good day trip from Iloilo City.

Among the attractions is **Daliran Cave**, just outside Buenavista. The walk to get there is better than the cave itself. You can only go by tricycle between Jordan (pronounced Hordan) and Buenavista; this should cost about P50. On **Bondulan Point**, about 40 minutes on foot from Jordan, there is a giant cross which attracts many pilgrims during Easter week. You will get a good view from here of Iloilo City and the Iloilo Strait. The re-enactment of the crucifixion of Christ, Ang Pagtaltal sa Guimaras, which takes place on Good Friday, is now a growing tourist attraction in Jordan.

At the Barrio San Miguel, between Jordan and Nueva Valencia, is a small **Trappist monastery**. The monks have been busy cultivating kalamansi, which has become an important source of income for Guimaras. South-west of San Miguel is the **Isla Naburot**, a beautiful small beach resort. There is a fairly good swimming beach about a 45-minute walk south of Nueva Valencia.

Tourists rarely visit the small village of Cabalagnan, in the south of the island. A couple of idyllic islands lie offshore.

Top: Boracay (White Beach) (JP)
Bottom Left: Gigantes at the Zamboanga Hermosa Festival (JP)
Botton Right: T'boli ankle bracelets, South Mindanao (JP)

Top: Changing a flat tyre: a recurring problem in the Philippines (JP)
Bottom: Lake Cayangan, Coron Island, North Palawan (JP)

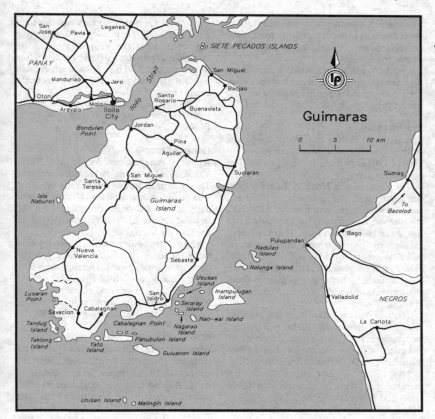

Boat Trip around Guimaras

The best way to do this trip is by outrigger boat, which can take two to three days, depending on the number of stops. It is essential to take along drinking water and food, and make sure your boat is equipped with a roof for sun protection.

The trip could start in Iloilo City and continue around the island in an anti-clockwise manner. All along the south-west coast, between Lusaran Point and Tandug Island, there are scores of tiny little bays which are perfect for snorkelling. Plans have been mooted to turn this coral-rich section of

coastline into a nature reserve. The various little coral islands with white sand beaches to the south and south east of Guimaras are well worth a visit, especially at high tide, because usually large areas dry out at low tide.

Malingin Island, a good 10 km south of Guimaras, is ideal for spending the night in the open air; Guiuanon Island (pronounced Giwanon) is good for hiking; Ususan Island (pronounced Usu-usan) which houses a handful of hermits, has a passable beach; and Nagarao Island, the location of the beach resort of the same name, run by Martin

Stummer, a German who has been active there for years in encouraging environmental protection and looking after endangered plants and species.

On the south coast, between San Isidro and Sebaste, primitive wind turbines have been constructed to pump sea water into flat basins from which salt is later extracted.

Places to Stay

The Gonzaga Family in Cabalagnan have a little guesthouse with only three rooms for about P150 per person, including meals. The cooking is good.

The *Colmenaras Hotel & Beach Resort* has rooms with fan and bath for P120 and rooms and cottages with bath for P100/200. It's pleasant and tidy, and has a restaurant and disco in a building on stilts. There are three swimming pools which are, however, usually empty or blocked with algae. Windsurfing is available, although the beach is not suitable for bathing. This place is about two km west of Jordan, halfway to Bondulan Point.

The *Isla Naburot Resort* on Isla Naburot Island has cottages for P2000 per person, including meals. This is a small, rustic establishment, without electricity. For further information, see the PAL office in Iloilo City.

The *Costa Aguada Island Resort* on Inampulugan Island has spacious and nicely decorated cottages with bath from P920 to P1400. This property on the white Bamboo Beach is well tended and covers a large area. There is an attractive restaurant, a swimming pool and tennis courts. There are outrigger sailboats for rent, and horseback riding is also available.

The *Nagarao Island Resort* on Nagarao Island has pleasant, spacious cottages with bath for P1250/2500, including meals. The resort has a restaurant and a swimming pool, and offers windsurfing and boat trips. For further information, ask at the Nagarao Island Office (☎ 78613; fax 71094) at 113 Seminario St, Jaro, in Iloilo City.

Getting There & Away

Several small ferries run daily from Iloilo City to Guimaras almost every hour between 5 am and 5 pm. They leave for Jordan from the wharf near the post office and for Buenavista from Rotary Park. The last return ferry leaves at 5.30 pm. Several small boats travel daily from the Ortiz wharf, near the central market, to Jordan.

The service charge in the resorts usually includes transfers, but it can cost up to P1000.

Getting Around

Jeepneys run between Jordan and Nueva Valencia, a few going as far as Cabalagnan. They return to Jordan only in the morning. You can go to Valladolid on Negros by boat daily. It leaves Cabalagnan at 3 or 4 am and stops at several islands. You can also board the boat on Nagarao Island.

Once a day at about noon, a jeepney runs from Jordan to San Isidro, where you can cross to Nagarao Island. The ride costs P10, but the asking price for a Special Ride is at least P250. There's a small signal post in San Isidro which you have to wave to get the boat to come across. The crossing costs P40.

SOUTH COAST

Although there are several beach resorts with cottages along the south coast, between Arevalo and San Joaquin, the beaches are no good. A good base for short trips to other coastal places or the Nadsadan Falls near Igbaras is the *Coco Grove Beach Resort* at Tigbauan. It has cottages from P150 to P200.

Buses from the Seventy Six Company run daily from Iloilo to San Jose de Buenavista, leaving about every hour from 5 am to 5.30 pm from M H del Pilar St, Molo, in Iloilo City. The trip takes two hours, unless the bus gets a flat tyre, in which case it could take more than six hours. Although buses travel along the south coast, they don't go via Anini-y and Dao (see Anini-y & Nogas Island later in this section).

Guimbal

'Home of the sweetest mangoes in Iloilo province', Guimbal has a sandstone church dating back to the time of the Spaniards. It also has three watchtowers built in the 16th century, from which smoke signals used to be sent to warn against pirates.

Miagao

Miagao, 40 km west of Iloilo, has a mighty church resembling a fortress that dates back to 1787. It has unusual reliefs on the façade mixing European elements (St Christopher) and Philippine plants (coconut palms and papaya trees).

San Joaquin

The most 'military' church in the Philippines is in San Joaquin. The façade, built of blocks of coral, shows the battle of the Spanish against the Moors in Tetuan, Morocco, in 1859. Every second Saturday in January water buffalo fights are held in San Joaquin.

Places to Stay The *Talisayan Beach Resort* has cottages with bath for P300/400 and cottages for five people with fan and bath for P500. It's a pleasant resort and the staff can arrange meals for you.

Anini-y & Nogas Island

Anini-y has a massive old church of white coral built by Augustinian monks during the Spanish colonial period. Private overnight accommodation is available with Mrs Magdalena Cazenas.

From Anini-y you can go to Nogas Island, which has white beaches and excellent diving areas. Although there is no regular service, you can get a paddle banca to take you across for about P50.

Getting There & Away There is a daily bus through Anini-y that goes as far as Dao, leaving from the corner of Fuentes and De Leon Sts in Iloilo at 7 am. There may also be others leaving at 11 am and noon. The trip takes three hours. The return bus leaves Anini-y at 12.30 pm; there are sometimes others at 4.30 and 6.30 am.

A daily jeepney goes from San Joaquin to Anini-y at 10 am, taking one hour and possibly going on to Dao. The return jeepney from Anini-y leaves at 1 pm.

SAN JOSE DE BUENAVISTA

San Jose de Buenavista is the capital of Antique Province, so Filipinos know the town not by its official name but as San Jose Antique. Unfortunately, the Binirayan Festival may no longer be held because of financial problems.

Places to Stay

The *Susana Guest House*, across from the Seventy Six Bus Terminal, has basic rooms with fan and bath for P50/100 and a restaurant. The *Annavic Hotel* (☎ 558) has rooms with fan and bath for P170/225 and with air-con and bath for P400/450.

Places to Eat

The handful of restaurants closes very early in the evening. After 7 pm the only place open is *Nina's Pizza & Restaurant* near the Seventy Six Bus Terminal. It is possible that the good *Diamond Garden Restaurant* will still be open; it's 500 metres outside of town in a northerly direction.

Getting There & Away

There are few jeepneys and buses from San Jose de Buenavista to Culasi and Pandan. As the road is in poor condition it takes four hours to reach Culasi and seven hours to reach Pandan. Some jeepneys only go as far as Culasi. From Pandan you can get connections to Malay and Kalibo.

CULASI

You may like to break the trip along the west coast of Panay at Culasi and spend a few days on Mararison Island. Although there is no regular boat service there, one or two crossings a day are possible. A Special Ride costs around P100 and takes 30 minutes.

A boat makes the trip from Lipata, about five km north of Culasi, once or twice a week to San Jose, Mindoro, via the Semirara Islands. A tricycle takes 10 minutes and costs P5.

Places to Stay

The *Balestramon Lodging House* in Culasi is a simple place and has rooms for P60/120.

There is only private accommodation on Mararison Island, at about P150 per night, including three meals.

Getting There & Away

From Culasi to San Jose the last bus departs daily at 1.30 pm.

NORTH-EAST COAST
Concepcion, San Dionisio & Pan de Azucar Island

Concepcion and San Dionisio are small places on the coast with quite big markets. There is a string of beautiful islands lying offshore which you can reach quickly by outrigger boat.

The most conspicuous island is Pan de Azucar – its 573-metre-high 'sugar loaf' can be seen a long way off. Because of its scenic attractions and friendly people, this island promises to become very popular before long. For the time being, it will only attract visitors who are prepared to put up with basic amenities. **Little Agho Island**, too, a little farther south-east, is among the more attractive of the islands. Surprisingly, there is not even the beginning of any tourist development here.

Places to Stay In Concepcion, the *SBS Iyang Beach Resort* has passable cottages with fan and bath for P200. It also has a restaurant, and the owners, Sandy and Betty Salcedo, will organise islands trips on request. You can only stay in private houses in San Dionisio, for example, with the Esteban Juanico family on J M Basa St; it's about P50 per person.

On Pan de Azucar Island you also have to depend on private hospitality, but as the locals are friendly, this should not be too difficult. You could ask for Anidlina and Avelino de Julian who like to accommodate travellers (about P50 per person). They run a small store and don't mind preparing the fish you bought from the fishermen at the beach for your meal.

Getting There & Away From Iloilo City to Concepcion, there are a few Ceres Liner buses, taking 2½ hours. The last departure is at 3 pm. There is no direct bus from Iloilo City to San Dionisio. The best way to get there is by Ceres Liner bus from the Tanza bus terminal on Rizal St to Estancia. They leave every hour from 4 am to 4 pm. To go to San Dionisio, get off no later than the turn-off in Deveria and wait for a jeepney coming from the larger town of Sara. As an alternative, you can get off at Sara, which is more pleasant than Deveria.

Outrigger boats leave from Dionisio to Pan de Azucar Island between 9 and 11 am. The fare is P10. Apparently the boats leave on Thursday from Concepcion, where there is a market on that day. A Special Ride should cost from P100 to P150. The trip takes 45 minutes.

Estancia

This unattractive little town serves mainly as a jumping-off point for the offshore islands. Boats cross from here to the Sicogon and Gigante islands and other destinations.

Places to Stay The *Terry & Em Lodge* (☎ 388) on Cement St, has simple rooms for P60/120 and with fan for P70/120. The *Fuentes Lodging House* on Inventor St offers basic accommodation with rooms with fan and bath for P80/160. The *Vila Lily Beach Resort* (☎ 429) is a fairly large establishment on a hill near Estancia. It has rooms with fan and bath for P225/335 and cottages with air-con and bath for P560.

The *Pa-on Beach Resort*, just a bit out of town, has clean rooms with fan and bath for P210/295 and with air-con and bath for P400/485. There is a restaurant.

Places to Eat Estancia's few restaurants close very early. Only *Melbert Restaurant* in Reyes Ave stays open after 8 pm. The *Together Restaurant* across from the Ceres Liner Bus Terminal is good and fairly inexpensive.

Getting There & Away Ceres Liner buses go daily from Iloilo City to Estancia every hour between 4 am and 4 pm. They leave from the

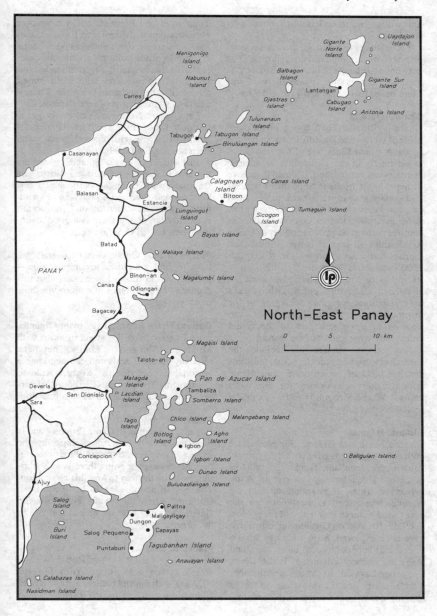

North-East Panay

0   5   10 km

Tanza bus terminal on Rizal St and take over five hours.

From Roxas to Estancia, there are several jeepneys or minibuses every morning. You may have to change at President Roxas. The trip takes three hours. Apparently two Ceres Liner buses leave between 7.30 and 9 am.

Sicogon Island

On the idyllic island of Sicogon, on the magnificent white sand Bantill Beach, stands the Sicogon Island Club, one of the first beach resort hotels in the Philippines to achieve international recognition. It's hard to believe it, but this luxurious establishment with its 120 cottages, swimming pool, tennis court etc, has been closed for quite some time. Amongst many factors contributing to its demise, perhaps its peculiar policy of trying to minimise all contact between locals and tourists had a lot to do with it. (Sicogon's 3000 inhabitants were strictly forbidden to let rooms to tourists. They also were not allowed to sell anything either, so the island's only restaurant was that belonging to the resort. To cap it all, locals were not even allowed to bring strangers to the island unless they were guests of the resort.)

Any touristic venture that excludes the locals has to end up creating social tensions, not the kind of background considerate holidaymakers are looking for. But, who knows? Maybe Sicogon Island will soon be seeing happier days again..

Gigante Islands

Gigante Norte and Gigante Sur islands are both very rugged. Massive rocks, commonly known as the 'enchanted rocks', contain lots of caves which have given rise to many mysterious tales. It is rumoured that the complex system of tunnels between the caves used to serve as a hide-out for pirates.

Of the 10 caves on Gigante Sur, only three have been explored. Most islanders are too scared and superstitious to enter them and many are just not interested. **Turtle Cave**, also called Pawikan, has a huge antechamber where white monkeys swing on roots hanging down from the top of the opening.

Tiniphagan and Elephant caves have been even less explored than Turtle Cave and they may have connecting tunnels to other caves. A good departure point for visiting the caves is Barrio Lantangan. It's recommended that you hire a guide and take stout shoes, torches, candles and drinking water. There is a natural swimming pool near the caves.

On Gigante Norte you can easily get to **Langub Cave** from the Barrio Piagao. A beautiful beach with crystal clear water stretches all along the barrio.

Just south of the two Gigante Islands are the small islands of **Cabugao Norte** and **Cabugao Sur**. Cabugao Norte has a few huts, a small cave and a pretty good swimming beach. The settlement on Cabugao Sur is slightly larger and there is a good swimming beach with very fine sand.

Places to Stay On the Gigante Islands you have to find your own accommodation – possibly at the Barrio Lantangan – but this shouldn't be a problem. It's up to you how much you pay.

Getting There & Away To go to the Gigantes from Estancia, you'd best get in touch with Mr Rustum Tan and his family. They have relatives on the islands and can negotiate a reasonable price for the Special Ride to Gigante Sur. The trip takes 2½ hours. Apparently, there is also a regular daily connection.

ROXAS

Roxas is the capital of Capiz Province and is therefore usually just called Capiz by the natives. There are no tourist attractions and the only reason for going there is as a stopping point on the way to Manila or Romblon. The best time of year to be there is in October, when the locals celebrate the Halaran Festival with music and dancing in the streets.

Places to Stay

The *Beehive Inn* (☎ 418) on Roxas Ave is a simple place with rooms with fan for P75/100, with fan and bath for P100/170 and with air-con and bath for P260. There is also a restaurant. The *River Inn* (☎ 809) on Lapu Lapu St has rooms with fan for P80/100 and with air-con for P230. It's unpretentious and quiet, and the doors close at 9 pm.

The *Halaran Avenue Pension* (☎ 675) on Roxas Ave has rooms with fan for P130/160, with fan and bath for P160/200 and with air-con and bath for P280/330. It's a pleasant place with a restaurant. The *Halaran Plaza* (☎ 649) on Rizal St, opposite the City Hall, is also quite good and has a restaurant. Rooms with fan and bath cost P180/230 and with air-con and bath P275/330.

Well located on Baybay Beach (P15 by tricycle from Roxas) between the airport and Culasi port is *Marc's Beach Resort* (☎ 103). It has rooms with fan and bath for P340 and with air-con and bath for P450. It's a comfortable place with a restaurant and a tennis court. Another good place in Baybay is *Villa Patria Cottages* (☎ 180). Singles with with air-con and bath cost P475 and doubles with air-con and bath cost P600 and P750.

Places to Eat

Of the few restaurants in Roxas only two are worth mentioning. *John's Fast Foods* on Roxas Ave, opposite Halaran Avenue Pension, is remarkably cheap and has a large selection of Filipino and Chinese dishes. *Halaran Restaurant* in the Halaran Avenue Pension serves well-priced comida (the daily special) but no beer. There are a few beer gardens and eateries with live music near the church: from Roxas Ave, go over the river, then go off to the right when you come to the church.

Getting There & Away

Air PAL has an office at Roxas Airport (☎ 210244) and on Plaridel St (☎ 210618).

Bus From Iloilo City to Roxas, Ceres Liner buses leave every 30 minutes from 4 am to 5.30 pm from the Tanza bus terminal on Rizal St. The trip takes four hours.

The last bus for Iloilo usually leaves Roxas at about 11 am.

Several buses go from Roxas to Kalibo daily, departing between 5 am and noon, taking 3½ hours.

Getting Around

To/From the Airport Roxas Airport is about four km west of Roxas. If you come by plane from Manila and want to travel to Boracay the same day, take the next bus from the airport to Kalibo. Then there's a chance of catching the last bus or jeepney to Caticlan, where you can catch a boat to Boracay.

Boat Culasi Port is about six km west of Roxas. The ride by tricycle from there to the city takes 10 minutes and costs P15.

KALIBO

The oldest town in Aklan, Kalibo is also the capital of the province. Well known for the piña textiles and intricately woven abaca shoes and handbags it manufactures, Kalibo is even more renowned for the annual Ati-Atihan Festival held in January. This is the Mardi Gras of the Philippines. Long before the show begins, the people of Aklan think of nothing but the vibrant Tam-Tam, which is the sound of the drums that dominate the festival's activities from the beginning to the end. Other villages and towns in the Philippines hold similar festivals but the one in Kalibo is the most popular.

About 20 km north-west of Kalibo are the **Jawili Falls**, which cascade down the valley, forming several basins where you can have a refreshing swim. To get there, take a bus or jeepney from Kalibo going to Nabas or Caticlan, get off at Tangalan and go on by tricycle.

In **Banga**, a few km south of Kalibo, you can visit the Aklan Agricultural College with its well-equipped experimental station. If you want to stay, there is a guesthouse.

Places to Stay

During the Ati-Atihan Festival, prices in Kalibo may be tripled and it can be almost impossible to find a hotel room.

Gervy's Lodge (☎ 3081) on R Pastrana St has basic, clean rooms for P60/120, and there is a restaurant. *RB Lodge* (☎ 2604), on the

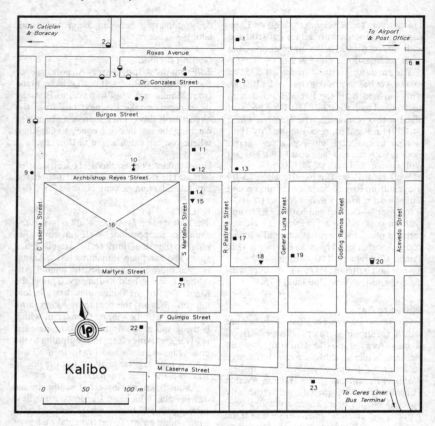

To Caticlan & Boracay →

To Airport & Post Office →

Roxas Avenue

Dr Gonzales Street

Burgos Street

Archbishop Reyes Street

C Laserna Street

S Martelino Street

R Pastrana Street

General Luna Street

Goding Ramos Street

Acevedo Street

Martyrs Street

F Quimpo Street

M Laserna Street

Kalibo

0   50   100 m

To Ceres Liner Bus Terminal

same street, has rooms with fan for P75/120, with fan and bath for P160 and with air-con and bath for P250.

The *LM Plaza Lodge* on Martyrs St has simple and tidy rooms with fan for P100/140, with fan and bath for P150/200 and with air-con and bath for P300/400. The *Apartel Marietta* (☎ 3302) on Roxas Ave has rooms with fan for P100/150, with fan and bath for P150/200 and with air-con and bath for P300/350. The accommodation is basic and there is a restaurant, but the place is noisy.

The *Green Mansions* (☎ 2244) on M Laserna St has dorm beds with fan for P60, rooms with fan for P100/150 and with fan and bath for P160/220. It's a reasonably good, quiet place.

There are a couple of passable hotels on S Martelino St. The *Glowmoon Hotel* (☎ 3193, 3247) has pleasant, clean rooms with fan for P200/300, with fan and bath for P350/550 and with air-con and bath for P500/600. It also has a restaurant. The *Casa Alba Hotel* (☎ 3146) has rooms with fan for P300/400 and with air-con and bath for P700/800. This is a fairly basic hotel with slightly overpriced rooms.

■ PLACES TO STAY

1   R B Lodge
6   Apartel Marietta
11 Glowmoon Hotel
14 Casa Alba Hotel
17 Gervy's Lodge
19 Lemon Lodge
21 LM Plaza Lodge
22 Glowmoon Pension House &
    LM Lodge
23 The Green Mansions

▼ PLACES TO EAT

15 Bistro
18 Peking House Restaurant

    OTHER

2   Jeepneys & Buses to
    Caticlan & Malay
3   Jeepneys to Dumaguit &
    New Washington
4   Gothong Lines
5   William Lines
7   Market
8   Buses to Roxas
9   Aboitiz Lines
10 Church
12 Aklan Museum
13 Philippine National Bank (PNB)
14 PT&T Office
16 Plaza
20 Great Minds Pub

restaurant also has a warm and friendly bar. It serves excellent Filipino and international dishes, European specialities and desserts like vanilla ice cream with mango flambé.

Getting There & Away
Air PAL has an office at Kalibo Airport (☎ 2409). The flights from Kalibo to Manila are often hopelessly overbooked. This could also happen on flights to Cebu City, so you would be well advised to confirm your return flight or connecting flight at the PAL counter as soon as you arrive. There is also a PAL office on Boracay which will deal with reconfirmations and changes of flight.

Bus From Iloilo City to Kalibo, Ceres Liner buses leave every hour from 3 am to 3 pm and take four hours. An express bus leaves at 7 am, taking three hours.

From Kalibo, several Ceres Liner buses go to Iloilo daily. The last trip may be at about 2 pm. Express buses leave at 7 and 11 am and 1 pm, taking three hours.

Buses run from Kalibo to Roxas at 8 and 11 am and 2 pm from C Laserna St, taking 3½ hours. Minibuses run in between.

After the flight from Manila arrives, jeepneys and comfortable air-con buses leave the airport for Caticlan, where boats for Boracay leave. The trip to Caticlan takes about 1½ hours. Tickets for the air-con buses are on sale at the airport, and include the boat transfer which costs P12.50. The fares are: air-con bus P150 and jeepneys P50.

Several jeepneys make the trip from Kalibo to Caticlan daily from Roxas Ave. The fare costs P30.

Getting Around
To/From the Airport It's only a few km from the airport to town. Normally, a tricycle costs P4 per person, and a Special Ride for two people P10 (however, you could be asked for P50 or more).

Bus The Ceres Liner Bus Terminal is at the south-eastern edge of town. A tricycle from there to the departure point of the jeepneys for Caticlan/Boracay costs P2 per person.

The pleasant and well-looked after *Hibiscus Garden Club* in Andagao, about 10 minutes away from Kalibo (a tricycle costs P20), has quite comfortable rooms with fan for P300/400 and with fan and bath for P600/700. There is a restaurant and a swimming pool, and airport service is free.

Places to Eat
You can enjoy good Chinese meals at the *Peking House Restaurant* on Martyrs St, and, with some reservations, the same can be said of the *Bistro* next to the Casa Alba Hotel on S Martelino St. The *Hibiscus Garden* in Andagao (see Places to Stay) is like a sanctuary. This romantically decorated garden

Boat Jeepneys ply between Dumaguit port and Kalibo.

IBAJAY

Ibajay (pronounced Eebahi) is a little town halfway between Kalibo and Caticlan. Each year on the weekend after the Kalibo festival, the 'really original' Ati-Atihan Festival (according to the locals) is held here. It is more authentic and traditional than the commercialised Kalibo festival. Sunday is the main day. The festival is very colourful and offers great opportunities for photos.

Places to Stay

The *R L A Hotel*, just across from the petrol station is simple, clean and comfortable. It has rooms with fan and bath for P125/225 and with air-con and bath for P160/260.

CATICLAN

This little town in the north-west corner of Panay is the starting point for outrigger boats to offshore Boracay Island. Before boarding, you have to register at the ticket counter. As it has no pier, you will have to wade through the water to get to the boats. Apart from the wharf, Caticlan also has an airstrip for small planes, which are being used increasingly to go to and from Manila.

The best day for day trips from Boracay to Caticlan is Sunday, when the market and the cockfights take place.

Places to Stay

The *Twin Pagoda Inn* is the big house near the pier. It has rooms for P150/250 and is friendly and well kept.

Getting There & Away

Bus There is a direct daily Ceres Liner bus to Iloilo via Kalibo departing from Caticlan at around 6.30 am and noon. It takes 1½ hours to reach Kalibo and five hours to reach Iloilo. The last bus from Kalibo to Iloilo leaves at about 2 pm. There are also several jeepneys from Caticlan to Kalibo daily. The trip takes two hours or more.

Several air-con buses go daily from Caticlan to Kalibo airport. Tickets are on sale on Boracay.

Boat Several large outrigger boats make the trip from Caticlan to Boracay daily until late in the afternoon. They tie up at three places, the so-called boat stations, on White Beach designed for them by the tourist office. The crossing takes 30 minutes. There is a set fare of P12.50 per person.

Getting Around

To/From the Airport A tricycle between the small Caticlan Airport and the wharf is P10 to P20.

BORACAY

Boracay Island is a great place for just lazing around. Seven km long, it is only one km wide at its narrowest point. Boracay's largest villages or *barangays* are Yapac, Balabag and Manoc-Manoc. They, and several smaller hamlets called *sitios*, are connected by a confusing network of paths and tracks, so the map of Boracay can only serve as a general guide.

There is a beautiful beach on the west coast with very fine white sand, particularly near Balabag. The water is quite shallow, however. For snorkelling the east coast is better but beware of rips. There are scores of little sandy bays scattered around the island; they make an attractive alternative to the ever popular White Beach. Boracay is also well known for its now very rare gleaming white puka shells, said to be the best in the world. For years puka shells were dug out of the beach at Yapak and then sold.

It cannot be denied that the island has lost its innocence. But, in spite of the odd incident and various sins against the environment, it still has that certain something about it. Amongst its good points, are the friendly locals being one of them, are the carefully tended gardens, the individually designed resorts, and the tastefully decorated cottages.

Every day seems to be a holiday on Boracay - all you need to do is relax and enjoy yourself. Long before you get up,

Boracay

0   1   2 km

Yapak Beach

Puka Shell Beach

Punta-Ina ●

Punta-Ina Beach

Bat Caves

Ilig-Iligan

● Yapak

Ilig-Iligan Beach

1

Banyugan Beach

Punta-Bunga

■ 2

Santoyo Beach

Punta-Bunga Beach

■ 3

Sanbaloron Beach

Balinghai Beach

Pinaungan

Lupuz-Lupuz Beach

Lapuz-Lapuz ●

● Diniwid

Diniwid Beach

SIBUYAN SEA

White Beach

The Rock

Bulabog ●

● Balabag

4 ■

5 ■

Bulabog Beach

6 ■

7 ■

Boracay Rock

● Mangayad

White Beach

Dead Forest

Fish Pond

Tulubhan ●

TABLAS STRAIT

Malabunot ●

Angol ●

Bantud

■ 8

Manoc-Manoc

9 10 ■

Manoc-Manoc Beach

Crocodile Island

Laurel Island

Cacpan Beach

Tabon Strait

PANAY

Caticlan

1 Kar-Tir Shell Museum
2 Club Panoly Resort Hotel
3 Balinghai Resort
4 Sinag Village Resort
5 Boracay Island Garden Resort
6 Palomar Beach Club
7 Laguna de Boracay Village Resort
8 Lorenzo South Beach Resort
9 Boracay Beach & Yacht Club
10 Villa Beach Resort

someone has swept around the cottages and put thermos flasks with hot water on the balcony tables. You can even have fresh bread rolls delivered in the morning. Just make some coffee and decide whether to go sailing, windsurfing or perhaps snorkelling and looking at corals. If you're curious you may get as far as the **Yapak Caves** on the other side of the island, where there are still fishermen who have nothing to do with tourism, except that they too have to pay higher prices in the stores.

For many people, Boracay is the typical Pacific island paradise. Whether this will change in the foreseeable future depends on the Department of Tourism, which is thinking of making Boracay into South-East Asia's leading beach resort with all the usual luxuries. The mind boggles, especially when you think of the irreparable damage caused by similar developments in other countries. The fact that Boracay is an attraction because of its lack of development does not seem to impress the powers that be. So far these plans are still in the discussion stages and the inhabitants and guests of the island hope they will go no further.

It wouldn't be a bad idea if somebody were to get rid of the algae that has been turning the water green regularly for the last few years from January to April. Here's a suggestion: if every resort would take one single peso per cottage per day in the high season and contribute that to a kitty, the money could be used to hire a dozen workers who could gather the algae together at low tide and cart it away. That would at least keep the algae from spreading in the first place. At the same time, a sewage plant could be built, because it's obvious that the cesspits used at the moment just aren't big enough to handle the 100,000 guests the resort receives each year.

Information

Tourist Office The Department of Tourism runs a small office in Mangayad, at about the middle of White Beach.

Money The Allied Bank next to the PAL office in Angol will change travellers' cheques and cash.

Post & Telecommunications There is a small post office in Balabag on the basketball court. It would be a good idea to have some change on you. Better still, bring your own stamps with you, from Manila for example.

Long-distance calls (national and international) can be made from the RCPI office in Angol, where fax facilities are also available. In the meantime, several resorts have their own radio telephone.

Massage Both next to the Titay Restaurant in Mangayad and behind the Summer Palace in Balabag there is the Shiatsu Center. For about P200 an hour well-trained, licensed blind masseurs will provide acupressure and reflexion zone massages. These professional massages should not be compared with the ones available at the beach!

Warning The influx of tourists has attracted a few shady characters who want their share in the boom. Keep an eye on your valuables and lock your cottage, especially at night. If possible, use your own lock. It's a sad fact that, in security as in other things, Boracay may be approaching the end of its time as the second Garden of Eden.

The tap water on Boracay is not suitable for drinking. I even avoid brushing my teeth with it. Nearly every store carries drinking water in plastic bottles, but be careful, make sure the seal hasn't been broken before you buy any! The best alternative is to have your own water bottle and to treat the water with iodine. This is 100% safe. See the Health section in the earlier Facts for the Visitor chapter for information on iodine treatment.

Things to See & Do
The list of sports and other leisure time facilities available on the holiday island of Boracay is gradually getting longer.

Dead Forest Next to the fishponds in the south of the island there are scores of dead trees. Their silhouettes jut eerily into the air in a horribly fascinating way (especially at the witching hour on the night of a full moon).

Museum The Kar-Tir Shell Museum in Ilig-Iligan has a small collection of sea shells on display as well as arts-&-crafts works and various woven products. Admission is P20.

Boat Trips An unhurried trip around the island by outrigger boat can be arranged for about P500. A day trip, including the nearby Carabao Island with its equally beautiful white sand beaches – still unspoiled by tourism – would cost a bit more. There are skilful artisans on Carabao who not only build snazzy *paraw* (a small, fast outrigger sailboat given to capsizing), but also have mastered the art of sailing them well.

Now and then, boat trips to interesting snorkelling areas are available, for example, with the MB *Blue Dolphin*, which costs P150 per person for four hours.

Diving A diving trip, including one dive, the boat and equipment, will cost you P500; four-day diving courses are available for US$250. For further information, see Beach Life Diving Center, Calypso Diving, Boracay Scuba Diving School, Far East Scuba Diving Institute, Ocean Deep Diver Training Center, Lapu-Lapu Diving Center, Victory Divers and the Inter Island Dive Center.

Horseback Riding A one-hour ride, with a guide if necessary, costs about P300 at the Boracay Horse Riding Stables, Balabag, near Friday's. Riding lessons are available.

Sailing On White Beach you can hire a paraw. It costs P100 an hour, or P500 per day.

Snorkelling There are good snorkelling areas at Ilig-Iligan Beach in the north-east and at little Crocodile Island just off the south-east coast. But beware of the strong currents that can often be encountered on the east coast of Boracay. Especially off Croco-

dile Island and Laurel Island the undertow has been known to put the wind up even strong swimmers.

Tennis Tennis is available at the Tirol-Tirol Beach Club, Mangayad (next to the tourist office) for P150 an hour, including rackets and balls.

Windsurfing It costs P250 an hour to rent a board. One-week courses cost around P2000. Rental and courses are available at the Green Yard Seasports Centre and Richie's Mi tral Windsurfing.

Places to Stay
In the last few years, many fine cottages have been added to the accommodation available. Most of them are on White Beach, between Balabag and Angol. They are all equipped with either two single beds or a double bed, and nearly always have their own veranda and bathroom. If you are staying on your own, you may get the price lowered in the off season. But to save embarrassing your landlord, keep quiet about the prices you get – especially to other landlords! Prices can vary, depending on how successful the season is. Especially around Christmas time price hikes are possible, while the off season from June until November is good for, at times, big discounts.

Out of about 170 beach resorts, a selection has been made of some 50 clean and comfortable places to stay. Each of the villages along White Beach is represented in the different price brackets. The prices shown are for cottages or rooms with fan and bathroom for two people. If the price is P2000 and more it can be assumed there is air-con. It would be worthwhile comparing the resorts, because sometimes there is a big difference in what is being offered for the same money (size, furnishing and setting of a cottage, for instance).

Places to Stay – bottom end
There are several good, relatively cheap places in Angol. *Hei-dio Cottages* has cottages for P200 to P300, *Moreno's Place* has

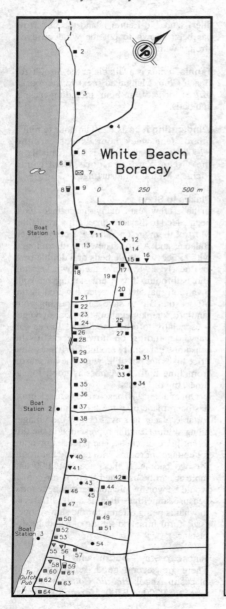

■ PLACES TO STAY

1 Diniwid Beach Resort,
  Laughing Water Cottages &
  Sundance Resort
2 Boracay Terraces
3 Costa Blanca Resort,
  Costa Hills Resort ,
  Naro's Place, Friday's &
  Moonshiner's
5 Cocomangas Beach Resort &
  Pearl of the Pacific
6 Willy's Place &
  V I P Lingau
9 Sea Breeze Cottages
  The Cliff Hanger Inn &
  Jony's Place
13 Boracay Beach Club Hotel
15 Nena's Paradise Inn
17 LSM Square
18 Bans Beach House
19 Vangie's Cottages
20 Mistral Resort
21 Sunshine Cottages,
   Fiesta Cottage, Jomar's Place,
   Serina's Place & Sand Castles
22 Galaxy Cottages
23 Crystal Sand Beach Resort
24 La Reserve Resort
25 Lion's Den
26 Red Coconut
27 Jackson's Place,
   Villa Arcontisz & Romaga's
28 Sea Lovers
29 Nora's Cottages
31 Blue Moon Beach Resort
32 Nirvana Beach Resort &
   Casa Filipina
35 Aqua Blue Cottages,
   Dalisay Village, Bahay Kaibigan
   & Diamond Head
36 Family Cottages & Summer Place
37 Jopines Place & Vista del Mar
38 Tirol-Tirol Beach Club
39 Sunset Beach Resort &
   Nigi Nigi Nu Noos
42 Rainbow Villa Resort
44 Saint Vincent Cottages &
   Shangrila Oasis Cottages
45 Morimar Beach Resort
46 Palm Beach Club,
   Bamboo Cottages &
   Dalisay Cottages
47 Lorenzo Beach Resort
48 Tonglen Homes & Magic Palm
49 Holiday Homes, Lea Homes &
   Paradise Garden Resort

50	Casa Pilar Cottages & Fernando's Place	36	Chez Deparis Restaurant
51	Trafalgar Lodge	39	Boracay Garden Restaurant
52	Paradise Lodge & La Isla Bonita	40	Green Yard Restaurant & Happy Homes Restaurant
53	Queen's Beach Resort	41	Tito's Place
57	A-Rock Resthouse, Highland Spring Resort & Faith Village	47	Titay Restaurant
		55	Sulu Tha Thai Restaurant & Swiss Inn Restaurant
60	Pearl of the Pacific	56	Da Baffo Pizza Restaurant
61	Roy's Rendezvous	58	Starfire Restaurant
62	Discovery Cottages & South Sea Beach House	64	Dada's Restaurant, English Bakery Outlet & Jolly Sailor Restaurant
63	Moreno's Place & Melinda's Garden	65	Da Mario Restaurant, Fischfang Restaurant & Sundown Restaurant
64	Villa Camilla Apartel		

50 Casa Pilar Cottages &
      Fernando's Place
51 Trafalgar Lodge
52 Paradise Lodge &
      La Isla Bonita
53 Queen's Beach Resort
57 A-Rock Resthouse,
      Highland Spring Resort &
      Faith Village
60 Pearl of the Pacific
61 Roy's Rendezvous
62 Discovery Cottages &
      South Sea Beach House
63 Moreno's Place &
      Melinda's Garden
64 Villa Camilla Apartel
65 Austrian Pension House,
      Dublin Resthouse,
      Judy's Cottages,
      Lorenzo South Beach Resort,
      Vanessa Cottages,
      Villa Beach Resort,
      Hei-dio Cottages,
      Boracay Beach & Yacht Club &
      Floremar's Place

▼   PLACES TO EAT

9 Jonah's Restaurant &
      Lion City Restaurant
10 The Hump
11 Boracay Steak House
13 El Toro Restaurant &
      Harrigan Sunset Bar & Grill
16 English Bakery & Tea Room
18 Zorbas Restaurant
20 Kobayashi Japanese Restaurant
29 Family Restaurant &
      Zur Kleinen Kneipe
30 Hard Rock Café,
      Mango Ray &
      True Foods Indian Restaurant
32 Viking Inn Restaurant

36 Chez Deparis Restaurant
39 Boracay Garden Restaurant
40 Green Yard Restaurant &
      Happy Homes Restaurant
41 Tito's Place
47 Titay Restaurant
55 Sulu Tha Thai Restaurant &
      Swiss Inn Restaurant
56 Da Baffo Pizza Restaurant
58 Starfire Restaurant
64 Dada's Restaurant,
      English Bakery Outlet &
      Jolly Sailor Restaurant
65 Da Mario Restaurant,
      Fischfang Restaurant &
      Sundown Restaurant

OTHER

4 Boracay Horse Riding Stables
7 Post Office
8 Beachcomber Bar
12 Doctor, GP
14 Island Delight
21 Calypso Diving
30 Bazura Disco &
      Lapu-Lapu Diving
31 Bowling Lanes
33 The Shop (Delicatessen)
34 Swiss Bakery
36 Shiatsu Center
38 Tourist Office
40 Calypso Diving
43 Police Station
47 Boracay Diving & Shiatsu Center
54 Talipapa Market
55 Sulu Bar & Kodak Photo Shop
59 Benny's Bar
62 Allied Bank, PAL &
      International Telephone & Telefax
64 Sand Bar, Lapu-Lapu Diving &
      Inter Island Dive Center

---

cottages for P250 to P350, *Melinda's Garden* has cottages for P300 to P500 and *Villa Camilla Apartel* has rooms with cooking facilities for P300 to P600.

In Mangayad, you will find *Lea Homes* with cottages for P300 to P400. The *Magic Palm* has cottages for P300 and the *Aqua Blue Cottages*, *Country Inn* and *Trafalgar Lodge* have cottages for P350. *Holiday Homes* has cottages for P350 to P450, and both *Shangrila Oasis Cottages* and *Family Cottages* have cottages for P350 to P500.

Balabag also has several places in this price range. *Sunshine Cottages* has cottages for P250 to P350. *Bans Beach House* has cottages for P350 to P400 and *Serina's Place*, *Vangie's Cottages* and *Nena's Paradise Inn* have cottages for P300 to P450.

There are many places that charge around P600. *Roy's Rendezvous* in Angol has cottages for P450 to P500 and *A-Rock Resthouse* has cottages for P400 to P600.

Mangayad offers the most choice. *La Isla Bonita Cottage* has cottages for P350 to P600, *Tito's* has cottages for P400 to P500, *Bamboo Cottages* has cottages for P500 to P600 and *Tonglen Homes*, *Vista del Mar* and *Mango Ray* have cottages for P600 to P700. In Balabag, *Galaxy Cottages* has cottages for P400 to P500, *Lion's Den* has cottages for P450 to P600 and *LSM Square* has rooms for P450 to P550. The *VIP Lingau* has cottages for P600 and *Willy's Place* has cottages for P500 to P700.

In Din Iwid the *Laughing Water Cottages* has cottages for P200 to P300 and the *Sundance Resort* has cottages on the hillside for P400 to P600.

Places to Stay – middle

Again, Mangayad has many places in this price range. *Casa Pilar Cottages* has cottages for P700 to P800, *Lorenzo Beach Resort* has cottages for P700 to P1000 and *Morimar Beach Resort* has cottages for P700 to P1000.

In Balabag, the *Red Coconut* has cottages for P800 to P1500, the *Cocomangas Beach Resort* has cottages for P700 to P1000, *Costa Blanca Resort* has cottages for P700 to P1100 and *Boracay Terraces* has cottages for P1000 to P1500.

In Bulabog, the *Palomar Beach Club* has cottages for P800 to P1600.

Places to Stay – top end

The *Pearl of the Pacific* in Angol and Balabag has cottages for P1000 to P1800, including breakfast.

In Balabag, the *Boracay Beach Club Hotel* has cottages for P1500 to P1800, Crystal Sand Beach Resort has rooms for P1600 to P1900, *Costa Hills Resort* has cottages for P1500 to P2200, including breakfast, and *Friday's* has cottages for P2750 to P4800.

In Mangayad, *Nirvana Beach Resort* has rooms for P1400 to P1800, *Paradise Garden Resort* has rooms with bath for P2000/3000

and *Palm Beach Club* has cottages for P2200 to P3000, including breakfast.

The *Boracay Beach & Yacht Club* in Manoc Manoc has cottages for P3800, including meals. The *Club Panoly Resort Hotel* in Punta Bonga has rooms from P5000 to P6000.

Places to Eat

There are now so many restaurants here that some have to tempt customers with surprisingly inexpensive, yet quite sumptuous buffets, while others have concentrated on one particular kind of food to do the same.

In Balabag, the modest *Family Restaurant* next to the little bridge serves an excellent bulalo, a strong- tasting vegetable soup with beef shank, as well as other outstanding Filipino dishes. *The Hump* is a pleasant little restaurant on a hill, with steps leading up to it. On clear days you can enjoy a romantic evening up there on the terrace, under a canopy of stars and with a magnificent view of the sea. The *Zorbas* has good Greek and Filipino food, *La Reserve* serves real French cuisine (wines and cognac too), while the *El Toro Restaurant* offers Spanish food like paella and sangria by the carafe for about P100. The *Boracay Steak House* prepares steaks in a variety of ways on a charcoal grill. The *Red Coconut* serves Chinese and European dishes, *Jony's Place* has Mexican food, while *Jonah's Restaurant* is popular for its fruit juices. The *English Bakery & Tea Room* is a good tip for breakfast; there is a branch in Angol.

Mangayad seems to have more European restaurants than anything else. The *Boracay Garden Restaurant* is tastefully decorated and has good German and Chinese food. *Chez Deparis* is the place for French food, and the *Bamboo Restaurant* for Swiss. According to its advertising, the *Green Yard* is 'your schnitzel haus'. *Tito's Place*, an unpretentious, but clean restaurant with inexpensive Filipino dishes, is popular and always busy – especially at happy hour. *Happy Homes* is another popular place.

In Angol the *Starfire* can be recommended for its inexpensive menu of the day.

Melinda's Garden Restaurant is a pleasant place specialising in seafood, but also with excellent Filipino cooking and typical European dishes. The fruit salads and fruit juices are particularly good in the *Jolly Sailor*, which seems to be the place to swap travel information. Next door, in *Dada's Restaurant*, the fish can be recommended. The restaurants *Da Baffo* and *Da Mario* both compete for the title of 'Best Ristorante Italiano on Boracay'. The *Sundown Restaurant* has good German, Austrian and Swiss food (their dinner buffet seems to be very popular), while the *Swiss Inn*, not surprisingly, offers almost exclusively Swiss food.

Imported delicacies and red or white wines are available at the *Island Delight* and *The Shop*.

Entertainment

There are lots of opportunities for entertainment and diversion on Boracay. Now that there is also the possibility of using a motorbike-taxi, for example from the Sulu Bar to the Beachcomber, even those of us too lazy to walk can indulge in the pleasure of 'barhopping'.

After dinner many guests like to listen to music or go dancing at their favourite place. Many like the *Beachcomber* at Balabag, where the dancing can become very animated when things warm up. Others prefer the big *Bazura* disco one km farther south, with the adjoining *Hard Rock Café*, which is particularly busy at weekends. Two of the popular places in Angol are the *Sulu Bar*, with billiards and videos, and the *Sand Bar*, which is beginning to show its age. Just for a change the *Titay Restaurant* in Mangayad offers free cultural shows every evening together with a dinner buffet.

Getting There & Away

Air The quickest (and dearest) connection between Manila and Boracay via Caticlan is by Aerolift, Boracay Air and Pacific Airways; the one-way fare is about P1700.

On peak days during the high season, Interisland Travel & Tours offer a Manila-Caticlan flight of their own for P1950. The Manila office is at 1322 Roxas Blvd, Ermita (☎ 5221405); on Boracay bookings can be made at the Red Coconut in Balabag.

Aerolift bookings can be made at the Lorenzo Beach Resort, Mangayad, and at the Red Coconut, Balabag.

Pacific Airways bookings can be made at the Dublin Resthouse, Angol, and on the Red Coconut, Balabag.

The little PAL office is next to the South Sea Beach House in Angol. Apart from taking care of changes in itinerary and flight confirmations PAL also sells tickets for P150 for the air-con bus from Caticlan to Kalibo, which includes the boat trip from Boracay to Caticlan. The office is open from 8.30 am to noon and 2 to 4 pm.

PAL flies from Manila to Kalibo on Panay and Tugdan on Tablas Island, in Romblon Province. The connection from Kalibo t Boracay via Caticlan is better than the one from Tugdan to Boracay via Santa Fe. After the aircraft arrives there are jeepneys and air-con buses from Kalibo to Caticlan. PAL also flies from Cebu City to Kalibo.

Boat & Bus Many boats cruise along White Beach heading for Caticlan; just wait at one of the boat stations if you want to go there. The first boat comes along at about 6.30 am. On arrival in Caticlan, you can get a jeepney or bus to Kalibo. The trip takes two hours or more.

A bus leaves Caticlan for Iloilo City via Kalibo at around 6.30 am. The trip takes six hours. Anyone wanting to take this bus will have to take either the first boat at 6 am or a Special Ride for about P175 from Boracay.

Air-con buses make special trips from Caticlan to Kalibo Airport, timed to catch the departures of PAL flights. Tickets are available at the PAL office on Boracay.

There are shipping services between Manila, New Washington and Dumaguit, both are near Kalibo on Panay. (See the section on getting to Panay in the Getting There & Away section of the Manila chapter.)

Getting Around

Boat There are three so-called boat stations on White Beach for boats to and from Caticlan: Boat Station 1 at the Boracay Beach Club Hotel, Boat Station 2 at the tourist office and Boat Station 3 at the Sulu Bar. From June to November, during the south-west monsoons, the sea on the west side of Boracay can grow too rough for outrigger boats. They then have to drop anchor on the east coast in the bay near the Dead Forest, and/or near Bulabog.

As almost all passengers have to wade through the water to get to the boats or back to shore, patent-leather boots and well-pressed long trousers are definitely not the things to wear.

Tricycle Several tricycles ride along the narrow road which runs through the middle part of the island from Manoc-Manoc in the south to Yapak Beach in the north. They charge P10 to P15 per person.

Bicycle Various resorts along White Beach rent out bikes, for example, Jony's Place and the Boracay Beach Club Hotel, both in Balabag, and Melinda's Garden in Angol. A mountain bike costs P30 to P50 an hour, or P150 per day.

Romblon

Almost in the centre of the Philippine archipelago, Romblon Province is made up of about 20 islands and islets, the largest of which are Tablas, Sibuyan and Romblon. All three are hilly and Sibuyan is thickly forested.

Because of its large marble deposits, Romblon is also called 'Marble Country'. Experts consider that Romblon marble is at least equal in quality to Italian marble. It is usually sold as large blocks, but several families make a few pesos by selling handmade ashtrays, chess pieces, vases and statues. When passenger ships visit, people set up stalls on the wharf of Romblon town to sell marble souvenirs.

GETTING THERE & AWAY

You can get to Romblon from Luzon, Masbate, Mindoro and Panay (see the Getting There & Away section of the Manila chapter and the relevant Getting There & Away sections of this chapter and the chapters on the other islands).

Air

To/From Luzon PAL flies on Tuesday, Thursday and Saturday from Tugdan on Tablas Island to Manila.

Boat

To/From Luzon There is a boat four times a week from Magdiwang on Sibuyan Island to Lucena which takes 12 hours.

From Odiongan to Batangas, a Viva Shipping Lines' boat sails once a week, taking 10 hours.

From Romblon town to Batangas, the MV *Socorro* leaves on Tuesday and Saturday at 7 pm, taking 10 hours.

From Romblon town to Lucena, the MV *Don Rosario* and the MV *Transmar* leave on Monday, Wednesday and Friday, taking 12 hours.

From Romblon town to Manila, the Negros Navigation Lines' MV *Santa Maria* leaves on Sunday at 8 am, taking 13 hours

From San Agustin to Batangas, the MV *Socorro* leaves on Friday at 2 pm, taking 10 hours.

From San Agustin to Lucena, the MV *Kalayaan* leaves on Tuesday, Wednesday and Thursday, taking 10 hours.

To/From Masbate A big outrigger boat goes from Cajidiocan (on Sibuyan Island) to Mandaon three times a week, taking five hours.

To/From Mindoro A big outrigger boat goes from Romblon town to Bongabong on Tuesday at 9 am, taking six hours, and from Looc on Tablas Island to Roxas on Saturday at 10.30 am, taking four hours. Additional

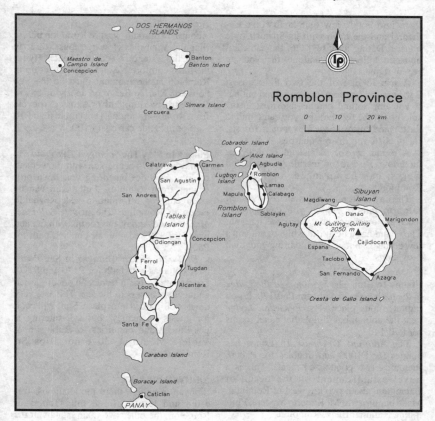

Romblon Province

trips may be run on Monday and Thursday and even daily if required. Sometimes it may run from Odiongan, also on Tablas Island, instead of Looc.

To/From Panay A big outrigger boat goes from Looc on Tablas Island to Boracay about twice a week, taking two hours.

A big outrigger boat goes from Santa Fe on Tablas Island to Boracay on Tuesday, Thursday and Saturday, soon after the Manila plane's arrival in Tugdan. The boat then waits for the jeepney from the airport

and goes on to Caticlan. The trip takes 1½ hours.

ROMBLON ISLAND
Romblon

The small port town of Romblon is the capital of Romblon Province. In the typhoon season, ships often take cover in its sheltered bay. The two forts of San Andres and Santiago Hill were built by the Spaniards in 1640 and are said to have underground passages leading to the coast. Today, San Andres is used as a weather station. From the forts there is a good view of San Joseph's Cathedral and the town with its Spanish-style houses. Dating back to 1726, the cathedral houses a collection of antiques that you can see on request.

A trip to one of the two lighthouses, **Sabang** and **Apunan**, makes a good outing. If you don't mind heights and trust in the stability of the lighthouses, you can climb to the top and enjoy the view over palm forests, rocky cliffs and marble quarries.

A round trip of the island by tricycle, including a vista of marble quarries and works, can be arranged for P200 in Romblon.

The bay of Romblon is sheltered by small **Lugbon Island**, which you can quickly reach by outrigger boat from the harbour. The island has a beautiful white beach and a few cottages, but you should bring your own provisions.

Places to Stay The *Moreno Seaside Lodge* at the harbour has rooms for P60/120. It's an unpretentious place. The *Feast-Inn Lodge* near the church has simple but clean rooms for P70/140.

The *Aniniput Treehouse* in Lonos has singles for P1000 and doubles for P1800, including two good-sized meals. This is a novel establishment on the beach of Batangtan, about two km west of Romblon. Make enquiries to Mr Roberto Madera, Philippine National Bank, Romblon.

Places to Eat The *Tica Inn* at the harbour is better than the well-known *Kawilihan Food House*, also at the harbour. The *Marble Dust Restaurant* is also good.

Getting There & Away A boat does about four trips a week between Romblon and Magdiwang on Sibuyan Island. Fairly reliable departure times are from Romblon on Friday at 1 pm and from Sibuyan on Saturday at 9 am. The trip takes two hours.

Outrigger boats leave daily from San Agustin on Tablas Island for Romblon at 8 am and 1 pm, taking 45 minutes.

Agnay

About 10 km south-west of Romblon before Mapula, Agnay has a few tree houses directly above the water on a beautiful beach. By far the most comfortable and pleasant set up in Romblon at the moment must be the tree house on Marble Beach on an idyllic bay in San Pedro, two km south of Agnay. A tricycle from Romblon shouldn't cost more than P10 – a Special Ride can cost P100.

Places to Stay The *Selangga Tree House* in Agnay costs P75 per person with shower and cooking facilities but bring your own provisions from Romblon. Full board can be arranged. For information, ask Reynaldo Festin in Romblon. The private *Villa del Mar*, outside Agnay, has rooms with fan and bath for P350 and with air-con and bath for P550.

D'Marble Beach Cottages in San Pedro have cottages with bath for P170 and P220. Every cottage has a terrace, a small garden and its own access to the sea. This is a very quiet, well-looked after place. Staff will cook for guests on request, but self-catering is possible. Make enquiries to Robinson & Violeta Montojo, Governor Rios St, Romblon.

SIBUYAN ISLAND

Sibuyan is wilder, more mountainous, forested and less explored than Tablas or Romblon, the other two main islands in the Romblon archipelago. It has several waterfalls, such as the Cataga and Lambigan falls near Magdiwang, and the Kawa-Kawa Falls in Lumbang Este near Cajidiocan, the most densely populated town on the island.

Mt Guiting-Guiting, 2050 metres high, is very hard to climb because of its thick covering of moss. It was first climbed in mid-1982. There are numerous legends and myths about the mountain's many waterfalls.

One of these is that the souls of rich landowners and corrupt politicians are gathered on the mountain, where they wait fruitlessly for the day when the proverb about the camel passing through the eye of a needle comes true. The scriptures say that it is easier for a camel to go through the eye of a needle than for a rich man to enter the kingdom of heaven. The long wait is causing them great pain and their tears flow down to the living in majestic waterfalls. These souls cannot leave the mountain as their evil deeds have encouraged the growth of impenetrable moss and mud.

Another myth says that a giant magnet inside the mountain attracts climbers who then get caught in the moss and die of hunger. It also makes the instruments of aircraft go haywire, causing them to crash on the mountain.

Offshore, the coral reefs around Cresta de Gallo Island with its white sands are well known for the good diving they offer.

A boat runs about four times a week between Magdiwang on Sibuyan Island and Romblon on Romblon Island, taking two hours.

Magdiwang
Magdiwang is a clean little town on the north coast of Sibuyan Island. The natural pool with crystal-clear water at nearby **Lambigan Falls** is ideal for a dip.

Places to Stay You can only stay in private houses in Magdiwang, such as the Muros family's house on Rizal St, which is basic but has a beautiful terrace right above the Dulangan River. They charge about P50 per person. Other places are the Ransay residence, also P50, and Mrs Geneva Rivas' place.

Taclobo
Taclobo, on the south-west coast of Sibuyan Island, is a good starting point for trips into the hilly jungles of the interior, such as the wild **Cantingas River Valley**. About 15 minutes outside of Taclobo (head from the main road and follow the sign 'Christ in the Mountain') there are the little **Lagting Falls** with a natural pool, where you can have a refreshing dip. A simple guest house at the waterfall offers accommodation for P50 per person.

San Fernando
San Fernando, like Taclobo, is a good base for exploring the interior. You can also make trips from there to the little island of **Cresta de Gallo**, although you could also arrange such trips in Azagra at the southerly point of Sibuyan Island, for example, in the shop belonging to the friendly Mangarin family.

Places to Stay In the village, *Jenmar Lodge* has rooms for P60/120. *Bernie's Inn* on the edge of the village has rooms for P60/120. This is a comfortable and pleasant inn built of bamboo, with four bedrooms, a living room and a kitchen. It is also known as *Bernie's Nipa Huts*.

TABLAS ISLAND
Tablas is the largest island in the Romblon archipelago. Anybody with any experience travelling around the Philippines won't take long to realise that travelling on Tablas Island is comparatively dear. And more often than not, you get the impression that it is mostly tourists who are being asked to dig deep into their pockets. So it wouldn't do any harm to ask a local first what fares normally cost.

Outrigger boats go daily from Romblon town to San Agustin on Tablas Island at 8 am and 1 pm, taking 45 minutes.

San Agustin
San Agustin is a pleasant little town and has a wharf for boats to and from Romblon town. You can also do day trips to the **Bitu Falls** near Dabdaban and the **Cajbo-aya Ruins**.

Places to Stay The *S & L Lodge* is a simple place which has rooms for P40/80. As an alternative, private accommodation would not be a bad idea. The Montessa family charge P100 for a double room.

Getting There & Away Several jeepneys run from Looc to San Agustin daily, taking three hours. The 6 am jeepney from Looc connects with the boat to Romblon.

Calatrava & San Andres
Near Calatrava, in Kabibitan, you will find Tinagong Dagat, the 'hidden lake', where the

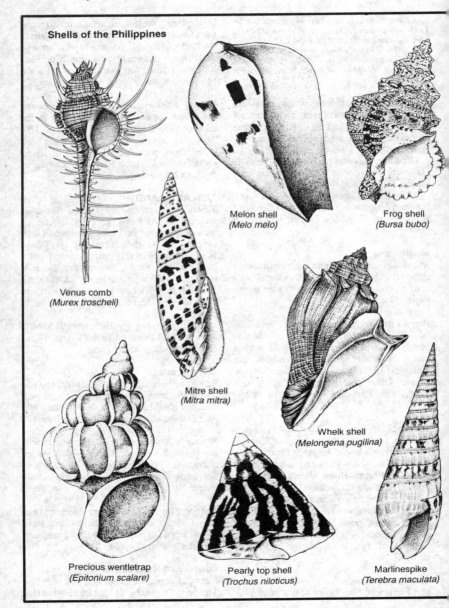

Shells of the Philippines

Venus comb
(*Murex troscheli*)

Melon shell
(*Melo melo*)

Frog shell
(*Bursa bubo*)

Mitre shell
(*Mitra mitra*)

Whelk shell
(*Melongena pugilina*)

Precious wentletrap
(*Epitonium scalare*)

Pearly top shell
(*Trochus niloticus*)

Marlinespike
(*Terebra maculata*)

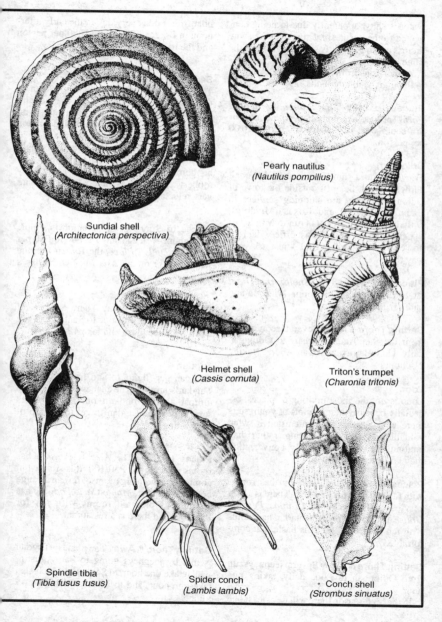

Sundial shell
(*Architectonica perspectiva*)

Pearly nautilus
(*Nautilus pompilius*)

Helmet shell
(*Cassis cornuta*)

Triton's trumpet
(*Charonia tritonis*)

Spindle tibia
(*Tibia fusus fusus*)

Spider conch
(*Lambis lambis*)

Conch shell
(*Strombus sinuatus*)

water is salty, apparently due to being connected to the ocean somehow. Not far away there is another, slightly smaller lake with the same properties.

A track runs from San Andres (Despujols) to the high Mablaran Falls.

Places to Stay The *Balogo Fernandez Farm* (private accommodation), about four km south-west of Calatrava, charges P100 per person.

Odiongan

Tricycles run a shuttle service to the small harbour which lies just outside the town of Odiongan. There are shipping services to Batangas (Luzon) and Roxas (Mindoro). Only large outrigger boats run to Mindoro.

Odiongan has a small post office which is, however, a bit hard to find – just ask your way there.

Places to Stay The *Shellborne Hotel* (☎ 591265) has simple rooms with fan and bath for P70/140.

Getting There & Away Several jeepneys run from the San Agustin wharf to Odiongan daily, via Calatrava and San Andres, taking 2½ hours.

Looc

Looc is not the most inviting of places, especially because there are lots of youngsters there who appear more interested in what valuables visitors are wearing, rather than continuing with the friendly conversation they had struck up.

Places to Stay The *Plaza Inn* has rooms with fan and bath for P90/180. There is a boat service to Boracay. The *Tablas Pension House* just across from the market has rooms with fan for P100/200. It is basic, but comfortable.

Getting There & Away Several jeepneys run from Odiongan to Looc daily, taking one hour.

In the high season there will be at least one boat from Looc every day in the early afternoon to Boracay. The fare is P80 per person and the trip takes 2½ hours.

Santa Fe

There is a daily outrigger boat from Santa Fe to Caticlan on Panay, via Carabao and Boracay islands. It picks up passengers who are coming from the airport in Tugdan and takes two hours. The fare to Boracay is P70 per person. If you charter a boat, it should not cost more than P400, but up to P800 may be demanded. This smacks of highway robbery, especially as the boat operators are very reluctant to bargain.

Places to Stay Accommodation is simple throughout. You can stay for P40 to P60 per person at *Dolly's Place*, the *Tourist Inn*, the *White House* or the *Asis Inn*, which has a restaurant.

Getting There & Away There are several jeepneys daily from Looc to Santa Fe. They leave from the plaza and take 45 minutes.

Tugdan

You can get flights to and from Manila at Tugdan's airport. The planes to Manila are almost always booked out and it takes several days in Tugdan to get to the top of the waiting list.

Places to Stay The *Airport Pension* has rooms with fan for P50/100. It is simple but comfortable with big rooms. You can arrange board on request. *Monte Carlo Lodging* has simple but pleasant rooms with fan for P50/100, and there is a restaurant.

Getting There & Away The plane in Tugdan is met by jeepneys going to San Agustin, which take one hour, to Santa Fe, which also take one hour, and to Looc, which take 45 minutes.

Samar

The second biggest island in the Visayas, Samar lies between South Luzon and Leyte and is connected with Leyte by the two-km long San Juanico Bridge, which spans the San Juanico Strait. The island is divided into the three provinces of Eastern, Northern and Western Samar and is surrounded by about 180 small islands. One of these is Homonhon, where Ferdinand Magellan is reputed to have set foot for the first time on Philippine soil on 16 March 1521. Samar's landscape is hilly and steep and the greater part of the island is thickly wooded. Plains exist only along the coast and in the north, around Catarman.

Samar's climate is different from that of other islands in the Philippines, with dry periods only occurring occasionally in May and June. Apart from that, rainfall is possible throughout the year, although never for long periods. Most rain falls from the beginning of November until February. In early October to December there are fierce typhoons. The best and sunniest time to visit Samar is from May to September.

The main crops are rice, maize and sweet potatoes, although Samar does not produce near enough of these to be self-sufficient. On the other hand, there are plentiful harvests of abaca and coconuts, and Borongan, in Eastern Samar, is the leading copra producer.

Sohoton National Park, near Basey in Southern Samar, is Samar's outstanding natural attraction. The best way to reach it is from Tacloban on Leyte (see the Sohoton National Park in the Leyte section earlier in this chapter for further information). Rather less exciting are the Blanca Aurora Falls near Gandara, between Calbayog and Cat balogan. The potential tourist attractions of Northern Samar should not be underestimated, although the infrastructure will have to be improved before people start taking notice of them.

Central and Eastern Samar are regarded as problem areas as fighting often breaks out there between government troops and the NPA. Find out what the situation is before you venture there, although Northern Samar and the west coast are OK.

The inhabitants of Samar are Visayans who call themselves Waray and speak the Waray-Waray dialect.

GETTING THERE & AWAY

You can get to Samar from Cebu, Leyte, Luzon and Masbate (see the Getting There & Away section of the Manila chapter and the relevant Getting There & Away sections of this and the Around Luzon chapter earlier in this book).

Air

To/From Luzon PAL flies daily except Wednesday and Sunday from Calbayog to Manila and on Tuesday, Thursday, Friday and Sunday from Catarman to Manila.

Bus

To/From Leyte Several Philtranco and Philippine Eagle buses run daily from Catarman, Calbayog and Catbalogan to Tacloban along the west coast of Samar, either to Tacloban only or on the way to Ormoc or Mindanao. The buses leave Catbalogan at 4, 10 and 11 am and 2 pm from the Petron service station. In between, other buses leave about every 30 minutes.

The trip takes two hours from Catbalogan to Tacloban.

To/From Luzon Air-con Philtranco buses and Inland Trailways buses (the better of the two, because it has fewer stops) go from Catarman to Manila daily at 8 am. It takes about 24 hours, including the Allen-Matnog ferry. The trip finishes at Pasay City (Edsa) in Manila.

Philtranco air-con buses run from Catbalogan and Calbayog to Manila daily. The bus comes from Mindanao or Leyte and is mostly full. The trip takes 25 and 26 hours respectively, including the San Isidro-Matnog ferry.

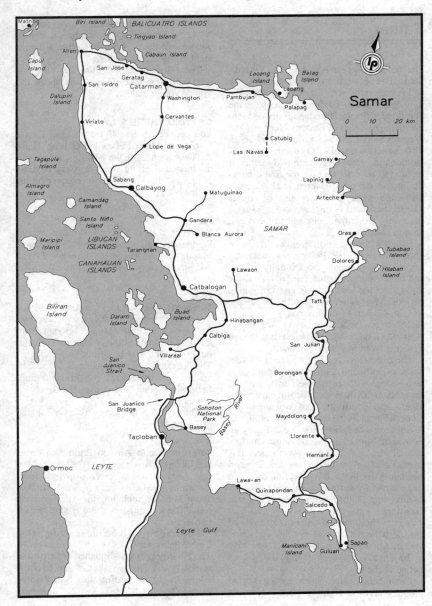

Boat

To/From Cebu The Western Samar Shipping Lines' MV *Elizabeth Lilly* sails from Allen to Cebu City on Sunday at 5 pm, taking 14 hours, and from Catbalogan to Cebu City on Thursday at 5 pm, taking 12 hours.

The Palacio Shipping Lines' MV *Don Martin Sr* leaves Calbayog for Cebu City on Tuesday, Thursday and Saturday at 8 pm, taking 12 hours.

To/From Leyte The Sulpicio Lines' MV *Cebu Princess* leaves Calbayog for Ormoc on Saturday at 10 pm, taking eight hours.

From Catbalogan to Tacloban, the William Lines' MV *Masbate I* leaves on Tuesday at 1 pm, taking four hours. The Sulpicio Lines' MV *Tacloban Princess* leaves on Thursday at noon, taking four hours. The Carlos Gothong Lines' MV *Don Calvino* leaves on Sunday at 7 am, taking four hours.

The K & T Shipping Lines' MV *Stacey* leaves Guiuan for Tacloban every other day at 10 pm, taking six hours.

To/From Luzon The ferries MV *Michelangelo* and MV *Northern Samar* sail daily at 6 am and 1 pm from Allen to Matnog. The crossing takes 1½ hours. The ferry MV *Marhalika I* of St Bernard Services leaves San Isidro for Matnog daily at 9 am and 4.30 pm, taking two hours. The Matnog and San Isidro terminal fee is P7 per passenger.

The Sulpicio Lines' MV *Cebu Princess* leaves Calbayog for Manila on Tuesday at 10 pm and goes via Masbate, taking 40 hours.

The William Lines' MV *Masbate I* leaves Catbalogan for Manila on Wednesday at 3 pm, taking 26 hours. The Sulpicio Lines' MV *Tacloban Princess* leaves Catbalogan for Manila on Friday at 7 pm, taking 22 hours.

To/From Masbate The Sulpicio Lines' MV *Cebu Princess* leaves Calbayog for Masbate on Masbate on Tuesday at 10 pm, taking four hours.

ALLEN

Allen has a wharf for ferries to and from Matnog on Luzon. There are also boats for Capul and Dalupiri islands, which lie offshore to the west. On Dalupiri Island, near San Antonio, you will also find the *Flying Dog Resort*.

Places to Stay

The *Bicolana Lodging House* has rooms for P35/70. It is an unpretentious place with a restaurant. *Angie's Eatery & Lodge* at the market and *El Canto Lodging House* both have simple rooms for P35 to P80. The *Buenos Aires Beach Cottages* are available for P80 and P120 per cottage. It is on the beach about three km south of Allen, halfway to Victoria.

Getting There & Away

Several buses go from Catbalogan to Allen via Calbayog daily, such as the Philippine Eagle buses at 9 and 10 am, which continue on to Catarman. The trip takes 3½ hours from Catbalogan and 1½ hours from Calbayog.

GERATAG & SAN JOSE

Three km west of Geratag lies San Jose, from where several boats leave daily for the Balicuatro Islands offshore. They go to San Antonio on Tingyao (Tinau) Island and Biri on Biri Island, and possibly other islands as well.

Places to Stay

The *House Schiefelbein (Mendoza)* near the beach at Geratag offers family-style accommodation. The rooms are basic, but clean and comfortable and cost P120/150. Food can be supplied on demand.

Getting There & Away

Several buses and jeepneys depart from Allen daily and go through San Jose and Geratag on the way to Catarman and Rawis (for Laoang). The trip takes one hour.

BALICUARTRO ISLANDS

Biri and Bani islands are reckoned to be two of the most attractive diving areas in the eastern Philippines. With an eye to the effect

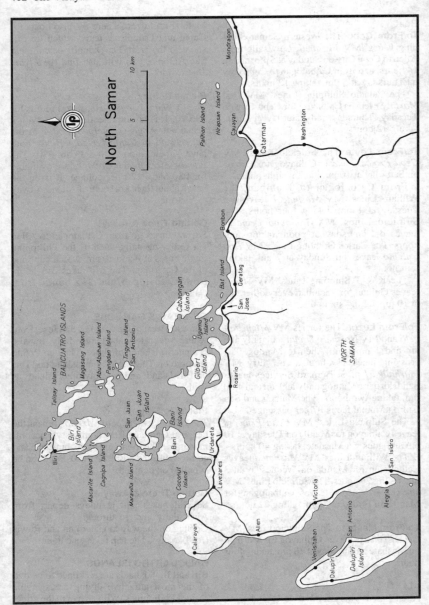

of publicity on tourists, the Northern Samar Tourism Council has applied to the Philippine Congress to have the Balicuatro Islands declared a protected area. In addition, the northern section of the Biri Island coast, with its small offshore limestone islands jutting out of the water by up to 37 metres, is to be declared a national marine park. During WW II, Biri Island had a Japanese garrison whose job was to observe the maritime traffic in the San Bernardino Straits.

If you want to spend a few days in the picturesque village of San Antonio on Tingyao (Tinau) Island, you can organise an overnight stay at House Schiefelbein (Mendoza) in Geratag. See Places to Stay in the previous Geratag & San Jose section for further information.

CATARMAN

Catarman, the capital of Northern Samar Province, is the starting point for travel in the north-east, for example, to the Laoang or Batag islands.

An easy river cruise is to go along the Catarman River from Catarman as far as Washington. A boat leaves at 1 pm and takes less than two hours for the nine-km trip. You can go back to Catarman by jeepney.

Owing to the possibility of skirmishes between the military and the NPA, trips inland on Northern Samar can not always be recommended for obvious security reasons. The coastal regions never present any problems to travellers in this respect.

The airport manager has tourist information about the sights of Northern Samar and photos of the most attractive places in this province.

Places to Stay

The *J & V Hotel* has basic rooms for P40/80, and there is a restaurant and a disco. It is at the White Beach in Cawayan, next to the University of Eastern Philippines (UEP), about four km east of Catarman.

The *Pahuwayan Lodging House* on Bonifacio St has simple rooms for P45/90.

Joni's Lodging House at the market has clean and fairly good rooms with fan for P80/160.

The *Diocesan Catholic Center (DCC)* (☎ 491), next to the Catholic church, has pleasant rooms with fan for P75/150, and there is a restaurant.

Getting There & Away

Air PAL has an office at Catarman Airport and on Bonifacio St.

Bus Several minibuses run from Catarman to Rawis (for Laoang) daily until about 5 pm, taking 1½ hours.

CALBAYOG

Calbayog is at one end of what is probably one of the most scenic coastal roads in the Philippines; at the other end is Allen. The road runs along almost the entire length of the coast and is especially impressive near the village of **Viriato** (about halfway between Calbayog and Allen), with mountains, steep cliffs, distant islands and little bays with colourful boats.

There is a large **waterfall** near Viriato that can be seen as far back as the bridge near the river mouth. The area around Viriato is good for a day trip and could include a hike along the coast. Getting back to Calbayog or Catarman shouldn't be a problem. The next jeepney will be coming round the corner any minute.

Approximately 50 km south-east of Calbayog are the **Blanca Aurora Falls**, the best known on Samar. To get there take the bus going to Catbalogan from Calbayog. Get out at the little community of San Gorge (pronounced San Horhay) about five km beyond Gandara. A river boat for Buenavista leaves at 10 am and noon, taking one hour. From Buenavista it is three km on foot to the village of Blanca Aurora. Keep on walking and after about 10 minutes you will get to the falls. There might be a boat leaving San Gorge at 11 am for Blanca Aurora, which comes back in the late afternoon. It's best to check in Gandara whether the waterfall area is still a stronghold of the NPA.

Places to Stay

The *Calbayog Hotel* has basic rooms with fan for P60/120 and also has a restaurant. The *San Joaquin Inn* (☎ 387), on the corner of Nijaga and Orquin Sts, has rooms with fan for P90/180 and with fan and bath for P140/280, and there is a restaurant. This place is simple, with less than clean sanitary facilities.

The best hotel in Calbayog is the *Seaside Drive Inn* (☎ 234) in Rawis. It has rooms for P80/160, with fan and bath for P200 and with air-con and bath for P350. It is tidy and pleasant, and has a restaurant.

Getting There & Away

Air PAL has an office (☎ 242) on Navarro St.

Bus Philippine Eagle buses run almost every hour between 5 and 9 am from Catarman to Calbayog via Allen daily. The trip takes 2½ hours to Catarman and 1½ hours to Allen. The buses go on to Ormoc on Leyte.

There are also several jeepneys daily, taking 3½ hours to Catarman and two hours to Allen.

Several buses go from Catbalogan to Calbayog daily. You can get a Philippine Eagle bus at 9 or 10 am going to Allen and Catarman. The trip takes two hours.

There are also several jeepneys travelling between Catbalogan and Calbayog daily, taking an hour or more.

CATBALOGAN

Catbalogan, the capital of Western Samar Province, hasn't all that much to offer travellers, so most people head straight for Tacloban. You can, however, get buses from here that go across the island to the east coast.

Places to Stay

The Hotel Saint Bartholomew on San Bartolome St has simple but fairly good rooms with fan for P100/190, with fan and bath for P150/260 and with air-con and bath for P350, and there is a restaurant.

Kikay's Hotel (☎ 664) on Curry Ave has singles/doubles with fan for P70/140 and one double room with air-con and bath for P240. It is simple and clean, and has a restaurant

Tony's Hotel on Del Rosario St, has singles with fan for P100, doubles with fan and bath for P180 and singles/doubles with air-con and bath for P180/250, and there is a restaurant. The *Fortune Hotel* (☎ 680), also on Del Rosario St, has rooms with fan for P100/160, with fan and bath for P220 and with air-con and bath for P350. There is also a restaurant.

Places to Eat

You can get good meals at the *Fortune Restaurant* in the hotel of the same name. *Tony's Kitchen* is another cheap restaurant where you can eat well.

Getting There & Away

Several buses and jeepneys run daily from Catarman to Catbalogan via Allen and Calbayog, such as the Philippine Eagle buses, which leave almost every hour between 5 and 9 am. Going to Catbalogan, the trip takes five hours from Catarman, four hours from Allen and two hours from Calbayog.

BORONGAN

Borongan, the capital of Eastern Samar, is an important trading post for copra, rattan and bamboo.

The *Domsowir Hotel* on Real St has singles with fan for P100 and doubles with fan and bath for P200. It also has a restaurant.

Getting There & Away

A daily SBL Lines bus runs from Catbalogan to Borongan at 9 am from Pier 1. The trip takes five hours.

GUIUAN

A friendly little town on a peninsula in south-east Samar, Guiuan is fairly easy to reach by boat from Tacloban on Leyte. The Americans started their aerial attacks on the Japanese from here and the giant airport at the eastern edge was once one of the biggest US bases in the Pacific. Today grass grows on the unused runways.

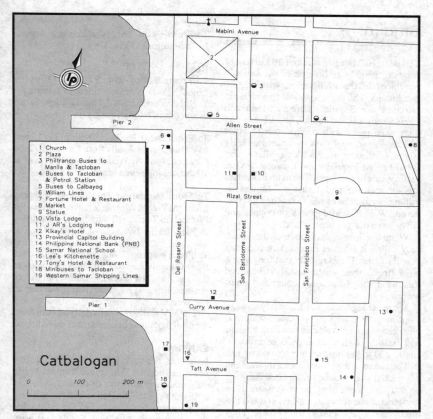

1 Church
2 Plaza
3 Philtranco Buses to Manila & Tacloban
4 Buses to Tacloban & Petrol Station
5 Buses to Calbayog
6 William Lines
7 Fortune Hotel & Restaurant
8 Market
9 Statue
10 Vista Lodge
11 J AR's Lodging House
12 Kikay's Hotel
13 Provincial Capitol Building
14 Philippine National Bank (PNB)
15 Samar National School
16 Lee's Kitchenette
17 Tony's Hotel & Restaurant
18 Minibuses to Tacloban
19 Western Samar Shipping Lines

Catbalogan

0   100   200 m

Near Guiuan are a couple of beautiful beaches which are hardly ever visited, as well as numerous small islands west of Guiuan in Leyte Gulf.

Places to Stay
The *Arcenos Boarding House* on Managantan St has simple rooms for P50/100 and with fan for P60/120.

The *Bluestar Lodging House* on Concepcion St has rooms for P50/100 and with fan for P60/120. It's a reasonable place with a sing-along disco. The *Villa Rosario Lodging House* on Concepcion St has dorm beds with fan for P50, rooms for P50/100 and with fan for P80/160. It is basic, clean and comfortable.

Places to Eat
You can get very cheap meals at the clean *Sherly Tan Restaurant* on Concepcion St. The *Bluestar Eatery* in the lodging house of the same name serves meals if you order them in advance.

Siquijor

The island of Siquijor is about 20 km east of southern Negros and is one of the smallest provinces in the Philippines, with 75,000 inhabitants. The main towns of this pleasant province are Siquijor, Larena, Maria and Lazi. Siquijor is the capital, and Larena and Lazi have ports with connections to other islands. A surfaced road encircles this hilly island, connecting its well-kept villages and small towns; jeepneys and tricycles are the main means of transport. The main industries are agriculture and fishing. Manganese mining north-west of Maria reached its peak before WW II, and deposits of copper and silver have not yet been mined.

When the Spaniards discovered the island, they called it Isla del Fuego, which means island of fire. This suggests that they saw a large fire as they sailed past. It is believed that what they saw were countless glow-worms.

There is a legend that millions of years ago Siquijor lay completely under water. It emerged from the sea amid crashing thunder and flashing lightning. Fossils of mussels, snails and other underwater creatures can still be found in the mountainous interior and are quoted as evidence for this belief.

You can sense that there is something mysterious about Siquijor when you tell Filipinos that you intend to travel there. They will warn you of witches and magicians and healers with wondrous powers. Many strange events take place on this singular island and are enhanced by the practice of voodoo and black magic. Filipinos will warn you that it is better to avoid it for your own safety's sake...

GETTING THERE & AWAY

You can get to Siquijor from Bohol, Cebu, Mindanao and Negros (see the relevant Getting There & Away sections of this and the Mindanao & Palawan chapter).

Air
To/From Cebu PAL is planning a service from Siquijor to Cebu City.

Boat
To/From Bohol The Palacio Shipping Lines' MV *Don Martin 6* leaves Larena for Tagbilaran on Tuesday, Thursday and Saturday at 6 pm, taking four hours.

To/From Cebu The Palacio Shipping Lines' MV *Don Martin 7* sails from Larena to Cebu City on Monday, Wednesday and Friday at 10 pm, taking seven hours.

To/From Mindanao The Palacio Shipping Lines' MV *Don Martin 6* leaves Larena for Plaridel on Tuesday, Thursday and Saturday at 3 am, taking five hours.

To/From Negros A big outrigger boat goes from Cangalwang or Larena to Dumaguete daily at 7 am and takes 2½ hours. For safety reasons, this service is not recommended in bad weather.

The MV *Catherine* sails daily at 7 am from Siquijor to Dumaguete and takes three hours.

LARENA
Larena is a pretty little place with a few beautiful houses. The place comes to life only when a boat docks or departs.

If you walk to Congbagsa and go on along the road that branches off to the right, past the large white National Food Authority building, you will reach a beautiful bay with a white beach. If there weren't so many sharp-edged stones in the water, the place would be perfect. There is a very refreshing spring in the rocks here.

Places to Stay
Larena The *Luisa & Son's Lodge* at the wharf has rooms with fan for P80/120. Luisa and Douglas are very helpful and have some good information. They have a restaurant and you can hire a motorbike for P300 and a jeep for P800 a day. The *Larena Pension House*, just a few minutes' walk uphill from the wharf, has simple but fairly good rooms

Top: Coron Island, North Palawan (JP)
Middle: Off-road crossing by jeepney, Palawan (JP)
Bottom: Badjao (sea gypsies) of the Sulu Islands (JP)

Top: Badjao woman (JP)
Bottom: T'boli woman (JP)

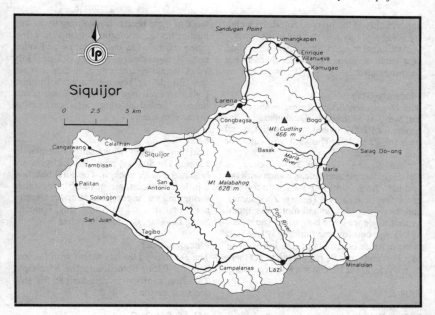

with fan for P100/200 and with air-con for P300.

Around Larena The *Paradise Beach* at Sandugan has pleasant accommodation on a quiet, deserted beach (shallow water), six km north of Larena, some 400 metres off the ring road. Cottages with bath are P150 and P250 and double rooms with bath are P200. Only three weeks are charged for a four-week stay. It belongs to an Englishman, Brian, and his Filipina wife, Lucki; Nick Buca still remains the spirit behind the place. They have an excellent restaurant. Paddle boats can be obtained for P25 a day.

The *Hidden Paradise* at Bitaog has cottages with bath for P150. A discount is given for longer stays. This is a friendly little place on an out-of-the-way bay with an attractive beach for swimming. It is nine km north of Larena, just before Enrique Villanueva, about 300 metres off the ring road. You will find delicious cooking in a family-style res-

taurant. They don't call the owner, Eleuterio Sumalpong, 'Eater' for nothing! He is also a tricycle driver and charges fair prices, for a trip around the island for example.

Places to Eat
There is a fairly large restaurant near the market, where jeepneys wait for passengers. A few smaller places are near the wharf.

Getting There & Away
Numerous jeepneys leave the market in Larena to go to various places around the island. Always ask about the last trip back or you may have to walk, hire a tricycle or stay the night. A tricycle should not cost more than P200 a day.

SIQUIJOR
The small town of Siquijor is the capital of the island. It has a Provincial Capitol Building, a church, a hospital and a post office. You can get Filipino sardines, called *ihala-*

son, cheaply at the market. Another speciality is *tognos*, tiny fish that are eaten raw.

At Cangalwang, a little west of Siquijor, is a small airstrip. The beach there is not recommended.

Places to Stay

The *Dondeezco Beach Resort* is about two km west of Siquijor in Dumanhug. It has rooms for P200/280 and rooms with fan and bath for P280/350. The staff will cater for you on request.

The *Beach Garden Mini Hotel* in Catalinan has pleasant, clean rooms with fan and bath from P240 to P360. A discount is given for longer stays. There is a restaurant, and they offer bicycle and motorbike rental as well as jeepney and boat trips. The owner of this big, comfortable building is Dutch. It is on a white beach about one km west of Siquijor, and costs P2 per person to get there by tricycle; from Larena it's P5 per person.

SAN JUAN

One of the best beaches on the island is **Paliton Beach**, about two km north-west of San Juan.

The *Coco-Grove Beach Resort* has rooms with fan and bath for P300 and with air-con and bath for P500. There is a restaurant, and a jeepney and outrigger boat can be hired.

SAN ANTONIO

San Antonio is in the mountainous centre of the island and is supposed to be the place for the nature healers, also known as *mananambals*. The road there is bad and not easy for tricycles to pass through. Don't expect to find a devil's kitchen there. The work of these healers has nothing to do with magic, but is an original attempt to effect cures through the use of herbs and other natural ingredients. A visit during Holy Week would be interesting, as this is when the 'druids' of the southern Philippines gather to exchange information and create dubious herbal mixtures after performing mysterious rites.

LAZI

Lazi has a small wharf and is similar to Larena. On Sunday, popular cockfights are held in the rustic cockpit. The coral beaches, a little to the east, are unsuitable for either swimming or snorkelling. **Lapac Beach**, north-east of Lazi on Maria Bay, opposite Salag Do-Ong, is said to be better.

Places to Stay

The *Traveler's Den* has rooms with fan and bath for P150. Someone in the Municipal Treasurer's office is responsible for this accommodation.

SALAG DO-ONG

Salag Do-Ong is on the northernmost point of Maria Bay. With its small swimming beach it is probably the most popular holiday resort of the Siquijodnons. There is no regular jeepney service and you have to walk the two km from the road to the beach. The last trip back to Larena is at about 4 pm.

Places to Stay

The *Tourist Cottage* has rooms for P140. It is self-catering and has a small kitchen. The manager lives at the turn-off from the main road and looks after the water supply.

Mindanao & Sulu

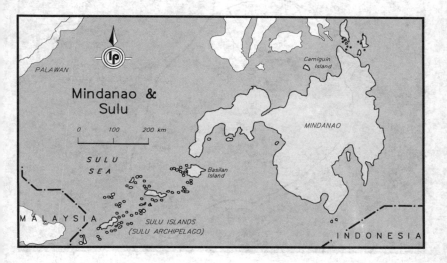

South of the Visayas is the large island of Mindanao, second in size only to Luzon. Smaller islands associated with Mindanao include the tiny island of Camiguin, off the north coast, the island of Basilan, off Zamboanga, and the Sulu Islands – the archipelago pointing towards Borneo.

Camiguin

Camiguin lies off the north coast of Mindanao. Though relatively small, it has no less than seven volcanoes, as well as springs and waterfalls. The best known volcano is Hibok-Hibok, which last erupted in 1951. The volcanoes seem to attract clouds like magnets, and from December to mid-March short rain showers can be expected. The sunniest months are April, May and June. Camiguin is well known for its sweet *lanzones* fruit (called 'buahan' on Cami-

guin), which grows on the slopes of Hibok-Hibok and is the best in the Philippines. The colourful Lanzones Festival, a sort of thanksgiving festival, takes place every year in late October, usually 24 and 25 October, in Mambajao. The Camiguinos are well known for their hospitality. Certainly it is one reason why the comparatively few visitors who have so far discovered it like to come back. (Camiguin is pronounced almost like 'come again'...) Unlike on other islands, strangers here are greeted not with 'Hi Joe', but with 'Hi friends'. If you can do without luxury, you will definitely enjoy your stay on Camiguin.

GETTING THERE & AWAY
You can get to Camiguin from Cebu, Leyte and Mindanao (see the Mindanao Getting There & Away section in this chapter and the Cebu and Leyte Getting There & Away sections in the Visayas chapter).

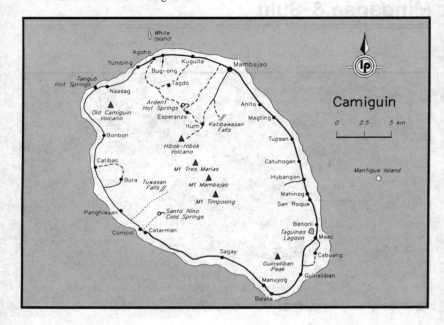

Air

To/From Cebu PAL has flights from Mambajao to Cebu City on Monday and Saturday. These flights are not very reliable and cancellations are frequent due to lack of demand.

Apart from Mambajao, the nearest airports for flights to Cebu City are in Butuan and Cagayan de Oro on Mindanao. Bookings can be made in Mambajao at the PAL agents in the General Merchandise Caves Hardware & Auto Supply. Staff will also arrange the charter of a small aircraft for three or four passengers; the price from Mambajao to Cebu City should be around P3500.

To/From Luzon PAL has flights from Butuan and Cagayan de Oro, both on Mindanao, to Manila.

Boat

To/From Cebu From Mambajao to Cebu City, the Georgia Shipping Lines' MV *Luzille* leaves on Wednesday at 6 pm and takes 14 hours, going via Maasin on Leyte. The Cokaliong Shipping Lines' MV *Filipinas Siargao* leaves on Wednesday at 7 pm and takes 13 hours, going via Maasin on Leyte.

From Benoni to Cebu City, the Tamula Shipping Lines' MV *Ruperto* leaves twice monthly, taking 12 hours.

To/From Leyte From Mambajao to Maasin, the Georgia Shipping Lines' MV *Luzille* leaves on Wednesday at 6 pm, taking five hours. The Cokaliong Shipping Lines' MV *Filipinas Siargao* leaves on Wednesday at 7 pm, taking five hours.

To/From Mindanao From Benoni to Balingoan, the Tamula Shipping Lines' MV *Ruperto Jr*, MV *Hijos* or MV *Anita* leaves at 6, 8 and 10 am, noon and at 2 pm, taking

1½ hours. At 6.30 and 10.30 am a boat sometimes leaves from Guinsiliban, south of Benoni.

From Guinsiliban to Cagayan de Oro, the MV *Yuhun* leaves at 2 or 3 pm and takes three hours.

GETTING AROUND

You can travel right around the island, which has a circumference of about 65 km, in about three hours, if you don't make too many stops. For the best connections, go in an anticlockwise direction, as there are not many vehicles between Yumbing and Catarman – the road between Benoni and Mambajao is most travelled by jeepneys and buses and is your best prospect for getting transport on the return trip. Plenty of jeepneys also travel between Catarman, the second largest town on the island, and Benoni. Along the west coast, however, be prepared to walk a few km, as only a few jeepneys run from Mambajao to Catarman and back, and the last jeepney from Catarman leaves at about 3 or 4 pm.

For short distances you may be able to use tricycles but the service is only good in and around Mambajao. A trip around the island – of course by rented motorbike – is a great idea. Although there is no commercial rental, some motorbike owners in Mambajao are willing to hire out their machines for P250 or P300 a day. Many resorts will arrange motorbike hire on request.

MAMBAJAO

The little town of Mambajao is the capital of Camiguin, which has been a province since 1966.

There is a tourist information centre in the Provincial Capitol Building. Mambajao also has a branch of the Philippine National Bank (PNB); you can change travellers' cheques there, although the rate is not as good as in Cagayan de Oro or Cebu City, for instance.

Good, freshly grilled fish is sold at the market. You might find a bit of social life in the Parola Disco.

Places to Stay & Eat

Tia's Pension House is a nice big house near the town hall. It has rooms with fan for P100/150 and is quite good. You can order meals or use the kitchen to prepare your own meals for a small charge.

Tia's Beach Cottages in Tapon, a few minutes from the town centre, has cottages with bath for P250. They are clean and quiet and have electricity from 6 to 11 pm. It's a friendly, pleasant place.

The *Tree House* at Bolok-Bolok, about one km north-west of Mambajao, right on the seafront, has rooms with bath for P150/200 and tree houses big enough for two people for P250. There is a restaurant, and windsurfing, paddle bancas and mountain bikes are available.

AROUND MAMBAJAO
Hibok-Hibok Volcano

Hibok-Hibok (1320 metres) is the most active of Camiguin's seven volcanoes. On 5 December 1951 it erupted without warning, killing over 2000 people. A small collection of photos and newspaper clippings can be seen at the Comvol Station which monitors volcanic activity. This is about 400 metres up the mountain and takes a good hour to reach on foot. The staff at the station are happy to show you around and explain the use of the seismographic instruments. They appreciate small gifts like bread, sweets and cigarettes.

For trips to the volcano, the tourism office in the Provincial Capitol Building in Mambajao or any resort can arrange an experienced guide for about P300. The climb is via Esperanza and takes about four hours. It begins with a gentle slope and takes you first through high cogon grass and fern groves, leading to a steeper section which takes you over scree, lava and rock faces to the summit.

Once at the top, you can climb down to a moss-encircled crater lake. This takes about 45 minutes. If you start early, you won't need to spend the night up there, but if you decide to go down to the lake, it would be wise to spend the nights before and after the trek at the Comvol Station. Alternatively, you can take a tent and camp beside the lake.

Katibawasan Falls

These falls are a great place to swim; they are about 50 metres high and have refreshingly cool water. There is a resthouse, but you have to take your own food. The best time to go there is from 10 am to 2 pm, when the sun is high. Admission costs P3.

Getting There & Away To get to the falls, go from Mambajao to Pandan, which is on the edge of town, by tricycle. You have to do the remaining two km to the falls on foot.

Ardent Hot Springs

The crystal clear water in the beautifully designed swimming pool is around 40°C warm. The surrounding area is well tended and there are sheltered picnic places. It's a favourite for weekend outings; the pool is cleaned out on Monday. Admission costs P25; Filipinos pay only P10.

The *Ardent Hot Spring Resort* has dorm beds for P120 and cottages with bath for P400. There is a restaurant, and the food is good.

Getting There & Away Including a few hours waiting time, the trip from Mambajao by tricycle and back costs around P150.

White Island

White Island is a small island about three km north of Agoho. It consists of nothing but coral and sand and offers good swimming and snorkelling but no shade. A sun umbrella or a tent would be really useful here.

Getting There & Away To get to White Island, go by tricycle or jeepney from Mambajao to Yumbing, Naasag or Agoho, then charter a boat. At the White Island terminal in Agoho and in the resorts there, you can organise a round trip for P200.

AROUND THE ISLAND
Kuguita

The sandy beach at Mahayahay and Turtles Nest Beach, which has a few corals, are in Kuguita, three km west of Mambajao.

Places to Stay & Eat The *Turtles Nest Beach Cottages* has rooms with bath for P225/300. The cottages are fairly large duplexes. The establishment is pleasant, well tended, and it has a garden and restaurant. Mountain bikes and motorbikes are available for hire.

Agoho & Bug-ong

A few km west of Kuguita are Agoho and Bug-ong, two small coastal towns which are popular with most travellers; both have accommodation. At Agoho you can get a boat to the offshore White Island for P200.

Places to Stay & Eat The clean and peaceful *Camiguin Seaside Lodge* in Agoho, also known as Agohay Cottage, has dorm beds for P100 and P150 and cottages with bath for P250 and P300. It has a restaurant and motorbikes are available for hire. The *Morning Glory Cottages* in Agoho has rooms for P100/200 and cottages with bath for P350. It is fairly comfortable and has a restaurant as well as good cooking facilities. The comfortable *Caves Resort* in Agoho has rooms for P100/200 and cottages with bath for P250 and P350. It has a restaurant and a tennis court; windsurfing equipment, a dive shop (Splash Diving Centre) and mountain bikes can be hired.

Jasmine by the Sea in Bug-ong is a pleasant place which has cottages with bath for P250 and P350 (more spacious), and there is a restaurant.

Getting There & Away The trip from Mambajao to Agoho by tricycle costs P2.75 per person; a Special Ride costs P25. A Special Ride by jeepney from Benoni to Agoho costs P150 to P250.

Bonbon

Bonbon has some interesting ruined churches and a cemetery sunk under the sea. Some years ago grave stones could be seen at low tide. Later a large cross was put in the sea to indicate where the Sunken Cemetery was, but it has since toppled over.

Catarman

Just under two km north-west of Catarman there is a turn-off leading to the **Tuwasan Falls**, about four km from the ring road. When you get to the Dinangasan River, you have to head upstream a bit to find them. The local people compare the two main falls with two different women: one, Katibawasan, who wears lots of make-up; the other, Tuwasan, who has a natural, unspoilt beauty.

The nearby **Santo Nino Cold Springs** are refreshingly cool and you can swim in a nice large pool that is one to two metres deep; the pool is cleaned out on Wednesday. There are toilets and a picnic shelter. The place is also known as the Kiyab Pool and is over two km off the main road.

In Catarman you can stay in rooms at the high school for P50 per person.

Guinsiliban

There is a ferry route between Guinsiliban in the south of the island and Balingoan and Cagayan de Oro, both on Mindanao. The roughly 300-year-old Moro watchtower stands behind the elementary school. It looks as if the Tamula Beach Cottages never got past the planning stage.

Benoni

Benoni has a wharf for ferries going to and from Balingoan on Mindanao. From here boats also go to Mantigue (Magsaysay) Island, which lies offshore and is a favourite diving place. South of Benoni is a beautiful artificial lake, **Taguines Lagoon**.

Places to Stay The *Travel Lodge Lagoon* has rooms with fan and bath for P300 and with air-con and bath for P450. Cottages with bath cost P200. The simple, but appealing cottages with their large verandas stand on stilts in the water. This place has an excellent restaurant which specialises in crabs which are cultivated on the premises. It is a quiet place right on the lagoon, about one km from Benoni; it costs P15 by tricycle to go there.

Mahinog & Mantigue Island

Mahinog lies on the east coast of Camiguin, almost opposite Mantigue (Magsaysay) Island. The beach there is pebbly but Mantigue Island has a white sandy beach and usually offers good snorkelling. Unfortunately the rubbish lying around on the island has detracted from its original beauty. If you want to stay for a few days, bring your own provisions and drinking water. The round trip from Mahinog costs about P200.

Place to Stay The *Mychellin Beach Resort* in Mahinog has rooms with fan and bath for P150, and there are cooking facilities. It appears like this place has already seen its heyday.

Tupsan

Near Tupsan, about one km from the ring road, you can take a refreshing dip in the cold water of the **Macao Cold Spring**. The turn-off is signposted.

Mindanao

Mindanao is the second largest island of the Philippines. Its landscape is dominated by mountain chains running north-south. Close to Davao is Mt Apo, the highest mountain in the Philippines. Mindanao is one of the Philippines' richest islands, even though little of its mineral wealth has yet been tapped. There is an occasional gold rush sparked off by rumours of a sizeable find, but at present most of the island's income comes from agriculture, with large pineapple plantations in the north near Cagayan de Oro and banana groves in the south near Davao.

It is not quite true that all of the Mindanao population is Muslim but certainly most of the Muslim Filipinos live there and on the neighbouring Sulu Islands. The area around Lake Lanao in central Mindanao is predominantly Muslim.

Warning There has been an on-going struggle for an autonomous Muslim state on the

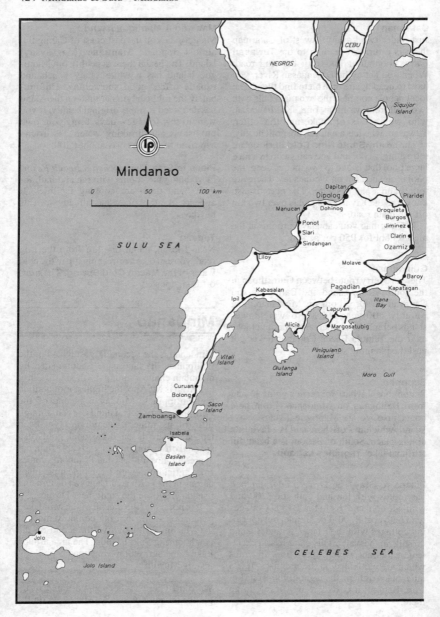

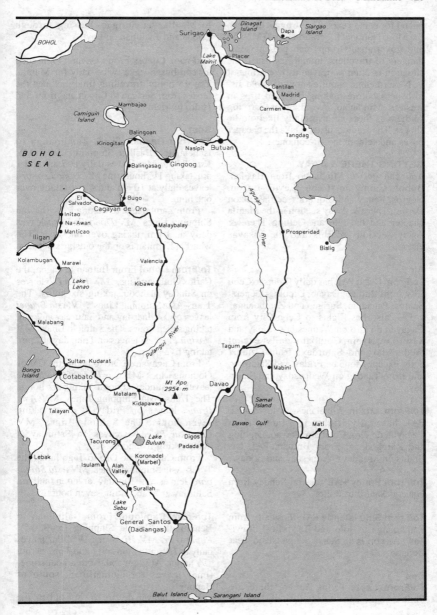

island for some years. The struggle between the Moro National Liberation Front (MNLF) and government troops can present some dangers to travellers, though, as usual, the situation is often portrayed as worse than it is. Nevertheless, enquire about possible disturbances before making overland trips in western Mindanao. Avoid buses carrying soldiers as these are especially likely to be shot at. The soldiers usually take the cheaper buses and seldom the air-con ones.

GETTING THERE & AWAY

You can get to Mindanao from Basilan, Bohol, Camiguin, Cebu, Leyte, Luzon, Negros, Panay and Siquijor (see the Luzon Getting There & Away section in the Manila chapter and the relevant Getting There & Away sections of this and the Visayas chapter).

Air

To/From Cebu PAL has daily flights to Cebu City from Butuan, Davao, Dipolog, General Santos, Pagadian, Surigao and Zamboanga.

PAL also has flights to Cebu City from Cagayan de Oro on Wednesday, Friday and Saturday; from Cotabato daily except Wednesday and Saturday; from Ozamiz daily except Monday, Friday and Saturday; and from Tandag on Wednesday and Saturday.

To/From Luzon All planes go to Manila. PAL has daily flights to Manila from Cagayan de Oro, Cotabato, Davao, Dipolog and Zamboanga. From Butuan, PAL has flights on Monday, Wednesday and Friday.

To/From Panay PAL flies on Sunday from General Santos to Iloilo.

To/From Sulu Islands PAL flies daily from Zamboanga to Jolo and Tawi-Tawi. Tawi-Tawi Airport is on Sanga Sanga Island, near Bongao.

Bus

To/From Leyte From Davao, there are Philtranco air-con buses twice daily heading to Manila via Surigao, passing through Liloan and Tacloban on Leyte.

To/From Luzon From Davao, Philtranco air-con buses leave twice daily for Manila. The 45 hours' travelling time includes the ferries from Surigao to Liloan and from San Isidro to Matnog.

Boat

To/From Basilan From Zamboanga to Isabela, the Basilan Shipping Lines' MV *Estrella del Mar* leaves daily at 7 am and 1 pm, taking 1½ hours; the MV *Doña Leonora* leaves daily at 10 am and 4 pm, taking over one hour.

From Zamboanga to Lamitan, the Basilan Shipping Lines' MV *Doña Ramona* leaves daily at 3 pm, taking over one hour. The wharf at Lamitan is on the outskirts of town.

To/From Bohol From Butuan to Jagna, the Carlos Gothong Lines' MV *Doña Lili* leaves on Sunday at noon, taking six hours. The Trans-Asia Shipping Lines' MV *Asia Brunei* leaves on Wednesday and Saturday at 7 pm, taking seven hours. The Sulpicio Lines' MV *Nasipit Princess* leaves on Thursday at 2 pm, taking five hours.

From Cagayan de Oro to Jagna, the Carlos Gothong Lines' MV *Our Lady of Guadalupe* leaves on Sunday at noon, taking six hours. The Trans-Asia Shipping Lines' MV *Asia Brunei* leaves on Friday at noon, taking seven hours. The Sulpicio Lines' MV *Cagayan Princess* leaves on Saturday at noon, taking five hours.

From Cagayan de Oro to Tagbilaran, the Trans-Asia Shipping Lines' MV *Asia Singapore* leaves on Tuesday at noon and on Saturday at 7 pm, taking seven hours.

To/From Camiguin From Balingoan to Benoni, the Tamula Shipping Lines' MV *Ruperto Jr*, MV *Hijos* or MV *Anita* leaves daily at 7, 9 and 11 am and 1 and 3 pm, taking 1½ hours. At 9 am and 1 pm a boat sometimes leaves for Guinsiliban, south of Benoni.

From Cagayan de Oro to Guinsiliban, the

MV *Yuhum* leaves at 7 or 8 am and takes three hours.

To/From Cebu Several ships go to Cebu City from various towns on Mindanao.

From Butuan, the Carlos Gothong Lines' MV *Doña Lili* leaves on Monday, Wednesday and Friday at 6 pm, taking 12 hours; the MV *Our Lady of Lourdes* leaves on Thursday at 6 pm, taking 9 hours. The Sulpicio Lines' MV *Nasipit Princess* leaves on Tuesday, Friday and Sunday at 8 pm, taking 10 hours.

From Cagayan de Oro, the Carlos Gothong Lines' MV *Our Lady of Guadalupe* leaves on Monday, Wednesday and Friday at 7 pm, taking 9 hours. The Sulpicio Lines' MV *Cagayan Princess* leaves on Tuesday, Thursday and Sunday at 7 pm, taking 12 hours. The Trans-Asia Shipping Lines' MV *Asia Japan* leaves on Tuesday, Thursday and Saturday at 7 pm; the MV *Asia Thailand* leaves on Wednesday, Friday and Sunday at 7 pm. Both take 10 hours.

From Dapitan, the Cokaliong Shipping Lines' MV *Filipinas Dumaguete* leaves on Tuesday, Thursday and Saturday at 4 pm and takes 14 hours, going via Dumaguete on Negros.

From Davao, the Sulpicio Lines' MV *Manila Princess* leaves on Wednesday at 8 pm, taking 25 hours.

From Iligan, the Carlos Gothong Lines' MV *Doña Cristina* leaves on Tuesday, Friday and Sunday at 7 pm, taking 11 hours. The William Lines' MV *Misamis Occidental* leaves on Thursday at 8 pm; the *Iligan City* leaves on Sunday at 7 pm. Both take 10 hours.

From Ozamiz, the Carlos Gothong Lines' MV *Our Lady of Mount Carmel* leaves on Monday, Wednesday, Friday and Sunday at 7 pm, taking 10 hours. The William Lines' MV *Iligan City* leaves on Tuesday and Thursday at 7 pm and the MV *Tacloban City* leaves on Sunday at 7 pm. Both take 10 hours.

From Surigao, the Cokaliong Shipping Lines' MV *Filipinas Siargao* leaves on Monday at 9 pm, taking 11 hours (this boat departs at 3 pm from Dapa on Siargao Island). The MV *Filipinas Maasin* leaves on Wednesday at 9 pm and Sunday at 7 pm; and the MV *Filipinas Surigao* leaves Thursday and Saturday at 7 pm. They all take 10 hours.

To/From Leyte From Surigao to San Juan, Kasamahan Shipping Lines has one ship weekly, which leaves on Wednesday at midnight and takes five hours.

From Surigao to Liloan, the MV *Maharlika II* of Bernard Services leaves at 5 pm from Lipata, 10 km north-west of Surigao, and takes three hours.

From Surigao to Maasin, the Sulpicio Lines' MV *Surigao Princess* leaves on Tuesday at 10 pm. It takes six hours and continues on to Palompon and Calubian. The Cokaliong Shipping Lines' MV *Filipinas Surigao* leaves on Tuesday at 7 pm, taking 4½ hours. The Trans-Asia Shipping Lines' MV *Asia Singapore* leaves on Thursday at 7 pm, taking three hours.

To/From Luzon There are several ships that go to Manila from Mindanao.

From Butuan, the Carlos Gothong Lines' MV *Our Lady of Lourdes* leaves on Saturday at 6 pm, taking 35 hours.

From Cagayan de Oro, the Aboitiz Lines' MV *Superferry 1* leaves on Tuesday at 4 pm and takes 40 hours, going via Iloilo on Panay. The Negros Navigation Lines' MV *Princess of Negros* leaves Wednesday at 4 pm and takes 42 hours. It goes via Bacolod on Negros. The William Lines' MV *Doña Virginia* leaves on Wednesday at 11 pm and takes 32 hours, going via Dumaguete on Negros.

From Davao, the William Lines' MV *Maynilad* leaves on Monday at noon. It goes via Zamboanga and takes 64 hours.

From Dipolog, the William Lines' MV *Misamis Occidental* leaves on Saturday at 10 pm, taking 31 hours.

From Ozamiz, the William Lines' MV *Tacloban City* leaves on Tuesday at 7 pm, taking 36 hours.

From Surigao, the Sulpicio Lines' MV *Surigao Princess* leaves Tuesday at 10 pm, taking 51 hours and going via Maasin, Palompon and Calubian on Leyte. The Aboitiz Lines' MV *Legaspi* leaves on Friday at 9 pm and takes 43 hours and goes via Ormoc on Leyte.

From Zamboanga, the William Lines' MV *Maynilad* leaves on Tuesday at 4pm, taking 33 hours.

To/From Negros From Cagayan de Oro to Dumaguete, Negros Navigation Lines' the MV *Princess of Negros* leaves on Wednesday at 4 pm, taking 16 hours. The William Lines' MV *Doña Virginia* leaves on Wednesday at 11 pm, taking six hours.

From Dapitan to Dumaguete, the MV *Dumaguete Ferry*, MV *Georich*, MV *Palauan Ferry* or MV *Don Victorino* of George & Peter Lines leaves daily, taking five hours. The harbour for Dapitan and Dipolog lies between both cities and is called Dapitan Port. A tricycle from Dipolog or Dapitan costs about P10.

To/From Panay From Cagayan de Oro to Iloilo, the Aboitiz Lines' MV *Superferry 1* leaves on Tuesday at 4 pm, taking 16 hours. The Negros Navigation Lines' MV *Santa Ana* leaves on Sunday at 4 pm, taking 14 hours.

From Zamboanga to Iloilo, the Trans-Asia Shipping Lines' MV *Asia Korea* leaves on Wednesday at 2 pm, taking 18 hours. The Sulpicio Lines' MV *Philippine Princess* leaves on Saturday at 8 pm, taking 14 hours (this boat departs on Friday at 8 pm from General Santos).

To/From Siquijor From Plaridel to Larena, the Palacio Shipping Lines' MV *Don Martin 6* leaves on Tuesday, Thursday and Saturday at noon and takes five hours.

To/From Sulu Islands SKT Shipping Lines has three ships going from Zamboanga to Sitangkai. The MV *Lady Ruth* leaves on Tuesday at 8 pm and takes 45 hours, going via Jolo (10 hours), Siasi (22 hours) and Bongao (36 hours).

The MV *Lady Helen* leaves on Wednesday at 6 pm and takes 44 hours, going via Jolo, Siasi and Bongao.

The MV *Doña Isabel II* leaves on Saturday at 6 pm and takes 45 hours, going via Jolo, Siasi and Bongao.

The Sampaguita Shipping Corporation also has three ships going from Zamboanga to Sitangkai. The MV *Sampaguita Grandeur* leaves on Monday at 8 pm and takes 42 hours, going via Jolo (nine hours), Siasi (18 hours) and Bongao (33 hours).

The MV *Sampaguita Laei* leaves on Thursday at 8 pm and takes 42 hours, going via Jolo, Siasai and Bongao.

The MV *Sampaguita Blossom* leaves on Sunday at 7 pm and takes 45 hours, going via Jolo, Siasi and Bongao.

The Zamboanga-based Magnolia Shipping Lines also has numerous ships on this route or parts of this route.

SURIGAO

Surigao, the capital of Surigao del Norte Province, is the starting point for trips to offshore islands like Dinagat and Siargao. What must be the best beach in the Surigao area, **Mabua Beach**, 12 km outside the city, is a favourite weekend resort. Here the water is clear and the swimming is great, although the beach itself has black pebbles instead of sand.

It's always a bit rainy in north-east Mindanao and in December and January be prepared for heavy downpours. If you can put up with a few drops, however, you will be well rewarded by the magnificent landscape of the east coast. The best time to visit Surigao and its surroundings is from April to June.

Places to Stay

The *Tavern Hotel* (☎ 87300) on Borromeo St is the best place in town. It has rooms with fan for P60/90, with fan and bath from P100 to P190 and with air-con and bath from P340 to P570. It is pleasant and has a restaurant. You can arrange for the hotel boat to take you to the offshore islands.

The *Flourish Lodge* on Borromeo St, Port

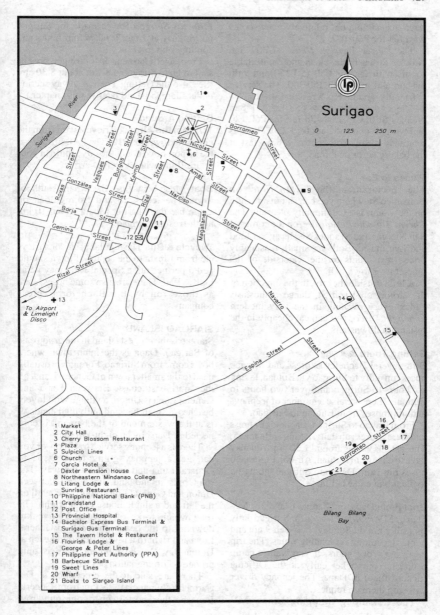

Surigao

0   125   250 m

1 Market
2 City Hall
3 Cherry Blossom Restaurant
4 Plaza
5 Sulpicio Lines
6 Church
7 Garcia Hotel &
   Dexter Pension House
8 Northeastern Mindanao College
9 Litang Lodge &
   Sunrise Restaurant
10 Philippine National Bank (PNB)
11 Grandstand
12 Post Office
13 Provincial Hospital
14 Bachelor Express Bus Terminal &
   Surigao Bus Terminal
15 The Tavern Hotel & Restaurant
16 Flourish Lodge &
   George & Peter Lines
17 Philippine Port Authority (PPA)
18 Barbecue Stalls
19 Sweet Lines
20 Wharf
21 Boats to Siargao Island

Area, has simple but relatively good rooms with fan for P60/100.

The *Dexter Pension House* at 309 San Nicolas St has basic, clean and comfortable rooms with fan for P50 to P150 and with air-con and bath for P250/300. The service is friendly, and there's a restaurant.

The *Garcia Hotel* (☎ 658) at 311 San Nicolas St has rooms with fan for P60/120 and with air-con and bath for P220/240. It is relatively clean. You can have breakfast at the bakery across the road.

Places to Eat

The restaurant at the *Tavern Hotel* on Borromeo St, where you can sit outside right on the water, is exceptionally pleasant. The *Cherry Blossom Restaurant*, on the corner of San Nicolas and Vasques Sts, has good food and live music. Both are small, reasonably priced restaurants on the waterside of the market near town hall.

A little outside the city, in the direction of the airport on Rizal St, dance enthusiasts gather every evening in the very modern *Limelight Disco*; you can eat cheaply in the restaurant downstairs.

Getting There & Away

Bus Several Bachelor Express and Surigao buses run daily to Surigao via Butuan, taking six hours to Surigao and over two hours to Butuan. There are also a number of jeepneys and minibuses from Butuan to Surigao.

From Davao to Surigao, Bachelor Express and Ceres buses run daily, taking eight hours. The last bus leaves around 1.30 pm. You may have to change in Butuan. Air-con Philtranco buses run from Davao to Surigao, going on to Tacloban and Manila.

Boat From Dapa, on Siargao Island, the MV *Dua* or MV *Philippe* leaves for Surigao daily (possibly not on Sunday) between 9 am and noon, depending on loading times. The trip takes over four hours. If you want a camp bed, get your ticket early at the Officina (ticket office) in Dapa. The jeepney driver will stop there on request.

The Cokaliong Shipping Lines' MV

Filipinas Siargao leaves Dapa for Surigao on Monday at 3 pm. It takes four hours and continues on to Cebu City.

From Del Carmen, an outrigger boat is said to go to Surigao daily at about 8.30 am. (See also the Getting There & Away section under Siargao Island later in this chapter.)

Getting Around

To/From the Airport Tricycles run from the airport to town for P10. The PAL office is at the airport now, not in the city; confirm your return flight when you first arrive.

Boat Most boats use the wharf south of town. The ferries to and from Liloan on Leyte use the wharf at Lipata, about 10 km north-west of Surigao.

Tricycle & Bus The regular price for a tricycle from Lipata to the centre of town should be P5 per person; a Special Ride may be as high as P50. There are also some buses, such as those run by the Bachelor Express company.

SIARGAO ISLAND

Siargao is the biggest island in the group east of Surigao. Dapa is the main town where boats come from Surigao. Foreigners usually head to the smaller town of General Luna, on the south-east coast. Between Dapa and General Luna is Union, a village with lovely beaches, a small bay and outlying islands. It is at the western end of the bay and is connected to Dapa by an eight-km road.

There is a jeepney service to Union, or you can get a jeepney going from Dapa to General Luna and get off on the way. The road runs inland and, on a rise between Union and General Luna, you'll see a hill on the left and a single house on the right. The road which forks off here goes five km downhill to the beach, then left to General Luna and right to a lovely, deserted beach at Union Bay. At the moment there is only private accommodation at Union.

There are said to be crocodiles at Del Carmen (Numancia), 25 km from General Luna, but the reports seem to come only from

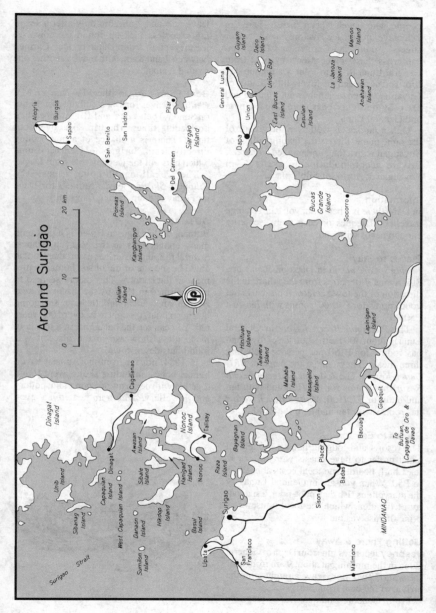

Around Surigao

people who haven't been there! There are extensive mangrove swamps with 'water streets' around Del Carmen and Pilar. You can cross these water streets by boat from General Luna to go to Pilar – a unique day trip. You can reach the lovely little islands of Guyam, La Janoza, Anahawan, Mamon and Daco by outrigger boat from Dapa, Union and General Luna.

On La Janoza, as well as in the village of the same name, there's the fishing village of Suyangan with a long undamaged coral reef. Private accommodation is available in Suyangan at Aurio Murillo's place.

Information
In Dapa there is a bank, but you can't change travellers' cheques or cash there, so bring enough pesos with you.

Places to Stay
Lucing's Carenderia in Dapa on Juan Luna St is about 300 metres from the wharf, in the direction of the town centre. It has basic but good rooms for P40/60, rooms with fan cost P50/80.

The *Pisangan Beach Resort* in General Luna is about 300 metres outside of town and has rooms for P150 per person, including three meals. They charge the same at *BRC Beach Resort*. The *Jadestar Lodge & Beach Resort* has rooms for P50/100 and with fan and bath for P75/150. *Maite's Beach Resort* has rooms with fan and bath for P100.

Places to Eat
The resorts and lodging houses in General Luna prefer to have guests with full, or at least half, board. One meal costs about P25 to P50. When you are in General Luna, try the marvellous fish dish poot-poot, a speciality of the area, which the local housewives pride themselves on.

Getting There & Away
Jeepney Jeepneys run from Dapa to General Luna in the morning at about 9 am from near the wharf. Two more leave straight after the arrival of the boat from Surigao.

From General Luna to Dapa, jeepneys leave at 6 and 7 am, but only after a seemingly endless pick-up round the town. A jeepney goes from Dapa to Del Carmen between 7 and 8 am, with maybe another one around 9 am.

Boat From Surigao, the MV *Dua* or MV *Philippe* leaves for Dapa daily (possibly not on Sunday) between 8 and 10 am, depending on loading times. The trip takes over four hours. There is a chance of a boat sailing directly from Surigao to General Luna, which cuts out the jeepney ride from Dapa.

The Cokaliong Shipping Lines' MV *Filipinas Siargao* leaves Surigao for Dapa on Friday at 8 am, taking four hours.

BUTUAN
Butuan, on the Agusan River, is a port with many connections to the Visayan Islands. Several Filipino historians assert that Butuan could be the site of the oldest human settlement in the country. This theory seemed to be confirmed in 1976 by the discovery near Butuan of a *balanghai* (a large sea-going outrigger boat) thought to be over 1000 years old. You can see the balanghai in a specially made glass showcase in the place it was found outside the town.

In 1984, not far from the Agusan River, human bones, including skulls, were found together with death masks, porcelain, pottery and jewellery, which indicated an even

Balanghai

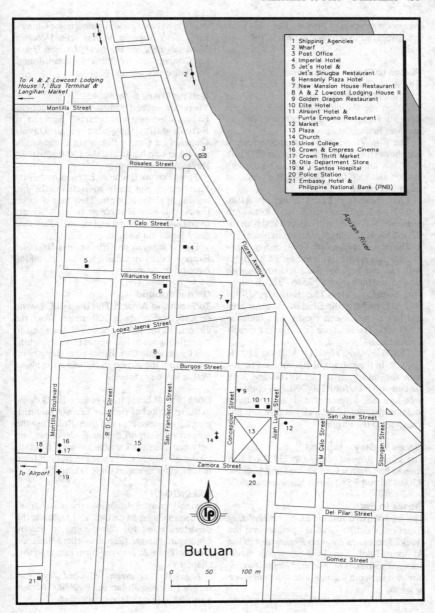

1 Shipping Agencies
2 Wharf
3 Post Office
4 Imperial Hotel
5 Jet's Hotel &
  Jet's Sinugba Restaurant
6 Hensonly Plaza Hotel
7 New Mansion House Restaurant
8 A & Z Lowcost Lodging House II
9 Golden Dragon Restaurant
10 Elite Hotel
11 Alrsont Hotel &
   Punta Engano Restaurant
12 Market
13 Plaza
14 Church
15 Urios College
16 Crown & Empress Cinema
17 Crown Thrift Market
18 Otis Department Store
19 M J Santos Hospital
20 Police Station
21 Embassy Hotel &
   Philippine National Bank (PNB)

To A & Z Lowcost Lodging
House 1, Bus Terminal &
Langihan Market

Montilla Street

Rosales Street

T Calo Street

Villanueva Street

Lopez Jaena Street

Burgos Street

Montilla Boulevard

R D Calo Street

San Francisco Street

Concepcion Street

Juan Luna Street

M. M. Calo Street

Silongan Street

San Jose Street

Zamora Street

To Airport

Del Pilar Street

Gomez Street

Flores Avenue

Agusan River

Butuan

0   50   100 m

earlier occupation of Butuan. The 1984 finds are displayed in a museum next to the town hall.

Places to Stay – bottom end

The *A & Z Lowcost Lodging House I* on Langihan Rd has basic rooms for P30/60 and with fan for P40/80. The *A & Z Lowcost Lodging House II* is on the corner of Burgos and San Francisco Sts.

The *Elite Hotel* (☎ 3133) on San Jose St has rooms for P60/80, with fan for P80/100, with fan and bath for P100/130 and with air-con and bath for P150/200. It is plain but relatively clean.

The *Hensonly Plaza Hotel* (☎ 3196, 52040) on San Francisco St has rooms with fan for P75/100 and with air-con and bath for P200/280. It is a simple but clean place.

The *Imperial Hotel* (☎ 2199) on San Francisco St has singles with fan for P85, singles with fan and bath for P125 and rooms with air-con and bath from P175 to P320. It is tidy and comfortable. The *Embassy Hotel* (☎ 3737) on Montilla Blvd is in a quiet area and has clean air-con rooms with bath for P300/400. The staff are friendly and there's a restaurant.

The *New Narra Hotel* (☎ 3145) at 1100 R Calo St, in the suburb of Bading, has rooms with fan and bath for P130/160 and with air-con and bath for P210/290. It is comfortable and has a restaurant. It is in a quiet location just outside the city centre and has transport to the airport.

Places to Stay – top end

The clean *Almont Hotel* (☎ 3332) on San Jose St has rooms with air-con and bath for P300/420 and P580 and it has a restaurant.

Places to Eat

The inexpensive restaurant in the *Embassy Hotel* on Montilla Blvd is open around the clock. The *Punta Engano Restaurant* in the Almont Hotel, San Jose St, serves international dishes. The *Nicolite Restaurant & Bar*, not far from there, is also a decent place to go to.

The *Golden Dragon Restaurant* on Con-cepcion St has a good reputation for Chinese food. *Jet's Sinugba* in the Jet's Hotel on Villanueva St, and the *New Mansion House* on Concepcion St (both air-conditioned) specialise in seafood.

Getting There & Away

There are several Philtranco and Bachelor Express buses running from Surigao to Butuan daily; they also go to Davao, Cagayan de Oro or Iligan via Butuan. The trip takes two hours and the last bus usually leaves at about 6 pm.

From Davao, Bachelor Express and Ceres Liner buses run daily to Butuan, the last leaving at about 1.30 pm. They take over six hours. Air-con Philtranco buses also run from Davao to Butuan and go on to Tacloban and Manila via Surigao.

From Cagayan de Oro, several Bachelor Express buses run daily to Butuan, taking three hours or more.

Getting Around

To/From the Airport The Butuan-Cagayan de Oro road is about 200 metres from the airport. To the left it goes to Butuan and to the right it goes to Balingoan (for Camiguin) and Cagayan de Oro. Buses pass along here. A taxi from the airport to Butuan costs about P60; a jeepney costs P2.

Boat Not all boats from other islands come to the river port of Butuan. Trans-Asia Shipping Lines' vessels to and from Bohol use the seaport of Nasipit/Lumbacan. Jeepneys run between Nasipit/Lumbacan and Butuan, taking 30 minutes. They leave Butuan from the shipping agencies on R D Calo St.

BALINGOAN

A small coastal town on the road from Butuan to Cagayan de Oro, Balingoan is the departure point for ships going to nearby Camiguin Island. (See also the Mindanao Getting There & Away section earlier in this chapter.)

Ligaya's Restaurant & Cold Spot has simple rooms with fan for P40/80. There is a similar lodging place opposite it.

CAGAYAN DE ORO

Cagayan de Oro has a population of around 400,000 and is a clean and friendly university city with numerous schools. An old legend tells how the name Cagayan is derived from the word 'kagayha-an', which means shame. The legend tells of an attack on a Manobo tribe by another tribe. The defeated villagers planned to retaliate, but, before they could, their chieftain fell in love with the daughter of the enemy chieftain and married her. His disgusted subjects referred to their village as a place of shame or 'kagayha-an'. The Spaniards pronounced it Cagayan and, after they discovered gold in the river, it became Cagayan de Oro.

The Xavier University Folk Museum (Museo de Oro) on Corrales Ave is worth seeing.

Information

Tourist Office The tourist office (☎ 3340) is in the Pelaez Sports Complex on Velez St. Farther south in the Golden Friendship Park (also called Divisoria) is the Tourist Information Center.

Money The Interbank on Borja St (next to the Cogon Market) will change American Express travellers' cheques. The Equitable Bank, on the corner of Borja and Tiano Brothers Sts, will give a cash advance on Visa or MasterCard.

Places to Stay – bottom end

The *New Golden Star Inn* (☎ 4079) on Borja St has simple rooms with fan for P130/170, with fan and bath for P150/200, and with air-con and bath for P200/300. The *Sampaguita Inn* (☎ 2640, 2740) on Borja St has rooms with fan and bath for P200/250 and with air-con and bath for P350. It is basic and comfortable, but the bedrooms don't live up to the standard of the lobby.

The *Oro United Inn* (☎ 4884) on Gomez St has rooms with fan and bath for P155 and with air-con and bath for P235/315.

The *Mabini Lodge* (☎ 3539) on the corner of Mabini and Velez Sts, has rooms with fan for P150 and with air-con and bath for P300.

The accommodation, above a loud disco, is clean and fairly good, and there is a restaurant.

The *Bonair Inn* (☎ 5431), east of town on Don Sergio Osmeña St, has passable singles with fan and bath for P130 and rooms with air-con and bath for P220/300. Suites are P420 and P480.

The *Parkview Lodge* (☎ 5869, 4678) on Tirso Neri St has good rooms with fan for P150/190, with fan and bath for P250 and with air-con and bath for P360. It is in a quiet area next to the Golden Friendship Park.

Nature's Pensionne (☎ 3985, 723718; fax 726033) on T Chavez St has rooms with air-con and bath from P460 to P790. The rooms are clean and passable, with wide beds. It has a restaurant.

Places to Stay – middle

The *VIP Hotel* (☎ 3629, 5873; fax 6441), near the corner of Velez and J R Borja Sts, has singles with air-con and bath from P620 to P720, doubles with air-con and bath from P750 to P860, and suites from P880 to P2700. It has a restaurant and the dearer rooms have a fridge and TV.

The *Philtown Hotel* (☎ 726295, 723089; fax 723104) on Makahambus St near the corner of Velez St, has clean, comfortable rooms with TV, air-con and bath from P870 to P1170, and there is a restaurant and a disco.

Places to Stay – top end

The 1st-class *Pryce Plaza* (☎ 722791- 93; fax 726687) at Carmen Hill, about four km west of the town centre, has singles with air-con and bath for P1950, doubles with air-con and bath for P2450 and suites for P3620, and there is a restaurant and a swimming pool.

Places to Eat

In Cagayan de Oro, probably the best restaurant for Filipino food is the *Kagay-Anon* at Lapasan, roughly north-east from the town centre. The *Singkil Restaurant & Coffee Shop* on the ground floor in the VIP Hotel is open 24 hours a day and the lunch and dinner

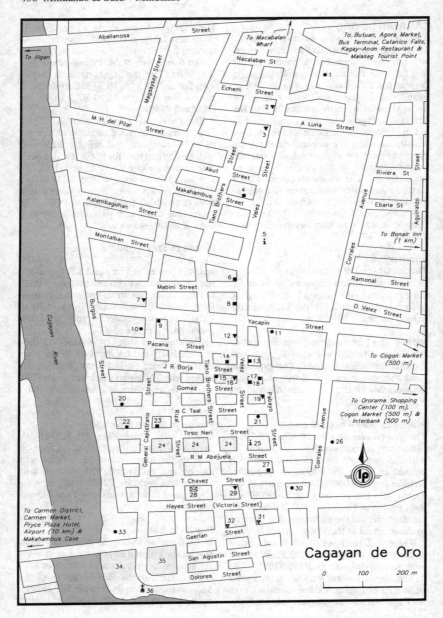

To Iligan

Abellanosa Street

Magsaysay Street

To Macabalan Wharf

To Butuan, Agora Market,
Bus Terminal, Catanico Falls,
Kagay-Anon Restaurant &
Malasag Tourist Point

Nacalaban St

● 1

Echem Street

2 ▼

M H del Pilar Street

3 ▼

A Luna Street

Riviera St

Aguinaldo

Akut Street

Makahambus Street

Tiano Brothers Street

Velez Street

4 ■

Ebarle St

Corrales Avenue

To Bonair Inn
(1 km)

Kalambagohan Street

Montalban Street

5 i

Ramonal Street

D Velez Street

Mabini Street

6 ■

Burgos Street

7 ▼

8 ■

To Cogon Market
(500 m)

10 ●

9 ●

12 ▼

Yacapin Street

● 11

Pacana Street

To Ororama Shopping
Center (100 m),
Cogon Market (500 m) &
Interbank (500 m)

J R Borja Street

14 ■

13 ■

Velez Street

15 ●

16 ■

17 ●
18 ■

Gomez Street

Tiano Brothers Street

19 ▼

Pabayo Street

20 ●

Rizal Street

C Taal Street

Tirso Neri Street

21 ■

● 26

22 ■

23 ■

General Capistrano Street

24 ■

24 ■

24 ■

i 25

R M Abejuela Street

27 ■

T Chavez Street

⊠ 28

29 ▼

● 30

Hayes Street (Victoria Street)

● 33

32 ▼

31 ▼

Gaerlan Street

San Agustin Street

To Carmen District,
Carmen Market,
Pryce Plaza Hotel,
Airport (10 km) &
Makahambus Cave

Cagayan River

34

35

Dolores Street

■ 36

Cagayan de Oro

0   100   200 m

■ PLACES TO STAY		OTHER	
4	Philtown Hotel	1	Provincial Capitol Building
6	Mabini Lodge	3	Phillipine National Bank (PNB)
8	Excelsior Hotel	5	Tourist Office &
13	VIP Hotel		Pelaez Sports Complex
14	New Golden Star Inn	9	Thrives Disco
17	Sampaguita Inn	10	Alabama Disco
18	Oro United Inn	11	Shinding Disco
23	Parkview Lodge	15	Equitable Bank
27	Nature's Pensionne	20	Sunflower Disco
		21	Love City Disco
▼ PLACES TO EAT		22	PAL
		24	Golden Friendship Park
2	Caprice Steak House		(Divisoria)
3	Salt & Pepper Restaurant	25	Tourist Information
7	The Bungalow Restaurant	26	Xavier University Folk
12	Bagong Lipunan Restaurant		Museum
16	Persimmon Fastfoods &	28	Post Office
	Bakeshoppe	30	Greenhills Memorial Garden
19	Dante's Restaurant	33	City Hall
27	Hotfoods Plaza	34	Riverside Park
29	Blueberry Coffee Shop	35	Gaston Park
31	Paolo's Ristorante	36	San Agustin Cathedral
32	Consuelo Restaurant		

specials are really worth the money. You get big meals which are very good value at the *Bagong Lipunan Restaurant* on Velez St, between the VIP and the Excelsior hotels.

About 100 metres south is the *Persimmon Fastfoods & Bakeshoppe*, an inexpensive self-service restaurant with sandwiches and good, standard Filipino dishes like caldereta, kare-kare and sinigang. At the north end of Velez St is the air-con *Caprice Steak House* and the small *Salt & Pepper Restaurant*, which has a limited menu but cheap beer.

In *Dante's*, on the corner of Pabayo and Gomez Sts, you will find the lighting a bit dim, but the service is extremely attentive and the food surprisingly good and not unreasonably priced. *Paolo's Ristorante*, on Velez St near the corner with Gaerlan St, is a popular garden restaurant with not only a good variety of pizzas and pastas, but also Spanish and Japanese food, seafood, steaks and sandwiches.

The *Consuelo Restaurant*, on the corner of Tiano Brothers and Gaerlan Sts, specialises in steaks and sizzling spaghetti. *Sugbahan sa Josefina's* is a seafood grill restaurant near the swimming pool in the Pryce Plaza Hotel, where the view of Cagayan de Oro is magnificent. If you have a sweet tooth, then the *Blueberry Coffee Shop*, on Velez St near the corner with Chavez St, is well worth the visit. It specialises in coffee and cakes and the menu runs from blueberry pie to cappucino.

Entertainment

If you want nightlife, Cagayan de Oro has plenty of discos, as well as 20 bars and eight cinemas. The most popular are the *Alabama Disco* on Capistrano St, the *Shinding Disco* on the corner of Pabayo and Yacapin Sts and the *Sunflower Disco* on C Taal St, all three with live music. It appears that *Thrives*, on the corner of Capistrano and Yacapin Sts, only hires 1st-class bands. The *Love City Disco* on C Taal St has live shows.

The Pelaez Sports Complex on Don Velez St is well equipped; its facilities include a large public swimming pool.

Getting There & Away
Air PAL has return flights between Cotabato and Cagayan de Oro daily except Friday and Sunday. Flying time is 20 minutes. PAL also has flights from Davao to Cagayan de Oro on Tuesday, Thursday, Saturday and Sunday and back on Monday, Wednesday, Thursday and Saturday. Flying time is 35 minutes.

PAL has an office at Lumbia Airport (☎ 3701) and at 21 Tirso Neri St.

Bus Bachelor Express buses leave Butuan almost hourly from 4.30 to 11.30 am for Cagayan de Oro; after that the intervals are longer. The buses go via Balingoan, which is the berth for boats to and from Camiguin. The trip takes over an hour to Balingoan and over three hours to Cagayan de Oro.

From Davao several Ceres Liner and Bachelor Express run daily to Cagayan de Oro, taking 10 hours.

Several Bachelor Express and Fortune Liner buses go daily between Iligan and Cagayan de Oro, taking 1½ hours. Jeepneys and minibuses also cover this route.

From Pagadian, Bachelor Express and Fortune Liner buses leave daily for Cagayan de Oro, hourly between 4.30 am and 1 pm, taking over four hours.

From Zamboanga four or five Fortune Liner and Almirante buses leave daily for Cagayan de Oro, between 4.30 and 6.45 am. Each one leaves as soon as it's full, so you should get to the bus terminal early, or book your seat a day in advance. It's a 16-hour trip. Express buses – the ones with indicators saying 'Non Stop' or 'Five Stops' – are about three hours faster and cost only a little more.

Getting Around
To/From the Airport Lumbia Airport is barely 10 km from town. PU-Cabs may ask up to P100, but you can do the trip for P50.

Bus The bus terminal is on the outskirts in the north-east of the city, next to the Agora Market. There is a jeepney service to the town centre, three km away. Jeepneys going to the centrally located Golden Friendship Park have the sign 'Divisoria'. Jeepneys going from the town to the bus terminal will have the sign 'Gusa/Cugman'.

Boat The Macabalan Wharf is three km from the town centre. There is a jeepney service, which usually goes direct to the bus terminal. The trip by taxi shouldn't cost more than P10.

Tricycle Tricycles here run on a sort of fixed route and they usually leave only when they're full. The most central interchange is Cogon Market. If you go somewhere that isn't on the fixed route, for instance, from the bus terminal to a hotel off the route, it always counts as a Special Ride.

Car Avis-Rent-a-Car has an office at the Pryce Plaza Hotel at Carmen Hill.

Warning The jeepneys and tricycles travelling from the bus terminal to the city are favourite haunts of pickpockets who travel in twos and often change seats to make the most of their opportunities.

AROUND CAGAYAN DE ORO
The **Makahambus Cave** is about 14 km south of Cagayan de Oro and can be reached by jeepneys going to Talacag. Make sure you take a powerful torch with you.

Even visitors who are not remotely interested in agriculture will enjoy a trip to the huge **pineapple plantations** at Camp Phillips, 34 km out of Cagayan. Bachelor minibuses go there and if you're lucky you may get to go on a tour of the plantations. On Wednesday and Saturday, jeepneys run the extra five km from Camp Phillips to the Del Monte Club House, where you can get very good, if not exactly cheap, meals in the Golf Club. The Del Monte Canning Factory is at Bugo, 15 km east of Cagayan de Oro, where the finished products are shipped away.

For a day at the beach, try **Raagas Beach** near Bonbon and **San Pedro Beach** in Opol, seven km west of Cagayan de Oro. They're nothing special but are OK for a quick dip.

MALAYBALAY

The capital of Bukidnon, which is the largest province in the northern Mindanao region, Malaybalay lies surrounded by mountain ranges in the valley of a tributary of the Pulangi River. Once a year there's the Kaamulan Festival, usually in November, but, if the weather's bad, it may be held either in May or September. The members of the various cultural minorities living in and around Malaybalay get together to celebrate. They meet in Pines View Park, dressed in traditional costumes and play music, dance, and put on craft demonstrations.

Places to Stay

The *Haus Malibu* (☎ 5714), on the corner of Bonifacio Drive and Comisio St, has rooms for P140/200 and rooms with fan and bath for P240/300. It has a coffee shop, is comfortable and the staff offer real hospitality.

Getting There & Away

Bachelor Express and Ceres Liner buses run daily between Cagayan de Oro and Malaybalay, leaving hourly. The trip takes two hours.

ILIGAN

Iligan is an industrial town surrounded by factories. The nearby **Maria Cristina Falls** will be the main source of power for the surrounding districts as far as Zamboanga, once the plant there is operating at full capacity. The power station so dominates the landscape that it's more likely to appeal to the technically minded than to nature lovers.

To get to the falls, take a jeepney from the pier to Agus Bridge, about seven km away, turn left behind the bridge and walk for about half an hour. You can't swim in the pool and, as the river is a raging torrent, it's too dangerous; the attraction is to look down on the falls from above by going about 200 metres back towards Iligan from the Agus Bridge, where a path and concrete steps lead straight to the waterfall.

On the other hand, the **Tinago Falls** – also known as the Hidden Falls – have been left in their beautiful natural state and are not marred by construction. They must be amongst the most beautiful waterfalls on Mindanao. It is a real pleasure to go for a dip in the big, natural pool there, and admission is free. The easiest way to get to the Tinago Falls is with a PU-Cab (you have to walk the last 50 metres down to the pool), or with the jeepney as mentioned above. If you do take the jeepney, then go past the Agus Bridge for another two km to the turn-off (which is signposted) and cover the next couple of km on foot.

About 30 km north of Iligan on the Cagayan de Oro road is Initao, where there's a cave which you can explore, near the hospital. You'll need a good, powerful torch. There are cottages available for around P100 about 300 metres away on a white beach which will appeal to guests wanting peace and quiet.

Information

Money The Interbank on Quezon Ave will change American Express travellers' cheques.

Places to Stay

The *Iligan Star Inn* (☎ 20601) on Quezon Ave has basic rooms with fan for P140/175, with fan and bath for P180/200 and with air-con and bath for P360. The rooms are good but those facing Quezon Ave are noisy.

The *MC Tourist Inn* (☎ 5194) on Tibanga Highway is a reasonable place north of the town centre on Baslayan Creek. It has singles with fan for P150, doubles with fan and bath for P250 and doubles with air-con and bath for P350.

The *Maria Cristina Hotel* (☎ 20645, 21082), near the intersection of Aguinaldo and Mabini Sts, has rooms with air-con and bath for P500/650 and suites for P1200. It also has a restaurant. It is pleasant and attractive and is the best hotel in the town centre.

The *Iligan Village Hotel* (☎ 21752), east of town in Pala-o, has very comfortable

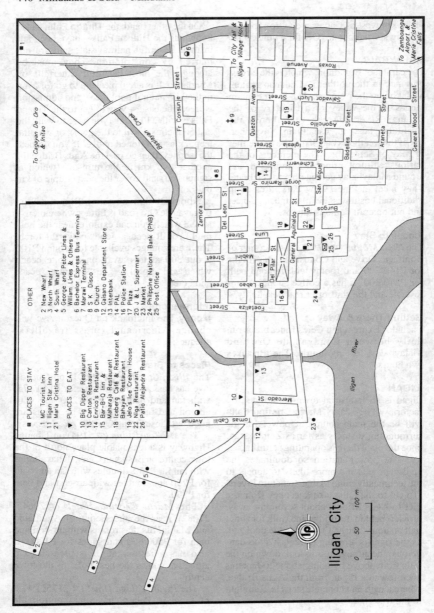

PLACES TO STAY
■ 1 MC Tourist Inn
11 Iligan Star Inn
21 Maria Cristina Hotel

▶ PLACES TO EAT
10 Big Dipper Restaurant
13 Canton Restaurant
14 Enrico's Restaurant
15 Bar-Q Inn &
   Maharaja Restaurant
18 Iceberg Café & Restaurant &
   Bahayan Restaurant
19 Jelo's Ice Cream House
22 Niga Restaurant
26 Patio Alejandra Restaurant

OTHER
2 New Wharf
3 North Wharf
5 South Wharf
6 George and Peter Lines &
   William Lines & Others
7 Marawi Terminal
8 S K Disco
9 Church
12 Gaisano Department Store
13 Interbank
16 Police Station
17 Plaza
20 J & L Supermart
23 Market
24 Philippine National Bank (PNB)
25 Post Office

Iligan City

0   50   100 m

rooms with air-con and bath for P650/850 and suites for P1400. It is the best hotel near Iligan. It has a restaurant, fish ponds and an orchid garden.

Places to Eat

Iligan has quite a few bakeries and restaurants, though most of them close at about 9 pm. You have a choice of reasonably priced Chinese or regular meals at the *Big Dipper Restaurant* and the *Canton Restaurant*, both on Quezon Ave. *Enrico's Restaurant*, next to the PAL office, is clean. It has excellent food and the service is friendly. The *Bar-B-Q Inn* on the plaza is great for an evening meal.

In the mid-range category are the *Iceberg Café & Restaurant* and the *Bahayan Restaurant*, both serving Filipino food. The only problem with the well-run *Patio Alejandra*, on the corner of San Miguel and Luna Sts, is making your mind up from the wide choice of food and cuisines available; the seafood festival is highly recommended. The partly open-air *Terrace Garden Restaurant* by the fish pond of the Iligan Village Hotel is a pleasant place.

Amongst others, the *S K Disco* will make sure your nightlife is well taken care of.

Getting There & Away

Air PAL has return flights daily from Cotabato to Iligan. Flying time is 35 minutes.

PAL has an office at Iligan Airport and on Quezon Ave (☎ 2037).

Bus From Cagayan de Oro, several Bachelor Express and Fortune Liner buses run daily to Iligan, taking 1½ hours. There are also jeepneys and minibuses.

From Pagadian several Bachelor Express and Fortune Liner buses run daily to Iligan, taking three hours. The last bus usually leaves in the early afternoon.

From Zamboanga four or five Fortune Liner and Almirante buses leave daily between 4.30 and 6.45 am for Cagayan de Oro, going via Iligan. (See also the Getting There & Away section under Cagayan de Oro earlier in this chapter.)

Boat The William Lines' MV *Misamis Occidental* sails from Dipolog on Thursday at 7 am to Iligan, taking six hours.

Getting Around

To/From the Airport The airport is located 17 km south of Iligan, about 600 metres off the road to Marawi. It's best to take a taxi there, as the jeepneys that travel between Marawi and Iligan are filled to the brim. The taxi to Iligan will cost you P70.

MARAWI & LAKE LANAO

Marawi on Lake Lanao is the spiritual and cultural centre for the Filipino Muslims. The Mindanao State University, usually referred to as 'Misyu' because of its initials, MSU, is here, as is the RP-Libya Hospital, the biggest and most modern hospital on Mindanao. Take a jeepney from Marawi to MSU, where there is a tourist office in Ford Guest House No 2. On the campus, there is a small but interesting Aga Khan Museum, featuring the Muslim culture of Mindanao. It is open Monday to Thursday from 9 to 11.30 am and 1.30 to 5 pm, and on Friday from 9 to 10.30 am and 1.30 to 5 pm. It is closed on weekends and public holidays.

Don't expect a mysterious oriental bazaar in Marawi – there is a big market over towards the lake where you can buy brass ware, tapestries and Indonesian textiles. Good handwoven tapestries at fixed prices are for sale at the Dansalan College Art Shop at MSU. You may give offence if you photograph a Muslim woman without first asking permission.

Lake Lanao is the second biggest inland lake in the Philippines. During normal conditions the lake would be 112 metres deep, but it has often been considerably lower than this in recent years. More than 500,000 Maranao who live in one of the 30 towns around or near the lake, and whose lives depend on it, feel their way of life is being threatened. The culprit is apparently a power station in Marawi, run by the National Power Corporation (Napocor), which draws water from the lake (located 700 metres above sea level) to generate power. Napocor runs another five power stations along the Agus River, which drains naturally from Lake Lanao. They make use of the river current to generate power.

The region around Lake Lanao is a crisis area, so think twice before visiting the town of Tugaya, famous for its brass ware, or making boat trips to the small islands of Nusa-Nusa and Silangan.

Places to Stay & Eat
The *Marawi Resort Hotel* on the MSU campus has rooms with bath for P420/500 and cottages with bath for P350/450. This place is clean, comfortable and pleasantly furnished. It has a restaurant and a swimming pool, which are located on a hill outside of Marawi from where you can get a beautiful view of Lake Lanao.

Getting There & Away
Several jeepneys and shared taxis, costing about P20 each for four to six people, leave the Marawi Terminal in Iligan daily for Marawi. The jeepneys cost P10 and go to the MSU campus, taking 45 minutes. They wait opposite the Marawi Terminal in Iligan and have a sign 'Iligan-MSU'. The last departure from Marawi to Iligan is at about 4 pm.

OZAMIZ
There's not much for the traveller in Ozamiz, a sea port in the south-east of Misamis Occidental Province. It is simply the port for ships to Cebu. (See also the Mindanao Getting There & Away section earlier in this chapter.)

Places to Stay
The *Cebuana Lodge* on the Port Rd has basic rooms for P50/100. The *Grand Hotel*, opposite the post office at 55 Abanil St, near the corner with Ledesma St, has rooms with fan for P100/120 and rooms with fan and bath for P150/200. It is simple but quite good.

The *Surigao Pension House* (☎ 21114) on Mabini St Extension has rooms with fan and bath for P85/125 and with air-con and bath for P185/275. It's clean, quiet and fairly good.

The *Country Lodge*, near the Lilian Liner bus terminal on the Ledesma St Extension, has rooms with fan and bath for P180/230 and with air-con and bath for P250/320. It is tidy and quiet.

The *Holiday Tourist Inn* (☎ 20073) on Blumentritt St has comfortable rooms with fan and bath for P150/200 and with air-con and bath for P300/350.

Getting There & Away
From Dipolog, Lilian Liner buses go daily to Ozamiz via Oroquieta, leaving almost hourly. The trip takes over two hours to Dipolog and one hour to Oroquieta.

From Pagadian, several Lilian Liner buses run daily to Ozamiz, taking two hours. The last bus leaves in the early afternoon.

From Iligan, several Bachelor Express and Fortune Liner buses run daily to Kolambugan, some finishing there and some going on to Pagadian. The trip takes one hour. There is a ferry service between Kolambugan and Ozamiz almost every hour, between 7 am and 5 pm.

OROQUIETA
Oroquieta, on Iligan Bay, in the north-east of the Zamboangan Peninsula, is the provincial capital of Misamis Occidental, but most of the region's trade and industry is centred farther south in Ozamiz.

Places to Stay
The *Joy Lodge* in Oroquieta has simple rooms with fan for P70/120 and with air-con and bath for P180/260. The *Beach Resort Elvira* on Orbita St, on the beach at Plaridel, about 20 km north of Oroquieta, has dorm beds for P80 and rooms with fan for P240. It's comfortable and you can use the kitchen.

Getting There & Away
Several Lilian Liner buses run daily from Dipolog to Oroquieta, either finishing there or going on to Ozamiz or Plaridel. The trip takes 1½ hours.

From Ozamiz several Lilian Liner buses run daily to Oroquieta, some going on to Dipolog. They take one hour.

DIPOLOG & DAPITAN

Dipolog, the capital of Zamboanga del Norte Province, seems very clean and neat. The offshore **Aliguay Island** has white beaches and extensive undamaged coral reefs good for snorkelling and diving; you can reach it in about 45 minutes by outrigger boat. There's a chance of getting a lift out there with the boats that come in daily to Dipolog and Dapitan to get fresh water.

Dapitan, 15 km north-east of Dipolog, is a quiet, clean town. The national hero, Jose Rizal, lived in exile here from 1892 to 1896. He made the big relief map of Mindanao in the town plaza, near St James Church. From the bridge over the river on the way to Rizal Park, you can catch a boat every 20 minutes going to **Dakak Bay**, which has a white beach and the luxurious, well-designed Dakak Park & Beach Resort. There is a road, which in the meantime should have been completely widened, from Dapitan to the bay. A service for hotel guests has already been introduced. There are minibuses between Dapitan and Dipolog.

Places to Stay & Eat

There are several places you can choose from in Dipolog. *Ranillo's Pension House* (☎ 3030, 56299) on Bonifacio St has good rooms with fan for P80/100, with fan and bath for P200/220 and with air-con and bath for P250/300.

The *Ramos Hotel* (☎ 3299) on Magsaysay St has singles/doubles with fan for P120/240, with fan and bath for P250/300 and with air-con and bath for P360/500.

The *CL Inn* (☎ 3491, 4293) on Rizal Ave is the best hotel in the centre of town. Very comfortable, spacious and clean rooms with air-con and bath cost P300/450, and suites with TV and fridge cost P780. There is also a restaurant.

The *Hotel Arocha* (☎ 3397, 2332) on Quezon Ave has rooms with fan and bath for P365 and with air-con and bath for P520. It is fairly good, although most of the rooms are a bit on the loud side. It has a restaurant and coffee shop.

The *Village Hotel* (☎ 56154) at Sicayab has passable, clean rooms of various sizes with fan and bath for P200 and with air-con and bath for P400. It is in a quiet area, about three km outside of Dipolog towards Dapitanl shortly after the airport. A tricycle into town costs P3. It's only a few minutes

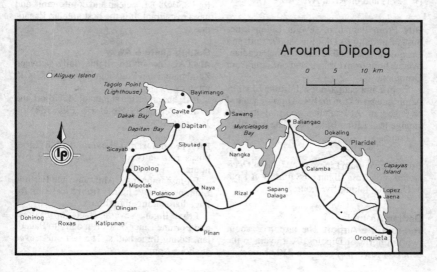

Around Dipolog

on foot from the hotel to the long, fairly clean beach.

The *Dakak Park & Beach Resort* (☎ 3147; fax 7222463) on Dakak Bay has singles with air-con and bath for P2000 and P2850 and doubles with air-con and bath from P2500 to P5000. It has tastefully furnished cottages in well-organised grounds, and also has a restaurant, open-air bar, swimming pool, whirlpool, sauna, and tennis court, and there is diving and horse riding.

The airport transfer costs P750 (there and back). Admission for day visitors is P200 (without cover charge). Anybody wanting, for instance, to make a short trip from Cebu City to Dakak would be well advised to make the reservation through a travel agent. Southwind Travel & Tours in the Cebu Plaza Hotel offers this resort for P2200: three days/two nights, including breakfast and airport transfer.

Getting There & Away

Air PAL has return flights daily except Thursday and Sunday between Zamboanga and Dipolog. Flying time is 50 minutes.

PAL has an office at Dipolog Airport (☎ 2271) and on Rizal Ave (☎ 2171).

Bus From Pagadian, several Lilian Liner buses run daily to Dipolog via Ozamiz and Oroquieta. It takes five hours from Pagadian, over an hour from Ozamiz and one hour from Oroquieta.

From Zamboanga, a few Fortune Liner or Almirante buses run daily to Dipolog via Ipil or Pagadian. At Pagadian you may have to change to a Lilian Liner bus. The trip takes 13 hours.

Boat The William Lines' MV *Misamis Occidental* sails from Iligan on Saturday at 1 pm to Dipolog, taking five hours.

Getting Around

To/From the Airport The airport is about two km north of Dipolog. A tricycle to the centre of town will cost you P10 or more.

PAGADIAN

The image of the province of Zamboanga del Sur is best captured by the Department of Tourism of Pagadian as a 'land of lakes, caves and waterfalls'. What may also interest the traveller is that the small town of Lapuyan, 40 km from Pagadian, and other parts of the two Zamboangan provinces, are the home of the Subanon, which means 'river people'. American Protestant missionaries brought Christianity and the English language to this isolated mountain world.

Places to Stay

The *Zamboanga Hotel* (☎ 437) on Jamisola St has passable rooms with fan and bath for P140/190 and with air-con and bath for P250/320. The *Peninsula Hotel* (☎ 52115), also on Jamisola St, has clean, comfortable rooms for P150/200, with fan and bath for P200/250 and with air-con and bath for P350/400.

Pagadian City Hotel (☎ 285) on Rizal Ave has quite comfortable rooms with air-con and bath for P360/420. The *Guillermo Hotel* (☎ 42062) also on Rizal Ave has singles/doubles with air-con for P550/650 and rooms with TV, fridge, air-con and bath for P850/950. It's clean and comfortable and has a restaurant. It is the best hotel in Pagadian.

Getting There & Away

Air PAL has return flights daily between Zamboanga and Pagadian. Flying time is 45 minutes.

PAL has an office at Pagadian Airport and in the Peninsula Hotel (☎ 199, 338) on Jamisola St.

Bus From Ozamiz, several Lilian Liner buses run daily to Pagadian, taking two hours.

From Zamboanga, Almirante and Fortune Liner buses leave hourly from 5 to 10 am for Pagadian, taking eight hours.

From Iligan, several Bachelor Express and Fortune Liner buses run daily to Pagadian, taking three hours. The last one leaves at about 2 pm.

Boat Three SKT Shipping Lines' ships sail from Zamboanga to Pagadian taking 12 hours. The MV *Lady Helen* leaves on Monday at 6 pm, the MV *Doña Isabel II* on Thursday at 6 pm and the MV *Lady Ruth* on Saturday at 7 pm.

The road from Cotabato to Pagadian passes through a crisis area and can be interrupted by broken bridges. It's better to take the daily ship that leaves Cotabato at about 6 pm (eight hours).

ZAMBOANGA

It's hard to see why Zamboanga has been praised as 'the exotic pearl of the south Philippines'. A few Muslims in an otherwise Filipino-populated city hardly make it exotic, and the colourful – and very expensive – sails of the Vintas are only seen at festivals or when one of these boats is chartered. Plain sails are normally used. The popular description of City of Flowers comes from the Malay word 'jambangan', meaning 'land of flowers' and may have been used when the first Malays settled here. It is more likely that the name comes from 'samboangan', a word made up of 'samboang', meaning 'boat pole', and 'an', meaning 'place'.

As well as speaking English, Filipino, Cebuano, Tausug and Samal, the locals in Zamboanga also speak Chavacano, a mixture of Spanish and Philippine languages ironically known as Bamboo Spanish.

Fort Pilar & Rio Hondo

On the outskirts of town, to the east of Zamboanga, are Fort Pilar and the Muslim water village of Rio Hondo. The fort was built in 1635 by Jesuit priests as protection against Muslim, Dutch, Portuguese and English attacks. It was then called Real Fuerza de San Jose, but was renamed Fort Pilar after its overthrow by the Americans at the end of last century. For many years the only part of the ruins worth seeing was the altar on the outside, but in 1986 restoration was begun to make the building usable. A visit to the very instructive **Marine Life Museum** is worth the effort. They have also set up botanical, archaeological, anthropological and historical departments. The museum is open daily except Saturday from 9 am to noon and 2 to 5 pm.

About 200 metres east of Fort Pilar, past a shining silver mosque, is a bridge leading to a village built on piles in the mouth of the river. This is Rio Hondo. The houses are linked by footbridges, many looking none too secure. The locals here are very friendly, however for your own safety, it's probably not a good idea to visit Rio Hondo after nightfall.

Information

The tourist office (☎ 3931, 3247) is at the Lantaka Hotel on Valderozza St. The Interbank on Mayor Climaco Ave will change American Express travellers' cheques.

Things to Buy

You can shop cheaply at the market in the Alta Mall Building, Governor Alvarez Ave Extension, in the suburb of Tetuan. Receipts are checked at the exits. Amongst other things they sell batik, which has been made in Mindanao and is not really up to the quality of Indonesian work.

The fish market at the docks is very lively and colourful in the late afternoons. In the alleys of the public markets next door, between the fish market and J S Alano St, there are lots of little shops – flea-market style. Here and on the waterside of the Lantaka Hotel, you can buy shells, but you will get a better deal from a wholesaler like the Rocan Shell Shop on San Luis St.

Salva's Orchids (☎ 2613) at 300 Tumaga Rd will appeal to flower lovers.

Places to Stay – bottom end

The *Unique Hotel* (☎ 9911598) on Corcuera St near the wharf has basic singles with fan for P75, with fan and bath for P90 and doubles with fan and bath for P165/190. It is quite noisy.

The simple but fairly clean *Imperial Hotel* (☎ 9911648) on Campaner St has rooms with fan for P90/120, with fan and bath for

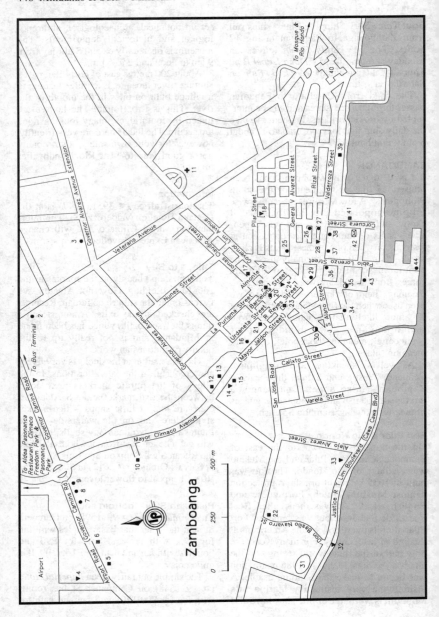

Zamboanga

■ PLACES TO STAY

5	Garden Orchid Hotel
6	Hotel Marcian Garden
10	Atilano's Pension House
12	Zamboanga Hermosa Hotel
13	Hotel Preciosa
15	New Astoria Hotel
17	New Pasonanca Hotel
19	Platinum 21 Pension House
20	Paradise Pensionhouse
21	Imperial Hotel
22	Mag-V Royal Hotel
23	Hotel Paradise
39	Lantaka Hotel
41	Unique Hotel

▼ PLACES TO EAT

1	Quostaw Restaurant
4	Lutong Pinoy
5	Village Zamboanga
13	Savoury Restaurant
14	Abalone Restaurant
18	Sunburst Fried Chicken
19	Café Blanca
23	Food Paradise
24	Dunkin Donut & Shakey's Pizza
28	Sunflower Restaurant
32	Boulevard Restaurant by the Sea
33	Alavar's House of Seafood
41	Welcome Bakery Snack Shop

OTHER

2	Santa Cruz Market
3	Alta Mall Building
4	Airlanes Disco
7	Love City Disco
8	Yagbulls Disco
9	Latin Quarter Disco
11	Zamboanga General Hospital
16	Fire Department
25	Sulpicio Lines
26	S K T Shipping Lines
27	Immigration Office & George & Peter Lines
29	Interbank
30	Buses to San Ramon
31	Athletic Field
34	Public Market
35	Jeepneys to Pasonanca Park & Taluksangay
36	Philippine National Bank
37	City Hall
38	Basilan Shipping Lines
39	Tourist Office
40	Fort Pilar
42	Post Office
43	Fish Market
44	Wharf

P160/190 and with air-con and bath for P230/300.

Atilano's Pension House (☎ 4225), on a side street off Mayor Climaco Ave, is good value with rooms with fan for P130, with fan and bath for P140/160 and with air-con and bath for P250/270. It's a comfortable place with big rooms and spacious grounds. The food is good – the family run a catering service.

The *Mag-V Royal Hotel* (☎ 4614), on the corner of San Jose Rd and Don Basilio Navarro St, slightly out of town, has singles with fan for P100, singles/doubles with fan and bath for P150/180 and with air-con and bath for P250/350. It is clean and has a restaurant. The rooms are spacious, but not all of them have windows. The arrival of the

morning is announced by very loud jeepneys!

The *New Pasonanca Hotel* (☎ 2201, 4579), on the corner of Almonte and Tomas Claudio Sts, has singles with fan and bath for P190 and singles/doubles with air-con and bath for P250/400. The rooms are small, but it is comfortable and has a restaurant and disco.

The *Hotel Paradise* (☎ 2026-28) on R Reyes St is central and has clean rooms with air-con and bath for P360/450. It has a restaurant.

Places to Stay – middle

The *Paradise Pension House* (☎ 3005-08), on the corner of Barcelona and Tomas Claudio Sts, is central and has good rooms with air-con and bath for P370/450. It also has a restaurant.

The *Zamboanga Hermosa Hotel* (☎ 9912040-42) on Mayor Climaco Ave has rooms with fan and bath for P200/250 and with air-con and bath for P370/450. It is well maintained and has a restaurant.

The *New Astoria Hotel* (☎ 2075-77) on Mayor Climaco Ave has reasonable rooms with fan and bath for P280 and with air-con and bath for P380/470. The best rooms are on the 2nd floor.

The *Hotel Marcian Garden* (☎ 9912519-21; fax 9911874) on Governor Camins Rd has rooms with air-con and bath from P390 to P480. Located near the airport, this hotel is clean and has a restaurant. It gives you value for your money.

The *Platinum 21 Pension House* (☎ 9912514-16; fax 9912709) on Barcelona St has comfortable and clean rooms with air-con and bath for P500 and P560. The rooms have TV; the more expensive ones also have a fridge. There is a restaurant which is open 24 hours.

Places to Stay – top end

The *Hotel Presiosa* (☎ 2910, 2919; fax 6226) on Mayor Climaco Ave has good rooms with TV, air-con and bath for P650. Suites with a fridge and TV cost P1100, and there is a restaurant.

The *Lantaka Hotel* (☎ 9912033-36; fax 9911626), on Valderroza St on the waterfront, has rooms with air-con and bath for P750/900, and suites for P1500. It is comfortable and has a restaurant and swimming pool.

The *Garden Orchid Hotel* (☎ 9910031-34; fax 9910035) on Governor Camins Rd, near the airport, is the best hotel in town. It has pleasant and comfortable rooms with air-con and bath for P1220/1490, and it has a restaurant.

Places to Eat

You can eat cheaply and well at the *Flavorite Restaurant*, opposite the George & Peter Lines' office, and nearby at the *Sunflower Restaurant*, where, apart from the regular menu, you can eat good goat meat. Young Zamboangans meet in the popular *Food Paradise* where there are milk shakes and fast food on the ground floor and Chinese meals upstairs. In the Plaza Mall Building not far from there, *Dunkin Donut* is the place if you have a sweet tooth, and they're open round the clock. Right next door there is a *Shakey's Pizza*. *Sunburst Fried Chicken*, on Corcuera St near the intersection with Pilar St, specialises in chicken meals.

Alavar's House of Seafood is known for good Filipino and Chinese dishes, especially seafood, but is rather dear. Equally good and in the mid-price range is the *Abalone Restaurant*, beside the New Astoria Hotel on Mayor Climaco Ave. *Café Blanca* in the Platinum 21 Pension House on Barcelona St, is open day and night and offers good Filipino and international food at reasonable prices.

A little farther out of town is the *Boulevard Restaurant by the Sea*, where you sit right on the water – a good spot for sunset freaks. There are also numerous food stalls that open in the late afternoon along the Justice Lim Blvd. You can also sit out by the water, by torch light in the evenings, at the *Lantaka Hotel Restaurant*, where a reasonably priced buffet dinner is served; breakfast there is also pleasant. The *Aldea Pasonanca Restaurant* at the Pasonanca Park had the original idea of converting railways cars into a restaurant. It has excellent Filipino food.

Entertainment

Zamboanga, like most Philippine cities, has the best nightclubs on the outskirts of town. In Zamboanga there are some near the airport. Most clubs have a cover charge of P30 or P40 to get in. This often includes a drink.

There is a generally cheery atmosphere in the *Lutong Pinoy* open-air restaurant, which has a bar and live music. The *Lutong Pinoy Airlanes Disco* is right next door. Also at the airport you will find the *Village Zamboanga*, a beer garden with fast food, just right for night owls. About 500 metres east from there, the *Love City Disco*, *Yagbulls Disco* and the *Latin Quarter Disco* all provide evening entertainment. If you carry on in the direction of the Santa Cruz Market you will come to the *Quostaw Restaurant* and the *Kiss Me Disco*, both of which round off the entertainment on offer.

In the city itself, there's a noisy band at the *King's Palace Disca*, on the corner of La Purisma and Tomas Claudio Sts. And if it all gets too exhausting, you can always recover in the soothing atmosphere of the open-air *Talisay Bar* at the waterside of the Lantaka Hotel, which is also a perfect place for a sundowner.

Getting There & Away
Air PAL has flights to Zamboanga from various towns in Mindanao. There are daily return flights from Cotabato, (one hour); from Davao (1½ hours); from Dipolog (50 minutes); and from Pagadian (45 minutes).

PAL has an office at Zamboanga Airport (☎ 2021, 2779).

Bus From Cagayan de Oro, four buses run daily to Zamboanga via Iligan, leaving between 4.30 and 7 am, and taking 15 hours from Cagayan de Oro and 13 hours from Iligan.

From Dipolog, an early morning bus runs daily to Zamboanga via Ipil, taking 15 hours.

From Pagadian, buses run about every hour from 4.30 to 10 am to Zamboanga, taking eight hours.

Boat The Sulpicio Lines' MV *Cotabato Princess* leaves Cotabato for Zamboanga on Tuesday at 10 pm, taking nine hours.

The Sulpicio Lines' MV *Philippine Princess* leaves General Santos on Friday at 8 pm for Zamboanga, taking 14 hours.

The William Lines' MV *Maynilad* leaves Davao for Zamboanga on Monday at noon, taking 22 hours.

Three SKT Shipping Lines' ships sail from Pagadian to Zamboanga, all leaving at 7 pm and taking 12 hours. The MV *Lady Helen* goes on Tuesday, the MV *Doña Isabel II* on Friday and the MV *Lady Ruth* on Sunday.

Getting Around
To/From the Airport The airport is two km from the city centre. The regular fare for the jeepney marked 'ZCPM' or 'Canelar – Airport' is P1.50, or P10 by tricycle, but you rarely get a tricycle under P20, and up to P40 is sometimes asked. Taxi drivers, presumably without a licence, demand up to P60.

Bus The bus terminal for trips to and from Cagayan de Oro, Dipolog, Iligan and Pagadian is on the National Highway in the Guiwan District of town, about four km north of the city centre. A tricycle costs P10.

AROUND ZAMBOANGA
Pasonanca Park & Climaco Freedom Park
If the houses of the early settlers were really surrounded by a carpet of flowers, the nickname City of Flowers can today only belong to Pasonanca Park, about seven km, or 15 minutes by jeepney, north of the city centre.

On the way there you pass prize-winning gardens, and in the 58-hectare park itself there are three swimming pools, an amphitheatre and a tree house, where honeymooners can spend one night free. Since the demand is not great, tourists can also stay there by applying to the City Mayor's office. It's complete with two beds, a stereo, fridge, fan, bath and telephone, but remember, it's for one night only and open to all visitors during the day.

Not far from Pasonanca Park is Climaco Freedom Park, which used to be called Abong-Abong Park. It is now named in memory of a popular mayor, Cesar Climaco, who was murdered by political opponents. From the big cross on Holy Hill, you get a wonderful view over Zamboanga and the Basilan Strait. Jeepneys heading for Pasonanca Park leave from the fish market near the wharf and cost P2.

Santa Cruz Islands
Great Santa Cruz Island has a lightly coloured sandy beach, peppered with fine, red pieces of coral. Drinks are available at a small kiosk. Not far from the main beach are

a small Samal cemetery tucked away in the bush, and, in a mangrove lagoon, a Muslim village built on piles. Nearby Little Santa Cruz Island is off limits to visitors. A few soldiers are stationed there and there is an army guesthouse.

Sea gypsies try to sell shells and coral to tourists from their outrigger canoes beside the Lantaka Hotel. From here you can also hire boats to go over to Great Santa Cruz Island. It takes 15 minutes and the return fare is about P200 per boat. They also charge a landing fee of P5 per person.

San Ramon & Yakan Weaving Village
About 20 km west of Zamboanga is San Ramon Prison & Penal Farm – a good place to buy handicrafts made by the prisoners. You can get there by bus.

At Pulanlupa, eight km north-west of San Ramon, there is said to be a magnificent coral reef, but it is only suitable for diving from March to June. At other times heavy

seas cause poor visibility. On the San Ramon road, seven km from Zamboanga on the right-hand side, is a weaving village of seven Yakan families who make and sell traditional fabrics, which you can see on the looms. You can get a bus there from Governor Lim Ave, near the corner of Mayor Climaco Ave.

Taluksangay
This Muslim town, 19 km north-east of Zamboanga, is partly built over the water. The Badjao live in houses on piles, while the Samal have settled on land centred around a minareted mosque. Their modest income comes mainly from fishing and collecting firewood. The children there can get quite aggressive if their begging doesn't produce results. Jeepneys leave Zamboanga for Taluksangay from the public market and the last one back is likely to leave before dark.

DAVAO
The fastest growing city in the Philippines

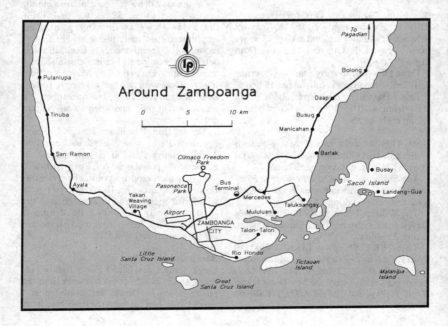

after Manila, Davao, with its population of 900,000, is also the second largest. Its cosmopolitan population of settlers from all over the country is spread over 2440 sq km, one of the most sprawling cities in the world.

You can't miss the Chinese influence here, especially west of the wharf, where numerous businesspeople have set up little stores. Muslims have also set up the so-called Muslim Fishing Village, not far from the wharf and the nearby Magsaysay Park. It can be reached by a footbridge.

Information
Tourist Office The tourist office (☎ 74861, 71534) is in the Apo View Hotel on J Camus St.

Money The Equitable Bank on T Monteverde St and on Claro M Recto Ave will give you a cash advance on your Visa or MasterCard.

The Interbank on T Monteverde and J Rizal Sts will change American Express travellers' cheques.

Things to See & Do
Next to the Insular Hotel Davao, near the airport, is the **Dabaw Museum**, featuring the cultural minorities of south Mindanao, such as the Mansaka and the Bagobo; the latter are known as a proud and warlike people. The museum is open Tuesday to Sunday from 9 am to 5 pm. Behind the Insular Hotel Davao in Etnika Dabaw, Mandaya people demonstrate their traditional skills in dyeing abaca fibres, weaving, and decorating textiles.

The **Lon Wa Temple** on Cabaguio Ave, three km in the direction of the airport, is the biggest Buddhist temple in Mindanao; the Taoist temple is not far away. Jeepneys to the temple leave from San Pedro St.

From the **Shrine of the Holy Infant Jesus of Prague**, there's a good view over the town and the Davao Gulf. This small shrine is in the suburb called Matina, about six km west of Davao. It stands on a hill behind the Davao Memorial Park and can be reached by a road which branches off the

MacArthur Highway. Take a jeepney from the NCCC department store, Magsaysay Ave, to the Bankerohan Market and change there to a jeepney heading for Matina. The turn-off to the shrine is easy to miss, so the best thing to do is use the Matina cockpit (cockfighting arena) on the left-hand side as an orientation point. The ride by tricycle up to the shrine costs P2.

Also around the city are numerous **banana plantations** and **orchid farms** you can visit, like the Lapanday Banana Plantation near Buhangin, 14 km north-west of Davao, and the Derling Orchid Farm near Toril, 12 km south-west of Davao.

The Tamolo Beach and Times Beach, south-west of Davao, are not worth a visit, but the white **Paradise Island Beach** on Samal Island makes a good day trip from Davao, as do Talikud Island and Eagle Camp.

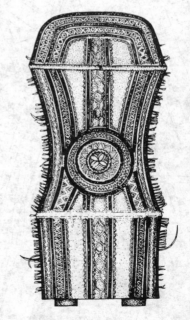

Bagobo Shield

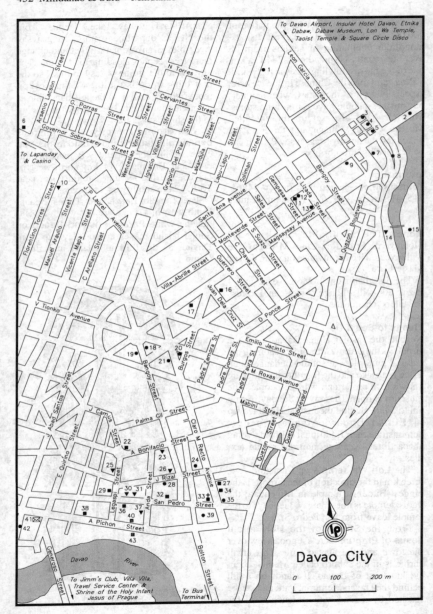

To Davao Airport, Insular Hotel Davao, Etnika Dabaw, Dabaw Museum, Lon Wa Temple, Taoist Temple & Square Circle Disco

N Torres Street

C Cervantes Street

G Porras Street

Governor Sobrecarey Street

Arsenio Lacson Street

To Lapanday & Casino

Leon Garcia Street

Bangoy Street

M Quezon Boulevard

Santa Ana Avenue

T Monteverde

Villa-Abrille Street

Guerrero Street

S Suazo Street

Magsaysay Avenue

C Chavez Street

D Ponce Street

Emilio Jacinto Street

V Tionko Avenue

Juan Dela Cruz St

Juna Street

Burgos Street

Padre Zamora St

Padre Gomez St

Padre Faura St

M Roxas Avenue

Mabini Street

M Quezon Boulevard

A Quezon Boulevard

J Camus

Palma Gil Street

Claro M Recto Street

A Bonifacio Street

J Rizal Street

San Pedro Street

Anda Street

Legaspi Street

A Pichon Street

E Quirino Street

Abad Santos Street

J Quirino Street

Fiorentino Torres Street

JP Laurel Avenue

Manuel Araullo Street

Vicente Mapa

C Arellano Street

Ignacio Villamar

Gregorio Del Pilar

Lakandula

Lapu-Lapu

Soliman

Wenceslao Vinzon

Gempesaw Street

Seles Street

C Lizada Street

Bonifacio Boulevard

Davao River

Generoso Street

Baton Street

To Jimm's Club, Villa Villa, Travel Service Center & Shrine of the Holy Infant Jesus of Prague

To Bus Terminal

Davao City

0   100   200 m

PLACES TO STAY

6	Durian Hotel
11	B S Inn
16	Trader's Inn
17	Fortune Inn
22	Apo View Hotel
27	Royale House
29	El Mimar Tourist Lodge
32	Le Mirage Family Lodge
34	Hotel Maguindanao
36	Men Seng Hotel
38	Manor Pension House
40	Pension Felisa
43	El Gusto Family Lodge

▼ PLACES TO EAT

10	Bistro Rosario, Harana Restaurant, Mongolian Garden, Peter Pan Pie Shop & Sarung Banggi Restaurant
14	Eateries
17	Shanghai Restaurant
23	Davao Majestic Restaurant
25	Dencia's Kitchenette
26	Molave Restaurant
30	New Sunya Restaurant & Kusina Dabaw
31	Merco Restaurant
36	Men Seng Restaurant
37	Sunburst Fried Chicken

OTHER

1	Agdao Market
2	Wharf
3	William Lines
4	Sweet Lines
5	Sulpicio Lines
7	Immigration Office
8	Magsaysay Park
9	Equitable Bank
11	Interbank
12	Interbank
13	NCCC Department Store
15	Muslim Fishing Village
18	PAL
19	Madroza Fruit Center
20	Aldevinco Shopping Center
21	Equitable Bank
22	Tourist Office
24	Interbank
28	Bronco Disco
33	St Peter's Cathedral
35	Philippine National Bank (PNB)
36	J R Super Club Disco
39	City Hall
41	Post Office
42	Bankerohan Market

Davao boasts of quite a few attractive markets and shopping centres which have a wide variety of goods on offer. Fruit, vegetables, meat and fish are all sold at the Bankerohan Market near Generoso Bridge, and at the Agdao Market on Lapu-Lapu St. The stalls of the Madrazo Fruit Center on Bangoy St offer a wide selection of tropical fruits including, naturally, the infamous durian – a specialty of Davao. There is even a monument to it in Magsaysay Park. This prickly fruit that 'stinks like hell and tastes like heaven', has such a strong smell that it is banned from most hotel rooms, and PAL won't allow it on its planes.

The NCCC is Davao's leading department store and is better and less expensive than Gaisano.

Places to Stay – bottom end

El Gusto Family Lodge (☎ 73662) at 51 A Pichon St has rooms with fan for P100/200, with fan and bath for P140/250 and with air-con and bath for P250/350. It's a clean, quiet place with a nice enclosed garden and a small restaurant.

Le Mirage Family Lodge (☎ 63811) on San Pedro St is a good place. It has singles with fan for P95, singles/doubles with fan and bath for P160/200 and with air-con and bath for P260/325.

The *Men Seng Hotel* (☎ 75185, 73101; fax 64994) on San Pedro St has rooms with fan and bath for P175/240 and with air-con and bath for P250/350. It is basic, not particularly appealing and has a restaurant.

The *Trader's Inn* (☎ 73578; fax 64976) on

Juan Dela Cruz St has good singles with fan and bath for P200 and singles/doubles with air-con and bath for P280/380.

The *Royale House* (☎ 73630, 64537) at 34 Claro M Recto Ave has rooms with fan for P150/240 and with air-con and bath for P320/460. It is clean and has a restaurant.

The *B S Inn* (☎ 2213980-89; fax 221 0740), on the corner of Monteverde and Gempesaw Sts, has singles with air-con and bath for P450 and P520 and doubles with air-con and bath for P540 and P585. The rooms are clean and of varying sizes; they're good value.

Places to Stay – middle

The *Manor Pension House* (☎ 2212511) on A Pichon St has rooms with air-con and bath for P585/695. This place is clean and good, with pleasantly furnished rooms. The service is friendly and there is a restaurant. It is in a quiet little street which leads off A Pichon St.

The *Hotel Maguindanao* (☎ 78401; fax 2212894) at 86 Claro M Recto Ave, opposite the cathedral, has rooms with TV, air-con and bath from P850 to P1190. Suites cost P1430. It's pleasant, comfortable and has a restaurant.

Places to Stay – top end

The *Apo View Hotel* (☎ 74861-65; fax 63802) on J Camus St has very good rooms with air-con and bath for P1300/1500, and suites for P2000 and P2600. There is a restaurant and swimming pool. The tourist office is in the same building.

The *Durian Hotel* (☎ 72721-25; fax 2211835) on J P Laurel Ave has singles with air-con and bath from P1400 to P1600, doubles with air-con and bath from P1700 to P1900 and suites from P2400 to P4500. The rooms have TVs and fridges. It is very comfortable, tastefully decorated and there's a restaurant. Although the hotel is not directly in the town centre, transport is no problem (there are lots of jeepneys).

The *Insular Hotel Davao* (☎ 76051, 76061; fax 62959) at Lanang has pleasant and comfortable rooms with air-con and bath for P2000/2500 and suites from P3000 to P5500. The hotel complex of several two-storey houses in a beautiful garden setting has its own beach, boats to Samal and Talikud islands, swimming pool, basketball, tennis and squash courts and golf. It is on the north-east edge of the city towards the airport.

Places to Eat

Good cheap Chinese meals are available in *Dencia's Kitchenette* on Legaspi St, in the *Shanghai Restaurant* on Magsaysay Ave, which closes at 8 pm, and in the *Men Seng Restaurant*, in the hotel of the same name on San Pedro St, which is open round the clock.

Other good restaurants on San Pedro St are the *Kusina Dabaw* which serves Chinese and Filipino dishes, the ever crowded *New Sunya Restaurant* and the *Merco Restaurant*, which also has good ice cream.

The Chinese food in the *Davao Majestic Restaurant* on Bonifacio St is very popular. If it's fried chicken you're after, then *Sunburst Fried Chicken* on Anda St is the place to go to. You could also try the pleasant little *Molave Restaurant*, on Bangoy St close to the intersection with J Rizal St, where they specialise in 'greaseless chicken'.

There is a whole row of different restaurants on Florentino Torres St near the corner of J P Laurel Ave. Worth mentioning are the *Harana* which has good barbecues and Filipino food, the *Sarung Banggi* which is renowned for its steaks, prawns and salads, the *Mongolian Garden* which specialises in Mongolian barbecue and spare ribs, the *Bistro Rosario* with its excellent steaks, and the *Peter Pan Pie Shop* which has wonderful cakes.

The *Eateries* at the Muslim Fishing Village near Magsaysay Park are strong on grills of almost anything that swims, mainly tuna and squid. A good spot for those who enjoy rustic life.

Entertainment

For a reasonable nightclub with live music and a floor show that is not too expensive, try *Jimm's Club*, a bit outside the city centre on the MacArthur Highway. Also out of town, in the direction of the airport, on a side street to the right, 300 metres before the Taoist temple, is the *Square Circle Disco*, which has go-go dancers. The *Casino* on Laurel St on the north-west outskirts of the city is open every night.

Bronco on Rizal St has live and disco music, and there's a good lively atmosphere at the *Spam's Disco* downstairs in the Apo View Hotel (the entrance is at the back). By contrast, the *J R Super Club Disco* on San Pedro St is quite simple, as is the *Hang Out* just next door.

Things to Buy

The Aldevinco Shopping Center on Claro M Recto Ave offers artwork, antiques, products from cultural minorities, batik and lots more.

Getting There & Away

Air PAL has flights from Cagayan de Oro to Davao on Monday, Wednesday, Thursday and Saturday. There are flights from Davao to Cagayan de Oro on Tuesday, Thursday, Saturday and Sunday. Flying time is 35 minutes.

PAL has return flights daily between Zamboanga and Davao. Flying time is 1½ hours.

PAL has an office at Davao Airport (☎ 78802, 64060) and in the Villa-Abrille Building (☎ 73774, 73785) on Banyoy St.

Bus Several Bachelor Express and Ceres Liner buses leave Butuan for Davao daily, taking six hours or more. The last bus leaves around noon.

From Cagayan de Oro, several Bachelor Express and Ceres Liner buses run to Davao daily, taking 10 hours. The last one may leave quite early in the morning.

From Cotabato, numerous Mintranco buses run daily to Davao, taking six hours.

From General Santos, numerous Yellow Bus Company buses run daily to Davao, taking four hours. The last bus leaves at about 3 pm.

There are four Bachelor Express buses from Surigao to Davao daily between 4 and 9 am, taking over eight hours.

Boat The William Lines' MV *Maynilad* sails from Zamboanga to Davao on Saturday at noon, taking 20 hours.

Motorbike Motorbikes can be hired at the Travel Service Center in Villa Viva (☎ & fax 2971411) at Willow St, Matina Heights. A 125cc bike costs P450 a day.

Getting Around

To/From the Airport The airport is 12 km north-east of Davao, between the districts of Lanang and Panacan. A taxi shouldn't cost more than P50 to P70. It's cheaper to take a tricycle (P1.50), 1½ km along the Airport Rd to the main road, then a jeepney marked marked 'San Pedro' or 'Bajuda' to Davao (P3.50); you may have to wait a few minutes. The jeepney travelling from the town centre to the airport has the sign 'Sasa'.

Bus The bus terminal for trips to and from Butuan, Cagayan de Oro, Cotabato, General Santos, Manila and Surigao is in the Ecoland District, about two km south of the town centre. Taxis charge P50 and jeepneys cost about P5.

Boat There are two piers you can use: Santa Ana Wharf next to Magsaysay Park and Sasa Pier a few km out of town. A jeepney from Sasa to the town centre costs P3.50.

AROUND DAVAO
Samal Island

A romantic pearl diving atmosphere is missing on Samal, as the prosperous times of the Aguinaldo Pearl Farm are over. Nowadays, a 1st-class hotel complex – the Pearl Farm Beach Resort – sticks out into the picturesque bay, where only a few years ago thousands of oysters produced cultured pearls.

The white **Paradise Island Beach** on the north-west coast is the best beach on Samal; north of it are the cottages of the Coral Reef Beach Resort.

Big and Little Cruz islands, north-east of Samal, are good for diving. They used to be called the Liquid Islands. There is another

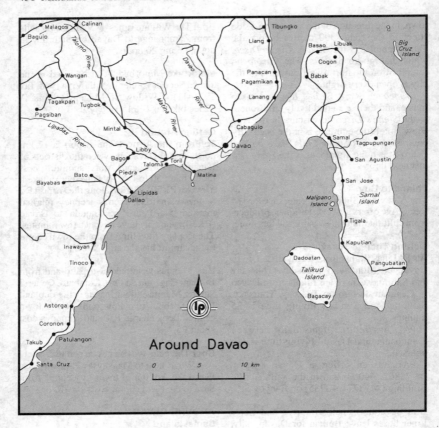

Around Davao

good diving area near the Pearl Farm Beach Resort at Malipano Island, where the wrecks of two WW II ships lie 30 metres below water.

Places to Stay The *Paradise Island Beach Resort*, which has very friendly staff and good service, has cottages with fan for P450 and with fan and bath for P600 and P720. As an alternative, it is possible to get a private cottage at the nearby *Coral Reef Beach Resort*.

The *Pearl Farm Beach Resort* has cosily furnished rooms with fridge, air-con and bath for P2400 and spacious suites for P5300. It has a restaurant, swimming pool, tennis courts, water skiing, windsurfing and diving facilities on its extensive property. It also provides free transport to the airport for guests.

Getting There & Away To get from Davao to Paradise Island Beach, go by jeepney towards the airport and Sasa. Get out shortly before Lanang before the Sasa bridge (the bridge is small and easy to miss) and walk to the right along the river to the Caltex oil tanks. From there you can get a boat to take you over to Paradise Island Beach; it costs P3.50 per person, or P40 for the boat. The last return trip leaves around 5.30 pm.

Tours to Paradise Island Beach and to the Pearl Farm Beach Resort are sometimes arranged at the Insular Hotel Davao.

Talikud Island

This little island south-west of Samal has a cave with reputedly well-fed pythons and a couple of nice beaches with very hungry sharks. At least that's the story told by the friendly islanders. You can stay overnight with the mayor. It should be possible to go across from here to the Pearl Farm Beach Resort on Samal.

Getting There & Away You can expect problems if you want to go to Talikud, but if you do decide to go there, get the boat in Davao from the left-hand side of Santa Ana Wharf. It leaves daily at about 10 am, but sometimes not until 2 pm and the return trip may not be possible until the next day.

Eagle Camp

This camp has been set up near Calinan in the Bagio District of the Malagos region, about 36 km north-west of Davao by road. It makes a good day trip (not only for ornithologists). The camp people, who are observing the nesting habits of the Philippine eagle, are very friendly and can provide a fund of information about these birds. For a fee, it may be possible to stay overnight and go trekking in the area, for instance, to Mt Apo National Park. You should bring a sleeping bag, provisions and warm clothing, as it gets much colder up there than in Davao.

Getting There & Away Several jeepneys leave for Calinan daily from Bankerohan Market in Davao, costing P10. Take a tricycle for the remaining five km or so from Calinan to Malagos. The trip costs P5 and entrance to Eagle Camp is P10. The last jeepney from Calinan to Toril and Davao leaves at about 3 pm.

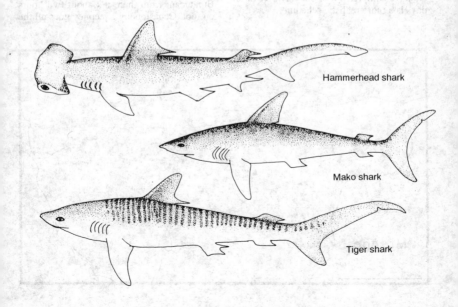

Hammerhead shark

Mako shark

Tiger shark

Mt Apo National Park

The tourist office in Davao has detailed information about Mt Apo National Park, the various routes up the mountain, and recommended equipment. The personnel is competent to advise whether the climb is responsible and feasible. In April 1989 when around 300 local and foreign climbers took part in the annual organised climb, members of the NPA made it blatantly clear to the public who was boss on the mountain by seizing the whole group in a surprise raid, only to free them again shortly after.

In Digos, south of Mt Apo, you can obtain further information about climbing and security from the Mt Apo Climber Association at the office of the *Digos Times*. Guides and porters can be hired in Kidapawan for about P250 a day. A water canteen and boots are essential. A warm sleeping bag is also necessary as the nights are cool – temperatures around freezing point are not uncommon. Take your own provisions, not forgetting salt, to prevent dehydration.

The climb is not easy. Even though sprinters have completed it in one day, five or six days is a more realistic schedule.

Kidapawan Route This recommended four-day schedule includes travel to and from Davao:

Day 1 – Go from Davao to Kidapawan by Mintranco bus headed either for Kidapawan itself or Cotabato. This takes over two hours. Leave early as the last jeepney from Kidapawan to Lake Agco, via Ilomavis, usually leaves at about 3 pm. From Lake Agco it's a good three hours uphill on foot to the Marbel River Campsite, where you can stay overnight in the shelter.

Day 2 – This is six to eight hours' hard climbing; it's about five hours to Lake Venado. You will have to sleep outside, so take a plastic sheet, or better still a small tent, as it's uncomfortable if it rains.

Day 3 – Allow for two hours to reach the summit, then return to Lake Venado or the Marbel River Campsite.

Day 4 – Return to Kidapawan or Davao.

New Israel Route As well as the popular Kidapawan/North Cotabato route, there is the alternative New Israel route. The mountain village of New Israel is the home of the Alpha & Omega sect, widely known in the region for its faith healer.

From Kidapawan, take a jeepney to Bulatucan; from there it's about two hours on foot. Occasionally a jeepney goes all the

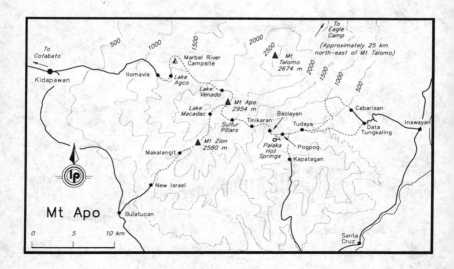

way, but in bad weather this would be almost impossible. For a small donation, you can stay overnight in the sect's guesthouse and you can hire guides and porters there.

The climb from New Israel up Mt Apo takes about 13 hours altogether. The members of the sect make the climb once a year and have built overnight shelters on the way up. In Makalangit a capacious store camp has even been provided; a small donation is expected for its use. From there it takes five hours.

An alternative descent would be down the North Cotabato route, via Lake Venado and Ilomavis to Kidapawan, which would take about 12 hours.

GENERAL SANTOS (DADIANGAS)

Maguindanao Muslims and B'laans were the sole inhabitants of this city up to the beginning of the 20th century. The first influx of immigrants arrived between 1914 and 1915 and more followed in the 1930s. In 1939 pioneers from Luzon and the Visayas led by General Paulino Santos established a settlement on the Silway River in Sarangani Bay. In 1965 Dadiangas was renamed General Santos in his honour. The old name is also used today.

The city's economy depends mainly on pineapple, bananas (Dole Pineapple Plantation and Stanfilco Banana Plantation) and cattle (Sarangani Cattle Co).

The two islands of Balut and Sarangani, which still belong to the Philippines, lie off the coast of Mindanao, south of General Santos. Indonesia's territorial waters begin only a few miles away. Although there is a shipping route between Balut Island and Manado in the north of Sulawesi/Indonesia, they will only accept Filipinos and Indonesians as passengers. Other nationalities are not allowed on board, even with a valid Indonesian visa. The Indonesian border officials who check everybody before they leave Balut Island stick to the rules exactly. The outrigger boat from General Santos to Balut Island only goes at night, and the trip can be damp and cold. It takes seven hours.

Information

Money The Interbank on Pioneer Ave will change American Express travellers' cheques.

Places to Stay – bottom end

The *Concrete Lodge* (☎ 4876) on Pioneer Ave has rooms with fan and bath for P130/160 and with air-con and bath for P250. It is unpretentious and pleasant. The *South Sea Lodge I* (☎ 5146, 2086) on Pioneer Ave has rooms with fan for P140/190, with fan and bath for P190/230 and with air-con and bath for P300/360. It is clean and relatively good, and has a restaurant. The *South Sea Lodge II* is on the corner of Salazar St and Magsaysay Ave.

The *Pioneer Hotel* (☎ 2422, 3543) on Pioneer Ave has rooms with fan and bath for P300/320, with air-con and bath for P350/400 and suites for P750. It is comfortable and has a restaurant and coffee shop. The *Matutum Hotel* (☎ 4901, 2711) on P Acharon Blvd has clean and passable rooms with fan and bath for P200/280, with air-con and bath for P340/440 and suites are P630. It has a restaurant and disco.

Places to Stay – top end

Pietro's Hotel (☎ 4333, 4831) on the National Highway, on the edge of town, has clean rooms with fan and bath for P230/340, with air-con and bath for P350/460 and suites for P700. It also has a restaurant and disco.

The *Phela Grande Hotel* (☎ 2950, 4925; fax 2990) on Magsaysay Ave has pleasant rooms with air-con and bath for P550/750 and suites for P1500. It has a restaurant and coffee shop. *Oscar's Club & Country Inn* (☎ 2313, 3042) on the National Highway has comfortable rooms with air-con and bath for P720/990 and suites from P1000 to P1800. It is pleasant and attractive, and has a restaurant and music lounge.

Getting There & Away

Air PAL has an office at Buayan Airport (☎ 5019) and in the Angkalian Building on the National Highway (☎ 5282).

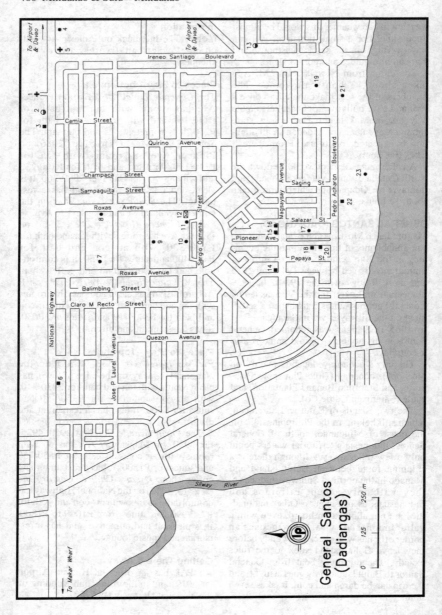

General Santos
(Dadiangas)

0   125   250 m

■ PLACES TO STAY

3   Oscar's Club &
    Country Inn
6   Pietro's Hotel
14 Phela Grande Hotel
15 Concrete Lodge
16 South Sea Lodge II
18 South Sea Lodge I
20 Pioneer Hotel
22 Matutum Hotel

OTHER

1   Doctor's Hospital
2   Yellow Bus Terminal
4   PAL
5   St Elizabeth Hospital
7   Mindanao State University
8   Immigration Office
9   Police Station
10 City Hall
11 Philippine National Bank (PNB)
12 Post Office
13 Bus Terminal
17 Interbank
19 Market
21 Fish Market
23 Magsaysay Park

Bus From Davao numerous Yellow Bus Company buses run daily to General Santos, taking four hours. The last bus is likely to leave at about 3 pm.

From Koronadel (Marbel) numerous Yellow Bus Company buses run daily to General Santos, some going on to Davao; the trip takes one hour. There are also minibuses.

Boat The Sulpicio Lines' MV *Philippine Princess* leaves Zamboanga for General Santos on Thursday at 6 pm. It takes 11 hours.

Getting Around

To/From the Airport The Buayan Airport is about six km east of General Santos. A tricycle to the centre of town costs P20.

KORONADEL

Koronadel, also known as Marbel, is the capital of South Cotabato Province. Mainly Maguindanao and B'laan, members of the original native ethnological groups, live here, but there are also immigrants from other parts of the Philippines. The Maguindanao call the town Koronadel, while the B'laan call it Marbel. It is a good starting point for a trip to Lake Sebu.

Places to Stay

The rather old *Samahang Nayon Home* (☎ 272), on the corner of Osmeña and Roxas Sts, has rooms with fan and bath for P120/200 and with air-con and bath for P220/280. It is plain but relatively comfortable.

Alabado's Home, on the corner of Alunan and Rizal Sts, is a reasonable place; it has rooms with fan and bath for P120/220 and with air-con and bath for P280/330.

Places to Eat

The Chinese meals at the *Capitol Restaurant* on Roxas St, just around the corner from the Samahang Nayon Home, are good value. The *D'Breeze Restaurant* a little farther on has good Chinese and Filipino dishes.

Getting There & Away

From Davao several Yellow Bus Company buses run daily to Koronadel via General Santos, some going on to Tacurong. It takes four hours from Davao and one hour from General Santos. From General Santos there are also minibuses to Koronadel.

To go from Lake Sebu to Koronadel via Surallah, you go first by jeepney to Surallah, then to Koronadel in a Yellow Bus Company bus bound for General Santos. It takes two hours or more.

SURALLAH

Surallah is a small town in the south of the Alah Valley. It provides access to Lake Sebu, perhaps the loveliest inland sea in the Philippines.

About 15 km south of Surallah are the impressive **Seven Falls**, which are surrounded by tropical rainforest. These thundering falls can be reached on foot in less than an hour along a well-cleared path which begins at the road from Surallah to Lake Sebu and leads through dense jungle.

The following day trips from Surallah can be recommended: to Buluan, and from there to **Lake Buluan** with its swamp areas – especially interesting for ornithologists; and to the **Kimato gold mines** in the mountains of the Tiruray Highlands, where the metal of kings is mined under hair-raising conditions.

Places to Stay & Eat

Bonns Haus in Surallah has basic rooms for P50/100. The *V I P Trading* has rooms for P80/160. The accommodation is clean and there is a family atmosphere. Meals are provided on request. The owner, Ruth Lagamayo, is happy to put guests in touch with the Fernandez family, who will provide trips with their jeep to Lake Buluan and Kimato. They even organise trips lasting several days on horseback through the mountains and the rainforest.

LAKE SEBU

Lake Sebu, which is teeming with fish, and the two, smaller neighbouring lakes Sultan and Lahit, are nested into the southern Tiruray Highlands at an altitude of almost 300 metres. Around Lake Sebu live the tribespeople called the T'boli. They live in almost total seclusion and produce rice, maize and sugar cane. They are well known for the quality of their brass ware and weaving. (For more details, see the section on Cultural Minorities in the Facts about the Country chapter.)

Try to arrange your schedule so as to include the colourful Saturday market, or, even better, the annual Lem-Lunay T'boli Festival on the second Friday in September, which lasts several days and includes wild horse fights as a high point.

You will only enjoy visiting the Lake Sebu area if you are interested in the traditional life and culture of the T'boli. Those after more modern attractions, such as discos, will soon

be bored and will not be welcomed by the locals.

Places to Stay & Eat

The *Ba-ay Village Inn* by the lake has rooms for P40/80. The owner, Bao Ba-ay, is a pure T'boli and can tell you a great deal about the T'boli culture. His wife, Alma, is an Ilokana and is a good cook. They also have their own fish farm and can arrange boats and horses for outings.

The *Lakeview Tourist Lodge* near the market has basic cottages for P40 and rooms for P50/100. At the *Hillside View Park & Lodge* (also called the Municipal Guesthouse) rooms cost P40/80.

The *Santa Cruz Mission* on Lake Sebu has rooms for P40/80. Board can be arranged for an agreed price. The guesthouse is equipped with a small kitchen and you can bring provisions from Surallah, though there is a small store with not much choice in the town. There are some small eating places about 30 minutes' walk away.

If the few beds in the guesthouse are taken, you can use your own tent or arrange private accommodation through the Santa Cruz Mission.

Getting There & Away

Jeepney Several jeepneys go from the market at Surallah to Lake Sebu daily, taking an hour or more. You can ask to be dropped off at the Santa Cruz Mission. The last jeepney from Surallah usually leaves at about 3 pm.

COTABATO

Cotabato is on the Rio Grande de Mindanao, one of the country's longest rivers. The town appears to be predominantly Muslim, but statistics show that the population is 60% Christian and only 40% Muslim. The people here are known as Maguindanao. Islam came to Cotabato in 1371, when the Arab Sharif Muhammad Kabungsuwan, who is said to be the founder of Cotabato, arrived. The Jesuits didn't arrive until 1872 and settled in Tamontaka, seven km south-west, to build a church and establish Christianity in the area.

Places to Stay

The *Padama Pension House* on Quezon Ave, near the bus terminal, has simple rooms with fan for P100/120 and with fan and bath for P150/180, but the rooms facing the street are noisy.

The *Hotel Filipino* (☎ 2307) in the city plaza on Sinsuat Ave has reasonable rooms for P170/200, with fan and bath for P220/300 and with air-con and bath for P340/460. Some rooms have a good view over the city.

El Corazon Inn on Makakua St has comfortable rooms with fan and bath for P240/290 and with air-con and bath for P340/400. Suites cost P580.

The *New Imperial Hotel* (☎ 212075-79) at 51 Don Rufino Alonzo St has rooms with air-con and bath for P700/800. It is comfortable and has a restaurant and disco.

Places to Eat

The *Jay Pee's Dan Restaurant & Snack House* on Don Rufino Alonzo St has a reputation for good, reasonably priced food.

Entertainment

The disco upstairs in the *New Imperial Hotel* is relatively expensive and has a rather austere décor. The disco on the 1st floor of the *Sampaguita Hall* is better and you can listen to folk music on the 2nd floor.

Getting There & Away

Air PAL has return flights from Cotabato to Cagayan de Oro daily except Wednesday and Saturday. Flying time is 20 minutes.

PAL has return flights between Zamboanga and Cotabato daily except Wednesday and Saturday. Flying time is one hour.

PAL has an office at Cotabato Airport (☎ 2086) and on Don Roman Vilo St.

Bus There are numerous Mintranco buses from Davao to Cotabato daily, taking over five hours.

From Koronadel many Maguindanao Express and J D Express buses run daily to Cotabato, taking three hours. Yellow Bus Company buses go at least as far as Tacurong, from where jeepneys run to Cotabato.

The bus trip from Pagadian to Cotabato by land is not advisable even if one is available. (See the Getting There & Away section under Pagadian earlier in this chapter.)

Boat A boat leaves Pagadian for Cotabato daily at 5 pm, taking eight hours.

The Sulpicio Lines' MV *Cotabato Princess* leaves Zamboanga for Cotabato on Monday at 8 pm, taking 11 hours.

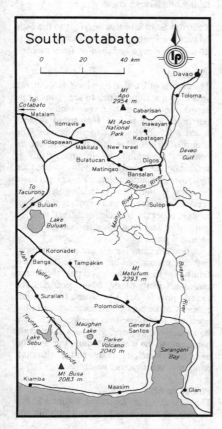

South Cotabato

Basilan

The southern end of Basilan meets the northern end of the Sulu Islands, and its northern end is just across the Basilan Strait from Mindanao. Since 1973, Basilan has been a province, comprising a main island and numerous smaller ones. About 230,000 people live here, roughly one-third of whom are Yakan, an ethnic minority found only on Basilan, except for some families living near Zamboanga on Mindanao. They are peace-loving Muslim farmers and cattle raisers, who are well known for their hospitality towards visitors and for their colourful and elaborate ceremonies, festivals and weddings. As well as the Yakan, Basilan is inhabited by the Chavacano, Visayan, Samal, Tausug and a few Badjao tribespeople.

Basilan is hilly and rugged and its centre is virtually unexplored. In the north of the island, the climate is fairly stable and there is no obvious dry or wet season, but rain may fall at any time of the year. The southern part, by contrast, has a fairly dry season from November to April.

The area's main industry is the processing of caoutchouc for rubber. Basilan rubber is considered among the best in the world, and large international companies have invested in the plantations. Other crops are coffee, cocoa, pepper, African oil (a plant oil extracted from the dates of the African palm tree) and abaca; copper is also mined. Because the waters around Basilan abound with fish, mussels and seaweed, the province is one of the most important suppliers of seafood in the southern Philippines.

Warning Throughout 1993, Basilan frequently hit the headlines in the Philippine press owing to kidnappings and other acts of violence. Many people lost their lives in shoot-outs between the military and members of the MNLF who had set up camp in the Basilan mountains. For your own safety you would be wise to think twice

about visiting Basilan. Check with the tourist office in Zamboanga for the latest news on the situation there.

GETTING THERE & AWAY
Boat
To/From Mindanao From Isabela to Zamboanga, the Basilan Shipping Lines' MV *Doña Leonora* leaves daily at 7 am and 1 pm; the MV *Estrella del Mar* leaves daily at 10 am and 4 pm. Both take 1½ hours.

From Lamitan to Zamboanga, the Basilan Shipping Lines' MV *Doña Ramona* leaves daily at 8 am from the wharf outside town, taking one hour or more.

To/From Sulu Islands Services to the Sulu Islands are irregular. It is probably better to go to Zamboanga and then on from there.

ISABELA
The capital of Basilan Province, Isabela, is a small town with not much to see. You can go across the harbour in a few minutes in an outrigger boat to see **Malamaui Island**, where a few Badjao live in pile houses. The beautiful **White Beach** is the best known beach on the island, but, in spite of this, is practically deserted. It's about an hour on foot from the landing place. You can get there by tricycle but there is no regular return service, so you either have to ask the driver to wait, order the tricycle for a fixed time, or walk. The last boat back to Isabela leaves around 4 pm.

A few km from Isabela are coffee, pepper and date plantations belonging to the Menzi family. On the way there you pass the **Menzi manufacturing plant**, where you can see exactly how rubber is produced from caoutchouc. Coffee beans are roasted there in the open air. It is closed on weekends. Before you reach the factory, you pass a mansion belonging to the wealthy Allano family, who own the electricity plant and a shipping company, among other enterprises.

Places to Stay
The *New Basilan Hotel* on J S Alano St has rooms with fan for P80/160 and with fan and

Basilan

bath for P140/280; it has a restaurant. It is not far from the wharf and is better than the nearby *Selecta Hotel*.

Places to Eat

The restaurant in the *New Basilan Hotel* is well run but you can eat better and more economically at the *New International Restaurant*. The food at *Awin's Icecream House* on Valderossa St is not exactly cheap, but the price of the beer makes up for it.

LAMITAN

Lamitan is a small town that is slightly inland but connected to the sea by an estuary. Every Thursday and Saturday from 6 to 11 am there is a large market that's really worth seeing. Ragged Badjao come with their boats to sell seafood, while Yakan bring farm produce and animals down from the hillside villages. Chinese merchants vie with local Chavacano and Visayan merchants in selling household goods and textiles.

In March 1983, the first Lami-Lamihan Festival took place. It was a pure Yakan folk festival to which the Yakan from the surrounding hills came in droves, dressed in their colourful costumes. The festival now takes place every year at the end of March or beginning of April.

Just off the main road, 12 km from Lamitan, you will find the **Buligan Falls**, which have a big, deep, natural pool – ideal for swimming.

The *Traveller's Inn* has rooms for P75/150.

Getting There & Away

Several buses leave the market in Isabela for Lamitan from 5 am, taking 45 minutes. There is also a white nonstop bus which does the 27-km stretch in 20 minutes.

Sulu Islands

The Sulu Islands are at the southernmost tip of the Philippines. They stretch about 300 km from Basilan to Borneo, dividing the Sulu and Celebes seas. A well-known pirate haunt, these waters are avoided by wary sailors whenever possible. Even commercial trading ships have been boarded and plundered. Frequent bloody battles also occur between pirates and smugglers.

The Sulus consist of a group of 500 islands, which is subdivided into smaller groups: Jolo (pronounced Holo), Samales, Pangutaran, Tapul, Tawi-Tawi, Sibutu and Cagayan de Tawi-Tawi (Cagayan Sulu). There are two provinces: Sulu, the capital of which is Jolo, and Tawi-Tawi, the capital of which is Bongao.

Attempts by the Spaniards to gain a foothold on these islands failed and the Americans were no more successful. At present government troops are trying to prevent the MNLF from realising its aim of political autonomy.

Among the most significant cultural minority groups are the Samal and the Badjao. Both seem very gentle and peaceful. The main islands inhabited by the Samal are Siasi, Tawi-Tawi and Sibutu islands. These people are Muslim and make their living predominantly from fishing, agriculture and small-scale trading. Their houses are always close to the water, often standing in the water on piles.

The Badjao live on boats throughout the entire archipelago, but are concentrated around Tawi-Tawi and Sibutu. They are sea gypsies and their religion is generally thought to be animism. A lot of them, especially those who have ceased to be nomads and live in houses on piles like the Samal, have accepted the new way of life and converted to Islam. Of all the inhabitants of the Sulu Islands, the Badjao are on the lowest rung of the social ladder. Like the Samal, they feel oppressed by the Tausug, the largest and most politically and economically advanced tribe.

The Tausug are Muslim and are considered powerful, aggressive and independent. Quite a few generations have lived by piracy, smuggling and slave-trading. The original inhabitants of the Sulu Islands, the Buranun, are said to have been the forefathers of the Tausug. They too were converted to Islam and their descendants have remained so, except for small communities of Catholics and Buddhists.

From 1974 until the end of 1981, the Sulu Islands were totally out of bounds to tourists. You could sail there from Zamboanga but were not permitted to disembark without a permit. Now, however, foreigners are allowed into the area without permits or restrictions on where they go or how long they stay. This sounds good, but in fact many islands or parts of the islands are still inaccessible because of constant tension, such as that between Tawi-Tawi and Jolo. There are other islands like Laa, near Simunul, or Sipangkot, near Tumindao, which no boat operators will visit because they fear or dislike the inhabitants.

It is essential to take warnings seriously. When I wanted to cross from Bongao to Bilatan, the boatman only gave a discouraging 'Maybe tomorrow'. That evening there was a real shoot out on Bilatan. A few

SULU SEA

Tuburan
Lamitan
Isabela
Bojelebung
Maluso
Basilan Island

Pilas Island

TAPIANTANA GROUP

Tanquil Island

PANGUTARAN GROUP

Pangutaran Island

Taglibi
Patikul
Luuc
Pananaw
Jolo
Maimbung
Jolo Island
Parang
JOLO GROUP

Pata Island

Tapul Island
Cabingaan Island

Cap Island

Lugus Island
TAPUL GROUP

Laparan Island

Siasi
Lapac Island
Siasi Island

CELEBES SEA

Bubuan Island

Tawi-Tawi Island

Tandubas Island

TAWI-TAWI GROUP

Sanga Sanga Island
Bato Bato
Bongao
Bongao Island
Simunul Island

Manuk Mankaw Island

Sibutu Island

Sitangkai
SIBUTU GROUP

Sulu Islands

0   25   50 km

Birds of the Philippines

Palawan hornbill
(*Anthracoceros marchei*)

Philippine eagle
(*Pithecophaga jefferyi*)

Philippine trogon
(*Harpactes ardens*)

Seleputo owl
(*Strix seloputo wiepkeni*)

Philippine kingfisher
(*Halcyon chloris qullaris*)

Palawan peacock pheasant
(*Polyplectron emphanum*)

days earlier I had been refused a ride from Bongao to Laa through fear of an ambush. That night you could clearly hear a long fusillade of shots from across the water. There was probably a good reason, too, for the marine escort given to our boat from Sitangkai to Bongao.

Added to this are accommodation and water shortages. Commercial accommodation is available only in Jolo, Bongao and Sitangkai. Elsewhere you have to find private lodgings and you should pay a reasonable price for them. On the southern islands, like Bongao, Sibutu, Tumindao and Sitangkai, there is a severe water shortage. You get a guilty conscience even brushing your teeth! Any washing is done in sea water polluted with sewage and refuse. You can almost feel the hepatitis threatening your liver.

Nevertheless, a trip to the Sulu Islands is a unique experience. The impressions gained are many and varied and well worth the effort. However, before going there it would be advisable to enquire about the current situation in areas of possible unrest. The tourist office in Zamboanga or Southern Command Headquarters should be able to help.

GETTING THERE & AWAY
You can get to the Sulu Islands from Mindanao and probably also from Basilan. (See the Mindanao Getting There & Away section earlier in this chapter.)

Air
To/From Mindanao PAL flies daily to Zamboanga from Tawi-Tawi (the airport is on Sanga Sanga Island, near Bongao) and Jolo.

Boat
To/From Basilan Connections to Basilan from the Sulu Islands are irregular. However, merchant ships, which will also take passengers, are said to leave Jolo quite often for Isabela.

To/From Mindanao See the timetable for SKT ships and the Sampaguita Shipping Corporation in the following Getting Around section in this chapter.

To/From Palawan If you have time, you could try the following route: go from Jolo to Pangutaran Island, then on to Cagayan de Tawi-Tawi, where you can occasionally get a freighter to Rio Tuba or Brooke's Point in southern Palawan.

GETTING AROUND
Ships, ranging from vile little tubs to quite passable freighters that take passengers, ply more or less regular routes between almost all of the larger islands. The better ships on the route from Zamboanga via Jolo, Siasi, and Bongao to Sitangkai and back are those of the SKT Shipping Lines and the Sampaguita Shipping Corporation.

SKT Shipping Lines Timetable:

MV Lady Ruth

Destination	Arrives	Departs
Zamboanga	Sat 5 pm	Tue 6 pm
Jolo	Wed 4 am	Wed 12 pm
Siasi	Wed 4 pm	Wed 10 pm
Bongao	Thu 6 am	Thu 11 am
Sitangkai	Thu 3 pm	Thu 12 am
Bongao	Fri 4 am	Fri 6 pm
Jolo	Sat 6 am	Sat 9 am

MV Lady Helen

Destination	Arrives	Departs
Zamboanga	Mon 5 am	Wed 6 pm
Jolo	Thu 4 am	Thu 12 pm
Siasi	Thu 5 pm	Thu 8 pm
Bongao	Fri 5 am	Fri 10 am
Sitangkai	Fri 2 pm	Fri 12 am
Bongao	Sat 4 am	Sat 6 pm
Siasi	Sun 2 am	Sun 1 pm
Jolo	Sun 5 pm	Sun 9 pm

MV Doña Isabel II

Destination	Arrives	Departs
Zamboanga	Thu 4 am	Sat 6 pm
Jolo	Sun 2 am	Sun 12 pm
Siasi	Sun 4 pm	Sun 6 pm
Bongao	Mon 4 am	Mon 11 am
Sitangkai	Mon 3 pm	Tue 1 am
Bongao	Tue 5 am	Tue 6 pm
Siasi	Wed 2 am	Wed 2 pm
Jolo	Wed 6 pm	Wed 8 pm

Sampaguita Shipping Corporation Timetable:

MV *Sampaguita Grandeur*

Destination	Arrives	Departs
Zamboanga	Fri 6 pm	Mon 8 pm
Jolo	Tue 5 am	Tue 10 am
Siasi	Tue 2 pm	Tue 6 pm
Bongao	Wed 3 am	Wed 10 am
Sitangkai	Wed 2 pm	Wed 8 pm
Bongao	Wed 12 am	Thu 7 pm
Jolo	Fri 6 am	Fri 9 am

MV *Sampaguita Lei*

Destination	Arrives	Departs
Zamboanga	Mon 6 pm	Thu 8 pm
Jolo	Fri 5 am	Fri 10 am
Siasi	Fri 2 pm	Fri 6 pm
Bongao	Sat 3 am	Sat 10 am
Sitangkai	Sat 2 pm	Sat 8 pm
Bongao	Sun 12 am	Sun 7 pm
Jolo	Mon 6 am	Mon 9 am

MV *Sampaguita Blossom*

Destination	Arrives	Departs
Zamboanga	Thu 10 pm	Sun 7 pm
Jolo	Mon 7 am	Mon 11 am
Siasi	Mon 4 pm	Mon 6 pm
Bongao	Tue 6 am	Tue 11 am
Sitangkai	Tue 4 pm	Tue 8 pm
Bongao	Wed 3 am	Wed 7 pm
Jolo	Thu 7 am	Thu 10 am

JOLO

Jolo is the capital of the island of the same name and also of Sulu Province. It is the only place in the entire archipelago where the Spaniards, after a relatively short period of 20 years, finally gained a foothold and built a fortress. This was at the end of the 19th century, about 300 years after they first reached the Philippines.

In February 1974, Jolo was partly destroyed in fighting between Muslims and government troops. Even today the military is still present in the city. Although no permit is required for the city itself, foreigners need a military permit to travel around this volcanic island. It is remarkable to see the many trishaws standing around the great mosque. Don't miss the colourful fish market and the Barter Trade Market in the halls next to the harbour, where goods that come mainly from Borneo are sold. The lovely, sandy **Quezon Beach** is about three km north-east of Jolo.

If it's not off limits for security reasons, you can get there by jeepney, getting out before Patikul. A little farther east in Taglibi is another wide, sandy beach with crystal clear water.

Places to Stay

Helen's Lodge (☎ 104) on Buyon St has rooms with fan for P70/120 and with fan and bath for P150/250. It is simple and relatively clean and has a restaurant. Travellers passing through can use the sanitary facilities for a small charge.

Places to Eat

If you have just arrived from Zamboanga, you will have your first experience of the island's coffee shops in Jolo. Whether you order coffee or a Sprite (the popular soft drink in Sulu), you will be offered a large tray of all sorts of cakes.

Good restaurants are the *Bee Gees* on Sanchez St, the *Plaza Panciteria* on Sevantes St, where they serve a mean milkshake among other things, and the *Plaza Restaurant* that has quite passable toilet facilities.

SIASI

This island is a crisis area according to locals. I must admit, the little harbour town of the same name didn't make a particularly good impression on me either. It has lots of damaged or totally burnt-out houses, a boarded-up Sultan Hotel, and few restaurants with little food. People are rather unforthcoming and language difficulties could be a problem.

BONGAO

Bongao, on Bongao Island, is the most important town in the Tawi-Tawi Island group. It's bigger than Siasi but smaller than Jolo, and has two harbours, a market, two cinemas and a main street with several side streets. The Provincial Capitol Building stands out like a mosque on the hillside. The Badjao village of Tungkalang, on the southwest tip of Sanga Sanga, which has been described in some old travel books, no longer

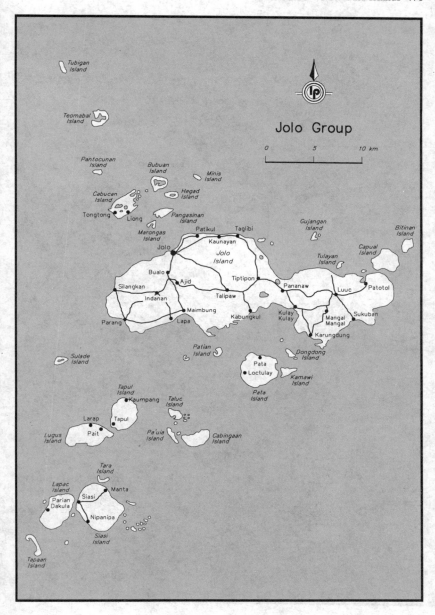

Jolo Group

0   5   10 km

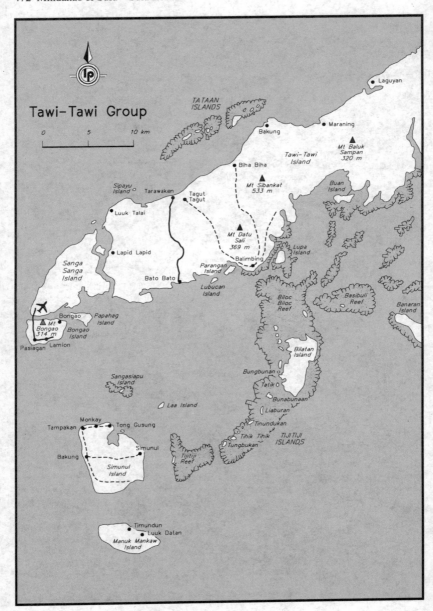

exists. Sea gypsies have settled near Bongao, in the bay by the hospital, and Notre Dame College. As far as these friendly people are concerned, an 'Americo' isn't a 'Joe' (a holdover from 'GI Joe', popular after American troops helped liberate the islands from Japanese invaders in 1944 to 1945) but 'Milikan'.

Orientation
The military camp, Philippine National Bank and PAL are all on the outskirts of town. Beyond them, you come to quite a nice swimming place, where the road meets the shore. At low tide you can walk across to a sandbank that is good for snorkelling.

Mt Bongao
The little village of Pasiagan is five km from Bongao. This is the start of the trail leading up Mt Bongao, a 314-metre mountain worshipped by both Christians and Muslims. Anjaotals, a member of an old royal family, is buried on the summit. Prayers said in the four-sq-metre enclosure with its wall draped in white cloth are said to be more powerful than any medicine. (If you visit the enclosure, you must take off your shoes.) Paths right and left of the grave lead to good lookout points that are clear of trees. The climb takes about an hour and is hot and tiring.

As this is a holy mountain, you should not defile it in any way and offensive behaviour like swearing should be avoided. It is believed that people who touch a monkey here will soon die or lose their wits. It's as well to take some bananas for these inquisitive animals. There are numerous snakes, though they're not easy to see, so don't grab blindly at trees or vines. In early October, Bongao has a fiesta and the hill is alive with people.

Places to Stay
The *Southern Inn* on Datu Halun St, opposite the mosque, has basic rooms for P250 and with fan and bath for P350. It has a restaurant and two pleasant balconies.

It is possible to find really comfortable accommodation in Bongao, including three meals, for about P200.

Getting There & Away
From Bongao you can catch small boats to the islands of Bilatan, Simunul and Manuk Mankaw. Bunabunaan is the burial island of the Badjao and can only be reached by a Special Ride. When in Bongao, I was constantly advised not to visit Tawi-Tawi.

Getting Around
To/From the Airport The Tawi-Tawi Airport is on Sanga Sanga Island, north of Bongao. The jeepney trip to the town costs P5, or P50 by tricycle.

SITANGKAI
It is said that more than 6000 people live in this 'Venice of the Far East', in houses built on piles on the giant reef. The water is so shallow that big ships have to anchor three km away in the Tumindao Channel and ferry their freight and passengers across in small boats (P25 per person).

There are more Badjao villages built on piles scattered over a large area west of Sitangkai. The largest, and furthest away, is called Tong Tong and is made up of 50 houses. It's not far from the Meridian Channel, which is 50 to 100 metres deep. Here as elsewhere the Badjao have laid out underwater seaweed fields; sea cucumbers are another main source of income. A day trip there by boat can be arranged for P300 to P500.

From Sitangkai small boats run to the two bigger islands of Tumindao and Sibutu.

Warning
Because of the many people who travel illegally on the smugglers' boats from Sitangkai to Sempora on Borneo (in the state of Sabah, East Malaysia), for many years tourists were only allowed to leave the ship at Sitangkai after showing a passport and a valid visa, as well as a permit from the Tawi-Tawi Task Force (TTTF). The TTTF Permit

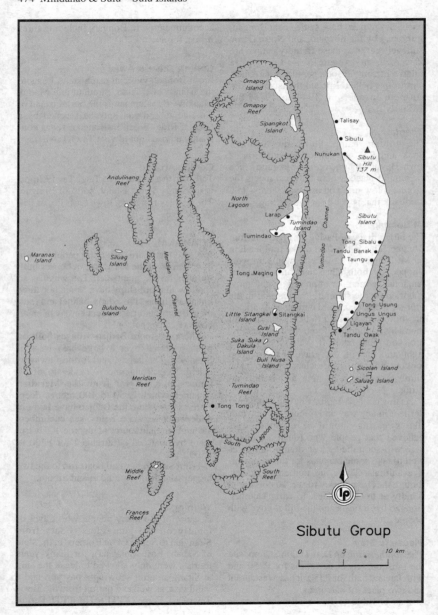

Sibutu Group

0   5   10 km

was issued by the appropriate authorities in Bongao, where showing a return ticket (eg, from Zamboanga to Manila) cut down the interrogation considerably. Apparently these checks have been discontinued in the meantime. Nevertheless, it would be worth the effort asking in Bongao whether it is possible to travel to Sitangkai without going through red tape first.

Places to Stay

The Plaza Hotel has been converted into a hospital, so you will have to look for private accommodation. If you have the chance to stay with the Badjao for a few days, do so but be generous with food and supplies, as these friendly people don't have much. Hadji Musa Malabong, the teacher at Sitangkai, and his brother, Hadji Yusof Abdulganih, can arrange private accommodation.

Palawan

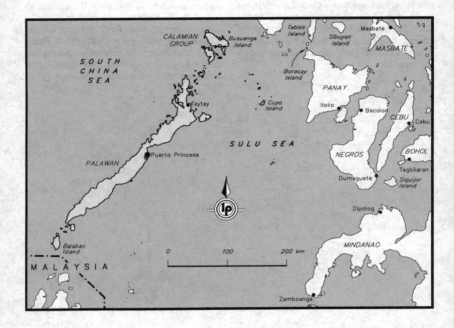

Palawan, in the south-west of the Philippines, is 400 km long but only 40 km wide and separates the Sulu Sea from the South China Sea. Beautiful empty beaches, untouched natural scenery and friendly inhabitants make this a very attractive island. A further 1768 islands make up Palawan Province, the most important being Busuanga, Culion, Coron, Cuyo, Dumaran, Bugsuk and Balabac. Most of Palawan consists of mountainous jungle. At 2086 metres, Mt Mantalingajan is the highest mountain.

The El Nido cliffs and the limestone caves of Coron and Pabellones islands, off Taytay, are home to countless swallows' nests. Hotels and Chinese restaurants all over the country get their supplies from these places to make that oriental delicacy, birds' nest

soup. If you like fish, you will think this is paradise, as the fruits of the sea are really plentiful here. You could try a different fish dinner every day, choosing from crayfish, mussels, sea urchin, lobster and many others. The jungles harbour plants and animals which are found nowhere else in the Philippines. These include the iron tree, the mouse deer (chevrotain), the king cobra and many rare parrots and butterflies.

With the exception of the Underground River and the Tabon Caves, Palawan has no sights worth talking about. On the other hand, what makes the island so attractive and pleasant to visit are the friendly inhabitants, unspoilt nature and the outstanding, deserted beaches. Palawan also offers a wide variety of activities for the more adventurous visitor:

you can try jungle expeditions, searching for gold, cave exploring, diving, trekking, searching for shipwrecks or living like Robinson Crusoe, among other things.

ECONOMY

Only a few coastal regions can be used for agriculture. The main crops are rice, coconuts, bananas, groundnuts and cashew nuts. For the economy, however, fishing is by far the most important activity. The richest fishing grounds in the Philippines are off Palawan's northern coast. About 60% of Manila's staple food is caught between Coron, Cuyo and Dumaran islands and especially in Taytay Bay.

Since the discovery of oil off Palawan's north-west coast, the development of that industry looks promising. Another important industry is forestry, which is almost exclusively dominated by Pagdanan Timber Products (PTP) and Nationwide Princesa Timber (NPT). Both companies are controlled by one person. Up to 1989, when the Aquino government imposed a logging ban, Palawan had lost 20,000 hectares of forests every year since 1979. That is about 2½% of the total forest reserves of this island, which has such rich flora & fauna. It is becoming increasingly obvious, however, that the law is not being observed. As so often in the Philippines, the letter of the law and practical reality are two different things. This stripping of Palawan is likely to frustrate the promising plans of the Department of Tourism. In a few years there will be dead coral reefs caused by fishing with explosives and barren hillsides because of uncontrolled deforestation. These will so alter the face of the island that nature lovers will no longer have any reason for visiting.

PEOPLE

Palawan is thinly populated, with most inhabitants coming from several islands in the Visayas. The Batak and Pala'wan are among the aboriginal inhabitants of Palawan. The Batak are very shy. If you want to find them and visit their villages, you need plenty of time and a competent guide.

The Negrito, nomads who live by hunting, are found in the north. Attempts to convince them of the benefits of agriculture and of settling the land have nearly always failed. Some of them go to school but then disappear into the jungle again.

In the extreme north of Palawan are the Tagbanua, a seafaring people who rarely settle in one place. On the other hand, the Tagbanua who live near the coast and along the rivers of central Palawan live in settled village communities. Like the Hanunoo on Mindoro, they use a syllabic writing system.

The Tau't Batu in the south of Palawan were only discovered in 1978. They live in caves in the Singnapan Basin, a few km east of Ransang, as they have done for about 20,000 years. Their habitat has been declared a protected area and is absolutely off limits. This prohibition must obviously be respected.

HEALTH
Warning

Outside of the capital, medical services are inadequate. Even if you can find a doctor, there won't be a pharmacy which stocks the necessary medication. In case of illness, head straight for Puerto Princesa.

Malaria is widespread on Palawan, so it's important to take antimalarial tablets, always sleep under mosquito netting, and use insect repellent. (See the section on Health in the Facts for the Visitor chapter.) If you get a fever, remember that it could be malaria and head straight for Puerto Princesa. The doctors there know more about malaria and how to treat it than doctors in Manila. On a more positive note, you won't see a mosquito during the dry season in large parts of Palawan. This is also when most people visit. Mosquitoes are usually only a problem in the rainy season, especially in the south.

During the summer months, deadly jellyfish called *salabay* may be found in the coastal waters.

Unfortunately many Palawan beaches are also a popular home for 'nik-niks': tiny sandflies which often take pleasure in stinging lightly-clad sun worshippers. An

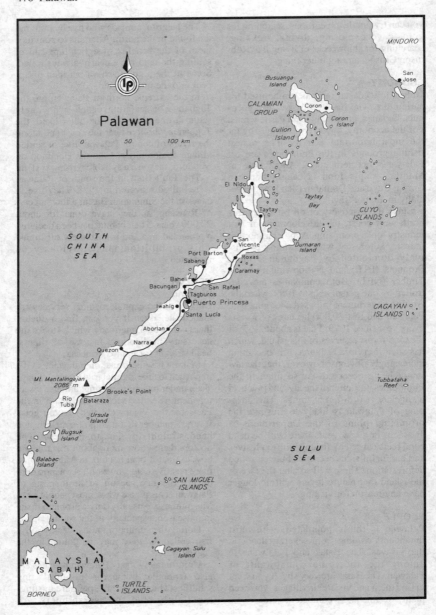

effective way of warding off these annoying little insects is to rub on coconut oil combined with a dash of insect repellent such as Autan or Off.

GETTING THERE & AWAY

You can get to Palawan from Cebu, Lubang, Luzon and Panay. (See the Getting There & Away section in the Luzon section of the Manila chapter and the relevant Getting There & Away section of the Visayas chapter.)

Air

To/From Cebu PAL flies on Monday, Wednesday and Saturday from Puerto Princesa to Cebu City via Iloilo City on Panay.

To/From Luzon From Busuanga to Manila, Pacific Airways flies daily; Aerolift flies on Monday, Wednesday, Friday and Sunday; Air Link flies on Monday, Thursday and Saturday; and PAL flies on Friday and Sunday.

Pacific Airways has flights from Cuyo to Manila on Monday, Wednesday and Friday. Aerolift has daily flights from El Nido to Manila and PAL has daily flights from Puerto Princesa to Manila.

To/From Panay PAL has flights on Monday, Wednesday and Saturday from Puerto Princesa to Iloilo City.

Boat

To/From Lubang For information about ships to Lubang, see the following To/From Luzon section. The trip from Coron to Tilik takes 16 hours.

To/From Luzon From Puerto Princesa to Manila, the William Lines' MV *Sugbu* leaves on Monday at 7 pm, taking 19 hours.

From Coron to Batangas, the Viva Shipping Lines' MV *Love Boat* leaves Monday at noon, taking 15 hours.

The Asuncion Shipping Lines has several ships going to Manila. The MV *Asuncion X* leaves Culion on Tuesday at 6 am and Coron

at 4 pm for Manila, via Tilik on Lubang, taking 26 hours from Coron.

The MV *Catalyn A* leaves Culion on Friday at 4 am and Coron at 3 pm for Manila, via Tilik on Lubang, taking 27 hours from Coron.

The MV *Asuncion XI* leaves Culion on Sunday at 4 am and Coron at 4 pm for Manila, via Tilik on Lubang, taking 26 hours.

The MV *Asuncion IV* leaves Liminangcong on Saturday at noon and El Nido on Sunday at 6 pm for Manila, taking 29 hours from El Nido.

The MV *Asuncion VI* leaves Puerto Princesa for Manila once a week, via Caramay, Roxas and Dumaran, taking 78 hours from Puerto Princesa, 68 hours from Roxas and 38 hours from Dumaran.

To/From Panay The Milagrosa Shipping Lines' MV *Milagrosa-J-Dos* leaves Puerto Princesa for Iloilo City, via Cuyo, on the 1st, 11th and 21st of the month at noon. It takes 38 hours, including an eight hour stopover in Cuyo. Departure from Cuyo is on the 2nd, 12th and 22nd of the month at 6 am. The MV *Milagrosa-J-Tres* sails on the 7th, 17th and 27th of the month, leaving Puerto Princesa at 4 pm.

GETTING AROUND THE ISLAND

Touring is a little bit difficult in Palawan. The roads between the villages are only good in parts but road works are progressing. There is only one 'highway', which is partly surfaced, leading from Brooke's Point via Puerto Princesa, Roxas and Taytay to El Nido. If you want to travel on side roads, you either need lots of time or lots of money. Jeepney drivers and boat operators always try to make you pay for a Special Ride. If you agree because you can't wait, you will certainly be paying for all the other passengers, too, so everybody will get in and enjoy the free ride.

It's difficult and sometimes impossible to travel by road in the rainy season as some of the routes become impassable after a few days' rain. If, as a result, you can only travel

Swords

Single and double-edged swords of various designs are an integral part of the arts and crafts of the Muslims in the south of the Philippines. In Mindanao and the Sulu Islands in particular, the art of forging blades and shaping handles remains important. In Sulu, the classical type is the *kris*, called *kalis seko*, and the *kampilan*. Although they are rarely used in battle these days, swords are still of social and symbolic significance to the wearer.

1 Barong: a leaf-shaped, single-edged blade
2 Kampilan: the handle is supposed to represent the open mouth of a crocodile
3 Kris: a wavy-shaped blade
4 T'boli-bolo: the handle is decorated with brass curls
5 Dagger-kris: a weapon preferred by women
6 Talibong: a sabre with a single-edged, curved blade

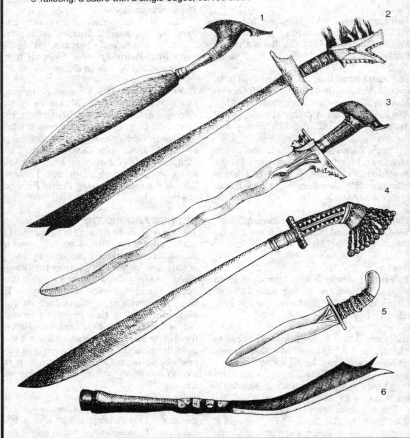

by boat, you will have to pay through the nose to get anywhere.

Travel to North Palawan has been made considerably easier with the introduction of a boat service between Coron-El Nido in early 1992. With the addition of regular flights between Manila-Busuanga and Manila-El Nido round trips are now possible without hassle, in an area where up until recently almost every trip ended up in a dead end.

Boat Tours

More and more visitors are discovering the pleasures of extended boat trips to Palawan's more interesting places and islands. So it is not surprising to find out that more and more large boats are being built.

A 10-day tour could look something like this: Puerto Princesa – Coco-Loco Island – Flowers Island – Elephant Island – El Nido – Port Barton – Underground River. This would cost around US$35 per day per person, with full board.

Mark Bratschi from Switzerland offers trips with his MB *Moonshadow*. The boat is 21 metres long and has five cabins for eight to 10 passengers. Contact Mark at PO Box 107, 5300 Puerto Princesa. He can also be contacted at the Sonne Gasthaus in Puerto Princesa. Martin and Flora from the Swissipini Lodge in Port Barton also offer trips on the large outrigger, MB *Palawan Beauty* (30 metres long, with cabins for 12 passengers). You can write to them at the following address: International Guest House, PO Box 49, 5300 Puerto Princesa.

The Coco-Loco Island Resort offers two-day trips to and from El Nido on a large outrigger (25 metres long, accommodates 15 passengers). Contact the Coco-Loco office opposite the Palawan Hotel, Rizal Ave, 5300 Puerto Princesa for reservations.

The Cruise & Hotel Center (☎ 8153008, 8190290; fax 8190289), Maripola Building, 109 Perea St, Legaspi Village, Makati, offers three and six-day trips on the catamaran MV *Lagoon Explorer*. This extremely well-equipped ship (10 air-con cabins for 36 passengers in all) sails from Coron to El Nido and back, with frequent stops at anchor. Flights can be booked at the same time for Manila-El Nido and Manila-Busuanga (and vice versa). A three-day trip in a double cabin, including return flight and full board, costs US$640 per person.

Central Palawan

PUERTO PRINCESA

Puerto Princesa is a relatively new city with about 100,000 inhabitants. Although more houses are being built, you can still find beautiful buildings in the traditional style. The main buildings are the cathedral and the Provincial Capitol. At the waterfront there are fishers' huts built right over the water.

Puerto Princesa is remarkable for its cleanliness, something the mayor is deservedly praised for. He managed to enthuse the locals with the idea of keeping their city clean. Refuse disposal and street cleaning both function immaculately, and many tricycles even have an ashtray in them (throwing away cigarette butts on the streets is a fineable offence!).

The scene on the wharf at sunset is good fun. Puerto Princesa Bay also has some interesting places for diving. For about P300 you can hire an outrigger boat for a few hours and sail, swim, dive and fish in the bay.

White Beach on the eastern edge of town is good for sunbathing but swimming is only possible at high tide; admission costs P5. Keep a good look out for pickpockets, who have been encouraged by unwary tourists. You can get to White Beach by tricycle by going in the direction of the airport and getting off at the Ice Plant. Just before the Ice Plant is an old gate – this is where the track to the beach starts. It's about 10 minutes' walk down to the beach. In the dry season you can go right to the beach by tricycle.

Each year there is a week-long festival which starts on 7 December. It includes concerts in Mendoza Park, Caracol boat processions, a beauty contest, quizzes, competitions, and so on.

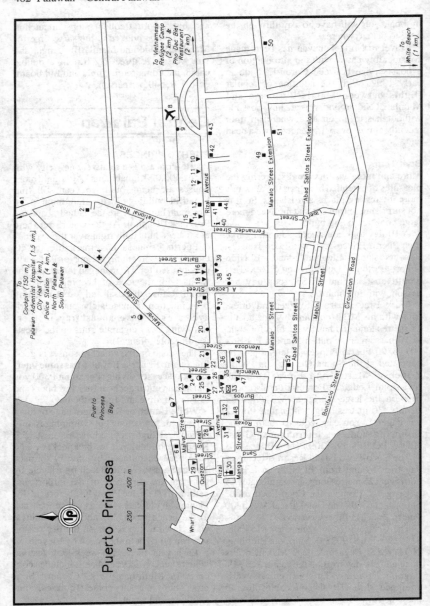

Puerto Princesa

■ PLACES TO STAY

2	Asiaworld Resort Hotel Palawan
3	Emerald Hotel
6	Puerto Pension
13	Trattorio Terrace Pensionhouse
19	Garcellano Tourist Inn
35	Circon Lodge
41	Badjao Inn
42	Palawan Hotel
43	Puerto Airport Hotel
44	Casa Linda
48	Abelardo's Pensionne
49	International Guest House
50	Sonne Gasthaus
51	Yayen's Pension
52	Duchess Pension House

▼ PLACES TO EAT

10	Crystal Forest Grill Park & Disco
11	Pink Lace Grill Garden Restaurant
12	Kalui Restaurant
13	Trattorio Terrace Restaurant
14	Dragon King Seafood Restaurant
15	Bavaria Restaurant
17	Café Puerto
18	Palawan Chef Restaurant
19	Zum Kleinen Anker
22	Edwin's Food Palace & Disco
27	Roadside Pizza Inn & Folkhouse
28	Pink Lace Restaurant
29	Ignacio Restaurant
34	Café Nostalgia
38	Kamayan Folkhouse & Restaurant
41	Kubo Restaurant
47	Swiss Bistro Valencia

OTHER

1	Nightclubs
4	Provincial Hospital
5	Charing Bus Lines & Jeepney Terminal
7	Puerto Royale Bus Lines
8	Airport
9	Caparii Dive Camp Office & Pacific Airways
11	Paradise Nightclub
12	Island Divers
16	William Lines
19	PCI Bank
20	RPCI (Long Distance Calls)
21	PT&T Office
22	Metrobank
23	Market
24	Bowling Lanes & Cinema
25	Jeepneys to Iwahig
26	Philippine National Bank (PNB)
30	Cathedral
31	Piltel (Long Distance Calls)
32	City Tourist Office
33	Post Office
35	Bang-Bang Disco
36	Mendoza Park
37	Karla's Antiques
39	AS Money Changer, Culture Shack & Nikki's
40	Provincial Tourist Office & Provincial Capitol Building
41	Bottle Ground Disco & Gold Mine Spirituosen
45	NCCC
46	Museum

Information

Tourist Office There is an information counter at the airport. A City Tourist Office on Rizal Ave, near the corner of Roxas St specialises mainly in information on Puerto Princesa and transport connections to and from there; and a Provincial Tourist Office in the Provincial Capitol Building on Rizal Ave, on the corner of Fernandez St, has information on the whole province.

The monthly bulletin *Bandillo ng Palawan*, written and published by local environmentalists, has interesting articles about ecotourism and conservation on Palawan. It costs P5 and is available at the Kalui Restaurant and the Culture Shack, both on Rizal Ave.

Money The Metrobank and the Philippine National Bank change travellers' cheques and US dollars as does the A S Money Changer (but cash and American Express travellers' cheques only). Outside of Puerto Princesa there are practically no money-changing facilities on Palawan. This is especially true in El Nido, where many travellers have had to leave early because of lack of available funds.

Medical Services The treatment, nursing care and medication are apparently much better in the Palawan Adventist Hospital than in the Provincial Hospital.

Activities

Diving Palawan is becoming more and more popular with underwater enthusiasts.

The Queen Ann Divers diving shop has a 23-metre-long outrigger diving boat with 10 complete sets of diving equipment. It offers diving instruction as well as one-day or more diving trips with two dives daily for US$45 per day per person, including equipment. For bookings, contact Martin Gugi and Urs Rechsteiner, c/o Zum Kleinen Anker, Rizal Ave, 5300 Puerto Princesa.

The Palawan Diving Corporation offers one-way or more diving trips on its 20-metre-long diving boat ML *Vicky*. It can handle trips of up to three weeks on demand.

The boat has three four-bed cabins, shower and toilet. There is diving equipment for 15 people on board. The price of US$60 per day per person includes two dives daily (night diving is possible), equipment and full board. From July until October, the price is reduced to US$35. Contact Bernd Henke, c/o Zum Kleinen Anker, Rizal Ave, 5300 Puerto Princesa. The MB *Moonshadow* and the MB *Palawan Beauty* also have diving equipment on board (see Boat Tours earlier in this chapter).

For information about good diving places, you could also ask Norman Songco of Island Divers on Rizal Ave. This diving shop runs organised trips. Hiring a complete outfit costs US$30 a day and you can get goggles and a snorkel for P125 a day. Diving tours for two or more divers cost US$55 per person a day. This includes transport, two tanks, a belt, a backpack, two dives a day and a meal. You can do a one-week diving course for US$300.

Plane Charter At the airport, Pacific Airways has a six-seater Cessna for charter at P7000 an hour. However, the organisation is not exactly reliable. A pre-booked aircraft may be chartered to someone else at short notice, or a reserved seat given to another passenger.

Things to Buy

Typical Palawan artwork is available in the Culture Shack and Karla's Antiques, both on Rizal Ave. Also on sale is the tape *Palawan: At Peace with Nature*, which makes an excellent souvenir. It is 'A Musical Journey to the Last Frontier' by Sinika, a group using mostly native instruments.

Places to Stay – bottom end

The *Duchess Pension House* (☎ 2873) on Valencia St has singles/doubles with fan for P80/130 and doubles with fan and bath for P250. It is unpretentious but good. The owners, Joe and Cecille, are friendly and the atmosphere is pleasant. They have a garden restaurant serving breakfast and snacks. Girls from the local 'scene' are not allowed in.

Abelardo's Pensionne (☎ 2049) at 63 Manga St has fairly good rooms with fan for P150/200, doubles with fan and bath for P275 and with air-con and bath for P450.

The *Garcellano Tourist Inn* (☎ 2314, 2553) at 257 Rizal Ave has basic, small singles with fan and bath for P100 and doubles with fan and bath for P150. It is plain and has a large courtyard.

Yayen's Pension (☎ 2261) at 294 Manalo St Extension has singles/doubles with fan for P75/120, doubles with fan and bath for P175 and with air-con and bath for P375. It is a pleasantly run place with a coffee shop and a garden.

Puerto Pension at 35 Malvar St has singles with fan for P135 and doubles with fan for P165 (there is one bath for every two rooms). Doubles with fan and bath cost P200. It is simple and clean, and has a restaurant. The building was tastefully designed using natural materials.

The *Sonne Gasthaus* is a quiet place at 366 Manalo St Extension. It has clean rooms with fan for P170/200 and cottages with fan and bath for P280, as well as a restaurant.

The *International Guest House* (☎ 2540)

located at 263 Manalo St Extension has singles/doubles with fan for P150 and doubles with fan and bath for P180 (there is one bath for two rooms). It has a friendly, family atmosphere.

The *Trattoria Terrace Pensionhouse* (☎ 2719) at 353 Rizal Ave has decent rooms with fan for P140/200 and with air-con and bath for P390. There is a restaurant, bar and a terrace with lots of plants.

Places to Stay – middle

Badjao Inn (☎ 2761, 2380; fax 2180) at 350 Rizal Ave has singles with fan and bath for P180 and doubles with fan and bath for P260. Singles with air-con and bath cost P450 and P595 and doubles with air-con and bath cost P510 and P660. The air-con rooms are neat and comfortable, the more expensive ones are tastefully furnished and have a fridge and TV. There is a nice big garden with a restaurant. Girls from the local 'scene' are not allowed in.

Casa Linda (☎ 2606) on Trinidad Rd has clean singles/doubles with fan and bath for P300/350 and with air-con and bath for P450/500. This is a pleasant place with a well-kept garden. The service is attentive and friendly. All in all, a well-run establishment in a quiet area.

Palawan Hotel (☎ 2326), a comfortable place with a restaurant, is near the airport on Rizal Ave. It has singles/doubles with air-con and bath for P450/540.

Places to Stay – top end

The *Puerto Airport Hotel* (☎ 2177) at 442 Rizal Ave has cozy rooms with air-con and bath for P465/550 and comfortable suites with fridge and TV for P1000 and P1200. There is a restaurant, a coffee shop and a small swimming pool. It is handy for the airport.

The *Emerald Hotel* (☎ 2611, 2263) on Malvar St has rooms with air-con and bath for P500/650 and suites for P850. It is pleasant and attractive and has a restaurant and swimming pool, as well as transport to the airport.

Asiaworld Resort Hotel Palawan (☎ 202,

2111, 2212) on National Rd has singles with air-con and bath for P2500 and doubles with air-con and bath for P2650. The rooms are well kept, although a bit on the expensive side. This is the biggest and best hotel in town. It has a restaurant, swimming pool and disco.

Places to Eat

There are lots of restaurants on the side streets, but Rizal Ave alone offers a bewildering range of places to eat, reflecting the cosmopolitan range of tourists in Puerto Princesa and Palawan generally.

You can enjoy a good meal in an attractive setting at the *Café Puerto*, on Rizal Ave, where the English chef Andrew prepares excellent French dishes. It is open from 11.30 am to 2 pm and from 5.30 pm to midnight. Italian food is also available at the *Roadside Pizza Inn & Folkhouse*.

The cuisine at the friendly *Pink Lace Restaurant* includes Filipino, Chinese, Indian, Mexican and Vietnamese dishes and cakes. The Filipino dishes at the *Kamayan Folkhouse & Restaurant* are good and you can eat on the terrace or in the tree house.

The unassuming *Ignacio Restaurant* on Quezon St also serves good value Filipino dishes. The *NCCC Fast Food Restaurant*, on the ground floor in the shopping mall of the same name on A Lacson St, is always busy. It offers a wide choice of Filipino dishes and it is self-service.

At the rustic cellar bar *Zum Kleinen Anker*, Achim and Honey serve Filipino and German meals and cold beer from 8 am to 10 pm. The friendly *Sonne Gasthaus* on Manalo St Extension also serves good Filipino and German meals as well as tasty breakfasts. The pleasant and busy, *Swiss Bistro Valencia* on Valencia St has good steaks and European dishes, together with what must be the best music in town. At the *Trattoria Terrace* on Rizal Ave the menu features steaks and a good choice of pasta dishes.

The *Kubo Restaurant* in the green backyard of the Badjao Inn, Rizal Ave, offers an excellent breakfast menu. About 100 metres farther, in the direction of the airport, right next door to Island Divers, you will find the charmingly rustic *Kalui Restaurant*. In addition to having a refreshingly original look about it, there is an area in the restaurant where guests can simply read and relax. It is open daily except Sunday, from 11 am to 2 pm and 5.30 to 11 pm. Instead of a menu, it has a meal of the day, always seafood. What it is depends on the catch, and it is served with vegetables and rice.

At the entrance to the Vietnamese refugee camp, about two km out of town behind the airport, you will find the *Pho Dac Biet Restaurant*. You can eat good cheap Vietnamese meals there as well as French-style bread from the camp bakery.

The sophisticated *Yoko Restaurant* in the Asiaworld Resort Hotel Palawan specialises in Japanese food.

Entertainment

Edwin's Food Palace & Disco shows films all day on a large screen. At around 9 pm this spacious Chinese restaurant is transformed into a disco where until midnight the guests can enjoy a mixture of music ranging from sweet music to techno. The popular *Bang-Bang Disco* across the street is open three hours longer and has live music. Late at night the *Crystal Forest Grill Park & Disco* opposite the Palawan Hotel also seems to attract plenty of night birds.

One of the most popular dance clubs is the *Prism Disco* in the Asiaworld Resort Hotel Palawan. You have to pay P45 to get into the *Bottle Ground Disco* next to the Badjao Inn where they have go-go girls. It is quite possible you may also have to pay a service charge and a table charge!

The *Café Nostalgia* entertains its guests with golden oldies, while the *Kamayan Folkhouse & Restaurant* has male and female folk singers.

Several nightclubs, such as *Mina-Vic*, *Mena Rosa* and *Nenette's*, are on the northern edge of town.

Getting There & Away

Air PAL has an office at Puerto Princesa Airport (☎ 2356, 2561). If you are flying back to Manila, Iloilo City and Cebu City, you should reconfirm your flight in advance as soon as possible as flights are often hopelessly booked out.

Getting Around

To/From the Airport The airport is on the eastern edge of town, about three km from the town centre. A tricycle trip into town costs P4 per person or P15 to P20 if it's not shared .

Tricycle A trip in town by tricycle costs P2 per person. Chartering a tricycle should not cost more than P80 an hour. The normal price by tricycle from the wharf to a hotel in the centre of town should be P4 but P10 is often charged.

Bicycle At Nikki's on Rizal Ave you can rent a mountain bike for P25 per hour.

AROUND PUERTO PRINCESA
Irawan

Irawan, halfway between Puerto Princesa and Iwahig, is the location of the **Irawan Crocodile Farming Institute**. The goal of this project, financed by Japanese money, is supposed to be to protect endangered species of the Philippine crocodile from extinction. Only time will tell whether the laudable idea of this facility will be amended, as is the case with other Asian crocodile farms, to include the export of some of the animals in the form of handbags, shoes, belts, wallets etc. It is open Monday to Friday from 1 to 4 pm and on Saturday and public holidays from 8 am to noon; it's closed on Sunday. Admission is free.

Getting There & Away Buses and jeepneys for South Palawan go via Irawan. A tricycle from Puerto Princesa to Irawan costs around P50.

Balsahan

There is a resort by the river in Balsahan where the local Filipinos like to visit on short holidays to relax and celebrate family occasions.

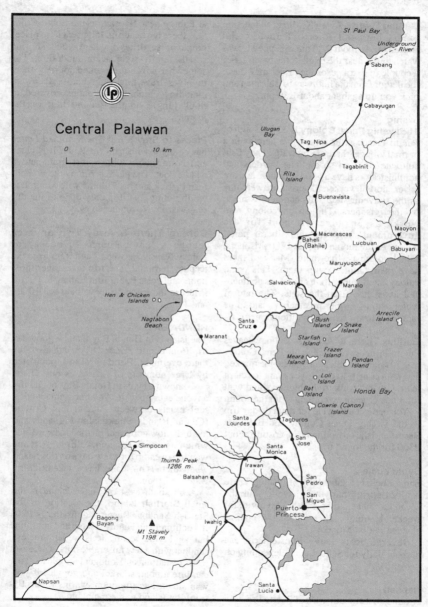

Central Palawan

Getting There & Away No direct connection exists between Puerto Princesa and Balsahan. At about 9.30 am a jeepney leaves Valencia St, near the market, for Iwahig. For a couple of extra pesos the driver may make the detour from the highway to Balsahan and pick you up again at about 1.30 pm.

Iwahig

The **Iwahig Penal Colony** is 23 km south of Puerto Princesa. Prisoners live here as in a normal village; there are no walls. They fish, cultivate rice and so on. The warders and administrators have a good time here and are never short of workers. Tourists are welcome as the souvenir shop sells handicrafts made by the prisoners. The prison colony also works as an advertisement for the government's modern and liberal penal policy. At the moment about 1700 prisoners, called colonists, live there. Many of them have their families with them. This penal colony is self-supporting and needs no financial assistance from the state. The rate of recidivism of former prisoners is said to be markedly lower than in traditional prisons.

Getting There & Away A jeepney leaves Puerto Princesa for the Iwahig Penal Colony at 9.30 am from Valencia St, near the market, and returns at 1.30 pm. If you want to return later, you can walk to the highway and wait for a bus or jeepney coming from the south.

You can get a tricycle for the half-day trip to the Iwahig Penal Colony, the Balsahan Resort and the crocodile farm, costing about P300 for the round trip.

Santa Lucia

Santa Lucia is a subcolony of Iwahig. There is a **hot spring** but you'll have to walk the seven km there and back. It's a favourite for weekend outings, after which the pool is cleaned out on Monday.

Several boats leave Puerto Princesa harbour daily for Santa Lucia (depending on demand).

Napsan

Around 70 km south-west of Puerto Princesa at Labtay near Napsan on the South China Sea, there is a beautiful long beach (in places home of sandflies!) where you can find small, family-style accommodation. The somewhat adventure-packed journey there involves travelling right across Palawan, including climbing mountains covered in thick jungle on the second half of the journey.

Places to Stay & Eat The *Kiao Sea Lodge* has cottages with bath for P300. It is clean and comfortable with a restaurant and a paddle boat. The place is run by the Frenchman Patrick and his Filipina wife Mary. It is worth noting that it is only open in the dry season from November to May.

Getting There & Away Two or three jeepneys leave Puerto Princesa for Labtay/Napsan between 7 and 9 am from the jeepney terminal. The trip takes over three hours and costs P35. From Labtay to Puerto Princesa the jeepneys leave between 10 am and 1 pm.

HONDA BAY

The islands in Honda Bay make a good day trip from Puerto Princesa. You can also stay there overnight. **Pandan Island**, populated by large numbers of fishers, is one of the best-known islands in Honda Bay, but hardly anyone ever visits it. An almost intact coral reef exists between Pandan and Cowrie (Canon) islands. **Snake Island** is sandy and has a shallow coral reef on the landward side which is ideal for snorkelling. Anyone wanting to camp for a few days on this island where there is no shade, has to take drinking water and food.

A bit south-west of Snake Island is the small **Starfish Island**, the location of the Starfish Sandbar Resort; admission is P20. It's definitely no Fantasy Island and anything but an idyllic resort. It is a flat, treeless sandbar with a few miserable huts, a modest, rustic restaurant and loungers for guests. You can hire a boat, snorkel and goggles if you want. In the late afternoon swarms of bats fly from Bat Island to the mainland.

Places to Stay & Eat
Meara Marina Island Resort (☎ 2575) on Meara Island is under Austrian management and has doubles for P450 and cottages with bath for P650. The price includes breakfast and there is a restaurant. You can go water skiing, windsurfing and diving (courses for beginners and diving equipment are available). For bookings, you can write to: Franz and Jane Urbanek, PO Box 4, 5300 Puerto Princesa.

Getting There & Away
You can go from Puerto Princesa to Santa Lourdes Pier (on the highway, north of Tagburos) by any jeepney or bus going north. They leave from the jeepney terminal or from the market. Get off at the big Caltex tank and walk towards the waterfront, where you can hire a boat for about P500 a day.

A tricycle from Puerto Princesa market to Santa Lourdes Pier costs about P50.

NAGTABON BEACH
White Nagtabon Beach lies on a beautiful calm bay on Palawan's west coast looking out on Hen & Chicken islands.

Places to Stay & Eat
Pablico's Beach Resort has singles for P175 and doubles for P250, as well as a restaurant.

Georg's Place has singles with fan for P150 and cottages with fan and bath for P380. There is a good restaurant with Filipino and European cuisine. Georg and Lucy Bauer are a German-Filipino couple. Their postal address is PO Box 67, 5300 Puerto Princesa.

Getting There & Away
Two or three jeepneys are supposed to go from Puerto Princesa to Nagtabon Beach, but this route is not reliable. They leave around 7.30 am, 10 am and noon, taking more than one hour. If there are not enough passengers, the trip may finish at Maranat. From Maranat it's about an hour's walk down to the beach (four km). A Special Ride from Puerto Princesa to Nagtabon Beach costs P800.

There may be a jeepney from Nagtabon Beach to Puerto Princesa between 11 am and 1 pm.

UNDERGROUND RIVER
The Underground River, or St Paul Cave to give it its proper name, counts as Palawan's most fascinating network of caves. Carved out by an underground river, the cave meanders for over eight km. Nature has provided it with a bewildering variety of enormous stalactites, fragile-looking columns, smooth-walled pipes, jagged caverns and big, impressive chambers. The entrance to the Underground River is set in a picturesque lagoon on the west coast of Central Palawan. You could almost overlook this deeply fissured, yawning opening in the grey limestone face, through which you can enter the dark maw of the cave in small paddle bancas. The flickering light of the kerosene lamps reveals countless bats in the cave. You would need a powerful flash to take photographs here.

Getting There & Away
For years, Baheli and Macarascas have been the favourite starting points for trips to the Underground River by outrigger boat. The journey to the cave entrance takes about three hours and costs about P1200. It is worth noting that the trip from there is not possible during the south-west monsoon season from June to November, which can get quite stormy, as the waves of the South China Sea are simply too large for outrigger boats at this time.

Day trips are also possible from Port Barton and San Vicente. However, the easiest and best way to make a short trip to the Underground River is from Sabang.

Leaving Sabang by foot, head along the long, palm-lined white sand beach to the right in an easterly direction. After about two km, or one hour, through the jungle and over a little mountain, you will come to the Park Ranger Station. It is about another two km, or just over an hour, on foot from the Park Ranger Station to the cave entrance, either along the jungle trail or along the so-called 'monkey trail'. At the entrance the permit for the journey into the Underground River will be given. Admission costs P150, including the river trip with a paddle boat.

A boat from Sabang to the Underground River costs P300.

SABANG

The introduction of a regular jeepney service from Puerto Princesa brought to an end the role of the tiny community of Sabang as a kind of Sleeping Beauty. Sabang is situated near the **St Paul Subterranean National Park**, supported by the World Wild Fund for Nature (WWF); this beautiful piece of nature with its thick covering of jungle lies at the feet of the 1028-metre Mt St Paul. The main attraction of this extremly well-looked after national park is, as the name would suggest, a subterranean one: the Underground River. There is another relatively unknown cave with impressive dripstone deposits which was only discovered recently, called the **Ren-Pat Cave**. This can be reached from Sabang by outrigger boat, provided the sea is calm enough.

If you head out from Sabang by foot along the beach in a westerly direction, after about 30 minutes you will come to a gorgeous waterfall, arching into the sea from a height of about 10 metres. You would be well advised to wear sturdy shoes as the beach is quite stony around this side.

Another fascinating trip from Sabang is by boat up the river, the mouth of which is near the national park.

Places to Stay & Eat

The modest little *Robert's Beach & Cottages* has cottages for P150 and cottages with bath for P200, and there is a restaurant. Right next door is the Coco Grove Canteen, a simple, but clean and inexpensive restaurant.

The *Villa Sabang* has dorm beds for P75 and cottages with bath for P150 and P175. It is basic but comfortable, and has a restaurant. Horse-back riding and guided mountain trekking is available.

Mary's Cottages has some small cottages with bath for P200 and a bigger one for P250.

There is a restuarant. It is east of Sabang, just before the entrance to the national park.

The *Bambua Jungle Cottages* has cottages for P75 per person and a tastefully designed cottage with bath for P250; there is an excellent restaurant. The place is about 20 minutes on foot from Sabang, in a dream setting at the foot of a mountain with jungle all around. A couple (German and Filipina) have carved themselves out a little paradise here with loads of animals and useful plants.

If you want to have a more intensive look at the rugged countryside around the national park, you can spend the night next to the Park Ranger Station in a tent or simple but clean room for P75 – although only for up to three days. You will have to take food and supplies with you.

Getting There & Away

Jeepneys from Puerto Princesa to Sabang via Baheli, Macarascas and Cabayugan leave at 8 and 11 am, taking four hours. This dusty route could cause problems during the rainy season because of the unfavourable state of the road. From Sabang to Puerto Princesa, jeepneys leave at 7 am and 1 pm.

You can also get to Sabang from San Rafael by a three-day walk right across Palawan.

South Palawan

NARRA

Narra makes a good stop on the way to South Palawan. The **Estrella Waterfalls** are six km north at the foot of the Victoria Peak; admission is P3. Near Tigman, about 20 km north-east of Narra and 10 km north-west of Aborlan, there is a beautiful long beach with white sand and palm trees. The water is quite shallow, suitable for bathing.

Places to Stay

The *Tiosin Lodging House* on Panacan Rd has rooms with fan for P50/100. It is a simple place and has good, well-priced meals.

The *Gardeña Boarding House* on Panacan

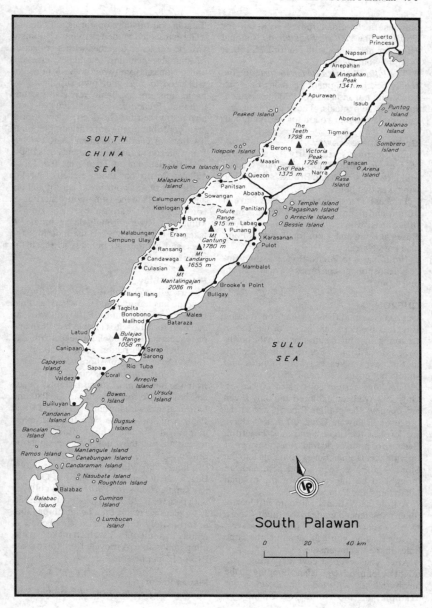

South Palawan

0   20   40 km

Rd has fairly clean rooms with fan for P60/120. The *Victoria Peak Inn* on National Highway has rooms with fan for P75/150. It is simple, but clean.

The *Villa Christina Beach Resort* is on the lonely beach of Tigman. There are nice cottages with fan and bath for P700 per person, including two meals. There is also a restaurant. It's about two km for the main road.

Getting There & Away

Many jeepneys run daily from Puerto Princesa to Narra as do several buses, some going on to Quezon and Brooke's Point. The trip takes two hours.

Princess Transport air-con buses leave at 10 am and 4 pm from the William Lines' office on Rizal Ave. The trip takes two hours. Buses at 8 am and 1 pm for Brooke's Point also pass Narra.

From Narra to Puerto Princesa, the Princess Transport air-con buses leave at 8.30 am and 4 pm.

QUEZON

Quezon is a small fishing village on Malanut Bay. It is the departure point for the **Tabon Caves**, whose main entrance is on the northwest side of Lipuun Point. The boat trip to the caves takes only 30 minutes and should not cost more than P250.

This huge system consists of 200 caves. Only 29 have been explored and only seven are open to the public. Tabon Cave is the biggest and Diwata Cave, 30 metres above sea level, is the highest and most beautiful. Because of prehistoric finds, they are of great importance. Human bones going back to the Stone Age have been found here and are thought to be the remains of the original inhabitants, the Pala'wan.

Ask at the National Museum in Quezon for an experienced guide to the Tabon Caves. Don't expect too much from the caves, however, as all you can see are some large holes in the mountainside.

After you've gone cave exploring, you might be tempted to go island hopping on the nearby islands with the white beaches, for example, on the islands of Sidanao or

Tataran. Far offshore on Tamlagun Island is a German called Frederick living a Robinson Crusoe existence together with a collection of animals, including sea eagles, chickens and goannas. If you want to visit him, you will need to take your own supplies. Two basic huts are available for visitors, and although Frederick does not have a fixed charge for their use, he does expect a moderate contribution towards the completion of his tropical Garden of Eden. A round trip from Quezon to Tamlagun Island costs P500.

A Belgian named Theo runs the Tabon Village Resort on Tabon Beach, four km north-east of Quezon. From here it's about an hour's walk to the Tumarbon Waterfall, or for P300 you can go by boat on the Tumarbon River through dense jungle. It takes 45 minutes to reach the mouth of the river and another 30 minutes to reach the waterfall.

Places to Stay

The friendly *New Bayside Lodging House* is near the bus terminal and the wharf, and has small rooms with fan for P100 and with fan and bath for P120. It is simple but clean and on request staff will cook for guests. You can also obtain information about boats to the Tabon Caves and to offshore islands.

The *Villa Esperanza* is about 300 metres from the bus terminal towards Tabon Beach and has simple rooms with fan for P80 and basic cottages with fan and bath for P300 and P350, which seems to be a little bit overpriced. It's a well-kept place with a restaurant but they don't serve alcoholic drinks.

The *Tabon Village Resort* on Tabon Beach, about four km north-east of Quezon, has simple rooms for P90/110 and cottages with bath for P220/310. There is a restaurant. It's a pleasant resort on a beautiful bay, but unfortunately the water at the beach is muddy and full of rocks which makes swimming impossible. A tricycle from town costs P15 or P5 per person.

Places to Eat

The *Bayside Restaurant* and *Paganiban Res-*

taurant are both basic but serve good and reasonably priced meals. The tastefully designed and decorated *Mutya ng Dagak* (Pearl of the Sea) is a bit dearer but has very good food. It is part of the Tabon Village Resort and is on an artificial island that is connected to the beach by a bridge.

Getting There & Away

Charing Bus Lines buses run daily from the Puerto Princesa jeepney terminal to Quezon at 6, 7 and 9 am and 1 pm. The trip takes over three hours.

From Quezon to Puerto Princesa, the buses leave at 7, 8, 9 and 11 am and 1 pm.

Several jeepneys leave early in the morning from both Quezon and Puerto Princesa.

BROOKE'S POINT & URSULA ISLAND

On nautical charts and in mariners' handbooks the light at Sir James Brooke Point is listed as a navigational aid. The township of Brooke's Point on the cape at the northern end of Ipolote Bay is, however, more important in terms of the growth of trading. No-one can guess what made the British explorer Sir James Brooke move to the south of Palawan, where he settled and erected the striking watchtower which finally gave the place its name.

Several km inland is a range of forested mountains with peaks around 1500 metres. Mt Matalingajan, Palawan's highest mountain at 2086 metres, is roughly 25 km west of Brooke's Point.

About 10 km north-west of Brooke's Point, near Mainit, are a small waterfall and hot sulphur springs. You can get there by tricycle for P50.

The area to the south-west of Brooke's Point may be a crisis area and dangerous for travellers.

Thousands of birds used to nest on beautiful Ursula Island, where they would return in swarms in the evening after foraging on other islands. However, too many shotguns (hunters) has caused most birds to shift their nests, mainly to the faraway Tubbataha Reef.

Ursula Island is uninhabited and there is no drinking water.

Places to Stay

The *Sunset Travel Lodge & Garden* has rooms for P70/140, with fan and bath for P200, and with air-con and bath for P350. Although simple, it is clean and fairly good, with a restaurant, disco and rather extensive grounds.

The *Silayan Lodge* has singles/doubles with fan for P50/100, with fan and bath for P150, and with air-con and bath for P300. It is unpretentious but good and has friendly owners.

The *Villasenor Lodge* has singles/doubles with fan for P180. It is plain but fairly pleasant. Staff will prepare meals if you order them in advance.

The *Cristina Beach Resort* on Tagusao Shore has singles/doubles for P100 and cottages with fan and bath for P200/250. This is a pleasant, generously appointed resort on a grey beach with a restaurant, about seven km north-east of Brooke's Point (1.5 km off the main road).

Places to Eat

Most of the few restaurants in town close early at night, but the *Islander* on the main road serves very good Filipino food until 10 pm.

Getting There & Away

A few Puerto Royale buses run from the market at Puerto Princesa to Brooke's Point in the morning; last departure is at 1 pm. There is also a Mic Mac Trail air-con bus which leaves in the morning. Princess Transport air-con buses leave at 8 am from the Williams Lines office, Rizal Ave. The trip takes four to five hours.

Princess Transport air-con buses leave Brooke's Point for Puerto Princesa at 6.30 am and 1.30 pm.

In addition, there are jeepneys which travel between Puerto Princesa and Brooke's Point, taking five hours.

A Special Ride on an outrigger boat from

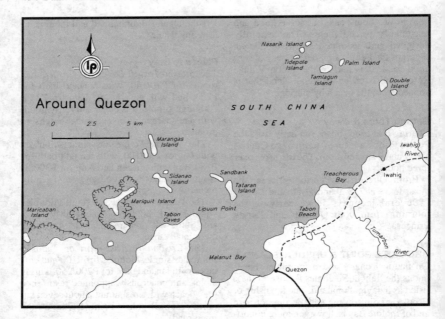

Around Quezon

0   2.5   5 km

SOUTH CHINA SEA

Nasarik Island
Tidepole Island
Tamlagun Island
Palm Island
Double Island
Marangas Island
Sidanao Island
Sandbank
Tataran Island
Iwahig River
Treacherous Bay
Iwahig
Mariquit Island
Maricaban Island
Tabon Caves
Lipuun Point
Tabon Beach
Tumarbon River
Malanut Bay
Quezon

Brooke's Point, Bataraza or Rio Tuba to Ursula Island costs at most P2000.

RIO TUBA
Apparently, freighters occasionally sail from Brooke's Point or Rio Tuba to Cagayan de Tawi-Tawi Island (Cagayan de Sulu Island), where there are sometimes opportunities for onward travel to Jolo or Zamboanga via Pangutaran Island.

You can stay overnight at Rio Tuba in basic hostels at the wharf. The price is a matter for negotiation.

Getting There & Away
Between 6 am and 1 pm, four jeepneys run from Brooke's Point to Rio Tuba via Bataraza, taking two hours. Puerto Royale buses and jeepneys run from Puerto Princesa to Brooke's Point, possibly going on to Rio Tuba. Outrigger boats travel between Rio Tuba and Balabac on Balabac Island.

North Palawan

SAN RAFAEL
San Rafael has only a few huts, which are strung out along the highway, a school and two small shops, where you can't buy much anyway. From San Rafael you can visit the Batak with a guide. Whether you want to visit the Batak is something you will have to decide for yourself. The few remaining tribes of these nomadic people certainly do not need any contact with travellers.

The Duchess Beachside Cottages together with the adjacent Coral Island can be recommended for those seeking peace and quiet and is also a good starting point for longer hikes, for example, right across Palawan to Sabang with its St Paul National Park and the Underground River. This takes three days and a guide costs P300 a day plus food.

Places to Stay

The *Duchess Beachside Cottages* has cottages for P120/150. Accommodation is simple and clean. The cottages themselves are built in a row on the beach. The grounds are well looked after and there is a restaurant.

The *Tipanan sa Palawan Resort* on Tanabag beach, two km east of San Rafael, is a little place with cottages with fan and bath for P250. There is a restaurant. From the highway to the beach it's about 200 metres.

Getting There & Away

Between 5 and 7 am, three Puerto Royale buses run daily from the market in Puerto Princesa to San Rafael, going on to Roxas or Taytay. The trip takes two hours. In the morning there are also several jeepneys from the market or the jeepney terminal.

ROXAS & COCO-LOCO ISLAND

Roxas is a pleasant little place right by the sea. Fish and fruit are on sale in the relatively large market at reasonable prices. If you want to stay on a desert island in the north of Palawan, Roxas is the last opportunity to buy equipment. You can get things like canisters and buckets in out-of-the-way places such as El Nido, but not less common items like cookers. The extensive bay beyond Roxas has several small islands, including beautiful Coco-Loco Island (Reef Island) surrounded by a coral reef, that are worth seeing. The friendly lady who owns the restaurant Tito's Canteen has a lot of information about the Coco-Loco Island Resort and Port Barton.

Places to Stay

Gemalain's Inn is a basic place in Roxas, by the market, with rooms for P50/100. There is a restaurant which doubles as a disco at night.

About three km north of Roxas, the *Retac Beach Resort* has comfortable rooms with fan and bath for P400 and cottages with fan and bath from P500 to P700, and there is a restaurant. A tricycle from Roxas costs P10.

The *Coco-Loco Island Resort* has cottages for P180 and cottages with bath for P300. It is comfortable and has a restaurant. It also has diving, water skiing, windsurfing, outrigger boats, paddle bancas, billiards and table tennis.

Getting There & Away

Puerto Royale buses leave the Puerto Princesa market for Roxas daily at 3 and 5 am and 1 pm taking four hours. In case of demand there may be another one at about 9 am. In the morning between 6 and 10 am several dusty jeepneys also make the run. The trip takes five hours.

Every day around 9 to 11 am and 2 to 3 pm, the Coco-Loco Island Resort's outrigger boat returns to the island after buying supplies in Roxas. The trip takes 45 minutes. You can get a ride for P65 per person. A Special Ride costs P500.

The first boat from Reef Island to Roxas leaves at 7 am.

PORT BARTON

Port Barton is a small community on the picturesque Pagdanan Bay with a fairly good, long drawn-out beach. It has developed into a popular little meeting place in the north of Palawan. In the country around Port Barton there are several **waterfalls**. On the way to Caruray is **Honeybee Valley**.

You can hire outrigger boats and visit the nearby islands, some of which have really beautiful white beaches. You can enjoy good snorkelling off **Inadawan Island** (formerly Tomas Tan) and in the so-called aquarium. The colourful coral reefs off Exotica and Albaguin islands have unfortunately been largely destroyed by dynamite fishing.

At the time of this book's publication the following prices were being charged: island hopping P500, San Vicente, Boayan and Albaguin P700, Baheli P2000, El Nido P2500 and Underground River P1500. The charge for waiting time for the boat is P600 per day.

The boat trip from Port Barton to the Underground River takes at least four hours. It is important to leave early or you'll have no time to see the river.

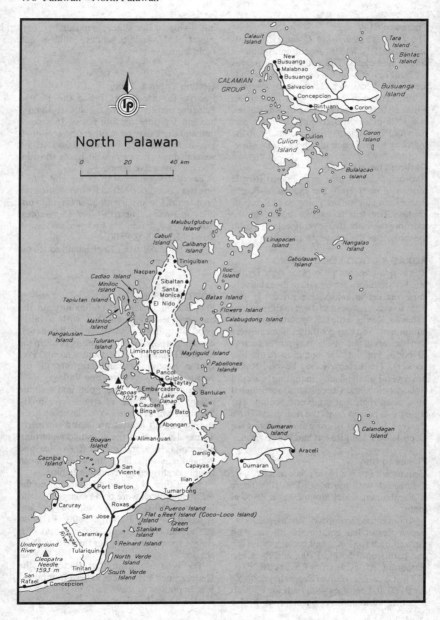

North Palawan

0   20   40 km

Places to Stay

Elsa's Place has rooms for P100/150 and cottages with bath for P250/300, as well as a restaurant. The accommodation is pleasant here. The *Swissippini Cottages* has cottages for P150 and cottages with bath for P250 to P350. There is a restaurant and it has billiards and diving facilities. This is a well-run resort.

The *El Busero Inn* has rooms for P100/150 and cottages with bath for P250. It has a restaurant.

At the eastern edge of Port Barton, the *Shangri-La of Scandinavian* has cottages with bath for P200. There is a restaurant, and you can hire snorkel and paddle boats.

The *Manta Ray Island Resort* on Capsalay Island has cottages for P1700 per person, including meals. There is a seasonal surcharge of around P300 from mid-December to mid-January. It has three tastefully designed cottages on attractive grounds with a well-kept garden. The resort is run by an Italian woman by the name of Paola. Reservations can be made in Puerto Princesa at the Swiss Bistro Valencia (☎ 2609) on Valencia St.

Places to Eat

The places just mentioned serve good and generous meals but the owners appreciate prior notice. The village itself has a small, inexpensive restaurant called *Evergreen* on the main road. The restaurant/bar *Ginger's Cave* serves drinks until quite late. It also shows video clips and movies.

Getting There & Away

Several jeepneys run daily between 7 and 9 am to Port Barton from the jeepney terminal in Puerto Princesa, taking six hours. Occasionally there are faster jeepneys with relatively few passengers and ample space for luggage, but they cost double the normal fare. You can also go first to Roxas by bus or jeepney and then catch a jeepney going to Port Barton.

Several jeepneys leave Roxas market for Port Barton daily, taking one hour or more. The first one leaves at 9 am.

A jeepney runs daily to Puerto Princesa from Port Barton at 6 am; a Special Ride costs P2500. Two jeepneys go to Roxas daily from Port Barton between 6.30 and 8 am.

SAN VICENTE

San Vicente lies on a peninsula, about 18 km north-east of Port Barton. On the other side is a long beach that you will like if you want to be alone. A good idea for a day trip would be to hike to the **Little Baguio Waterfall**, about six km inland from San Vicente.

Places to Stay

The *Caparii Dive Camp* has comfortable duplex cottages with singles/doubles with fan and bath for P560 and with air-con and bath for P980/1100. The camp has its own restaurant and offers boat trips (including to the Underground River), bicycle hire (mountain bikes), windsurfing (P125 an hour) and diving (including diving courses).

This is a well-run resort on a small bay, two km north-west of San Vicente. There is a booking office at the airport in Puerto Princesa.

Getting There & Away

The road from Port Barton to San Vicente is open again, but no-one knows for how long. The trip by outrigger boat is faster than by jeepney and takes one hour.

A jeepney goes from Roxas to San Vicente two or three times daily, taking over one hour. If requested, the driver will take passengers to Caparii Dive Camp.

ABONGAN & TABUAN

Abongan is a tiny place on the Abongan River. The trip from Roxas leads through a beautiful landscape, some of it dense jungle. The track to Taytay turns off just before Abongan. It takes about 30 minutes to walk from Abongan to Tabuan, a small river port which is also on the Abongan River.

From Tabuan you can get a boat to Liminangcong and Embarcadero near Taytay. A boat leaves for Liminangcong on Friday, Saturday and Sunday at about 11 am, costing P100 per person. The departure times are not completely reliable and you may

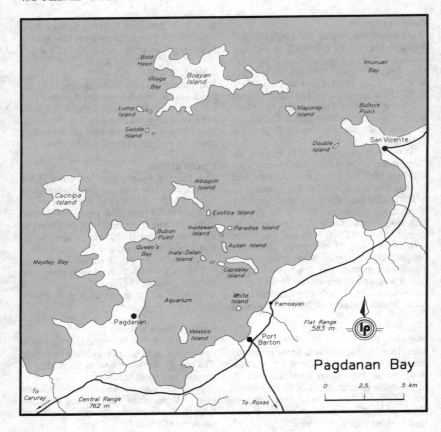

Pagdanan Bay

have to charter a boat; a Special Ride to Liminangcong costs about P1000. The trip takes four hours.

You can also go to El Nido by boat, which costs P200 per person and P1800 for a Special Ride. The trip down the Abongan River is beautiful and lively – the river still has crocodiles! Further on you go through Malampaya Sound, which is a giant fish trap.

Places to Stay

In Tabuan there is only private accommodation. Baby and Manuel Padernilla, who live by the footbridge over the river, charge P50 per person.

Getting There & Away

A few jeepneys leave Roxas market daily for Abongan, taking three hours or more.

TAYTAY & EMBARCADERO

Taytay is the old capital of Palawan. You can still visit the **fort** which was built by the Spaniards in 1622 and of which only ruins remain. The church is about 300 years old.

There is a hospital and numerous shops which have an astonishing range of goods.

From Taytay you can go to the **Pabellones Islands** by outrigger boat, which takes about one hour. These are three small islands with sheer limestone cliffs. The many caves and cracks yield birds' nests for bird's nest soup. **Elefante Island** has a lagoon which is good for snorkelling. A round-trip costs about P500.

Only a few km south of Taytay is **Lake Danao**, which is 62 hectares in size. It has small islands and is surrounded by primeval forest. It takes about 30 minutes to get there by jeepney.

Embarcadero is about six km west of Taytay. Outrigger boats go almost daily, but at least twice a week, down the mangrove river to Malampaya Sound and on to Liminangcong or Tabuan, near Abongan.

Tricycles ply between Embarcadero and Taytay for P10 per person or P50 for the tricycle; now and then jeepneys also travel the route.

Places to Stay

Publico's International Guest House in Taytay has rooms for P100. It is simple, clean and comfortable, and has a restaurant. *Pem's Pension House* in Taytay on Taytay Bay, near the fort, has quite good rooms with fans for P50/80 and cottages with fan and bath for P120, P200 and P500 as well as a good restaurant.

The *Embarcadero Riverview Guesthouse* in Embarcadero has rooms for P30/60. It is simple but pleasant and the cuisine is delicious, especially seafood.

Getting There & Away

A Puerto Royale bus leaves daily at 5 am from Puerto Princesa to Taytay via Roxas. The trip takes nine hours. The bus leaves Roxas for Taytay at 11 am, taking four hours. Occasionally a jeepney leaves from Roxas market at noon. From Taytay the bus to Roxas and Puerto Princesa leaves at 3 am.

The trip from El Nido to Embarcadero by outrigger boat costs P150 per person or P1500 for a Special Ride. The trip takes four

hours. During the day several jeepneys make the trip in three hours and cost P100.

The MB *Dioniemer*, a big outrigger boat, leaves from Coron on Busuanga for Taytay every Monday at 10 am. The trip takes nine hours and costs P400. During heavy seas the trip is interrupted in San Miguel on Linapacan Island and continues the next morning. The boat leaves Taytay on Saturday at 10 am.

FLOWERS ISLAND

Flowers Island is a dream of a small island, around 50 km north-east of Taytay, with a white sandy beach and a still-intact reef. A Frenchman and his Filipina wife run pleasant beach resort here with only five cottages. For information on accommodation, check with Pem's Pension House in Taytay.

Places to Stay

The *Flowers Island Beach Resort* has roomy, pleasantly decorated cottages for P600 per person, full board. It has a restaurant and paddleboats are available.

Getting There & Away

An outrigger boat from Taytay to Flowers Island costs P800, or P150 per person. The trip takes three hours.

LIMINANGCONG

During the north-east monsoons, Liminangcong becomes a fishing centre. People there are friendly and helpful and the place itself is surprisingly peaceful as there are no cars. There is a cinema, for a change, and a small restaurant.

From Liminangcong you can go to the small offshore **Saddle and Camago islands**. You can also get boats to islands farther north. Apart from that, there are always irregular shipping connections to Manila. The shopkeepers often know more about departure times than the coastguard.

Places to Stay

There is only private accommodation. Mr Abrina, who lives opposite the school, charges P50.

Butterflies of the Philippines

Demoleus demoleus

Graphium anthipathes itamputi

Troides magellanus

Papilio idaeoides

Papilion doson gyndes

Zeuxidia semperi

Graphium agamemnon agamemnon

Papilio trojana

Pantoporia maenas semperi

Salatura genutia

Getting There & Away

From Tabuan several outrigger boats leave for Liminangcong weekly, almost certainly on Friday, Saturday and Sunday at 11 am, taking four hours. The fare is P100 per person and a Special Ride costs about P1000.

From Embarcadero several outrigger boats leave for Liminangcong weekly. The fare is P100 per person. A Special Ride costs P800.

To travel to El Nido costs P80 per person, but you usually have to charter a boat. A Special Ride to El Nido should cost about P600.

EL NIDO & BACUIT ARCHIPELAGO

Picturesque El Nido is on a beautiful part of the coast, surrounded by rugged, steep limestone cliffs. The houses and streets are clean and well looked after. There are scarcely any vehicles. More and more travellers have been attracted to this beautiful little town in the north of the 'Last Frontier' (as Palawan is often called) since the roads and transport were improved. Inevitably, some of these people will have been disappointed, because the transport and accommodation require not only flexibility, but also a willingness not to expect too much.

When in El Nido you can take a trip to the fascinating islands of the Bacuit archipelago just offshore. Almost all of these grey islands jut steeply out of the crystal-clear water and have small, sandy bays. It costs around P600 per day to hire a boat, including petrol. A small paddleboat costs P50 a day.

Anyone who finds it too expensive to hire a boat for one or more days or to join an excursion group, but who wants to go snorkelling or to the beaches outside of El Nido, would be best advised to go to Corong-Corong Bay, about three km south. From there it is possible to get a fisher to drop you off on one of the sandy beaches on the southwest coast of the peninsula (for about P20). But careful – even deserted beaches have their fair share of thieves these days.

El Nido's most important claim to fame for tourists is its living coral reefs and the multicoloured fish of the Bacuit archipelago.

So, if no-one manages to put an end to irresponsible fishers dynamiting vast areas of the underwater world into oblivion, then tourism in El Nido has no chance of having a future.

Islands of the Bacuit Archipelago

Cadlao Island Cadlao is the biggest, and at almost 600 metres, also the highest island in the Bacuit archipelago. Its massive cliff face, in places covered with thick green vegetation, is riddled with caves and fissures.

Miniloc Island Miniloc, south-west of El Nido, is the island where the well-known El Nido Resort is located. The deeply indented coast, a little to the north of this establishment, leads to a beautiful lagoon in the island's interior which is only accessible by boat. There are said to be barracudas in the deep centre part of the lagoon, which could possibly be dangerous to snorkellers. Turtles have also been occasionally sighted there.

Matinloc Island Matinloc has numerous little bays along its long coast, with sandy beaches and corals worth seeing. Calmung Bay on the east side of the island is worth a mention.

Tapiutan Island Tapiutan runs for half of its length almost parallel and fairly closely to Matinloc Island. On this part of the island there is an attractively situated beach with a reef well suited for snorkelling. The extremely picturesque Binangculan Bay in the north-west of the island has a beach with some vegetation. Occasionally, sailboats use this for anchoring. The cliffs jutting out south of the bay signal one of the best diving areas in the waters around El Nido. There are several tunnels, archways and fissures that can be swum through; turtles, groupers and barracudas are quite common.

North Guntao Island This is the most westerly island of the archipelago. The climb to the top is rewarded with a breath-taking panorama. The little beaches on the west coast

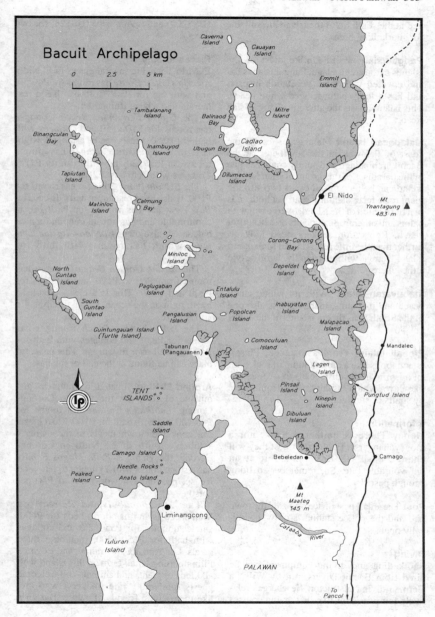

Bacuit Archipelago

0   2.5   5 km

and at the south tip of the island are suitable for snorkelling breaks.

Pangalusian Island Unlike most of the islands in the archipelago, Pangalusian is flat and covered with thick vegetation in parts and has a long, palm-fringed white beach. This island boasts the attractive Pangalusian Resort.

Malapacao Island Malapacao lies off the coast of Palawan in the south-east of the Bacuit archipelago and surely counts as one of the paradises of this group of islands. This island can be recognised by its two striking giant rock-faces standing sentry at both ends of a flat section of the island, overgrown with palms and other tropical plants on a beautiful beach. Relaxation seekers need look no further than the little resort called Malapacao Island Retreat with its friendly, family-style atmosphere.

Inabuyatan Island With its white sandy beach and its palms, Inabuyatan is also one of the South Seas dream islands of the archipelago.

Pinsail Island From a distance, Pinsail Island looks like a modest lump of rock until an opening in the cliffs leads to a cathedral-like cave, which is illuminated from above by shafts of sunlight.

Information
Money There is neither a bank, nor a moneychanger in El Nido. At best they will change cash US dollars, albeit at an unfavourable rate. So, remember to bring enough pesos!

Post The small post office opposite the town hall and the police station is only sporadically open.

Diving
Snorkelling and diving equipment can be hired from Bacuit Divers, run by Willy, a German diving instructor. He charges relatively fair prices for five-day diving courses (US$200) and diving trips (US$28; for two dives).

Places to Stay
El Nido There are several places in El Nido. *Austria's Guest House* has rooms for P40/50, and with fan for P50/70. It also has a restaurant and a beautiful garden.

The *Gloria Fernandez Beach Cottages* has rooms for P100/150 and cottages with bath for P250. Meals can be arranged. Right next to it, *Tandikan Cottages* has simple rooms for P60/120 and with bath for P175. Cottages with bath cost P250.

The *El Nido Plaza Cottages* has rooms for P100. It also has a restaurant and a disco. The *Bay View Inn* has rooms for P80/100, is comfortable and has a restaurant and a nice balcony. It also owns *El Nido Cliffside Cottages* which has rooms with bath for P150/200.

The *Marina Garden Beach Cottages* has rooms from P60 to P120 and cottages for P200 and P300. This is a clean establishment, right on the ocean, with a family-style atmosphere.

The *Lally & Abet Beach Cottages* has rooms for P250 and cottages with bath for P400 as well as a restaurant. This peaceful place can be found at the end of the bay.

Around El Nido Situated in Maligaya, just outside of town on the way to Corong-Corong, *Lualhati's Cottage* has rooms for P80/100 and with bath for P100/120. Guests can cook their own meals in the owner's kitchen. South of El Nido in Corong-Corong, the *Victor & Belia Magos Family* has a stone house with a kitchen to let; good for six people as it works out to P50 per person.

The *Malapacao Island Retreat* on Malapacao Island has dorm beds for P400, singles/doubles for P550/900 and cottages with bath for P650/1300, including three meals. Lee Ann, an Australian, and Edgar, a Filipino, run a small farm on this island with all kinds of plants and animals and welcome guests (preferably non-smokers) who are, like themselves, friends of nature. Bar girls and nightclubbers as well as friends of loud music and strong drink are absolutely persona non grata in this resort! Thanks to solar energy, the God-given peace is not even disturbed by sputtering generators. The Leegar Farm boat leaves daily at 9 am from El Nido for several different islands of the archipelago (P100 per person). At around 6 pm it leaves El Nido for Malapacao Island (P50 per person). The trip takes an hour.

The *Pangalusian Resort* on Pangalusian Island has comfortable, tastefully furnished cottages with air-con and bath for US$110 and US$135. It is a sophisticated establishment with an attractively decorated restaurant. Bookings can be made through Stettler Hotels Inc, Manila (☎ 8190282; fax 8190281).

The *El Nido Resort* on Miniloc Island has good cottages for US$190/300, including meals, diving gear and diving trips. There is a small beach and you can go water skiing and windsurfing. The boat trip from El Nido to Miniloc Island takes just less than one hour.

Places to Eat

The modest, but clean, *Vicenta's Eatery* offers excellent food and generous portions, all at a good price. It is recommended to order the evening meal at lunchtime. Highly recommended also is the *Countryside Restaurant* owned by Mr Austria with its tasty dishes ranging from banana pancake to lobster. Also popular are the excellent *Elm's Café*, *Lunings Restaurant* on the 1st floor next to the Bayview Inn, and the *Tia Bodin Restaurant*, where the guests are occasionally entertained with short musical interludes. After dinner many guests prefer the tastefully decorated *Shipwreck* for a drink and to listen to the good music.

Getting There & Away

At least one jeepney leaves Puerto Princesa daily in the early morning for El Nido. The trip takes 10 hours and costs P200. It is also possible to take the Puerto Royale bus at 5 am for Taytay and then take a jeepney from there to El Nido. Apparently, there is also a direct bus from Puerto Princesa to El Nido and return. It leaves at 3 am and costs P180.

Several jeepneys travel between Taytay and El Nido daily – at least in the dry season. The trips take three hours (P100). From Embarcadero near Taytay you can also go to El Nido by boat, which costs P150 per person and P1500 for a Special Ride.

Outrigger boats leave irregularly from Tabuan to El Nido via Liminangcong. The fare is P200. A Special Ride costs about P1800. Jeepneys go to Tabuan from Roxas.

Outrigger boats run from Port Barton to El Nido for P2500, taking five hours one way.

The big outrigger MB *Sea Fun* leaves from Coron on Busuanga for El Nido on Mondays at 6 am. The trip takes eight to 12 hours, including a one-hour break. Depending on the weather and the stops requested or required by passengers, the trip can take up to two days and costs P650. The boat departs from El Nido on Wednesday at 6 am. Note: during the rainy season this route is possibly cancelled.

Getting Around

To/From the Airport The small airport is about four km north of El Nido. Boats and jeepneys go into town after the arrival of a scheduled flight. The fare is P50, although locals only pay about P20.

Anyone arriving on a chartered flight can have a jeepney ordered by radio from El Nido. This is a Special Ride and shouldn't cost more than P200.

It is only possible to go along the beach from the airport to El Nido at low tide, and should not be attempted with heavy baggage.

Calamian Group

The northernmost part of Palawan consists of the Calamian Group, whose main islands are Busuanga, Culion and Coron. The improvements made to the travel links with other islands and towns, together with the expansion in overnight accommodation, have brought about a modest upsurge in

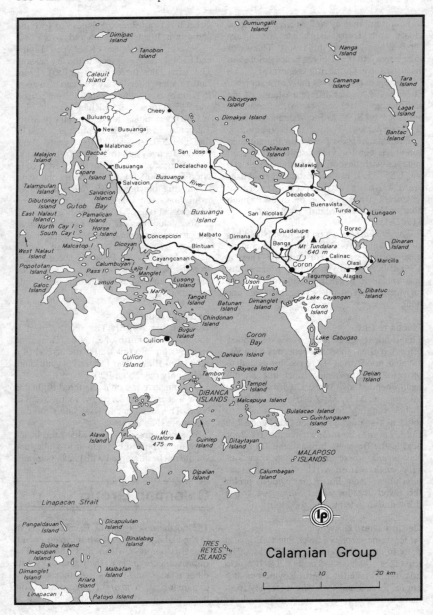

Calamian Group

tourism in this beautiful island world. But so far people still live mostly from fishing and selling *kasoy* (cashew nuts), which are mainly harvested on Busuanga and Culion.

Kasoy (Cashew Nuts)

BUSUANGA ISLAND

Busuanga is the largest island in the Calamian Group. A partly surfaced road runs from Coron through Concepcion and Salvacion to New Busuanga. The amount of traffic on the roads is minimal. Around noon two rickety buses, and the occasional jeepney, leave Coron for Salvacion, returning the next morning. That makes Busuanga an ideal spot for nature lovers and bushwalkers.

In the centre of the island is the Yulo King Ranch, which is said to be the largest cattle station in Asia.

The wharf is in Tagumpay, just outside Coron. It takes about 20 minutes on foot to get there or for P2 per person you can take a tricycle.

Getting Around

To/From the Airport Tiny Busuanga Airport is near Decalachao in the north of the island. Aerolift, Pacific Airways and PAL aircraft land and take off from there. Some resorts, for example, Club Paradise, pick up their guests with their own vehicles, or else the airlines organise jeepneys to Coron. The trip takes over one hour and costs P50 (PAL) or P70 (Aerolift). A roof seat guarantees an uninterrupted view of the magnificent scenery. Air Link planes take off and land directly in Coron on an airstrip behind the hospital.

Another airport is being built in the north-west of the island and should be operational in 1994. Aerolift will then probably transfer their flight operations to the new airport.

CORON

Coron is a small town with 25,000 inhabitants, a market, a fishing school, a hospital, two cinemas and a few shops. There are a few more shops and simple restaurants at the wharf in Tagumpay.

To get to the **Makinit Hot Spring**, go from Coron past the wharf to the ice plant, then go towards the water, not along the creek. The path soon leads away from the water through a cashew-nut plantation to a narrow beach. Turn left here.

Information

Money You would be best advised to take as many pesos with you as you will need. In an emergency, PYY Hardware will exchange US dollars in cash and travellers' cheques, however, their rate is below the official one.

Diving

For many people diving is the only reason to go to Busuanga; the waters between Busuanga and Culion islands are an El Dorado for wreck explorers. In Coron you will be charged P450 per dive; day trips (with two dives) and diving courses are available at Sea Diving in the Sea Breeze Coron Lodging House and Asia Divers in the Bayside Divers Lodge.

Places to Stay & Eat

Darwin's Tulay Lodging House has rooms for P70/120. It's a simple place with a restaurant; food has to be ordered beforehand.

The *Sea Breeze Coron Lodging House* has singles/doubles with fan for P75/150 and with fan and bath for P200. The rooms here are simple, the best of them have their own small veranda. This is a pleasant, family-style place to stay, built on stilts over the water. It has a restaurant and diving facilities.

The attractive *L & M Lodging House*, also built on stilts over the water, has simple, very small rooms for P100/200 and a cozy veranda. It is right next to the market. Food must be ordered beforehand.

The *Bert Lim Lodging House* (☎ 361 1728) is a private house with a few rooms for P260 per person, including three meals.

Next to the market, the *Bayside Divers Lodge* has simple and clean singles/doubles with fan for P225 and with bath for P275. There is a good restaurant. They have a big terrace with a sea view and diving facilities are available. Reservations can be made in Manila with Swagman Travel (☎ 5223650; fax 5223663), 1133 L Guerrero St, Ermita.

The *Kokosnuss Resort* has cottages for about P200 and cottages with bath for P500. There is a restaurant and swimming pool in quiet grounds with a garden, right next to the hospital. It is only 10 minutes on foot to Coron itself. At the time of publication, this establishment was still being built; it plans to offer motorbike hire, boat trips and diving trips.

Getting There & Away

Air PAL and Pacific Airways have an office next to the Shell petrol station in Tagumpay, near the wharf.

Aerolift has an office in Coron opposite the Baptist Church, and Air Link has an office next to the fishdealer Neri Lim, near the market.

Boat Three ships of the Asuncion Shipping Lines ply between Coron and Culion, leaving Coron every Monday, Thursday and Saturday at noon and Culion every Tuesday, Friday and Sunday at 4 am. The trip takes two hours.

The big outrigger MB *Sea Fun* leaves El Nido for Coron on Wednesday at 6 am. The trip takes eight to 12 hours, including a one-hour break. Depending on the weather and the stops requested or required by passengers, the trip can take up to two days and costs P650. The boat leaves Coron on Monday at 6 am. Note: during the rainly season this route is possibly cancelled.

The MB *Dioniemer*, a big outrigger boat, leaves from Taytay for Coron every Saturday at 10 am. The trip takes nine hours and costs P400. During heavy seas the trip is interrupted in San Miguel on Linapacan Island and continued the next morning. The boat departs from Coron on Monday at 10 am.

CONCEPCION

This pleasant little place with only a few houses on a mangrove-lined bay, is a good starting point for boat trips to the offshore islands of Gutob Bay. On the way out of town heading towards Salvacion, just off the road, there is a small waterfall with a natural pool, where you can have a relaxing swim.

Places to Stay & Eat

The *Sea Side Highway Lodging House* has simple, but clean rooms for P60/120. Food has to be ordered beforehand; the cooking is good. A day of island hopping costs about P600 per boat.

Pier House Lodging has rooms for P100/120 and a cottage with fan and bath for P350. The simple, quiet accommodation at the pier is run by an Englishman, Andy. Their *Happy Edith Restaurant* is cosy. Diving (P450 per dive) is available.

Getting There & Away

Two buses leave the cinema in Coron for Concepcion at around noon. The trip takes two hours. During the day the occasional jeepney will make the trip, which costs around P150 by motorbike.

From Concepcion the buses and jeepneys leave between 6 and 7 am for Coron.

BUSUANGA

The small town of Busuanga is at the mouth of the Busuanga River in the north-west of Busuanga Island. A long beach stretches south of the river mouth, and there you will find the Las Hamacas Resort. A trip up the river in an outrigger boat is a wonderful way to experience nature and can be highly recommended if you are staying in the area. Busuanga is also handy as a base for a short trip to Calauit Island.

Places to Stay & Eat

The *Las Hamacas Resort* has comfortable duplex cottages with singles/doubles with fan and bath for P1760/2700, including three meals. It is a pleasant place run by the Frenchman Daniel and his Filipina wife, Belen. They have a restaurant and can organise boat trips.

Getting There & Away

To get from Coron to Busuanga, first take a bus or a jeepney to Salvacion, from there it is only a few minutes by outrigger boat to the Las Hamacas Resort. The bus leaves Coron around noon.

The bus leaves Salvacion for Coron between 5.30 and 6.30 am.

CALAUIT ISLAND

Large African animals are being raised on this small island, north of Busuanga Island, as an experiment which started in 1977 with eight African species and was carried on for 10 years in strict seclusion. The project has been successful: almost 500 African wild animals, including giraffes, zebras and gazelles, live together with rare Philippine animals such as the mouse deer, bear cat and Philippine crocodile in the 3700-hectare large **Calauit Island Wildlife Sanctuary**. Visitors are welcome. The manager is happy to drive guests around the national park in his jeep for a nominal fee (at the most P100). Admission costs P300.

DIMAKYA ISLAND

There is a group of beautiful little rocky islands north of Busuanga Island, partially covered with various kinds of vegetation. If palms grew there, they would be veritable treasure islands. One of them is Dimakya Island. It is surrounded by a magnificent coral reef and boasts a beach with blindingly white sand which makes a seductive contrast to the turquoise, crystal clear water. This island is home to the exclusive Club Paradise which, amongst others, offers trips to Calauit Island and diving trips.

Places to Stay & Eat

The beautiful *Club Paradise* has singles/doubles with fan and bath for US$100/180 and with air-con and bath for US$150/240. It has cosy, comfortable cottages and offers full board. The price also includes Busuanga Airport service, Hobie

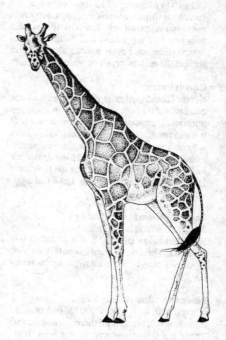

Giraffe

Cat sailing, windsurfing, diving instruction (one hour) and a trip around the island in a speedboat. The management is German-Filipino and reservations can be made in Manila at Euro-Pacific Resorts Inc (☎ 873454; fax 8167685), Suite 302, Erechem Building, Herrera St, Legaspi Village, Manila.

CORON BAY

The best way to explore the islands of Coron Bay is from Coron and Culion. Tiny Cagbatan Island, better known as CYC Island, is ideal for picnics, as is the slightly larger Dimanglet Island; both of them are near Coron. I especially liked the small Malcapuya Island amongst those east of Culion Island. If it had been a little closer to Busuanga Island it would propably have a resort on it by now.

In 1944 a convoy of 12 Japanese naval and merchant ships was sunk in Coron Bay in the north-west, most of them in the waters between Lusong Island and Tanglat Island, where there are seven wrecks altogether in around 30 metres depth of water.

Coron Island

Coron Island is almost uninhabited and can be reached by boat from Coron in about 30 minutes. It consists of steep limestone cliffs with caves and numerous lonely sandy bays where you may meet Tagbanua semi-nomads with Negrito blood. In the centre are hidden mountain lakes such as the turquoise Lake Cayangan and the large Lake Cabugao which has two islands.

Tending Island

This little island is snuggled between Marily and Chindonan islands. It is also called Isla Migrosa. The coarse sandy beach is only of moderate quality but is all right for snorkelling.

Places to Stay At *Isla Migrosa Cottages* a cottage with bath costs P500 for two people, including full board, and there is a restaurant. There are only three simple cottages, built well apart from each other on the side of the hill, with a beautiful view. There is a res-

taurant. This place is for those who like to be alone.

GUTOB BAY

There are lots of lovely and deserted islands in Gutob Bay, between Culion and Busuanga islands. **Dibutonay Island**, **Maltatayoc Island** and **Horse Island** are only three amongst the many idyllic spots available.

The larger **Talampulan Island** is a complete contrast, with a town of 2000 people straggling along the east coast. There are two cinemas, and big ships often drop anchor off the town. Talampulan is a fishing centre, where the catches are brought and shipped to Manila two or three times a week. Note the chance of a ride! It is odd here to see the number of very young fishers with bleached straw-blond hair.

Calumbuyan Island

Calumbuyan Island can be reached from Concepcion on Busuanga Island by boat in about 30 minutes (P150). There is a pearl farm near this island which makes dynamite fishing impractical. This is fortunate for the CIA Resort, as this means the reef is protected.

Places to Stay & Eat The *CIA Resort* has simple and clean cottages for P250 and cottages with bath for P400. It has a restaurant, a billiard bar with good music, boat trips, diving, water skiing, and windsurfing. The management is German. CIA stands for Calumbuyan Island Adventures, and is not affiliated with the American organisation of the same name. Divers in particular will appreciate this place. A dive costs P500; a diving course P7000; and one-week trips with two dives daily cost P6000.

Treasure Island

A little north of Popototan Island, in the southern part of Gutob Bay, the lovely little island of Manguenguey has lately become known as Treasure Island. Day guests are not encouraged unless they are willing to pay P250 admission, which gets them a drink as well.

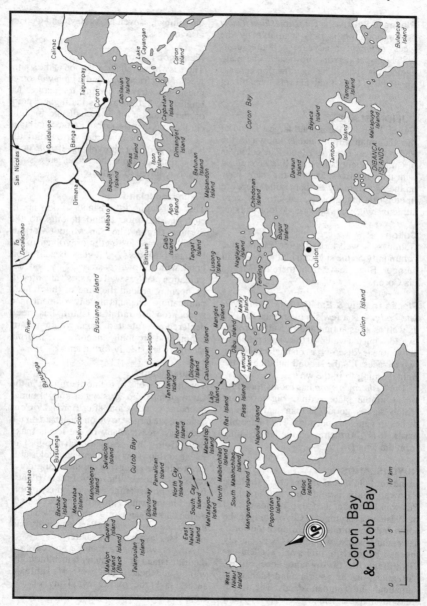

Coron Bay
& Gutob Bay

Places to Stay At the *Treasure Island Resort* accommodation is only available by the week, payment in advance: a double costs US$1195 per person, full board. The management is Swiss. The big attraction here are the Polaris Ultra-light aircraft (capable of landing on water).

CULION ISLAND

Culion Island is the second largest island of the Calamian Group and is known in the Philippines as Leprosy Island. The colony is in Culion; about 600 lepers live here along with their relatives. Most of the many bays on the island, many of them quite deep, are lined with mangroves and are not very attractive when you take a good look at them.

Culion

Culion is a well-looked after, picturesque community on the side of a hill, with a small harbour. Boats leave from there for Manila via Coron.

Places to Stay & Eat The *New Luncheonette Lodge* has a few simple rooms for P75 as well as a restaurant and two airy terraces overlooking the water. At the weekends there is live music (disco-type) on the larger of the two terraces. It's the second building on the right, coming from the wharf.

The *Fishermen's Inn* has rooms for P100. It's a simple place with a big restaurant which serves good German and Filipino dishes in generous portions. They have billiards. It is 150 metres on the left, coming from the wharf.

CUYO ISLANDS

In the north Sulu Sea, set apart from the large Palawan main islands but still part of Palawan Province, the Cuyo Islands consist of 40 islands, forming the Cuyo Group in the south and the Quiniluban Group in the north. This island world, which has been scarcely touched by tourism, offers an excellent environment for diving and snorkelling, particularly in the reefs around Manamoc, Pamalican and Tinituan islands. The diving areas around the islands of Alcisiras and Quiniluban, as well as Agutaya and Oco are also impressive.

Manamoc Island

There is a broad, shallow lagoon in the southwest of this friendly island which welcomes guests who have a feeling for nature. Mt English, at 220 metres, is the highest point on the island; a bit of a challenge for hill-climbers, as there is no trail for the final stage of the climb. The coral reef surrounding the island is good for snorkelling. It runs quite some distance from the beach, so a small boat is required to get there.

Pamalican Island

This enchanting little island six km northeast of Manamoc Island belongs to the Soriano Group (the San Miguel Corporation) who are just getting involved in the tourism business. A 1st-class beach resort hotel with its own power supply and de-salination plant, as well as a small airport will be opening around the time of this book's publication. The marine environment in a wide area around the island has been declared a protected area, which means fishing and dropping anchor in this marine sanctuary are strictly forbidden.

Tinituan Island

This island is one of the northernmost in the Cuyo archipelago. It is better known under the name Concepcion, after Barangay Concepcion, the largest town on the island on the south-east coast. Many of the locals make their living by seaweed farming. The seaweed flourishes in underwater fields cultivated in the extensive neighbouring coral reefs. To protect these profitable plants, fishing with dynamite and poison is not tolerated in the waters around Tinituan Island. So the underwater world can be viewed in all its pristine glory; snorkellers especially can enjoy 1st-class conditions here.

Anyone wishing to spend a few days on the little island of **Taytay** with its blindingly white sand beach, just west of Tinituan, should ask the owner Mr Tony de los Angeles, for permission first.

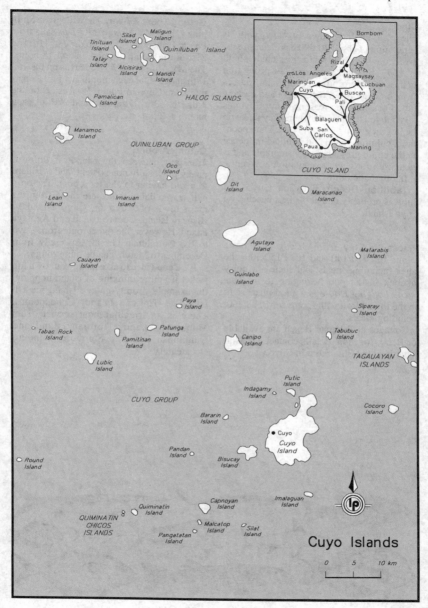

Cuyo Islands

Cuyo

The pleasant little town of Cuyo with its population of about 30,000 has clean streets, lovely old houses and a fortress-church built in 1677 by the Spaniards as protection against the Moro pirates. The main sources of income are dried fish, copra and cashew nuts. For economic reasons many Cuyonos have moved to Palawan where they make up the largest group of immigrants. Their economic, cultural, social and political influence on the entire province is considerable and is the reason for Cuyo's reputation as a centre of traditional culture.

Tabunan Beach, between Cuyo and Suba, is probably one of the best beaches on Cuyo Island.

Places to Stay *Ireen's Lodge* has basic rooms for P70/140 and for P150/300, the latter including meals, but there's a noisy jukebox in the pub belonging to it. *Rene Lucas Lodging House* is a good place right on the town plaza with rooms for P180/360, including meals.

Cottages at Tabunan Beach are available for P100; for more details contact Mr Milo Agustin at the Elda Store in Cuyo.

Getting There & Away The Milagrosa Shipping Lines' MV *Milagrosa-J-Dos* sails from Puerto Princesa to Cuyo on the 1st, 11th and 21st of the month at noon, taking 18 hours. The MV *Milagrosa-J-Tres* leaves on the 7th, 17th and 27th of each month at 4 pm. Departure from Cuyo to Puerto Princesa is on the 3rd, 7th, 13th, 17th, 23rd and 27th of each month at 2 pm.

Getting Around

Transport between the islands is unfortunately practically nonexistent, and it is hard to avoid having to charter a boat. The only half-way reliable routes are those from the main town of Cuyo on Cuyo Island to Bisucay Island, Cocoro Island and Agutaya Island. However, the direct route from Cuyo to the Quiniluban Group, especially from December to March, can be quite rough.

It's a good idea to take along your own life jacket if you're thinking of island hopping, for example, from Agutaya Island via Dit Island to Tinituan Island (Concepcion). There is an irregular boat service from Manamoc Island, Tinituan Island and Quiniluban Island to San Jose, Mindoro Occidental.

Index

ABBREVIATIONS

Ba – Basilan
BI – Batanes Islands
Bo – Bohol
Ca – Camiguin
Ce – Cebu
Ct – Catanduanes
L   – Luzon
Le – Leyte

Lu – Lubang
Ma – Masbate
Mi – Mindanao
Mo – Mondoro
Mq – Marinduque
N   – Negros
NL – North Luzon
Pw – Palawan

Py – Panay
R   – Romblon
Sa – Samar
SL – South Luzon
SI – Sulu Islands
Sq – Siquijor

MAPS

Abra Province (NL) 234
Albay Province (SL)266
Alona Beach (Bo) 312
Angeles (L) 176-177

Bacolod (N) 365
    Goldenfield Commercial
        Complex 367
Bacuit Archipelago (Pw) 503
Baguio (NL) 212
    Baguio City 214
Baler, Around (NL) 248
Banaue (NL) 227
    Around Banaue 229
Bantayan Island (Ce) 341
Batanes Islands 272
Benguet Province (NL) 209
Bohol 306
    North Bohol 307
Boracay (Py) 395
    White Beach Boracay 398
Butuan (Mi) 433

Cagayan de Oro (Mi) 436
Cagayan Province (NL) 245
Calamian Group (Pw) 506
Camiguin 420
Catanduanes 274
Catbalogan (Sa) 415
Cebu 318
    Cebu City 324-325
    North Cebu 338
Coron Bay & Gutob Bay (Pw)
    511
Cuyo Islands (Pw) 513

Dau (L) 179
Davao City (Mi) 452
    Around Davao 456
Dipolog, Around (Mi) 443

Dumaguete (N) 373

General Santos (Dadiangas)
    (Mi) 460
Guimaras (Py) 385

Iligan City (Mi) 440
Ilocos Norte Province (NL) 236
Iloilo (Py) 382
Isabela Province (NL) 247

Jolo Group (SI) 471

Kalibo (Py) 392

Laoag (NL) 238
Legaspi (SL) 259
    Legaspi City 261
Leyte 350
Lingayen Gulf (NL) 200
Lubang 278

Mactan Island (Ce) 336
Manila (L)
    Adriatico & Mabini Streets 148
    Around Manila 171
    Binondo & Santa Cruz 120
    Bus Destinations from Manila
        158
    Chinese Cemetery 119
    Ermita, Malate & Paco 138
    Intramuros & Rizal Park 116
    Makati 130
    Makati Avenue & Burgos Street
        144
    Metro Manila 112-113
    Metro Manila Reference Map
        110
    Metrorail Stations & Bus
        Terminals 161

Parañaque & Pasay City 126
    Quezon City 134
Marinduque 280
Masbate 284
Mayon Volcano (SL) 264
Mindanao & Sulu 419
Mindanao 424-425
Mindoro 287
Mt Apo (Mi) 458

Naga (SL) 256
Negros 361
North Luzon 194
    North Luzon Mountain
        Provinces 219

Ormoc (Le) 358

Pagdanan Bay (Pw) 498
Palawan 478
    Central Palawan 487
    North Palawan 496
    South Palawan 491
Panay 378
    North-East Panay 389
Pandan Bay (Mo) 301
Philippines 10-11
    Aerolift & Pacific Airline
        Routes 101
    Airline Routes 102
    Cultural Minorities 30
    Climatic Zones 19
    Diving Places 82
    Main Shipping Routes 105
    National Parks 24
    Provinces & Regions 26
Puerto Galera (Mo) 289
    Around Puerto Galera 291
Puerto Princesa (Pw) 482

Quezon, Around (Pw) 494

Romblon Province 403

Sagada (NL) 221
Samar 410
    North Samar 412
San Fernando, Around &
    Bauang (NL) 204
San Fernando (La Union) (R)
    207

San Jose (Mo) 298
San Miguel Bay (SL) 254
Sibutu Group (SI) 474
Siquijor 417
Sorsogon Province (SL) 268
South Luzon 252-253
South Zambales (NL) 196
Sulu Islands 467
Surigao (Mi) 429
    Around Surigao 431

Tacloban (Le) 354
Tagbilaran (Bo) 309
Tawi Tawi Group (SI) 472

Vigan (NL) 232
Virac (Ct) 276
Visayas 304-305

White Beach (Mo) 295
Zamboanga (Mi) 446
    Around Zamboanga 450

TEXT

Map references are in **bold** type

Abongan (Pw) 497-498
Abongan River (Pw) 497
Accommodation 85-86
Agho Island (Py) 388
Agnay (R) 404
Agoho (Ca) 422
Agoo (NL) 202
Agus (Ce) 337
Agusan River (Mi) 432
Air Travel
    To/From the Philippines 95-98
    Within the Philippines 100-101
Alaminos (L) 189
Alaminos (NL) 197-198
Aliguay Island (Mi) 443
Allen (Sa) 411
Alligator Lake (L) 188
Almeria (Le) 356
Alona Beach (Bo) 312-314, **312**
Anda (Bo) 311-312
Andagao (Py) 393
Angeles (L) 174-180, **176-177**
    Entertainment 178
    Getting Around 180
    Getting There & Away 178-180
    Information 174-175
    Places to Eat 178
    Places to Stay 175, 178
Angol (Py) 397, 400
Anilao (L) 187
Anini-y (Py) 387
Aninuan Beach (Mo) 296
Antequera (Bo) 310-311
Aparri (NL) 239, 241-244
Apayao People 31
Apo Island (Mo) 299-300
Apo Island (N) 376
Apo Reef (Mo) 299-300
Apuao Grande Island (SL)
    251-255
Aquino, Cory 15-16

Ardent Hot Springs (Ca) 422
Arevalo (Py) 380
Argao (Ce) 348-349
Aringay (NL) 202
Ati-Atihan Festival (Kalibo)
    (Py) 61, 391
Atimonan (SL) 251

Babuyan Claro Volcano (NL)
    241
Babuyan Island (NL) 241
Bacarra (NL) 239
Baclayon (Bo) 311
Bacolod (N) 364-369, **365, 367**
Bacuit Archipelago (Pw)
    502-505, **503**
Badian (Ce) 346-347
Badian Island (Ce) 346-347
Bading (Mi) 434
Badjao People 31-32, 466
Bagalangit (L) 187
Baguio (NL) 210-218, **212, 214**
    Baguio Botanical Gardens 213
    Bell Church 213-215
    Burnham Park 211
    Camp John Hay 211-213
    City Market 211
    Easter School 211
    Entertainment 217
    Faith Healers 215
    Getting Around 218
    Getting There & Away 217-218
    Information 211
    Lourdes Grotto 211
    Mines View Park 213
    Mountain Provinces Museum
        211
    Places to Eat 217
    Places to Stay 216
    St Louis Filigree 211
    Wright Park 213
Baheli (Pw) 489
Balabag (Py) 394, 397, 399, 400

Balanacan (Mq) 281
Baler (NL) 248-249, **248**
Balicasag Island (Bo) 314
Balicuatro Islands (Sa) 411-413
Balingoan (Mi) 434
Balsahan (Pw) 486-488
Balthazar Island (Mq) 283
Banaue (NL) 226-228, **227, 229**
Banga (L) 185
Banga (Py) 391
Banga'an (NL) 222
Bangaan (NL) 230
Bangued (NL) 235
Bani (NL) 197
Banilad (N) 374
Banks, see Money
Bantayan (Ce) 340, 342
Bantayan (N) 372
Bantayan Island (Ce) 340-342,
    341
Banua (NL) 239
Bargaining, see Money
Barrio Barretto (L) 173
Barrio Lantangan (Py) 390
Barrio Piagao (Py) 390
Barrio San Miguel (Py) 384
Basco (BI) 272
Basey (Le) 355-356
Basilan 464, 465-466
Basketball 40, 150
Bataan Peninsula (L) 170
Batac (NL) 240
Batad (NL) 228-230
Batak People 32, 477, 494
Batan Island (BI) 272
Batanes Islands (BI) 271,
    272-273, **272**
Batangas (L) 186-187
Bato (Ce) 347
Bato (Ct) 277
Bato (Le) 359
Bauang (NL) 202-206, **204**
Bayawan (N) 377

Baybay (Le) 359
Baybay Beach (Py) 391
Benoni (Ca) 423
Bicycling, see Cycling
Big La Laguna Beach (Mo) 293, 295
Biliran (Le) 356-357
Biliran Volcano (Le) 356
Binalbagan (N) 376
Binoclutan (NL) 195
Biri Island (Sa) 413
Bitaog (Sq) 417
Bitu-on Beach (Ma) 285
Black Market, see Money
Blanca Aurora Falls (Sa) 413
Boac (Mq) 280-281
Bohol 304-317, 306, 307
Bolinao (NL) 198-199
Boliney (NL) 233
Bolok-Bolok (Ca) 421
Bonbon (Ca) 422
Bongabong (Mo) 297
Bongao (SI) 470-473
Bontoc (NL) 222-224
Bontoc People 32-33
Bonuan (NL) 199, 201
Books 66-67
Bool (Bo) 310-311
Boracay (Py) 394-402, 395, 398
    Entertainment 401
    Getting Around 402
    Getting There & Away 401
    Places to Eat 400-401
    Places to Stay 397-400
    Things to See & Do 396-397
    Tourist Information 396
Borongan (Sa) 414
Botolan (NL) 195
Boxing 40
Brooke's Point (Pw) 493-494
Buenavista (Mq) 282
Bug-ong (Ca) 422
Bugnay (NL) 224
Bulabog (Py) 400
Bulan (SL) 269
Bulusan (SL) 269
Bunabunaan Island (SI) 473
Bus Travel 101-103
Business Hours 60
Busuanga Island (Pw) 507, 509
Butuan (Mi) 432-434, 433
Buyong (Ce) 337

Cabalagnan (Py) 384, 386
Cabilao Island (Bo) 315
Cabugao Norte (Py) 390
Cabugao Sur (Py) 390
Cadlao Island (Pw) 502
Caganhao (Mq) 281

Cagayan de Oro (Mi) 435-438, 436
Cagsawa (SL) 263-265
Cajidiocan (R) 404
Calabidogan Cave (SL) 265
Calamba (L) 188
Calamian Group (Pw) 505-514, 506
Calapan (Mo) 296
Calatrava (R) 405-408
Calauit Island (Pw) 509
Calbayog (Sa) 413-414
Calesas 108
Caliraya Reservoir (L) 192
Callao Caves (NL) 244
Calubian (Le) 357
Calumbuyan Island (Pw) 510
Camalig (SL) 265
Cambulo (NL) 228-230
Camera Island (NL) 193
Camiguin 419-423, 420
Camotes Islands (Le) 357
Camp Phillips (Mi) 438
Canezares Beach (Ce) 343
Caplonga (SL) 251
Capones Island (NL) 193
Capsalay Island (Pw) 497
Capul Island (Sa) 411
Car Rental 103-104, 168
Carabao Island (Py) 397
Caridad (Le) 359
Carlatan (NL) 208
Carmen Hill (Mi) 435
Casinos (L) 150
Cataingan (Ma) 285
Catalinan (Sq) 418
Catanduanes 273-278, 274
Catarman (Ca) 423
Catarman (Sa) 413
Catbalogan (Sa) 414, 415
Catholicism 42
Caticlan (Py) 394
Cauayan (NL) 246
Caving (1) 81
Cavite (L) 183
Cawit (Mq) 281
Cebu 317-349, 318, 338
Cebu City 323-334, 324-325
    Basilica Minore del Santo Niño 328
    Carbon Market 329
    Caretta Cemetery 329
    Casa Gorordo Museum 328
    Cebu Heavenly Temple of Charity 329
    Cebu Zoo 329
    Entertainment 333
    Fort San Pedro 328
    Getting Around 334

    Getting There & Away 334
    Magellan's Cross 328
    Orientation 323
    Places to Eat 332-333
    Places to Stay 329-332
    Shopping 334
    Taoist Temple 329
    Tops 329
    Tourist Information 323-328
    University of San Carlos Museum 328-329
Central Palawan (Pw) 481-490
Chess 40
Children's Island National Park (NL) 198
Chocolate Hills (Bo) 315-316
Christianity 42
Cinema 40, 150
Claveria (NL) 239, 240
Climaco Freedom Park (Mi) 449
Climate 17-20
Climbing 81
Coco Beach (Mo) 295
Concepcion (Pw) 508
Coral Cove Beach (Mo) 294
Coron (Pw) 507-508
Coron Bay (Pw) 510, 511
Coron Island (Pw) 510
Corong-Corong (Pw) 504
Corregidor Island (L) 182-183
Costs, see Money
Cotabato (Mi) 462-463
Credit Cards, see Money
Cresta de Gallo Island (R) 405
Cuernos de Negros (N) 375
Culasi (Py) 387-388
Culion (Pw) 512
Culion Island (Pw) 512
Cultural Minorities 29-39
    Apayao 31
    Badjao 31-32, 466
    Batak 32, 477, 494
    Bontoc 32-33
    Ifugao 33-34
    Ilokano 34
    Kalinga 35, 225, 226,
    Mandaya 35-36
    Mangyan 36
    Mansaka 35-36
    Maranao 36
    Negrito 36-37
    Pala'wan 37
    Samal 466
    T'boli 38, 462
    Tasaday 37
    Tau't Batu 38, 477
    Tausug 37-38, 466
    Yakan 38-39, 464
Currimao (NL) 235

Customs Regulations 56
Cuyo (Pw) 514
Cuyo Islands (Pw) 512-514, **513**
Cycling 104

Daet (SL) 251-255
Dagupan (NL) 199-201
Dakak Bay (Mi) 443, 444
Dalupiri Island (Sa) 411
Dangay (Mo) 297
Dapa (Mi) 432
Dapitan (Mi) 443-444
Daraga (SL) 263-265
Davao (Mi) 450-455, **452, 456**
    Entertainment 454-455
    Getting Around 455
    Getting There & Away 455
    Places to Eat 454
    Places to Stay 453-454
    Shopping 455
    Things to See & Do 451-453
    Tourist Information 451
Del Carmen (Mi) 431, 432
Departure Tax 99
Digos (Mi) 458
Dimakya Island (Pw) 509-510
Din Iwid (Py) 400
Dipolog (Mi) 443-444, **443**
Diving 81-84
    Alona Beach (Bo) 313
    Anilao (L) 187
    Bacuit Archipelago (Pw) 504
    Boracay (Py) 397
    Cabilao Island (Bo) 315
    Coron (Pw) 507
    Moalboal (Ce) 346
    Puerto Princesa (Pw) 484
    Samal Island (Mi) 455
    Santa Cruz (Mq) 281
    Silliman Beach (N) 371
Drinks 91
Dumaguete (N) 371-374, **373**
Dumanhug (Sq) 418

Eagle Camp (Mi) 457
Economy 28-29
El Nido (Pw) 502-505
Elefante Island (Mq) 282
Elefante Island (Pw) 499
Embarcadero (Pw) 498-499
English 43
Estancia (Py) 388-390

Fatima (Mo) 301
Fauna 20-25
Fiestas & Festivals 60-64
    Ati-Atihan (Ibajay) 61
    Ati-Atihan (Kalibo) 61
    Black Nazarene Procession 61
    Feast of Our Lady 61
    Good Friday Crucifixions 62
    Moriones Festival 62
    Muslim Festivals 64
    Peñafrancia Festival 63
    Sinulog Festival 61, 323, 376
Flora 20-25
Flowers Island (Pw) 499
Food 86-91
Fort Pilar (Mi) 445

Gasan (Mq) 283
Gaspar (Mq) 283
Gaspar Island (Mq) 283
Gattaran (NL) 244
General Luna (Mi) 430, 432
General Santos City (Dadiangas)
    (Mi) 459-461, **460**
Geography 16-17
Geratag (Sa) 411
Gigante Islands (Py) 390
Gigmoto (Ct) 277
Gold Hunting 84-85
Golf 41
Government 25-28
Governor's Island (NL) 198
Great Santa Cruz Island (Mi) 450
Gubat (SL) 267-269
Guimaras Island (Py) 384-386,
    385
Guimbal (Py) 386-387
Guinsiliban (Ca) 423
Guiuan (Sa) 414-415
Gumaca (SL) 251
Gumtob Bay (Pw) 510-512, **511**

Hanunoo People 36
Health 68-78
Hibok-Hibok Volcano (Ca) 421
Hidden Valley, Alaminos (L) 189
Hilongos (Le) 359
Hinoba-an (N) 376-377
History 12-16
Honda Bay (Pw) 488-489
Hondura Beach (Mo) 290
Horse Racing 41, 150
Horseback Riding
    Boracay (Py) 397
Hoyop-Hoyopan Caves (SL) 265
Hundred Islands (NL) 198
Hundred Islands National Park
    (NL) 197

Iba (NL) 195
Ibajay (Py) 394
Ibayat Island (BI) 273
Ifugao People 33-34
Iguig (NL) 244
Iligan (Mi) 439-441, **440**

Ilin Island (Mo) 299
Iloilo City (Py) 380-384, **382**
Ilokano People 34
Inabuyatan Island (Pw) 504
Inadawan Island (Pw) 495
Inampulugan Island (Py) 386
Initao (Mi) 439
Irawan (Pw) 486
Iraya Volcano (1) 272
Iriga (SL) 258
Irosin (SL) 269
Isabela (Ba) 464-465
Isla Naburot (Py) 384
Islam 42
Iwahig (Pw) 488

Jagna (Bo) 311
Jao Island (Bo) 317
Jawili Falls (Py) 391
Jeepneys 107, 167-168
Jolo (SI) 470, **471**
Jordan (Py) 384

Kabankalan (N) 376
Kabayan (NL) 218
Kahawangan (NL) 197
Kalibo (Py) 391-394, **392**
Kalinga People 35, 225
Kalinga Villages (NL) 225
Katibawasan Falls (Ca) 422
Kawasan Falls (Ce) 347
Kidapawan (Mi) 458
Koronadel (Mi) 461
Kuguita (Ca) 422
Kumintang Ibana (L) 186

La Janoza (Mi) 432
La Paz (NL) 240
Lagting Falls (R) 405
Lahug (Ce) 332
Lakawon Island (N) 370
Lake Buhi (SL) 258
Lake Danao (Pw) 499
Lake Lanao (Mi) 441-442
Lake Sebu (Mi) 462
Lake Taal (L) 184, 188
Lambigan Falls (R) 405
Lambug (Ce) 347
Lamitan (Ba) 465-466
Language 42-54
Laoag (NL) 235-239, **238**
Laoang Island (Sa) 413
Lapu-Lapu (Ce) 335
Larena (Sq) 416-417
Las Piñas (L) 183
Lazi (Sq) 418
Legaspi (SL) 258-263, **259, 261**
Lemery (L) 187-188
Leynes (L) 184

Leyte 349-360, **350**
Leyte National Park (Le) 358
Ligpo Island (L) 187
Ligpo Point (L) 187
Ligtasin (L) 185
Liloan (Ce) 340, 347-348
Liloan (Le) 360
Limasawa Island (Le) 360
Liminangcong (Pw) 499-502
Lingayen (NL) 199
Lingayen Beach (NL) 199
Loay (Bo) 311
Loboc (Bo) 311
Lodpond (Mo) 297
Lonos (R) 404
Looc (R) 408
Loon (Bo) 310
Los Baños (L) 188-189
Lubang 278-279, **278**
Lubuagan (NL) 225-226
Lucap (NL) 197-198
Lucban (L) 192
Lucban (SL) 250
Lucena (SL) 250-251

Ma-ao (N) 369
Maasin (Le) 359-360
Mabua Beach (Mi) 428
Macarascas (Pw) 489
Mactan Island (Ce) 335, **336**
Magdapio Waterfalls (L) 190
Magdiwang (R) 405
Magellan, Ferdinand 12
Magnesia (Ct) 275
Mahagnao Volcano National
    Recreation Area (L) 25
Mahinog (Ca) 423
Mainit (NL) 224-225
Mainit (Ce) 348
Malamaui Island (Ba) 464
Malapacao Island (Pw) 504
Malapascua Island (Ce) 342-343
Malaybalay (Mi) 439
Malbog (Mq) 282
Malbog Hot Springs (Mq) 282
Malegcong (NL) 224
Maligaya (Pw) 504
Malilipot (SL) 265-267
Malingin Island (Py) 385
Malipano Island (Mi) 456
Maluay (N) 375-376
Mambajao (Ca) 421
Mambucal (N) 369
Mamburao (Mo) 300-302
Manamoc Island (Pw) 512
Mandaon (Ma) 285
Mandaya People 35-36
Mangayad (Py) 399, 400
Mangnao (N) 374

Mangyan (Mo) 297
Mangyan People 36
Manila (L) 109-169, **110,
    112-113, 148, 158, 161, 171**
    Chinatown 119
    Chinese Cemetery 118-119, **119**
    Cultural Center of the
        Philippines 121
    Entertainment 150-153
    Faith Healers 122
    Forbes Park 121
    Fort Santiango 118
    Getting Around 164
    Getting There & Away 154-164
    Information 111-115
    Intramuros 117-118, **116**
    Malacañang Palace 119-121
    Manila Cathedral 118
    Markets 123-124
    Museums 122-123
    Nayong Pilipino 121
    Orientation 109-111
    Places to Eat 137-147, 149
    Places to Stay 124-137
    Quiapo Church 118
    Rizal Park 115-116, **116**
    San Agustin Church 118
    Shopping 153-154
    US Military Cemetery 121-122
    Zoological & Botanical Gardens
        151
Maniuayan Island (Mq) 281
Manoc Manoc (Py) 400
Mansaka People 35-36
Mansalay (Mo) 297
Mantigue Island (Ca) 423
Maps 67
Maranao People 36
Maranlig (Mq) 282
Mararison Island (Py) 388
Marawi (Mi) 441-442
Marbel River Campsite (Mi) 458
Marcos, Ferdinand 14-15
Maria Cristina Falls (Mi) 439
Maribago (Ce) 337-339
Maribojoc (Bo) 310
Marigondon (Ce) 337
Marigondon Beach (Ce) 337
Marinduque 279-283, **280**
Maripipi Islands (Le) 356-357
Masbate 285, **284**
Masbate Island (Ma) 283-285
Masinloc (NL) 195-197
Matabungkay (L) 185-186
Matahan (Le) 359
Mateo Hot & Cold Springs (SL)
    269
Matinloc Island (Pw) 502
Matnog (SL) 270

Matutinao (Ce) 347
Mayon Volcano (SL) 263, **264**
Meara Island (Pw) 489
Media 67
Melchor Island (Mq) 283
Mercedes (SL) 251
Miagao (Py) 387
Mindanao 423-463, **419,
    424-425**
Mindoro 285-302, **287**
Miniloc Island (Pw) 502, 505
Moalboal (Ce) 343-346
Mobo (Ma) 285
Mogpog (Mq) 281
Momo Beach (Bo) 313, 314
Money 56-58
Montalongan (Ce) 348
Motorbike Travel 104
    Motorbike Rental 168
Mt Apo National Park (Mi) 25,
    458-459, **458**
Mt Banahaw (L) 190
Mt Batulao (L) 185
Mt Bongao (SI) 473
Mt Bulusan (SL) 269
Mt Guiting-Guiting (R) 404
Mt Ilig-Mt Baco National Wild-
    life Sanctuary (Mo) 23-25
Mt Kanlaon National Park (N)
    25, 369
Mt Makiling (L) 189
Mt Makiling Forest Reserve (L)
    23
Mt Malindig (Mq) 282
Mt Manunggal National Park
    (Ce) 334-335
Mt Matalingajan (Pw) 493
Mt Pinatubo (L) 180-182
Mt Sungay (L) 184

Naga (SL) 255-258, **256**
Nagarao Island (Py) 386
Nagtabon Beach (Pw) 489
Naguilian (NL) 203
Napo Cove (Le) 356
Napsan (Pw) 488
Narra (Pw) 490-492
Nasugbu (L) 185-186
National Parks, Reserves &
    Sanctuaries 23-25
    Children's Island NP (NL) 198
    Hundred Islands NP (NL) 197
    Leyte NP (Le) 358
    Mahagnao Volcano National
        Recreation Area (L) 25
    Mt Apo NP (Mi) 25, 458-459
    Mt Ilig-Mt Baco National
        Wildlife Sanctuary (Mo)
        23-25

Mt Kanlaon NP (N) 25, 369
Mt Makiling Forest Reserve (L) 23
Mt Manunggal NP (Ce) 334-335
Quezon National Recreation Area (SL) 23
Sohoton NP (Le) 355-356
St Paul's Subterranean NP (Pw) 25, 490
Nauhang (N) 376
Naval (Le) 357
Negrito People 36-37
Negros 360-377, **361**
New Israel (Mi) 458-459
New People's Army (NPA) 224, 225, 226, 250, 355, 360, 458
Nogas Island (Py) 387
North Guntao Island (Pw) 502
North Luzon 193-249, **194, 219**
North Palawan (Pw) 494-505
North Pandan Island (Mo) 300

Odiongan (R) 408
Olango Island (Ce) 337, 339-340
Old San Roque (SL) 258
Olongapo (L) 172-173
Ormoc (Le) 357-359, **358**
Oroquieta (Mi) 442
Ozamiz (Mi) 442

Pabellones Islands (Pw) 499
Paete (L) 192
Pagadian (Mi) 444-445
Pagsanjan (L) 190-192
Pagudpud (NL) 239, 240
Pala'wan People 37
Pala-o (Mi) 439
Palawan (Pw) 476-514, **478, 487, 491, 496**
Paliton Beach (Sq) 418
Palo (Le) 356
Palompon (Le) 357
Pamalican Island (Pw) 512
Pamilacan Island (Bo) 315
Pan de Azucar Island (Py) 388
Panay 377-402, **378, 389**
Pandan Island (Pw) 488
Pangalusian Island (Pw) 504, 505
Pangi (Mq) 283
Panglao Island (Bo) 312-314
Paoay (NL) 240
Paradise Island Beach (Mi) 455
Pariaan Cave (SL) 265
Paringao (NL) 203
Paskuhan Village (L) 170
Pasonanca Park (Mi) 449
Pasuquin (NL) 239
Pavia (Py) 381

Penablanca (NL) 244
Pescador Island (Ce) 343
Photography 67-68
Pilar (Mi) 432
Pili (SL) 258
Pinamalayan (Mo) 296-297
Pinatubo Lake (L) 174
Pinsail Island (Pw) 504
Plaridel (Mi) 442
Poctoy (Mq) 282
Population 29
Poro Island (Le) 357
Poro Point (NL) 204
Port Barton (Pw) 495-497
Post 64-65
PU-Cabs 107
Puerto Galera (Mo) 288-293, **289, 291**
Puerto Princesa (Pw) 481-486, **482**
Pulanlupa (Mi) 450
Pundaquit (NL) 193-195
Punta Bonga (Py) 400
Punta Engaño (Ce) 339
Puraran (Ct) 277-278

Quezon (Pw) 492-493, **494**
Quezon Beach (SI) 470
Quezon Island (NL) 198
Quezon National Recreation Area (NL) 23

Ramos, Fidel 16
Rawis (Sa) 414
Reef Island (Pw) 495
Rio Hondo (Mi) 445
Rio Tuba (Pw) 494
Rizal, Dr Jose 14
Romblon 403-404
Romblon Island (R) 403-404
Romblon Province 402-408, **403**
Roxas (NL) 246
Roxas (Mo) 297
Roxas (Pw) 495
Roxas (Py) 390-391

Sabang (Mo) 293
Sabang (Pw) 490
Sabang Beach (Mo) 294
Sablayan (Mo) 300
Sabtang Island (BI) 273
Sagada (NL) 218-221, **221**
Sailing 85
    Boracay (Py) 397
Saint Paul's Cave (Pw) 489
Salag Do-Ong (Sq) 418
Salinas (NL) 246
Sallapadan (NL) 233
Salomague Island (Mq) 282

Samal Island (Mi) 455-457
Samal People 466
Samar 409-415, **410, 412**
Sampaloc Lake (L) 189
San Agustin (R) 405
San Andres (R) 405-408
San Antonio (Sa) 413
San Antonio (Sq) 418
San Carlos (N) 370-371
San Dionisio (Py) 388
San Fabian (NL) 201-202
San Fernando (La Union) (NL) 206-210, **204, 207**
San Fernando (Pampanga) (L) 170-172
San Fernando (R) 405
San Isidro (Le) 357
San Joaquin (Py) 387
San Jose (Mo) 297-299, **298**
San Jose (N) 375
San Jose (Sa) 411
San Jose de Buenavista (Py) 387
San Juan (Sq) 418
San Miguel (NL) 193-195
San Nicolas (L) 188
San Nicolas (NL) 240
San Pablo (L) 189-190
San Rafael (Pw) 494-495
San Ramon (Mi) 450
San Salvador (NL) 195
San Sebastian (Ce) 347
San Vicente (Pw) 497
Sandugan (Sq) 417
Santa Cruz (Mq) 281-282
Santa Cruz Islands (Mi) 449-450
Santa Fe (NL) 246-248
Santa Fe (Ce) 342
Santa Fe (R) 408
Santa Lucia (Pw) 488
Santo Domingo (SL) 265
Santo Nino Cold Springs (Ca) 423
Sarrat (NL) 240
Sea Travel
    To/From the Philippines 98
    Within the Philippines 104
Seksi Beach (NL) 239
Shopping 92-94
Siargao Island (Mi) 430-432
Siasi (SI) 470
Sibulan (N) 374
Sibuyan Island (R) 404-405
Sibuyao (Mq) 282
Sicayab (Mi) 443
Sicogon Island (Py) 390
Sierra Madre (NL) 244
Silay (N) 369-370
Sinulog Festival 61, 323, 376
Sipaway Island (N) 370

Siquijor 417-418, **417**
Siquijor Island 416-418
Sitangkai (SI) 473-375
Small La Laguna Beach (Mo)
　293-294
Snake Island (Pw) 488
Snorkelling
　Anilao (L) 187
　Bacuit Archipelago (Pw)
　　502-504
　Balicasag Island (Bo) 314
　Boracay (Py) 397
　Honda Bay (Pw) 488
　Maniuayan Island (Mq) 281
　Masinloc (NL) 195
　Panglao Island (Bo) 312
　Puerto Galera Beaches (Mo)
　　288-290
　Tabangao (NL) 186
　Tres Reyes Islands (Mq) 283
　White Beach (NL) 203
　White Beach, Torrijos (Mq) 282
Sogod (Ce) 340
Sohoton National Park (Sa)
　355-356, 409
Sorsogon (SL) 267-269, **268**
South Luzon 250-270, **252-253**
South Palawan (Pw) 490-494
Spanish 42
St Paul's Subterranean National
　Park (Pw) 25, 490
Starfish Island (Pw) 488
Suba Beach (NL) 237, 240
Subic (L) 173
Sulu Islands 466-475, **419, 467**
Sumilon Island (Ce) 348
Surallah (Mi) 461-462
Surigao (Mi) 428-430, **429, 431**
Suyangan (Mi) 432

T'boli People 38, 462
Tabaco (SL) 267
Tabangao (L) 186
Tablas Island (R) 405-408
Tabon Beach (Pw) 492
Tabon Caves (Pw) 492
Tabuan (Pw) 497-498
Tabunan Beach (Pw) 514
Tacloban (Le) 352-355, **354**

Taclobo (R) 405
Tagaytay (Taal Volcano) (L)
　183-184
Tagbilaran (Bo) 308-310, **309**
Taggat (NL) 241
Taglibi (SI) 470
Talampulan Island (Pw) 510
Talibon (Bo) 316-317
Talikud Island (Mi) 457
Talipanan Beach (Mo) 296
Talisay (L) 184-185
Talisay (Ce) 342, 343
Taluksangay (Mi) 450
Tampi (N) 375
Tanlagan Waterfalls (NL) 244
Tapiutan Island (Pw) 502
Tapon (Ca) 421
Tasaday People 37
Tau't Batu People 38, 477
Tausug People 37-38, 466
Taxis 107, 165, 167
Taytay (Pw) 498-499, 512
Telephone 65-66
Tending Island (Pw) 510
Tennis 41
Terejo (N) 375
Ternate (L) 183
Theatre 151
Tiaong (L) 190
Ticlin (SL) 270
Tigbauan (Py) 386
Tilik (Lu) 279
Tinago Falls (Mi) 439
Tinglayan (NL) 225
Tingyao Island (Sa) 413
Tinituan Island (Pw) 512
Tipping, see Money
Tiwi (SL) 267
Toledo (Ce) 343
Torrijos (Mq) 282
Tourist Offices 59-60
Train Travel 103
Travellers' Cheques, see Money
Treasure Island (Pw) 510-512
Trekking 85
Tres Reyes Islands (Mq) 283
Tricycles 108
Trishaws 108
Tubigon (Bo) 316

Tugdan (R) 408
Tuguegarao (NL) 244-246
Tungonan (Le) 357
Tupsan (Ca) 423
Tuwasan Falls (Ca) 423
Twin Lakes (N) 375

Ubay (Bo) 316
Underground River (Pw)
　489-490
Union (Mi) 430
Urbiztondo (NL) 208
Ursula Island (Pw) 493-494

Valencia (Bo) 311
Valencia (N) 375
Victorias (N) 370
Viga (Ct) 277
Vigan (NL) 230-234, **232**
Villa (Py) 381
Villa Escudero (L) 190
Virac (Ct) 275-277, **276**
Viriato (Sa) 413
Visas 55
Visayas 303-418, **304-305**
Volleyball 41

White Beach, Catarman (Sa) 413
White Beach, Isabela (Ba) 464
White Beach, Puerto Galera
　(Mo) 294-296, **295**
White Beach, Puerto Princesa
　(Pw) 481
White Beach, Torrijos (Mq) 282
White Island (Ca) 422
Windsurfing
　Boracay (Py) 397
Women Travellers 78

Yakan People 38-39, 464
Yakan Weaving Village (Mi) 450

Zambales Coast (NL) 193-197,
　196
Zamboanga (Mi) 445-449, **446,
450**
Zamboanguita (N) 375-376

Update – April 1996

INTRODUCTION

Despite growing disillusionment with the government, the economy is set to grow at a high 5% for the third year in a row and the army seems no longer to be a threat to government stability.

A militant Muslim insurgent organisation, the Moro Islamic Liberation Front (MILF), seems set to establish an independent Islamic state in the areas it controls on Mindanao. The group is distancing itself from the Moro National Liberation Front (MNLF), which is the only Islamic rebel group currently talking with the government. The MNLF hopes for a formal treaty by the end of 1996, which would have the blessing of the Organisation of Islamic Countries.

However, the MNLF has lost a lot of support to the MILF and, while loosely co-operating with it, has squabbles over territory. The MILF claims 180,000 troops, although the government says it has fewer than 10,000. If the government is right, it's hard to see why it has deployed half the Filipino army on Mindanao and is no closer to ending the rebellion.

Mindanao is crucial to the country, as it is having an economic boom, especially around cities such as Cagayan de Oro.

VISAS & PERMITS

The immigration office has changed its name to Bureau of Immigration & Deportation.

A traveller reports difficulties in extending her stay beyond two months. She had to go to the immigration building in Manila, and getting an extension took two weeks. Even the 'express' service (US$10) takes a week. Each month costs US$10 or more for a maximum of two months.

Manila is reportedly a good place to apply for Australian visas. Allow two days.

MONEY

Cirrus money machines can be found at almost any PCI bank branch. Travellers report that when changing travellers'

cheques you might need to show your receipt of purchase and the 'back-up paper' as well as your passport.

In April 1996, $US1 = P26.

TELEPHONE

Although there are more public phones, it's still difficult to find one which works. At Manila airport, after immigration but before customs clearance, there is a table selling PLDT Fonkard and a working phone from which you can make long distance calls.

DANGERS & ANNOYANCES

In Manila, sedatives put into the food or drink of potential robbery victims is an increasing problem. Pickpocketing from daypacks (while you're wearing them) is also rife. One traveller suggests talking to the police in the Tourism Building in Manila for advice on current dangers.

The area around San Fernando is still heavily affected by *lahar* (volcanic mudflow) from Mt Pinatubo. The rainy season can bring dramatic changes to the landscape, so check the situation with the registration centre at Sapangbato near Angeles City before attempting hikes towards the volcano.

GETTING THERE & AWAY
Air
Brunei Airlines flies twice a week from Manila to Darwin via Bandar Seri Begawan, where you have to overnight.

A traveller advises arriving in Cebu City rather than Manila, if you have a choice – it's safer and more central to the rest of the country.

Boat
There is reportedly a 'legitimate' ferry (that is, not a smuggling operation) between Sandakan (Sabah) in Malaysia and Zamboanga City (Mindanao). From Sandakan it departs at 3 pm on Thursday and arrives at 9 am on Friday. From Zamboanga City it departs at 3 pm on Tuesday. The fare is P1000 (M$100) for a bunk bed. The ship is the MV *Lady Mary Foy* and is operated by Alison Shipping Lines.

GETTING AROUND
Air
Grandair is in competition with PAL, reducing fares on some routes. Aerolift has ceased operations, but there are some new airlines, such as Star Asia Airways Corp, flying to Caticlan and San Jose, Soriano Aviation, flying to El Nido and Grand Air, and Makati, flying to Cebu and Davao.

Motorcycle
If you're looking to buy a bike, check *Buy and Sell*, a weekly ad paper available at major bookstores Bear in mind that motorcycles are not allowed on the North and South Luzon Tollways (Dau-Manila-Calamba). Finding secondary roads is not an easy task.

Boat
Many boats have changed their timetables, so check well in advance, preferably at the dock rather than at a ferry company office.

Ferry sinkings continue, although after the disaster in early 1996 there were calls for the death penalty for ferry owners whose vessels sink because of negligence. If you're visiting Marinduque for the Moriones Festival at Easter, consider flying back or staying on the island for a few days after the festival, as the Lucena/Balanacan ferry is extremely overloaded, especially on the last night when everyone heads back to Manila.

On many routes, services seem to be improving, with travellers reporting new and faster services. For instance, the trip from Cebu City to Tagbilaran (Bohol) can now be made by the Bullet Xpress, which has air-con and costs P200 for the trip of 90 minutes.

A traveller reports a new route from Puerto Princesa to Antique and Iloilo City on Panay and says that a route from Puerto Princesa to Mindanao is planned.

DESTINATIONS
Boracay (Panay)
There is now a large, helpful tourist centre on White Beach, which also handles airline bookings and confirmations.

Cebu
There don't seem to be any shuttle buses to the airport now. Taxis, at about P100 to Matacan, are the only option.

The PAL office on General Maxilom Ave is due to move to Plaridel St, opposite the Centrepoint Hotel.

Manila
The Ermita area has suffered because the government closed down many bars and clubs to prepare for a revamping that has yet to begin. There's a distinct air of sleaze. Malate has fared better, and you'll still find some legitimate nightlife. The remaining upmarket hotels in the Bay area can offer good deals, although you might have to ask.

At the international airport there are two information counters, one with maps and information on hotels; the other, run by the Department of Tourism (DOT), has general tourist information.

Travellers report that the Museum of Arts & Sciences at the University of Santo Tomas on Espana Blvd in Sampaloc is worth visiting. It has ethnographic items from around the country and many stuffed birds and animals. It's open from Tuesday to Saturday from 9 am to noon and 2 to 5 pm.

Getting Around Traffic continues on its crazy way (or crazy standstill). Despite soaring sales of new cars, new roads aren't being built (although some are planned), and an odds-and-evens system of regulating cars at peak times doesn't seem to have had any affect. Allow almost two hours to get between the Bay area and Makati at peak times.

Taxis 2000 now operate from the arrivals area of Manila international airport. Fares to Ermita/Malate are about P250. It's safest to arrange a taxi through the DOT counter. Cheaper taxis from the airport to downtown can be found down from the main entrance, some 100 m on the right. Jeepneys are also available to Divisoria and from there to Mabini.

A traveller recommends taxis carrying a sign saying DZRN or DZXL; they are equipped with mobile telephones and are in contact with base.

There are no more Love Buses through Ermita. The major bus route in the Tourist Belt area is along Taft Ave, in Makati along Sen Gil Puyat and Ayala Ave. To get to the bus station for provincial buses to the north, go to Taft Ave and catch a city bus displaying Ayala, Cubao signs. Since this ride is time consuming, taking the LRT to the nearest stop is worth considering. It is packed with commuters throughout the day, however.

A bus station for provincial buses to the south was supposed to go into operation in late 1995 at the Food Terminal Inc (FTI). This is about 30 km from town, and there were supposed to be shuttle buses to get you there. However, buses currently still depart from the old bus terminals and stop at FTI.

Marinduque Island

In April 1996 a mine's storage dam spilled possibly toxic waste into the Boac River. Officials say that livestock and crops were killed, and thousands of villagers were trapped by the torrent.

Pagsanjan (Luzon)

Readers report thefts and other hassles with *banqueros* they had met on the bus from Manila. They recommend finding your own way to a guesthouse and then using the guesthouse's recommended boatmen. If you let outside boatman lead you to a guesthouse, the owner won't be able to let you take local boatmen, or he will face 'problems'.

Sagada

The Crystal Cave has been closed because visitors were breaking and stealing the crystals.

Sitangkai Island

Smugglers and pirates are still very active in this area. If you do want to travel around, you must check first with the local security forces. They will probably insist that you take an escort of around six soldiers, for whom you pay about P200 per day.

TRAVELLERS' TIPS & COMMENTS

When you arrive at Kalibo airport (Panay) en route to Boracay Island, there are a few companies offering AC buses to Caticlan and boats to Boracay for P150. A much cheaper way to get there is to get from the airport to Calibo City by tricycle (P10), take a jeepney to Caticlan (departing about hourly, P30) and take a boat to Boracay (P15). It is not as complicated as it sounds, and we got to Boracay only 30 minutes after the group who took the AC bus deal. The same thing can be done on the way back, at least for the afternoon flight.

Itay Lusky

The biggest disappointment of our trip, Malapascua Island bore no resemblance to the description in the LP guide. True, the beach is nice and white, but there is plenty of seagrass around which, when it decomposes, reduces visibility. The fishermen have reduced their net holes down to tea-strainer size, therefore killing anything and everything that's around. The charming locals also sign their names in the sand next to their faeces. Walking around the island wasn't any better than the miserable snorkelling. The locals seem to abandon their rubbish everywhere.

John Mitchell

Last November I took off with some friends to the Philippines. The trip was intended to be primarily a surf mission, although seasoned travelling surfers will know that November to May is certainly not the time to visit the Philippine Pacific Coast for surf. Strong NE trade winds – on shore for all but a few Pacific surf locations – blow relentlessly during these months, so basically there is no point in visiting the east coast then. During May, the winds usually swing around and lighten, producing lovely clean surf.

Between November and April, the best bet for clean surf in the Philippines is in the South China Sea. The swell is obviously smaller and less reliable, as it relies largely on typhoons travelling NW across the northern tip of Luzon. We spent quite some time in San Fernando (La Union), where the best waves are at Urbiztondo. Lubben's Point is a mellow right-hand reef break at the front of Mona Lisa cottages and usually attracts the most swell.

There are also waves further north at the charming Spanish towns of Vigan, Laoag and Pagudpud, but they are difficult to reach without independent transport. Travelling with a surfboard was mostly hassle free but some bus companies aren't keen to take them. In addition, it's a good idea to learn the different dialects for 'Don't sit on my surfboard, it's fragile'.

Paul Harvey

Travel in the Philippines, especially by boat from island to island, is time-consuming. Therefore you should plan well ahead what you want to see and whether it can be done without too much hurry. Certainly everybody has their own ideas of which places to visit, but after having travelled in the Philippines for the past seven years, I would like to give you my idea of an itinerary.

If you have one month, I suggest some quick sightseeing in Manila and visiting some nearby places such as Las Pinas, Tagaytay and Pagsanjan, and then head towards the Mt Province to see Banaue, Batad, Bontoc and Sagada. If road conditions permit, return via Baguio, then you may want some days at the beach; depending on your budget, it could be either Puerto Galera or Boracay. If you are real quick, you could still take in Mt Mayon.

If you have two months, you could do the same route to the north but add maybe Igan and Hundred Islands and return via Zambales with the chance to get an idea of the Mt Pinatubo area. Then you could bus all the way south to Leyte with stops at Lake Buhi, Mt Mayon and Sorsogon, before continuing through Samar and across the San Juanico Bridge to Leyte to visit Palo. From Leyte travel via Bohol (Chocolate

Hills), Cebu City and Iloilo, with its famous nearby churches, to Boracay. Unless you do not mind really rushing it, you would probably have to fly some sectors such as Cebu City to Iloilo and/or Caticlan or Kalibo to Manila.

If you have three months or more you could do this trip in a much more relaxed way and add a few places such as Camiguin or return from Boracay via Tablas and Mindoro. Another alternative is to visit Palawan – the last frontier – but count on one month unless you fly, for example from Iloilo to Puerto Princesa and from El Nido to Manila.

Alexander Winter

INTERNET INFO

For the latest travel information, check out Lonely Planet's award-winning web site, which contains updates, recent travellers' letters and a useful bulletin board:

http://www.lonelyplanet.com

Silkroute has useful practical information for travellers to the Philippines, from currency regulations and local transport to tipping etiquette and duty-free shopping:

http://silkroute.com/silkroute/travel/ essn/ph.html

The Soc.Filipino Homepage offers an eclectic intro to Filipino culture, but unfortunately does not have much travel-specific information:

http://www.mozcom.com/SCF/SCF.html

The Philippines Page is a pleasant site purporting to offer a virtual trip to the Philippines, but is really an introduction to aspects of Filipino art:

http://www.europa.com/ria/pinoy.html

ACKNOWLEDGMENTS

The information in this Update was compiled from various sources, including a contribution from Lonely Planet author Paul Greenway, and reports by the following travellers:

Wim & Garyfallia Achramme; Cynthia Balaberda; Don & Theresa Benoit; Michael Bolton; Art Hacker; Bob & Elaine Howlett; Niels Janssen; Steve Lidgey; Jose M Lomas; John Mitchell; Ian Queen; Tatjana Steinecke; Mrs Sietske A Op het Veld; Gerhard Willinger; Alexander Winter; and David Yu.

LONELY PLANET PRODUCTS

Lonely Planet is known worldwide for publishing practical, reliable and no-nonsense travel information in our guides and on our web site. The Lonely Planet list covers just about every accessible part of the world. Currently there are eight series: *travel guides*, *shoestring guides*, *walking guides*, *city guides*, *phrasebooks*, *audio packs*, *travel atlases* and *Journeys* – a unique collection of travellers' tales. .

EUROPE

Austria • Baltic States & Kaliningrad • Baltic States phrasebook • Britain • Central Europe on a shoestring • Central Europe phrasebook • Czech & Slovak Republics • Denmark • Dublin city guide • Eastern Europe on a shoestring • Eastern Europe phrasebook • Finland • France • Greece • Greek phrasebook • Hungary • Iceland, Greenland & the Faroe Islands • Ireland • Italy • Mediterranean Europe on a shoestring • Mediterranean Europe phrasebook • Poland • Prague city guide • Russia, Ukraine & Belarus • Russian phrasebook • Scandinavian & Baltic Europe on a shoestring • Scandinavian Europe phrasebook • Slovenia • St Petersburg city guide • Switzerland • Trekking in Greece • Trekking in Spain • Ukranian phrasebook • Vienna city guide • Walking in Switzerland • Western Europe on a shoestring • Western Europe phrasebook

NORTH AMERICA

Alaska • Backpacking in Alaska • Baja California• California & Nevada • Canada • Hawaii • Honolulu city guide • Los Angeles city guide • Mexico • Pacific Northwest USA • Rocky Mountain States • San Francisco city guide • Southwest USA • USA phrasebook

CENTRAL AMERICA & THE CARIBBEAN

Central America on a shoestring • Costa Rica • Eastern Caribbean • Guatemala, Belize & Yucatán: La Ruta Maya • Jamaica

SOUTH AMERICA

Argentina, Uruguay & Paraguay • Bolivia • Brazil • Brazilian phrasebook • Buenos Aires city guide • Chile & Easter Island • Colombia • Ecuador & the Galápagos Islands • Latin American Spanish phrasebook • Peru • Quechua phrasebook • Rio de Janeiro city guide • South America on a shoestring • Trekking in the Patagonian Andes • Venezuela

ALSO AVAILABLE:

Travel with Children • Traveller's Tales

AFRICA

Arabic (Moroccan) phrasebook • Africa on a shoestring • Cape Town city guide • Central Africa • East Africa • Egypt & the Sudan • Ethiopian (Amharic) phrasebook • Kenya • Morocco • North Africa • South Africa, Lesotho & Swaziland • Swahili phrasebook • Trekking in East Africa • West Africa • Zimbabwe, Botswana & Namibia • Zimbabwe, Botswana & Namibia travel atlas

MAIL ORDER

Lonely Planet products are distributed worldwide. They are also available by mail order from Lonely Planet, so if you have difficulty finding a title please write to us. North American and South American residents should write to Embarcadero West, 155 Filbert St, Suite 251, Oakland CA 94607, USA; European and African residents should write to 10 Barley Mow Passage, Chiswick, London W4 4PH; and residents of other countries to PO Box 617, Hawthorn, Victoria 3122, Australia.

NORTH-EAST ASIA

Beijing city guide • Cantonese phrasebook • China • Hong Kong, Macau & Canton • Hong Kong city guide • Japan • Japanese phrasebook • Japanese audio pack • Korea • Korean phrasebook • Mandarin phrasebook • Mongolia • Mongolian phrasebook • North-East Asia on a shoestring • Seoul city guide • Taiwan • Tibet • Tibet phrasebook • Tokyo city guide

INDIAN SUBCONTINENT

Bengali phrasebook • Bangladesh • Delhi city guide • Hindi/Urdu phrasebook • India • India & Bangladesh travel atlas • Karakoram Highway • Kashmir, Ladakh & Zanskar • Nepal • Nepali phrasebook • Pakistan • Sri Lanka • Sri Lanka phrasebook • Trekking in the Indian Himalaya • Trekking in the Nepal Himalaya

SOUTH-EAST ASIA

Bali & Lombok • Bangkok city guide • Burmese phrasebook • Cambodia • Ho Chi Minh city guide • Indonesia • Indonesian phrasebook • Indonesian audio pack • Jakarta city guide • Java • Laos • Lao phrasebook • Malaysia, Singapore & Brunei • Myanmar (Burma) • Philippines • Pilipino phrasebook • Singapore city guide • South-East Asia on a shoestring • Thailand • Thailand travel atlas • Thai phrasebook • Thai audio pack • Thai Hill Tribes phrasebook • Vietnam • Vietnamese phrasebook • Vietnam travel atlas

AUSTRALIA & THE PACIFIC

Australia • Australian phrasebook • Bushwalking in Australia • Bushwalking in Papua New Guinea • Fiji • Fijian phrasebook • Islands of Australia's Great Barrier Reef • Melbourne city guide • Micronesia • New Caledonia • New South Wales & the ACT • New Zealand • Outback Australia • Papua New Guinea • Papua New Guinea phrasebook • Queensland • Rarotonga & the Cook Islands • Samoa • Solomon Islands • South Australia • Sydney city guide • Tahiti & French Polynesia • Tonga • Tramping in New Zealand • Vanuatu • Victoria • Western Australia

Travel Literature: Islands in the Clouds • Sean & David's Long Drive

MIDDLE EAST & CENTRAL ASIA

Arab Gulf States • Arabic (Egyptian) phrasebook • Central Asia • Iran • Israel • Jordan & Syria • Middle East • Turkey • Turkish phrasebook • Trekking in Turkey • Yemen

Travel Literature: The Gates of Damascus

ISLANDS OF THE INDIAN OCEAN

Madagascar & Comoros • Maldives & Islands of the East Indian Ocean • Mauritius, Réunion & Seychelles

THE LONELY PLANET STORY

Lonely Planet published its first book in 1973 in response to the numerous 'How did you do it?' questions Maureen and Tony Wheeler were asked after driving, bussing, hitching, sailing and railing their way from England to Australia.

Written at a kitchen table and hand collated, trimmed and stapled, *Across Asia on the Cheap* became an instant local bestseller, inspiring thoughts of another book.

Eighteen months in South-East Asia resulted in their second guide, *South-East Asia on a shoestring*, which they put together in a backstreet Chinese hotel in Singapore in 1975. The 'yellow bible', as it quickly became known to backpackers around the world, soon became *the* guide to the region. It has sold well over half a million copies and is now in its 8th edition, still retaining its familiar yellow cover.

Today there are over 180 titles, including travel guides, walking guides, language kits & phrasebooks, travel atlases and travel literature. The company is one of the largest travel publishers in the world. Although Lonely Planet initially specialised in guides to Asia, we now cover most regions of the world, including the Pacific, North America, South America, Africa, the Middle East and Europe.

The emphasis continues to be on travel for independent travellers. Tony and Maureen still travel for several months of each year and play an active part in the writing, updating and quality control of Lonely Planet's guides.

They have been joined by over 70 authors and 170 staff at our offices in Melbourne (Australia), Oakland (USA), London (UK) and Paris (France). Travellers themselves also make a valuable contribution to the guides through the feedback we receive in thousands of letters each year.

The people at Lonely Planet strongly believe that travellers can make a positive contribution to the countries they visit, both through their appreciation of the countries' culture, wildlife and natural features, and through the money they spend. In addition, the company makes a direct contribution to the countries and regions it covers. Since 1986 a percentage of the income from each book has been donated to ventures such as famine relief in Africa; aid projects in India; agricultural projects in Central America; Greenpeace's efforts to halt French nuclear testing in the Pacific; and Amnesty International.

'I hope we send the people out with the right attitude about travel. You realise when you travel that there are so many different perspectives about the world, so we hope these books will make people more interested in what they see. These are guidebooks, but you can't really guide people. All you can do is point them in the right direction.'
— Tony Wheeler

LONELY PLANET PUBLICATIONS

Australia
PO Box 617, Hawthorn 3122, Victoria
tel: (03) 9819 1877 fax: (03) 9819 6459
e-mail: talk2us@lonelyplanet.com.au

USA
Embarcadero West, 155 Filbert St, Suite 251,
Oakland, CA 94607
tel: (510) 893 8555 TOLL FREE: 800 275-8555
fax: (510) 893 8563
e-mail: info@lonelyplanet.com

UK
10 Barley Mow Passage, Chiswick,
London W4 4PH
tel: (0181) 742 3161 fax: (0181) 742 2772
e-mail: 100413.3551@compuserve.com

France:
71 bis rue du Cardinal Lemoine, 75005 Paris
tel: 1 44 32 06 20 fax: 1 46 34 72 55
e-mail: 100560.415@compuserve.com

World Wide Web: http://www.lonelyplanet.com